SO-BKT-278

Hien Dang

New Perspectives on

MICROSOFT®
WINDOWS XP

Comprehensive

JUNE JAMRICH PARSONS

DAN OJA

JOAN & PATRICK CAREY
Carey Associates

LISA RUFFOLO

THOMSON
™
COURSE TECHNOLOGY   Australia • Canada • Mexico • Singapore • Spain • United Kingdom • United States • Japan

THOMSON

COURSE TECHNOLOGY

New Perspectives on Microsoft® Windows XP—Comprehensive

is published by Course Technology.

Managing Editor:
Rachel Crapser

Senior Editor:
Donna Gridley

Senior Product Manager:
Kathy Finnegan

Product Manager:
Melissa Hathaway

Technology Product Manager:
Amanda Young

Marketing Manager:
Sean Teare

Developmental Editor:
Kim Crowley

Production Editor:
Kristen Guevara

Composition:
GEX Publishing Services

Text Designer:
Meral Dabcovich

Cover Designer:
Efrat Reis

COPYRIGHT © 2002 Course Technology, a division of Thomson Learning, Inc. Thomson Learning™ is a trademark used herein under license.

Printed in the United States of America

1 2 3 4 5 6 7 8 9 BM 04 03 02 01

For more information, contact Course Technology, 25 Thomson Place, Boston, Massachusetts, 02210.

Or find us on the World Wide Web at: www.course.com

ALL RIGHTS RESERVED. No part of this work covered by the copyright hereon may be reproduced or used in any form or by any means—graphic, electronic, or mechanical, including photocopying, recording, taping, Web distribution, or information storage and retrieval systems—without the written permission of the publisher.

For permission to use material from this text or product, contact us by
Tel (800) 730-2214
Fax (800) 730-2215
www.thomsonrights.com

Disclaimer
Course Technology reserves the right to revise this publication and make changes from time to time in its content without notice.

Some of the product names and company names used in this book have been used for identification purposes only and may be trademarks or registered trademarks of their respective manufacturers and sellers.

Microsoft and the Office logo are either registered trademarks or trademarks of Microsoft Corporation in the United States and/or other countries. Course Technology is an independent entity from the Microsoft Corporation, and not affiliated with Microsoft in any manner.

ISBN 0-619-04462-4

New Perspectives

Preface

Course Technology is the world leader in information technology education. The New Perspectives Series is an integral part of Course Technology's success. Visit our Web site to see a whole new perspective on teaching and learning solutions.

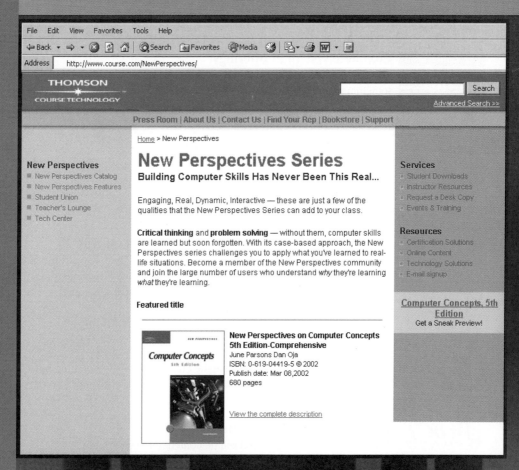

New Perspectives—Building Computer Skills Has Never Been This Real

Why New Perspectives will work for you.

Critical thinking and **problem solving**—without them, computer skills are learned but soon forgotten. With its **case-based** approach, the New Perspectives Series challenges students to apply what they've learned to real-life situations. Become a member of the New Perspectives community and watch your students not only **master** computer skills, but also **retain** and carry this **knowledge** into the world.

New Perspectives catalog
Our online catalog is never out of date! Go to the Catalog link on our Web site to check out our available titles, request a desk copy, download a book preview, or locate online files.

Brief
Introductory
Comprehensive
Advanced

Complete system of offerings
Whether you're looking for a Brief book, an Advanced book, or something in between, we've got you covered. Go to the Catalog link on our Web site to find the level of coverage that's right for you.

Instructor materials
We have all the tools you need—data files, solution files, figure files, a sample syllabus, and ExamView, our powerful testing software package.

SAM XP and TOM

How well do your students know Microsoft Office?
Experience the power, ease, and flexibility of SAM XP and TOM. These innovative software tools provide the first truly integrated technology-based training and assessment solution for your applications course. Click the Tech Center link to learn more.

APPROVED COURSEWARE

Get certified
If you want to get certified, we have the titles for you. Find out more by clicking the Teacher's Lounge link.

Interested in online learning?
Enhance your course with rich online content for use through MyCourse 2.0, WebCT, and Blackboard. Go to the Teacher's Lounge to find the platform that's right for you.

Your link to the future is at
www.course.com/NewPerspectives

What you need to know about this book.

"This text provides a thorough understanding of basic concepts through the use of step-by-step instruction, coverage of practical tasks, and case-based lessons. I especially liked the writing assignments and critical thinking skills factored into the end-of-chapter projects."

Risa Blair,
Champlain College

"I am personally impressed with the New Perspectives style, as it promises to give the student an above average coverage of the subject."

Eric Johnston,
Vatterott College

"The greatest strength of the book is that you have chosen meaningful case studies to exemplify the concepts."

Risa Blair,
Champlain College

- Student Online Companion takes students to the Web for additional work.

- ExamView testing software gives you the option of generating a printed test, LAN-based test, or test over the Internet.

- New Perspectives Labs provide students with self-paced practice on computer-related topics.

- Students will appreciate the contemporary, realistic scenarios that place them in the context of a computer lab and a distance-learning course.

- The step-by-step instructions and screen illustrations guide students as they tour the Windows XP desktop, practice using the mouse, and explore Windows XP online Help.

- Students will gain confidence with Windows XP by working with files and folders in both My Computer and Windows Explorer, personalizing the Windows environment, bringing the Web to their desktops, searching for information, working with object linking and embedding, and using administrator tools.

- This text provides a comprehensive overview of working with Windows XP. It moves quickly and is suitable for both beginning students and experienced students, who can use it as a review.

CASE	TROUBLE?	SESSION 1.1	QUICK CHECK	RW
Tutorial Case Each tutorial begins with a problem presented in a case that is meaningful to students. The case sets the scene to help students understand what they will do in the tutorial.	**TROUBLE? Paragraphs** These paragraphs anticipate the mistakes or problems that students may have and help them continue with the tutorial.	**Sessions** Each tutorial is divided into sessions designed to be completed in about 45 minutes each. Students should take as much time as they need and take a break between sessions.	**Quick Check Questions** Each session concludes with conceptual Quick Check questions that test students' understanding of what they learned in the session.	**Reference Windows** Reference Windows are succinct summaries of the most important tasks covered in a tutorial. They preview actions students will perform in the steps to follow.

www.course.com/NewPerspectives

BRIEF CONTENTS

TABLE OF CONTENTS

Acknowledgments

Many thanks to everyone on the New Perspectives team for their guidance, insight, and good humor, including Rachel Crapser, Jessica Engstrom, and Kristen Guevara. Special thanks to Kathy Finnegan, whose common sense and dedication to the reader informs this book, and Kim Crowley, who approached each draft with freshness and improved the book with every edit. I also appreciate the careful work of Harris Bierhoff, Quality Assurance tester, and Risa Blair, Hilda Wirth Federico, and Eric Johnston, who reviewed these tutorials. Special thanks to June Parsons, Dan Oja, and Joan and Patrick Carey, on whose previous work this book is based.

—Lisa Ruffolo

www.course.com/NewPerspectives

New Perspectives on

MICROSOFT®

WINDOWS XP

Read This Before You Begin

To the Student

Data Disks

To complete the Level I tutorials, Review Assignments, and Projects, you need three Data Disks. Your instructor will either provide you with the Data Disks or ask you to make your own.

If you are making your own Data Disks, you will need **three** blank, formatted high-density disks. You will need to copy a set of files and/or folders from a file server, standalone computer, or the Web onto your disks. Your instructor will tell you which computer, drive letter, and folders contain the files you need. You could also download the files by going to **www.course.com** and following the instructions on the screen.

The information below shows you the Data Disks you need so that you will have enough disk space to complete all the tutorials, Review Assignments, and Projects:

Data Disk 1

Write this on the disk label:
Windows XP Tutorial 2 Data Disk

Data Disk 2

Write this on the disk label:
Windows XP Disk 1 Data Disk Copy

Data Disk 3

Write this on the disk label:
Windows XP Tutorial 2, Assignment 4

When you begin each tutorial, Review Assignment, or Project, be sure you are using the correct Data Disk. Refer to the "File Finder" chart at the back of this text for more detailed information on which files are used in which tutorials. See the inside front or inside back cover of this book for more information on Data Disk files, or ask your instructor or technical support person for assistance.

Course Labs

The Windows XP Level I tutorials feature three interactive Course Labs to help you understand how to use a keyboard and a mouse, and how to work with files. There are Lab Assignments at the end of Tutorial 1 and Tutorial 2 that relate to these Labs.

To start a Lab, click the **Start** button on the Windows taskbar, point to **Programs**, point to **Course Labs**, point to **New Perspectives Course Labs**, and then click the name of the Lab you want to use.

Using Your Own Computer

If you are going to work through this book using your own computer, you need:

- **Computer System** Microsoft Windows XP must be installed on your computer. This book assumes a typical installation of Microsoft Windows XP Professional.

- **Data Disks** You will not be able to complete the tutorials or exercises in this book using your own computer until you have your Data Disks.

- **Course Labs** See your instructor or technical support person to obtain the Course Lab software for use on your own computer.

Visit Our World Wide Web Site

Additional materials designed especially for you are available on the World Wide Web.
Go to **www.course.com/NewPerspectives**.

To the Instructor

The Data Disk Files and Course Labs are available on the Instructor's Resource Kit for this title. Follow the instructions in the Help file on the CD-ROM to install the programs to your network or standalone computer. For information on creating Data Disks or the Course Labs, see the "To the Student" section above.

You are granted a license to copy the Data Files and Course Labs to any computer or computer network used by students who have purchased this book.

OBJECTIVES

In this tutorial you will:

- Start and shut down Windows XP

- Identify the objects on the Windows XP desktop

- Practice mouse functions

- Run software programs, switch between them, and close them

- Identify and use the controls in a window

- Use Windows XP controls, such as menus, toolbars, list boxes, scroll bars, option buttons, tabs, and check boxes

- Explore Windows XP Help

EXPLORING THE BASICS

Investigating the Windows XP Operating System

Your First Day at the Computer

You walk into the computer lab and sit down at a desk. There are computers in front of you, and you find yourself staring dubiously at the screen. Where to start? As if in answer to your question, your friend Steve Laslow appears.

"You start with the operating system," says Steve. Noticing your puzzled look, Steve explains that the **operating system** is software that helps the computer carry out operating tasks, such as displaying information on the computer screen and saving data on disks. (Software refers to the **programs**, or **applications**, that a computer uses to perform tasks.) Your computer uses the **Microsoft Windows XP** operating system—**Windows XP** for short.

Steve explains that much of the software created for use with Windows XP shares the same look and works the same way. This similarity in design means that once you have learned to use one Windows program, such as Microsoft Word (a word-processing program), you are well on your way to understanding how to use other Windows programs. Windows XP allows you to use more than one program at a time, so you can easily switch between your word-processing program and your address book program, for example. Windows XP also makes it very easy to access the **Internet**, the worldwide collection of computers connected to one another to enable communication. All in all, Windows XP makes your computer an effective and easy-to-use productivity tool.

In this tutorial you will start Microsoft Windows XP and practice some basic computer skills.

LABS

Using a Keyboard

Using a Mouse

SESSION 1.1

In this session, you will learn some basic Windows terminology. You will use a pointing device, start and close a program, and switch between programs that are running at the same time.

Starting Windows XP

Using a Keyboard

Windows XP automatically starts when you turn on your computer. Depending on the way your computer is set up, you might be asked to enter your username and password.

To start Windows XP:

1. Turn on your computer. After a moment, Windows XP starts and displays the Windows XP Welcome screen.

TROUBLE? If you are asked to select an operating system, do not take action. Windows XP should start automatically after a designated number of seconds. If it does not, ask your instructor or technical support person for help.

TROUBLE? If this is the first time you have started your computer with Windows XP, messages might appear on your screen informing you that Windows is setting up components of your computer. Wait until the Welcome screen appears, and then continue with Step 2.

2. On the Welcome screen, click your user name. The Windows XP screen appears, as shown in Figure 1-1.

TROUBLE? If your user name does not appear on the Welcome screen, ask your instructor which name you should click.

TROUBLE? If prompted to do so, type your assigned user name, press the Tab key, type your password, and then click OK or press the Enter key to continue.

Figure 1-1	THE WINDOWS XP DESKTOP

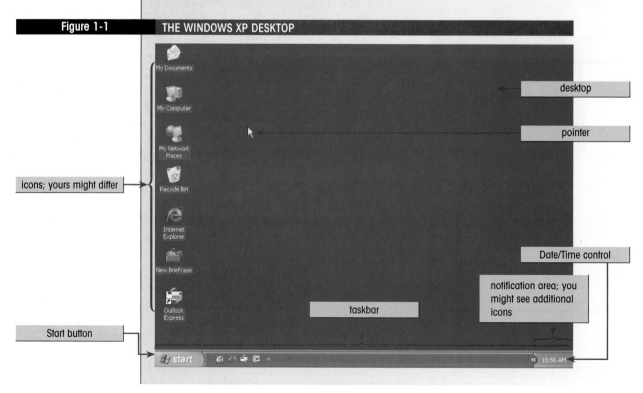

3. Look at your screen and locate the objects labeled in Figure 1-1. The objects on your screen might appear larger or smaller than those in Figure 1-1, depending on your monitor's settings. Figure 1-2 describes the function of each of these objects.

Figure 1-2	ELEMENTS OF THE WINDOWS XP DESKTOP

ELEMENT	DESCRIPTION
Icon	A small picture that represents an object available to your computer
Pointer	A small object, such as an arrow, that moves on the screen when you move the mouse
Desktop	Your workplace on the screen
Date/Time control	Shows the current date and time and lets you set the clock
Taskbar	Contains buttons that give you quick access to common tools and the programs currently running
Start button	Provides access to Windows XP programs, documents, and information on the Internet
Notification area	Displays icons corresponding to services running in the background, such as an Internet connection

TROUBLE? One default setting for your computer might be to use a screen saver, a program that causes the monitor to go blank or to display an animated design after a specified amount of idle time. If a blank screen or animated design replaces the Window XP desktop, you can press any key or move the mouse to restore the Windows XP desktop.

The Windows XP desktop uses a **graphical user interface** (**GUI**, pronounced "gooey"), which displays **icons**, or pictures of familiar objects, such as file folders and documents, to represent items stored on your computer, such as programs and files. Windows XP gets its name from the rectangular work areas, called "windows," that appear on your screen as you work. No windows should be open right now. You will learn more about windows in Session 1.2.

The Windows XP Desktop

In Windows terminology, the area that appears on your screen when Windows XP starts represents a **desktop**—a workspace for projects and the tools that you need to manipulate your projects. When you first start a computer, it uses **default settings**, those preset by the operating system. The default desktop you see after you first install Windows XP, for example, might have a plain blue background. However, Microsoft designed Windows XP so that you can easily change the appearance of the desktop. You can, for example, change color, or add patterns, images, and text to the desktop background.

Many organizations design customized desktops for their computers. Figure 1-1 shows the default Windows XP desktop. Figure 1-3 shows two other examples of desktops, one designed for a business, North Pole Novelties, and one designed for a school, the University of Colorado. Although your desktop might not look exactly like any of the examples in Figure 1-1 or Figure 1-3, you should be able to locate similar objects on your screen.

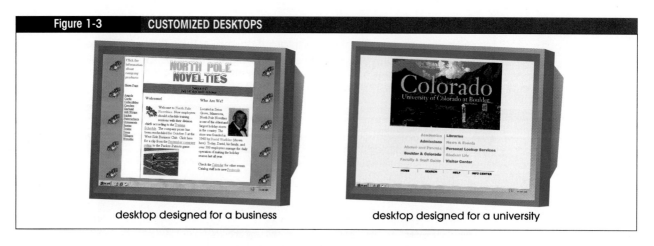

Figure 1-3	CUSTOMIZED DESKTOPS

desktop designed for a business   desktop designed for a university

Using a Pointing Device

Using a Mouse

A **pointing device** helps you interact with objects on your computer screen. Pointing devices come in many shapes and sizes; some are designed to ensure that your hand won't tire while using them. Some attach directly to your computer via a cable, whereas others function like a TV remote control and allow you to access your computer without being right next to it. Figure 1-4 shows examples of common pointing devices.

Figure 1-4	POINTING DEVICES	HOW TO HOLD A MOUSE

traditional two-button mouse

touch pad pointing devices have no moving parts; you slide your finger to move the pointer and tap to click

place your forefinger over the left mouse button and place your thumb on the left side of the mouse

your ring and small fingers should be on the right side of the mouse

traditional three-button mouse

trackball pointing devices feature a ball that you roll with your finger

mouse designed especially to prevent hand fatigue

trackballs and touchpads are often embedded into notebook computers

some mice include a "wheel" that you can use to move through documents more easily

use your arm, not your wrist, to move the mouse

The most common pointing device is called a **mouse**, so this book uses that term. If you are using a different pointing device, such as a trackball, substitute that device whenever you see the term *mouse*. Because Windows XP uses a GUI, you need to know how to use the mouse to manipulate the objects on the screen. In this session, you will learn about pointing and clicking. In Session 1.2, you will learn how to use the mouse to move objects.

You can also interact with objects by using the keyboard; however, the mouse is more convenient for most tasks, so the tutorials in this book assume that you are using one.

Pointing

You use a pointing device to move the mouse pointer over objects on the desktop. The pointer is usually shaped like an arrow ⬉, although the pointer will change shape depending on its location and on the tasks you are performing. Most computer users place the mouse on a **mouse pad**, a flat piece of rubber that helps the mouse move smoothly. As you move the mouse on the mouse pad, the pointer on the screen moves in a corresponding direction.

You begin most Windows operations by positioning the pointer over a specific part of the screen. This is called **pointing**.

To move the pointer:

1. Position your right index finger over the left mouse button, as shown in Figure 1-4, but don't click yet. Lightly grasp the sides of the mouse with your thumb and little finger.

   TROUBLE? If you want to use the mouse with your left hand, ask your instructor or technical support person to help you use the Control Panel to swap the functions of the left and right mouse buttons. Be sure to find out how to change back to the right-handed mouse setting, so that you can reset the mouse each time you are finished in the lab.

2. Place the mouse on the mouse pad, and then move the mouse. Watch the movement of the pointer.

   TROUBLE? If you run out of room to move your mouse, lift the mouse and place it in the middle of the mouse pad. Notice that the pointer does not move when the mouse is not in contact with the mouse pad or another surface.

When you position the mouse pointer over certain objects, such as the objects on the taskbar, tips appear. These tips are called **ScreenTips**, and tell you the purpose or function of the object to which you are pointing.

To view ScreenTips:

1. Use the mouse to point to the **Start** button on the taskbar. After a few seconds, you see the ScreenTip "Click here to begin," as shown in Figure 1-5.

Figure 1-5	VIEWING SCREENTIPS

ScreenTip

pointer

2. Point to the time displayed in the notification area at the right end of the taskbar. Notice that a ScreenTip for today's date (or the date to which your computer's time clock is set) appears.

Clicking

Clicking refers to pressing a mouse button and immediately releasing it. Clicking sends a signal to your computer that you want to perform an action on the object you click. In Windows XP you perform most actions with the left mouse button. If you are told to click an object, position the mouse pointer on it and click the left mouse button, unless instructed otherwise.

When you click the Start button, the Start menu opens. A **menu** is a list of options that you can use to complete tasks. The **Start menu** provides you with access to programs, documents, and much more. Try clicking the Start button to open the Start menu.

To open the Start menu:

1. Point to the **Start** button ![start] on the taskbar.

2. Click the left mouse button. The Start menu opens. Notice the arrow ▷ following the All Programs option on the Start menu. This arrow indicates that you can view additional choices by navigating to a **submenu**, a menu extending from the main menu. See Figure 1-6.

Figure 1-6	START MENU

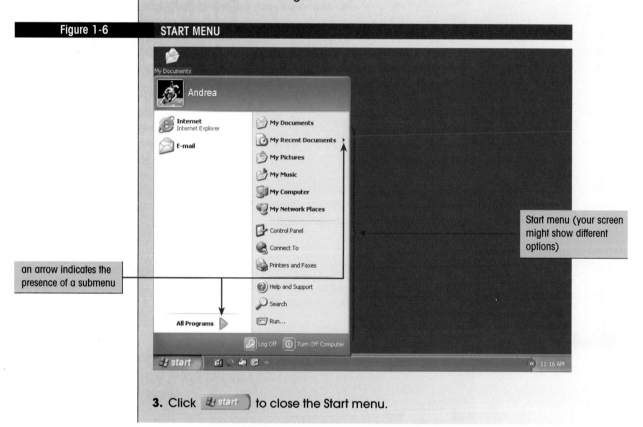

an arrow indicates the presence of a submenu

Start menu (your screen might show different options)

3. Click ![start] to close the Start menu.

Next you'll learn how to select items on a submenu.

Selecting

In Windows XP, you point to and then click an object to **select** it. You need to select an object to work with it. Windows XP shows you which object is selected by highlighting it, usually by changing the object's color, putting a box around it, or making the object appear to be pushed in, as shown in Figure 1-7.

Figure 1-7	SELECTED OBJECTS

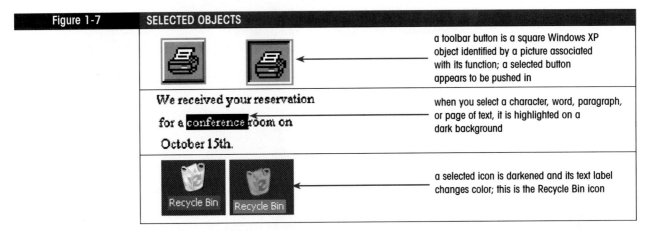

a toolbar button is a square Windows XP object identified by a picture associated with its function; a selected button appears to be pushed in

We received your reservation for a conference room on October 15th.

when you select a character, word, paragraph, or page of text, it is highlighted on a dark background

a selected icon is darkened and its text label changes color; this is the Recycle Bin icon

In Windows XP, depending on your computer's settings, you can select certain objects by pointing to them and others by clicking them. Try pointing to the All Programs option on the Start menu to open the All Programs submenu.

To select an option on a menu:

1. Click the **Start** button *start* on the taskbar, and notice how it appears to be pushed in, indicating that it is selected.

2. Point to (but don't click) **All Programs** on the Start menu. When you first point to the All Programs option, it is highlighted to indicate it is selected. After a short pause, the All Programs submenu opens. See Figure 1-8.

   TROUBLE? If a submenu other than the All Programs menu opens, you pointed to the wrong option. Move the mouse so that the pointer points to All Programs.

Figure 1-8   **ALL PROGRAMS SUBMENU**

All Programs submenu
(your options
might differ)

these options display
additonal submenus

point to an option to
open its submenu

3. Click **start** to close the Start menu. You return to the desktop.

Double-Clicking

In addition to clicking an object to select it, you can double-click an object to open or start the item associated to it. For example, you can double-click a folder icon to open the folder and see its contents. Or you can double-click a program icon to start the program. Double-clicking means to click the mouse button twice in quick succession.

You can practice double-clicking now by opening the My Documents folder. **My Documents** is your personal folder, a convenient place to store documents, graphics, and other work.

To open the My Documents folder:

1. Click and then point to the **My Documents** icon on the desktop. After a few moments, a ScreenTip appears describing the My Documents folder.

TROUBLE? If you don't see the icons for My Computer or My Documents, you can add them to the desktop. Click Start, click Control Panel, click Switch to Category New, if necessary, click Appearance and Themes, and then click Change the desktop background. In the Desktop Items dialog box, click to insert checks in the boxes for My Computer and My Documents to add these icons to the desktop. You can also add icons for My Network Places and Internet Explorer. Click OK to close each dialog box.

2. Click the left mouse button twice quickly to double-click the **My Documents** icon. The My Documents window opens, as shown in Figure 1-9.

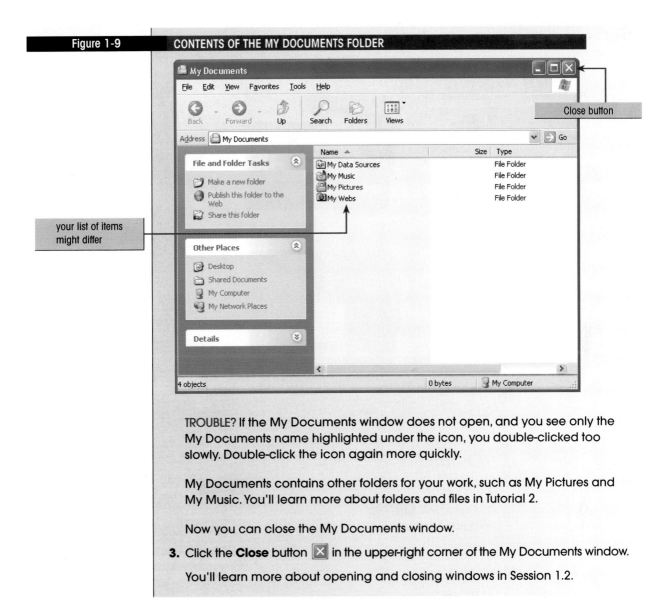

Figure 1-9 | **CONTENTS OF THE MY DOCUMENTS FOLDER**

TROUBLE? If the My Documents window does not open, and you see only the My Documents name highlighted under the icon, you double-clicked too slowly. Double-click the icon again more quickly.

My Documents contains other folders for your work, such as My Pictures and My Music. You'll learn more about folders and files in Tutorial 2.

Now you can close the My Documents window.

3. Click the **Close** button ☒ in the upper-right corner of the My Documents window.

You'll learn more about opening and closing windows in Session 1.2.

Right-Clicking

Pointing devices were originally designed with a single button, so the term "clicking" had only one meaning: you pressed that button. Innovations in technology, however, led to the addition of a second and even a third button (and more recently, options such as a wheel) that expanded the pointing device's capabilities. More recent programs—especially those designed for Windows XP—take advantage of additional buttons, especially the right button. However, the term "clicking" continues to refer to the left button; clicking an object with the *right* button is called **right-clicking**.

In Windows XP, right-clicking both selects an object and opens its **shortcut menu**, which is a list of options directly related to the object that you right-clicked. You can right-click practically any object—the Start button, a desktop icon, the taskbar, and even the desktop itself—to view options associated with that object. For example, the illustration in the top portion of Figure 1-10 shows what happens when you click the Start button with the left mouse button to open the Start menu. Clicking the Start button with the right button, however, opens the Start button's shortcut menu, as shown in the second illustration.

Figure 1-10	CLICKING WITH THE LEFT AND RIGHT MOUSE BUTTONS

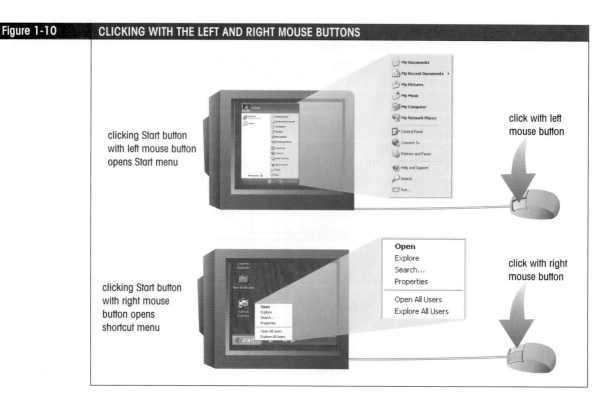

Try right-clicking to open the shortcut menu for the Start button.

To right-click an object:

1. Position the pointer over the Start button on the taskbar.

2. Right-click to open the Start button's shortcut menu. This menu offers a list of options available to the Start menu.

   TROUBLE? If you are using a trackball or a mouse with three buttons or a wheel, make sure you click the button on the far right, not the one in the middle.

   TROUBLE? Your menu may look slightly different from the one in Figure 1-11. Different computers often have different options and commands.

Figure 1-11	START BUTTON SHORTCUT MENU

shortcut menu

click the Start button with the right mouse button

these options appear if you work on a network or on a multiuser computer

3. Press the **Esc** key to close the shortcut menu. You again return to the desktop.

Starting and Closing a Program

To use a program, such as a word-processing program, you must first start it. With Windows XP you start a program by clicking the Start button and then locating and clicking the program's name in the submenus.

The Reference Window below explains how to start a program. Don't do the steps in the Reference Window now; they are for your reference later.

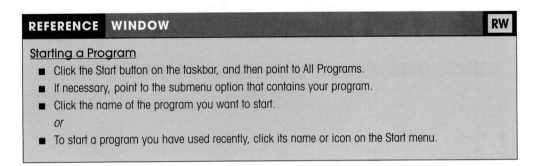

REFERENCE WINDOW RW

Starting a Program
- Click the Start button on the taskbar, and then point to All Programs.
- If necessary, point to the submenu option that contains your program.
- Click the name of the program you want to start.
  or
- To start a program you have used recently, click its name or icon on the Start menu.

Windows XP includes an easy-to-use word-processing program called WordPad. Suppose you want to start the WordPad program and use it to write a letter or report. You open Windows XP programs from the Start menu. Programs are usually located on the All Programs submenu or on one of its submenus. To start WordPad, for example, you navigate to the All Programs and Accessories submenus.

To start the WordPad program from the Start menu:

1. Click the **Start** button [*start*] on the taskbar to open the Start menu.

2. Point to **All Programs** to display the All Programs submenu.

3. Point to **Accessories**. Another submenu opens. Figure 1-12 shows the open menus.

| Figure 1-12 | START MENU AND RELATED SUBMENUS |

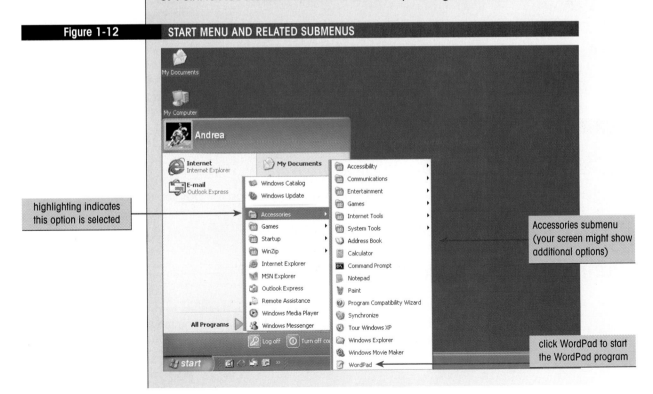

highlighting indicates this option is selected

Accessories submenu (your screen might show additional options)

click WordPad to start the WordPad program

TROUBLE? If a different menu opens, you might have moved the mouse too slowly so that a different submenu opened. Move the pointer back to the All Programs option, and then move the pointer up or down to point to Accessories. Once you're more comfortable moving the mouse, you'll find that you can eliminate this problem by moving the mouse quickly.

4. Click **WordPad** on the Accessories submenu. The WordPad program window opens, as shown in Figure 1-13. Depending on your computer settings, the WordPad program window may fill the entire screen. You will learn how to manipulate windows in Session 1.2.

Figure 1-13	THE WORDPAD PROGRAM WINDOW

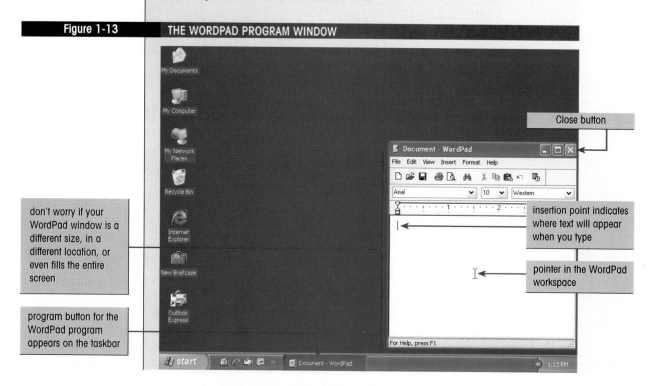

don't worry if your WordPad window is a different size, in a different location, or even fills the entire screen

program button for the WordPad program appears on the taskbar

Close button

insertion point indicates where text will appear when you type

pointer in the WordPad workspace

When you start a program, it is said to be **open** or **running**. A **program button** appears on the taskbar for each open program. You click a program button to switch between open programs. When you finish using a program, you can click the Close button located in the upper-right corner of the program window.

To exit the WordPad program:

1. Click the **Close** button ⊠ on the WordPad title bar. You return to the Windows XP desktop.

Running **Multiple Programs**

One of the most useful features of Windows XP is its ability to run multiple programs at the same time. This feature, known as **multitasking**, allows you to work on more than one project at a time and switch quickly between projects. For example, you can start WordPad and leave it running while you then start the Paint program.

To run WordPad and Paint at the same time:

1. Start WordPad again and then click the **Start** button start .

2. Point to **All Programs** and then point to **Accessories**.

3. Click **Paint**. The Paint program window opens, as shown in Figure 1-14. Now two programs are running at the same time.

Figure 1-14	THE PAINT PROGRAM

the mouse pointer is a pencil when positioned in the drawing area

WordPad window might appear behind the Paint window

WordPad program button is not pressed in, indicating that WordPad is running but is not the active program

Paint program button is pressed in, indicating that Paint is the active program

TROUBLE? The Paint program may fill the entire screen. You will learn how to manipulate windows in Session 1.2.

What happened to WordPad? The WordPad program button is still on the taskbar, indicating that WordPad is still running even if you cannot see its program window. Try to imagine that the WordPad program window is stacked behind the Paint program window, as illustrated in Figure 1-15. Paint is the active program because it is the one with which you are currently working.

Figure 1-15	PROJECTS STACKED ON A DESK

screen is main work area of your desk

another project, such as a letter you're writing, might be hidden under the drawing you are working on

project you are currently working on, a drawing, is on top

Switching Between Programs

The easiest way to switch between programs is to use the program buttons on the taskbar.

To switch between WordPad and Paint:

1. Click the program button labeled **Document - WordPad** on the taskbar. The WordPad program window moves to the front, and now the Document - WordPad button looks as if it has been pushed in, indicating that it is the active program.

2. Click the program button labeled **untitled - Paint** on the taskbar to switch to the Paint program. The Paint program is again the active program.

Using the Quick Launch Toolbar

The Windows XP taskbar displays buttons for programs currently running. The taskbar also can contain **toolbars**, sets of buttons that give single-click access to programs or documents that aren't running or open. For example, the Windows XP taskbar can display the **Quick Launch toolbar**, which gives quick access to Internet programs and to the desktop. Your taskbar might contain additional toolbars or none at all.

When you are running more than one program but you want to return to the desktop, perhaps to use one of the desktop icons, such as My Computer, you can do so by using one of the Quick Launch toolbar buttons. Clicking the Show Desktop button returns you to the desktop. The open programs are not closed; they are simply inactive and reduced to buttons on the taskbar.

To return to the desktop:

1. Click the **Show Desktop** button ⊞ on the Quick Launch toolbar. The desktop displays, and both the Paint and WordPad programs are temporarily inactive. See Figure 1-16.

   TROUBLE? If the Quick Launch toolbar is not visible on your taskbar, right-click the taskbar, point to Toolbars, and then click Quick Launch. Then try Step 1 again.

| Figure 1-16 | ACCESSING THE DESKTOP |

Quick Launch toolbar (yours might show more or fewer buttons)

Show Desktop button

neither of these buttons appears pressed in, indicating that both programs are inactive

your taskbar might show additional toolbars

Closing Inactive Programs from the Taskbar

You should always close a program when you finish using it. Each program uses computer resources, such as memory, so Windows XP works more efficiently when only the programs you need are open. You've already seen how to close an open program using the Close button on the title bar of the program window. You can also close a program, whether active or inactive, by using the shortcut menu associated with the program button on the taskbar.

To close WordPad and Paint using the program button shortcut menus:

1. Right-click the **untitled – Paint** button on the taskbar. Remember that to right-click something, you click it with the right mouse button. The shortcut menu for the Paint program button opens. See Figure 1-17.

Figure 1-17	PROGRAM BUTTON SHORTCUT MENU

shortcut menu opens when you right-click a program button

click to close the inactive program

2. Click **Close** on the shortcut menu. (Recall that "click" means to use the left mouse button.) The Paint program closes and the program button labeled "untitled – Paint" disappears from the taskbar.

3. Right-click the **Document – WordPad** button on the taskbar, and then click **Close** on the shortcut menu. The WordPad program closes and its program button no longer appears on the taskbar.

Shutting Down Windows XP

You should always shut down Windows XP before you turn off your computer. If you turn off your computer without shutting it down correctly, you might lose data and damage your files.

Typically you will use the Turn Off Computer option on the Start menu when you want to turn off your computer. However, your school might prefer that you select the Log Off option on the Start menu. This option logs you off of Windows XP but leaves the computer on, allowing another user to log on without restarting the computer. Check with your instructor or technical support person for the preferred method at your lab.

To shut down Windows XP:

1. Click the **Start** button (start) on the taskbar.

2. Click **Turn Off Computer**, located at the bottom of the menu. The Turn Off Computer dialog box opens. See Figure 1-18.

TROUBLE? If you are supposed to log off rather than shut down, click Log Off instead and follow your school's logoff procedure.

Figure 1-18 **SHUTTING DOWN THE COMPUTER**

3. Click the **Turn Off** button.

4. Wait until you see a message indicating that it is safe to turn off your computer. If your lab procedure includes switching off your computer after shutting it down, do so now; otherwise leave the computer running. Some computers turn themselves off automatically.

In this session, you have started Windows XP, become familiar with the desktop, and learned how to use the mouse to select menu items. In the next session, you will learn how to work with windows.

Session 1.1 QUICK CHECK

1. What is the purpose of the taskbar?

2. The _____ feature of Windows XP allows you to run more than one program at a time.

3. The _____ is a list of options that provides you with access to programs, documents, submenus, and more.

4. What should you do if you are trying to move the pointer to the left edge of your screen, but your mouse bumps into the keyboard?

5. Even if you cannot see an open program on your desktop, the program might be running. How can you tell if a program is running?

6. Why should you close each program when you finish using it?

7. Why should you shut down Windows XP before you turn off your computer?

SESSION 1.2

In this session you will manipulate windows using controls that are available in Windows XP. You will move a window, and you will also change the size and shape of a window. You will use program menus, toolbars, and controls, such as list boxes and scroll bars, available in windows and dialog boxes. Also in this session, you will use Windows XP Help to gain access to program-related information and tasks.

Anatomy of a Window

Recall from Session 1.1 that when you run a program in Windows XP, the program appears in a window. A **window** is a rectangular area of the screen that contains a program, text, graphics, or data. "Windows," spelled with an uppercase "W," is the name of the Microsoft operating system. The word "window" with a lowercase "w" refers to one of the rectangular areas on the screen. A window also contains **controls**, which are graphical or textual objects used for manipulating the window and for using the program. Figure 1-19 describes the controls you are likely to see in most windows.

Figure 1-19	WINDOW CONTROLS
CONTROL	**DESCRIPTION**
Menu bar	Contains the titles of menus, such as File, Edit, and Help
Sizing buttons	Let you enlarge, shrink, or close a window
Status bar	Provides you with messages relevant to the task you are performing
Title bar	Contains the window title and basic window control buttons
Toolbar	Contains buttons that provide you with shortcuts to common menu commands
Window title	Identifies the program and document contained in the window
Workspace	Part of the window you use to enter your work—to enter text, draw pictures, set up calculations, and so on

The WordPad program is a good example of a typical window. Start WordPad and identify its window controls.

To look at the window controls in WordPad:

1. Make sure that Windows XP is running and the Windows XP desktop is displayed.

2. Start WordPad.

   TROUBLE? To start WordPad, click the Start button, point to All Programs, point to Accessories, and then click WordPad.

3. On your screen, identify the controls that are labeled in Figure 1-20. Your WordPad program window may fill the entire screen or differ in size. You'll learn to change window size shortly.

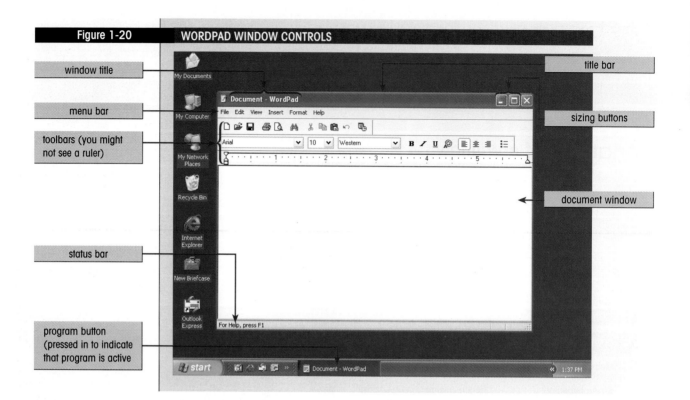

Figure 1-20   WORDPAD WINDOW CONTROLS

window title

menu bar

toolbars (you might not see a ruler)

status bar

program button (pressed in to indicate that program is active

title bar

sizing buttons

document window

Manipulating a Window

On the right side of the title bar are three buttons. You are already familiar with the Close button. The Minimize button, the first of the three buttons, hides a window so that only its program button is visible on the taskbar. The other button changes name and function depending on the status of the window. (It either maximizes the window or restores it to a predefined size.) Figure 1-21 shows how these buttons work.

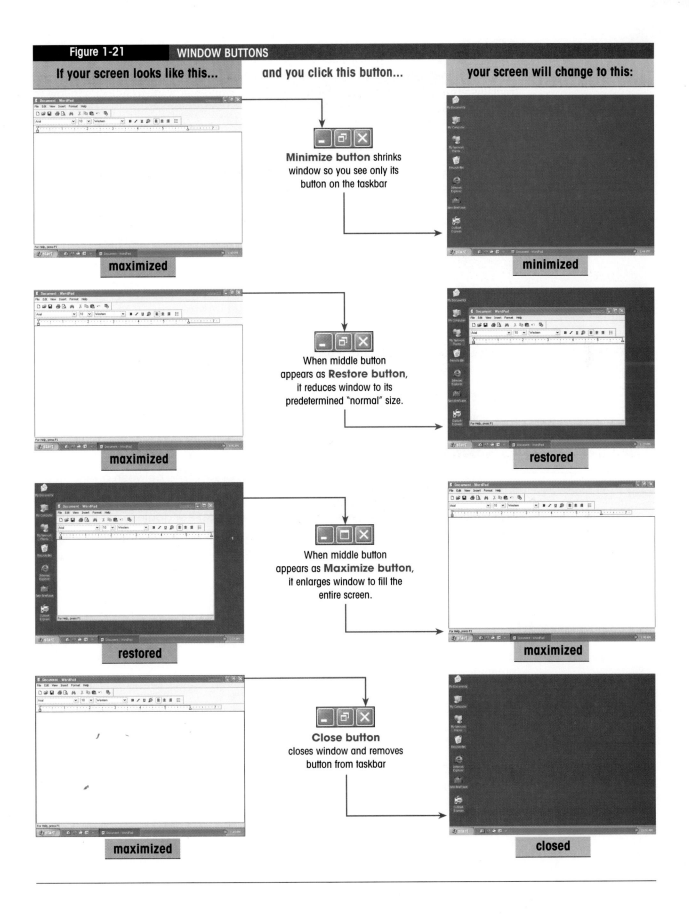

Figure 1-21   WINDOW BUTTONS

If your screen looks like this...   and you click this button...   your screen will change to this:

Minimize button shrinks window so you see only its button on the taskbar

maximized   minimized

When middle button appears as **Restore button**, it reduces window to its predetermined "normal" size.

maximized   restored

When middle button appears as **Maximize button**, it enlarges window to fill the entire screen.

restored   maximized

Close button closes window and removes button from taskbar

maximized   closed

Minimizing a Window

The Minimize button hides a window so that only the program button on the taskbar remains visible. You can use the Minimize button when you want to hide a window temporarily but keep the program running.

To minimize the WordPad window:

1. Click the **Minimize** button [ ] on the WordPad title bar. The WordPad window reduces so that only the Document - WordPad button on the taskbar is visible.

   TROUBLE? If you accidentally clicked the Close button and closed the WordPad program window, use the Start button to start WordPad again, and then repeat Step 1.

Redisplaying a Window

You can redisplay a minimized window by clicking the program's button on the taskbar. When you redisplay a window, it becomes the active window.

To redisplay the WordPad window:

1. Click the **Document - WordPad** button on the taskbar. The WordPad window is restored to its previous size. The Document - WordPad button looks pushed in— a visual clue that WordPad is now the active window.

   The taskbar button provides another means of switching between a window's minimized and active states.

2. Click the **Document – WordPad** button on the taskbar again to minimize the window.

3. Click the **Document – WordPad** button once more to redisplay the window.

Maximizing a Window

The Maximize button enlarges a window so that it fills the entire screen. You will probably do most of your work using maximized windows because they allow you to see more of your program and data.

To maximize the WordPad window:

1. Click the **Maximize** button [ ] on the WordPad title bar.

   TROUBLE? If the window is already maximized, it will fill the entire screen, and the Maximize button won't appear. Instead, you'll see the Restore button [ ]. Skip Step 1.

Restoring a Window

The Restore button reduces the window so that it is smaller than the entire screen. This feature is useful if you want to see more than one window at a time. Also, because the window is smaller, you can move the window to another location on the screen or change the dimensions of the window.

To restore a window:

1. Click the **Restore** button 🗗 on the WordPad title bar. Notice that once a window is restored, 🗗 changes to the Maximize button 🗖.

Moving a Window

You can use the mouse to move a window to a new position on the screen. When you click an object and then press and hold down the mouse button while moving the mouse, you are **dragging** the object. You can move an object on the screen by dragging it to a new location. If you want to move a window, you drag the window by its title bar. You cannot move a maximized window.

To drag the WordPad window to a new location:

1. Position the mouse pointer on the WordPad title bar.

2. Press and hold down the left mouse button, and then move the mouse up or down a little to drag the window. The window moves as you move the mouse.

3. Position the window anywhere on the desktop, and then release the left mouse button. The WordPad window appears in the new location.

4. Drag the WordPad window to the upper-left corner of the desktop.

Changing the Size of a Window

You can also use the mouse to change the size of a window. Notice the sizing handle 🔲 at the lower-right corner of the window. The **sizing handle** provides a visible control for changing the size of a window.

To change the size of the WordPad window:

1. Position the pointer over the sizing handle 🔲. The pointer changes to ↘. See Figure 1-22.

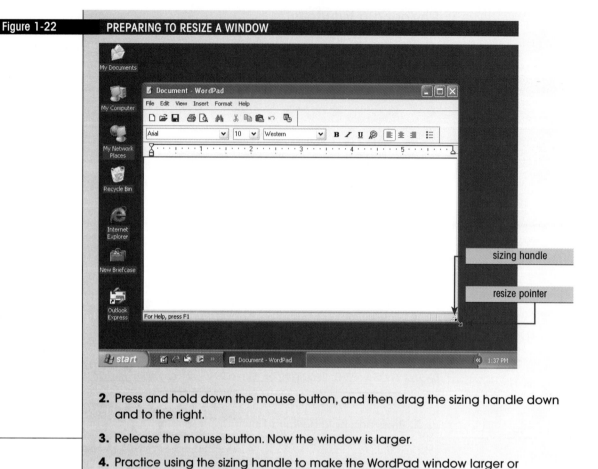

Figure 1-22   PREPARING TO RESIZE A WINDOW

2. Press and hold down the mouse button, and then drag the sizing handle down and to the right.

3. Release the mouse button. Now the window is larger.

4. Practice using the sizing handle to make the WordPad window larger or smaller, and then maximize the WordPad window.

You can also drag the window borders left, right, up, or down to change a window's size.

Using **Program Menus**

Most Windows programs use menus to organize the program's features and available functions. The menu bar is typically located at the top of the program window and shows the names of the menus, such as File, Edit, and Help. Windows XP menus are relatively standard—most programs designed for Windows include similar menus. Learning new programs is easy because you can make a pretty good guess about which menu contains the task you want to perform.

Selecting Options from a Menu

When you click any menu name, the choices for that menu appear below the menu bar. These choices are referred to as **menu items** or **commands**. To select a menu item, you click it. For example, the File menu, a standard menu in most Windows programs, contains the items and commands typically related to working with a file: creating, opening, saving, and printing.

To select the Page Setup menu command from the File menu:

1. Click **File** on the WordPad menu bar to open the File menu. See Figure 1-23.

Figure 1-23	FILE MENU

your menu may show additional options

Page Setup command

TROUBLE? If you open a menu and then decide not to select any of its commands, you can close the menu by clicking its name again.

2. Click **Page Setup** to open the Page Setup dialog box. A **dialog box** is a special kind of window where you enter or choose settings for how you want to perform a task. You use the Page Setup dialog box to set margins and some printing options.

TROUBLE? If a printer has not been installed for your computer, a message appears indicating that you must install a printer. (Click the Yes button, and then ask your instructor or technical support person for help with installing a printer.)

3. After examining the dialog box, click the **OK** button to close the Page Setup dialog box.

TROUBLE? If you close WordPad by mistake, restart it.

Not all menu items and commands immediately carry out an action—some show submenus or ask you for more information about what you want to do. The menu gives you visual hints about what to expect when you select an item. These hints are sometimes referred to as **menu conventions**. Figure 1-24 shows examples of these menu conventions.

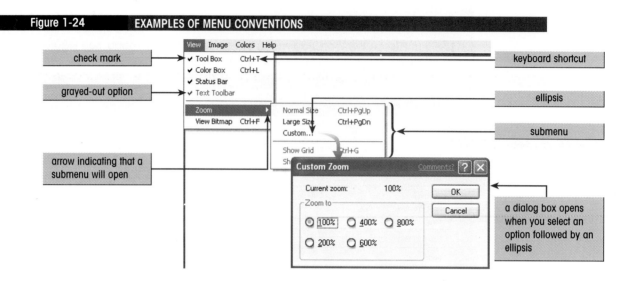

Figure 1-24	EXAMPLES OF MENU CONVENTIONS

Figure 1-25 describes the Windows XP menu conventions.

Figure 1-25	MENU CONVENTIONS
CONVENTION	**DESCRIPTION**
Check mark	Indicates a toggle, or "on-off" switch (like a light switch) that is either checked (turned on) or not checked (turned off).
Ellipsis	Three dots that indicate you must make additional selections after you select that option. Options without dots do not require additional choices—they take effect as soon as you click them. If an option is followed by an ellipsis, a dialog box opens that allows you to enter specifications for how you want a task carried out.
Triangular arrow	Indicates the presence of a submenu. When you point at a menu option that has a triangular arrow, a submenu automatically appears.
Grayed-out option	Option that is not currently available. For example, a graphics program might display the Text Toolbar option in gray if there is no text in the graphic to work with.
Keyboard shortcut	A key or combination of keys that you can press to select the menu option without actually opening the menu.

Using Toolbars

Although you can usually perform all program commands by using menus, you also have one-click access to frequently used commands on the toolbars in the program window. You can quickly access common commands using the buttons on the toolbars. As task-related menu items and commands provided on menus, the buttons on a toolbar are also grouped and organized by tasks.

In Session 1.1 you learned that Windows XP programs often display ScreenTips, which indicate the purpose and function of a window component, for example, a button. Explore the WordPad toolbar buttons by looking at their ScreenTips.

To determine the names and descriptions of the buttons on the WordPad toolbar:

1. Position the pointer over any button on the toolbar, for example, the Print Preview button . After a short pause, the ScreenTip for the button appears below the button, and a description of the button appears in the status bar just above the Start button. See Figure 1-26.

| Figure 1-26 | TOOLBAR BUTTON AIDS |

toolbar button ScreenTip

toolbar button description also appears in status bar

2. Move the pointer to each button on the toolbar to display its name and purpose.

To perform a command, you select the toolbar button by clicking it. When you pointed to each button on the WordPad toolbar, you found one called the Undo button. Clicking the Undo button reverses the effects of your last action.

To use the Undo button on the toolbar:

1. Type your name in the WordPad window.

2. Click the **Undo** button on the toolbar. WordPad reverses your last action by removing your name from the WordPad window.

Using List Boxes and Scroll Bars

As you might guess from its name, a **list box** displays a list of available choices from which you can select. In WordPad, you can choose a date and time format from the Available formats list box in the Date/Time dialog box. List box controls usually include arrow buttons, a scroll bar, and a scroll box.

To use a list box in the Date/Time dialog box:

1. Click the **Date/Time** button on the toolbar to open the Date and Time dialog box. See Figure 1-27.

Figure 1-27   **DATE AND TIME DIALOG BOX**

list box shows the available date formats

click the scroll up arrow to move toward the top of the list

a scroll bar appears when the list of available options is too long to fit in the list box

drag the scroll box up or down to view different parts of the list

click the scroll down arrow to move toward the bottom of the list

2. To scroll down the list, click the **scroll down arrow** button until you see the bottom of the list.

3. Drag the **scroll box** to the top of the scroll bar. Notice how the list scrolls back to the beginning.

TROUBLE? To drag the scroll box up, point to the scroll box, press and hold down the mouse button, and then move the mouse up.

4. Find a date format similar to "July 14, 2004" in the Available formats list box, and then click that date format to select it.

5. Click the **OK** button to close the Date and Time dialog box. The current date is inserted in your document.

A list box is helpful because it includes only options that are appropriate for your current task. For example, you can select only dates and times in the available formats from the list box in the Date and Time dialog box—no matter which format you choose, WordPad will recognize it. Sometimes, however, a list might not include every possible option, so it lets you type the option you want to select. In this case, the list box includes a **list arrow** on its right side. You can click the list arrow to view options and then select one, or you can type appropriate text.

Buttons can also have list arrows. The list arrow indicates that there is more than one option for that button. Rather than crowding the window with lots of buttons, one for each possible option, including a list arrow on a button organizes its options logically and compactly. Toolbars often include list boxes and buttons with list arrows. For example, the Font Size list box on the WordPad toolbar includes a list arrow. To select an option other than the one shown in the list box or on the button, you click the list arrow and then click the option that you want to use.

To select a new font size from the Font Size list box:

1. Click the **list arrow** for the Font Size list box 10 ⌄ on the toolbar. See Figure 1-28.

Figure 1-28	FONT SIZE LIST ARROW

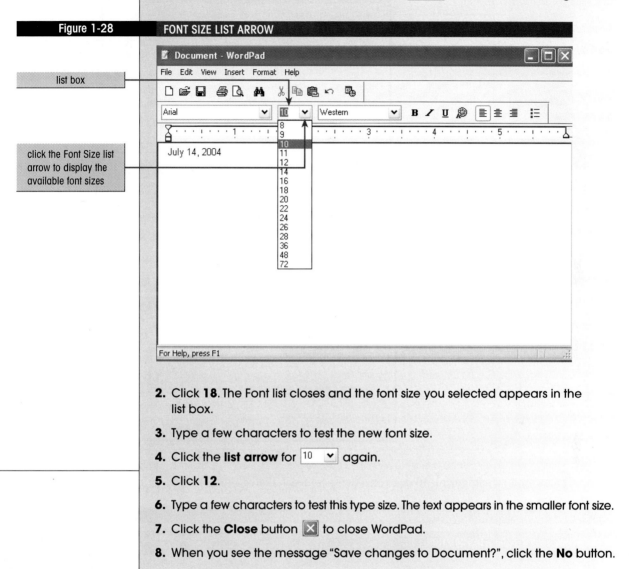

list box

click the Font Size list
arrow to display the
available font sizes

2. Click **18**. The Font list closes and the font size you selected appears in the list box.

3. Type a few characters to test the new font size.

4. Click the **list arrow** for 10 ⌄ again.

5. Click **12**.

6. Type a few characters to test this type size. The text appears in the smaller font size.

7. Click the **Close** button ☒ to close WordPad.

8. When you see the message "Save changes to Document?", click the **No** button.

Using **Dialog Box Controls**

Recall that when you select a menu command or item followed by an ellipsis, a dialog box opens that allows you to provide more information about how a program should carry out a task. Some dialog boxes group different kinds of information into bordered rectangular areas called **panes**. Within these panes, you will usually find tabs, option buttons, check boxes, and other controls that the program uses to collect information about how you want it to perform a task. Figure 1-29 displays examples of common dialog box controls.

Figure 1-29	EXAMPLES OF DIALOG BOX CONTROL

click a tab to view a group of controls whose functions are related

option buttons appear in groups; you click one option button in a group, and a black dot indicates your selection

click in the text box, and then type an entry

pane

click a check box to turn an option off (not checked) or on (checked)

click the up or down spin arrow to increase or decrease the number in the spin box

Options

Options | Text | Rich Text | Word | Write | Embedded

Word wrap
- ○ No wrap
- ○ Wrap to window
- ● Wrap to ruler

Toolbars
- ☑ Toolbar
- ☑ Format bar
- ☑ Ruler
- ☑ Status bar

OK   Cancel

Print

General

Select Printer

Add Printer   HP LaserJet 4   HP LaserJet 4/4M PostScript

Status: Ready
Location:
Comment:

☐ Print to file   Preferences
Find Printer...

Page Range
- ● All
- ○ Selection ○ Current Page
- ○ Pages: 1-65535

Enter either a single page number or a single page range. For example, 5-12

Number of copies: 1 ▲▼

☑ Collate

Print   Cancel   Apply

Figure 1-30 describes these common dialog box controls.

Figure 1-30	DESCRIPTION OF DIALOG BOX CONTROLS

CONTROL	DESCRIPTION
Tabs	Modeled after the tabs on file folders, tab controls are often used as containers for other Windows XP controls such as list boxes, option buttons, and check boxes. Click the appropriate tabs to view different pages of information or choices.
Option buttons	Also called radio buttons, option buttons allow you to select a single option from among one or more options.
Check boxes	Click a check box to select or deselect it; when it is selected, a check mark appears, indicating that the option is turned on; when deselected, the check box is blank and the option is off. When check boxes appear in groups, you can select or deselect as many as you want; they are not mutually exclusive, as option buttons are.
Spin boxes	Allow you to scroll easily through a set of numbers to choose the setting you want
Text boxes	Boxes into which you type additional information

Using Help

Windows XP **Help** provides on-screen information about the program you are using. Help for the Windows XP operating system is available by clicking the Start button on the taskbar, and then selecting Help and Support from the Start menu. If you want Help for a particular program, such as WordPad, you must first start the program and then click Help on the program's menu bar.

When you start Help for Windows XP, a Windows Help and Support Center window opens, giving you access to Help files stored on your computer as well as Help information stored on Microsoft's Web site. If you are not connected to the Web, you only have access to the Help files stored on your computer.

To start Windows XP Help:

1. Click the **Start** button **start** on the taskbar.

2. Click **Help and Support**. The Help and Support Center window opens. See Figure 1-31.

   TROUBLE? If the Help and Support window does not display the information you see in Figure 1-31, click the Home icon on the navigation bar to view Help contents. The navigation bar is located at the top of the window.

| Figure 1-31 | WINDOWS XP HELP AND SUPPORT CENTER WINDOW |

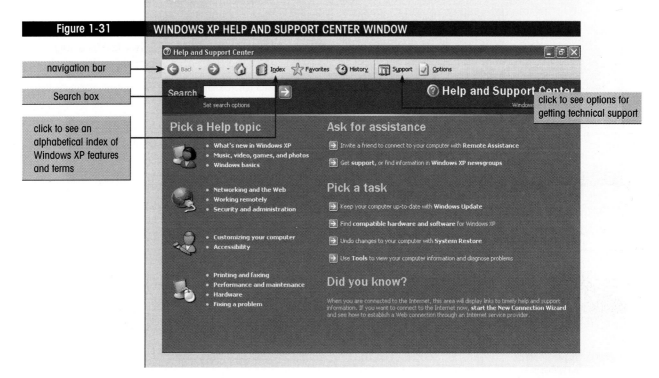

The Windows XP Help and Support window organizes the vast amount of help and support information into **pages**. These six pages of information—the Home, Index, Favorites, History, Support, and Options pages—are designed to aid users in locating help on a particular topic quickly. To open one of these pages, click its icon on the navigation bar. The **Home page** lists common tasks under the heading "Pick a Help topic" in the left pane on the page. Click a task to see detailed information or instructions about that task in the right pane of the page. The right pane of the Home page lists common tasks, tips, and ways you can ask for assistance. For example, you can contact a support professional or download the latest version of Windows XP. The **Index** page displays an alphabetical list of all the Help topics from which you can choose. The **Favorites** page shows Help topics you've added to your Favorites list. To add a topic to the Favorites list, open the topic, and then click the

Favorites button on the Help window. The **History** page lists links you've recently selected in Help. The **Support** page includes links that you can click to connect to the Microsoft Web site, if possible, for additional assistance. The **Options** page provides ways you can customize Help. For example, you can change the appearance of the navigation bar.

If you cannot find the topic you want listed on any of the six Help and Support Services pages, the word that you are using for a feature or topic might differ from the word that Windows XP uses. You can use the **Search box** to search for all keywords contained in the Help pages, not just the topic titles. In the Search box, you can type any word or phrase, click the Start Searching button, and Windows XP lists all the Help topics that contain that word or phrase.

Viewing Topics on the Windows XP Help and Support Center Home Page

Windows XP Help includes instructions on using Help itself. You can learn how to find a Help topic by using the Help and Support Center Home page.

To use the Help and Support Center Home page:

1. On the Home page, click **Windows basics**. A list of topics related to using Windows XP appears in the left pane of the Help and Support Center window.

2. Click **Tips for using Help**. A list of Help topics appears in the right pane of the Help window.

3. Click **Change fonts in Help and Support Center**. The instructions appear in the right pane of the Help and Support Center window, as shown in Figure 1-32.

| Figure 1-32 | FINDING A HELP TOPIC ON THE HOME PAGE |

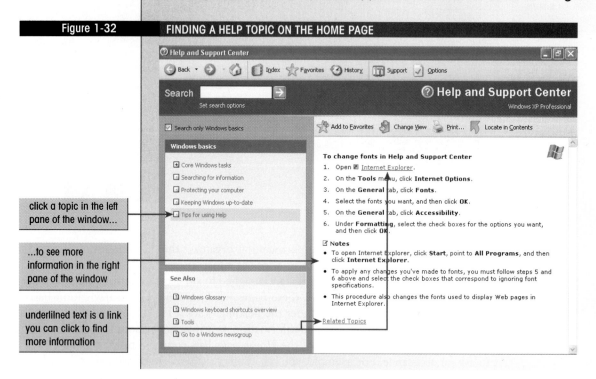

click a topic in the left pane of the window...

...to see more information in the right pane of the window

underlilned text is a link you can click to find more information

Besides listing the pages in the Help and Support Center window, the navigation bar contains two buttons—the Back button [⬅] and the Forward button [➡]. You use these buttons to navigate the pages you've already opened. You'll use the Back button next to return to the previous page you viewed. Once you do, you activate the Forward button, which you can click to go to the next page of those you've opened.

4. Click the **Back** button [⬅]. You return to the Tips for using Help page.

Selecting a Topic from the Index

The Index page allows you to jump to a Help topic by selecting a topic from an indexed list. For example, you can use the Index page to learn how to arrange open windows on your desktop.

To find a Help topic using the Index page:

1. On the navigation bar, click **Index** [📑]. A long list of indexed Help topics displays in the left pane.

2. Drag the **scroll box** down to view additional topics in the list box.

You can quickly jump to any part of the list by typing the first few characters of a word or phrase in the box that appears above the Index list.

3. If necessary, click in the **Type in the keyword to find** text box above the Index list, and then type **windows**. As you type each character in the word, the list of Index topic scrolls and eventually displays topics that relate to windows.

4. Under the "windows and panes on your computer screen" topic, click the topic **reducing windows to taskbar buttons**, and then click the **Display** button. When there is just one topic, it appears immediately in the right pane; otherwise, the Topics Found window opens, listing all topics indexed under the entry that interests you.

The information you requested displays in the right pane. See Figure 1-33. Notice this topic has two underlined phrases, "taskbar" and "Related Topics." You can click underlined words or phrases to view definitions or additional information.

Figure 1-33   **USING THE INDEX TO LOCATE INFORMATION**

type some or all of the characters in the word you want to look up in the index

click to display more information about the selected topic

5. Click the underlined phrase **taskbar**. A ScreenTip shows the definition of "taskbar." See Figure 1-34.

Figure 1-34   **VIEWING ADDITIONAL INFORMATION**

click an underlined word to view a definition or additional information

6. Click a blank area of the Help and Support Center window to close the ScreenTip.

If you have an Internet connection, you can use another Help page, Support, to contact Microsoft Support or get in touch with other users of Windows XP. The Support page works like the Home page. To get support on a particular feature, you click a support option and then click the topic for which you need help. Continue clicking topics, if necessary, until you get help from a Microsoft support person or an experienced Windows XP user.

Searching the Help Pages

If you can't find the topic you need by using the Home or Index pages, or if you want to quickly find Help pages related to a particular topic, you can use the Search box. Suppose you want to know how to exit Windows XP, but you don't know if Windows refers to this as exiting, quitting, closing, or shutting down. You can search the Help pages to find just the right topic.

To search the Help pages for information on exiting Windows XP:

1. Click in the Search box. A blinking insertion point appears.

2. Type **shutdown** and then click the **Start Searching** button ➡. A list of Help pages containing the word "shutdown" displays in the left pane of the Help and Support window. The ones listed under Suggested Topics are topics where "shutdown" has been assigned as a keyword—meaning the topics have to do with shutting something down.

3. Click the **Full-text Search Matches** button. The text of these topics includes the word *shutdown*.

4. Click the **Suggested Topics** button, and then click **Turn off the computer**. A Help topic displays in the right pane of the Help and Support Center window, as shown in Figure 1-35.

Figure 1-35	USING SEARCH TO FIND A HELP PAGE

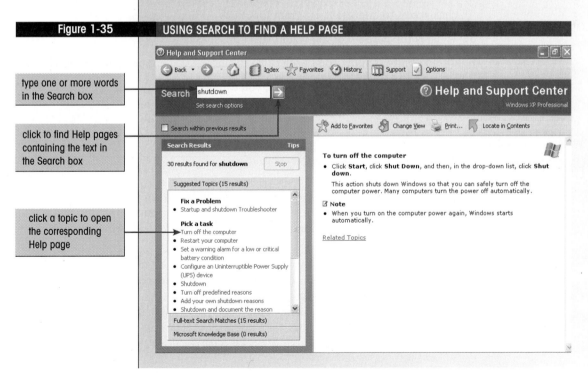

type one or more words in the Search box

click to find Help pages containing the text in the Search box

click a topic to open the corresponding Help page

If the text of this topic were longer than the Help and Support Center window, you could use the scroll bar to read all the text.

5. Click the **Close** button ☒ to close the Help and Support Center window.

Now that you know how Windows XP Help works, don't forget to use it! Use Help when you need to perform a new task or when you forget how to complete a procedure.

You've finished the tutorial, and as you shut down Windows XP, Steve returns from class. You take a moment to tell him all you've learned: you know how to start and close programs and how to use multiple programs at the same time. You have learned how to work with windows and the controls they employ. Finally, you've learned how to get help when you need it. Steve congratulates you and comments that you are well on your way to mastering the fundamentals of using the Windows XP operating system.

Session 1.2 QUICK CHECK

1. What is the difference between the title bar and a toolbar?

2. Provide the name and purpose of each button:
   a. ▣   b. ▣   c. ▣   d. ☒

3. Explain each of the following menu conventions:
   a. Ellipsis (...)
   b. Grayed-out
   c. ▷
   d. ▼

4. A (n) _____ consists of a group of buttons, each of which provides one-click access to important program functions.

5. What is the purpose of the scroll bar?

6. Option buttons allow you to select _____ option(s) at a time.

7. To learn how to perform new tasks, you can use _____.

REVIEW ASSIGNMENTS

Case 1. Running Two Programs and Switching Between Them In this tutorial you learned how to run more than one program at a time, using WordPad and Paint. You can run other programs at the same time, too. Complete the following steps, and write your answers to Questions b through f:

a. Start the computer. Enter your username and password if prompted to do so.
b. Click the Start button. How many menu options are on the Start menu?

Explore
c. Run the Calculator program located on the Accessories menu. How many program buttons are now on the taskbar? (Don't count toolbar buttons or items in the notification area.)
d. Run the Paint program and maximize the Paint window. How many programs are running now?
e. Switch to Calculator. What are two visual clues that tell you that Calculator is the active program?

Explore

f. Multiply 576 by 1457 using the Calculator accessory. (*Hint*: Click the numbers and arithmetic operators on the Calculator keypad.) What is the result?

g. Close Calculator and then close Paint.

Explore

Case 2. WordPad Help In Tutorial 1 you learned how to use Windows XP Help. Just about every Windows XP program has a Help feature. Many computer users can learn to use a program just by using Help. To use Help, you start the program and then click the Help menu at the top of the program window. Try using WordPad Help:

a. Start WordPad.

b. Click Help on the menu bar, and then click Help Topics.

c. The Index tab in WordPad Help works like the Index page in Windows XP Help. Using the Index tab in WordPad Help, write out your answers to Questions 1 through 4.

1. How do you create a bulleted list?

2. How do you set the page margins in a document?

3. How do you undo a mistake?

4. How do you change the font style of a block of text?

d. Close Help and then close WordPad.

Case 3. The Index Page versus the Search Box You might have heard that Windows XP makes it possible to speak to your computer and have it carry out your voice commands. This feature is called **speech recognition**. You could browse through the Help and Support Home page, although you might not know where to look to find information about speech recognition. You could also use the Index page to search through the indexed entries. Or you could use the Search box to find all Help topics that mention speech recognition.

a. Start Windows XP Help and use the Index page to find information about the topic of speech recognition. How many topics are listed? What is their primary subject matter?

b. Use the Search box to find information about the topic of speech recognition. How many topics are listed?

c. Write a paragraph comparing the two lists of topics. You don't have to view them all, but in your paragraph, indicate which tab seems to yield more information. Close the Help and Support Center window.

Case 4. Discover Windows XP Windows XP Help lets you access articles that provide more detailed information about common features or introduce new features. You can find and read an article about one new feature Windows XP offers—playing music and making music CDs on your computer.

a. Start Windows XP Help, open the Home page, click What's new in Windows XP, and then click Windows XP Articles: Walkthrough ways to use your PC.

b. Click Walkthrough: Making Music.

c. Read the Getting Started page. Note that the box in the upper-left corner of the window lists the contents of the article. Each topic is a link you can click to go to another page in the article.

d. Click the links in the contents box, and then answer the following questions using the information you find:

1. How can you listen to music using Windows XP?

2. What is a playlist? What is the first step you take to create one?

3. What is the advantage of listening to the Internet radio?

e. Close Help and then close WordPad.

PROJECTS

1. Many types of pointing devices are on the market today. Research the types of available devices. Consider what devices are appropriate for these situations: desktop or laptop computers, connected or remote devices, and ergonomic or standard designs. (Look up the term *ergonomic*.)

   To locate information, use up-to-date computer books, trade computer magazines (such as *PC Computing* and *PC Magazine*), or the Internet (if you know how). Your instructor might suggest specific resources you can use. Write a one-page report describing the types of devices available, the differing needs of users, special features that make pointing devices more useful, price comparisons. Finally, indicate what you would choose if you needed to buy a pointing device.

2. Locate information about the release of Windows XP, using the resources available to you, either through your library or the Internet (if you know how). Trade computer magazines are an excellent source of information about software. Read several articles about Windows XP, and then write a one-page essay discussing the features that seem most important to the people who evaluate the software. If you find reviews of the software, mention the features to which reviewers had the strongest reaction, pro or con.

3. **Upgrading** is the process of placing a more recent version of a product onto your computer. When Windows XP first came out, people had to decide whether they wanted to upgrade their computers to Windows XP. Interview at least three people you know who are well-informed Windows computer users. Ask them whether they use Windows XP or an older version of Windows. If they use an older version, ask why they chose not to upgrade. If they use Windows XP, ask why they chose to upgrade. Ask such questions as:

   a. What features convinced you to upgrade or made you decide to wait?
   b. What role did the price of the upgrade play?
   c. Would you or did you have to purchase new hardware to make the upgrade? How did this affect your decision?
   d. If you did upgrade, are you happy with that decision? If you didn't, do you intend to upgrade in the near future? Why or why not?
      Write a single-page essay summarizing what you learned from these interviews about making the decision to upgrade.

4. Choose a topic you'd like to research using the Windows XP online Help system. Look for information on your topic using the Help and Support Home page, Index page, and Search box. Once you find all the information you can, compare the three methods (Home page, Index page, Search box) of looking for information. Write a paragraph that discusses which method proved most useful. Did you reach the same information topics using all three methods? In a second paragraph, summarize what you learned about your topic. Finally, in a third paragraph, indicate under what circumstances you'd use which method.

LAB ASSIGNMENTS

Using a Keyboard

Using a Keyboard To become an effective computer user, you must be familiar with your primary input device—the keyboard. See the Read This Before You Begin page for information on installing and starting the lab.

1. The Steps for the Using a Keyboard Lab provides you with a structured introduction to the keyboard's layout and the functions of special computer keys. Click the Steps button and begin the steps. As you work through the Steps, answer all of the Quick Check questions that appear. When you complete the steps, you will see a Summary Report of your performance on the Quick Checks. Follow the directions on the screen to print the Summary Report.

2. You can develop your typing skills using the typing tutor in Explore. Start the typing tutor in Explore. Take the typing test and print your results.

3. In Explore, try to increase your typing speed by 10 words per minute. For example, if you currently type 20 words per minute, your goal is 30 words per minute. Practice each typing lesson until you see a message indicating that you can proceed to the next lesson. Create a Practice Record, as shown here, to keep track of how much you practice. When you reach your goal, print the results of a typing test to verify your results.

Practice Record

Name:

Section:

Start Date:	Start Typing Speed:	wpm
End Date:	End Typing Speed:	wpm
Lesson #:	Date Practiced/Time Practiced	

Using a Mouse

Using a Mouse A mouse is a standard input device on most of today's computers. You need to know how to use a mouse to manipulate graphical user interfaces and to use the rest of the Labs. See the Read This Before You Begin page for information on installing and starting the lab.

1. The Steps for the Using a Mouse Lab show you how to click, double-click, and drag objects using the mouse. Click the Steps button and begin the steps. As you work through the steps, answer all Quick Check questions that appear. When you complete the steps, you will see a Summary Report of your performance on the Quick Checks. Follow the directions on the screen to print the Summary Report.

2. In Explore, create a poster to demonstrate your ability to use a mouse and to control a Windows program. To create a poster for an upcoming sports event, select a graphic, type the caption for the poster, and then select a font, font styles, and a border. Print your completed poster.

QUICK | CHECK ANSWERS

Session 1.1

1. The taskbar contains buttons that give you access to commands and programs.

2. multitasking

3. Start menu

4. Lift up the mouse and move it to the right.

5. Its button appears on the taskbar.

6. to conserve computer resources such as memory

7. to ensure you don't lose data and damage your files

Session 1.2

1. The title bar identifies the window and contains window controls; toolbars contain buttons that provide you with shortcuts to common menu commands.

2. a. The Minimize button shrinks the window so you see its button on the taskbar.
    b. The Maximize button enlarges the window to fill the entire screen.
    c. The Restore button reduces the window to a predetermined size.
    d. The Close button closes the window and removes the program button from the taskbar.

3. a. Ellipsis indicates a dialog box will open.
    b. Grayed out indicates that the option is not currently available.
    c. Arrow indicates that a submenu will open.
    d. Check mark indicates a toggle option.

4. toolbar

5. Scroll bars appear when the contents of a box or window are too long to fit; you drag the scroll box to view different parts of the contents.

6. one

7. online Help

OBJECTIVES

In this tutorial you will:

- Format a disk
- Enter, select, insert, and delete text
- Create and save a file
- Open, edit, and print a file
- View the list of files on your Data Disk and change view options
- Navigate a hierarchy of folders
- Move, copy, delete, and rename a file
- Make a copy of your Data Disk

LAB

Using Files

WORKING WITH FILES

Creating, Saving, and Managing Files

CASE

Distance Learning

You recently purchased a computer to gain new skills and stay competitive in the job market. You hope to use the computer to enroll in a few distance learning courses. **Distance learning** is formalized education that typically takes place using a computer and the Internet, replacing normal classroom interaction with modern communications technology. Distance learning instructors often make their course material available on the **World Wide Web**, also called the **Web**. The Web is a network of **Web pages**, which are electronic documents stored on the Internet that people can access and explore using **hyperlinks**. Hyperlinks are text or graphical elements embedded in the Web pages. You click the hyperlinks in a Web page to navigate to related Web pages and **Web sites**, computers connected to the Internet that store collections of Web pages.

Your computer came with the Windows XP operating system already installed. Your friend Shannon suggests that before you enroll in any online course, you should become more comfortable with your computer and with Windows XP. Knowing how to save, locate, and organize your files will make the time you spend working with your computer much more productive. A **file** is a collection of data that has a name and is stored on a computer. Once you create a file, you can open it, edit its contents, print it, and save it again—usually using the same program you used to create it.

In this tutorial, you will learn how to perform some basic tasks in Windows XP programs, such as formatting a disk and working with text and files. You will also learn how to view information on your computer in different ways. Finally, you'll spend time learning how to organize your files.

SESSION 2.1

In Session 2.1 you will format a disk so you can store files on it. You will create, save, open, and print a file. You will learn more about the difference between the insertion point and the mouse pointer. You also will learn the basic skills for working with text, such as entering, selecting, inserting, and deleting text. For the steps in this tutorial, you will need two blank 3½" disks.

Formatting a Disk

Before you can save files on a disk, the disk must be formatted. When the computer **formats** a disk, the magnetic particles on the disk's surface are arranged so data can be stored on the disk. Today, many disks are sold preformatted and can be used right out of the box. However, if you purchase an unformatted disk or if you have an old disk you want to completely erase and reuse, you can format the disk using the Windows XP Format command. This command is available through the **My Computer window**, a feature of Windows XP that you use to view, organize, and access the programs, files, and drives on your computer. You open My Computer by using its icon on the desktop. You'll learn more about the My Computer window in Session 2.2.

The following steps explain how to format a 3½" high-density disk using drive A. Your instructor will explain how to revise the instructions given in these steps if the procedure is different for your lab equipment.

Make sure you are using a blank disk (or one that contains data you no longer need) before you perform these steps.

To format a disk:

1. Start Windows XP and log on using your user name, if necessary.

2. Write your name on the label of a 3½-inch disk, and then insert your disk in drive A. See Figure 2-1.

Figure 2-1   INSERTING A DISK INTO A DISK DRIVE

edge with the notch goes into the drive first

floppy disk drive

edge with the label goes in last

TROUBLE? If your disk does not fit in drive A, put it in drive B, and then substitute drive B for drive A in all of the steps for the rest of the tutorial.

3. Double-click the **My Computer** icon on the desktop. See Figure 2-2. The My Computer window on your screen might be maximized.

TROUBLE? If you see a list of items instead of icons like those in Figure 2-2, click View on the My Computer menu bar, and then click Tiles. Your toolbar may not exactly match the one in Figure 2-2; it may have fewer or more buttons.

| Figure 2-2 | MY COMPUTER WINDOW |

My Computer icon (don't worry if the icon on your screen looks different)

your window might contain different icons

3½ Floppy (A:) icon

4. Right-click the **3½ Floppy (A:)** icon to open its shortcut menu, and then click **Format**. The Format 3½ Floppy (A:) dialog box opens. See Figure 2-3.

| Figure 2-3 | FORMATTING A FLOPPY DISK |

storage capacity is 1.44MB

file system is FAT

if you are using a disk that has already been formatted, you can check the Quick Format box

to format a disk you can use to start MS-DOS, check this box

5. Make sure your dialog box settings match those in Figure 2-3. These settings describe a disk's characteristics and format options. The capacity of a floppy disk indicates how much data it can hold—a 3½-inch floppy disk can hold 1.44MB of data. By default, Windows XP uses the FAT (File Allocation Table) file system for floppy disks. A **file system** is the way files are organized on the disk. Windows XP supports other file systems such as FAT32 and NTFS. Selecting a file system, allocation unit size, volume label, and creating an MS-DOS startup disk are advanced topics, so you can accept the defaults for these options. If you have a disk that has been previously formatted, and you're sure the disk is not damaged, you can use the Quick Format option. In this instance, you will do a full format, so this box should remain unchecked.

6. Click the **Start** button to begin formatting the disk.

TROUBLE? If you are using a disk that contains data, you will see a warning that formatting will erase all the data on the disk. Click OK to continue.

A bar at the bottom of the Format window shows you how the formatting is progressing.

7. When the formatting is completed, a Format Complete message box appears. Click the **OK** button.

8. Click the **Close** button to close the Format 3½ Floppy (A:) dialog box, and then close the My Computer window to return to the desktop.

Now that you have formatted a disk, you can create a document and save it as a file on your disk. To create a document, you first need to learn how to enter text into a document.

Working with Text

To accomplish many computing tasks, you need to type text where text is required, whether it is in a document or in a text box. Entering text involves first learning how to place the mouse pointer so the text will appear where you want it. Then you can insert new text between existing words or sentences, select text, and delete text.

For example, when you start WordPad, a white area will appear below the menu bar, toolbars, and ruler. This area is called the **document window**. In the upper-left corner of the document window, there is a flashing vertical bar, called the **insertion point**. The insertion point indicates where the characters you type will appear.

When you type sentences of text, you do not need to press the Enter key when you reach the right margin of the page. Most programs contain a feature called **word wrap**, which automatically continues your text on the next line. Therefore, you should press the Enter key only when you have completed a paragraph.

If you make a typing error, you can use the Delete key or the Backspace key. If you type the wrong character, you can press the **Backspace key** to delete the character immediately to the left of the insertion point. You can press the **Delete key** to delete the character immediately to the right of the insertion point. You can also use the mouse to select the text you want to delete and then press either the Delete or Backspace key.

Now you will type some text in the WordPad document window.

To type text in WordPad:

1. Start WordPad and locate the insertion point in the WordPad document window.

TROUBLE? If the WordPad window does not fill the screen, click the Maximize button on the WordPad title bar.

TROUBLE? If you cannot find the insertion point, move the I pointer over the WordPad window and then click the mouse button. The insertion point will appear in the upper-left corner of the document window.

2. Type your name, just as you would on a typewriter, pressing the Shift key as you type uppercase letters and using the spacebar to enter spaces.

3. Press the **Enter** key to end the current paragraph and to move the insertion point down to the next line.

4. Type the following sentences, watching what happens when the insertion point reaches the right margin of the page:

This is a sample typed in WordPad. See what happens when the insertion point reaches the right edge of the page. Note how the text wraps automatically to the next line.

TROUBLE? If you make a mistake, delete the incorrect character(s) using the Backspace key or Delete key. Then type the correct character(s).

TROUBLE? If your text doesn't wrap, your screen might be set up to display more information than the screen used for the figures in this tutorial, or your WordPad program might not be set to use Word Wrap. To set the Word Wrap option, click View on the menu bar, click Options, click the Rich Text tab in the Options dialog box, click the Wrap to window option button, and then click the OK button.

The Insertion Point Versus the Pointer

The insertion point is not the same as the pointer. When the pointer is in the document window, the pointer is called the **I-beam pointer**. Figure 2-4 explains the difference between the insertion point and the I-beam pointer.

Figure 2-4	THE INSERTION POINT VS. THE POINTER

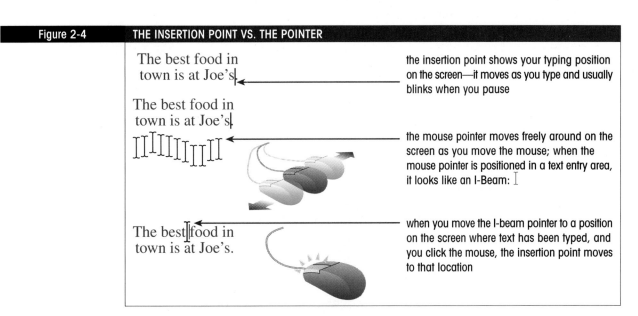

The best food in
town is at Joe's|

the insertion point shows your typing position on the screen—it moves as you type and usually blinks when you pause

The best food in
town is at Joe's|

the mouse pointer moves freely around on the screen as you move the mouse; when the mouse pointer is positioned in a text entry area, it looks like an I-Beam: I

The best food in
town is at Joe's.

when you move the I-beam pointer to a position on the screen where text has been typed, and you click the mouse, the insertion point moves to that location

When you enter text, the insertion point moves as you type. If you want to enter text in a location other than where the insertion point is positioned, you can use the pointer to move the insertion point to a different location. Move the I-beam pointer to where you want to type, and then click. The insertion point moves to where you clicked. In most programs, the insertion point blinks so you can locate it easily on a screen filled with text.

Try moving the insertion point to different locations in the sample text in the WordPad document window.

To move the insertion point to a new location in the sample text:

1. Locate the insertion point and the I-beam pointer in the WordPad document window. The insertion point should be at the end of the sentence you typed in the last set of steps. The easiest way to find the I-beam pointer is to move your mouse gently until you see the pointer. The pointer will look like ⌖ until you move it into the document window; then the pointer will change to ⌶.

2. Use your mouse to move the I-beam pointer just to the left of the word "sample," and then click. The insertion point should now be just to the left of the "s" in the word "sample."

TROUBLE? If you have trouble clicking just to the left of the "s," try clicking in the word and then using the left arrow key to move the insertion point one character at a time.

3. Move the I-beam pointer to a blank area near the bottom of the document window, and then click. Notice the insertion point does not jump to the location of the I-beam pointer. Instead the insertion point jumps to the end of the last sentence or to the point in the bottom line directly above where you clicked. The insertion point can move only within existing text. In most programs, the insertion point cannot be moved out of the existing text.

Selecting Text

Many text-editing operations are performed on a **block of text**, which is one or more consecutive characters, words, sentences, or paragraphs. Once you select a block of text, you can delete it, move it, replace it, underline it, and so on. To deselect a block of text, click anywhere outside the selected block.

If you want to delete the phrase "See what happens" in the text you just typed and replace it with the phrase "You can watch word wrap in action," you do not have to delete the first phrase one character at a time. Instead, you can select the entire phrase and then type the replacement phrase.

To select and replace the block of text "See what happens":

1. Move the I-beam pointer just to the left of the word "See."

2. Click and then drag the I-beam pointer over the text to the end of the word "happens." The phrase "See what happens" should now be highlighted, indicating it is selected. See Figure 2-5.

TROUBLE? If the space to the right of the word "happens" is also selected, that means your computer is set up to select spaces in addition to words. You can continue with Step 3.

Figure 2-5	SELECTING TEXT

position the I-beam pointer here

press and hold the left mouse button while you drag the I-beam pointer over text

Andrea Conti

This is a sample typed in WordPad. See what happens when the insertion point reaches the right edge of the page. Note how the text wraps automatically to the next line.

3. Release the mouse button.

TROUBLE? If the phrase is not selected correctly, repeat Steps 1 through 3.

4. Type **You can watch word wrap in action** and then press the **spacebar**, if necessary, to insert a space between "action" and "when." The text you type replaces the selected text. You do not have to delete selected text before you type the replacement text.

In addition to replacing existing text with new material, you can also insert text into an existing block of text.

Inserting Text

Windows XP programs usually operate in **insert mode**—when you type a new character, the characters to the right of the insertion point automatically move over to make room.

Insert the word "page" before the word "typed" in the sample text.

To insert text:

1. Position the insertion point just before the word "typed".

2. Type **page** and then press the **spacebar**. The letters in the first line are pushed to the right to make room for the new characters. When you insert text and a word is pushed past the right margin, the word wrap feature moves the word down to the beginning of the next line.

Now that you have practiced typing, you can save the file.

Saving a File

Using Files

As you type text, it is held temporarily in the computer's memory and is erased when you turn off or restart the computer. For permanent storage, you need to save your work on a disk. In the computer lab, you will probably save your work on a floppy disk in drive A.

When you save a file, you must give it a name, which then becomes its **filename**. Windows XP allows you to use up to 255 characters in a filename—this gives you plenty of room to name your file accurately so that you'll know the contents of the file just by looking at the filename. You can use spaces and certain punctuation symbols in your filenames. You cannot use the symbols \ / ? : * " < > | in a filename, but other symbols such as & ; - and $ are allowed.

When naming a file, you should also consider whether you might use your files on a computer that is running older programs. Programs designed for the Windows 3.1 or DOS operating systems (which were created before 1995) require that filenames have eight characters or less and no spaces. When you save a file with a long filename in Windows XP, Windows XP also creates an eight-character filename that can be used by older programs. The eight-character filename is created from the first six nonspace characters in the long filename, with the addition of a tilde (~) and a number. For example, the filename Car Sales for 2004 would be converted to Carsal~1.

Most filenames have an extension. An **extension** (a set of no more than three characters at the end of a filename, separated from the filename by a period) is used by the operating system to identify and categorize the files by their file types. The characters also indicate the program in which the file was created. In the filename Car Sales for 2004.doc, for example, the file extension "doc" identifies the file as one created with Microsoft Word. You might also have a file called Car Sales for 2004.xls—the "xls" extension identifies the file as one created in Microsoft Excel, a spreadsheet program. When pronouncing filenames with extensions, say "dot" for the period, so that you pronounce the filename Resume.doc as "Resume dot doc."

You usually do not need to add an extension to a filename because the program that you use to create the file adds the file extension automatically. Also, Windows XP keeps track of extensions, but not all computers are set to display extensions. The steps in these tutorials refer to files using the filename without its extension. So if you see the filename Practice Text in the steps, but "Practice Text.doc" on your screen, both names refer to the same file. Also, you do not have to use lowercase and uppercase letters consistently when naming files. Usually the operating system doesn't distinguish between them. Be aware, however, that some programs are case-sensitive—that is, they check for case in filenames.

Now you can save the document you typed.

To start saving your document:

1. Click the **Save** button 🖫 on the toolbar. The Save As dialog box opens, as shown in Figure 2-6.

Figure 2-6	SAVING A FILE

You use the Save As dialog box to specify where you want to save your file (on the hard disk or on a floppy disk, in a folder or not, and so on). Before going further with the process of saving a file, examine some of the features of the Save As dialog box so that you learn to save your files exactly where you want them.

Specifying the File Location

In the Save As dialog box, Windows XP provides the **Places Bar**, a list of important locations on your computer. When you click the different icons in the Places Bar, the contents of those locations will be displayed in the white area of the Save As dialog box. You can then save your document directly to those locations. Figure 2-7 identifies the icons in the Places Bar and gives their function.

Figure 2-7	ICONS IN THE PLACES BAR

ICON	DESCRIPTION
My Recent Documents	Displays a list of recently opened files, folders, and objects
Desktop	Displays a list of files, folders, and objects on the Windows XP desktop
My Documents	Displays a list of files, folders, and objects in the My Documents folder
My Computer	Displays a list of files, folders, and objects in the My Computer window
My Network Places	Displays a list of computers and folders available on the network

To see this in action, try displaying different locations in the Save As dialog box.

To use the Places Bar:

1. Click the **Desktop** icon in the Places Bar.

2. The Save As dialog box now displays the contents of the Windows XP desktop. See Figure 2-8.

Figure 2-8   USING THE PLACES BAR

click to display the contents of the Windows XP desktop

contents of the Windows XP desktop; yours may differ

3. Double-click the **My Documents** icon to display the contents of the My Documents folder.

Once you've clicked an icon in the Places Bar, you can open any file displayed in that location, and you can save a file in that location. The Places Bar doesn't have an icon for every location on your computer, however. The Save in list box (located at the top of the dialog box) does. Use the Save in list box now to save your document on your floppy disk.

To use the Save in list box:

1. Click the **Save in** list arrow to display a list of drives.

2. Click **3½ Floppy (A:)**.

Now that you've specified where you want to save your file, you can specify a name and type for the file.

Specifying the File Name and Type

After choosing the location for your document, you have to specify the name of the file. You should also specify (or at least check) the file's format. A file's **format** determines what type of information you can place in the document, the document's appearance, and what kind of programs can work with the document. You can save a WordPad document in one of four file formats: Rich Text Format (RTF), Text, Text for MS-DOS, and Unicode Text. In addition, you can open a document in the Word for Windows 6.0 or Windows Write formats. The Word, Write, and RTF formats allow you to create documents with text that can use boldfaced or italicized fonts as well as documents containing graphic images and scanned photos. However, only word-processing programs like WordPad or Microsoft Word can work with those files. The four text formats allow only simple text with no graphics or special formatting, but such documents are readable by a wider range of programs. The default format for WordPad documents is RTF, but you can change that, as you'll see shortly.

Continue saving the document, using the name "Practice Text" and the file type Text Document.

To finish saving your document:

1. Select the text **Document** in the File name text box, and then type **Practice Text.** The new text replaces "Document."

2. Click the **Save as type** list arrow, and then click **Text Document** in the list. See Figure 2-9.

Figure 2-9	COMPLETED SAVE AS DIALOG BOX

select the floppy drive for the file's location

if this check box is selected, future documents will use Text Document format as the default

the file's name

save the document in Text Document format

3. Click the **Save** button in the lower-right corner of the dialog box.

4. If you are asked whether you are sure that you want to save the document in this format, click the **Yes** button.

Your file is saved on your Data Disk, and the document title, "Practice Text," appears in the WordPad title bar.

Note that after you save the file, the document appears a little different. What has changed? By saving the document in Text Document format rather than RTF, you've changed the format of the document slightly. One change is that the text is wrapped differently in Text Document format. A Text Document file does not wrap text when it reaches the right margin.

What if you try to close WordPad before you save your file? Windows XP will display a message—"Save changes to document?" If you answer "Yes," Windows XP will display the Save As dialog box so you can give the document a name. If you answer "No," Windows XP will close WordPad without saving the document. Any changes you made to the document will be lost. Unless you are absolutely sure you don't need to keep the work you just did, answer "Yes."

After you save a file, you can work on another document or close WordPad. Because you have already saved your Practice Text document, you'll continue this tutorial by closing WordPad.

To close WordPad:

1. Click the **Close** button ☒ to close the WordPad window.

Opening a File

Now that you have saved and closed the Practice Text file, suppose you now want to revise it. To revise a file you must first open it. When you open a file, its contents are copied into the computer's memory. If you revise the file, you need to save the changes before you close the file or close the program. If you close a revised file without saving your changes, you will lose them.

You can use one of several methods to open a file. If you have opened the file recently, you can select the file from the My Recent Documents list on the Start menu. The My Recent Documents list contains the 15 most recently opened documents. You can also locate and open a file using the My Computer window (or **Windows Explorer**, another Windows XP file management tool). Or you can start a program and then use the program's Open button (or Open command on the File menu) to locate and open the file. Each method has advantages and disadvantages.

Using one of the first two methods for opening the Practice Text file simply requires you to click the file in the My Recent Documents list or locate and select it from the My Computer window or Windows Explorer window. With these methods, the document, not the program, is central to the task; hence, these methods are sometimes referred to as **docucentric**. You only need to remember the name of your file—you do not need to remember which program you used to create it.

Opening a File from the My Computer Window

You can open a file by selecting it from the My Computer window or Windows Explorer window. Windows XP uses the file extension (whether it is displayed or not) to determine which program to start so you can work with the file. Windows XP starts the program and then opens the file. The advantage of this method is simplicity. The disadvantage is that Windows XP might not start the program you expect. For example, when you select Practice Text, you might expect Windows XP to start WordPad because you used WordPad to create it. Depending on the programs installed on your computer system, however, Windows XP might start Notepad or Microsoft Word instead. Notepad works with simple text files, such as those that have a .txt extension, and Word works with a wide range of documents that can include formatting, graphics, and other elements. Word files have a .doc extension. Using any word-processing program to open a text file is not usually a problem. Although the program might not be the one you expect, you can still use it to revise your file.

To open the Practice Text file by selecting it from My Computer:

1. Double-click the **My Computer** icon on the desktop to open the My Computer window.

2. Double-click the **3½ Floppy (A:)** icon in the My Computer window.

3. Double-click the **Practice Text** file icon. Windows XP starts Notepad and then opens the Practice Text file. You could edit the document at this point, but instead, you'll close all the windows on your desktop so you can try another method for opening files.

TROUBLE? If Windows XP starts Microsoft Word or another word-processing program instead of NotePad, continue with Step 4.

4. Close all open windows on the desktop.

Windows XP opened Practice Text in Notepad because you saved it as a text document—and Windows is usually setup to open text documents with Notepad. If you want to be sure to edit Practice Text in WordPad, first open WordPad and then use the Open button. You will try that next.

Opening a File from Within a Program

The advantage of opening a file from within a program is that you can specify the program you want to use to modify the file—WordPad, in this case. This method, however, involves more steps than the method you tried previously.

You can take advantage of the Places bar to reduce the number of steps it takes to open a file from within a program. Recall that the Places Bar contains the My Recent Documents icon, which when clicked, provides a list of recently opened files. One of the most recently opened files was the Practice Text file, so you should be able to open it using this method.

Open the Practice Text file using the Open button in WordPad.

To open a list of recent files and then save a WordPad document:

1. Start **WordPad** and maximize the WordPad window.

2. Click the **Open** button 🖼 on the toolbar.

3. In the Open dialog box, click **My Recent Documents** in the Places bar.

The Practice Text file doesn't appear in the list. Why not? Look at the Files of Type list box. The selected entry is "Rich Text Format (rtf)". What this means is that the only files listed in the Open dialog box are those saved as Rich Text files—they all have an .rtf file extension. Limiting the types of files displayed frees you from having to deal with the clutter of unwanted or irrelevant files. The downside is that unless you're aware of how the Open dialog box will filter the list of files, you may mistakenly think that the file you're looking for doesn't exist. You can change how the Open dialog box filters this file list. Try this now by changing the filter to show only .txt documents.

To change the types of files displayed:

1. Click the **Files of type** list arrow. Note that WordPad can open files with a .doc or .wri extension, in addition to the file types it can save. Click **Text Documents (*.txt)**. The Practice Text file now appears in the list.

2. Click **Practice Text** in the list box. See Figure 2-10.

Figure 2-10   SELECTING THE FILE

list only files in Text Documents format

3. Click the **Open** button. The document opens in the WordPad window. Note that you could also open the Practice Text file by double-clicking its name in the file list.

Saving the file as a Text Document did not preserve the word wrap. To restore word wrap, you can save the file in the Rich Text Format.

4. Click **File** on the menu bar, and then click **Save As**. You use the Save As command when you want to save the current file with a different name, file type, or location.

5. Click the **Save as type** list arrow, and then click **Rich Text Format (RTF)**.

6. Click the **Save** button. A message appears indicating that a file named Practice Text already exists in the selected location. You want to replace this file with one in the RTF format.

7. Click the **Yes** button. The word wrap in the Practice Text document is restored.

Now that you have opened and saved the Practice Text file as an RTF file, you can print it.

Printing a Document

Windows XP provides easy access to the printers connected to your computer. You can choose which printer to use, you can control how the document is printed, and you can control the order in which documents print. You also can preview your document before printing it to see how it will appear when it is printed.

Previewing Your Document Before Printing

Before you send a document to the printer, you should always preview it using Print Preview. **Print Preview** shows your document exactly as it will appear when printed on paper. You can check your page layout so you don't waste paper printing a document that is not quite the way you want it.

Preview and print the Practice Text document. Your instructor might supply you with additional instructions for printing in your lab.

To preview the Practice Text document:

1. Click the **Print Preview** button 🔍 on the WordPad toolbar.

   TROUBLE? If an error message appears, printing capabilities might not be set up on your computer. Ask your instructor or technical support person for help, or skip this set of steps.

2. Look at your document in the Print Preview window. Before you print the document, you should make sure the font, margins, and other document features are the way you want them.

   TROUBLE? If the document does not look the way you want it to, click the Close button, edit the document, and then click the Print Preview button again.

   TROUBLE? If you can't read the document text on screen, click the Zoom In button as many times as necessary to read the text.

3. Click the **Close** button on the Print Preview toolbar to close Print Preview, and return to the document.

Now that you've verified that the document looks the way you want, you can print it.

Sending Your Document to the Printer

There are three ways to send your document to the printer. One way is to click the Print button 🖨 on your program's toolbar. This method will send the document directly to your printer—you do not need to take any further action. It's the quickest and easiest way to print a document, although it does not allow you to change settings such as margins and number of copies. What if you have access to more than one printer? In that case, Windows XP sends the document to the default printer, the one set up to handle your print tasks.

If you want to select a different printer or control how the printer prints your document, you can select the Print command from the File menu. Selecting the Print command opens the Print dialog box, allowing you to choose which printer to use and how that printer will print the document.

You can also print your document directly from the Print Preview window by clicking the Print button on the Print Preview toolbar. Clicking the Print button in Print Preview also opens the Print dialog box so you can verify or change settings.

Print the Practice Text document using the File menu.

To print the document using the Print command on the File menu:

1. Click **File** on the menu bar, and then click **Print**. The Print dialog box opens, as shown in Figure 2-11.

Figure 2-11 **PRINTING A FILE**

to print a range of pages, click the Pages option button and then enter the starting and ending page numbers

specify to print all the pages in a document or part of a document

enter the number of copies you want to print

2. Make sure your Print dialog box shows the Print range set to **All** and the number of copies set to **1**.

3. Click the **Print** button to print your document.

TROUBLE? If your document does not print, make sure the printer is turned on and contains paper. If your document still doesn't print, ask your instructor or technical support person for help.

4. Close WordPad.

TROUBLE? If you see the message "Save changes to Document?", click the No button.

You've now learned how to create, save, open, and print word-processed files—essential skills for students in distance learning courses that rely on word-processed reports transmitted across the Internet. Shannon assures you that the techniques you've just learned apply to most Windows XP programs.

Session 2.1 QUICK CHECK

1. A(n) _____ is a collection of data that has a name and is stored on a disk or other storage medium.

2. _____ erases the data on a disk and arranges the magnetic particles on the disk's surface so the disk can store data.

3. True or False: When you move the mouse pointer over a text entry area, the pointer's shape changes to an I-beam I.

4. What shows you where each character you type will appear?

5. _____ automatically moves text down to the beginning of the next line when you reach the right margin.

6. How do you select a block of text?

7. In the filename New Equipment.doc, doc is a(n) _____.

SESSION 2.2

In this session you will change the settings in the My Computer window to control its appearance and the appearance of desktop objects. You will use My Computer to manage the files on your Data Disk; view information about the files on your disk; organize the files into folders; and move, delete, copy, and rename files.

Using My Computer

The My Computer icon on the desktop represents your computer, its storage devices, printers, and other objects. The My Computer icon opens the My Computer window, which contains an icon for each of the storage devices on your computer, as shown in Figure 2-12. These icons appear in the right pane of the My Computer window. On most computer systems, the My Computer window also has a left pane, which shows icons and links to other resources. You'll learn more about the left pane shortly.

Figure 2-12 | RELATIONSHIP BETWEEN COMPUTER AND MY COMPUTER WINDOW

hard drive on your computer

3½-inch floppy drive

hard drive on network computer

CD-ROM drive

Each storage device you have access to on your computer has a letter associated with it. The first floppy drive on a computer is usually designated as drive A. (If you add a second floppy drive, it is usually designated as drive B.) The first hard drive is usually designated drive C. (If you add additional hard drives, they are usually designated as D, E, and so on.) If you have a CD or DVD drive, it will usually have the next letter in the alphabetic sequence. If you have access to hard drives located on other computers in a network, those drives will sometimes (although not always) have letters associated with them as well. In the example shown in Figure 2-12, the network drive has the drive letter E.

You can use the My Computer window to keep track of where your files are stored and to organize your files. In this session, you will move and delete files on your Data Disk, which is assumed to be located in drive A. If you use your own computer at home or work, you will probably store your files on drive C instead of drive A. However, in a school lab environment you usually don't know which computer you will use, so you need to carry your files with you on a floppy disk that you can use in drive A on any computer. In this session, therefore, you will learn how to work with the files on drive A. Most of what you learn will also work on your home or work computer when you use drive C (or other drives).

Now you'll open the My Computer window.

To explore the contents of your Data Disk using the My Computer window:

1. Make sure your Data Disk is in the floppy drive. If necessary, remove the disk you formatted—the one that contains only the Practice Text file—and then insert your Data Disk in the floppy drive.

2. Open the My Computer window. See Figure 2-13.

Figure 2-13	MY COMPUTER WINDOW

Figure 2-14 identifies and describes the elements of the My Computer window.

Figure 2-14	ELEMENTS OF THE MY COMPUTER WINDOW

ELEMENT	DESCRIPTION
System Tasks	Click a System Tasks link to view system information, such as the capacity of your hard drive, add or remove programs, or change a system setting.
Other Places	Click an Other Places link to open the My Documents or Shared Documents folder or the Network Places or Control Panel Window.
Control Panel	Click this link to view or change your computer settings.
Details	If you are viewing the contents of a folder, click a Details link to see more information about the folder or device, such as its size and the date it was created on.
Right pane	Shows the folders, drives, and devices on your computer; double-click an icon to open the object.
Standard Buttons toolbar	Contains buttons for performing common tasks, such as navigating your computer or changing the icon view.
Address Bar	Shows the name and location of the current device or folder; you can enter a different location in the Address Bar to open a different folder or other object.

3. Double-click the **3½ Floppy (A:)** icon. A window opens showing the contents of drive A; maximize this window if necessary. See Figure 2-15.

| Figure 2-15 | CONTENTS OF DATA DISK |

TROUBLE? Your window might look different from Figure 2-15; for example, you might see only files, and not the additional details under the filenames.

TROUBLE? If you see a list of filenames instead of icons, click View on the menu bar, and then click Tiles.

TROUBLE? If you do not see the status bar, click New on the menu bar, and then click Status Bar.

Changing the Appearance of the My Computer Window

Windows XP offers several options that control how toolbars, icons, and buttons appear in the My Computer window. To make the My Computer window look the same as it does in the figures in this book, you need to ensure three things: that only the Standard and Address toolbars are visible; that files and other objects appear as Tiles, which displays files as large icons, and that the configuration of Windows XP uses the default setting. Setting your computer to match the figures makes it easier for you to follow the steps in these tutorials.

Controlling the Toolbar Display

The My Computer window, in addition to featuring a Standard toolbar, allows you to display the same toolbars that can appear on the Windows XP taskbar, such as the Address toolbar or the Links toolbar. You can use these toolbars to access the Web from the My Computer window. In this tutorial, however, you need to see only the Address and Standard Buttons toolbars.

To display only the Address and Standard Buttons toolbars:

1. Click **View** on the menu bar, and then point to **Toolbars**. The Standard Buttons and Address Bar commands on the Toolbars submenu should be checked, indicating that they are displayed in the My Computers window. The Links option should not be checked.

2. If the Standard Buttons or Address Bar commands *are not checked*, click the command to select it. Or if the Links option *is checked*, click it to deselect it. Note that you must display the Toolbars submenu to select or deselect each option.

3. If necessary, click **View** on the menu bar, and then point to **Toolbars** to verify that your Toolbars submenu and the toolbars displayed in the My Computer Window look like Figure 2-16.

Figure 2-16	CHECKING VIEW OPTIONS

TROUBLE? If the check marks on the Toolbars submenu are distributed differently than in Figure 2-16, repeat Steps 1 and 2 until the correct options are selected.

TROUBLE? If your toolbars' arrangement differs from that shown in Figure 2-16 (for example, both the Standard Buttons and Address toolbars are on the same line or the Standard Buttons toolbar is above the Address toolbar), you can easily rearrange them. To move a toolbar, first make sure it is unlocked. Click View on the menu bar, point to Toolbars, and then click Lock the Toolbar to uncheck this command. Then drag the vertical bar at the far left of the toolbar left, right, up, or down.

TROUBLE? If there are no labels included on the toolbar buttons, click View on the menu bar, point to Toolbars, click Customize, click the Text options list arrow in the Customize Toolbar dialog box, click Show text labels, and then click the Close button.

4. Press the **Esc** key to close the Toolbars menu.

Changing the Icon Display

Windows XP provides five ways to view the contents of a disk—Thumbnails, Tiles, Icons, List, and Details. Figure 2-17 shows examples of these five styles.

Figure 2-17	VIEWING STYLES

The default view, **Tiles view**, displays a large icon, title, file type, and file size for each file. The icon provides a visual cue to the type of file, as shown in Figure 2-18. You also can find this same information with the smaller icons displayed in the **Icons** and **List views**, but in less screen space. In Icons and List views, you can see more files and folders at one time, which is helpful when you have many files in one location.

Figure 2-18	TYPICAL ICONS IN WINDOWS XP

FILE AND FOLDER ICONS

Text documents that you can open using the Notepad accessory are represented by notepad icons.

Graphic image documents that you can open using the Paint accessory are represented by drawing instruments.

Word-processed documents that you can open using the WordPad accessory are represented by a formatted notepad icon, unless your computer designates a different word-processing program to open files created with WordPad.

Word-processed documents that you can open using a program such as Microsoft Word are represented by formatted document icons.

Files created by programs that Windows does not recognize are represented by the Windows logo.

A folder icon represents folders.

Certain folders created by Windows XP have a special icon design related to the folder's purpose.

PROGRAM ICONS

Icons for programs usually depict an object related to the function of the program. For example, an icon that looks like a calculator represents the Calculator accessory.

Non-Windows programs are represented by the icon of a blank window.

All of the three icon views (Tiles, Icons, and List) help you quickly identify a file and its type, but what if you want more information about a set of files? **Details view** shows more information than the other three views. Details view shows the file icon, filename, file size, program used to create the file, and the date and time the file was created or last modified.

If you have graphic files, you can use **Thumbnails view**, which displays a small preview image of the graphic. In Thumbnails view, you can quickly see not only the filename, but also which picture or drawing the file contains. Thumbnails view is great for browsing a large collection of graphic files, but switching to this view can be time-consuming because Windows XP must first create all the preview images.

To practice switching from one view to another, start by displaying the contents of drive A in Details view. So far, you've used the View menu to change the window view. Now you can use the Views button, which displays the same commands for changing views as the View menu.

To view a detailed list of files:

1. Click the **Views** button ⊞ ˇ on the Standard Buttons toolbar, and then click **Details** to display details for the files on your disk. See Figure 2-19. Your files might be listed in a different order.

| Figure 2-19 | DETAILS VIEW |

click these buttons to sort the file list in a different order

date and time the file was created or last modified

file icon

filename

file size (1KB equals about 1000 characters)

file type

total size of all the objects in the window

total number of objects in the window

2. Look at the file sizes. Which files are the largest?

3. Look at the Type column. Which file is an Outlook Express Mail Message?

One of the advantages of Details view is that you can sort the file list by filename, size, type, or date. This helps if you're working with a large file list and you're trying to find a specific file.

To sort the file list by type:

1. Click the **Type** button at the top of the list of files. The files are now sorted in alphabetical order by type, starting with the Bitmap Image files and ending with the Windows XP Audio/Visual Media file.

   If you were looking for all the .rtf files (those created with WordPad, for example), sorting by type would be useful because the .rtf files would all be grouped together under "R" for Rich Text Format.

2. Click the **Type** button again. The sort order is reversed, with the Windows XP Audio/Visual Media file now at the top of the list.

3. Click the **Name** button at the top of the file list. The files are now sorted in alphabetical order by filename.

Now that you have looked at the file details, you can switch back to Tiles view.

To switch to Tiles view:

1. Click the **Views** button on the Standard Buttons toolbar, and then click **Tiles** to return to the Tiles view.

Restoring the My Computer Default Settings

Windows XP provides other options for working with your files and windows. These options fall into two general categories: Classic style and Web style. **Classic style** lets you interact with windows and files using techniques from earlier versions of the Windows operating system. **Web style** lets you work with windows and files in the same way you work with Web pages on the World Wide Web. For example, to open a file in Classic style, you can double-click the file icon or the filename, or you can click the file icon or filename once and press the Enter key. To open a file in Web style, you would point to a file icon until the pointer changed to 🖑, and then you would click the file icon once. The filenames would also appear underlined, indicating you can click once to open them. Underlined text is usually called a **hyperlink** or just **link**. You can also create your own style, choosing elements of both the Classic and Web styles, and add customized features of your own.

Try switching to the Web style to see how it works in the My Computer window. Then, to maintain consistency and make sure your screens match the ones in this tutorial, you'll return to the default style—the one Windows XP uses when it's initially installed. No matter what changes you make to the setup of Windows XP, you can always revert to the default style.

To switch to the Web style and back to the default style:

1. Click **Tools** on the menu bar, and then click **Folder Options**.

2. If necessary, click the **General** tab in the Folder Options dialog box. The General sheet includes options for working with files and windows.

3. In the Click items as follows section, click the **Single-click to open an item (point to select)** option button. When you select this option button, the Underline icon titles consistent with my browser option button is also selected. This means that filenames will always be underlined to indicate that you can click to open them.

4. Click the **OK** button. The filenames in the My Computer window are underlined as hyperlinks.

5. In the My Computer window, point to the **Agenda** icon. The icon is highlighted, indicating it is selected, and after a few moments, a ScreenTip appears. See Figure 2-20.

Figure 2-20	MY COMPUTER WINDOW IN WEB STYLE

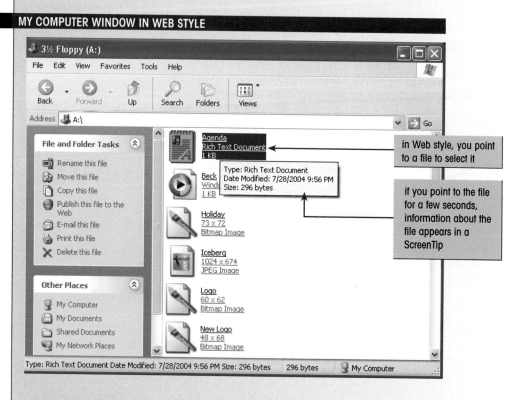

In Web style, when you move the pointer over an icon or underlined text, it appears as a hand, indicating the icon or text is a hyperlink. In Classic style, when you point to an icon or filename, the pointer is a selection arrow.

6. To restore the default style, click **Tools** on the menu bar, and then click **Folder Options**.

7. Click the **Restore Defaults** button in the Folder Options dialog box.

8. Click the **View** tab. The View tab includes options that control the appearance of files and other objects. You need to make sure these options are set to their default settings as well.

9. Click the **Restore Defaults** button.

10. Click the **OK** button to close the Folder Options dialog box.

Working with Folders and Directories

Up to now, you've done a little work with files and windows, but before going further, you should look at some of the terminology used to describe these tasks. Any location where you can store files on a computer is called a **directory**. The main directory of a disk is sometimes called the **root directory**, or the **top-level directory**. All of the files on your Data Disk are currently in the root directory of your floppy disk.

If too many files are stored in a directory, the directory list becomes very long and difficult to manage. You can divide a directory into **subdirectories**, also called **folders**. The number of files for each folder then becomes much fewer and easier to manage. A folder within a folder is called a **subfolder**. The folder that contains another folder is called the **parent folder**.

Windows XP arranges all of these objects—root directory, folders, subfolders, and files—in a **hierarchy**. The hierarchy begins with your desktop and extends down to each subfolder. Figure 2-21 shows part of a typical hierarchy of Windows XP objects.

Figure 2-21	PART OF A TYPICAL HIERARCHY OF WINDOWS XP OBJECTS

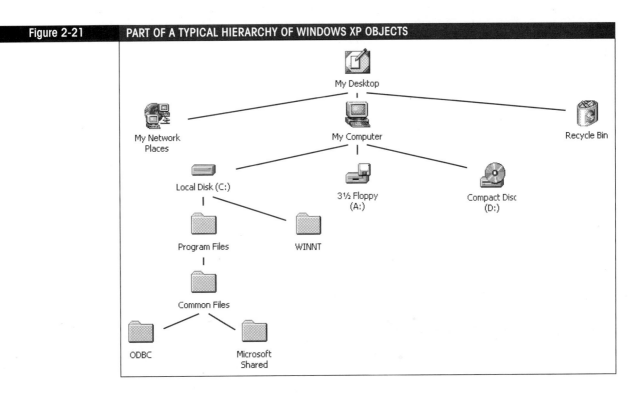

Creating a Folder

You've already seen folder icons in the windows you've opened. Now you'll create your own folder called Practice to hold your documents. This time, you can work in Icons view so you can see all the files on the Data Disk.

To create a Practice folder:

1. Click the **Views** button [icon] on the Standard Buttons toolbar, and then click **Icons**.

2. Click **File** on the menu bar, and then point to **New** to display the submenu.

3. Click **Folder**. A folder icon with the label "New Folder" appears in the My Computer window.

4. Type **Practice** as the name of the folder.

   TROUBLE? If nothing happens when you type the folder name, it's possible that the folder name is no longer selected. Right-click the new folder, click Rename on the shortcut menu, and then repeat Step 4.

5. Press the **Enter** key. The new folder is now named "Practice" and is the selected item on your Data Disk.

6. Click a blank area next to the Practice folder to deselect it.

Navigating Through the Windows XP Hierarchy

Now that you've created a folder, how do you move into it? You've learned that to view the contents of a file, you open it. To move into a folder, you open it in the same way.

To view the contents of the Practice folder:

1. Double-click the **Practice** folder. The Practice folder opens.

Because the folder doesn't contain any files, there's nothing listed in the right pane of the My Computer window. You'll change that shortly.

You've learned that to navigate through your computer, you open My Computer and then click the icons representing the objects you want to explore, such as folders and files. But what if you want to move back to the root directory? The Standard Buttons toolbar, which stays the same regardless of which folder or object is open, includes buttons that help you navigate the hierarchy of drives, directories, folders, subfolders, and other objects in your computer. Figure 2-22 summarizes the navigation buttons on the Standard Buttons toolbar.

Figure 2-22		NAVIGATION BUTTONS
BUTTON	**ICON**	**DESCRIPTION**
Back	◀	Returns you to the folder, drive, directory, or object you were most recently viewing. The button is active only when you have viewed more than one window in the current session.
Forward	▶	Reverses the effect of the Back button.
Up	⬆	Moves you up one level in the hierarchy of directories, drives, folders, and other objects on your computer.

You can return to your floppy's root directory by using the Back or Up buttons. Try both of these techniques now.

To move up to the root directory:

1. Click the **Back** button ◀ on the Standard Buttons toolbar. Windows XP opens the previous window, in this case, the root directory of your Data Disk.

2. Click the **Forward** button ▶ on the Standard Buttons toolbar. The Forward button reverses the effect of the Back button and takes you to the Practice folder.

3. Click the **Up** button ⬆ on the Standard Buttons toolbar. You move up one level in the hierarchy of Windows XP objects, to the root directory of the Data Disk.

Another way of moving around in the Windows XP hierarchy is through the Address Bar. By clicking the Address Bar list arrow, you can view a list of the objects in the top part of the Windows XP hierarchy, as illustrated in Figure 2-23. This gives you a quick way of moving to the top without navigating through the intermediate levels.

| Figure 2-23 | A HIERARCHY OF OBJECTS IN THE ADDRESS LIST BOX |

Now that you know how to move around your computer's hierarchy, you can practice manipulating files. The more organized the hierarchy of your computer, the easier it is to find the files you need.

Working with Files

As you've seen, the Practice folder doesn't contain any files. To add files to a folder or drive, you can move a file from one place to another or copy a file so you have duplicates in two locations. After you copy a file, you might want to rename it—that way, you won't confuse it with the original file. If you no longer use a file, you can delete it from your disk. You should periodically delete files you no longer need, so your folders and disks don't get too full and slow the performance of your system.

My Computer simplifies these tasks because you can move, copy, rename, and delete files using the My Computer window. Next, you will use My Computer to place a file from the root directory in the Practice folder.

Moving and Copying a File

If you want to place a file in a folder from another location, you can either move the file or copy it. **Moving** a file removes it from its current location and places it in a new location you specify. **Copying** leaves the file in its current location and places a copy in the new location. Windows XP provides several techniques for moving and copying files. One way is to make sure that both the current and the new location are visible on your screen and then hold down the right mouse button and drag the file from the old location to the new location. A menu appears, including options to move or copy the selected file to the new location. The advantage to this technique is that it is clear whether you are moving or copying a file. Try this technique now by moving the Logo file to the Practice folder.

To move the Logo file to the Practice folder:

1. Point to the **Logo** file in the root directory of your Data Disk, and then press and hold the *right* mouse button.

2. With the right mouse button still pressed down, drag the **Logo** file to the Practice folder. When the Practice folder icon is highlighted, release the button. A shortcut menu appears, as shown in Figure 2-24.

Figure 2-24	MOVING A FILE

3. Click **Move Here** on the shortcut menu with the left mouse button. The Logo file is removed from the window showing the files in the root directory.

TROUBLE? If you release the mouse button by mistake before dragging the Logo file to the Practice folder, the Logo shortcut menu opens. Press the Esc key, and then repeat Steps 1 through 3.

4. Double-click the **Practice** folder. The Logo file now appears in the Practice folder.

You can also copy a file from one folder to another, or from one disk to another. When you copy a file, you create an exact duplicate of a file in whatever disk or folder you specify. To copy a file from one folder to another on your floppy disk, you use the same procedure as for moving a file, except that you select Copy Here on the shortcut menu. Try copying the Agenda file into the Practice folder.

To copy the Agenda file into the Practice folder:

1. Click the **Up** button on the Standard Buttons toolbar. The root directory of your Data Disk is displayed.

2. Using the right mouse button, drag the **Agenda** file into the Practice folder.

> **3.** Using the left mouse button, click **Copy Here** on the shortcut menu. Notice this time the file is not removed from the root directory because you copied the file.
>
> **4.** Double-click the **Practice** folder. A copy of the Agenda file now appears in the Practice folder.

Note that the Move Here command was also on the shortcut menu. In fact, the command was in boldface, indicating that it is the default command whenever you drag a document from one location to another on the same drive. This means that if you were to drag a file from one location to another on the same drive using the left mouse button (instead of the right), the file would be moved and not copied.

Renaming a File

Sometimes you decide to give a file a different name to clarify the file's contents. You can easily rename a file by using the Rename command on the file's shortcut menu.

Practice this technique by renaming the Agenda file to give it a more descriptive filename.

> *To rename the Agenda file:*
>
> **1.** Make sure the right pane is set to Tiles view. If necessary, click the **Views** button ▦ ˙ on the Standard Buttons toolbar, and then click **Tiles**.
>
> **2.** Right-click the **Agenda** icon.
>
> **3.** Click **Rename** on the shortcut menu. The filename is highlighted and a box appears around it.
>
> **4.** Type **Practice Agenda** and press the **Enter** key. The file now appears with the new name.
>
> TROUBLE? If you make a mistake while typing and you haven't pressed the Enter key yet, you can press the Backspace key until you delete the mistake, and then complete Step 3. If you've already pressed the Enter key, repeat Steps 1 through 3 to rename the file again.

Deleting a File or Folder

You should periodically delete files you no longer need so that your folders and disks don't get cluttered. In My Computer, you delete a file or folder by deleting its icon. Be careful when you delete a folder, because you also delete all the files it contains! When you delete a file from a hard drive on your computer, the filename is deleted from the directory but the file contents are held in the Recycle Bin. The **Recycle Bin** is an area on your hard drive that holds deleted files until you remove them permanently; an icon on the desktop allows you easy access to the Recycle Bin. If you change your mind and want to retrieve a file deleted from your hard drive, you can recover it by using the Recycle Bin. However, after you empty the Recycle Bin, you can no longer recover the files that were in it.

When you delete a file from a floppy disk or another disk on your network, it does not go into the Recycle Bin. Instead, it is deleted as soon as its icon disappears—and you can't recover it.

Try deleting the Practice Agenda file from your Data Disk. Because this file is on the floppy disk and not on the hard disk, it will not go into the Recycle Bin. If you change your mind, you won't be able to recover it.

To delete the Practice Agenda file:

1. Right-click the **Practice Agenda** file icon.

2. Click **Delete** on the shortcut menu.

A message box appears, Windows XP asking if you're sure you want to delete this file.

3. Click the **Yes** button.

4. Click the **Close** button [X] to close the My Computer window.

Another way of deleting a file is to drag its icon to the Recycle Bin on the desktop. Be aware that if you're dragging a file from your floppy disk or network drive, the file will *not* be placed in the Recycle Bin—it will be permanently deleted.

Other Copying and Moving Techniques

As you become more familiar with Windows XP, you will probably settle on the copying and moving technique you like best. Figure 2-25 describes some of the other ways of moving and copying files.

Figure 2-25	METHODS FOR MOVING AND COPYING FILES	
METHOD	**TO MOVE**	**TO COPY**
Cut, copy and paste	Select the file icon. Click Edit on the menu bar, and then click Cut. Move to the new location. Click Edit and then click Paste.	Select the file icon. Click Edit on the menu bar, and then click Copy. Move to the new location. Click Edit and then click Paste.
Drag and drop	Click the file icon. Drag and drop the icon to the new location.	Click the file icon. Hold down the Ctrl key, and drag and drop the icon to the new location.
Right-click, drag and drop	With the right mouse button pressed down, drag the file icon to the new location. Release the mouse button, and click Move Here on the shortcut menu.	With the right mouse button pressed down, drag the file icon to the new location. Release the mouse button, and click Copy Here on the shortcut menu.
Move to folder and copy to folder	Click the file icon. Click Edit on the menu bar, and then click Move to Folder. Select the new location in the Browse for Folder dialog box.	Click the file icon. Click Edit on the menu bar, and then click Copy to Folder. Select the new location in the Browse for Folder dialog box.

The techniques shown in Figure 2-25 are primarily for document (data) files. Because a program might not work correctly if moved to a new location, the techniques for moving program files are slightly different. See the Windows XP online Help for more information on moving or copying a program file.

Copying an Entire Floppy Disk

You can have trouble accessing the data on your floppy disk if the disk is damaged, is exposed to magnetic fields, or picks up a computer virus. To avoid losing all your data, you should always make a copy of your floppy disk.

If you wanted to make a copy of a videotape, your VCR would need two tape drives. You might wonder, therefore, how your computer can make a copy of your disk if you have only one floppy disk drive. Figure 2-26 illustrates how the computer uses only one disk drive to make a copy of a disk.

Figure 2-26	USING ONE DISK DRIVE TO COPY A DISK

1. First, the computer copies the data from your original disk into memory.

2. Once the data is in memory, you remove your original disk from the drive and replace it with your copy disk.

Original Disk

3. The computer moves the data from memory onto your copy disk.

Memory Data

Memory

Memory Data

original disk

copy disk

copy disk

REFERENCE WINDOW   **RW**

<u>Copying a Disk</u>

- Insert the disk you want to copy in drive A.
- In My Computer, right-click the 3½ Floppy (A:) icon, and then click Copy Disk.
- Click Start to begin the copy process.
- When prompted, remove the disk you want to copy, place your second disk in drive A, and then click OK.

If you have an extra floppy disk, you can make a copy of your Data Disk now. Make sure you copy the disk regularly so that as you work through the tutorials in the book the disk stays updated.

To copy your Data Disk:

1. Write your name and "Windows XP Disk 1 Data Disk Copy" on the label of a blank, formatted disk.

   TROUBLE? If you aren't sure the disk is blank, place it in the disk drive and open the 3½ Floppy (A:) window to view its contents. If the disk contains files you need, get a different disk. If it contains files you don't need, you could format the disk now, using the steps you learned at the beginning of this tutorial.

2. Make sure your original Data Disk is in drive A, and then open and maximize the My Computer window.

3. Right-click the **3½ Floppy (A:)** icon, and then click **Copy Disk**. The Copy Disk dialog box opens.

4. Click the **Start** button to begin the copy process.

5. When the message "Insert the disk you want to copy from (source disk)" appears, click **OK**. Windows XP reads the disk in drive A and stores its contents in memory.

6. Click the **OK** button. When the copy is completed, you will see the message "Copy completed successfully."

7. Click the **Close** button to close the Copy Disk dialog box.

8. Close the My Computer window, and then remove your disk from the drive.

As you finish copying your disk, Shannon emphasizes the importance of making copies of your files frequently, so you won't risk losing important documents for your distance learning course. If your original Data Disk were damaged, you could use the copy you just made to access the files.

Keeping copies of your files is so important that Windows XP includes with it a program called **Backup** that automates the process of duplicating and storing data. In the Projects at the end of the tutorial you'll have an opportunity to explore the difference between what you just did in copying a disk and the way in which a program such as the Windows XP Backup program helps you safeguard data.

Session 2.2 QUICK CHECK

1. If you want to find out about the storage devices and printers connected to your computer, what Windows XP window can you open?

2. If you have only one floppy disk drive on your computer, the letter _____ usually identifies it.

3. The letter C typically designates the _____ drive of a computer.

4. What information does Details view supply about a list of folders and files?

5. The main directory of a disk is referred to as the _____ directory.

6. True or False: You can divide a directory into folders.

7. If you have one floppy disk drive and two floppy disks, can you copy the files on one floppy disk to the other?

REVIEW ASSIGNMENTS

1. **Opening, Editing, and Printing a Document** In this tutorial you learned how to create a document using WordPad. You also learned how to save, open, and print a document. Practice these skills by opening the document called **Resume** on your Data Disk. This document is a resume for Jamie Woods. Make the changes shown in Figure 2-27, and then save the document in the Practice folder with the name **Woods Resume** using the Save As command. After you save your revisions, preview and then print the document. Close WordPad.

Figure 2-27

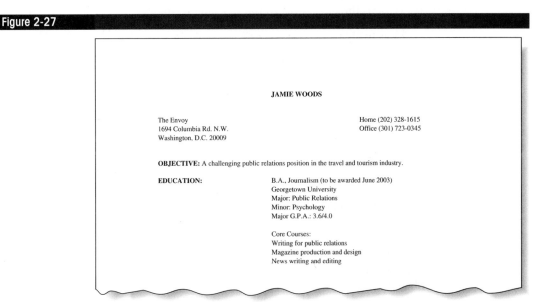

```
                              JAMIE WOODS


  The Envoy                            Home (202) 328-1615
  1694 Columbia Rd. N.W.               Office (301) 723-0345
  Washington, D.C. 20009


  OBJECTIVE: A challenging public relations position in the travel and tourism industry.

  EDUCATION:                    B.A., Journalism (to be awarded June 2003)
                                Georgetown University
                                Major: Public Relations
                                Minor: Psychology
                                Major G.P.A.: 3.6/4.0

                                Core Courses:
                                Writing for public relations
                                Magazine production and design
                                News writing and editing
```

2. **Creating, Saving, and Printing a Letter** Use WordPad to write a one-page letter to a relative or a friend. Save the document in the Practice folder on your Data Disk with the name **Letter**. Use the Print Preview feature to look at the format of your finished letter, then print it, and be sure to sign it. Close WordPad.

3. **Managing Files and Folders** Using the copy of the disk you made at the end of the tutorial, complete Steps a through f below to practice your file-management skills. Then answer Questions 1 through 5 below.

   a. Create a folder called "Documents" on the copy of your Data Disk.
   b. Move the files Agenda, Proposal, and Resume to the Documents folder.
   c. Create a folder called "Park Project."
   d. Move the files New Logo, Stationery, and Vinca to the Park Project folder.
   e. Delete the file called "Logo."
   f. Switch to Details view, and write out your answers to Questions 1 through 5:

      1. What is the largest file in the Park Project folder?

      2. What is the newest file in the Documents folder?

      3. How many files are in the root directory of your Data Disk? (Don't count folders.)

      4. How are the Salinas Family and Iceberg icons different? Judging from the appearance of the icons, what would you guess these two files contain?

      5. Which file in the root directory has the most recent date?

4. **More Practice with Files and Folders** For this assignment, you need a third blank disk. Complete parts a through g below to practice your file-management skills.

   a. Write "Windows XP Tutorial 2 Assignment 4" on the label of the blank disk, and then format the disk if necessary.
   b. Create another copy of your original Data Disk, using the Assignment 4 disk. Refer to the section "Copying an Entire Floppy Disk" in Session 2.2.
   c. Create three folders on the Assignment 4 Data Disk you just created: Documents, Meetings, and Graphics.
   d. Move the files Iceberg, Holiday, Logo, and New Logo to the Graphics folder.
   e. Move the files Resume and Salinas Family to the Documents folder.
   f. Move Agenda and Stationery to the Meetings folder.
   g. Switch to Details view, and write out your answers to Questions 1 through 5.

      1. What is the largest file in the Graphics folder?

      2. How many documents created with a word-processing program are in the root directory? (*Hint*: These documents will appear with the WordPad, Microsoft Word, or some other word-processing icon, depending on what software you have installed.)

      3. What is the newest file or files in the root directory? (Don't include folders.)

      4. How many files in all folders are 5KB in size?

      5. How many files in the root directory are JPEG images? (*Hint*: Look in the Type column to identify JPEG images.)

      6. Do all the files in the Graphics folder have the same icon? What type are they?

Explore

5. **Searching for a File** Windows XP Help includes topics that explain how to search for files on a disk without looking through all the folders. Start Windows Help and use one of the following methods to locate topics on searching for files.

   ■ On the Home page, click the Windows basics link. On the Windows basics page, click the Searching for information link, and then click the Search for a file or folder topic. In the article, click the Related Topics link, and then click Search for a file or folder.

   ■ On the Index page, type "files and folders" (no quotation marks) in the Type in the keyword to find text box and then click the Display button. In the list of entries for "files and folders," double-click "searching for." In the Topics found dialog box, double-click "To search for a file or folder."

   ■ In the Search box, type "searching for files and folders" and then press the Enter key. Click the Search for a file or folder link.

   Read the topic and click the Related Topics link at the end of the topic, if necessary, to answer Questions a through c:

   a. How do you display the Search window?
   b. Do you need to type the entire filename in the Search window to find the file?
   c. What are three file characteristics you can use as Search options?

6. **Help with Managing Files and Folders** In Tutorial 2 you learned how to work with Windows XP files and folders. Use the Index page in Windows XP Help and Support to find an overview of files and folders. Use the Related Topics link to find two procedures for managing files and folders that were not covered in the tutorial. Write out the procedures in your own words, and include the title of the Help page that contains the information.

Explore

7. **Formatting Text** You can use a word processor such as WordPad to **format** text, that is, to change its appearance by using bold, italic, and different fonts, and by applying other features. Using WordPad, type the title and words of one of your favorite songs, and then save the document on your Data Disk with the name **Song**. (Make sure to use your original Data Disk.)

   a. Select the title of the song, click the Center button ▤ on the toolbar, click the Bold button **B**, and then click the Italic button *I* .
   b. Click the list arrow for the Font button on the toolbar, and then select a different font. Repeat this step several times with different fonts until you locate a font that is appropriate for the song.
   c. Experiment with formatting options until you find a look you like for your document. Save and print the final version.

PROJECTS

1. Formatting a floppy disk removes all the data on a disk. Answer the following questions:

   a. What other method did you learn in this tutorial to remove data from a disk?
   b. If you wanted to remove all data from a disk, which method would you use? Why?
   c. What method would you use if you wanted to remove only one file? Why?

2. A friend who is new to computers is trying to learn how to enter text into WordPad. She has just finished typing her first paragraph when she notices a mistake in the first sentence. She can't remember how to fix a mistake, so she asks you for help. Write the set of steps that she should follow.

3. Computer users usually develop habits about how they access their files and programs. Take a minute to practice methods of opening a file, and then evaluate which method you would be most likely to use and why.

   a. Using WordPad, create a document containing the words to a favorite poem, and save it on your Data Disk with the name **Poem**.
   b. Close WordPad and return to the desktop.
   c. Open the document using a *docucentric* approach.
   d. After a successful completion of part c, close the program and reopen the same document using another approach.
   e. Write the steps that you used to complete parts c and d of this assignment. Then write a paragraph discussing which approach is most convenient when you are starting from the desktop, and indicate what habits you would develop if you owned your own computer and used it regularly.

Explore ▷ 4. The My Computer window gives you access to the objects on your computer. In this tutorial you used My Computer to access your floppy drive so you could view the contents of your Data Disk. The My Computer window gives you access to other objects, too. Open My Computer and write a list of the objects you see, including folders. Then double-click each icon and write a two-sentence description of the contents of each window that opens.

Explore

5. In this tutorial you learned how to copy a disk to protect yourself in the event of data loss. If you had your own computer with a 40GB hard drive that was being used to capacity, it would take many 1.44MB floppy disks to copy the contents of the entire hard drive. Is copying a reasonable method to use for protecting the data on your hard disk? Why, or why not?

   a. Windows XP includes an accessory called Backup that helps you safeguard your data. Backup doesn't just copy the data, it organizes the data so that it takes up much less space than if you simply copied it. This program might not be installed on your computer, but if it is, try starting it (click the Start button, point to all Programs, point to Accessories, point to System Tools, and then click Backup) and opening the Help files to learn what you can about how it functions. If it is not installed, continue with part b.

   b. Look up the topic of backups in a computer concepts textbook or in computer trade magazines. You could also interview experienced computer owners to find out which method they use to protect their data. When you have finished researching the concept of the backup, write a single-page essay that explains the difference between copying and backing up files, and that evaluates which method is preferable for backing up large amounts of data, and why.

LAB ASSIGNMENTS

Using Files In this Lab you manipulate a simulated computer to view what happens in memory and on disk when you create, save, open, revise, and delete files. Understanding what goes on "inside the box" will help you quickly grasp how to perform basic file operations with most application software. See the Read This Before You Begin page for instructions on starting the Using Files Course Lab.

1. Click the Steps button to learn how to use the simulated computer to view the contents of the memory and disk when you perform basic file operations. As you proceed through the Steps, answer all of the Quick Check questions that appear. After you complete the Steps, you will see a Quick Check Summary Report. Follow the instructions on the screen to print this report.

2. Click the Explore button and use the simulated computer to perform the following tasks:
   a. Create a document containing your name and the city in which you were born. Save this document as NAME.
   b. Create another document containing two of your favorite foods. Save this document as FOODS.
   c. Create another file containing your two favorite classes. Call this file CLASSES.
   d. Open the FOOD file and add another one of your favorite foods. Save this file without changing its name.
   e. Open the NAME file. Change this document so it contains your name and the name of your school. Save this as a new document called SCHOOL.
   f. Write down how many files are on the simulated disk and the exact contents of each file.
   g. Delete all the files.

3. In Explore, use the simulated computer to perform the following tasks.
   a. Create a file called MUSIC that contains the name of your favorite CD.
   b. Create another document that contains eight numbers, and call this file LOTTERY.
   c. You didn't win the lottery this week. Revise the contents of the LOTTERY file but save the revision as LOTTERY2.
   d. Revise the MUSIC file so it also contains the name of your favorite musician or composer, and save this file as MUSIC2.
   e. Delete the MUSIC file.
   f. Write down how many files are on the simulated disk and the exact contents of each file.

QUICK CHECK ANSWERS

Session 2.1

1. file
2. Formatting
3. True
4. insertion point
5. word wrap
6. Move the I-beam pointer to the left of the first word you want to select, and then drag the I-beam pointer over the text to the end of the last word you want to select.
7. file extension

Session 2.2

1. My Computer
2. A
3. hard
4. filename, size, type, and date modified
5. root or top-level
6. True
7. yes

New Perspectives on

WINDOWS XP

Read This Before You Begin

To the Student

Data Disks

To complete the Level II tutorials, Review Assignments, and Projects, you need three Data Disks. Your instructor will either provide you with these Data Disks or ask you to make your own.

If you are making your own Data Disks, you will need **three** blank, formatted high-density disks. You will need to copy a set of files and/or folders from a file server, standalone computer, or the Web onto your disks. Your instructor will tell you which computer, drive letter, and folders contain the files you need. You could also download the files by going to **www.course.com** and following the instructions on the screen.

The information below shows you the Data Disks you need so that you will have enough disk space to complete all the tutorials, Review Assignments, and Projects:

Data Disk 1

Write this on the disk label:
Data Disk 1: Windows XP Tutorial 3

Data Disk 2

Write this on the disk label:
Data Disk 2: Windows XP Tutorials 4 and 5

Data Disk 3

Write this on the disk label:
Data Disk 3: Windows XP Tutorial 6

When you begin each tutorial, Review Assignment, or Project, be sure you are using the correct Data Disk. Refer to the "File Finder" chart at the back of this text for more detailed information on which files are used in which tutorials. See the inside front or inside back cover of this book for more information on Data Disk files, or ask your instructor or technical support person for assistance.

Course Labs

The Windows XP Level II tutorials feature an interactive Course Lab to help you understand Internet concepts. There are Lab Assignments at the end of Tutorial 5 that relate to this Lab.

To start a Lab, click the **Start** button on the Windows taskbar, point to **Programs**, point to **Course Labs**, point to **New Perspectives Course Labs**, and then click the name of the Lab you want to use.

Using Your Own Computer

If you are going to work through this book using your own computer, you need:

- **Computer System** Microsoft Windows XP must be installed on your computer. This book assumes a typical installation of Microsoft Windows XP Professional.

- **Data Disks** You will not be able to complete the tutorials or exercises in this book using your own computer until you have your Data Disks.

- **Course Labs** See your instructor or technical support person to obtain the Course Lab software for use on your own computer.

Visit Our World Wide Web Site

Additional materials designed especially for you are available on the World Wide Web.
Go to **www.course.com/NewPerspectives**.

To the Instructor

The Data Disk Files and Course Labs are available on the Instructor's Resource Kit for this title. Follow the instructions in the Help file on the CD-ROM to install the programs to your network or standalone computer. For information on creating Data Disks or the Course Labs, see the "To the Student" section above.

You are granted a license to copy the Data Files and Course Labs to any computer or computer network used by students who have purchased this book.

OBJECTIVES

In this tutorial you will:

- View the structure of folders and files in Windows Explorer

- Select, create, and rename folders in Windows Explorer

- Navigate through devices and folders using navigation buttons

- Select a single file, a group of files, all files, or all files but one in a list of files

- Create a printout showing the structure of folders and files

- Move and copy one or more files from one location to another

- "Quick" format a floppy disk

- View files in the Favorites, Media, History, and Search Companion panes

ORGANIZING

FILES WITH WINDOWS EXPLORER

Structuring Information on a Disk for the Kolbe Climbing School

CASE

Kolbe Climbing School

Bernard Kolbe knew how to climb before he could ride a bike. In college he started what is now one of the most popular guide services in the Front Range, the Kolbe Climbing School, known to locals as "KCS." KCS offers guided climbs in the Front Range area, especially in Rocky Mountain National Park and nearby climbing areas such as Lumpy Ridge. While most clients simply want to learn rock and sport climbing, a few want guides for longer alpine climbs and ice climbing.

Until recently, Bernard maintained mostly paper records of his business activities, with some electronic records stored on the computer he used in college. When he graduated from college, his business took off, and he now has twice as many clients and employees as he did a year ago. In addition, conversations with his insurance agent and accountant have convinced him that he needs to keep more reliable and complete records on his employees, clients, and equipment. He bought a new computer and copied all his business files from his old computer to a floppy disk. Now he's ready to store and maintain these files on his new computer.

Not too long ago, Bernard asked if you could help him organize the KCS files on his floppy disk before he copies them to the new hard disk. You agreed (in exchange for some free climbing lessons) and got to work reviewing and organizing the files on his floppy disk. When Bernard first gave you the disk, all the files were stored together—you couldn't tell which files related to employee guides, for example, unless you opened them. Your first task was to create a folder structure on the disk, with separate folders for guides, clients, and gear.

This morning, you walked into the office and found that Bernard had spent yesterday evening at his new computer creating business files. You realize you need to show him the folder structure you created so he can learn to use it. You point out that an important part of electronic recordkeeping is creating and using a system that makes it easy to find important information. Bernard is willing to learn more (it's too cold to climb anyway), so you pull up a chair and offer to spend some time looking over Bernard's files.

SESSION 3.1

In this session, you will learn how Windows Explorer displays the devices and folders on your computer. Understanding how to manipulate this display is the first step in using Windows Explorer to organize files, which will make you a more productive Windows user. In this tutorial, you will work with files and folders on a floppy disk. If you have your own computer or are in a business environment, you will more likely work with files and folders on a hard disk. You will discover that file management techniques are practically the same for floppy disks and hard disks. For this tutorial, you will need the Windows XP Tutorial 3 Data Disk 1 and one blank 3½-inch disk.

Windows Explorer

Using Windows Explorer is one way to organize files. **Windows Explorer** is a program included with Windows XP that is designed to simplify file management tasks. Through an easy-to-navigate representation of the resources on your computer, Windows Explorer makes it easy to view, move, copy, or delete your files and folders.

If you have used the My Computer window, the Windows Explorer window will be familiar to you. Many of the techniques you use with the My Computer window apply to Windows Explorer—and vice-versa. Both let you display and work with files and folders. By default, however, Windows Explorer also lets you see the hierarchy of all the folders on your computer. Viewing this hierarchy makes it easier to navigate your computer, especially if it contains many files and folders.

The root directory of Bernard's floppy disk contains three folders—Clients, Gear, and Guides—plus the files he hasn't yet organized. You will use Windows Explorer to view the information stored on Bernard's disk.

Starting Windows Explorer

As with other Windows XP programs, you start Windows Explorer using the Start menu.

> *To start Windows Explorer:*
>
> **1.** Insert the Windows XP Tutorial 3 Data Disk 1 in drive A, click the **Start** button **start**, point to **All Programs**, point to **Accessories**, and then click **Windows Explorer**. The Windows Explorer window opens, as shown in Figure 3-1.

Figure 3-1	THE WINDOWS EXPLORER WINDOW

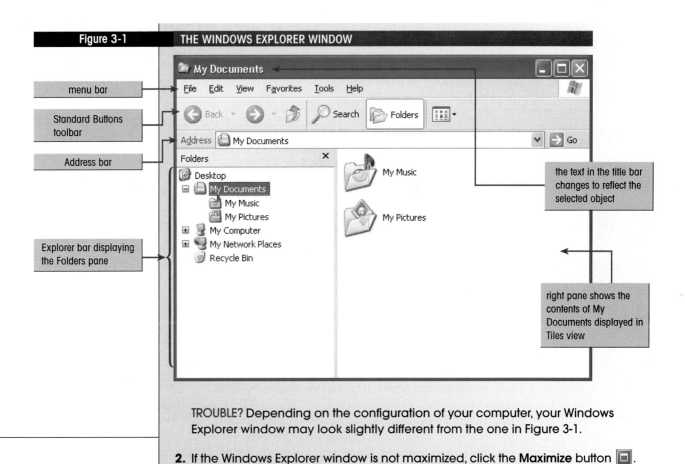

menu bar

Standard Buttons toolbar

Address bar

Explorer bar displaying the Folders pane

the text in the title bar changes to reflect the selected object

right pane shows the contents of My Documents displayed in Tiles view

TROUBLE? Depending on the configuration of your computer, your Windows Explorer window may look slightly different from the one in Figure 3-1.

2. If the Windows Explorer window is not maximized, click the **Maximize** button . Figure 3-2 describes the elements of the Windows Explorer window.

Figure 3-2	THE ELEMENTS OF THE WINDOWS EXPLORER WINDOW

WINDOWS EXPLORER WINDOW ELEMENT	DESCRIPTION
Title bar	Displays the name of the currently selected object in the Windows Explorer window
Menu bar	Contains commands for working with files and folders in the Windows Explorer window
Standard Buttons toolbar	Contains buttons that provide shortcuts to common commands
Address bar	Shows the location of the active folder; you can click the list arrow on the Address bar to select a different location
Explorer bar	Appears in the left pane and can be displayed in one of five ways: as a Search, Favorites, Media, History, or Folders Pane
Folders pane	Shows the folders and files on your computer; one of five panes you can display in the left pane, also called the Explorer bar
Right pane	Shows the contents of the object selected in the left pane

Like the My Computer window, the Windows Explorer window can display the Standard Buttons, Address, and Links toolbars and a status bar. For this tutorial, you need to make sure the window displays the Standard Buttons toolbar, the Address bar, and status bar. Also make sure the Lock toolbars option is selected. To match the figures in this tutorial, you should also display the files in the right pane in Tiles view unless the steps instruct you to use a different view.

To set up the appearance of Windows Explorer:

1. Click **View** on the menu bar, and then point to **Toolbars**. Change the settings, if necessary, so that the Standard Buttons toolbar and the Address bar are the only toolbars displayed.

2. Click **View** on the menu bar and point to **Toolbars** again. If the **Lock the Toolbar** option is not checked, click to select it.

3. Click **View** on the menu bar again, and then click **Tiles** to select this option, if necessary.

Displaying the Explorer Bar

Windows Explorer is divided into two sections called **panes**. The left pane, also called the **Explorer bar**, shows different ways of locating specific files or folders on your computer. The right pane lists the contents of these files and folders (similar to the view of files and folders you had using My Computer in Tutorial 2).

You can display the Explorer bar in one of five ways: as a Search, Favorites, Media, History, or Folders pane. The **Search** pane includes tools to help you search for a particular file or folder on your computer. The **Favorites** pane lists your favorite files and folders on your computer and sites on the World Wide Web. The **Media** pane lists multimedia files, such as videos and music. The **History** pane organizes the files and folders on your computer by the date you last worked with them. The **Folders** pane organizes your files and folders based on their location in the hierarchy of objects on your computer. To move between these different panes, you click the appropriate command on the View menu. You can also quickly open the Search and Folders panes by clicking either the Search button ⌕ or the Folders button 🗀 on the Standard Buttons toolbar. Note that the Explorer bar is available in any Windows XP window that displays files and folders. You can, for example, use the Explorer bar in the My Computer window.

You'll start working with Windows Explorer using the Folders pane.

To view the Folders pane:

1. Click **View** on the menu bar, and then point to **Explorer Bar**.

2. If necessary, click **Folders** to check that option; otherwise click a blank area of the screen to close the View menu. Your Windows Explorer window should now resemble Figure 3-3.

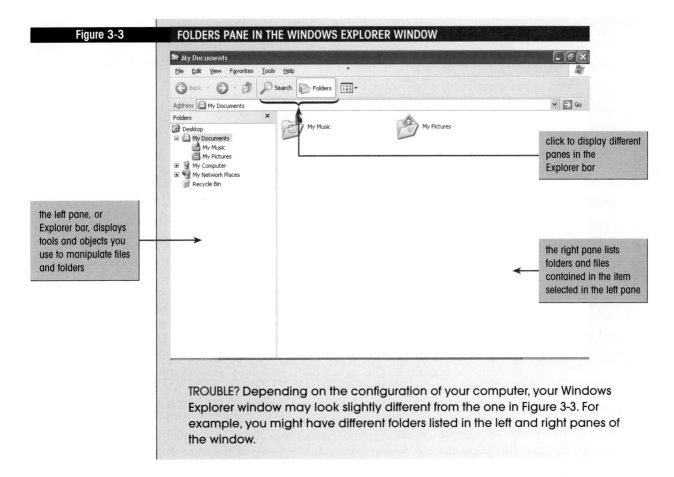

Figure 3-3 · **FOLDERS PANE IN THE WINDOWS EXPLORER WINDOW**

the left pane, or Explorer bar, displays tools and objects you use to manipulate files and folders

click to display different panes in the Explorer bar

the right pane lists folders and files contained in the item selected in the left pane

TROUBLE? Depending on the configuration of your computer, your Windows Explorer window may look slightly different from the one in Figure 3-3. For example, you might have different folders listed in the left and right panes of the window.

The Folders pane initially displays a list of the objects on your desktop: the My Documents folder, the My Computer window, the My Network Places window, and the Recycle Bin. If your desktop contains other folders or objects, the pane displays those as well. The right pane of the Windows Explorer window displays the contents of the object selected in the Folders pane. In this case, the My Documents folder is the selected object, and it contains two items—the My Music and My Pictures folders. Therefore, the right pane displays icons for these objects.

Working with the Folders Pane

The Folders pane displays the devices and resources available to your computer. (You may need to scroll the Folders pane to view the complete list of objects.) Each object in the list has a small icon next to it. In this session you will use the Folders pane to explore your computer's contents. Windows Explorer uses the icons shown in Figure 3-4, among others, to represent different types of storage objects.

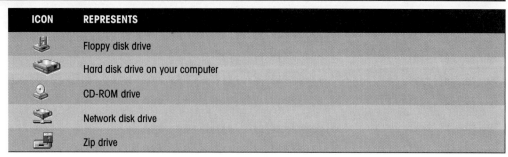

Figure 3-4 | STORAGE DEVICE ICONS

ICON	REPRESENTS
	Floppy disk drive
	Hard disk drive on your computer
	CD-ROM drive
	Network disk drive
	Zip drive

Opening an Object in the Folders Pane

Like a file cabinet, a typical storage device on your computer contains files and folders. These folders can contain additional files and one or more levels of subfolders. If Windows Explorer displayed all the storage devices, folders, and files on your computer at once, the list could be very long. Instead, Windows Explorer allows you to open devices and folders only when you want to see what they contain. Otherwise, you can keep them closed.

When the Folders pane is open in the left pane of the Windows Explorer window, it provides a view of the devices and folders on your computer and shows how these devices and folders are organized. The right pane is your work area. If you select a folder in the left pane, for example, the files stored in that folder appear in the right pane. Then you can move, copy, delete, and perform other tasks with the files in the right pane, referring to the left pane to see how your changes affect the overall organization.

To identify the objects in the Folders pane, look for the small icon next to each object in the list, called the **device icon** or **folder icon**; each icon represents a device or folder on your computer. Many of these icons also have a plus box or minus box next to them, which indicates whether the device or folder contains additional folders. The device and folder icons and the plus and minus boxes are controls that you can click to change the display in the Windows Explorer window. You click the plus box to display folders or subfolders, and you click the minus box to hide them. (You can also refer to clicking the plus box as "expanding" the view of the file hierarchy and clicking the minus box as "collapsing" the view of the file hierarchy.) When you click a device or folder icon, its contents appear in the right pane.

You begin assisting Bernard by showing him how you've structured the folders on drive A, which is located in the Windows XP hierarchy beneath the My Computer icon. You explain to him how he can use the plus and minus boxes to open the My Computer icon and then the drive icon for his floppy disk.

REFERENCE WINDOW | RW

Displaying or Hiding Objects in the Folders Pane
- Click the plus box next to a device or folder to display its next level of folders.
- Click the minus box next to a device or folder to hide all its subfolders.

To display or hide the levels of folders on drive A:

1. Click the plus box ⊞ to the left of the My Computer icon in the Folders pane.

2. Click to the left of the 3½ Floppy (A:) device icon. The folders in the root directory of drive A appear in the left pane, and the plus box in front of drive A changes to a minus box ⊟. See Figure 3-5.

Figure 3-5 | **THE FOLDERS PANE DISPLAYING FOLDERS ON DRIVE A**

TROUBLE? The 3½ Floppy (A:) device icon 💾 might appear with a different name on your computer. This is the icon representing the device that contains your Data Disk. In the steps in this tutorial, this icon is also called drive A.

TROUBLE? If you initially see a minus box to the left of the device icon for drive A, your drive A folders are already visible in the left pane. You don't need to click the icon in Step 2.

3. Click ⊟ to the left of 3½ Floppy (A:). Now the Folders pane shows only drive A; it does not show the folders it contains.

4. Click ⊞ to the left of 3½ Floppy (A:) one more time to redisplay the folders on the drive.

When you click the plus box ⊞ next to drive A, you do not necessarily see all the folders on the drive. You only see the first level of folders. If one of these folders contains subfolders, a plus box appears next to it. The Clients folder on drive A has a plus box next to it, indicating that it contains subfolders. When you originally created the structure for Bernard's disk, you grouped his clients into Advanced and Basic, and then grouped the Advanced clients by their primary interests—Alpine, Ice, and Sport.

To view the subfolders for Clients:

1. Click ⊞ next to the Clients folder. You see that Clients contains two subfolders: Advanced and Basic. Because ⊞ appears next to the Advanced folder, you know it contains subfolders as well.

2. Click ⊞ next to the Advanced folder. Now you see three additional subfolders: Alpine, Ice, and Sport. See Figure 3-6.

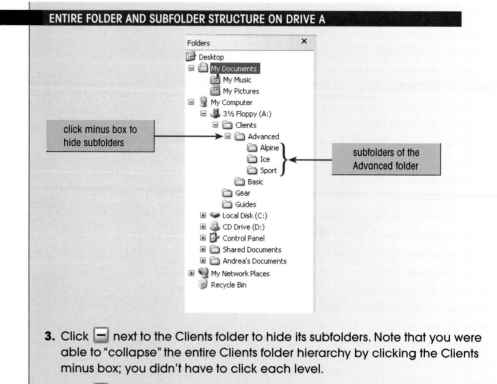

Figure 3-6   **ENTIRE FOLDER AND SUBFOLDER STRUCTURE ON DRIVE A**

3. Click ☐ next to the Clients folder to hide its subfolders. Note that you were able to "collapse" the entire Clients folder hierarchy by clicking the Clients minus box; you didn't have to click each level.

4. Click ☐ next to the Clients folder again. Note that the entire folder structure appears again—including the subfolders—because the last time you collapsed the Clients folder, you had all its subfolders displayed.

Using the plus and minus boxes does not select a device or folder. As you were clicking the plus and minus boxes next to the folders in drive A, the right pane still displayed the contents of the My Documents folder. To work with a device or folder in the Folders pane, you must first select its name or icon. Once selected, the device or folder appears highlighted, and the right pane displays its contents.

Selecting an Object in the Folders Pane

To select a device or folder, you must click its icon, not its plus or minus box. The selected device or folder is the one the computer uses when you take an action. For example, if you want to create a new folder on drive A, you first need to select drive A in the Folders pane. If you don't first select drive A, the new folder you create will be placed in whatever device or folder is currently selected—it could be a folder on the hard disk or network drive.

You can determine which device or folder is selected in four ways. First, it appears highlighted in the Folders pane, indicating it is selected. Also, its name appears in the Address bar and the title bar of the Windows Explorer window, and finally, its contents appear in the right pane.

You can experiment by selecting drive A and then selecting the Clients folder.

To select devices and folders:

1. Click **3½ Floppy (A:)**. Drive A is highlighted and its name appears in the Address bar and the Windows Explorer title bar. Its contents appear in the right pane.

2. Click **Clients** in the Folders pane. The computer highlights the folder name "Clients" and displays it in the Address bar and the title bar. Its contents appear in the right pane. See Figure 3-7.

Figure 3-7	THE SELECTED DEVICE OR FOLDER IN THE FOLDERS PANE

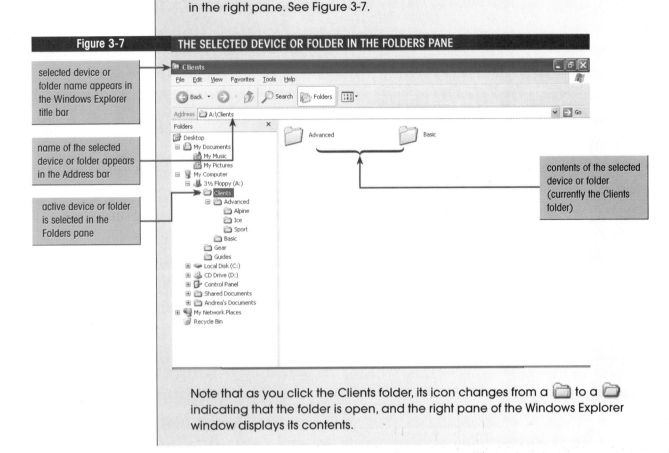

selected device or folder name appears in the Windows Explorer title bar

name of the selected device or folder appears in the Address bar

active device or folder is selected in the Folders pane

contents of the selected device or folder (currently the Clients folder)

Note that as you click the Clients folder, its icon changes from a 📁 to a 📂 indicating that the folder is open, and the right pane of the Windows Explorer window displays its contents.

Bernard tracks gear usage for ropes and other types of equipment such as karabiners, belay plates, and so on. His disk already contains a folder named Gear that contains files for each of the KCS ropes. Next, you decide to create two new subfolders within the Gear folder: one for all files having to do with ropes and the other for files having to do with hardware equipment.

Creating a New Folder

You can create a new folder using the New command on the File menu. You just have to make sure that you've first selected the location for the new folder in the Folders pane before creating the new folder.

REFERENCE WINDOW   **RW**

Creating a Folder in Windows Explorer
- In the Folders pane, click the device or folder that will contain the new folder.
- Click File, point to New, and then click Folder.
- Type a name for the new folder, and then press the Enter key.

The Clients folder is currently selected. If you create a new folder now, it will become a subfolder of Clients. Because you want to create the two subfolders in the Gear folder, you must first select the Gear folder.

To create the new subfolders within the Gear folder:

1. Click **Gear** in the Folders pane to select it.

2. Click **File** on the menu bar, point to **New**, and then click **Folder**. A folder icon labeled "New Folder" appears in the right pane. The folder name is selected. You can now type an appropriate name for the new folder.

   TROUBLE? If the folder name is not selected, you might have clicked to deselect it. Click the folder and then click it a second time to select the folder name.

3. Type **Hardware** as the title of the new folder, press the **Enter** key and then click a blank area of the right pane. Now create the second subfolder of the Gear folder for all the rope files.

   TROUBLE? If you pressed Enter twice by mistake, Hardware becomes the selected folder. Be sure the Gear folder is still selected.

4. Click **File**, point to **New**, click **Folder**, type **Ropes** as the name of the second folder, and then press the **Enter** key.

5. If necessary, click ➕ next to the Gear folder in the left pane to see the new folders in the left pane. See Figure 3-8.

| Figure 3-8 | CREATING NEW FOLDERS |

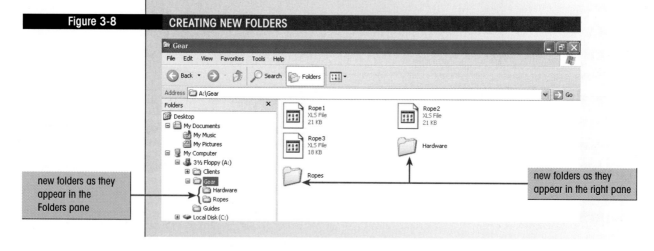

new folders as they appear in the Folders pane

new folders as they appear in the right pane

As you and Bernard go over the current folder structure, you realize that a complete inventory of the KCS gear also includes the harnesses climbers wear to attach themselves to the rope for protection in case they fall. Because harnesses aren't considered hardware, you decide that the harness inventory files should go in the same folder with the ropes. Thus, you need to rename the Ropes folder "Ropes and Harnesses." You rename a folder by right-clicking the folder icon in either the Folders pane or the right pane and then clicking the Rename command on the shortcut menu. You can also rename a folder by selecting the folder, clicking File on the menu bar, and then clicking Rename, or by clicking a folder name twice (more slowly than double-clicking) until a blinking insertion point appears in the folder name, indicating you can edit it. Then, you type the new text and press the Enter key.

To rename the Ropes folder, you'll try the right-clicking method.

To change the name of the Ropes folder:

1. Right-click **Ropes** in the Folders pane.

2. Click **Rename** on the shortcut menu. The folder name is selected and ready for you to rename.

3. Type **Ropes and Harnesses** as the new folder name, and then press the **Enter** key.

The new folder name now appears in both the left and right panes. If you cannot see the full name, you can adjust the width of the Explorer bar. You'll show Bernard how to do this next.

Adjusting the Width of the Explorer Bar

As you create or view more levels of folders, the Explorer bar might not be wide enough to display all the levels of folders in the Folders pane, especially if the folder names are long. As a result, you might not be able to see all the device and folder icons. You can change the width of the Windows Explorer window panes by dragging the dividing bar that separates the two panes.

REFERENCE WINDOW   **RW**

Adjusting the Width of the Explorer Bar

- Move the mouse pointer to the dividing bar between the left and right panes.
- When the arrow-shaped pointer ⬐ changes to a double-headed arrow ◄—►, hold down the left mouse button and drag the dividing line right or left, as necessary.
- When the dividing bar is in the desired position, release the mouse button.

To increase the width of the Explorer bar:

1. Move the mouse pointer to the vertical dividing bar between the two panes. The ⬐ pointer changes to a ◄—► pointer.

2. Hold down the left mouse button while you drag the dividing bar about one-half inch to the right, as shown in Figure 3-9.

Figure 3-9   **ADJUSTING THE WIDTH OF THE EXPLORER BAR**

3. Release the mouse button. The Explorer bar is now wider and will allow you to see more of the items listed in the Folders pane. The next time you open the Windows Explorer window, the Explorer bar will have the same width.

TROUBLE? If your instructor wants you to return the Explorer bar to its original width, drag the dividing bar about one-half inch to the left when you finish this tutorial.

4. Click the **Close** button ☒ to close the Windows Explorer window. You return to the Windows XP desktop.

You have now shown Bernard how to use Windows Explorer to view the files, folders, and devices on his computer, and how to create new folders for storing files. In the next session, you will show Bernard how the right pane in Windows Explorer can be used to organize the files and folders on his computer.

Session 3.1 QUICK CHECK

1. _____ is an alternative to using My Computer for file management tasks.

2. The Windows Explorer window is divided into two panes. Describe each pane, using one sentence for each pane.

3. True or False: If you see folders with the same names in both the right and left panes of the Windows Explorer window, the folders are duplicates and you should erase those in the right pane.

4. True or False: The Folders pane displays all the files in a folder.

5. A folder that is contained in another folder is referred to as a(n) _____.

6. You click the _____ to expand the display of folders in the Folders pane.

7. If you want to create a new folder on drive A, what should you first click in the Folders pane?

8. True or False: The Explorer bar exists only in Windows Explorer. You cannot use the Explorer bar in the My Computer window.

SESSION 3.2

In Session 3.2, you will work with the right pane of the Windows Explorer window, which you use to work with the files on your computer. You'll learn how to select multiple files in the right pane. You'll work with different methods of moving and copying files from one location to another. You'll also see how to print a copy of the Windows Explorer window to use as a reference.

Working with Files in the Right Pane of Windows Explorer

Now that you've worked with the Folders pane, it's time to put the right pane of Windows Explorer to use. Recall that the Folders pane shows how your devices and folders are arranged in a hierarchy on your computer. You've already used the Folders pane to create a folder structure for Bernard's files. The left pane, however, doesn't show files. When you want to manipulate files in your devices and folders—to move, copy, rename, or delete them, for example—you work in the right pane. You'll work in the right pane to move Bernard's files into different folders. To do this, you'll learn how to select and work with multiple files using the right pane of the Windows Explorer window.

Working with files listed in the right pane is exactly like working with files listed in the My Computer window or any Windows XP dialog box or window that displays a list of files. You can use the View command to determine the way the right pane displays files and objects, switching from Tiles view to Details or Thumbnails view. You can click the Back ⟵ , Forward ⟶ , and Up 🔼 buttons located on the Standard Buttons toolbar to navigate through the hierarchy of objects in your computer. (When you use these buttons, the view of your computer's contents changes in both the left and right panes.) You can open a file by double-clicking its icon. You can rename a file by right-clicking its icon and choosing the Rename command from the shortcut menu. You also use the same techniques to select files with which to work.

Selecting Multiple Files

You select a file by clicking the file's icon in the right pane of the Windows Explorer window. You can also select multiple files from the right pane, using one of several techniques. Suppose you want to select all the files in a folder or all the folders and files on your floppy disk. You can easily do this using the Select All command on the Edit menu.

To select all of the files in the root directory:

1. Make sure your Data Disk is in drive A, and then start Windows Explorer. Set up Windows Explorer so that the Standard Buttons toolbar, Address bar, and Folders pane are all visible.

2. Locate and click **3½ Floppy (A:)** in the Folders pane to display the contents of the root directory of drive A in the right pane.

3. Click **View** on the menu bar, and then click **Details** to display the file icons in Details view. In this view, you can see the complete contents of your Data Disk, so you'll know at a glance when everything is selected.

4. Click **Edit** on the menu bar, and then click **Select All**. (Note that you also can click Ctrl+A to select all the files in the list.) Windows Explorer highlights the files and folders on drive A to show that they are selected. See Figure 3-10.

Figure 3-10 | SELECTING ALL THE FILES IN A FOLDER

click Edit on the menu bar, and then click Select All to select all the files and folders in the selected folder

5. Deselect the files by clicking any blank area of the window. The highlighting is removed to indicate that no files are currently selected.

What if you want to work with more than one file, but not with all the files in a folder? For example, suppose Bernard wants to delete three of the files in a folder. In Windows Explorer, you can select a group of files in two ways. You can select files listed consecutively using the Shift key, or you can select files scattered throughout the right pane using the Ctrl key. Figure 3-11 shows the two different ways to select a group of files.

Figure 3-11 | TWO WAYS TO SELECT A GROUP OF FILES

press the Shift key and click the first file and the last file in a list to select consecutive files from a list of files

press the Ctrl key and then click each file you wish to select

REFERENCE   WINDOW   RW

Selecting Files

- Make sure the right pane displays the files you want to select.
- To select a single file, click the file.
- To select consecutive files in a list of files, select the first file and then press the Shift key while you select the last file in the list. The complete list of files is also selected. Release the Shift key.
- To select nonconsecutive files in a list, select the first file and then press the Ctrl key while you select each additional file. When you have selected all the files you want, release the Ctrl key.
- To select all the files and folders in the selected device or folder, click Edit and then click Select All.

First try selecting a set of consecutive files, and then select a set of nonconsecutive files listed within a folder.

To select groups of files:

1. Make sure the right pane displays the root directory of drive A, and then click the **Beckman** file.

2. Press the **Shift** key while you click the **Fuller** file. Release the **Shift** key. The Beckman and Fuller files and all files in between are selected. See Figure 3-12.

Figure 3-12   **SELECTING CONSECUTIVE FILES**

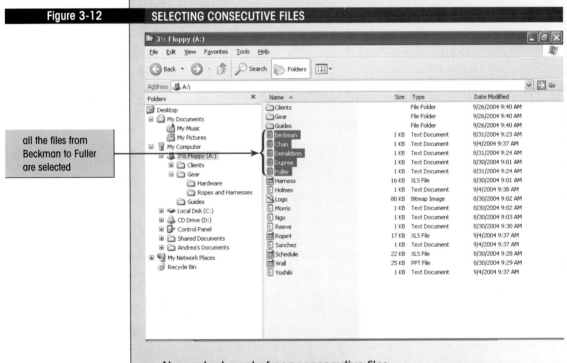

all the files from Beckman to Fuller are selected

Now select a set of nonconsecutive files.

3. Click the **Reeve** file. Notice that selecting this file automatically deselects any selected files.

4. Press the **Ctrl** key and select the **Morris** file and then the **Sanchez** file. Release the **Ctrl** key. All three files are now selected. See Figure 3-13.

Figure 3-13 SELECTING NONCONSECUTIVE FILES

press the Ctrl key as you click each file

TROUBLE? If you release the Ctrl key by mistake while selecting a set of noncon-secutive files, press it again and select the files you want.

While selecting multiple files with the Ctrl key, you can deselect any file by clicking it again while pressing the Ctrl key. You can also select more files by pressing the Ctrl key again, then selecting the additional files.

To select and deselect additional files:

1. Press the **Ctrl** key and click the **Chan** file to select it. Four files are now selected.

2. Continue to press the **Ctrl** key, and click the **Sanchez** file to deselect it. Release the **Ctrl** key. Now three files are selected: Chan, Morris, and Reeve.

Suppose you want to select all the files in a folder except one. You can use the Invert Selection menu option to select all the files that are not selected.

REFERENCE WINDOW **RW**

Selecting All Files Except Certain Ones
- Select the file or files you do not want selected. You can use the Shift or Ctrl key to select multiple files.
- Click Edit on the menu bar, and then click Invert Selection.

> ### To use Invert Selection to select all files except Dupree:
>
> **1.** Click the **Dupree** file.
>
> **2.** Click **Edit** on the menu bar, and then click **Invert Selection**. All the folders and files except Dupree are now selected.
>
> **3.** Click a blank area to deselect the files on drive A.

You are almost ready to start moving Bernard's files into the appropriate folders. Bernard first wants to identify the files that need to be moved. He wonders if there's a quick way to get a hard copy (that is, a paper copy) of the Windows Explorer window so he can write on it.

Printing the Windows Explorer Window

In Windows XP you can temporarily store an image of your computer screen in memory using the Print Screen key. Then you can start the WordPad program and paste the image into a blank WordPad document. Finally, you can print the document, which will contain an image of your screen. Bernard would like to have a hard copy of the hierarchy of files and folders currently on his floppy disk. You can use the Print Screen key to capture an image of the Windows Explorer window displaying the contents of the disk.

> ### To print the Windows Explorer window:
>
> **1.** In the Folders pane, click ⊞ next to 3½ Floppy (A:), Clients, Advanced, and Gear as necessary so that all the folders and subfolders on Bernard's disk are visible in the left pane.
>
> **2.** Press the **Print Screen** key. Although no visual cue appears on screen, an image of the Windows Explorer window is stored in your computer's memory.
>
> TROUBLE? If you cannot locate the Print Screen key, it might be accessible through another key on your keyboard or it might be labeled with an abbreviation such as "PrtScn." Ask your instructor or technical support person for help.
>
> **3.** Start WordPad.
>
> **4.** Maximize the WordPad window if necessary, type your name and the date on separate lines at the top of the WordPad window, and then press the **Enter** key twice.
>
> **5.** Click the **Paste** button 📋 to insert the image of the Windows Explorer window into the document, and then scroll to the top of the document (also scroll left, if necessary). The image of the Windows Explorer window appears in the WordPad document. See Figure 3-14.

Figure 3-14   **WINDOWS EXPLORER SCREEN IMAGE IN WORDPAD**

image of the
Windows Explorer
window in WordPad

6. Click the **Print** button 🖨. Because the WordPad document contains the graphic image of the Windows Explorer window, it might take longer than usual to print.

7. Close WordPad. When prompted to save changes to the document, click the **No** button.

Bernard annotates the printout of the Windows Explorer window as shown in Figure 3-15. His notes show you which files to move into folders on the root directory.

Figure 3-15   **BERNARD'S PRINTOUT**

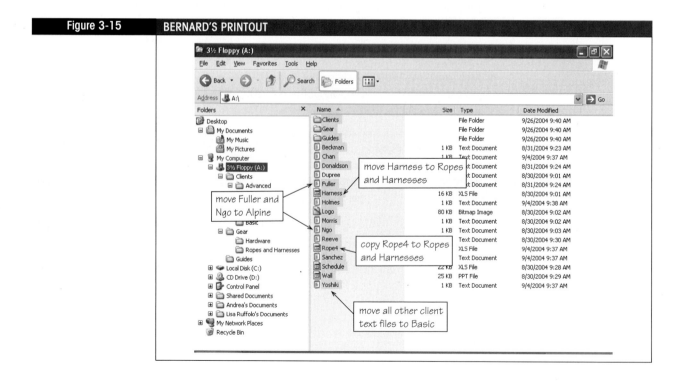

Moving Files in Windows Explorer

You've already had some experience in moving files. You saw in Tutorial 2 how you could right-click an object in My Computer and drag it into a folder on a floppy disk, choosing whether to copy or move the file. Moving files in Windows Explorer is exactly the same, except that you have the added benefit of using the Folders pane to navigate the hierarchy of Windows XP objects while still being able to view the files you are moving in the right pane. Because the Folders pane can display a detailed tree of folders and devices, you can easily move a file to almost any location on your computer.

Bernard has already marked the printout you created to show which files you need to move. You begin by moving the Harness file from the root directory to the Equipment folder.

To move the Harness file:

1. Make sure that the 3½ Floppy (A:) drive is selected in the Folders pane and that the Hardware and the Ropes and Harnesses subfolders of the Gears folder are also visible.

2. Hold down the right mouse button while you drag the **Harness** file icon from the right pane to the **Ropes and Harnesses** folder in the left pane, as shown in Figure 3-16.

Figure 3-16	MOVING A SINGLE FILE USING THE FOLDERS PANE

drag Harness with the right mouse button until the Ropes and Harnesses folder is selected

3. Release the right mouse button. Click **Move Here** on the shortcut menu that appears.

    TROUBLE? If you selected the wrong folder, click Cancel on the shortcut menu and repeat Steps 1 through 3.

    TROUBLE? If you moved the file to a different folder by mistake, click Undo Move from the Edit menu and then repeat Steps 1 through 3.

    The Harness file is moved to the new folder and no longer appears in the right pane showing the files on the root directory.

4. Click **Ropes and Harnesses** in the Folders pane. The Harness file appears in the right pane as a file in this folder.

Bernard recently purchased a fourth rope, and he is tracking its use in the file named Rope4. He wants a copy of the Rope4 file in the Ropes and Harnesses folder. You can also drag with the right mouse button to copy files.

To copy the Rope4 file into the Ropes folder:

1. Click 3½ **Floppy (A:)** in the Folders pane to display the files in the root directory in the right pane.

2. Hold down the right mouse button while you drag the **Rope4** icon from the root directory to the **Ropes and Harnesses** folder.

3. Make sure the Ropes and Harnesses folder is selected, and then release the right mouse button.

4. Click **Copy Here** on the shortcut menu. Rope4 is copied from the root directory to the Ropes and Harnesses folder. Notice that Rope4 is still listed in the right pane for drive A because you copied the file rather than moved it.

5. Click **Ropes and Harnesses** in the Folders pane, and notice that Rope4 now appears in this folder along with the Harness file.

Bernard wants to move the three rope files from the Gear folder to the Ropes and Harnesses folder. You can do this next using the cut-and-paste technique.

Moving Files with Cut and Paste

Although dragging works well when you can see the file in the right pane and its destination folder in the Folders pane, this is not always the case. You might need to navigate the folders in left pane first to find and open a subfolder, for example. Instead of dragging, you can use the Cut, Copy, and Paste buttons on the Standard Buttons toolbar to move or copy objects. The Cut, Copy, and Paste commands are also available on the Edit menu and on the selected objects' shortcut menus.

REFERENCE   **WINDOW**   **RW**

Moving or Copying Files with Cut, Copy, and Paste
- Select the file or files you want to copy or move.
- Click the Cut command on the Edit menu to move the files, or click the Copy command on the Edit menu to copy the selected file(s).
- Select the device or folder in which you want to place the copied or cut files.
- Click Edit on the menu bar, and then click the Paste command.
   or
- Select the file or files you want to copy or move.
- Right-click the selected file or files.
- Click the Cut command on the shortcut menu to move the files, or click the Copy command on the shortcut menu to copy the files.
- Right-click the device or folder into which you want to place the copied or cut files.
- Click the Paste command on the shortcut menu.

The rope files Bernard wants to move are listed consecutively, so you should use the Shift key to select these three files and move them as a group. You can then use the Cut and Paste commands to move the files.

To move the rope files to the Ropes and Harnesses folder:

1. Click the **Gear** folder in the left pane to select the Gear folder and view the other rope files, which also need to be moved into the Ropes and Harnesses folder. Switch to Details view, if necessary.

2. Select the three rope files, **Rope1**, **Rope2**, and **Rope3**.

3. Click **Edit** on the menu bar, and then click **Cut**.

4. Click the **Ropes and Harnesses** folder in the Folders pane.

5. Click **Edit** on the menu bar, and then click **Paste** to move the files to the Ropes and Harnesses folder. The Ropes and Harnesses folder now contains Harness, Rope1, Rope2, Rope3, and Rope4.

If you cut or copy a file or set of files but then neglect to paste them into a destination folder, you won't lose the files. Windows Explorer doesn't actually carry out the cut or copy until you paste. It stores the files on the Clipboard and in their original location until you finish moving or copying the files. If you close Windows Explorer without pasting a file, the file remains in its original position.

Using the Move To Folder and Copy To Folder Commands

Now that you've organized Bernard's gear files, it's time to look at the new client files he added. Mark Fuller and George Ngo are interested exclusively in alpine climbing, so you'll move the Fuller and Ngo client files into the Alpine folder. If you want to move these files without navigating many folders and subfolders in the Folders pane, you can do so with the Move To Folder and Copy To Folder commands. These commands open a dialog box you can use to navigate directly to the folder where you want to move or copy the files.

REFERENCE WINDOW   **RW**

Moving or Copying Files with the Move To Folder and Copy To Folder Commands
- Select the file or files you want to move.
- Click Edit on the menu bar, and then click Move To Folder.
- In the Move Items dialog box, locate and click the folder to which you want to move the files.
- Click the Move button.

  or
- Select the file or files you want to copy.
- Click Edit on the menu bar, and then click Copy To Folder.
- In the Copy Items dialog box, locate and click the folder to which you want to copy the files.
- Click the Copy button.

Try this technique now by moving the Fuller and Ngo files into the Alpine folder.

To move files using the Move To command:

1. Click **3½ Floppy (A:)** in the Folders pane to display the files on the floppy disk's root directory. Switch to Details view, if necessary.

2. Select the **Fuller** and **Ngo** files.

3. Click **Edit** on the menu bar, and then click **Move To Folder**.

   The Move Items dialog box opens and displays the hierarchy of objects and folders on your computer.

4. If necessary, click ⊞ next to the My Computer icon to display the contents of that object.

5. Move through the rest of the hierarchy of objects by clicking ⊞ next to the 3½ Floppy (A:) icon and then clicking the ⊞ boxes next to the Clients and the Advanced folders.

6. Click the **Alpine** folder to select it. The Move Items dialog box should look like the one shown in Figure 3-17.

Figure 3-17	MOVING FILES USING THE MOVE TO FOLDER COMMAND

if you click the Make New Folder button, you can create a new folder and then move files into that folder

7. Click the **Move** button to move the files into the Alpine folder. The Move Items dialog box closes, and you return to the Windows Explorer window.

8. Locate and click **Alpine** in the Folders pane to confirm that the Ngo and Fuller files have been moved to that location. (There should now be five files.)

You need to move the remaining client files from the root directory into the Basic folder. You can combine some of the methods you have already learned to complete this task most efficiently.

Moving Files of Similar Type

If you are working in Details view, you'll see that the client files (the ones with people's names) are all text files. If you arrange these files by type, they'll all be next to each other, so you can select them as a group and move them together to the Basic folder. You'll use the technique of cutting and pasting to accomplish this task.

To move a group of related files to a new folder:

1. Click **3½ Floppy (A:)** in the left pane to display the files of the floppy drive's root directory in the right pane.

2. If necessary, switch to Details view.

3. Click the **Type** button at the top of the file list. The client text files are now grouped together.

   TROUBLE? The Type button is at the top of the third column under the Address Bar in the right pane.

4. Select the **Beckman** and **Yoshiki** text files and all the files in between.

5. Right-click the selected files, click **Cut** on the shortcut menu, right-click **Basic** in the Folders pane, and then click **Paste** on the shortcut menu. The files move from the root directory into the Basic folder.

Bernard's disk is now reorganized, with the appropriate files in the Gear and Client folders.

Moving or Copying Files Between Drives

So far all the moving and copying you've done has been within a single drive—the floppy drive. Often you will want to move or copy files from one drive to another, for example, from your floppy drive to your hard disk, or from one floppy drive to another. You can do this using the same techniques you've learned so far: dragging with the right mouse button, using cut and paste, and so forth.

Bernard has one more file on his disk he needs to move—a PowerPoint file named Wall. This file contains a slide presentation for the local Parks and Recreation Department, proposing the construction of an indoor climbing wall. Bernard needs to fine-tune this presentation and also wants you to review it and make suggestions. Bernard wants to work with the file on his hard disk and also wants you to have a copy to work with on your home computer.

Moving Files from the Floppy to the Hard Disk

In addition to using Windows Explorer to copy and move files between folders, you can also use this tool to move and copy files from different devices on your computer, such as from the floppy disk to the hard disk. So that Bernard can work with the Wall file on his hard disk, you will show him how to move the file from his floppy disk to his hard disk. Also, you notice that none of the current KCS folders—Clients, Gear, or Guides—is appropriate for storing the climbing presentation. As you move Bernard's Wall file to the hard disk, you also will create a new folder named "Presentations."

To move a file from a floppy disk to a new folder on the hard disk:

1. If necessary, scroll the left pane to display the icon for drive C.

2. Click **My Documents** in the Folders pane.

3. Click **File** on the menu bar, point to **New**, and then click **Folder** to create a new folder in the My Documents folder.

> TROUBLE? If a message warns you that you cannot create a folder on drive C, you might be working on a computer that restricts hard disk access. Ask your instructor or technical support person about other options for working on a hard disk, and read through the rest of this section to learn how you would work on a hard disk if you had the opportunity.
>
> **4.** Type **Presentations** as the name of the new folder, and then press the **Enter** key.
>
> TROUBLE? If there is already a Presentations folder on the hard disk, you must specify a different name. Use the name "Presentation" with your initials, such as "PresentationJP." Substitute this folder name for the Presentations folder for the rest of this tutorial.
>
> **5.** Click **3½ Floppy (A:)** in the Folders pane (you might have to scroll to see it) to display its contents in the right pane.
>
> **6.** Right-click the **Wall** file in the right pane.
>
> **7.** Click **Cut** on the shortcut menu. Locate and then right-click the **Presentations** folder in the Folders pane. (You might have to scroll to see it.)
>
> **8.** Click **Paste** on the shortcut menu.
>
> **9.** Click the **Presentations** folder in the Folders pane, if necessary, to ensure that the Wall file was copied onto the hard disk.

Recall that Bernard wants to give you a copy of the Wall file on another floppy disk, so you can take it home and review it. To do this, you will need one 3½-inch floppy disk that is either blank or contains files you no longer need.

Preparing a Data Disk with Quick Format

When you want to erase the contents of a floppy disk, you can use the Quick format option rather than the Full format that you use on a new disk. A Quick format takes less time than a Full format because, instead of preparing the entire disk surface, a Quick format erases the file allocation table. The **file allocation table (FAT)** contains information that your operating system uses to track the locations of all the files on the disk. By erasing the FAT, you erase all the information that tells the computer about the files on the disk, and so the disk appears empty to the computer. Note that to delete only a few files from a floppy disk, you don't need to format the disk; you can just select the files (as you'll learn later in this tutorial) and delete them.

> *To Quick format a disk:*
>
> **1.** Write "Windows XP Tutorial 3 Data Disk—Disk 2" on the label of your disk.
>
> **2.** Place your disk in drive A.
>
> **3.** Right-click the **3½ Floppy (A:)** icon in the Folders pane.
>
> **4.** Click **Format** on the shortcut menu to open the Format 3½ Floppy (A:) dialog box.
>
> **5.** Click the **Quick Format** check box, as shown in Figure 3-18.

Figure 3-18   FORMAT DIALOG BOX

click to Quick format
a disk

6. Click the **Start** button.

TROUBLE? If an error message appears indicating you will lose the data on the floppy disk, click OK.

TROUBLE? If an error message appears indicating your disk capacity might be double-density, click OK, then replace the disk in the drive with a high-density disk, and repeat Steps 3 through 7.

7. Wait a few moments until an information box opens indicating that formatting is complete. Click the **OK** button and then click the **Close** button on the Format 3½ Floppy (A:) dialog box.

You can now copy Bernard's Wall file from the hard disk onto the newly formatted disk.

Copying a File from the Hard Disk to the Floppy Drive

To move a file from the hard disk to the destination disk, you can use the Send To command. The Send To command provides a simple one-click method of sending any file on your computer's hard disk to your floppy drive. (You can also use the Send To command to send files to other locations on your computer, such as the desktop.) Be aware, however, that the Send To command can only send files to the root directory of the floppy drive; you cannot direct a file to a specific folder within the floppy drive.

Now that you've moved the Wall file from Bernard's floppy disk to the hard disk, you can use the Send To command to copy the file to the floppy disk you just formatted.

To copy a file from the hard disk to a floppy disk:

1. Select the **Presentations** folder in the Folders pane of Windows Explorer, if necessary.

2. Right-click the **Wall** file in the right pane, and then point to **Send To** on the shortcut menu. See Figure 3-19.

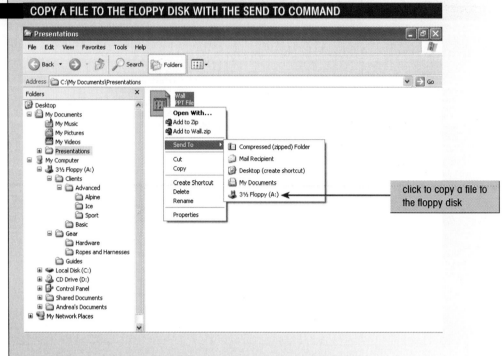

Figure 3-19   COPY A FILE TO THE FLOPPY DISK WITH THE SEND TO COMMAND

click to copy a file to the floppy disk

3. Click **3½ Floppy (A:)** on the shortcut menu. The file should now be copied onto the floppy disk.

4. Click **3½ Floppy (A:)** in the Folders pane, make sure the Wall file is safely on the disk, and then remove the Data Disk 2 from drive A.

5. Place your Windows XP Tutorial 3 Data Disk 1 back in drive A, click **View** on the menu bar, and then click **Refresh** to view the files on Data Disk 1.

You just showed Bernard how to move a file from a floppy disk to a hard disk and then copy the file to another floppy disk. Suppose you want to copy a file from one floppy disk to another. Most computers have only one floppy disk drive, so you cannot use Windows Explorer to drag a file from one floppy disk to another. If you worked through Tutorial 2, you learned how to copy the contents of one floppy disk to another using the Copy Disk command. However, that technique is useful only if you want to copy *all* the files from one floppy disk to another. To copy one file from a floppy disk to another, you first copy the file from the first floppy disk—the source disk—to a temporary location on the hard disk, and then you insert the second floppy disk—the destination disk—into drive A. Finally, you move the file from the hard disk to the destination floppy disk. You can use this same technique to copy more than one file from one floppy to another. Figure 3-20 shows this procedure.

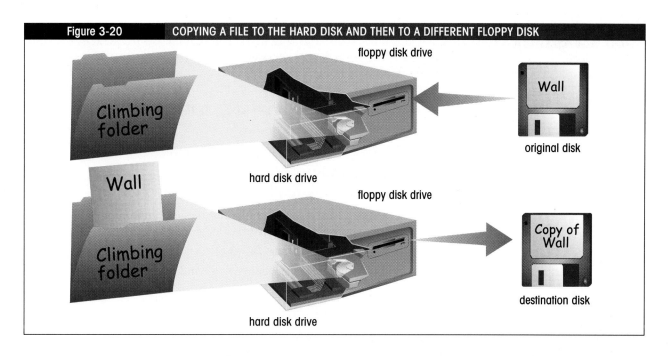

Figure 3-20 | **COPYING A FILE TO THE HARD DISK AND THEN TO A DIFFERENT FLOPPY DISK**

If you are working in a computer lab, you should delete the Presentations folder to avoid cluttering the hard disk with unnecessary files. You can do so easily by simply removing the Presentations folder from drive C. If you weren't able to move any files to drive C, you can skip these steps.

To delete the Presentations folder from drive C:

1. Right-click the **Presentations** folder in the Folders pane.

2. Click **Delete** on the shortcut menu. The Confirm Folder Delete message box opens.

   TROUBLE? If a message appears telling you that you cannot perform this operation, your system administrator might have restricted user privileges. Continue reading the rest of the instructions to understand the process.

3. Make sure the Confirm Folder Delete message indicates that the Presentations folder will be moved to the Recycle Bin, and then click the Yes button to delete the folder from the hard disk.

   TROUBLE? If a different filename appears in the Confirm Folder Delete dialog box, click the No button and repeat Steps 1 through 3.

4. Click the Close button ⊠ to close the Windows Explorer window. You return to the Windows XP desktop.

You look over the structure of folders and files on Bernard's disk and realize that, as his business increases, this structure will become increasingly useful. You've used the power of Windows Explorer to simplify tasks such as locating, moving, copying, and deleting files. You can apply these skills to larger file management challenges when you are using a computer of your own and need to organize and work with the files on your hard disk.

Session 3.2 QUICK CHECK

1. When you select files, you hold down the _____ key to select consecutive files, whereas you hold down the _____ key to select nonconsecutive files.

2. What is the difference between the left pane (the Folders pane) and the right pane in the Windows Explorer window?

3. How can you make a printout of your computer screen?

4. You can move files to a particular folder by using the _____ command on the Edit menu.

5. True or False: Using a hard disk for temporary storage, you can copy a file from one floppy disk to another even if you only have one floppy disk drive in your computer.

6. If you want to copy a file from your hard disk directly to the root directory of your floppy disk (without navigating the hierarchy of Windows XP objects), what command can you use?

SESSION 3.3

In this session, you'll learn how to use the Favorites, Media, History, and Search Companion panes in Windows Explorer. You'll learn how to add files to your Favorites list and view multimedia files in the Media pane. You'll view a list of recently opened files with the History pane and then search for a file you opened recently using the Search Companion pane.

Working with the Favorites Pane

If you want quick access to files and folders, such as those you use often, you can add them to the Favorites pane. Then you can open the Favorites pane in the Windows Explorer window and click a folder in the Favorites pane to see its contents in the right pane, or click a file in the Favorites pane to open the file. For example, if you frequently work with a to-do list file in a subfolder, you could add the to-do list to the Favorites pane. Instead of navigating from one folder to another until you find the to-do list, you can open the Favorites pane and then click the to-do list file to open it.

The Favorites pane is only an organizational tool. Unlike the Folders pane, which reflects the structure of the folders on your computer, the Favorites pane lists only links to files and folders, not the actual location of files and folders themselves. When you add a file to the Favorites pane, a link to the file is actually what appears in the Favorites pane; the file itself remains in its original location.

You can also organize the Favorites pane to make it easier to work with, especially if it lists many files. You can create a folder in the Favorites pane and then group the links to files within it.

Bernard is planning to devote some time next week to creating a spring schedule for Alpine climbing expeditions. You ask him to identify the folders and files he'll work with most often as he prepares the schedule. Then you will add links to these items in the Favorites pane of the Windows Explorer window.

Adding a Folder to the Favorites Pane

To add a folder to the Favorites pane, you open the folder in Windows Explorer, click Favorites on the menu bar, and then click Add to Favorites. After you open the folder, you can also open the Favorites pane, and then click the Add to Favorites button in the Favorites pane.

Bernard wants the Favorites pane to include a link to the Alpine folder. As he creates his schedule for spring climbing expeditions, he will reference this folder often because it contains files for clients who are most likely to participate. The Alpine folder is a subfolder of the Advanced folder, which is contained in the Clients folder. Adding the Alpine folder to the Favorites pane means Bernard can open the folder without navigating three levels of folders.

You explain to Bernard that you'll navigate to the Alpine folder first and then open the Favorites pane to get familiar with it. Then you'll use the Add to Favorites button to add the Alpine folder link to the Favorites pane.

To add a folder to the Favorites pane:

1. Make sure your Data Disk 1 is in the appropriate drive, and then open Windows Explorer.

2. Use the Folders pane to navigate to the Alpine folder on your Data Disk. Click the **Alpine** folder to see its contents in the right pane.

3. Click **View** on the menu bar, point to **Explorer Bar**, and then click **Favorites**. The Favorites pane opens in the Windows Explorer window, replacing the Folders pane. See Figure 3-21.

Figure 3-21	THE FAVORITES PANE IN THE WINDOWS EXPLORER WINDOW

Favorites pane

click the Add button to add a link to the Favorites pane; click the Organize button to organize links into folders

these links to Web pages appear in the Favorites pane by default

Note that the Favorites pane includes links to other objects your computer can access. For example, if you are connected to the Internet, you can click links to open Web pages.

4. In the Favorites pane, click the **Add** button. The Add Favorite dialog box opens with "Alpine" in the Name text box, indicating Windows Explorer will add the Alpine folder to the Favorites pane.

5. Click the **OK** button. The Alpine folder appears in the Favorites pane.

6. To test the new link in the Favorites pane, click the **Up** button 🔊 on the Standard Buttons toolbar until you return to the root directory of your Data Disk. Then click the **Alpine** folder link in the Favorites pane. The right pane of the Windows Explorer window displays the contents of the Alpine folder.

Now that Bernard can quickly access the files in the Alpine folder, he wants the Favorites pane to include links to individual files.

Adding a File to the Favorites Pane

Adding a file to the Favorites pane is different from adding a folder. Instead of opening the Add Favorite dialog box with a menu command or button, you drag one or more files from the right pane of the Windows Explorer window to the Favorites pane.

Emmy Zahn, a corporate trainer, is one of Bernard's clients and an expert Alpine climber. She has offered to accompany him on Spring Alpine expeditions and help train new climbers. Because Bernard will open the Zahn file frequently as he prepares the spring schedule, he wants to include a link to this file in the Favorites pane.

You'll drag the Zahn file from the right pane to add a link to this file in the Favorites pane.

To add a file to the Favorites pane:

1. Click the **Up** button 🔊 on the Standard Buttons toolbar to navigate to the Advanced folder on your Data Disk. Make sure A:\Clients\Advanced appears in the Address bar. The files in the Advanced folder appear in the right pane of the Windows Explorer window.

TROUBLE? If you cannot navigate to the Advanced folder with the 🔊 button, click the Back button 🔙 on the Standard Buttons toolbar to navigate.

2. Select the **Zahn** file.

3. Drag the **Zahn** file to the Favorites pane. A link to the Zahn file appears in the Favorites pane. See Figure 3-22.

Figure 3-22	ADDING FILES TO THE FAVORITES PANE

links to the Zahn file and Alpine folder appear in the Favorites pane

4. To test a link, click the **Zahn** file in the Favorites pane. The Zahn file opens in Notepad. Close the Notepad window.

Bernard mentions that he will add a few other files to the Favorites pane as he works on his schedule. You offer to show him how to organize the objects in the Favorites pane to make sure he can find links quickly.

Organizing the Favorites Pane

As you add links in the Favorites pane, you can organize them to make it easier to find the links. Because the Favorites pane is designed to provide quick access to objects such as files and folders, you should organize it logically to keep it uncluttered and easy to use.

To organize the links in the Favorites pane, you can group them in new or existing folders. When you no longer need quick access to a file or folder, you can delete its link from the Favorites pane. When you do, you delete the link only, not the file or folder itself.

You offer to create a folder in the Favorites pane called "Spring Climbs," and then move the links to the Schedule and Zahn files into it. Then Bernard can access those links by clicking the Spring Climbs folder in the Favorites pane.

To organize the Favorites pane:

1. In the Favorites pane, click the **Organize** button. The Organize Favorites dialog box opens. In this dialog box, you can create new folders and move files into the folders in the Favorites pane.

2. In the Organize Favorites dialog box, click the **Create Folder** button.

3. Type **Spring Climbs** as the name of the new folder, and then press the **Enter** key.

4. Select the **Zahn** file and then click the **Move to Folder** button.

5. Click the **Spring Climbs** folder in the Browse folder dialog box, and then click the **OK** button.

6. Click the **Close** button to close the Organize Favorites dialog box. The Spring Climbs folder appears in the Favorites pane.

7. Click the **Spring Climbs** folder to view its contents. See Figure 3-23.

| Figure 3-23 | ORGANIZING THE FAVORITES PANE |

the link to the Zahn file is now in the Sprint Climbs folder

8. Click the **Zahn** file again to make sure you can open it in Notepad. Then close the Notepad window.

Bernard can later use this same technique to move the Alpine folder link to the Spring Climbs folder in the Favorites pane. When he completes his schedule, he can delete the Spring Climbs folder. If you are in a lab environment, you should delete the Spring Climbs and Alpine folders now.

To delete folders from the Favorites pane:

1. In the Favorites pane, click the **Organize** button.

2. In the Organize Favorites dialog box, click the **Spring Climbs** folder.

3. Click the **Delete** button and then click the **Yes** button when prompted to confirm you want to delete the folder.

4. Click **Alpine**, click the **Delete** button, and then click the **Yes** button when prompted to confirm you want to delete the folder.

5. Click the **Close** button to close the Organize Favorites dialog box. The Spring Climbs and Alpine folders no longer appear in the Favorites pane.

The Explorer bar also can display the Media pane. You will work with that pane next.

Working **with the Media Pane**

You can use the Media pane in the Windows Explorer window to access **multimedia** files, which are files that use sound and images, such as music and video files. Using the Media pane, you can list the multimedia files stored on your computer or on a Web site. Then you can use the Media player to play the files, just as you do with a CD player or VCR. For example, to play a music file, you click the Play button. If you have a sound card and speakers on your computer, the music file plays until it finishes or until you click the Stop button in the Media player.

Bernard wants to find appropriate music to play at the beginning of his presentation to the Parks and Recreation Department. Because he'll show the presentation on a computer, he can play a music file on the hard disk. You suggest he use the Media pane to find music files that come with Windows XP. These are stored in the My Music folder on the hard disk, by default.

To view and play a music file in the Media pane:

1. In Windows Explorer, click **View** on the menu bar, point to **Explorer Bar**, and then click **Media**. The Media pane opens in the Windows Explorer window. See Figure 3-24.

Figure 3-24	OPENING THE MEDIA PANE

links to folders containing multimedia files

Media player, including Play and Stop buttons

TROUBLE? If a Connection dialog box opens, click the **Work Offline** button so you do not connect to the Internet.

TROUBLE? If the Media pane does not list media folders such as the ones shown in Figure 3-23, locate and open the My Documents folder in the right pane of Windows Explorer, and then double-click the My Music folder. Skip Step 2 and continue with Step 3.

2. Click **My Music** in the Media pane. The contents of the My Music folder appear in the right pane, including the Sample Music icon.

3. Double-click the **Sample Music** icon to access the music files that Windows XP provides by default.

TROUBLE? If the My Music folder on your computer does not include the Sample Music icon, navigate to a folder that contains music files.

4. Click a music file icon, such as **Beethoven's Symphony No. 9 (Scherzo)**, to select it.

5. In the Media pane, click the **Play** button ▸ to play the music file. The file plays through to the end.

TROUBLE? If your computer does not have a sound card, you won't be able to play music files. Close any message dialog boxes that appear. If your computer does not have speakers, you won't be able to hear the music when it plays.

TROUBLE? If the music file plays through to the end and then starts again, the file is set to loop, meaning it will play continuously until you click the Stop button. Click the Stop button ⬤ to stop playing the music.

Bernard can use the Beethoven music file to set the mood at the beginning of his presentation. He wonders if Windows Explorer offers any other organizational tools besides the ones you've shown him. You decide to introduce him to the History pane.

Viewing **Your File History**

Now that you've worked with the Folders, Favorites, and Media panes to organize and open files and folders, you show Bernard the History pane, which displays a history of the files and objects that you've opened recently (within the last three weeks). For example, if Bernard remembers opening a particular file last Tuesday or earlier today, but can't remember the file's location, he might still be able to locate it with the History pane by viewing a list of files opened on those days.

Displaying the History Pane

Like the Folders pane, the History pane is available on the Explorer Bar. You open the History pane using the View command on the menu bar.

To open the History pane:

1. Click **View** on the menu bar, point to **Explorer Bar**, and then click **History**.

Explorer displays the History pane, as shown in Figure 3-25.

Figure 3-25   DISPLAYING THE HISTORY PANE

the History pane lists the files you've recently opened organized by date

The History pane shows an icon for each of the last few days you've worked with the computer as well as icons for the last three weeks. Each icon displays a list of the files, folders, Web pages, and other objects that were opened during those times. Thus, if Bernard needs to locate the Zahn file that he worked on earlier today, he can do so by opening the Today icon in the History pane. Try this now.

To view files opened earlier today:

1. Click **Today** in the History pane.

   Under the Today icon are the various files and sites Bernard opened today. (Yours might be different.) For example, if he used this computer to access the Web, the Web sites he visited will be listed along with places on his computer, such as the My Computer window. Bernard is interested only in the files he's accessed on his computer.

2. Click the **My Computer** icon listed under Today in the History pane. See Figure 3-26.

Figure 3-26   FILES OPENED TODAY

click the View button on the History pane to set viewing options

files opened today (your file list will probably be different)

TROUBLE? Your list of files will probably be different. For example, if you opened other files today, they also appear in the Today list.

If Bernard wanted to open one of these files, he could do so by clicking the file icon. One important point: if you or anyone else moved the file since you last opened it, then you cannot open it from the Today list in the History pane—in that case, Windows XP looks for the file in its previous location.

Other Views in the History Pane

You have several choices of how to view the list of recently opened files. Figure 3-27 describes the ways you can view the recent file list.

Figure 3-27	HISTORY PANE VIEWS
VIEW OPTION	**DESCRIPTION**
By Date	View the files by the date that the files were opened (the default)
By Site	View the files according to location
By Most Visited	View the files by the number of times you've opened each file
By Order Visited Today	View the files by the order in which you've opened the files on the current day

Changing the view in the History pane can help you access files more quickly. For example, you opened the Zahn file more than once earlier today. Now Bernard wants to open it again to verify all the classes that Emmy Zahn has taken. He can view the History pane organized by the number of times each file has been opened. To do so, he could click View in the History pane and then click By Most Visited. The Zahn file would probably be near or at the top of that list. Bernard could click the Zahn file icon to open that file directly without having to know where the file is located within the Windows XP hierarchy of objects. The only limitation is that if the file is located on a CD or floppy disk, that disk must be in the corresponding drive before the file can be accessed.

Using the Search Companion Pane in Windows Explorer

Bernard finds the History pane a useful tool for locating the files he's recently worked with. But he wonders what he would do if he didn't know where the file was located, wasn't sure when he last accessed the file, or wasn't certain about a filename. For example, Bernard knows that he's opened a client's file sometime in the last week, but he cannot remember if the filename is spelled "Kranmmer," "Kranmar," "Kranmere," or "Kranmer," although he's sure it starts with "Kran." The best tool to use in this case is the Search Companion pane.

In the Search Companion pane, you can specify the name or part of a name of any file on your computer, and Windows Explorer will then locate the file for you. You show Bernard how to do this with the "Kran" file.

To locate the "Kran" file:

1. Click the **Search** button 🔎 on the Standard Buttons toolbar. Note that you could also click View on the menu bar, and then click Search to open the Search Companion pane. See Figure 3-28.

| Figure 3-28 | SEARCHING FOR FILES IN WINDOWS EXPLORER |

Search Companion pane →

2. Click **All files and folders**.

3. Type **Kran** in the All or part of the file name text box.

   By typing "Kran" you are limiting your search to only files with the text "kran" in their filenames, such as "Kranmer" or "Ckrank". By default, case doesn't matter—typing "kran" is the same as typing "Kran."

4. If necessary, click the **Look in** list arrow and then click **3½ Floppy (A:)** so that Windows XP searches only the files on your Data Disk.

5. Click the **Search** button.

   The Kranmer file is listed in the right pane, as shown in Figure 3-29. This is the file that Bernard is looking for.

Figure 3-29   LOCATING THE KRANMER FILE

the floppy disk has one file containing "Kran"

6. Click the **Close** button ⊠ to close Windows Explorer.

The Search Companion pane is a rich tool containing many features for complex and detailed searches. You can also open the Search Companion as a standalone tool from the Start menu. You'll get a chance to explore more of the Search Companion features in a later tutorial.

You've completed your work with Windows Explorer. You remind Bernard that each of the tools and techniques you've shown him can be used with most of the windows in Windows XP. For example, if he wants to use the History or Favorites panes in the My Computer window, he can do so.

Session 3.3 QUICK CHECK

1. True or False: If you delete a folder in the Favorites pane, you also delete the folder from your computer.

2. Why is it a good idea to organize the objects in the Favorites pane?

3. The Media pane shows the _____ files your computer can access, such as music and video files.

4. True or False: If a file is moved from its original location, the History pane will display the new file location.

5. To display a list of files you worked with earlier in the day, click the _____ icon in the History pane.

6. Under what circumstances would you use the Search Companion pane?

7. True or False: You can use the Search Companion pane to find any file on your computer.

REVIEW ASSIGNMENTS

1. *Copying Files to the Hard Disk* Bernard wants to place his sport-climbing client files (those in the Sport folder) on the hard disk to work with them on an advertisement campaign. The Sport folder is a subfolder of the Advanced folder, which is itself a subfolder of Clients.

   a. Start Windows Explorer and then create a new folder on the hard disk in the My Documents folder called Advertise.

   b. Copy the files in the Sport folder on your Data Disk to the Advertise folder on the hard disk.

   c. Open the Advertise folder on the hard disk to display the files it contains.

   d. Print the Windows Explorer window from WordPad, including your name and the date on the printout.

   e. Delete the Advertise folder from the hard disk when your printout is completed.

2. *Creating a New Folder and Copying Files* Bernard now wants a folder that contains all the clients he has because he'd like to mail flyers to all his clients advertising an expedition to the Tetons. (*Hint*: The client files are all text files, so consider viewing the files in the root directory by type. Don't forget that there are also client files in the Clients folder and its subfolders.)

   a. Create a folder called All Clients on the drive A root directory, and then copy any text files from the root directory into the All Clients folder.

   b. Open the Clients folder, open its subfolders one at a time, and then copy the text files from each of those folders into the new All Clients folder.

   c. Print the Exploring screen from WordPad (following the steps in Session 3.2 of this tutorial), showing the contents of the All Clients folder arranged by name. Be sure to include your name and the date on your printout.

   d. Delete the All Clients folder from the floppy disk when your printout is completed.

3. *Copying between Floppy Disks* Suppose someone who doesn't know how to use Windows Explorer wants to copy the Guides folder from her Data Disk to another floppy disk—but she doesn't want the entire contents of the Data Disk. Try this yourself, and as you go through the procedure, write each step so that this student will be able to follow the steps and make a copy of Guides. Keep in mind that she doesn't know how to use Windows Explorer.

4. *Restructuring a Disk*

   a. Create a folder called "Tutorial 3" in the My Documents folder on the hard disk. Copy all the folders on the Windows XP Tutorial 3 Data Disk 1 to the Tutorial 3 folder.

   b. Use Quick Format to format any disk that contains files you no longer need. You can use the disk you formatted in Session 3.3 (Disk 2, containing the Wall file).

   c. Copy all the files from the Tutorial 3 folder on your hard disk to the root directory of Disk 2. (Do not store the files on Disk 2 in folders.)

   d. Rearrange the files on the disk so they correspond to Figure 3-30. Delete any files or folders not shown in the figure.

Figure 3-30

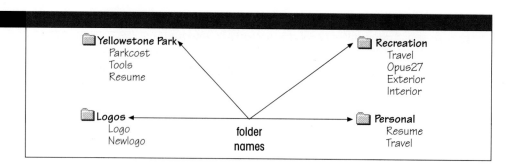

e. Print the Windows Explorer screen from WordPad that shows your new organization and the files in the Yellowstone Park folder arranged by size.

f. Delete the Tutorial 3 folder from the hard disk.

5. *Creating a Folder Structure* When you complete your computer class, you are likely to use a computer for other courses in your major and for general education requirements such as English and math. Think about how you would organize the floppy disk that would hold the files for your courses, and then prepare a disk to contain your files. If you're not a student, prepare a disk using fictitious data.

   a. Make a diagram of this organization.

   b. Use Quick Format to erase any disk containing files you no longer need, such as Disk 2.

   c. Create the folder structure on your Data Disk (even though you don't have any files to place in the folders right now). Use subfolders to help sort files for class projects. (Your composition course, for example, might have a midterm and a final paper.)

   d. Make sure the left pane displays all folders and subfolders, and then paste an image of the Windows Explorer window into WordPad. Be sure to include your name and the date, but don't print anything yet.

   e. Use WordPad to write one or two paragraphs after your name explaining your plan. Your explanation should include information about your major, the courses you plan to take, and how you might use computers in those courses. Print the document when it is finished.

6. *Exploring Your Computer's Devices, Folders, and Files* Answer each of the following questions about the devices, folders, and files on your lab computers. You can find all the answers using the Windows Explorer window. Note that your answers will vary from those of other students because different computers have different devices, folder hierarchies, and files.

   a. What are the names of three folders on drive C?

   b. Which folders on drive C have subfolders? What are the names of two or three of the subfolders?

   c. What is the size of the largest file in the My Documents folder on the hard disk?

   d. Does your computer have a CD drive? If so, what drive letter is assigned to the CD drive?

   e. Does your computer have access to a network storage device? If so, indicate the letter(s) of the network storage device(s).

7. *Separating Program and Data Files* Hard disk management differs from floppy disk management because a hard disk contains programs and data, whereas a floppy disk (unless it is an installation disk that you got from a software company) generally only contains data files. On a hard disk, a good management practice is to keep programs in folders separate from data files. Keeping this in mind, read the following description, draw a sketch of the folder structure described, and then make a sketch of how the current structure could be improved.

The Marquette Chamber of Commerce uses a computer to maintain its membership list and track dues. It also uses the computer for correspondence. All the programs and data used by the Chamber of Commerce are on drive C. The program for the membership database is in a folder called Members. The data file for the membership database is in a subfolder of Members called Member Data. The accounting program used to track income and expenditures is in a folder called Accounting Programs. The data for the current year is in a folder directly under the drive C icon called Accounting Data 2004. The accounting data from 2002 and 2003 is stored in two subfolders of the folder called Accounting Programs. The word-processing program is in a folder called Word. The documents created with Word are stored in the Member Data folder. Finally, Windows XP is stored in a folder called Windows, which has 10 subfolders.

8. *Using the Send To Command* The Send To command provides an efficient way to send files to the root directory of the floppy disk. You also can use this command to send a file on your floppy disk to the My Documents folder on your computer's hard disk. To see how this works, complete the following tasks:

   a. Insert the Windows XP Tutorial 3 Data Disk 1 in the floppy drive of your computer.
   b. Use the Send To command to move the Gonzalez file from the Advanced folder in the Clients folder to the My Documents folder on your hard disk.
   c. Use the Send To command to move the Gonzales file from the My Documents folder back to the root directory of your floppy disk.
   d. Delete the Gonzales file in the My Documents folder.

9. *Using the Favorites, Media, History, and Search Panes* Complete the following tasks and then answer each question about working with the Favorites, Media, History, and Search panes in the Windows Explorer window.

   a. Using the Windows XP Tutorial 3 Data Disk 1, add the Ygo and Tucker files to the Favorites pane, and then organize them in a new folder called "Tutorial 3." Open the Tutorial 3 folder in the Favorites pane, and then create a printout of this screen. Open the Ygo file and then close the Notepad window. Delete the Tutorial 3 folder in the Favorites pane.
   b. Use the Media pane to find at least one multimedia file on your hard disk. What is the size of that file?
   c. Open the History pane and view the files you opened today. Which files are on the list? Use the View button on the History pane to change the view. Which view did you choose? Which files now appear on the list?
   d. Use the Search Companion pane to find the Ramin and Ramirez files on the Data Disk. What did you type to find the files? Where is each located on the Data Disk?

PROJECTS

1. Shortly after graduation, you start working for your aunt and uncle, who own a thriving antique store. They hope to store data about their inventory and business on the computer they recently purchased. They have hired you to accomplish this task. Your Aunt Susan asks you to organize her client files and to prepare some financial statements. Your Uncle Gabe wants you to create customized forms for invoicing and inventory. Two part-time employees, Julia and Abigail, have asked you to help develop documents for advertising. You realize that a folder structure would help to keep things straight.

   a. Quick format a disk, such as Data Disk 2, and then create a folder on it named Antiques.
   b. Create the following subfolders: Customers, Finances, Invoices, Inventory, and Advertising.

   c. In WordPad, create each of the documents listed below and save them in the correct folders on your Data Disk:

Customers subfolder:	Inventory subfolder:
Harrington	Furniture
Searls	Art
Finances subfolder:	Advertising subfolder:
Budget	Anniversary Sale
Profit and Loss	Winter Clearance
Balance Sheet	
Invoices subfolder:	
Sales	
Vendors	

   d. In Windows Explorer, display the entire Antiques folder hierarchy in the left pane, and display the contents of the Finances subfolder in the right pane. Print an image of the Windows Explorer window showing your file structure.

2. Uncle Gabe decided to have his financial statements prepared by an accountant, so you need to copy the files in the Finances subfolder onto a different disk that you can give to the accountant. Use the folders and files you created in Project 1. You will need a blank floppy disk. You must also be able to access your computer's hard disk to complete this project. Uncle Gabe wants to know how to copy files to a new disk, so as you copy the files, write down in detail what you are doing so he can repeat this procedure by following your directions.

   a. Create a folder in the My Documents folder on your hard disk called Accountant.

   b. Copy the three files in the Finances folder on your Data Disk to the Accountant folder on your hard disk, using the drag technique.

   c. Copy the contents of the Accountant folder to the blank disk, using the copy-and-paste technique.

   d. Delete the Accountant folder from your hard disk.

3. Two of the methods you've learned for moving files between folders are the drag-and-drop method and the cut-and-paste method. Answer the following questions:

   a. Can you think of any situations in which you could not drag to move a file in Windows Explorer?

   b. In such a situation, what should you do instead?

   c. Which method do you prefer? Why?

Explore

4. Windows XP enables users to customize their working environment extensively. For each item, first write the steps you take to make the change, and then comment on the benefits or disadvantages of using the following options in the Windows Explorer window:

   a. Details view or List view

   b. Displaying or hiding the status bar

   c. Displaying or hiding the Folders pane

   d. Switching from the Folders pane to the Favorites pane

QUICK CHECK ANSWERS

Session 3.1

1. Windows Explorer

2. The left pane displays tools, such as the Folders pane, History pane, and Search pane, used to organize the files on your computer; the right pane displays the contents of the object selected in the right pane.

3. False

4. False

5. subfolder

6. plus box

7. the drive A device icon

8. False

Session 3.2

1. Shift, Ctrl

2. The Folders pane shows how devices and folders are arranged in a hierarchy on a computer, but does not show files. To move, copy, delete, and perform other tasks with files, you work in the right pane.

3. Press the Print Screen key, paste the image into WordPad, and print the WordPad document.

4. Move to Folder

5. True

6. the Send To command

Session 3.3

1. False

2. Because the Favorites pane is designed to provide quick access to objects such as files and folders, you should organize it logically to keep it uncluttered and easy to use.

3. multimedia

4. False

5. Today

6. If you didn't know details about a file, such as where the file is located, when you last accessed the file, or its complete filename, you can use the Search Companion to find the file.

7. True

OBJECTIVES

In this tutorial you will:

- Store a document on the desktop and use the Notepad time-date stamp

- Create and delete shortcuts to a drive, a document, and a printer

- Use the Control Panel to change the desktop appearance

- Configure your taskbar

- Create and modify taskbar toolbars

- Edit your Start menu

PERSONALIZING YOUR WINDOWS ENVIRONMENT

Changing Desktop Settings at Companions, Inc.

CASE

Companions, Inc.

Bow Falls, Arizona, is a popular Sun Belt retirement mecca that is also a college town with several distinguished universities. Beth Yuan, a graduate of Bow Falls University, realized that the unusual mix of ages in her town might be perfectly suited to a business in which college students and recent graduates offer personal care services to retirees. She formed Companions, Inc. to provide older residents with trained assistants who help with housecleaning, home maintenance, and errands. Many of Beth's employees are students at local colleges who like the flexible hours and enjoy spending time with the elderly people. In addition to employees who work directly with clients, Beth has hired office staff, often retirees themselves, who help manage the day-to-day tasks of running a business.

Companions, Inc. uses computers to maintain client records, schedule employees, manage company finances, develop training materials, and create marketing pieces. Beth recently upgraded the office computers to Windows XP. She heard that it's easy to change Windows XP settings to reflect the needs of her office staff. For example, she wants to customize her computers so she and her staff can easily access key documents and computer resources. She would also like the desktop itself to reflect her corporate image. She asks you to help her meet these goals.

SESSION 4.1

In this session, you will learn how to create and store a Notepad document on the desktop and how to "stamp" the document with the time and date. You will create shortcuts to the objects you use most often, including your computer's floppy drive, a document, and a printer. You will learn the difference between document icons and shortcut icons on the desktop, and how to restore your desktop to its original state.

Docucentric Desktops

As you know, when you start Windows XP, the large area you see on your screen is called the desktop. Because the desktop provides your first view of the computer and its contents, it should contain the items you want to access when you start your computer. These items include tools such as My Computer, programs you use often, and key documents. Desktop icons are the most visual and easiest way to access these resources. Figure 4-1 shows the types of icons you can include on the desktop and the objects they represent.

Figure 4-1	TYPES OF DESKTOP ICONS

ICON	DESCRIPTION
	Text document icon
	Shortcut icon
	Floppy drive
	Hard drive
	CD drive
	Printer
	Folder
	System tools

You are already familiar with some icons on your desktop that represent critical tools, such as My Computer and the Recycle Bin. As Figure 4-1 shows, you can place additional icons on the desktop that represent objects you want to access quickly and frequently, such as printers, disk drives, programs, and documents. These icons are **shortcuts**, quick ways to start a program or open a file, folder, or other object without having to go to its permanent location on your computer. Shortcut icons include a small arrow, as in 🗐, the shortcut icon for a Notepad document. The small arrow is a reminder that a shortcut icon points to an item that is stored elsewhere on the computer. When you delete a shortcut icon, the file or resource it represents remains in its original location.

Shortcut icons can simplify tasks you perform regularly. For example, you can create a shortcut icon to the floppy drive and then drag files to the shortcut icon to move them to a floppy disk. If you create a shortcut icon for your printer, you can print a file by dragging it to the printer's shortcut icon. You also can create a shortcut icon for a program you use often and then double-click the icon to start the program.

In some cases, instead of creating a shortcut, you might want to store a document right on the desktop. For example, if you move or copy a document often, you could store it on the desktop so you don't have to navigate your computer's file system every time you want to work with the document. Instead, when you want to move or copy the document, you could drag it from the desktop to a shortcut icon for a drive or folder.

When you store a document on the desktop, it appears as a **document icon**. A document icon is similar to a shortcut icon, except it doesn't include the shortcut arrow. For example, is the document icon for a Notepad document. Document icons represent documents that you create, open, change, and save on the desktop. When you delete a document icon, you send the document to the Recycle Bin.

Desktops that use shortcut icons and document icons to provide immediate access to documents are called **docucentric** desktops.

You offer to help Beth make her desktop more docucentric so she can work more efficiently. She mentions that she wants to create a phone log to track phone calls to her clients and take notes about the services they request. Before an employee visits a client, she wants to copy the phone log to a floppy disk so the employee can update the client notes. She also wants to print the phone log in case the employee wants to take notes during the visit. You'll show Beth how to create a phone log in Notepad and store it on the desktop as a document icon. Then you'll show her how to create shortcut icons for the floppy drive, a document, and the printer.

Creating and Storing a Document on the Desktop

You can create a document on the desktop by right-clicking the desktop and then selecting the type of document you want from a list. You also can create a document on Notepad or WordPad, for example, open the Save As dialog box, and then save the document on the desktop. In either case, a document icon appears on the desktop to represent your document. The appearance of the document icon depends on the type of document you create. For example, a Notepad document icon appears as , whereas a WordPad document icon appears as . When you open the document represented by the icon, Windows XP checks the filename extension to determine which program it should start.

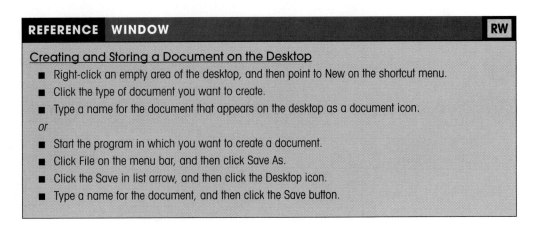

REFERENCE WINDOW **RW**

Creating and Storing a Document on the Desktop
- Right-click an empty area of the desktop, and then point to New on the shortcut menu.
- Click the type of document you want to create.
- Type a name for the document that appears on the desktop as a document icon.

or

- Start the program in which you want to create a document.
- Click File on the menu bar, and then click Save As.
- Click the Save in list arrow, and then click the Desktop icon.
- Type a name for the document, and then click the Save button.

You can use Notepad, an accessory included with Windows XP, to create phone logs and other documents that reflect the current time and date. Notepad, like WordPad, allows you to edit simple text documents, but because it does not include the formatting options provided by WordPad, it is used only for text documents with no formatting. Notepad includes a feature with which you can insert a time-date stamp that automatically inserts the time and date whenever you open the document. Figure 4-2 shows you a Notepad document with automatic time-date stamps.

Figure 4-2	NOTEPAD DOCUMENT WITH TIME-DATE STAMP

time and date automatically inserted each time you open the document

You suggest that Beth use Notepad to create a Companions, Inc. phone log and store it on her desktop. Then she and her employees can quickly access the phone log by double-clicking its icon on the desktop.

To create a Notepad document on the desktop:

1. Right-click a blank area of the desktop, and then point to **New**. The shortcut menu shown in Figure 4-3 opens.

Figure 4-3	CREATING A NEW TEXT DOCUMENT

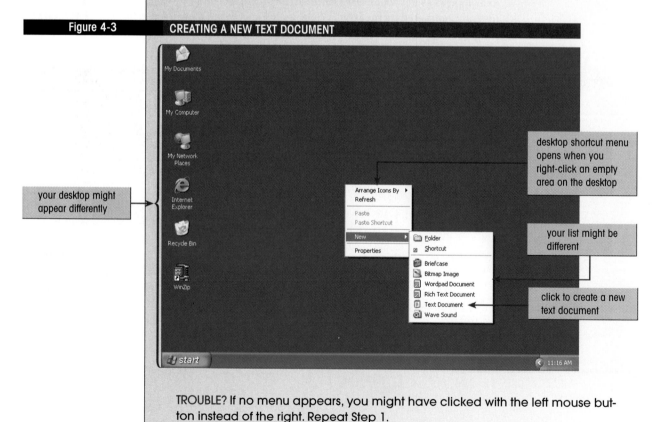

desktop shortcut menu opens when you right-click an empty area on the desktop

your desktop might appear differently

your list might be different

click to create a new text document

TROUBLE? If no menu appears, you might have clicked with the left mouse button instead of the right. Repeat Step 1.

TROUBLE? Your list of options on the New menu may differ from the one shown in Figure 4-3. The document types that appear on the New menu depend on the programs installed on your computer.

TROUBLE? Your monitor settings may differ, causing the objects on your screen to use more or less space than those shown in the figures.

2. Click **Text Document** on the shortcut menu. A document icon for your new text document appears on the desktop. See Figure 4-4. Its default filename, "New Text Document," is selected so you can type an appropriate name for the new file.

| Figure 4-4 | DOCUMENT ICON |

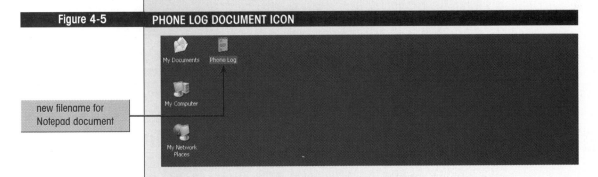

type filename here

TROUBLE? If you receive an error message when you try to create a new document on the desktop, your lab might not allow you to make any changes to the desktop. Ask your instructor which sections of this tutorial you will be able to complete using a lab computer.

3. Type **Phone Log** as the name of your document, and then press the **Enter** key. See Figure 4-5.

| Figure 4-5 | PHONE LOG DOCUMENT ICON |

new filename for Notepad document

TROUBLE? If nothing happens when you type the document name, you might have pressed a key or mouse button that deselected the document icon. Right-click the New Text Document icon, click Rename on the shortcut menu, and then type Phone Log.

TROUBLE? If you see a message about changing the filename extension, click the No button, type Phone Log.txt, and then press Enter. Your computer is set to display filename extensions, so you must provide an extension when you create a document on the desktop.

Now that you have created the Phone Log document on the desktop, you can use its icon to open it.

Opening a Document Stored on the Desktop

To open a document that is stored on the desktop, you double-click its icon. Windows XP then starts the appropriate program and opens the document.

To open the Phone Log document:

1. Double-click the **Phone Log** icon on the desktop. Windows XP starts Notepad. See Figure 4-6.

| Figure 4-6 | PHONE LOG DOCUMENT OPENS IN NOTEPAD |

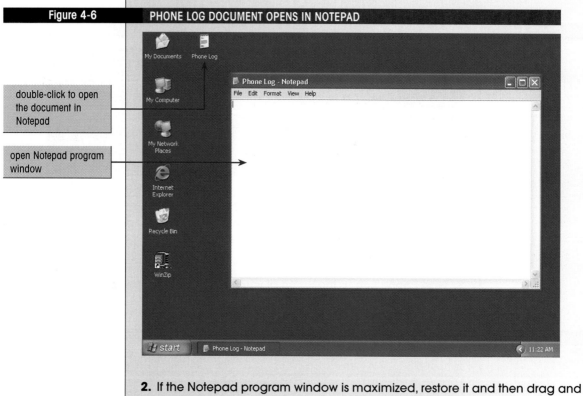

double-click to open the document in Notepad

open Notepad program window

2. If the Notepad program window is maximized, restore it and then drag and resize the window as necessary to view both the Notepad document icon on the desktop and the program window.

Now you can begin adding text to the phone log for Beth.

Creating a LOG File

Notepad automatically inserts the date when you open a document only if the document begins with .LOG, in uppercase letters. Your next step is to create a document with .LOG at the beginning and to enter some text. Then you will save the document and close it, so that the next time you open it, Notepad will automatically enter the time and date for you.

To set up the Phone Log document:

1. Type **.LOG**. Be sure to type the period first and to use uppercase letters. This text indicates that you want Notepad to enter the current time and date every time you open the document.

2. Press the **Enter** key to move the insertion point to the next line, type **Phone Log for**, and then type your name.

3. Press the **Enter** key. Now you are ready to use the Phone Log document to record names, phone numbers, and notes for phone calls you make. The time-date stamp Notepad inserts helps you track the calls by date and time.

4. Save the Phone Log document, and exit Notepad.

Now you will test the Phone Log document to ensure the automatic time-date stamp appears when you open it.

To test the Phone Log document:

1. Double-click the **Phone Log** icon on the desktop to open this document. Make sure your document contains a time-date stamp. See Figure 4-7.

Figure 4-7	TIME-DATE STAMP

typing .LOG in uppercase letters tells Notepad to insert a time-date stamp

time-date stamp; your date might be different

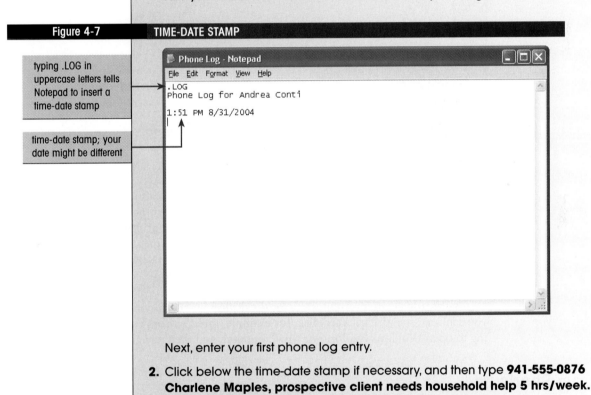

Next, enter your first phone log entry.

2. Click below the time-date stamp if necessary, and then type **941-555-0876 Charlene Maples, prospective client needs household help 5 hrs/week.**

3. Press the **Enter** key. See Figure 4-8.

Figure 4-8	FIRST PHONE LOG ENTRY IN NOTEPAD DOCUMENT

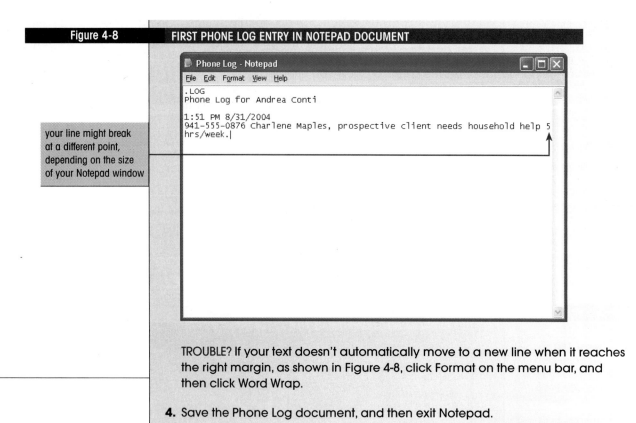

your line might break at a different point, depending on the size of your Notepad window

TROUBLE? If your text doesn't automatically move to a new line when it reaches the right margin, as shown in Figure 4-8, click Format on the menu bar, and then click Word Wrap.

4. Save the Phone Log document, and then exit Notepad.

You have created and edited a document stored on the desktop for easy access. You can also easily access existing documents from the desktop by creating a shortcut icon. A shortcut icon for a document works much the same way as a document icon—you can double-click the shortcut icon to open the document in the appropriate program. However, remember that a shortcut icon only points to the actual document. If you move the icon, for example, you move only the shortcut, not the document itself. One advantage of using shortcut icons is that if your desktop becomes cluttered, you can delete the shortcut icons without affecting the original document.

You can also create shortcut icons for the devices and drives on your computer. This way, you can access your local hard disk, for example, directly from the desktop, instead of having to open Windows Explorer or My Computer, and then navigate to the hard disk.

Using Shortcuts

You can create shortcuts to access drives, documents, files, Web pages, programs, or other computer resources such as a printer. Windows XP provides several ways of creating shortcuts. For example, you can right-click an object and select Create Shortcuts Here on the shortcut menu. Figure 4-9 summarizes the techniques you can use to create shortcuts. The one you choose is a matter of personal preference.

Figure 4-9	METHODS FOR CREATING SHORTCUTS
METHOD	**DESCRIPTION**
Drag	To create a shortcut on the desktop, use My Computer or Windows Explorer to locate the file icon, and then drag the icon to the desktop. For locations other than the desktop, hold down the Alt key as you drag.
Right-drag	Use My Computer or Windows Explorer to locate and select the file icon, hold down the right mouse button, and drag to a new location. Release the mouse button and click Create Shortcuts Here on the shortcut menu.
Right-click, Create Shortcut	Use My Computer or Windows Explorer to locate the file icon, right-click the icon, click Create Shortcut on the shortcut menu, and then drag the shortcut icon to a new location.
Right-click, Send To	To create a shortcut on the desktop, use My Computer or Windows Explorer to locate the file icon, right-click the icon, point to Send To, and then click Desktop (create shortcut).
Copy and paste shortcut	Use My Computer or Windows Explorer to locate and select the file icon. Click Edit on the menu bar, and then click Copy. Move to the new location. Click Edit on the menu bar, and then click Paste.
Create Shortcut command	Use My Computer or Windows Explorer to locate the file icon, Click File on the menu bar, click Create Shortcut, and then drag the shortcut icon to a new location.

Next you will create a shortcut to the floppy drive. You could use any technique listed in Figure 4-9, but you'll use the drag method because it involves the fewest steps.

Creating a Shortcut to a Drive

To create a shortcut to a drive, you can open the My Computer or Windows Explorer window, and then drag the drive icon from the window to the desktop. Windows XP creates a shortcut icon that looks like a hard disk or floppy disk, and includes an appropriate label, such as "Shortcut to 3½ Floppy (A)." When you create a shortcut to your floppy drive, you can double-click the shortcut to view the contents of your Data Disk, or you can move or copy documents to it without having to start Windows Explorer or My Computer.

Beth regularly copies the phone log to a floppy disk and wants to use a shortcut to simplify the task.

To create a shortcut to your floppy drive:

1. Double-click the **My Computer** icon on the desktop. If necessary, resize the My Computer window so you can see an empty area of the desktop. You need to see both the desktop and the My Computer window to drag effectively.

   TROUBLE? If the My Computer icon does not appear on your desktop, click the Start button on the taskbar, and then click My Computer.

2. Press and hold the left mouse button, and then drag the **3½ Floppy (A:) icon** from the My Computer window into an empty area of the desktop.

3. Release the mouse button. A shortcut labeled "Shortcut to 3½ Floppy (A)" now appears on the desktop. (Yours may be in a different location.) See Figure 4-10.

Figure 4-10 | SHORTCUT TO DRIVE A

other icons on your desktop might be different

shortcut to drive A (notice the small arrow)

TROUBLE? If you dragged with the right mouse button instead of the left, a shortcut menu appears when you release the mouse button. Click Create Shortcuts Here to add the Shortcut to 3½ Floppy (A) to the desktop.

If you drag a document icon from My Computer to the desktop, you move the document from its original location to the desktop. However, you cannot move a drive, program, or other computer resource—its location is fixed during installation—so when you drag a drive icon to the desktop, you automatically create a shortcut.

4. Close the My Computer window.

Now use the newly created shortcut to view the contents of your Data Disk in drive A.

To test the 3½ Floppy (A:) shortcut:

1. Make sure your Data Disk is in drive A, and then double-click the **3½ Floppy (A)** shortcut icon on the desktop. The My Computer window opens, showing the contents of the disk in your 3½ Floppy (A:) drive.

2. Click the **Close** button ☒ to close the My Computer window.

Beth often works at her home office, and she'd like to move the phone log to a floppy disk that she can carry back and forth. To copy the phone log to the floppy disk, you could drag the document icon to the 3½ Floppy (A:) shortcut icon. To move the log to a floppy disk, you can use the cut-and-paste method.

To move the document from the desktop to a floppy disk:

1. Right-click the **Phone Log** document icon on the desktop, and then click **Cut** on the shortcut menu.

2. Right-click the **3½ Floppy (A)** shortcut icon on the desktop, and then click **Paste** on the shortcut menu. The Phone Log icon disappears from the desktop, and the Phone Log document is now stored on your floppy disk.

When you moved the document icon to the drive A shortcut, the file itself was moved off your desktop and to the disk in drive A. Beth can now take the disk home with her and use a shortcut to drive A on her desktop there to open the file. You'll show her how to use the shortcut for the floppy drive you just created to access the Phone Log document stored on the floppy disk. (You could also open drive A from My Computer or Windows Explorer, but it is handier to use the drive A shortcut on the desktop.)

To open the Phone Log document using the shortcut to 3½ Floppy (A):

1. Double-click the **3½ Floppy (A)** shortcut icon on the desktop to open the My Computer window displaying the contents of drive A.

   TROUBLE? To switch to Details View, click View, and then click Details.

2. Scroll through the window, if necessary, to locate the Phone Log document on your Data Disk.

   TROUBLE? If you don't see the Phone Log document on your Data Disk, repeat the previous set of steps for moving a document to a floppy disk.

The Phone Log document is now on a floppy disk, as Beth requested; however, it no longer has an icon on the desktop. She realizes that she still might want to open the phone log on the office computer from the desktop. Recall that you can use shortcut icons to provide access to documents stored in other locations on your computer. In the next section, you will show her how to do this.

Creating a Shortcut to a Document

If you want to access the phone log document (now saved on your Data Disk) directly from the desktop, you can create a shortcut that opens the phone log from your Data Disk. Before you can use a shortcut icon that refers to a document on a floppy disk, you must make sure the floppy disk containing the document is in drive A.

You'll show Beth how to create a shortcut to a document using the right-click-and-drag method. (That is, you press and hold the right mouse button as you drag.)

To create a shortcut to the Phone Log document on your Data Disk:

1. Resize the 3½ Floppy (A:) window as necessary to see both the Phone Log icon in the window and a blank area of the desktop. Switch to Details View in the 3½ Floppy (A:) window, if necessary.

2. Press and hold the right mouse button, drag the **Phone Log** icon from the 3½ Floppy (A:) window onto the desktop, and then release the mouse button. A shortcut menu appears listing the tasks you can perform with this document. Note that you can use the shortcut menu to copy or move a document as well as create a shortcut to it.

3. Click **Create Shortcuts Here**.

An icon labeled "Shortcut to Phone Log" now appears on the desktop.

4. Rest your mouse pointer on the Shortcut to Phone Log icon, and note the ScreenTip that appears, indicating the location of the source document (in this case, on the root directory of drive A). See Figure 4-11.

Figure 4-11	CREATING A SHORTCUT TO THE PHONE LOG DOCUMENT ON DRIVE A

shortcut to the Phone Log document

ScreenTip indicates the location of the Phone Log document

source document

5. Click the **Close** button ⊠ to close the 3½ Floppy (A:) window.

Now you can test the shortcut to make sure it opens the Phone Log document.

To test the Phone Log shortcut:

1. Double-click the **Shortcut to Phone Log** icon. Windows XP starts Notepad and then opens the Phone Log document stored on your Data Disk.

2. Type: **941-555-7766 Trinity River Accounting** below the new time-date stamp, and then press the **Enter** key.

3. Click the **Close** button ⊠ to close Notepad.

4. Click the **Yes** button to save the changes.

The shortcut icon you just created and tested is different from the Phone Log icon you created at the beginning of this tutorial. That icon was not a shortcut icon, but a document icon representing a document stored on the desktop. The shortcut icon currently on your desktop represents a document located on your Data Disk.

You now have an efficient way to open the phone log and to access your floppy drive. Now you want to add a printer shortcut to the desktop so that Beth's employees can easily print their phone logs and other documents.

Creating a Shortcut to a Printer

You can create a printer shortcut in much the same way as you created a shortcut for the floppy drive: by locating the printer device icon in the Printers and Faxes window and then dragging the icon onto your desktop. You also can use the menu commands in the Printers and Faxes window to create a shortcut to a printer on the desktop. After you create a printer shortcut icon, you can print a document by dragging its icon to the printer shortcut icon on the desktop.

Beth and her employees often print phone logs and other documents before they visit prospective clients. Instead of starting Notepad or another program, opening the Print dialog box, selecting print settings, and then clicking OK, they can print by dragging a document to a printer shortcut icon. You'll show them how to create a printer shortcut using the menu commands in the Printers and Faxes window.

To create a printer shortcut:

1. Click the **Start** button (start) on the taskbar, and then click **Printers and Faxes**. The Printers and Faxes window opens. If necessary, resize the window so you can see both the window and a portion of the desktop.

2. Click the icon for the default printer (the one with the ✓) to select it.

   TROUBLE?If you are using a computer that is not connected to a network or printer, you will not be able to complete the steps in this section. Instead, read through the following steps to familiarize yourself with this process.

3. Click **File** on the menu bar, and then click **Create Shortcut**. A message appears, indicating that Windows cannot create a shortcut in the Printers and Faxes window. This is because the Printers and Faxes window shows the actual printers installed to work with your computer; you don't need a shortcut to a printer here. The message also asks if you want to place the shortcut on the desktop instead.

4. Click the **Yes** button. A shortcut icon for the printer you selected appears on the desktop. See Figure 4-12.

Figure 4-12   CREATING A SHORTCUT TO A PRINTER

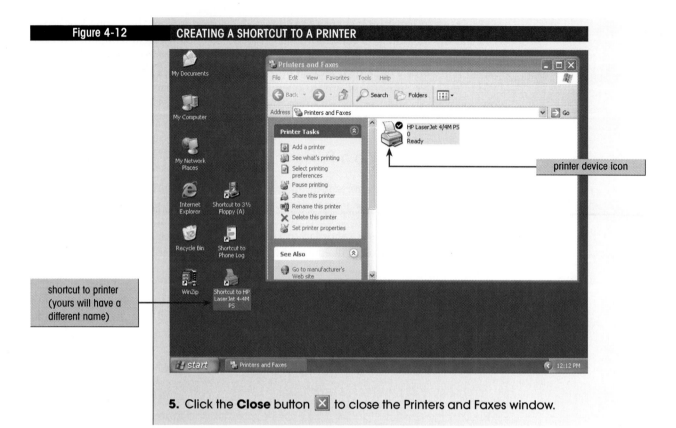

5. Click the **Close** button ⊠ to close the Printers and Faxes window.

Now you can show Beth how to print the Phone Log document on your Data Disk using the printer shortcut icon and the Phone Log document icon.

To print the Phone Log document using the printer shortcut icon:

1. Make sure your Data Disk is in drive A. Using the left mouse button, drag the **Shortcut to Phone Log** icon to the **Shortcut to Printer** icon that you just created on the desktop.

When you release the mouse button, Windows XP opens the Phone Log in Notepad and then prints the Phone Log. Normally Windows XP would simply close the program, but because your document has an automatic time-date stamp, the document is changed every time you open it. Thus, Windows XP asks if you want to save changes to the document before closing it. You don't need to save it because you don't have any new phone entries to log.

2. When prompted to save the changes to the Phone Log document, click the **No** button. Windows XP closes Notepad without saving the document.

If you are working on your own computer, you can leave the printer and drive icons in place, if you think you'll find them useful. Otherwise, you should delete all the shortcuts you created so that the desktop is restored to its original condition for the next user.

Deleting Shortcut Icons

If you delete a document icon, you also delete the document. If you delete a shortcut icon, however, you don't delete the document itself because it is stored elsewhere. You only delete the shortcut that points to the document. For example, if you removed your Data Disk from drive A, the shortcut to the Phone Log would no longer work because the source document would no longer be available.

To delete your shortcuts:

1. Click the **printer** shortcut icon to select it.

2. Press and hold down the **Ctrl** key, then click the **3½ Floppy (A:)** shortcut icon and the **Phone Log** shortcut icon, so that all three icons are highlighted. Make sure no other icons are highlighted. If they are, deselect them by clicking them while you hold down the Ctrl key.

3. Press the **Delete** key.

4. Click the **Yes** button if you are asked if you are sure you want to send these items to the Recycle Bin.

Your desktop is restored to its original appearance. You have learned how to create a docucentric desktop by creating and storing a document icon on the desktop, and by creating desktop shortcuts to a drive, document, and printer. You have also learned the difference between document icons and shortcut icons, and how to remove both from the desktop.

Session 4.1 QUICK CHECK

1. True or False: On a docucentric desktop, the quickest way to open a document is by locating the program that created the document, starting the program, and then using the Open command to locate and open the document.

2. True or False: You can create a document with an automatic time-date stamp in Notepad by typing "log" at the beginning of the document.

3. What happens if you delete a document icon on the desktop?

4. What happens if you delete a shortcut icon on the desktop?

5. Name three ways you can create a shortcut to the floppy drive on your desktop.

**SESSION
4.2**

In this session, you'll change the appearance of your desktop by working with a Windows XP tool called Control Panel. You'll experiment with your desktop's background and appearance, enable a screen saver, try different colors to see how they look, and modify desktop settings to explore your monitor's capabilities. As you proceed through this session, check with your instructor or technical support person before you change settings on a school lab computer, and make sure you change them back before you leave.

Using the Control Panel

In Session 4.1, you worked with document and shortcut icons to personalize your desktop. You can also personalize other parts of Windows XP using the Control Panel. The **Control Panel** is a window that contains specialized tools you use to change the way Windows looks and behaves. Some of these tools help you adjust settings that make your computer more fun to use. For example, you can use the Display tool to change the color of your desktop or display a graphic image in the background. You can also use the Sounds and Audio Devices tool to replace standard system sounds with sounds you choose. Other Control Panel tools help you set up Windows so that your computer is easier to use. For example, if you are left-handed, you can use the Mouse tool to switch the mouse buttons so that the button on the right performs the primary functions of selecting and dragging.

All of the Control Panel tools provide access to a dialog box that lets you select or change the **properties**, or characteristics, of an object. For example, to set or change the time of the clock shown on the taskbar, you open the Date/Time Properties dialog box, which you access from Control Panel.

To open the Control Panel:

1. Click the **Start** button ⟨ start ⟩ on the taskbar, and then click **Control Panel**. See Figure 4-13.

Figure 4-13 | CONTROL PANEL

click to switch to Classic View

the See Also list includes links related to your current task

the Appearance and Themes category contains options for customizing your desktop

Control Panel in Category View

point to a category icon to see a ScreenTip explaining the category's contents

The Control Panel window opens, showing tasks in the right pane and related links in the left pane. By default, the Control Panel opens in Category View, which groups similar tools into categories.

TROUBLE? If a message appears indicating that the Control Panel is not available, you might be in a computer lab with limited ability for customization. Ask your instructor or technical support person for options.

TROUBLE? If Control Panel opens in Classic View, click Switch to Category View in the left pane of the Control Panel window.

Figure 4-14 describes the Control Panel categories.

Figure 4-14	CONTROL PANEL CATEGORIES
CONTROL PANEL CATEGORY	**DESCRIPTION**
Appearance and Themes	Change the appearance of desktop items, apply a theme or screen saver, or customize the Start menu and taskbar
Network and Inrernet Connections	Connect to the Internet, create a home or small office network, configure network settings to work from home, or change the modem, phone, and Internet settings
Add or Remove Programs	Install and uninstall programs and Windows components
Sounds, Speech, and Audio Devices	Change the sound scheme or individual sounds on your computer and configure the settings for your sound devices
Performance and Maintenance	Schedule maintenance checks, increase the space on your hard disk, or configure energy-saving settings
Printers and Other Hardware	Change the settings for your printer, keyboard, mouse, camera, and other hardware
User Accounts	Change user accounts settings, passwords, and associated pictures (Windows XP Professional only)
Date, Time, Language, and Regional Options	Change the date, time, and time zone, the language you use on your computer, and the format for numbers, currencies, dates, and times
Accessibility Options	Change computer settings for vision, hearing, and mobility

If you are familiar with an earlier version of Windows, such as Windows 2000, and are more comfortable with the view that displays all of the tools individually, you can change to Classic View by clicking the Switch to Classic View link in the left pane. For now, however, you'll continue to explore the Control Panel in Category View.

To open a category and see its related tools, you click the appropriate link. For example, you can open the Appearance and Themes window to change the way the screen looks and behaves, or to set a **theme**, a collection of related colors, images, and effects for the desktop.

To open the Appearance and Themes category:

1. In the right pane of the Control Panel, click **Appearance and Themes**. The Control Panel window displays the tasks and tools related to changing your computer's appearance and setting themes. See Figure 4-15.

| Figure 4-15 | APPEARANCE AND THEMES OPTIONS IN THE CONTROL PANEL |

the left pane lists related links and troubleshooters

click a troubleshooter to solve a Windows XP problem

click a task to work with related Control Panel tools...

...or click a tool icon to open a Control Panel dialog box listing various options and settings

TROUBLE? Because some tools are optional, your Control Panel might display different tools from the ones shown in Figure 4-15.

The Appearance and Themes window, like the other Control Panel category windows, lists tasks and tools in the right pane and related links in the left pane. To change an element of the desktop, you click the appropriate task in the right pane. For example, when you click the Change the desktop background link, the Display Properties dialog box opens to the Background tab, where you can select or change a desktop background. You can also click the Display tool icon in the right pane to open the Display Properties dialog box to its default tab. The See Also section in the left pane lists links related to the Appearance and Themes tools. The left pane also lists **troubleshooters**, links you can click to solve problems with the display and sound on your computer.

Figure 4-16 lists the options in the Appearance and Themes window and describes their purposes.

Figure 4-16	APPEARANCE AND THEMES OPTIONS
APPEARANCE AND THEMES OPTION	**DESCRIPTION**
Change the computer's theme	Change the set of colors, images, and other effects for your desktop, or save the current set as a new theme
Change the desktop background	Change the color or background pattern or image of your desktop
Choose a screen saver	Select a moving image to display on the screen after the computer has been idle for a specified amount of time
Change the screen resolution	Change the sharpness of the screen and the quality of the color
Display icon	Open the Display Properties dialog box to change display properties for themes, the desktop background, screen saver, appearance, and other settings
Folder Options	Open the Folder Options dialog box to change the way folders look and behave
Taskbar and Start Menu	Open the Taskbar and Start Menu Properties dialog box to change the way the taskbar and Start menu look and behave
See Also	Set or change properties for fonts, mouse pointers, contrast, or user accounts
Troubleshooters	Open a series of dialog boxes that will help you solve ploblems with the display and sound on your computer

Beth wants her office computers to reflect the company image of Companions, Inc. She'd like the desktop itself to be more appealing to her and her employees. You suggest she work with the desktop properties to change the desktop background and other elements.

Changing Desktop Properties

In Windows XP, you can think of all the parts of your computer—the operating system, the programs, and the documents—as individual objects. For example, the desktop, taskbar, drives, programs, and documents are all objects. Each object has properties that you can examine and sometimes change to suit your needs and preferences. The desktop has many properties, including its color, its size, and the font it uses. You can change the properties of an object using the Properties command on the shortcut menu or the Control Panel. In this session, you will use Control Panel to change desktop properties.

Changing Your Desktop's Background

You can change the desktop background color, or you can select a graphic to display in the background of your desktop. When you change the background, you are not placing a new object on the desktop; you are simply changing the desktop's appearance.

Beth wants the staff computers in the Companions, Inc. offices to have a corporate look. You and Beth decide to change the desktop color to dark blue, which is one of Companions, Inc.'s corporate colors.

To change the desktop color:

1. In the Appearance and Themes window, click **Change the desktop background**. The Display Properties dialog box opens to the Desktop tab. See Figure 4-17.

Figure 4-17	DESKTOP SETTINGS IN THE DISPLAY PROPERTIES DIALOG BOX

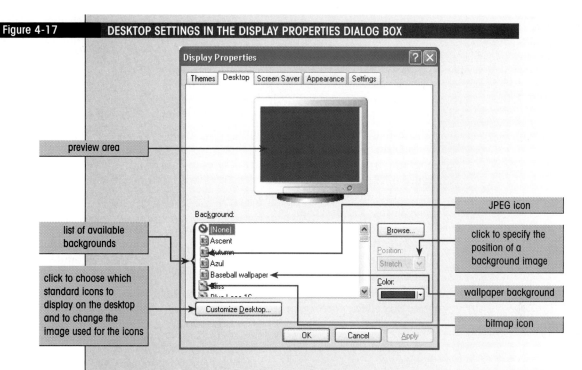

preview area

list of available backgrounds

click to choose which standard icons to display on the desktop and to change the image used for the icons

JPEG icon

click to specify the position of a background image

wallpaper background

bitmap icon

2. Minimize the Appearance and Themes window so you can see the Display Properties dialog box and the desktop at the same time.

3. Note the currently selected background color—you will restore this setting later.

4. If necessary, click **(None)** in the Background list if it is not already selected. The Preview window shows the background as the default color.

5. Click the **Color** list arrow, and then click **dark blue** (row 4, column 2) in the color palette. See Figure 4-18.

Figure 4-18	CHANGING THE COLOR OF THE DESKTOP

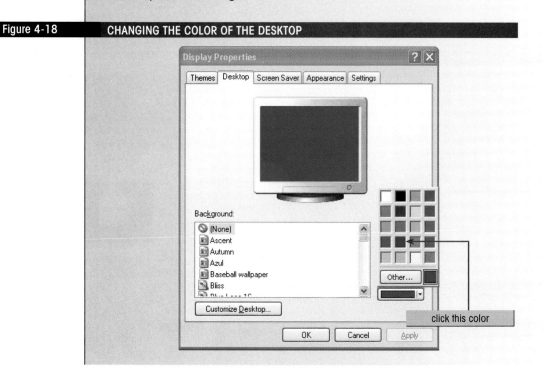

click this color

Right now, dark blue only appears in the Preview window. To change the desktop color but keep the Display Properties dialog box open to make other changes, you would click the Apply button. To change the desktop color and close the Display Properties dialog box, you would click the OK button. Before you do either one, you suggest to Beth that you continue to experiment.

Based on the preview, Beth thinks dark blue looks dull as a background on its own, but you suggest that placing an image against the blue might work well. If you choose a bitmap image from the Background list, you can set the position of the image. Recall that a bitmap image is a graphic that you can edit in Paint or another image-editing program. In the Background list, a bitmap image has a Paint icon 🖾, as shown in Figure 4-17. You can display a bitmap as a single image in the middle of the desktop, stretch the image across the width and height of the desktop, or repeat—or tile—the image across the desktop.

The Background list also includes two kinds of photographic images: JPEG images and wallpaper. Both have a 🖾 icon. The only differences are that wallpaper backgrounds are related to desktop themes, which you'll use later in this tutorial, and you can change the position of wallpaper backgrounds, but not other JPEG images.

Beth wants to see how an image looks if it has the dark blue desktop as its background. To create this effect, you display a bitmap image in the center of the desktop.

To select and position a bitmap image:

1. Scroll the Background list to locate and then click **Prairie Wind**. A pattern of blues and greens fills the preview window. Note that Tile is the default position for this image, so the pattern repeats across the screen.

   TROUBLE? If the Prairie Wind image isn't available, choose a different bit-map image.

2. Click the **Position** list arrow, and then click **Center** to preview a single copy of the Prairie Wind image in the middle of the desktop.

3. Click the **Apply** button to apply this effect to the desktop. See Figure 4-19.

Figure 4-19	PRAIRIE WIND IMAGE POSITIONED IN THE CENTER OF THE DESKTOP

your desktop might have different icons

Prairie Wind pattern

selected background

current position

Beth doesn't think the Prairie Wind image fits her company very well. You decide to experiment with other backgrounds. Recall that in the Background list, an image with a JPEG icon 🖾 indicates a photographic image. You decide to explore these backgrounds. Beth noticed a background named Home and thinks that might be appropriate for her business, which offers housecleaning and home maintenance services.

To select a photographic background:

1. Click **Home** in the Background list.

   TROUBLE? If the Home image is not available, choose a different JPEG image from the Background list.

2. Click the **Apply** button. See Figure 4-20.

Figure 4-20	USING A PHOTOGRAPHIC IMAGE AS THE DESKTOP BACKGROUND

current background image

This image doesn't reflect Companions, Inc.'s company image, so you return to the Background list.

3. Experiment with the other photographic backgrounds by clicking them in the Background list and then previewing them in the preview area. Click the **Apply** button to see each image on your desktop rather than only in the preview area.

As you experiment, you might notice the photographic images that include "wallpaper" in their names. Recall that you can change the position of wallpaper backgrounds.

To change the position of a wallpaper image:

1. In the Background list, click **Baseball wallpaper**. The image appears in the preview area in the Stretch position, which is the default.

TROUBLE? If the Baseball wallpaper is not available, click a different wallpaper background or a different photographic image.

2. Click the **Position** list arrow, and then click **Center**. Instead of reducing the photograph to a single small image in the middle of the screen, the center of the image—the batter and the catcher—enlarges to fill the entire screen. In effect, this brings the center of the photograph into focus.

3. Click the **Position** list arrow, and then click **Tile**. Now the batter and only part of the catcher appear. If the Baseball wallpaper photo were smaller than the screen, part of it would repeat on the right or bottom of the screen.

Besides using an image included in the Background list, you can also use any image you can access with your computer, including graphic images stored on a disk or those you find on the Web. Whereas the Background list includes only graphics in the bitmap (BMP) and JPEG formats, you can use graphics in other types of formats, such as GIF, a popular format for Web graphics.

None of the backgrounds that come with Windows XP suits Beth's corporate image, so you ask her if she would like to use a graphic of her company logo. She is enthusiastic; it would be great if clients who come to the offices could see the company logo on the office computers.

To use a graphic image as a custom desktop background:

1. If necessary, place your Data Disk in drive A.

2. Click the **Browse** button on the Desktop property sheet. The Browse dialog box opens, showing the contents of a folder on your hard drive.

The Companions, Inc. logo is on your Data Disk, however, so you'll display the contents of the floppy drive next.

3. Click the **Look in** list arrow, and then click **3½ Floppy (A:)**.

4. Click the file **Logo**.

TROUBLE? If Logo appears as Logo.bmp, click Logo.bmp. Your computer is set to display file extensions.

5. Click the **Open** button.

6. Click the **Position** list arrow, and then click **Center** to center the image on the screen.

7. Click the **OK** button to close the Display Properties dialog box. See Figure 4-21. The logo for Companions, Inc. appears in the middle of the desktop.

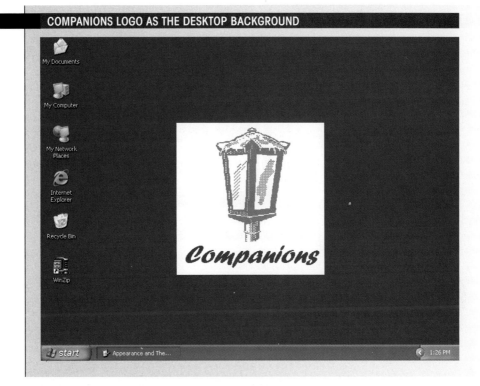

Figure 4-21 **COMPANIONS LOGO AS THE DESKTOP BACKGROUND**

Beth looks over your shoulder and comments that the blue in the background and the blue of the logo coordinate well. But she wants to use a contrasting color for window title bars and buttons. She asks you to change those elements to white or silver. Also, because some staff and volunteers are senior citizens, she wants to make the text of desktop elements and the icons themselves larger so they are easier to read and recognize.

Changing the Appearance of Desktop Elements

The Appearance property sheet on the Display Properties dialog box gives you control over the appearance of all the items on the desktop, including icons, title bars, borders, menus, and scroll bars. You also use the Appearance property sheet to change the window colors and font size.

To open the Appearance property sheet:

1. Click the **Appearance and Themes** button on the taskbar to restore the Appearance and Themes window, and then click **Display** to open the Display Properties dialog box. Minimize the Appearance and Themes window.

2. Click the **Appearance** tab in the Display Properties dialog box. The Appearance property sheet appears, as shown in Figure 4-22.

Figure 4-22   APPEARANCE PROPERTY SHEET

preview area

selected style; click the
list arrow to select a
different windows and
buttons style

click to select a different
color scheme

click to change the icon
size and other effects

click to change the font
size of screen text

The Appearance property sheet includes several list boxes from which you select options to change the desktop's appearance. Notice the Color scheme list box. A **color scheme** is a set of colors you can apply to the elements shown in the preview area. Windows XP includes a collection of color schemes, and the default scheme for the Windows XP style is blue. However, if your computer is in a lab, your technical support person might have designed and selected a different scheme. Before you experiment with the appearance of your desktop, you should write down the current scheme so you can restore it when you are finished working through the steps in this tutorial.

The preview area on the Appearance property sheet displays many of the elements you are likely to see when working with Windows XP. After you change an appearance setting, look in the preview area to see how the new setting will affect your windows and dialog boxes.

To change the color scheme of desktop elements:

1. Make a note of the current scheme, which is displayed in the Color scheme list box.

   TROUBLE? If your Color scheme list box is empty, your technical support person might have changed scheme settings without saving the scheme. Each time you change an object's color, write down the original color so you can restore that object's color when you are finished.

2. Note the style name in the Windows and buttons text box, and then click the **Color scheme** list arrow. The list shows the color schemes you can use for the style shown in the Windows and buttons text box.

3. Click **Silver**. The preview window shows how the silver color scheme looks in the Windows XP style.

   Now you want to increase the size of the text on the desktop elements.

4. Click the **Font size** list arrow, and then click **Large Fonts**. The preview window again shows the effects of this change.

5. To increase the size of the icons, click the **Effects** button. The Effects dialog box opens, as shown in Figure 4-23.

Figure 4-23   THE EFFECTS DIALOG BOX

click to use large icons instead of small ones

your dialog box might have different options selected

The Effects dialog box allows you to set visual effects for windows, menus, icons, and screen fonts.

6. In the Effects dialog box, click the **Use large icons** box to insert a check, and then click the **OK** button to close the Effects dialog box.

7. Click the **OK** button in the Appearance property sheet to apply your changes to the desktop. See Figure 4-24.

Figure 4-24   APPEARANCE OF THE MODIFIED DESKTOP

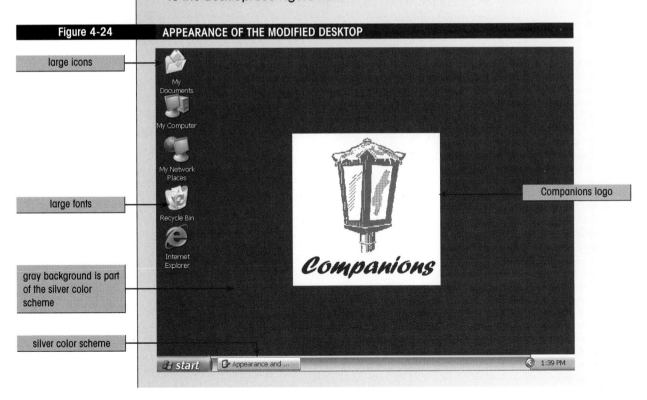

large icons

large fonts

Companions logo

gray background is part of the silver color scheme

silver color scheme

Because you applied a color scheme, Windows XP changed the color of many elements, including the taskbar, desktop icons, and icon labels. As you continue to work, you'll notice other elements have changed, including the text in shortcut menus and dialog boxes. Beth is pleased with how the desktop looks except for one thing—the background color you set earlier, the dark blue, has been replaced by a steel gray. This is because the gray desktop background is part of the silver color scheme. You can easily use the Display Properties dialog box again to change the desktop background back to blue. When you do, note the colors, fonts, and icons used on the desktop and in the dialog box.

To restore the dark blue desktop:

1. Click the **Appearance and Themes** button on the taskbar to restore the Appearance and Themes window, and then click **Change the desktop background** to open the Desktop property sheet of the Display Properties dialog box. Minimize the Appearance and Themes window.

   Note the silver color scheme applied to the title bar, tabs, and buttons in the Display Properties dialog box.

2. Click the **Color** list arrow, and then click **dark blue** (row 4, column 2) in the palette.

3. Click the **OK** button to apply the color to the desktop and close the Display Properties dialog box.

Now that you have customized the desktop, you can save the settings as a theme. Recall that a theme is a collection of customized elements, such as colors and graphics, that you apply to your desktop. If you save your current settings as a theme, you can apply all the changes—the dark blue background with the Companions logo, the silver color scheme, and large fonts—at the same time, without selecting the individual settings again. You can save the desktop settings you created for Beth as a theme called Companions.

To save the desktop settings as a theme:

1. Restore the Appearance and Themes window, and then click **Change the computer's theme** to open the Themes property sheet of the Display Properties dialog box. Minimize the Appearance and Themes window so you can see both the dialog box and portion of the desktop at the same time.

2. Click the **Theme** list arrow. See Figure 4-25.

Figure 4-25   **LIST OF THEMES**

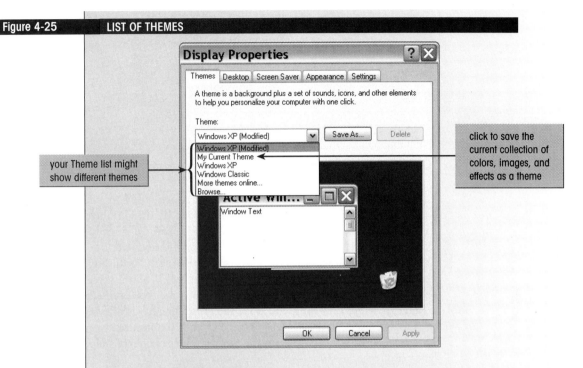

3. Click **My Current Theme**, if necessary. The My Current Theme option includes all the properties currently set in the Display Properties dialog box.

4. Click the **Save As** button.

5. In the Save As dialog box, navigate to your Data Disk. In the File name text box, type **Companions** as the name of this theme.

6. Click the **Save** button.

After you save the Companions theme on your Data Disk, restore the desktop colors and other appearance properties to their original settings.

To restore the desktop colors and appearance to their original settings:

1. Click the **Desktop** tab in the Display Properties dialog box.

2. In the Background list, locate and then click the desktop background that was in effect before you began this tutorial.

3. Click the **Appearance** tab.

4. Click the **Color scheme** list arrow, and then locate and click the color scheme you wrote down earlier, such as **Default (blue)**.

   TROUBLE? If your Color scheme list box was blank when you began working with the Appearance property sheet, skip Step 5 and instead restore each setting you changed to the original color you wrote down in the beginning of this section. Proceed to Step 6.

5. Click the **Font size** list arrow, and then click **Normal**.

6. Click the **Effects** button.

7. Click the **Use large icons** check box button to deselect it, and then click the **OK** button.

8. Click the **Apply** button. The original desktop is restored. Leave the Display Properties dialog box open.

Activating a Screen Saver

A **screen saver** blanks the screen or displays a moving design whenever you haven't worked with the computer for a specified period of time. In older monitors, a screen saver can help prevent "burn-in," or the permanent etching of an image into the screen, which occurs when the screen displays the same image for long periods of time. This is not a concern with newer monitors. However, screen savers are still handy for hiding your data from the eyes of passers-by if you step away from your computer. When a screen saver is on, you restore your desktop by moving your mouse or pressing any key on the keyboard.

You can select how long you want the computer to sit idle before the screen saver activates. Most users find settings between 3 and 10 minutes work best for them. You can change this using the options on the Screen Saver property sheet of the Display Properties dialog box.

Windows XP provides a wide variety of screen savers. Beth would like a screen saver that displays the name of the company. You decide to show her how to set up this screen saver.

To activate a screen saver:

1. Click the **Screen Saver** tab in the Display Properties dialog box. See Figure 4-26.

Figure 4-26 | THE SCREEN SAVER PROPERTY SHEET

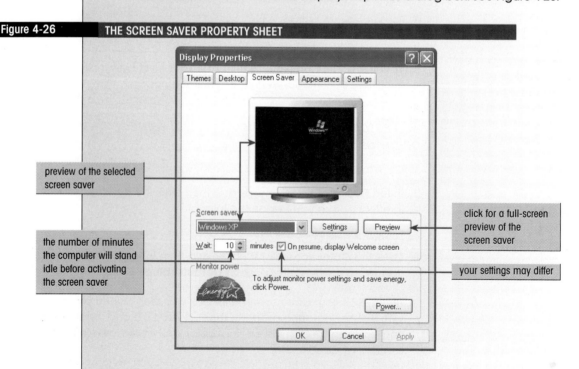

preview of the selected screen saver

the number of minutes the computer will stand idle before activating the screen saver

click for a full-screen preview of the screen saver

your settings may differ

2. Click the **Screen saver** list arrow, and then click **3D Text**.

TROUBLE? If the Screen Saver list box does not display 3D Text, you will not be able to complete these steps. Read through them to become familiar with the process.

3. Click the **Settings** button. The 3D Text Settings dialog box opens.

4. Select the text in the Custom Text box, and then type **Companions, Inc.** (including the final period). See Figure 4-27.

Figure 4-27	THE 3D SETTINGS DIALOG BOX

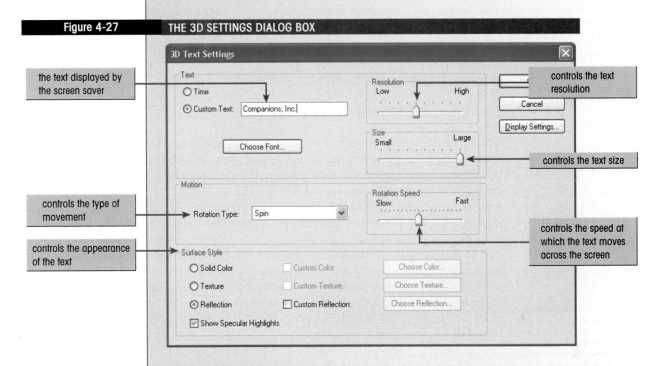

the text displayed by the screen saver

controls the text resolution

controls the text size

controls the type of movement

controls the appearance of the text

controls the speed at which the text moves across the screen

The 3D Text Settings dialog box contains several options you can set to control the screen saver. You can control the motion, the speed at which the text appears on the screen, the size of the text, the texture or color of the text, and also the way the text moves across the screen. You'll keep the defaults for all of these options.

5. Click the **OK** button.

The Preview window in the Screen Saver property sheet shows a preview of the screen saver. You can also view a full-screen preview of the screen saver.

6. Click the **Preview** button.

The screen saver fills the screen.

TROUBLE? If you move the mouse after clicking the Preview button, the screen saver will disappear, sometimes so quickly that you cannot even see it. Repeat Step 6, but make sure you don't move the mouse after you click the Preview button.

7. When you're finished previewing the screen saver move the mouse and then click the **Cancel** button to cancel your screen saver changes and close the Display Properties dialog box. If you were working on your own computer and wanted to save the changes, you would click the Apply button to save the changes or the OK button to save the changes and close the Display Properties dialog box.

Now that you have worked with the properties for the desktop background, theme, and screen saver, you are ready to explore the display properties that affect the computer monitor itself. The Settings property sheet lets you change the sharpness of the images on the desktop and the number of colors your monitor displays.

Changing **Display Settings**

The Settings property sheet allows you to control additional display settings that you might never need to consider. However, if you want to take full advantage of your monitor type, you should be aware of the options you have on the Settings property sheet. The settings you can change depend on your monitor type and on the **video card**, a piece of hardware inside your computer that controls visual information you see on the screen.

Changing the Size of the Desktop Area

The Settings property sheet has a Screen resolution slider bar that lets you display less or more of the desktop on your monitor. If you display less, objects will look bigger, while if you display more, objects will look smaller. You can drag the slider bar between these two extremes. When you do, you are actually increasing or decreasing the resolution, or sharpness, of the image. Resolution is measured by the number of individual dots, called **pixels**, short for "picture elements," that run across and down your monitor. The more pixels, the more you see on the screen at one time, and the smaller the objects look.

The 800 by 600 (800 pixels across and 600 pixels down) resolution shows the least information, but uses the largest text and is preferred by most users with 15-inch monitors. The 1024 by 768 resolution shows more information, but uses smaller text. Many users with 17-inch monitors prefer the 1024 by 768 resolution. The 1152 by 864 resolution shows the most information, but uses the smallest text. Most users find the 1152 by 864 resolution too small for comfortable use unless they are using a 17-inch or larger monitor. Users with limited vision might prefer the 800 by 600 setting even on larger monitors, because objects and text are bigger and easier to see. The software you use might also recommend you change the screen resolution to take advantage of special features in the software.

To change the screen resolution:

1. Open the Appearance and Themes window, and then click **Change the screen resolution** to display the Settings tab of the Display Properties dialog box. Minimize the Appearance and Themes window.

2. Make note of the original setting in the Screen resolution area so you can restore it once you finish this tutorial.

3. To select the 800 by 600 pixels resolution, if it is not already selected, drag the **Screen resolution** slider to the left. The preview monitor shows the relative size of the 800 by 600 display. See Figure 4-28.

Figure 4-28	800 BY 600 RESOLUTION

preview monitor; desktop practically fills the center part of the screen

drag to change the screen resolution

resolution shown in preview monitor

4. To select the 1024 by 768 resolution, drag the Screen area slider to the right. The preview monitor shows the relative size of the 1024 by 768 display.

5. Return the slider to the setting it was at the end of Step 2. Leave the Display Properties dialog box open.

While changing the screen resolution increases or decreases the sharpness of the images, the number of colors your monitor displays determines how realistic the images look. However, the higher the resolution and color settings, the more resources your monitor needs; the best settings for your computer balance sharpness and color quality with computer resources.

Changing the Color Settings

You can also use the Settings property sheet to change the color settings, which specify the number of colors available to your computer to create shading and other realistic effects. Beth's computers use High color, which includes up to 65,000 colors. Figure 4-29 provides additional information on common color settings. The color settings depend on your monitor, so your computer may have more or fewer settings.

Figure 4-29	COLOR SETTINGS

SETTING	DESCRIPTION
Medium (65,000 colors)	Relatively fast, requires a moderate amount of video memory, sufficient for most programs and adequate for the graphics in most games and educational programs. This is a good setting for general computer use.
High (16 million colors)	Requires higher-quality video card and additional video memory. This setting is useful for sophisticated painting, drawing, and graphics manipulation tasks.
Highest (over 4 billion colors)	Requires the most video memory and runs most slowly. This setting is useful for professional graphics tasks, but might not be available or might be too slow on some computer systems.

To view the color settings:

1. Click the **Color quality** list arrow to display the list of color palettes. See Figure 4-30.

Figure 4-30   CHANGING THE COLOR SETTINGS

list of available color palettes; your list might be different

2. Click **High (24 bit)**. Depending on your monitor, your screen can now display up to 16 million colors, which allows realistic shading and gradation.

TROUBLE? If High (24 bit) doesn't appear in your Color quality list, skip Step 2.

3. Click the **Cancel** button to close the Display Properties dialog box without accepting any changes.

4. If you are working in a school lab, make sure you have changed all settings back to their original state before moving on to Session 4.3.

5. Close the Appearance and Themes window.

You used the Control Panel and its tools to change the properties of Beth's desktop, including the background and the appearance of desktop elements, such as windows and icons. You added a graphic to the desktop background, saved her color scheme as a theme, activated a screen saver, and experimented with the display settings. Beth can now change the desktops of other computers in her office so they all reflect the corporate image of Companions, Inc.

Session 4.2 QUICK CHECK

1. True or False: The desktop is the on-screen work area where windows, icons, menus, and dialog boxes appear.

2. What is the Control Panel used for?

3. Name three desktop properties you can change from the Display Properties dialog box.

4. If you have a recently manufactured monitor, why might you use a screen saver?

5. What does it mean to say that a monitor's resolution is 800 by 600?

6. Users with limited vision might want to use which resolution: 800 by 600, 1024 by 768, or 1152 by 864? Why?

7. What is the disadvantage of using color settings with many colors, such as Highest Color?

SESSION 4.3

In this session, you'll work with the taskbar and Start menu objects on the desktop. You'll learn how to modify the appearance and location of the taskbar, and how to add items to it. You'll work with the properties of the Start menu, and learn how to add items to the menu and how to modify the existing menu items.

Modifying the Taskbar

As you know from previous tutorials, the bar that contains the Start button and appears by default at the bottom of the desktop is the taskbar. Besides the Start button, which you can click to open the Start menu, the taskbar shows the current time and buttons for any programs or documents that you currently have open. In addition, you can display toolbars on the taskbar. These toolbars can contain buttons for the icons on your desktop, for programs you use often, and for Web pages that you want to access quickly. Including these toolbars on the taskbar makes it easy to navigate your computer and open programs, documents, and Web pages without minimizing windows or closing dialog boxes that might be open on the desktop. Figure 4-31 shows some common items that can appear on the toolbar.

Figure 4-31	SOME ITEMS THAT CAN APPEAR ON THE TASKBAR

Besides displaying items on the taskbar, you can change the size and position of the taskbar itself, or even hide it altogether. For example, if you are editing a long document or creating a drawing and find that the taskbar gets in your way, you can hide the taskbar or move it to the sides or top of the desktop. If the taskbar becomes crowded with toolbars and program buttons, you can resize the taskbar to show more items.

So far you've shown Beth how to work with many properties of the Windows XP desktop. Now you can show her two other parts of the Windows XP desktop: the taskbar and the Start menu. You'll start by showing her how to work with the taskbar.

Moving and Resizing the Taskbar

When you first install Windows XP, the taskbar is locked in its position at the bottom of the desktop. That way, as you learn your way around Windows, you always have access to the Start menu, which you use to start programs and shut down Windows. Before you can move or resize the taskbar, however, you must unlock it. You can do so by right-clicking the taskbar to open its shortcut menu and then clicking the Lock the Taskbar command. Because this command is listed with a check mark by default to indicate it's selected, clicking it again removes the check mark, indicating the taskbar is no longer locked.

Beth's previous computer was a Macintosh, and she's used to seeing a menu bar at the top of the desktop. She wants to know how to change the position of the taskbar to create this familiar appearance. First, you will unlock the taskbar and then move it to the top of the desktop.

REFERENCE WINDOW   `RW`

Moving and Resizing the Taskbar
- Make sure the taskbar is unlocked. To do so, right-click any blank area on the taskbar, and then click Lock the Taskbar on the shortcut menu to remove the check mark.
- To move the taskbar, click a blank area on the taskbar, hold down the left mouse button, and drag the taskbar to a new location (the top, bottom, left, or right edge of the desktop).
- To resize the taskbar, move the mouse pointer over the taskbar border until the pointer changes to a ↕. Then drag the border to the desired width.

To move the taskbar:

1. Right-click any blank area on the taskbar, and then, if necessary, click **Lock the Taskbar** on the shortcut menu to remove the check mark.

   TROUBLE? If the Lock the Taskbar command is already unchecked, skip Step 1.

2. Drag the taskbar to the top of the desktop. See Figure 4-32. Notice that the icons currently on the desktop moved down slightly to make room for the newly placed taskbar.

Figure 4-32	MOVING THE WINDOWS XP TASKBAR TO THE TOP OF THE DESKTOP

taskbar relocated to the top of the desktop

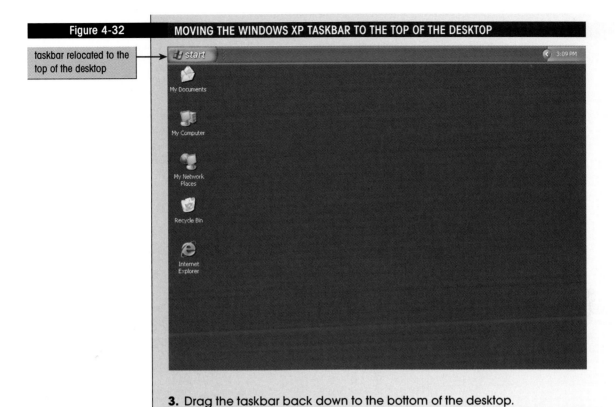

3. Drag the taskbar back down to the bottom of the desktop.

Beth has also noticed that when she has several programs running simultaneously, the icons for those programs fill the taskbar, sometimes to such an extent that the individual icons are compressed beyond recognition. You tell her that one way of dealing with that problem is to increase the size of the taskbar. This is easily accomplished by dragging the taskbar border to make the taskbar larger. Try this now.

To increase the size of the taskbar:

1. Move the mouse pointer over the top edge of the taskbar until the pointer changes to $\updownarrow$.

2. Drag the top border up, releasing the left mouse button when the taskbar has increased in height. See Figure 4-33.

Figure 4-33   RESIZING THE TASKBAR

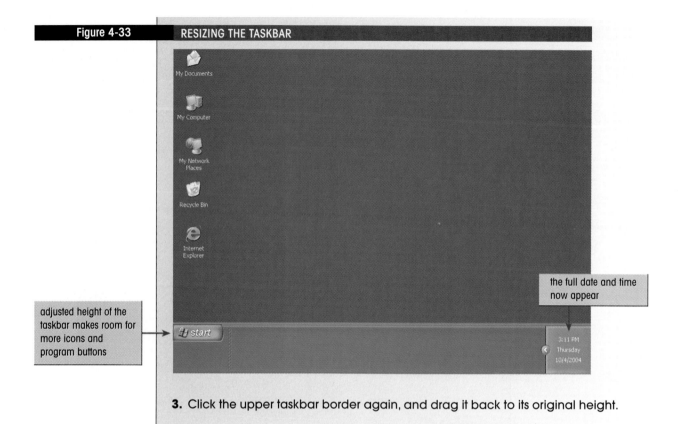

the full date and time now appear

adjusted height of the taskbar makes room for more icons and program buttons

3. Click the upper taskbar border again, and drag it back to its original height.

Resizing the taskbar is one way to change its appearance. You also can change other taskbar properties, such as those that determine when the taskbar appears.

Setting Taskbar Appearance Properties

In addition to resizing and relocating the taskbar, you can set taskbar appearance properties using the Taskbar and Start Menu Properties dialog box. Using this dialog box, you can increase the amount of screen space available for your program windows by hiding the taskbar. In this case, the taskbar is not closed, removed, or minimized, but is hidden either under the border of the desktop or under the program windows open on the desktop. It still remains active and accessible—you can use the mouse to point to the area of your screen where the taskbar is located to redisplay the taskbar.

By default, the taskbar appears on top of windows on the desktop, but you can change this setting in the Taskbar and Start Menu Properties dialog box so that program windows and dialog boxes cover the taskbar when necessary. Other taskbar appearance properties that you can set include whether to show the Quick Launch toolbar on the taskbar. The Quick Launch toolbar contains icons you can click to open programs quickly, show the desktop, or perform other tasks. You'll have a chance to add the Quick Launch toolbar to the taskbar later in this session.

Beth wants to see how to increase the amount of desktop space by hiding the taskbar or letting windows cover it. You'll show her how to change these taskbar appearance properties.

To set taskbar appearance properties:

1. Right-click a blank area in the taskbar, and click **Properties** on the shortcut menu.

   The Taskbar and Start Menu Properties dialog box opens, as shown in Figure 4-34.

Figure 4-34   **THE TASKBAR AND START MENU PROPERTIES DIALOG BOX**

locks or unlocks the taskbar in its current position

hides the task bar unless the mouse pointer is resting on it

places the taskbar on top of all other windows

shows or hides the clock and unused icon on the right side of the taskbar

if you have more than one document open in the same program, this option groups them on one taskbar button

shows the Quick Launch toolbar on the taskbar

2. Make note of the options currently selected in this dialog box, as you will need to restore these options when you are finished with this tutorial.

3. Click the **Auto-hide the taskbar** check box to select this option, and then click the **Apply** button. The taskbar disappears from the bottom of the desktop.

   TROUBLE? If the Auto-hide the taskbar check box is already selected, skip Step 3.

4. Move the mouse pointer over the location where the taskbar previously appeared, and note that the taskbar is visible as long as the mouse pointer is over its location.

5. Deselect the **Auto-hide the taskbar** check box, and then click the **Apply** button. Now the taskbar is visible again.

6. Click to deselect the **Keep the taskbar on top of other windows** check box, and then click the **Apply** button.

   TROUBLE? If the Keep the taskbar on top of other windows check box is already deselected, skip Step 6.

7. Drag the Taskbar and Start Menu Properties dialog box so that a portion of it appears over your taskbar. Note that the dialog box now appears over the taskbar.

8. Return the options in this dialog box to the state they were in Step 2, and then click the **OK** button to close the dialog box.

The Taskbar tab in the Taskbar and Start Menu Properties dialog box also includes options relating to toolbars, and you will learn about customizing those next.

Working **with Taskbar Toolbars**

One of the features of the taskbar is that you can use it to display toolbars. For example, you can display the Quick Launch toolbar, which contains icons for starting Internet Explorer and your e-mail software. When you are working with programs and documents that cover your desktop, you can access your e-mail, for example, without minimizing all the windows open on the desktop. Figure 4-35 describes the toolbars you can include on the taskbar.

Figure 4-35	TASKBAR TOOLBARS
TASKBAR TOOLBAR	**DESCRIPTION**
Quick Launch	Use to access icons you can click to quickly open programs, show the desktop, or perform other tasks.
Desktop	Use to access items on your desktop, such as the Recycle Bin and My Computer, from the taskbar. Open the Desktop toolbar by clicking the double chevron (»).
Links	Use to access links to product information on the Web and add Web links by dragging them to the toolbar. Open the Links toolbar by clicking the double chevron (»).
Address bar	Use to open any Web page you specify. Open the Address bar by double-clicking it.
New	Create a new taskbar toolbar to place a shortcut to a folder on the taskbar.

Displaying a Toolbar on the Taskbar

Two taskbar toolbars are especially helpful if you have shortcut and document icons on the desktop. The Quick Launch toolbar includes a desktop icon that you can click to show the desktop—then you can add or delete shortcut icons, for example, without minimizing or closing open windows. The Desktop toolbar has an icon for each object on the desktop, including system icons, such as My Computer and the Recycle Bin, shortcut icons, and document icons.

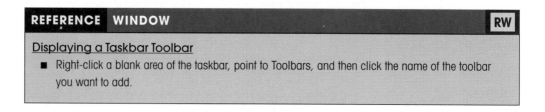

REFERENCE WINDOW   **RW**

Displaying a Taskbar Toolbar
- Right-click a blank area of the taskbar, point to Toolbars, and then click the name of the toolbar you want to add.

Beth often has several programs running at once, filling the screen and hiding the desktop. She has seen the benefit of placing icons on the desktop, but wants to be able to access those desktop icons without having to minimize all of her programs. You suggest that she place a Desktop toolbar on her taskbar. The Desktop toolbar includes double chevrons (>>) that you can click to display all of the icons that appear on the desktop. Beth also wants the toolbar itself to include an icon for the My Documents folder so she can quickly find the documents stored there. In addition, she occasionally wants to show the desktop itself so she can work with the shortcut and document icons. To do so, you'll show her how to add the Quick Launch toolbar to the taskbar.

To display the Quick Launch and Desktop toolbars:

1. Right-click a blank area of the taskbar.

2. On the shortcut menu, point to **Toolbars** and then click **Quick Launch**. A toolbar containing icons for your Web browser, e-mail software, and desktop appears on the left side of the taskbar. (Your Quick Launch toolbar might also contain other icons.) Now you can add the Desktop toolbar using the same shortcut menu.

TROUBLE? If the Quick Launch command is already checked, skip Step 2, and continue with Step 3.

3. Right-click a blank area of the taskbar.

4. On the shortcut menu, point to **Toolbars** and then click **Desktop**. See Figure 4-36.

| Figure 4-36 | DISPLAYING THE QUICK LAUNCH AND DESKTOP TOOLBARS |

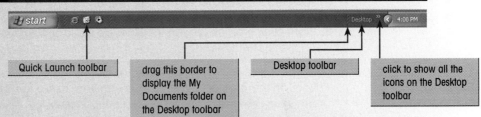

The Desktop toolbar first appears as a button with a "Desktop" label and double arrows you can click to see all the icons on the desktop. You can resize the toolbar to show more icons.

5. Point to the left border of the Desktop toolbar until the pointer changes to ◄──►. Then drag left until you see the My Documents folder.

6. To see all the icons on the desktop, click the **double chevrons (>>)** on the Desktop toolbar. See Figure 4-37.

| Figure 4-37 | MY DOCUMENTS ICON ON THE DESKTOP TOOLBAR |

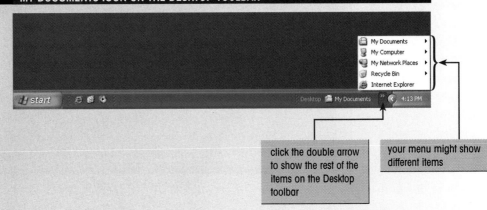

Beth likes having the icon for the My Documents folder on the Desktop toolbar, but wishes she could see more icons. She would like the toolbar to look more like the Quick Launch toolbar, with no names next to the icons and no title displayed for the toolbar. You explain that you can modify the toolbar's appearance by changing its properties.

Modifying the Appearance of a Taskbar Toolbar

You can modify the appearance of a taskbar toolbar by showing or hiding its title, and by showing or hiding the text labels for each icon. On the taskbar shortcut menu, these commands are checked by default. To hide the title and text labels, you remove the check mark from each command. You will modify the Desktop toolbar by hiding its title and text labels.

To modify the appearance of the Desktop toolbar:

1. Right-click a blank area in the Desktop toolbar.

2. On the shortcut menu, click **Show Text** to remove the check mark from this command.

    TROUBLE? If you don't see the Show Text entry on the shortcut menu, you may have right-clicked one of the buttons on the Desktop toolbar. Be sure to click a blank area on the toolbar. Also, be sure the Lock the Taskbar command is not selected on the Taskbar shortcut menu.

3. Right-click a blank area in the Desktop toolbar again, and deselect **Show Title** on the shortcut menu.

    Figure 4-38 displays the modified appearance of the toolbar. Note that each item on the desktop is matched by an item in the toolbar and that the icons are small, like those on the Quick Launch toolbar.

| Figure 4-38 | MODIFIED DESKTOP TASKBAR |

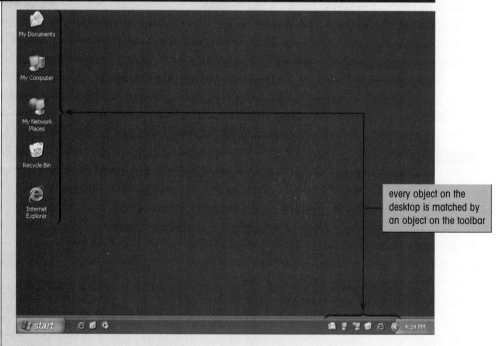

every object on the desktop is matched by an object on the toolbar

Now Beth can access all the items on her desktop without minimizing open windows.

Creating a Custom Toolbar

If the standard taskbar toolbars that Windows XP provides do not meet your needs, you can create your own taskbar toolbar. For example, if you often work with documents contained in folders in the My Documents folder, you could add each folder to a custom toolbar so you can access those documents quickly. To create a custom toolbar, you use the New Toolbar command on the taskbar shortcut menu.

REFERENCE WINDOW | **RW**

Creating a Custom Taskbar Toolbar

- To create a new toolbar, right-click a blank area of the taskbar, point to Toolbars, and then click New Toolbar.
- In the New Toolbar dialog box, click the folder or object you want to turn into a toolbar, and then click the OK button.

Beth is happy with the new appearance of the taskbar. However, she notices that when she clicks the My Computer icon on the Desktop toolbar it opens the My Computer window. Beth finds the My Computer window useful and wonders if you could create a taskbar toolbar displaying all of the icons in the My Computer window. This would give her even quicker access to all of the drives on her computer.

To create a toolbar for the My Computer window:

1. Right-click a blank area on the taskbar, point to **Toolbars**, and then click **New Toolbar** on the shortcut menu.

   The New Toolbar dialog box opens, showing the hierarchy of objects on your computer that is familiar to you from your work with My Computer and Windows Explorer. In the New Toolbar dialog box, you select a drive, folder, or object whose contents you want to display in a toolbar on the taskbar. You want to display the contents of the My Computer window, which appears near the top of the hierarchy.

2. Click **My Computer** in the New Toolbar dialog box, and then click the **OK** button.

   The My Computer toolbar appears on the taskbar. However, it makes the taskbar too crowded, so you will modify the appearance of the new toolbar by deselecting the Show Title and Show Text commands on the taskbar shortcut menu.

3. Right-click a blank area of the My Computer toolbar, and deselect **Show Text** on the shortcut menu.

4. Right-click a blank area of the My Computer toolbar again, and deselect **Show Title** on the shortcut menu.

   Figure 4-39 displays the new My Computer toolbar on your taskbar.

Figure 4-39 | TOOLBARS ON THE TASKBAR

Quick Launch toolbar

Desktop toolbar

My Computer toolbar
(your icons might be
different)

Having seen how to create and modify toolbars on the taskbar, you should now restore the taskbar to its original state, deleting the Quick Launch, Desktop, and My Computer toolbars. Note that this will not affect the desktop or the My Computer window. These toolbars contain shortcuts to those objects, not the objects themselves.

To remove a toolbar from the taskbar:

1. Right-click a blank area of the taskbar, and then point to **Toolbars** on the shortcut menu.

2. Click **Quick Launch** on the Toolbars submenu to deselect it.

   The menu closes and the Quick Launch toolbar is removed.

3. Use the same technique to remove the Desktop and My Computer toolbars from the taskbar.

Now the taskbar appears as it did when you started this tutorial.

Editing the Start Menu

The final component on your Windows XP desktop that you can customize is the Start menu. The Start menu lists the programs, tools, and windows you want to access quickly. For example, you can click an item on the Start menu to open the My Documents folder or the Help and Support Center window. You can also point to My Recent Documents to display a list of recently opened documents. To quickly access one of the documents in the My Recent Documents list, click a document name, and Windows XP locates and starts the program that created the document, and then opens the document. Most of the items on the Start menu are created for you by Windows XP or by the various programs you install. However, you also can determine the content and appearance of your Start menu, removing items you don't use and adding those you do. In addition, the left pane of the Windows XP Start menu automatically shows the programs you use most frequently. See Figure 4-40.

Figure 4-40	CUSTOMIZING THE START MENU

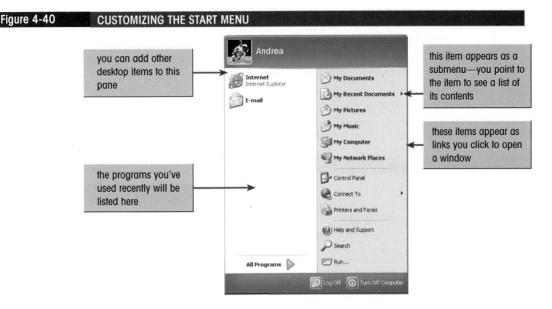

you can add other desktop items to this pane

this item appears as a submenu—you point to the item to see a list of its contents

these items appear as links you click to open a window

the programs you've used recently will be listed here

Controlling the Appearance of the Start Menu

One feature of the Start menu you can control is whether the menu displays small or large icons. The default is to use large icons, but you can save screen space by changing this to the smaller icon style.

Because the Start button is considered part of the taskbar, you change settings for the Start menu using the same dialog box you used earlier to control the appearance of the taskbar. This time, however, you can open the Taskbar and Start Menu Properties dialog box using the Control Panel.

To change the size of the icons on the Start menu:

1. Open the Control Panel, click **Appearance and Themes**, and then click **Taskbar and Start Menu**. Minimize the Appearance and Themes window.

   The commands for customizing the Start menu are available on the Start Menu tab of this dialog box.

2. In the Taskbar and Start Menu Properties dialog box, click the **Start Menu** tab.

3. Click the **Customize** button.

4. On the General tab of the Customize Start Menu dialog box, click the **Small icons** option button.

5. Click the **OK** button. The Taskbar and Start Menu Properties dialog box stays open. Next, you'll open the Start menu to view the small icons.

6. Click the **Start** button (**start**) on the taskbar. The Start menu shows small icons.

7. Click outside of the Start menu to close it.

Now that you have plenty of room on the Start menu, you can learn how to add items to it.

Adding an Item to the Start Menu

The Start menu lists shortcuts on the left and items you can change on the right. By default, the Internet Explorer and Outlook Express shortcuts appear at the upper-left of the Start menu. As you open other programs, Windows XP adds their shortcuts to the Start menu, listing them below the Internet Explorer and Outlook Express shortcuts. For example, after you opened Notepad in Session 4.1, Windows XP added a Notepad shortcut to the Start menu. The items on the right of the Start menu open dialog boxes or submenus. See Figure 4-41.

| Figure 4-41 | A TYPICAL START MENU |

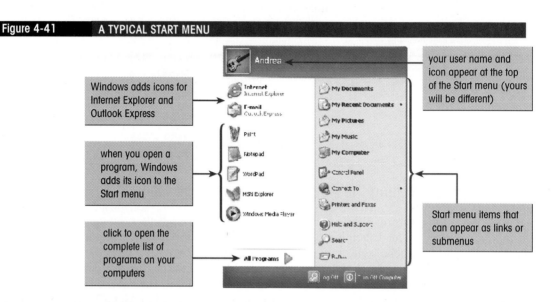

Most of the work you'll do to modify the Start menu will be to add, delete, and change the items on the right. For example, you can remove an item if you rarely use it, or change an item that displays a submenu to open a window instead. You can also add an item to access a feature not currently listed on the Start menu.

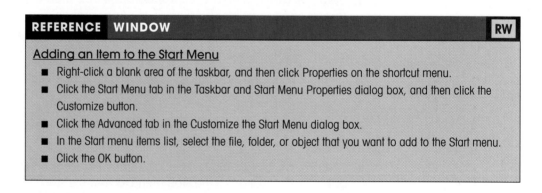

REFERENCE WINDOW   RW

Adding an Item to the Start Menu
- Right-click a blank area of the taskbar, and then click Properties on the shortcut menu.
- Click the Start Menu tab in the Taskbar and Start Menu Properties dialog box, and then click the Customize button.
- Click the Advanced tab in the Customize the Start Menu dialog box.
- In the Start menu items list, select the file, folder, or object that you want to add to the Start menu.
- Click the OK button.

Beth wants to see how she could use the Start menu to access the Favorites folder, which includes the same items that appear in the Favorites pane of Windows Explorer—folders, files, and Web pages to which you want quick access. You will add the Favorites item to the Start menu.

To add the Favorites item to the Start menu:

1. Make sure the Taskbar and Start Menu Properties dialog box is open to the Start menu tab.

   TROUBLE? If the Taskbar and Start Menu Properties dialog box is not open, right-click a blank area of the taskbar, click Properties, and then click the Start Menu tab.

2. Click the **Customize** button.

3. Click the **Advanced** tab in the Customize Start Menu dialog box.

4. Scroll the Start menu items, and then click the **Favorites menu** check box to select this option.

5. Click the **OK** button and then click the **Apply** button.

The Taskbar and Start Menu Properties dialog box remains open. Now view the modified Start menu to verify it contains a Favorites item.

To test the new Start menu item:

1. Drag the Taskbar and Start Menu Properties dialog box to the right, if necessary, so it will not be obstructed by the open Start menu.

2. Click the **Start** button 🐧 start on the taskbar. See Figure 4-42.

| Figure 4-42 | NEW ITEM ON THE START MENU |

small icons

new item on the Start menu

Note that the Start menu now includes a Favorites item.

Selecting Start Menu Settings

When you worked with the Advanced tab in the Customize Start Menu dialog box, you might have noticed that the Start menu items list includes settings for your Start menu. As you saw in the last section, you select check boxes to add items to the Start menu. Other settings let you display an item on the Start menu as a link or as a submenu. If you display an item as a link, you click it to open the appropriate dialog box or window. For example, the My Computer item appears on the Start menu as a link by default—you click My Computer to open its window. If you display an item as a submenu, you point to the item until a submenu appears, and then you click a command on the submenu. For example, you can also display the My Computer item as a submenu. When you point to My Computer, a submenu appears listing the contents of the My Computer window, including 3½ Floppy (A:) and your local hard disk. Figure 4-43 describes the settings you can select for your Start menu.

Figure 4-43	START MENU OPTIONS
START MENU	**DESCRIPTION**
Control Panel	Display this item as a link you click to open the Control Panel, as a submenu that lists individual tools or categories in the Control Panel, or don't display this item
Enable dragging and dropping	Drag and drop to change position or add to the Start menu
Favorites menu	Display this item to list your favorite Web sites, files, and folders
Help and Support	Display this item as a link to the Help and Support window
My Computer	Display this item as a link you click to open the My Computer folder, as a submenu that lists the contents of My Computer, or don't display this item
My Documents	Display this item as a link you click to open the My Documents folder, as a submenu that lists the contents of My Documents, or don't display this item
My Music	Display this item as a link you click to open the My Music folder window, as a submenu that lists the contents of My Music, or don't display this item
My Network Places	Display this item as a link you can click to open the My Network Places folder window, as a submenu that list the contents of My Network Places, or don't display this item
My Pictures	Display this item as a link you click to open the My Pictures folder window, as a submenu that lists the contents of My Pictures, or don't display this item
Network Connections	Display this item as a link you click to open the Network Connections folder window, as the "Connect to" submenu that lists the contents of Network Connections, or don't display this item
Printers and Faxes	Display individual printers and fax boards attached to your computer
Run command	Display the Run command as a link you click to open the Run dialog box
Scroll Programs	When you point to All Programs, display the programs as a list you can scroll
Search	Display the Search command as a link you click to open the Search window
System Administrative Tools	Display this item as a link you click to open the System Administrative Tools window, as a submenu that lists the contents of the window, or don't display this item

Beth wants to display the My Computer item as a submenu on the Start menu so she can easily access her floppy drive. The My Computer submenu will contain the 3½ Floppy (A:) shortcut icon that she can click to open her floppy drive quickly. You'll show her how to do this.

To change the My Computer command on the Start Menu to display a submenu:

1. In the Taskbar and Start Menu Properties dialog box, click the **Customize** button, and then click the **Advanced** tab on the Customize Start Menu dialog box.

2. Scroll the Start menu items list to locate My Computer, and then click the **Display as a menu** option button under the My Computer icon.

3. Click the **OK** button and then click the **Apply** button. Leave the Taskbar and Start Menu Properties dialog box open on the right side of your desktop.

Now verify that you can point to My Computer on the Start menu, and then click a command on the submenu to show the contents of the floppy drive.

To test the My Computer submenu on the Start menu:

1. Click the **Start** button ⊞ start and then point to **My Computer**. See Figure 4-44.

| Figure 4-44 | NEW SUBMENU ON THE START MENU |

My Computer displayed as a submenu

2. Click **3½ Floppy (A:)**. The contents of the floppy drive appear in the My Computer window.

3. Click the **Close** button ⊠ to close the window.

Beth feels the changes you made to the Start menu reflect the way she likes to work.

Removing an Item from the Start Menu

Now that you've seen how to add an item to the Start menu and change another, you should restore the Start menu to its default state by removing the Favorites icon and changing the My Computer item from a submenu back to a link. To remove an item, you use the same dialog box you opened to add and modify an item.

REFERENCE   WINDOW   **RW**

Removing a Start Menu Item

- Right-click a blank area of the taskbar, and then click Properties on the shortcut menu.
- Click the Start menu tab on the Taskbar and Start Menu Properties dialog box.
- Click the Customize button to open the Customize Start Menu dialog box.
- In the Start menu items list, deselect the item that you want to remove, and then click the OK button.

To restore the Start menu to its original state:

1. In the Taskbar and Start Menu Properties dialog box, click the **Customize** button on the Start menu tab.

2. On the General tab of the Customize Start Menu dialog box, click the **Large icons** option button.

3. Click the **Advanced** tab.

4. Click the **Favorites menu** check box to remove the check mark.

5. Under the My Computer icon, click the **Display as a link** option button.

6. Click the **OK** button to close the Customize Start Menu dialog box.

7. Click the **OK** button to apply your changes and close the Taskbar and Start Menu Properties dialog box.

8. To test your changes, click the **Start** button to confirm that My Computer appears as a link and the Favorites item has been removed from the Start menu, and then click outside the menu to close it.

Beth is impressed with how much she can personalize Windows XP to suit her needs and preferences. She customized the taskbar by adding taskbar toolbars and changing its appearance, and modified the Start menu to reflect her working style. Your ability to customize Windows XP in a lab setting is limited, and the settings are likely to be changed by the next user. But if you are running Windows XP on your own computer, you will find that designing a desktop that reflects your needs is time well spent.

If you are working in a lab setting, make sure you return all settings to their original state before leaving the lab.

Session 4.3 QUICK CHECK

1. How do you move the taskbar to the top of your computer screen?

2. To hide the taskbar, select _____ from the Taskbar and Start Menu Properties dialog box.

3. Why might you want to include the Desktop toolbar on the taskbar?

4. True or False: You can customize the Start menu by displaying the Control Panel item as having a submenu.

5. To modify the collection of objects and properties on your computer, you can open the _____.

REVIEW ASSIGNMENTS

1. *Creating Shortcuts* Practice placing a document on the desktop and printing it, using a printer shortcut icon.

   a. Create a shortcut on the desktop to the printer you use regularly.
   b. Open Notepad and create a new text document on your desktop, typing your name and the list of classes you currently are taking. Name this document **Classes**. Close Notepad.
   c. Drag the Classes document icon to the printer shortcut. Your document prints.
   d. Now use the techniques you learned in Tutorial 3 to print an image of your desktop. (Use the Print Screen key to save an image of the desktop, open WordPad, type your name and the date at the top of the document, paste the image into WordPad, and then print the image from WordPad.)
   e. When you are finished, delete both icons from your desktop.

2. *Create a Shortcut to a Folder* Beth recently assigned Sally Hanson, an undergraduate at one of the local colleges, to provide housekeeping for three clients. Sally plans to be out of the area over spring break, so Beth needs to write a memo to each client, asking if they need replacement help. Beth would like to be able to access the correspondence concerning Sally Hanson more easily.

   a. Start Windows Explorer and then create a new folder called Sally on your Data Disk.
   b. Start Notepad and then compose the three memos, typing your own text. Save the memos in the Sally folder on your Data Disk with the names **Smith**, **Arruga**, and **Kosta** (the names of the three clients). Close Notepad when you are finished.
   c. Drag the Sally folder from Windows Explorer to the desktop, using the left mouse button, to create a shortcut to the folder.
   d. Name the shortcut icon Sally.
   e. Test the shortcut icon by opening the Sally folder, and then open one of the memos. Use two different methods to open these two objects, and write down which methods you used.
   f. Arrange your desktop so you can see the open memo in Notepad, the open folder window, and the shortcut icon. You might need to resize the windows to make them smaller. Then print an image of the desktop. (See Step 1d.)
   g. Remove the desktop shortcut to the folder when you are done.

3. *Create a Bitmap on the Desktop* In this tutorial, you created a new text document directly on the desktop. In this review assignment, you'll create a new bitmap image document on your Data Disk. You'll use the mouse to write your signature. Then you'll use this bitmap image as your desktop background.

   a. Use My Computer to open drive A and display the contents of your Data Disk.
   b. Right-click an empty area of the drive A window, point to New, and then click Bitmap Image.
   c. Name the new file **My Signature**.
   d. Start Paint, and then open **My Signature**.
   e. Drag the mouse over the empty canvas to write your signature. (This will be awkward, even for experienced mouse users.)
   f. Exit the program and save your changes. Close the drive A window.
   g. Click Start, click Control Panel, click Appearance and Themes, and then click Change the desktop background to open the Desktop property sheet of the Display Properties dialog box.
   h. Click the Browse button and then use the Look in list arrow at the top of the dialog box to select the 3½ Floppy drive. Select the **My Signature** bitmap image on your Data Disk, and then click the Open button. Your signature appears as the wallpaper in the preview monitor.
   i. Print an image of the screen. (See Step 1d.)
   j. Click the Cancel button to preserve the desktop's original appearance.

4. *Explore Your Computer's Desktop Properties* Answer each of the following questions about the desktop properties on your lab computers.

   a. Open the Display Properties dialog box. What resolution is your monitor using? What other resolution settings are available for your monitor? Drag the slider to find out. If it's an older monitor, it might not have higher resolutions available.
   b. What color quality are you using?
   c. Is Windows XP using a screen saver on your machine? Which one? After how many minutes of idle time does it engage?
   d. What is your desktop's default color scheme?
   e. Does your computer use a desktop theme? If so, which one?
   f. Does your desktop display a special background? Which one?

   Explore g. On the Screen Saver tab, click the Power button to open the Power Options Properties dialog box. What power scheme is your computer using, if any? What settings are in effect for that power scheme?

   Explore h. In the Power Options Properties dialog box, click the Advanced tab. Turn on the option to show the power icon on the taskbar. A power icon, like a plug, appears on the taskbar. Point at the power icon. What ScreenTip appears? Go back to the Power Options Properties dialog box, turn this option off, and then close the Power Options Properties dialog box.
   i. Close the Display Properties dialog box and the Appearance and Themes window, if necessary.

5. *Customizing Your Desktop* The ability to place icons directly on the desktop gives you the opportunity to create a truly docucentric desktop. Figure 4-45 shows Beth's desktop after she's had a chance to create all the shortcuts you recommended and to add additional shortcuts for programs, folders, files, and other resources she uses regularly.

Figure 4-45

Notice that this desktop has shortcuts not just for drives and documents, but also for programs, tools, and other Windows XP objects. Also notice that some icons are document icons, not shortcuts. All the icons are arranged logically so they are easy to find. If you have your own computer, create a desktop that meets your needs.

Use the following strategy:

Explore

   a. Right-click the desktop, point to Arrange Icons By, and make sure Auto Arrange is not checked. If it is, click Auto Arrange to remove the check mark from this command.

   b. Use My Computer to locate the drives on your computer, and then create a shortcut on the desktop to each of the local or network drives you use regularly.

   c. If you haven't done so already, use My Computer to create folders for the work you usually do on your computer. You might want a folder for each class you're taking, letters you write, projects, or hobbies. Then create a shortcut on the desktop to each folder you use regularly. Use any method you learned in this tutorial to create the shortcuts.

   d. Create shortcuts for each document you use repeatedly. Avoid overcrowding your desktop.

   e. If you know how to locate program files, create shortcuts on the desktop to the programs you use most often.

   f. Group the icons on your desktop so that similar objects are in the same location.

   g. Print a copy of your desktop in its final form. (See Step 1d.)

6. *Customizing Your Start Menu* A simple way of adding items to your Start menu is to drag icons from the desktop or My Computer window to the Start menu. For example, you can click a file icon and drag it onto the Start menu, and Windows XP will automatically add that item to the Start menu. Similarly, you can remove any item from the Start menu by clicking the item and dragging it off the Start menu. For example, if you drag a Start menu item onto the desktop, it appears as a shortcut on the desktop. Dragging the same item off the Start menu and onto the Recycle Bin deletes the item.

Figure 4-46 shows a Start menu with a Recycle Bin item. While most Start menu items can be created using either the drag-and-drop technique or the Add method in the Taskbar and Start Menu Properties dialog box, you can only add a Recycle Bin item by dragging. Try this technique by performing Steps a through d below.

Figure 4-46

Explore

a. Drag the Recycle Bin icon to the Start button (you will have to point to the Start button for a few seconds to allow it to open), and drop the icon at the top of the left pane. An insert bar (a thick, dark horizontal line) appears to guide you.

b. Print a copy of the Start menu you created, showing the two new entries. (See Step 1d.)

c. When you click the Recycle Bin item on the Start menu, what do you see? What are the advantages and disadvantages of using the Start menu and Recycle Bin this way?

Explore

d. Remove the Recycle Bin item from the Start menu by right-clicking it and then clicking Remove From This List.

7. *Customizing a Taskbar Toolbar* You can also use the drag-and-drop technique to customize a taskbar toolbar. By dragging an icon from a folder or the desktop onto one of the toolbars on the taskbar, you can create additional buttons for quick one-click access to your favorite files and programs.

Figure 4-47 shows a modified Quick Launch toolbar with icons for Notepad, WordPad, and Windows Explorer added.

Figure 4-47

buttons for Notepad,
Windows Explorer, and
WordPad

the Quick Launch
toolbar

Make similar changes to your Quick Launch toolbar by performing Steps a through h below.

a. Add the Quick Launch toolbar to the taskbar. Make sure the taskbar is not locked, and then widen the Quick Launch toolbar so you can see most of its icons.

Explore

b. Open the Start menu so you can see the Accessories submenu, hold down the Ctrl key, and drag icons for Notepad, WordPad, and Windows Explorer from the Accessories submenu on your Start menu to the Quick Launch toolbar on your taskbar. Be sure to hold down the Ctrl key while dragging and dropping these icons, or you'll move the icons off the Start menu.

c. Modify the properties of the Quick Launch toolbar so that it shows the toolbar's title. Widen the Quick Launch toolbar again.

d. Print a copy of your screen showing the revised Quick Launch toolbar. (See Step 1d.)

e. Test each new button on the toolbar to verify that it opens the appropriate program.

f. Summarize what you've done and discuss the advantages of using the Quick Launch toolbar to launch your favorite programs. Which is easier, the Quick Launch toolbar or the Start menu, and why? What is the most effective use of the Quick Launch toolbar? Would you place all of your programs on the toolbar? Why or why not?

g. Delete the Notepad, WordPad, and Windows Explorer buttons from the Quick Launch toolbar by dragging them to your Recycle Bin.

h. Remove the title from the Quick Launch toolbar.

PROJECTS

1. Knowing that you have two years left in your college degree program, your parents decide to splurge and give you a computer, complete with Windows XP, for your birthday. Your parents spent hours getting everything loaded and configured for you, so when you pick it up this weekend you can get right to work on a major project due on Monday. You have about half an hour before your roommate returns with your car, so

take out an 8½ by 11-inch piece of paper, and draw the desktop that will give you the quickest access to all documents, devices, and/or programs needed to carry out the tasks listed below. Indicate shortcut icons with an arrow. Also draw a window showing your 3½-inch disk contents, using the information provided in the "To Do List."

To Do List

a. Finish typing paper for American History project, using WordPad.

_____currently saved on disk

_____will need to print

b. Finish lab report for Organic Chemistry, using WordPad.

_____currently saved on disk

_____will need to print

c. Insert bitmap image saved on disk into Organic Chemistry lab report.

d. Review outline for Office Procedures class test, created in WordPad.

_____currently saved on disk

_____will need to print

2. You provide computer support at Highland Yearbooks, a company that publishes high school and college yearbooks. Highland has just upgraded to Windows XP, and you'd like to get right to work customizing the desktops of Highland employees for optimal performance. You start with the computer belonging to John McPhee, one of the sales representatives. Create a desktop for John that takes the following circumstances into account. When you are done, print an image of the desktop. (See Step 1d in the Review Assignments.) Then make sure you remove any shortcuts you created, and restore the desktop to its original settings. On the back of your printout, write which options you changed to meet John's needs.

a. John keeps a Notepad file with a time-date stamp of long-distance phone calls stored on the desktop with a shortcut to that file on his Start menu.

b. John wants to be able to print the phone log file quickly, without having to open it first.

c. The company colors at Highland Yearbooks are blue and gold. John would like a blue desktop with gold title bars.

Explore

3. In this tutorial you learned how to use the Control Panel to customize display properties, such as the desktop background and theme. You can also use the Control Panel to customize other parts of your computer, such as the mouse and system sounds. Open the Control Panel, explore its contents to explain how to use the Control Panel to complete the following tasks, and then answer the questions below. (*Hint*: Use the Windows XP online Help, if necessary.)

a. What is a sound scheme? How can you change the sound scheme?

b. How can you find basic system information such as the version of your operating system and the speed of your computer?

c. How do you change the date and time? How can you have Windows XP automatically adjust the time during Daylight Savings Time?

d. What does "contrast" on your screen mean? How can you adjust the contrast to improve readability?

4. Your cousin, Joey, has Windows XP on his new computer but has not taken much time to learn about all of the customizable and timesaving features it offers him. In WordPad, type a letter to Joey, explaining three main features covered in this tutorial. Because you know that he is more likely to try to use these features if he has directions in front of him, include basic instructions on how to access them.

5. You just printed your letter to Joey in Project 4 and then remembered the concept of docucentric desktops you learned in this tutorial. You think that if Joey can conceptualize this, it will really expand his Windows XP horizons. You decide to add a note explaining the difference between the docucentric and program-centric desktop. Write a paragraph about this difference.

Explore

6. You are trying to save money on your electric bill and are wondering if you can take advantage of the Windows XP power management features. Open the Power Options Properties dialog box in the Control Panel, and print the screen you see, using the techniques you learned earlier in this book. On the printout, write a paragraph describing the power management features available specifically to your computer and how they can help save money.

Explore

7. You want to personalize your computer so that it reflects your interests or hobbies. One way to do this is to apply a desktop theme. Use the Display Properties dialog box to explore the themes you can use, and then select and apply one that seems best for you. Save the theme on your Data Disk as **Personal Theme**. Then open a dialog box, and print an image of the desktop. (See Step 1d in the Review Assignments.)

8. You have been asked to give a presentation at a *Computer Users with Special Needs* seminar on campus. You have a half hour to present participants with information on Windows XP Accessibility Options in the Control Panel. Using the online Help as a guide, write a handout describing the ways one can configure Windows XP for computer users with special needs. Include in your handout instructions for turning these features on and off.

Explore

9. You are having problems with your monitor—the display flickers and images are occasionally garbled. In addition, when you move the mouse or resize windows, the screen does not redraw to reflect your changes. Use a troubleshooter in the Control Panel to find the solution to your problems. When you find a solution, print the page in the troubleshooter that addresses your problems.

QUICK | CHECK ANSWERS

Session 4.1

1. False

2. False

3. You delete not only the icon but also the document.

4. You delete only the icon but not the document.

5. 1) Use the left mouse button to drag the floppy drive icon from the My Computer or Windows Explorer window to the desktop; 2) use the right mouse button to drag the floppy drive icon from the My Computer or Windows Explorer window to the desktop, and then click Create Shortcuts here; 3) click the floppy drive icon in the My Computer or Windows Explorer window, click File on the menu bar, click Create Shortcut, and then click Yes.

Session 4.2

1. True

2. You can use the Control Panel to change the way Windows looks and behaves.

3. Here are five: Themes, Background, Screen Saver, Appearance, Settings. You could also mention the properties on each of these sheets, such as color palette, resolution, and so on.

4. To display a moving image after a specified period so that you can keep your work private

5. There are 800 pixels across and 600 down.

6. 800 by 600, because it displays the largest objects

7. It requires extra video memory and runs more slowly.

QUICK CHECK ANSWERS

Session 4.3

1. Right-click the taskbar, click Lock the Taskbar to remove the check mark, if necessary, click a blank area on the taskbar, and then drag it to the top of the desktop.
2. Auto-hide the taskbar
3. For quick access to desktop icons without minimizing windows
4. True
5. Control Panel

OBJECTIVES

In this tutorial you will:

- Explore the structure of the Internet and the World Wide Web

- Open, view, navigate, and print Web pages in Internet Explorer

- Download a file from the World Wide Web

- Enable Active Desktop in order to add, move, resize, close, and remove Active Desktop items

- Schedule the automatic retrieval of data from the Web

- Use an HTML file as a desktop background

- Send and receive e-mail using Outlook Express

LABS

The Internet: World Wide Web

Web Pages & HTML

BRINGING THE WORLD WIDE WEB TO THE DESKTOP

Using Active Desktop at Highland Travel

CASE

Highland Travel

Highland Travel, a company that offers guided tour packages to Scotland, recently hired you as an advertising manager. During your first day at work, you meet with the company's technical support person, Scott Campbell. After describing the training you'll receive, Scott explains that Highland Travel uses the Internet and the World Wide Web to promote the company, to provide services to clients, and to improve communication among employees. The company recently upgraded its computers to Windows XP, and management wants all employees to be able to use its features to the fullest.

You tell Scott you've heard that one popular feature of Windows XP is its integration of the operating system with the Web. Scott reminds you that the Web is a set of linked documents residing on computers all around the world. He tells you that during your first week on the job, you'll go through a training program to familiarize yourself with Windows XP and particularly with its Web features. He explains that Windows XP brings the richness of the Web to your desktop with Active Desktop. **Active Desktop** is technology that transforms the Windows desktop into your own personal "communications central"—not only for launching programs and accessing files, but also for obtaining and displaying information you can find on the Web. The Windows XP desktop is called "active" because it allows you to access the Internet, particularly Web sites that provide frequently changing information, such as sports scores, stock prices, and weather maps.

Scott assures you that the training program will familiarize you with these and more features—-and will introduce you to Highland Travel's Web site.

SESSION 5.1

In this session, you will learn how to use Windows XP to bring the Internet and the World Wide Web to your desktop. You will learn to use Internet Explorer to view Web sites. You will activate a link, navigate a Web page with frames, print a Web page, and download a file. Finally you'll learn how to access your favorite Web pages quickly using the History pane and the Favorites folder. For this session you will need a blank 3½-inch disk.

The **Internet**

When two or more computers are connected together for the purpose of exchanging information and resources, they create a structure known as a **network**. Networks facilitate the sharing of data and resources among multiple users. Networks can also be connected to each other to allow computers on different networks to share information; when two or more networks are connected, they create an **internetwork**, or **internet**. "The Internet" (uppercase "I") has come to refer to the "network of networks" that is made up of millions of computers linked to networks all over the world. Computers and networks on the Internet are connected by fiber-optic cables, satellites, phone lines, and other communications systems, as shown in Figure 5-1. Data travels across these communication systems using whatever route is most efficient.

Figure 5-1	STRUCTURE OF THE INTERNET

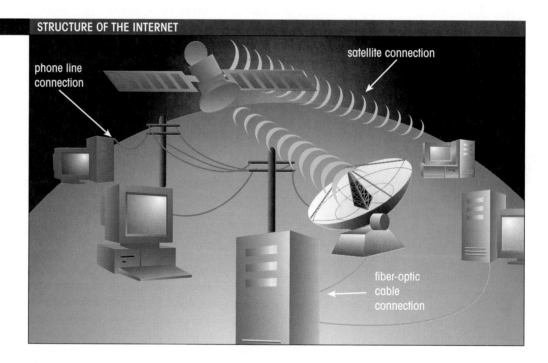

The Internet, by design, is a decentralized structure. There is no Internet "company." Instead, the Internet is a collection of different organizations, such as universities and businesses, each organizing its own information. There are no rules about where information is stored, and no one regulates the quality of information available on the Internet. Even though the lack of central control can make it hard for beginners to find their way through the resources on the Internet, decentralization has some advantages. The Internet is open to innovation and rapid growth, because different organizations and individuals have the freedom to test new products and services and make them quickly available to a global audience. One such service is the World Wide Web.

The **World Wide Web** makes it easy to share and access data stored on computers around the world with minimal training and support, and for this reason, Microsoft designed Windows XP to offer easy Web access. The Web is a system of **hypertext documents**— electronic files that contain elements known as **hyperlinks** or just **links**, which target other parts of a document or other documents altogether. A link can be a word or a phrase or a graphic image. Figure 5-2 shows a Colorado touring company hypertext document with several links. Each link targets a separate document that offers more information about the company. You can also connect to other file types, including scanned photographs, graphic images, film clips, sounds, online discussion groups, and computer programs.

| Figure 5-2 | WEB PAGE WITH LINKS TO WEB PAGES CONTAINING ADDITIONAL INFORMATION |

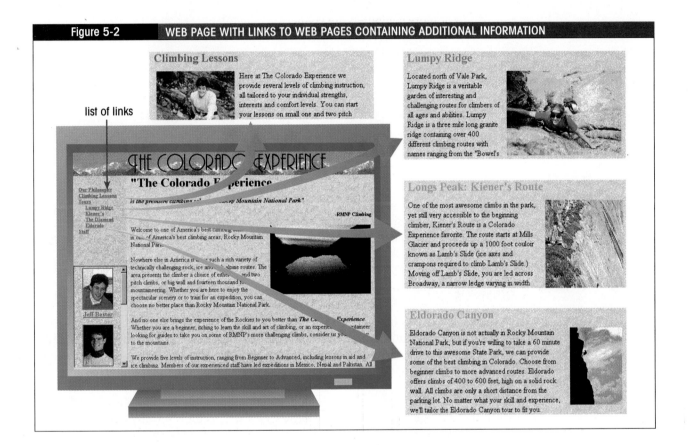

Each hypertext document on the Web is called a **Web page** and is stored on a computer on the Internet called a **Web server**. A Web page can contain links to other Web pages located anywhere on the Internet—on the same computer as the original Web page or on an entirely different computer halfway across the world. The ability to cross-reference other Web pages with links is one of the most important features of the Web.

Navigating Web pages using hypertext is an efficient way to access information. When you read a book, you follow a linear progression, reading one page after another. With hypertext, you progress through the pages in whatever order you want. Hypertext allows you to skip from one topic to another, following the information path that interests you, as shown in Figure 5-3.

Figure 5-3 FOLLOWING HYPERTEXT LINKS

3. Finally, from Canada you jump to the Natural History Museum in the U.K.

2. A quick jump from Hawaii and you are at the Royal Tyrrell Museum of Paleontology in Alberta, Canada, where additional Web pages on dinosaurs are stored.

1. Honolulu Community College maintains a Dinosaur exhibit. From this page you can jump to a page in Alberta, Canada.

Microsoft has taken advantage of this fact by designing its Windows XP operating system to incorporate your experience on the Internet. The techniques you'll learn in this tutorial to navigate Web pages are identical to those you learned in previous tutorials to navigate the objects on your computer. Microsoft's goal with Windows XP is to make the user's experience with local files, network files, and files on computers around the world as uniform as possible.

Browsers

To access documents on the Web, you need a **browser**—a program that locates, retrieves, displays, and organizes documents stored on Web servers. Your browser allows you to visit Web sites around the world; view multimedia documents; transfer files, images, and sounds to your computer; conduct searches for specific topics; and run programs on other computers. In Figure 5-3, the dinosaur Web documents that you see appear in a browser window. Windows XP includes a set of communications software tools called **Internet Explorer**, which includes the Internet Explorer browser, as well as tools for other Internet functions such as electronic mail, or **e-mail**, electronic messages sent between users over the Internet. Another popular communications software package is **Netscape Communicator**, which includes the Netscape Navigator browser. This tutorial assumes that you'll do your browsing with Internet Explorer. If you're using Netscape Communicator or another browser, talk to your instructor to resolve any difficulties in completing the steps in this tutorial.

Microsoft integrated the Internet Explorer browser into the Windows XP operating system to make its functions available to many Windows XP components. For example, the Windows Explorer utility that you used in Tutorial 3 to navigate files on your Data Disk uses Internet Explorer features so that it can function as a browser. The My Computer window works similarly. For example, when you are connected to the Internet, you can open the My Music folder in My Computer, and then click a link to shop for music online. The Internet Explorer window will open, showing a Web page where you can buy music CDs online. Using Windows Explorer, you can open the Favorites pane, for example, and click a link to MSN to open the MSN Web page, which contains links to news and general interest articles and to other Web pages.

In fact, Internet Explorer, Windows Explorer, and My Computer share many similarities. They have a common look and feel, with similar menu commands, toolbars, panes, and Address bar. For example, you can open the Favorites pane in Windows Explorer, My Computer, or Internet Explorer to access the same list of files, folders, and Web pages, no matter which window you have open. As you work through this tutorial, you'll learn more ways these three tools are integrated, making it easy to find information anywhere, whether on your computer, a network, or the Internet.

There are many advantages to using the same tools to access information regardless of its location. Computer users in the past had to use one tool to access local files, another to access network files, and many additional products such as e-mail, files, and other computers to access information on the Internet. The Windows XP operating system allows you to view information anywhere with a single set of techniques.

When you attempt to view a Web page, your browser locates and retrieves the document from the Web server and displays its contents on your computer. As shown in Figure 5-4, the server stores the Web page in one location, and browsers anywhere in the world can view it.

| Figure 5-4 | USING A BROWSER TO VIEW A WEB DOCUMENT ON A SERVER |

satellite connects the two computers

server in Florida stores the Web document, which browsers all over the world can access

Internet Explorer browser

Juggling Information Service

browser in California locates and displays document stored on server in Florida

For your browser to connect to the World Wide Web, you must have an Internet connection. In a university setting, your connection might come from your campus network. If you are working on a home computer and gaining Internet access from your modem over a phone line, your connection is called a **dial-up connection** and is maintained via an account with an **Internet service provider (ISP)**, a company that sells Internet access. See Appendix A, "Connecting Computers over a Phone Line," for more information. With a dial-up connection, you are connected to the Internet only as long as your modem "stays on the line," whereas on most institutional networks, you are always connected to the Internet because the network is actually a part of the Internet. If you are using a dial-up connection to connect to your institution's network, you have probably received instructions that help you establish this connection. Use these instructions any time you need to be connected to the Internet during this tutorial. If you are working from home, connect to the Internet using the instructions provided by your ISP.

Starting **Internet Explorer**

The Internet: World Wide Web

Scott suggests that you use Internet Explorer, the browser that comes with Windows XP, to start exploring the Web by connecting to the Highland Travel page. When you connect to the Internet without specifying a particular Web page, Windows XP automatically loads your **home page**—the Web page designated by the operating system as your starting point. Windows XP designates the Microsoft Network (MSN) pages as the default home page, but you can easily designate a different home page. If you are at an institution such as a university, a home page has probably already been designated for you. Note that "home page" can also refer to a personal Web page or to the Web page that an organization or business has created to give information about itself.

You'll notice a lot of similarities between Internet Explorer (designed to locate information on the Internet) and Windows Explorer (designed to locate information on your computer or network).

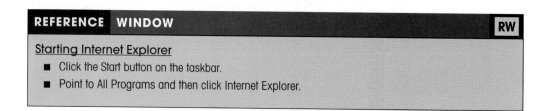

REFERENCE WINDOW	RW

Starting Internet Explorer
- Click the Start button on the taskbar.
- Point to All Programs and then click Internet Explorer.

To start Internet Explorer:

1. Click the **Start** button ![start], point to **All Programs**, and then click **Internet Explorer**. Note that the Internet Explorer icon might also appear in the upper-right section of the Start menu—you can also click that icon to start Internet Explorer.

   If you are in a university setting, you are probably already connected to the Internet, and your home page will appear immediately.

   TROUBLE? If you are working from a computer with a dial-up connection already set up and are not currently connected to the Internet, Windows XP will attempt to connect you. Wait and follow the prompts that appear. If you can't establish a connection, check with your technical support person in the lab, or if you are using your own computer, use Network Connections as instructed by your ISP, or call your ISP's technical support line for assistance. If an error message appears, it's possible that the server on which your home page is stored is temporarily busy or unavailable.

2. If necessary, click the **Maximize** button ![maximize] to maximize the Internet Explorer window. Figure 5-5 shows the MSN home page in the Internet Explorer window.

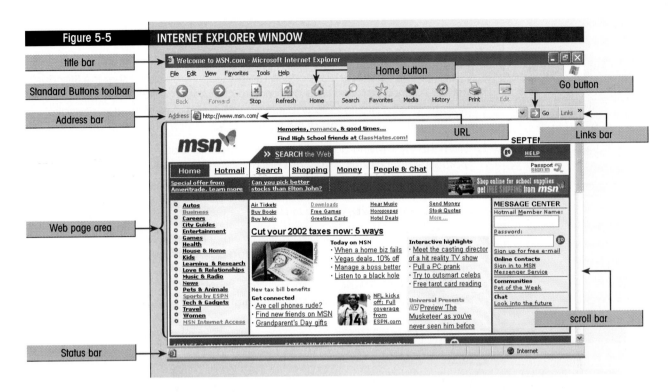

Figure 5-6 describes the elements of the Internet Explorer window.

Figure 5-6	ELEMENTS OF THE INTERNET EXPLORER WINDOW
FOLDER	**DESCRIPTION**
Title bar	Shows the name of the open Web page and includes the resizing buttons
Standard Buttons toolbar	Contains buttons you can click to perform common tasks, such as moving to the next or previous page and printing a Web page
Address bar	Shows the address of the current Web page; you can also type an address here
Web page area	Shows the current Web page
Status bar	Shows information about the browser's actions; for example, indicates that a page is loading or is done loading
Scroll bars	If a Web page is wider or longer than the browser window, use the scroll bars to move up and down or right and left
Home button	Click to open the Web page specified as the home page for your browser
Go button	After you type an address in the Address bar, you can click the Go button or press the Enter key to have the browser find the page at that address
Links bar	Contains links to Web pages you visit often
URL	Uniform Resource Locator; the address of the Web page you want to visit

The instructions in this tutorial will be easier to follow if your window matches those in the figures. The following steps help you set up the Internet Explorer window so it matches the one in the figures.

To set up the Internet Explorer window to match the figures in this tutorial:

1. Click **View** on the menu bar, point to **Toolbars**, and then make sure the **Standard Buttons**, **Address Bar**, and **Links** options are checked. The status bar in the Internet Explorer window provides valuable information about your actions, so make sure the status bar appears at the bottom of your Internet Explorer window.

2. Open the **View** menu again. Make sure **Status Bar** is checked and Lock the Toolbars is unchecked. If they are not checked, click the **Status Bar** command to check it and click the **Lock the Toolbars** command to uncheck it. Next, you can show text labels for each button on the Standard Buttons toolbar so that the toolbar is easier to use.

3. Open the **View** menu again, if necessary. Point to **Toolbars** and then click **Customize**. In the Customize Toolbar dialog box, click the **Text options** list arrow, and then click **Show text labels**, if necessary. Click the **Close** button to close the dialog box. Your Internet Explorer window should appear similar in form to that shown in Figure 5-7. (Your home page might be different.)

| Figure 5-7 | HOME PAGE DISPLAYED IN INTERNET EXPLORER |

Address bar indicates Web page address

Web page set up as home page

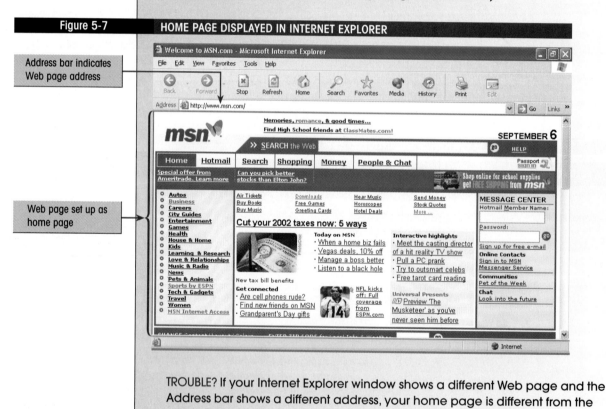

TROUBLE? If your Internet Explorer window shows a different Web page and the Address bar shows a different address, your home page is different from the one in Figure 5-7.

Now you can use Internet Explorer to open and view a Web page.

Opening a Page on the Web

Each page on the Web is uniquely identified by an address called a **URL**, or **Uniform Resource Locator**. A company may advertise its Web page by publishing the page's URL, such as "http://www.microsoft.com" in brochures, advertising pieces, and employees' business cards. A URL consists of three things: a protocol type, a server address, and a file pathname. Let's examine each of these items more closely.

A **protocol** is a standardized procedure used by computers to exchange information. Web documents travel between sites using **HyperText Transfer Protocol**, or **HTTP**. A Web page whose URL begins with the letters "http://" tells the Web browser to use the HTTP protocol when retrieving the page.

The **server address** gives the name of the Web server that is storing the Web page. You can usually learn a great deal about the Web server by examining the server address. For example, in the server address "www.northern.edu" the "www" indicates that the server is on the World Wide Web, "northern" indicates the name of the organization that owns the server (Northern University), and "edu" indicates that it's an educational site. Other common site types include "com" for commercial sites, "gov" for government agencies, and "org" for nonprofit organizations.

Finally, each file stored on a network server must have a unique pathname, just as files on a disk do. The **pathname** includes the folder or folders the file is stored in, plus the filename and its extension. The filename extension for Web pages is usually html, or just htm.

Try deciphering the following URL:

http://www.northern.edu/education/programs.html

The protocol is HTTP, the server address is www.northern.edu, the pathname is education/programs.html, and programs.html is the filename. So the Web browser knows it must retrieve the programs.html file from the /education folder located on the Web server at www.northern.edu, using the HTTP protocol.

Scott has given you the URL for the Highland Travel Web page, which is:

http://www.course.com/downloads/newperspectives/windowsxp/highland

You will access this Web page next using the URL that Scott has provided.

REFERENCE WINDOW   **RW**

Opening a Page Using a URL
- Select the contents of the Address box.
- Type the URL in the Address box, and then press the Enter key.

To open a page on the Web with a URL:

1. Click the **Address** box on the Address bar. The contents of the Address box, which should be the URL for your home page, are selected. Anything you type will replace the selected URL.

   TROUBLE? If the contents of the Address box are not selected, select the address manually by dragging the mouse from the far left to the far right of the URL. Be sure to select the entire URL.

2. Type **http://www.course.com/downloads/newperspectives/windowsxp/highland** in the Address box. Make sure you type the URL exactly as shown.

3. Press the **Enter** key. Highland Travel's Welcome page opens in the Internet Explorer window. See Figure 5-8.

| Figure 5-8 | CONNECTING TO HIGHLAND TRAVEL SITE |

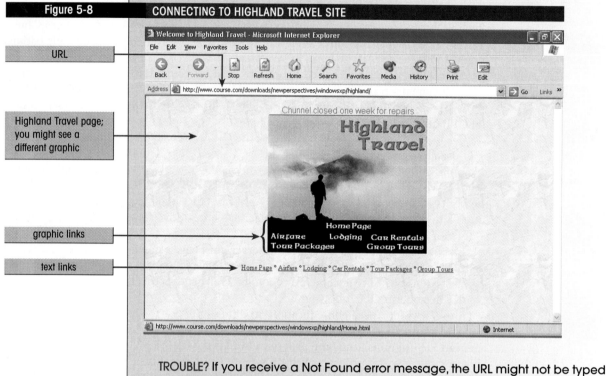

URL

Highland Travel page; you might see a different graphic

graphic links

text links

TROUBLE? If you receive a Not Found error message, the URL might not be typed correctly. Repeat Steps 1 through 3, making sure that the URL in the Address box matches the URL in Step 2. If you still receive an error message, ask your instructor or technical support person for help. If you see a different Web page from the one shown in Figure 5-8, click View on the menu bar and then click Refresh.

You can access information about the Highland Travel company by navigating through its Web pages. Spend some time doing that now.

Navigating the Web by Activating Links

Web Pages & HTML

A hypertext link on the Web, like a link in a chain, is a connector between two points. Links can appear in two ways: as text that you click or as a graphic that you click. A **text link** is a word or phrase that is usually underlined and often boldfaced or colored differently from the words around it. A **graphic link** is a graphic image that you click to jump to—or connect to—another location (note that graphic images can be or include text). When you aren't sure whether a graphic image is a link, point to it with the mouse pointer. When you move the mouse pointer over a link—text or graphic—the pointer changes shape from ⤹ to 🖑. The 🖑 pointer indicates that when you click, you will activate that link and jump to the new location. The destination of the link appears in the status bar, and, for some graphic links, a small ScreenTip appears next to your pointer.

The Highland Travel page contains both text and graphic links. The text links are at the bottom of the page, underlined, and in color. The graphic links are the words in a fancy font at the bottom of the Highland Travel photo, although graphic links are often images or photos. The links give your browser the information it needs to locate the page. When you activate a link, you jump to a new location. The target of the link can be another location on the current page (for example, you can jump from the bottom of the page to the top), a different page on the current Web server, or a different page located on an entirely different Web server. When you activate a link, there are three possible outcomes:

- You successfully reach the target of the link. The browser contacts the site you want, connects to the site, transfers the data from the site to your computer, and displays the data in your browser window.

- The link's target is busy, perhaps because the server storing the link's target is overwhelmed with too many requests. You can click the Stop button ▣ to prevent your browser from further attempting to make the connection. You'll have to try this link later or try a different link.

- The link points to a target that doesn't exist. Documents are often removed from Web servers as they become obsolete, or moved to new locations, and links that point to those documents are not always updated. If you click an obsolete link, a message box appears. If an error message box appears, click the OK button and try a different link. Otherwise click the Back button ◉ to return to the page you were previously viewing.

The amount of time it takes to complete a link, called the **response time**, can vary, depending upon the number of people trying to connect to the same site, the number of people on the Internet at that time, the site design, and the speed of your Internet connection. In fact, one of the differences you might notice between clicking links on your desktop (which target local objects, such as My Computer or a desktop document) and clicking those that target Web pages on the Internet is the difference in response time. Linking to local objects is usually instantaneous, whereas linking to pages on the Web can take many seconds, because of the time required for the data to be transferred over your Internet connection.

As you can see in Figure 5-9, activating a link starts a multistep process. When you point to a link, the status bar displays a message that the browser is connecting to the address of the link's target, its URL. When you click the link, the activity indicator animates. The status bar displays a series of messages indicating that your browser is connecting to the site, is waiting for a reply, is transferring data, and finally, is done.

| Figure 5-9 | ACTIVATING A LINK |

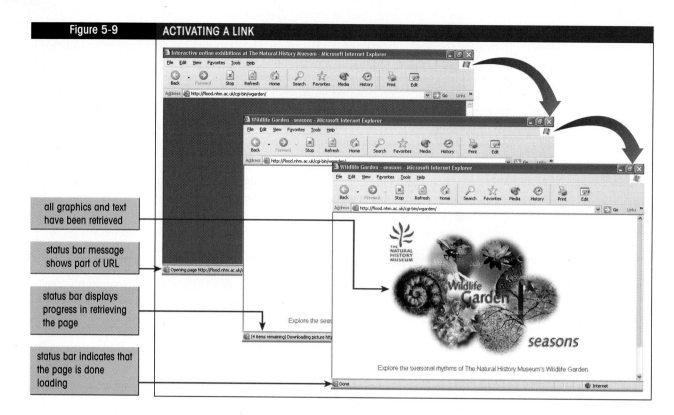

all graphics and text
have been retrieved

status bar message
shows part of URL

status bar displays
progress in retrieving
the page

status bar indicates that
the page is done
loading

You can see the Web page build as your browser transfers information to the screen in multiple passes. The first wave brings a few elements to the page, and with each subsequent pass, the browser fills in more detail, until the material is complete. Try activating one of the Highland Travel links to access the company's home page.

To activate a link:

1. Point to the text link **Home Page**—the one at the bottom of the page. (You could also point to the graphic link, the one with the fancy font; both links target the same page.) Notice that the pointer changes shape from ▷ to ↑, indicating that you are pointing to a hypertext link. The status bar shows the URL for that link. See Figure 5-10.

| Figure 5-10 | CLICKING A TEXT LINK |

graphics links

text links

link's target appears in
the status bar

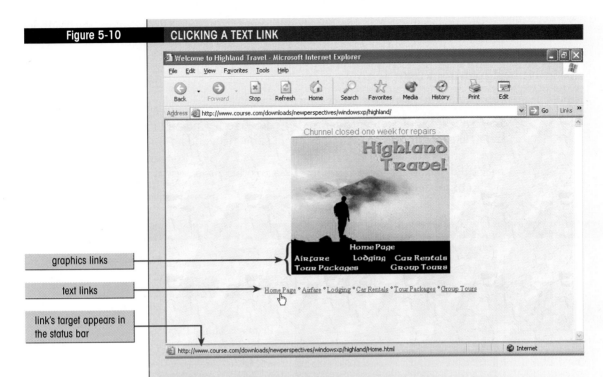

2. Click the **Home Page** text link to activate the link. The status bar notes the
progress of the link. When the status bar displays "Done," the link is complete,
and the Web page that is the target of the link appears. See Figure 5-11.

| Figure 5-11 | COMPLETED LINK |

You've opened the Highland Travel home page. Now you can explore the contents of
this page.

Scott mentions that if you spend time using Windows XP to explore the Web, you'll probably encounter Web pages with frames. You will learn about frames next.

Navigating with Frames

On a Web page, **frames** logically separate information into sections. For example, one frame might list the contents of the Web page, another might include links you can click to navigate related pages, and another might show the content. Each frame can have its own set of scroll bars, as shown in Figure 5-12. The NEC Products page is made up of two pages: the one on the left lists graphic links to other pages, and the one on the right displays the list of product categories.

Figure 5-12	WEB PAGE MADE UP OF FRAMES

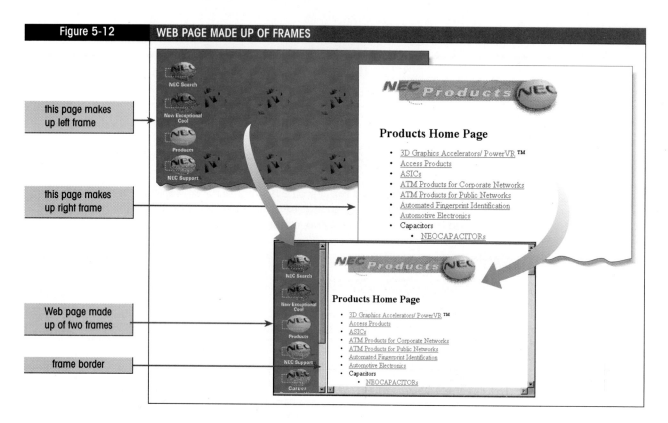

Many Web sites today use frames because they allow the user to see different areas of information simultaneously. When you scroll through the contents of one frame, you do not affect the other frames. Scott suggests you view the Tour Packages page, which uses frames, to learn about this season's Highland Travel tours.

To view a page with frames:

1. Click the **Tour Packages** text link, located in the yellow box on the left of the home page. The Tour Packages page opens. This page consists of four frames that contain (1) the Tour Packages heading at the top, (2) information on the left about the specified tour, (3) a scroll box on the right, listing the tour itinerary for each tour, and (4) graphic links to four different tours on the bottom. See Figure 5-13.

| Figure 5-13 | VIEWING A WEB PAGE WITH FRAMES |

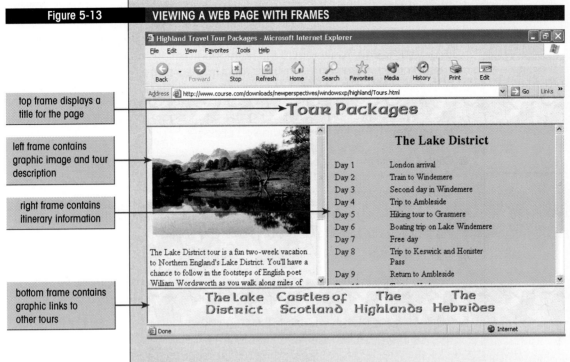

top frame displays a title for the page

left frame contains graphic image and tour description

right frame contains itinerary information

bottom frame contains graphic links to other tours

TROUBLE? If no scroll bars appear in the right frame, your screen resolution is so high that it is capable of displaying the entire itinerary. Skip Step 2 and note that in the rest of the steps it may not be necessary to scroll.

2. Scroll through the information in the right frame. The other three frames remain static while the right frame changes.

3. Click the **Castles of Scotland** graphic link in the bottom frame. The information in the left frame changes, and the itinerary in the right frame changes. Scroll through the information in the right frame, and again notice that the other frames are static.

4. Click **The Highlands** graphic link to view this tour's itinerary, and then click **The Hebrides** graphic link. You have now viewed information on all four tours.

By using frames, the designer of this Web page made it possible for you to view only the information you choose to view.

Returning to a Previously Viewed Page

You've already seen in earlier tutorials how Windows XP allows you to navigate the devices and folders on your local and network drives, using the Back 🔙 and Forward 🔜 buttons in Windows Explorer and My Computer. These buttons are also found on the Standard Buttons toolbars in most browsers. The Back button returns you to the Web page you were most recently viewing, and the Forward button reverses the effect of the Back button. Both the Back and Forward buttons contain lists of visited sites; you can return to those sites by clicking the list arrow to the right of either button and clicking the site from the drop-down list.

To return to a previously viewed Web page:

1. Click the **Back** button ⬅ repeatedly to navigate back through the tour itineraries you viewed. You return to the Highland Travel Home Page, the page you were visiting before you viewed the Tours framed page.

   TROUBLE? If you click the small down arrow (not the Forward button) to the right of the Back button, a list opens. Click the arrow again to close the list, and then repeat Step 1. This time make sure you click ⬅.

2. Click ⬅ until the Back button dims, indicating that you have reached your starting point, usually your home page. Now try moving forward again to return to the Tour Packages page.

3. Click the **Forward** button ➡ repeatedly until the Forward button dims, indicating that you are looking at the last page you visited.

4. Click the **Home** button 🏠 to return to your Home Page.

   Now you'll use the Back list to see how you can return to a page you've visited without having to navigate through all the pages you've seen in a given session.

5. Click the **Back button** list arrow (the small down arrow to the right of the Back button). The Back list opens. See Figure 5-14.

Figure 5-14	ACCESSING A PAGE VIA THE BACK BUTTON LIST ARROW

click to open the Back button list

Back button list

click to return to the Highland Travel Home Page

6. Click **Highland Travel Home Page** to return to the Highland Travel Home Page.

Scott explains that one limitation of the Back and Forward buttons is that they apply only to your current session in the browser. If you exit Internet Explorer and restart it, the Back list starts afresh. However, you can always use the History pane to access those pages quickly. Scott wants you to try this technique now.

Navigating with the History Pane

As mentioned earlier, Internet Explorer has a lot in common with Windows Explorer. Many of the menu commands and buttons are the same. In addition, Internet Explorer has the same Explorer bar that Windows Explorer has, allowing you to divide the Internet Explorer window into two panes. All of the tools you used in Tutorial 3 with the left pane in Windows Explorer apply to the left pane in Internet Explorer. For example, in Internet Explorer you can display the History pane, which lists the files, folders, and pages you've visited recently. This is the same History pane you opened in Windows Explorer, showing the same list of items. The History pane is particularly helpful in Internet Explorer because if you visit many sites on a certain day, you can quickly find one of those sites later in the History pane and revisit it.

You can change the setup in the History pane to view pages by date, by site, by the number of times visited, and in the order visited on the current day. You can also search the pages in the History pane to locate a specific Web site you've recently visited.

To use the History pane:

1. Click the **History** button on the Standard Buttons toolbar to open the History pane. (Note that you could also click View, point to the Explorer bar, and then click History to open the History pane.) See Figure 5-15.

Figure 5-15   DISPLAYING THE HISTORY PANE

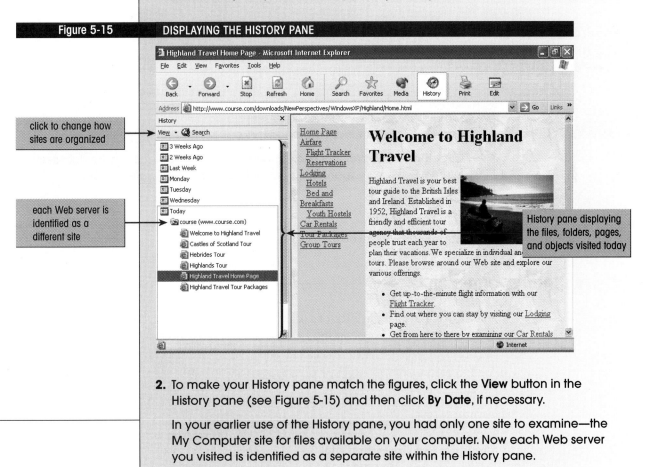

click to change how sites are organized

each Web server is identified as a different site

History pane displaying the files, folders, pages, and objects visited today

2. To make your History pane match the figures, click the **View** button in the History pane (see Figure 5-15) and then click **By Date**, if necessary.

In your earlier use of the History pane, you had only one site to examine—the My Computer site for files available on your computer. Now each Web server you visited is identified as a separate site within the History pane.

3. Click the **course (www.course.com)** icon in the History pane. Internet Explorer collapses the Course list so that only the course (www.course.com) heading appears. See Figure 5-16.

Figure 5-16 | WEB SERVERS VISITED

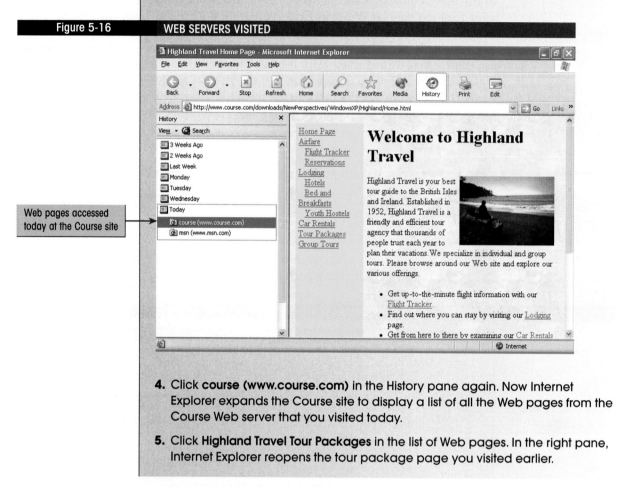

Web pages accessed today at the Course site

4. Click **course (www.course.com)** in the History pane again. Now Internet Explorer expands the Course site to display a list of all the Web pages from the Course Web server that you visited today.

5. Click **Highland Travel Tour Packages** in the list of Web pages. In the right pane, Internet Explorer reopens the tour package page you visited earlier.

As you explore the Web, you'll find pages that are your favorites, those you visit frequently. Internet Explorer allows you to track your favorite sites for frequent and easy access.

Using **the Favorites List**

Rather than retyping the URL of a page every time you want to visit it, you can save the location of your favorite pages in a list. In Windows XP, this is your **Favorites list**, and it contains shortcuts to the files, folders, objects, and Web pages that you visit most often. In Internet Explorer, My Computer, and Windows XP, you designate files, folders, and Web pages as your favorites—those which you want to organize for quick access—and Windows XP includes them in the Favorites list. When you want to retrieve a Web page, you can click an icon in the Favorites list and display the page in your browser.

Viewing the Favorites List

You can display your Favorites list in a variety of ways. You can use the Favorites menu available on the Internet Explorer menu bar or the Favorites button on the Standard Buttons toolbar. You can also display the contents of your Favorites list in the Explorer Bar for Internet

Explorer, Windows Explorer, and My Computer. You can even display the Favorites list on your Start menu. The method you use to access your favorites depends on your personal preference. In any case, the Favorites list includes any file, folder, or Web page you've added to it. If you use Internet Explorer to add the Web page of your favorite online travel site to the Favorites list, for example, the Web page also appears in the My Computer Favorites list.

Steve suggests you add the Highland Travel Web page to your Favorites list. First, you must open the Favorites list. You decide to display the Favorites pane in the Explorer bar.

To display the Favorites list:

1. Click the **Favorites** button ☆ on the Standard Buttons toolbar to open the Favorites list. (Note that you can also click View, point to the Explorer bar, and then click Favorites to open the Favorites list.) Internet Explorer displays the Favorites list in the Favorites pane, as shown in Figure 5-17.

| Figure 5-17 | DISPLAYING THE FAVORITES LIST |

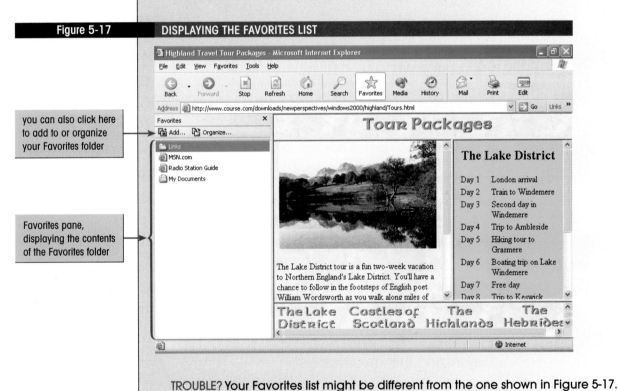

you can also click here to add to or organize your Favorites folder

Favorites pane, displaying the contents of the Favorites folder

TROUBLE? Your Favorites list might be different from the one shown in Figure 5-17.

The Favorites list shown in Figure 5-17 contains shortcuts to a Web page containing a radio station guide and a page for the Microsoft Network (MSN). Now you can add the home page for Highland Travel to your Favorites list.

Adding an Item to the Favorites List

To add a Web page, you must first access the page in Internet Explorer, and then you can use the Add to Favorites command. Windows XP adds the new page to the top of the Favorites list. You can add the page using the title of the Web page as its name, or you can change the name to something more meaningful to you.

If you are working on a network, you might not be able to change the content of the Favorites list. If that's the case, you will not be able to complete these steps or the ones that follow. Instead read through this material—if you've completed Tutorial 3, this information will be familiar to you.

REFERENCE WINDOW   **RW**

Adding a Web Page to the Favorites Folder
- Open the Web page in Internet Explorer.
- Click Favorites on the Internet Explorer menu bar, and then click Add to Favorites.
- Click the OK button.

To add the Highland Travel Home Page to the Favorites list:

1. Click the **Back** button ⬅ to return to the Highland Travel Home Page. This is the page you want to add to the Favorites list.

2. Click **Favorites** on the menu bar, and then click **Add to Favorites**. The Add Favorite dialog box opens.

   Note that you can also click the Add button in the Favorites pane to open the Add Favorite dialog box. The title of the Web page appears in the Name text box—in this case, the name is Highland Travel Home Page. To change this, you could enter a different name in the Name text box. Highland Travel Home Page is appropriate for this Web page, so you won't change it.

3. Click the **OK** button.

   An icon for the Highland Travel Home Page is added to the Favorites folder.

If you have many favorites in your Favorites list, you will want to organize them in a logical manner. Creating and using subfolders is one way of effectively organizing a long Favorites list.

Organizing the Favorites List

As you add more items to the Favorites list, you will find that you need to organize its contents: deleting some items and moving others to new folders. Using folders is an excellent way to organize your favorite files and pages.

REFERENCE WINDOW   **RW**

Organizing the Favorites List
- Click Favorites on the Internet Explorer menu bar, and then click Organize Favorites to open the Organize Favorites dialog box.
- To create a new folder, click the Create Folder button.
- To move an item into the Favorites folder, select the item, click the Move to Folder button, select the new folder for the item, and then click the OK button.
- To remove an item from the Favorites folder, select the item and then click the Delete button.

You decide to create a folder for the Highland Travel Web pages.

To organize your Favorites list:

1. Click **Favorites** on the Internet Explorer menu bar, and then click **Organize Favorites**. The Organize Favorites dialog box opens. You can also click the Organize button in the Favorites pane to open this dialog box.

2. Click the **Create Folder** button, type **Highland Travel** for the new folder name, and then press the **Enter** key. Now you'll move the Highland Travel Home Page into the new folder you created.

3. In the Organize Favorites dialog box, click the **Highland Travel Home Page** icon in the list box to select it.

4. Click the **Move to Folder** button. The Browse for Folder dialog box opens. You use this dialog box to find the folder in which you want to store the selected Web page.

5. Click the **Highland Travel** folder, and then click the **OK** button.

6. Click the **Close** button to close the Organize Favorites dialog box. A folder for Highland Travel now appears in the Favorites pane.

7. Click the **Highland Travel** folder in the Favorites pane. The contents of the folder appear as shown in Figure 5-18.

| Figure 5-18 | THE HIGHLAND TRAVEL FOLDER IN THE FAVORITES LIST |

Before completing your work with the Favorites list, you should remove the folder you created, and then close the Favorites pane.

To delete an item from the Favorites list:

1. Click the **Organize** button in the Favorites pane. The Organize Favorites dialog box opens.

2. Click the **Highland Travel** folder in the Organize Favorites dialog box. This is the folder you want to remove from the Favorites list.

3. Click the **Delete** button. A message box appears asking you to confirm you want to delete the folder and its contents.

4. Click the **Yes** button.

5. Click the **Close** button to close the Organize Favorites dialog box.

6. Click the **Close** button ⊠ in the Favorites pane to close the Favorites list.

Although reducing paper consumption is an advantage of browsing information online, sometimes you'll find it useful to print a Web page.

Printing **a Web Page**

You might want to refer to the information you find on the Web later when you don't have computer access. This is when printing a Web page becomes useful. Although Web pages can be any size, printers tend to use 8½ × 11-inch sheets of paper. When you print, your browser automatically reformats the text of the Web page to fit the paper dimensions. Because lines might break at different places or text size might be altered, the printed Web page might be longer than you expect. You can specify the number of pages you want to print in the Print dialog box. You decide to print the first page of the Highland Travel Web page.

To print a Web page:

1. Click **File** on the menu bar, and then click **Print**. The Print dialog box opens. In this dialog box, you can specify the print options you want. You only want to print the first page of the Highland Travel Web page.

2. In the Page Range section, click the **Pages** option button, and make sure the Pages text box shows 1.

TROUBLE? If a value other than 1 appears in the Pages text box, select the text in the text box, and then type 1.

3. Click the **Print** button to print the first page of the Highland Travel Home Page.

Some printers are set up to print headers and footers in addition to the Web page itself, so when you retrieve the page from your printer, you might find the page's title, its URL, the date, and other similar information at the top and bottom of the page.

Downloading a File

Scott explains that Windows XP also makes it easy to transfer files stored on the Internet to your computer. Although a Web page appears in your browser window and you can add the page to your Favorites list or find it in your History list, the page itself is still stored on a remote computer (a computer located elsewhere on the Internet.) To store the Web page on your computer, you must download it from the remote computer. **Downloading** is the process of saving a copy of a file located on a remote computer to your own computer. The method you use to download information you find on the Web depends on how the file appears on the Web page. If you want to save the Web page itself, you use the Save As command on the File menu. If you want to save a graphic image located directly on the Web page, you save it by right-clicking the object you want and then using the Save Picture As command that appears on the shortcut menu.

You liked the Lake District graphic on the Tours page, so you decide to download and use it as a background image on your desktop.

To download a file:

1. Click the **Forward** button ⊙ to return to the Lake District tour page.

2. Write "Windows XP Tutorial 5 Lake District graphic" on the label of a blank, formatted 3½-inch disk. Insert the disk into drive A.

3. Right-click the **Lake District** graphic to open its shortcut menu. See Figure 5-19.

| Figure 5-19 | SAVING A WEB GRAPHIC |

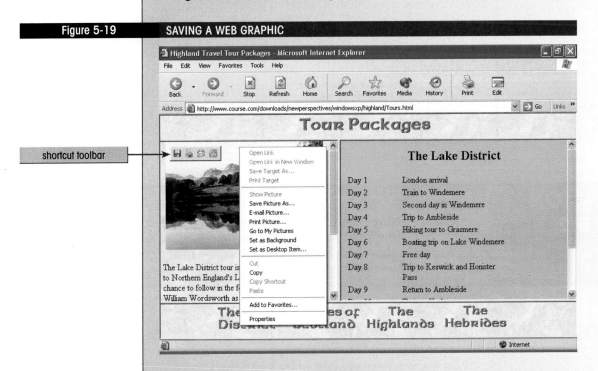

4. Click **Save Picture As** on the shortcut menu. Note that you could also click the Save as button on the shortcut toolbar. The Save Picture dialog box opens.

5. Click the **Save in** list arrow, and then click **3½ Floppy (A:)**. Make sure the name "lake" appears in the File name box and the type is JPEG, a common graphic image type used in Web pages.

> TROUBLE? If a name other than "lake" appears in the File name box, replace it with the name "lake." If a type other than JPEG appears in the Save as type text box, click the Save as type list arrow and then click JPEG (*.jpg).
>
> 6. Click the **Save** button. Windows XP transfers the file over the Internet from the Tour Packages Web page to your disk.
>
> 7. Close Internet Explorer.

The file is stored on your disk, and you could open it in a graphics program (such as Paint) and work with it there. Note that content appearing on Web pages is often copyrighted, and you should always make sure you have permission to use it before doing so. Since Highland Travel owns this graphic, Scott tells you that you can use it.

You have now used Internet Explorer to view information on the Web, navigate links, and print and save information from the Web.

Session 5.1 QUICK CHECK

1. What is a home page?

2. The address of a Web page is called a(n) _____.

3. If someone gives you the URL of an interesting Web page, how can you view the page?

4. What does a URL with "edu" in it tell you about that site's Web server?

5. Each Web server you visit appears as a different _____ in the History pane.

6. Describe how you could quickly locate a Web page that you viewed a few days earlier.

7. True or False: Only Web pages and folders can be stored in the Favorites folder.

8. How can you download a graphic image that you find on the Web?

SESSION 5.2

In this session, you will learn how to set up your computer so that it automatically delivers Web page content to your desktop. You'll add an Active Desktop item to your Windows XP desktop. You'll update the Active Desktop item using the Synchronize command, and you'll set up a schedule for automatic updates. Finally, you'll use a Web page as a background for your Windows XP desktop. For this session you need the Data Disk for Windows XP Tutorial 5.

Bringing the Web to Your Desktop

Scott now wants to show you how you can receive content from the Web without having to go look for it. When you connected to the Highland Travel Web page in Session 5.1, you had to go looking for it. You were told where to find the information (that is, you were given a URL), and then you went to that location and "pulled" information from the Web server onto your own computer.

Another way of retrieving data, called **push technology**, brings information to your computer without your having to go get it. True push technology occurs when the author of a Web site modifies the site so that it automatically sends information to users, without requiring the user to manually access the site and retrieve the data. Once the data has been retrieved, the user can view it without being connected to the Internet or any network. This is a technique known as **offline viewing** because the user is not "online" with the Web server.

Scott explains that you're going to begin your exploration of push technology and offline viewing by adding to the desktop content that changes frequently—Active Desktop items. An **Active Desktop** item is an object that you place on your desktop that receives updates from a Web page that pushes the updates to users on a set schedule. For example, you could place a selection of Active Desktop items on your desktop, as in Figure 5-20.

Figure 5-20	WINDOWS XP DESKTOP WITH ACTIVE DESKTOP ITEMS

CBS SportsLine features sports news

Epicurious FOOD allows you to view recipes for ingredient you specify

MSN MoneyCentral shows stock prices

MSNBC Weather Map features current temperatures around the country

Parent Soup offers parenting advice

You can set Active Desktop items to be updated each day, each hour, or on any schedule you choose. Every morning when the user of the computer shown in Figure 5-20 checks her desktop, for example, each active desktop item will have been automatically updated. The weather map will show the morning's weather instead of weather from the night before, the news service will display the most recent news, and other Active Desktop items are updated in a similar fashion. This user has created her own "mini-newspaper," made up of only the information that interests her.

Some Active Desktop items are interactive, allowing you to enter information and receive a response. The Epicurious FOOD Active Desktop item, for example, allows you to enter ingredients, such as beans and rice, and when you click the Get Recipes button, Internet Explorer starts (and connects to the Internet if you're not already connected) and displays recipes from the Epicurious site containing those ingredients. Microsoft maintains a collection of Active Desktop items at its Active Desktop Gallery Web site, which you'll access next.

Adding an Active Desktop Gallery Item to the Desktop

When you're connected to the Internet, you can add, update, and use Active Desktop items. If you specify that you want Active Desktop items to be available for offline viewing, you can view the items and their contents when you're not connected to the Internet, but you cannot update the items or add others.

Now you'll use the Customize Desktop button in the Display Properties dialog box to add Web content to your desktop. Although you can add any Web page to your desktop, you'll start by opening the Desktop Gallery on the Microsoft Web site. The Desktop Gallery contains popular Active Desktop items, including a weather map and sports scores.

To add a weather map from the Active Desktop Gallery to your desktop:

1. Right-click a blank area of the desktop, and then click **Properties** on the short-cut menu. The Display Properties dialog box opens.

2. Click the **Desktop** tab and then click the **Customize Desktop** button.

3. Click the **Web** tab in the Desktop Items dialog box. See Figure 5-21. In this dialog box, the Web pages box lists the Web pages you want to view on your desktop. To add a page to this list, you click the New button, and then enter the URL of the Web page you want, or open the Microsoft Desktop Gallery to select an Active Desktop item.

| Figure 5-21 | THE WEB TAB IN THE CUSTOMIZE ITEMS DIALOG BOX |

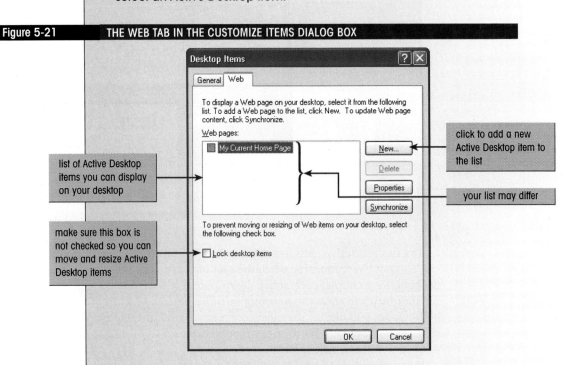

4. Click the **New** button.

5. In the New Desktop Item dialog box, click the **Visit Gallery** button. Windows XP opens the Active Desktop Gallery Web page in Internet Explorer.

    TROUBLE? If you are prompted to download a Stock Ticker from Microsoft, talk to your network manager or instructor to decide whether this program can be retrieved and loaded onto your computer.

6. Scroll the Desktop Gallery list to locate the MSNBC Weather Map, shown in Figure 5-22.

Figure 5-22   SELECTING THE MSNBC WEATHER MAP

this page might look
different if Microsoft has
updated it

click to add item to the
desktop

TROUBLE? If the MSNBC Weather Map doesn't appear in the list, select a different Active Desktop item.

7. Click the **Add to Active Desktop** button below the MSNBC Weather Map. Click the **Yes** button if an Internet Explorer message box appears asking if you want to add this item to your Active Desktop. A second message box appears that asks you to confirm the procedure.

8. Click the **OK** button to add the item to your desktop. The download process might take one or several minutes, depending on the speed of your Internet connection. If the Synchronization dialog box opens, wait until it closes before continuing.

9. Once the download is complete, close your browser. The item you added appears on your desktop. See Figure 5-23.

Figure 5-23   **ADDING AN ACTIVE DESKTOP ITEM**

weather map on your desktop (your desktop might look different)

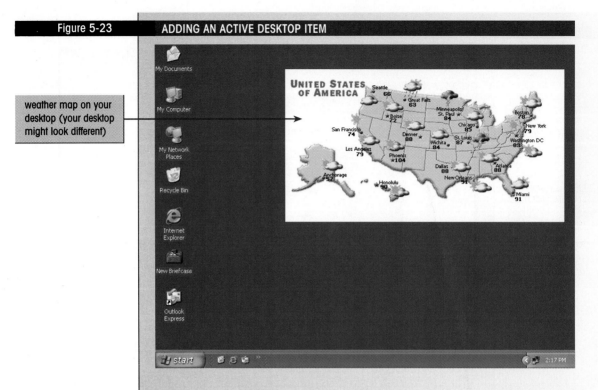

TROUBLE? If the Active Desktop item appears but doesn't look like a weather map, the MSNBC site might be busy. A desktop item will still appear, but it won't include the map. Continue with the steps, using the Active Desktop item.

TROUBLE? If scroll bars appear around your Active Desktop item or the item is off-center, you can move and resize the item; you'll learn how to do so in the next section.

When an Active Desktop item is on your desktop, it occupies a rectangular block that appears as part of the background. However, you can resize and move the Active Desktop item to suit your needs.

Resizing and Moving Active Desktop Items

To move or resize an Active Desktop item, you must first point to it to select it. When an Active Desktop item is selected, a title bar and border appear, which you can manipulate to move and resize the item just as you would any other Windows XP window (such as the My Computer window). You can move the Active Desktop item by dragging it. You can also resize the item using one of three techniques. You can use the sizing buttons on the item's title bar, you can use the sizing commands available from a menu by clicking the item's list arrow on its title bar, or you can drag the item's borders.

Practice moving Active Desktop items by moving the weather map.

To move the weather map:

1. Point to the top of the weather map. A border appears around the entire Active Desktop item, and a bar, similar to a window's title bar, appears at the top. This bar includes a Close Pane button ✕, sizing buttons, and a list arrow on the left that opens a menu for that item. See Figure 5-24.

Figure 5-24	SELECTING AN ACTIVE DESKTOP ITEM

click the arrow to open the weather map's menu

border appears when you move the pointer over the Active Desktop item

title bar

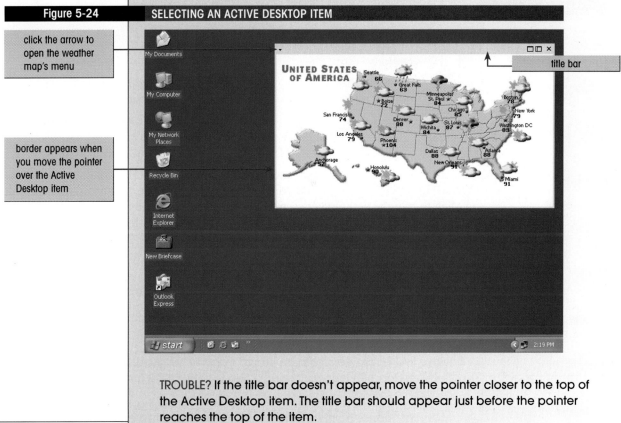

TROUBLE? If the title bar doesn't appear, move the pointer closer to the top of the Active Desktop item. The title bar should appear just before the pointer reaches the top of the item.

2. Drag the weather map to the center of the desktop, if yours was previously off-center. The entire weather map moves to this new location.

You can also use the border around the weather map to resize it. For example, you drag the left and right borders to widen the item or make it narrower, you drag the top and bottom borders to lengthen or shorten the item, and you drag any corner out to enlarge or reduce both dimensions proportionally.

To resize the weather map:

1. Point to the lower-right corner of the weather map. The gray border appears and the mouse pointer changes from ⤢ to ⤡.

2. Drag the corner border to the lower right. The Active Desktop item expands in size. If your map has scroll bars, drag down and to the right until the scroll bars disappear.

You can also change the size of a desktop item by clicking one of the buttons on the upper-right corner of the item border. Figure 5-25 describes the four buttons available on the border and how to use them to modify the desktop item. These sizing commands are also available on the window's menu, which you open by clicking the down arrow button in the left corner of the titlebar.

Figure 5-25	RESIZE BUTTONS FOR THE ACTIVE DESKTOP ITEM	
NAME		**DESCRIPTION**
Cover Desktop		Extend the item across the entire desktop
Split Desktop with Icons		Move all desktop icons to the far left and fill the remaining desktop with the item
Reset to Original Size		Reset the item to a window on the desktop
✕ Close Pane		Close the item

To see how these buttons work, you'll try resizing the image: first to fill the whole desktop, then to split the desktop between the icons and the item, and finally to restore the item to its original size and position. Note that you see only three of these buttons at a time. The middle button changes depending on the item's current size.

To use the sizing buttons:

1. Move your mouse pointer over the top border of the image to redisplay the title bar (if necessary), and click the **Cover Desktop** button ⬜. The weather map fills the entire desktop.

2. Move the mouse pointer to the top of the weather map, and then click the **Split Desktop with Icons** button ⬛. The weather map is reduced in size, moving to the right of the icons on the desktop.

3. Move the mouse pointer to the top of the weather map again, and click the **Reset to Original Size** button ▪. The weather map is restored to its original size on the desktop.

Figure 5-26 shows the weather map in each of the three sizes.

Figure 5-26	THE WEATHER MAP IN THREE SIZES

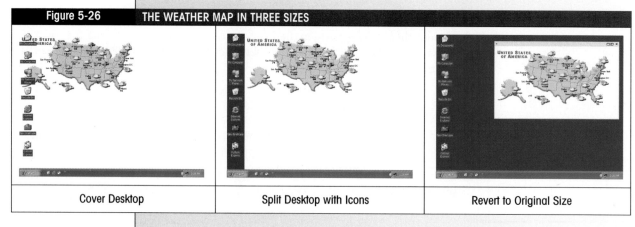

Cover Desktop	Split Desktop with Icons	Revert to Original Size

You might be wondering how you update the weather map to reflect current conditions. You will learn how to do that next.

Updating **Active Desktop Items**

The process of retrieving current information is called **synchronization**. When you synchronize an Active Desktop item, you refresh and update its content. For example, the weather map shows the weather that was current when you added the MSNBC Weather Map item to the desktop. To see how the weather has changed since you added that item, you must synchronize that Active Desktop item.

Windows XP allows you to synchronize not just Web content, but any information available over your network. For example, if you are working on a corporate network and are leaving on a trip, you can retrieve a file for offline viewing on your laptop. Windows XP will make a copy of that file available to you, but it might not be current with the network file when you return. You can change this by synchronizing your copy with the network version. Similarly, you can synchronize the weather map on your desktop with the map available on the Web server.

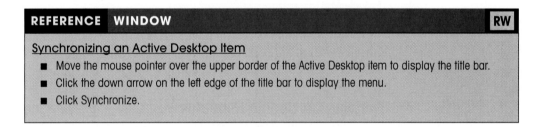

REFERENCE WINDOW   **RW**

Synchronizing an Active Desktop Item
- Move the mouse pointer over the upper border of the Active Desktop item to display the title bar.
- Click the down arrow on the left edge of the title bar to display the menu.
- Click Synchronize.

Now you can synchronize the weather map to show current weather conditions.

Synchronizing Active Desktop Items Manually

Files and Web pages can be synchronized on a fixed schedule or manually. When you manually synchronize, you use the Synchronize command on the Active Desktop item to connect to the original Web page and then transfer current information from that Web page to your desktop. After you synchronize, the Active Desktop item shows updated information.

To synchronize the weather map:

1. Move the mouse pointer over the upper border of the weather map to display the title bar.

2. Click the down arrow located on the left edge of the title bar, and then click **Synchronize** on the menu. See Figure 5-27.

Figure 5-27   SYNCHRONIZING THE WEATHER MAP

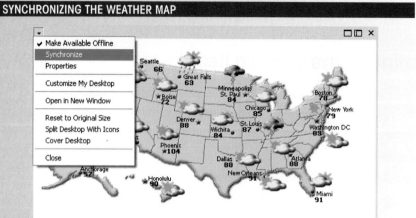

3. Windows XP connects to the Web server and updates the weather map with the latest weather information.

If you always had to update the weather map manually, having it on your desktop would not be much of an improvement over simply visiting the page on the Web. Windows XP allows you to schedule automatic updates.

Viewing an Update Schedule

The advantage of synchronization is the ability of Windows XP to access the page for you on a schedule. For example, you could have an Active Desktop item that downloads the latest stock market information every five minutes. By glancing at your desktop, you can view data that is no more than five minutes old.

Most Active Desktop items retrieved from the Active Desktop gallery have a schedule already set. The schedule is one of the properties of the Active Desktop item.

To view the schedule for the weather map:

1. Redisplay the title bar for the weather map, click the down arrow, and then click **Properties** on the menu. The MSNBC Weather Properties dialog box opens.

2. Click the **Schedule** tab. As shown in Figure 5-28, the weather map uses the MSNBC Weather Recommended Schedule.

Figure 5-28   THE MSNBC WEATHER PROPERTIES DIALOG BOX

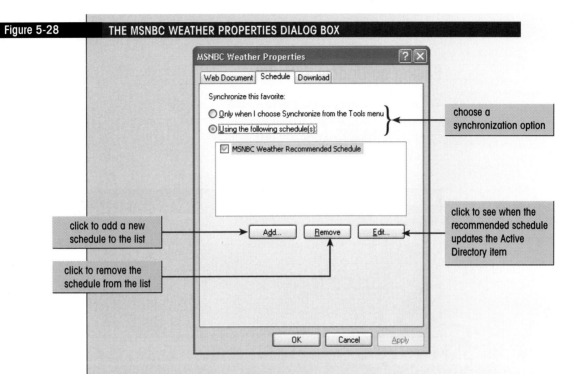

choose a synchronization option

click to add a new schedule to the list

click to remove the schedule from the list

click to see when the recommended schedule updates the Active Directory item

3. To see when the MSNBC Weather recommended schedule downloads updated weather maps, click the **Edit** button. As shown in Figure 5-29, under the recommended schedule the map is updated every night at 12:00 AM.

Figure 5-29   THE MSNBC WEATHER RECOMMENDED SCHEDULE

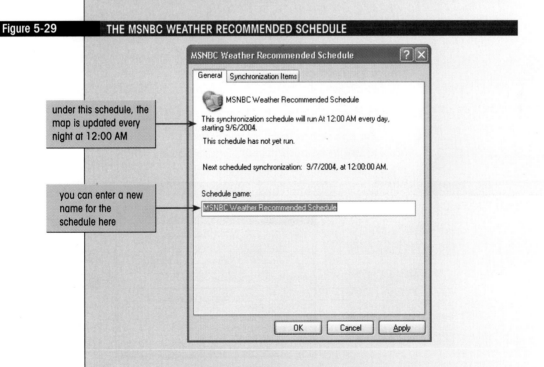

under this schedule, the map is updated every night at 12:00 AM

you can enter a new name for the schedule here

4. Click the **OK** button and leave the MSNBC Weather Properties dialog box open.

The recommended schedule may not be ideal for you. Fortunately, you can change it to suit your individual needs.

Editing an Update Schedule

You realize as you examine the current schedule that most of the time your computer will not be turned on at midnight to run the synchronization. A much better time would be 9:00 AM, shortly after you arrive at the office, and 3:00 PM, shortly before you leave. To make this change, you have to create two schedules: one for the morning and one for the afternoon.

REFERENCE WINDOW   RW

Scheduling an Update
- Click the down arrow on the Active Desktop item's title bar, and then click Properties.
- Click the Schedule tab.
- Click the Add button.
- Enter a time in the digital clock indicating when the update should occur, and then enter a name for the new schedule.

Now you can create an update schedule to synchronize the weather map once in the morning and once in the afternoon.

To create an update schedule:

1. Click the **Add** button in the MSNBC Weather Properties dialog box.

2. In the New Schedule dialog box, set the time value to **9:00 AM**. (You can set the time value by clicking the up and down arrows next to the digital clock or by double-clicking the hour or minutes digits, and then typing new values.)

3. Type **Morning Update** in the Name box.

4. Click the check box to allow Windows XP to connect to the Internet automatically to begin synchronization. Figure 5-30 shows the completed dialog box.

Figure 5-30   SCHEDULING THE MORNING UPDATE

5. Click the **OK** button. The Morning Update schedule is added to the list of schedules. Now Windows XP will synchronize the weather map Active Desktop item every morning at 9:00 AM.

6. Click the **Add** button again, and then add a new schedule named "Afternoon Update," which will update the map at 3:00 PM every day (automatically connecting to the Internet if needed).

7. Click the **OK** button to close the New Schedule dialog box. Figure 5-31 shows the new list of scheduled updates in the MSNBC Weather Properties dialog box.

Figure 5-31   **LIST OF UPDATE SCHEDULES**

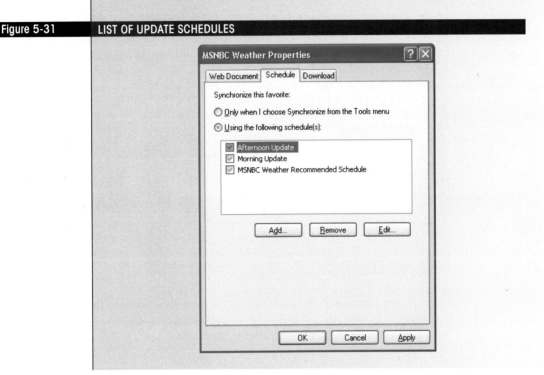

Now that you've seen how to work with Active Desktop items and update schedules, you should remove the weather map from your desktop.

Removing an Active Desktop Item

When you remove an Active Desktop item, you can either close the item (by clicking the down arrow button on the title bar) or delete it. Closing the item keeps the information about the item and its update schedule available for future use. You can restore the item later by opening the Display Properties dialog box and selecting the item on the Web property sheet. Deleting the item removes the file and all information about it from your computer. If you wanted to access the deleted Active Desktop item again, you would have to go back to the Web site and download the item again to reinstall it.

To delete the update schedules and weather map:

1. In the MSNBC Weather Properties dialog box, click **Morning Update** and then click the **Remove** button. When a message box appears, click the **Yes** button to confirm the deletion.

2. Remove the Afternoon Update schedule using the technique used in Step 1.

3. Click the **OK** button to close the MSNBC Weather Properties dialog box. Next you can remove the weather map Active Desktop item from the desktop and from the list of Web pages you can add to the desktop.

4. Right-click an empty area on the desktop, and then click **Properties** on the shortcut menu.

5. Click the **Desktop** tab in the Display Properties dialog box.

6. Click the **Customize Desktop** button, and then click the **Web** tab. The Web property sheet shows a list of all available Active Desktop objects for your desktop. Those that currently appear on the desktop have their check boxes selected.

7. Click **MSNBC Weather** and then click the **Delete** button. A message box appears asking you to confirm that you want to delete the item from your Active Desktop.

8. Click the **Yes** button and then click the **OK** button.

9. Click the **OK** button to close the Display Properties dialog box. You've restored the desktop to its original state.

TROUBLE? If you had to deselect your home page from the desktop earlier, open the Web property sheet in the Display Properties dialog box again, and then click the My Current Home Page check box.

An Active Desktop item provides a way for you to interact with your desktop by updating a weather map or receiving the latest sports scores. You can also use a Web page to interact with your desktop, as you'll see in the next section.

Using an HTML File as a Background

In Tutorial 4, you worked with the Display Properties dialog box to change your desktop's color and background, and then to display a graphic image on your desktop. Active Desktop technology extends your control over your desktop's background by allowing you to use Web pages as backgrounds. Like an Active Desktop item, you can also interact with a Web page you use as a desktop background. You can click any links the Web page contains, and Internet Explorer will start and open the corresponding Web page. However, unlike an Active Desktop item, after you select a Web page for the desktop background, you cannot update its contents by synchronizing. To use the new version of the Web page as the desktop background, you'd have to save and retrieve the new Web page as a new background. For this reason, if you want to include a frequently updated Web page on your desktop, add it as an Active Desktop item, not as a Web page background.

To create Web pages, you use a language called HTML, which stands for Hypertext Markup Language. HTML uses special codes to describe how the page should appear on the screen. Figure 5-32 shows a Web page as it appears on your computer screen and behind it, the underlying HTML code. It is this code that the browser interprets when a Web page is viewed.

Figure 5-32   WEB PAGE AND THE HTML CODE IT EMPLOYS

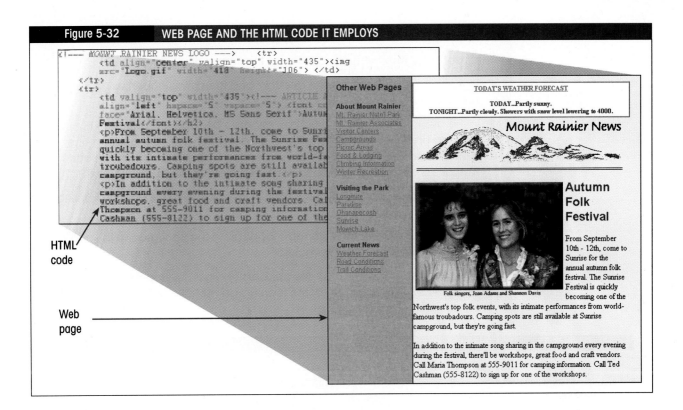

A document created using the HTML language is called an HTML file and is saved with the .htm or .html extension. Most Web pages are HTML files.

Because Windows XP enables you to use an HTML file as your desktop background, your Windows XP desktop background can feature text, clip art, photos, animated graphics, links, and multimedia objects such as sound and video. Your desktop can also include **applets**, programs attached to a Web page that extend its capabilities. Some applets add movement and interesting visual effects to your page, whereas others are capable of asking you questions, responding to your questions, checking your computer settings, and calculating data. There are even applets that allow you to play interactive games against the computer or against another person logged on to the Web.

You can use a word-processing program such as Microsoft Word to save a document as an HTML file, or you can create a new one using FrontPage Express, the Web page editor included with Windows XP. If you learn the HTML language, you can use a simple text editor (such as Notepad) to create a more complex and sophisticated HTML file. Alternately, you can use the Internet Explorer browser to save an existing Web page as an HTML file that you can then use as your wallpaper.

The added control Windows XP gives you over background wallpaper makes it possible to make the desktop a launchpad for your most important projects. A corporation, for example, might create an HTML file that contains important company information, an updatable company calendar, links to company documents, a company directory, and so on. Scott wants to show you a Web page he's designing to be used as a background for all Highland Travel computers. He has created an HTML file in his Web page editor and has placed it on a disk for you to examine. The Highland Travel desktop background Web page is on your Data Disk.

To use a Web page as a background:

1. If necessary, insert your Data Disk into the floppy drive.

2. Right-click a blank area of the desktop, and then click **Properties** on the shortcut menu.

3. In the Display Properties dialog box, click the **Desktop** tab and note the current Desktop background. You'll restore this background to your desktop after you learn how to use a Web page as the desktop background. The Highland Travel HTML file is on your Data Disk, so you need to navigate to drive A next.

4. Click the **Browse** button, click the **Look in** list arrow, click **3½ Floppy (A:)**, and then click the **Highland** file.

5. Click the **Open** button. The filename appears in the Background list, and a preview appears in the preview monitor.

6. Click the **OK** button. The HTML file appears on your desktop as a background. Figure 5-33 points out some of the features an HTML file allows you to employ on a desktop background.

| Figure 5-33 | PLACING AN HTML FILE ON THE DESKTOP |

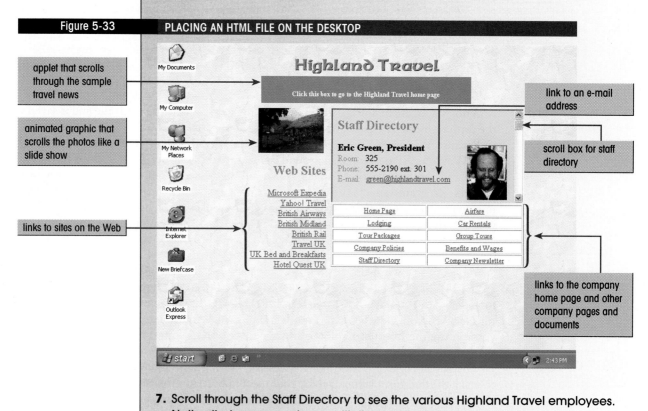

applet that scrolls through the sample travel news

animated graphic that scrolls the photos like a slide show

links to sites on the Web

link to an e-mail address

scroll box for staff directory

links to the company home page and other company pages and documents

7. Scroll through the Staff Directory to see the various Highland Travel employees. Notice that your experience with these objects is the same as it would be if you were working with this page in your Web browser.

The difference between using an HTML file as your desktop background and using a graphic file, as you did in Tutorial 4, is that a graphic is simply a picture that adds interest to your desktop background, whereas an HTML file allows you to interact with the information in your background. If the HTML file contains links, you can click those links to connect to the sites they target. Try clicking one of the links on the page.

To activate a desktop link:

1. Click the **Home Page** link in the first row of the table below the Staff Directory. Your browser starts and after a moment the link's target appears in the browser window—the familiar Highland Travel page.

2. Close your browser. You return to the desktop.

Scott explains that once he finishes developing his page, the company will place it on all company desktops as a background, so all employees have access to the information it contains. Because it isn't finished, he recommends that you remove it from your desktop.

To restore the desktop to its original appearance:

1. Right-click a blank area of the desktop, and then click **Properties** on the shortcut menu.

   TROUBLE? If you right-click an area of the Web page that has Web content, properties for that object appear, instead of desktop properties. Make sure the dialog box that opens is the Display Properties dialog box. If it isn't, try right-clicking a different area, and make sure it is blank.

2. Click the **Desktop** tab.

3. Scroll the Background list and then click the name of the original background, the one you noted in the previous steps.

4. Click the **OK** button.

You've completed your work with bringing Web content directly to your desktop. As you've seen, Windows XP provides a rich variety of tools to connect your computer with the Internet.

Session 5.2   QUICK CHECK

1. What is offline viewing?

2. What is push technology?

3. An object on the desktop that receives pushed content is called a(n) _____.

4. What is synchronization?

5. How would you schedule an object to be synchronized 24 times a day, once each hour?

6. What is HTML?

7. What are some advantages of using an HTML file for your desktop background?

SESSION 5.3

In this session, you'll learn about e-mail. You will learn how to start Outlook Express—the Windows XP e-mail program. You'll see how to customize Outlook Express, and you'll examine the properties of your mail account. You'll send and receive e-mail messages and reply to an e-mail message.

Getting Started with Outlook Express

Outlook Express, one of the tools that comes with Windows XP, allows you to send, receive, and manage **electronic mail** or **e-mail**—electronic messages transferred between users on a network. As more people connect to the Internet, communicating by e-mail is becoming more common. When you need to send information to someone else, an e-mail message saves time and money, because you don't need to wait for postal delivery nor make expensive long-distance phone calls. You can send e-mail to and receive e-mail from anyone in the world who has an e-mail address, regardless of the operating system or type of computer the person is using.

Just as you need an Internet account to browse the World Wide Web, you likewise need an account on a **mail server**, a computer that handles the storage and delivery of e-mail. Most Internet service providers also provide access to mail servers.

Scott informs you that the company's systems administrator has just established a mail server on the company network to handle all e-mail messages. He hands you a slip of paper with your account information, including your user ID, password, and e-mail address. A **user ID**, also called a **user name**, is the name that identifies you on the mail server. A **password** is a personal code that verifies that you have the right to read incoming mail and send mail. An **e-mail address** consists of the user ID, the @ symbol, and a host name. For example, Scott's e-mail address is:

scampbell@highlandtravel.com

Thus Scott's user name is scampbell, and the address of the company's mail server is highlandtravel.com. Like URLs, every e-mail address is unique. Many people might use the same host, but user IDs distinguish one e-mail address from another.

Customizing the Outlook Express Window

You use Outlook Express to compose, send, and receive e-mail messages. The Outlook Express window is divided into sections so that you can differentiate the messages you've received from those you've sent or are ready to send. To make Outlook Express suit your needs, you can customize the window by choosing to display or hide these sections and other elements. Now you can start Outlook Express and then explore the features you can customize. You start Outlook Express by clicking the Outlook Express button 🖼 on the Quick Launch toolbar, clicking the Outlook Express icon on the desktop, or using the Start menu.

To start Outlook Express:

1. Click the **Start** button *start* on the taskbar, point to **All Programs**, and then click **Outlook Express**. Note that the Outlook Express icon might also appear in the upper-right section of the Start menu.

TROUBLE? If more than one e-mail program is installed on your computer, and Outlook Express is not your current default mail program, a dialog box appears asking if you want Outlook Express to be your default mail program. If you are using your own computer and want to use Outlook Express as your mail program, click the Yes button. If you are using a school or institutional computer, click the No button or ask your technical support person for assistance.

TROUBLE? If the Identity Logon dialog box opens, you are using a version of Outlook Express that is configured for multiple users. If your name appears, click it and then enter the password as requested. Otherwise, ask your technical support person for assistance.

TROUBLE? If a connection dialog box appears, you are probably not connected to the Internet. Click the Connect button and follow the directions that appear on your screen. If you are prompted to enter your username and password and you do not know them, consult your technical support person.

TROUBLE? If the Internet Connection Wizard starts, click the Cancel button and the Yes button twice to exit the wizard. Contact your instructor or technical support person about setting up an Internet account on your computer.

2. If necessary, click the **Maximize** button . Figure 5-34 shows the maximized Outlook Express window.

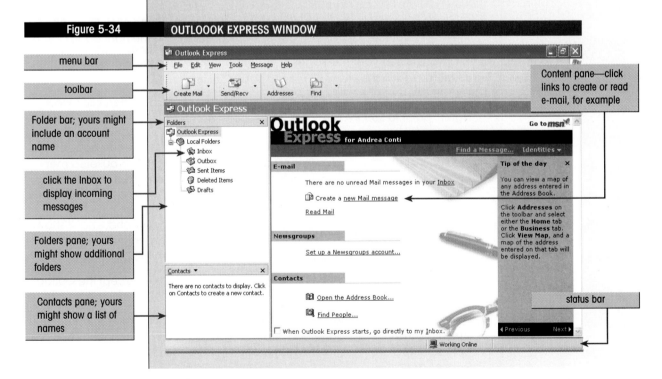

Figure 5-34	OUTLOOOK EXPRESS WINDOW

Figure 5-35 lists the components you can customize in the Outlook Express window.

Figure 5-35	COMPONENTS TO CUSTOMIZE IN THE OUTLOOK EXPRESS WINDOW
COMPONENT	**DESCRIPTION**
Contacts pane	Lists people whose e-mail addresses or other contact information you have saved
Folder bar	Identifies the current mail folder
Folders pane	Displays the hierarchy of mail folders that you can use to store and organize messages
Outlook bar	Contains icons for the folders in the Folders list (because this repeats the information in the Folders list, you don't need to view it unless you find it easier to use than the Folders list)
Status bar	Displays messages about the current folder
Toolbar	Displays the toolbar buttons used to accomplish most tasks
Info pane	An informational window at the bottom of the Outlook Express window, which may not be an available option for you, depending on how Outlook Express is installed on your computer
Content pane	Shows links you can click to perform typical Outlook Express tasks; can also show a list of messages you have sent or received

Before you start using Outlook Express, first ensure that your Outlook Express window matches the one shown in the figures.

To set up the Outlook Express window:

1. Click the **Inbox** icon in the Folders list.

   TROUBLE? If you see more than one Inbox on the Folders list, you might have more than one mail account. Click Inbox under Local Folders.

2. Click **View** on the menu bar, point to **Current View**, and then click **Show All Messages**, if necessary, so you can view all messages in the right pane.

   You want to sort your messages in the order they were received, in ascending order (newest first).

3. If necessary, click **View**, point to **Sort By**, click **Received**, and then click **View** again, point to **Sort By**, and click **Sort Ascending**.

   TROUBLE? If the Received and Sort Ascending options are already bulleted in the Sort By list, you can skip Steps 2 and 3. Note that clicking a bulleted menu option does not deselect it. Clicking a checked menu option, however, does deselect the option.

4. To change the arrangement of the Outlook Express window and what it shows, click **View** and then click **Layout**. The Window Layout Properties dialog box opens, listing the items you can hide or show in the Outlook Express window.

5. In the Basic area, make sure all check boxes are checked *except* the Outlook Bar and Views Bar.

6. In the Preview Pane area of the Window Layout Properties dialog box, make sure the **Show preview pane** and **Show preview pane header** check boxes are both selected and that the **Below messages** option button is selected. See Figure 5-36.

Figure 5-36	CHECKING OUTLOOK EXPRESS LAYOUT

only these two check boxes should not be selected; if the Info Pane is also an option in the Basic list, leave that unselected as well

Preview Pane options

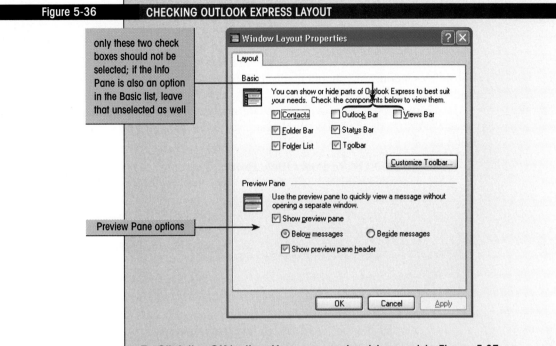

7. Click the **OK** button. Your screen should resemble Figure 5-37.

Figure 5-37	DEFAULT OUTLOOK EXPRESS WINDOW

message list appears here; yours might display messages you've already received

Preview pane displays contents of selected message; it is empty now because the message list contains no messages

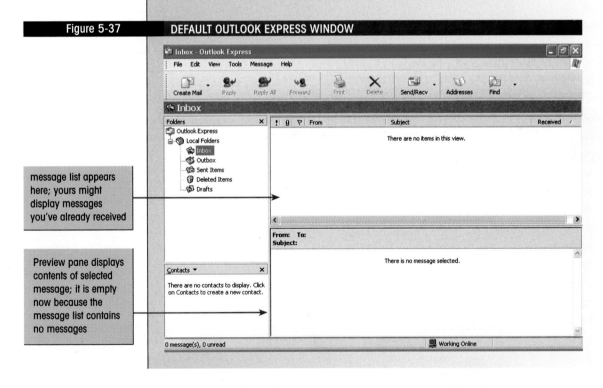

Now that you have ensured that your window matches the one shown in the figures, you are ready to check the status of your e-mail account using Outlook Express.

Setting Up an Outlook Express Account

Once you have an account with a mail service provider (usually this is your ISP), you add your account to Outlook Express. If you are in a university or other institution, this has probably been done for you, but if you are using your own computer, you will probably have to add it yourself.

Most Internet service providers include mail service as part of their Internet services package. What type of mail account you choose depends on how you plan to access your mail. Outlook Express supports POP, IMAP, and HTTP account types.

- With a **POP**, or **Post Office Protocol** account, your mail server receives incoming mail and delivers it to your computer. Once messages are delivered, they are usually deleted from the mail server. POP accounts work best when you have only a single computer, since POP is designed for offline mail access. To receive POP mail if you are away from your computer, you must be able to set up a POP mail account on a different computer—an impossibility in many places.

- With an **IMAP**, or **Internet Message Access Protocol** account, mail is stored on a mail server, not on your computer. Thus you can access your mail from any computer on which you have an account, without having to transfer files back and forth between computers.

- With an **HTTP** account, known as **Web-based e-mail**, you use the same HTTP protocol used on the Web. You set up an account with a Web-based e-mail provider, and your mail is stored on that provider's mail server. You can access your messages from any Web browser. Libraries, hotels, airports, and banks are increasingly making computers with Web access available to the public, so you don't need to own a computer to use Web-based e-mail. Moreover, Web-based e-mail accounts are often free. However, because messages are stored on a server and not on your local computer, mail retrieval is limited by the speed of your Internet connection. Web-based accounts currently don't offer the same breadth of features you find with a traditional e-mail program. The largest provider of free Web-based e-mail is **Hotmail**, a Microsoft service that is made available from Internet Explorer via the Links toolbar or from Outlook Express when you set up a new mail account. Outlook Express allows you to add a Hotmail account to your Folders list, and it treats incoming mail just as it would in a POP account. Hotmail also allows you to check POP mail.

Before you can send and receive e-mail messages, you need an e-mail account with an ISP or other provider, and then you need to provide Outlook with the appropriate information to access this account.

REFERENCE WINDOW | **RW**

Setting Up an E-Mail Account
- In the Outlook Express window, click Tools and then click Accounts.
- Click the Add button.
- Click Mail. Follow the steps in the Internet Connection Wizard.

The following steps will help you determine whether or not you already have a mail account. If you don't, you will need to set one up before you can continue with this tutorial. Outlook Express can help you with this task. You can set up a Hotmail account almost instantaneously, but to set up a POP or IMAP account, you will need to provide the account information, such as your incoming and outgoing mail server address and type, your username and password, and your e-mail address.

To examine your mail account:

1. Click **Tools** on the menu bar, and then click **Accounts** to open the Internet Accounts dialog box.

2. Click the **Mail** tab, if necessary. See Figure 5-38, which shows one mail account already set up.

Figure 5-38	MAIL ACCOUNTS

accounts that have been set up appear here (you might not have any, or you might have several)

click to set up a new mail account

3. Click the account you want to use.

TROUBLE? If no account with your name is listed, no account has been set up for you. You can set up an account yourself by clicking the Add button and then clicking Mail to start the Internet Connection Wizard. This Wizard walks you through the steps of setting up a mail account. If you do not know the answers to all the questions the Wizard asks, you will need to get further assistance from your technical support person or your Internet service provider.

4. Click the **Properties** button. Your name and e-mail address should appear in the account Properties dialog box; Outlook Express uses this information when you send and receive e-mail. See Figure 5-39.

Figure 5-39   CONFIGURING E-MAIL PROPERTIES

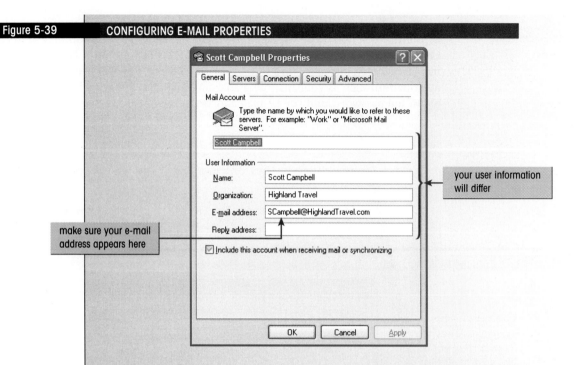

make sure your e-mail address appears here

your user information will differ

TROUBLE? If your new mail account doesn't appear in the list of accounts, click the Close button in the Internet Accounts dialog box, click No to answer the question about downloading services and then repeat Steps 1 through 4. Your account should appear. If the name and e-mail address boxes are blank, ask your instructor or technical support person what to enter in them.

5. Click the **Servers** tab (your tab may be labeled "server") to check your mail server information. Your account name (userID) and password should appear, along with information about your mail server. (Your password will appear as a series of bullets for security.) For an HTTP account such as Hotmail, you would see the URL of the mail provider's Web page, but Highland Travel uses POP accounts, so each account must identify the incoming and outgoing mail server address, as shown in Figure 5-40.

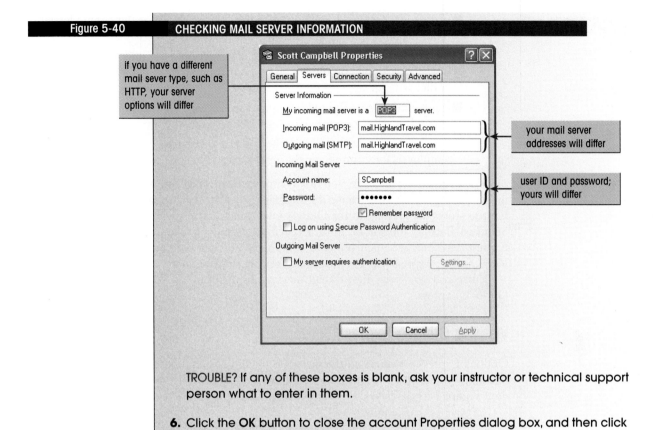

Figure 5-40   CHECKING MAIL SERVER INFORMATION

if you have a different mail sever type, such as HTTP, your server options will differ

your mail server addresses will differ

user ID and password; yours will differ

TROUBLE? If any of these boxes is blank, ask your instructor or technical support person what to enter in them.

6. Click the **OK** button to close the account Properties dialog box, and then click the **Close** button in the Internet Accounts dialog box.

Now that you have ensured that Outlook Express can handle your e-mail, you're ready to send e-mail messages.

Sending E-Mail

An e-mail message uses the same format as a standard memo: it typically includes From, Date, To, and Subject lines, followed by the content of the message. The **To line** indicates who will receive the message. Outlook Express automatically supplies your name or e-mail address in the **From line** and the date you send the message in the Date line (as set in your computer's clock). The **Subject line**, although optional, alerts the recipient to the topic of the message. Finally, the **message area** contains the content of your message. You can also include additional information, such as a **Cc line**, which indicates who will receive a copy of the message, or a Priority setting, which indicates the importance of the message.

When you prepare an e-mail message, you should remember some common-sense guidelines:

■ Think before you type; read before you send. Your name and your institution's name are attached to everything you send.

■ Type both uppercase and lowercase letters. Using all uppercase letters in e-mail messages is considered shouting, and messages in all lowercase letters are difficult to read and decipher.

■ Edit your message. Keep your message concise so the reader can understand your meaning quickly and clearly.

■ Send appropriate amounts of useful information. Like junk mail, e-mail messages can pile up quickly. If you must send a longer message, attach it as a file.

■ Find out if personal e-mail messages are allowed on a work account. E-mail is not free. (Businesses pay to subscribe to a server.)

■ E-mail at your workplace or school is not necessarily confidential. Your employer, for example, might be able to access your e-mail.

To send an e-mail message, you first compose the message and then click the Send button in the message window. Because it's inefficient to send the message immediately, Outlook Express stores the message in the Outbox folder until you click the Send/Recv button on the Standard Buttons toolbar or until a specified period of time has passed. Then Outlook Express sends the message from your computer to the network, which routes it to the recipient. Outlook Express lists the messages it sent in the Sent folder.

Before you send your first e-mail message in this tutorial, you'll explore the folders in Outlook Express.

Viewing Outlook Express Folders

Outlook Express organizes all the messages it handles, outgoing and incoming, into folders that allow you to sort your messages, located in the Folders list in the Outlook Express window. Figure 5-41 describes the Outlook Express folders that you can use to store mail.

Figure 5-41	OUTLOOK EXPRESS FOLDERS
FOLDER	**DESCRIPTION**
Inbox	Stores messages that have just been delivered and messages that you've read but haven't discarded or filed
Outbox	Stores messages that you've finished composing and plan to send as soon as you connect to your mail server
Sent Items	Stores a copy of every message you've sent until you discard or file them
Deleted Items	Stores the messages you've discarded; they remain in this folder until you delete them from here, and then they are irretrievable
Drafts	Stores messages that you have written but not finished

When a folder contains one or more messages that you have not sent or read, the folder name appears in boldface and Outlook Express places the number of new or pending messages in that folder within parentheses.

The name of any folder that contains subfolders is preceded by a plus box ⊞ or minus box ⊟ in the Folders list. When ⊞ appears in front of a folder's name, its subfolders are hidden. When ⊟ appears, its subfolders are visible. Outlook Express automatically starts with Local Folders open. To see the contents of a folder, you click its name in the Folders list.

To work with Outlook Express folders:

1. Click **Outbox** in the Folders pane. It will probably be empty, unless you have other outgoing mail. See Figure 5-42.

| Figure 5-42 | VIEWING THE OUTBOX FOLDER |

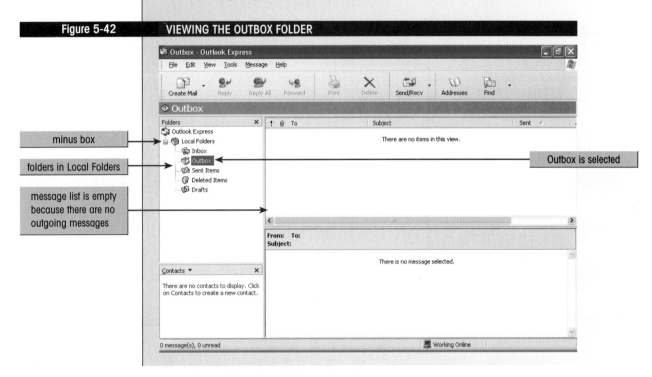

Now you're ready to compose and send your first message.

REFERENCE WINDOW — **RW**

Sending an E-Mail Message

- Click the Create Mail button.
- Enter the e-mail address of the recipient in the To box.
- Press the Tab key until you reach the Subject box, and then type the subject of the message.
- Press the Tab key and then type the content of the message in the message area.
- Click the Send button.

After you compose a message and click the Send button, Outlook Express places the message in the Outbox and then sends it immediately if you're connected to your mail server and if you haven't changed Outlook's default settings. Because you've opened the Outbox, you'll be able to watch this happen. Remembering that Scott wanted you to contact Katie Herrera about a Highland Travel golf tour as soon as you got settled, you decide to compose your first message to her. Her e-mail address is kherrera@highlandtravel.com.

To send an e-mail message:

1. Click the **Create Mail** button 📭. The New Message window opens, which allows you to compose a new message. See Figure 5-43.

Figure 5-43   **THE NEW MESSAGE WINDOW**

click the Send button when you're ready to send the message to the Outbox

type the recipient's e-mail address in the To text box

type a subject to describe the message

type your message here

TROUBLE? If you receive an error message at any point during these steps, check your mail server properties using the procedure you learned in the previous section. Write down your settings and then ask your instructor or technical support person for help.

TROUBLE? If you have more than one account, be aware that in the outgoing message, Outlook Express identifies the sender for the currently selected account. If, for example, you want to send a message from your Hotmail account, click Hotmail in the Folders list before you click the New Mail button.

2. Type **kherrera@highlandtravel.com** in the To text box, and then press the **Tab** key.

3. Type your own e-mail address in the Cc text box, and then press the **Tab** key. Note that normally you would not copy yourself on an e-mail sent to another person. You are sending a copy to yourself only to ensure that you will receive mail later for practice in other sections of this tutorial.

4. Type **Golf Tour** in the Subject text box, and then press the **Tab** key.

5. Type the following message in the content area:

Scott Campbell suggested I contact you regarding the new St. Andrews Golf Tour we're starting next summer.

Thank you,

(your name)

As you send the message, make sure you are watching the Outbox. Read all of Step 6 before you perform it, so you know what to watch for.

6. Click the **Send** button 🔲. Outlook Express moves your message into the
Outbox; the Outbox is briefly boldfaced and followed by a (1) in the Local
Folders list, indicating there is one outgoing message. See Figure 5-44.

Figure 5-44	SENDING A MESSAGE

Outlook Express sends the message. The message and the (1) disappear, the
Outbox is empty, and the Outbox is no longer boldfaced in the list.

TROUBLE? If Outlook Express does not send the message immediately and the
(1) does not disappear, Outlook Express might be configured only to send
messages when you click the Send/Recv button 🔲. Click 🔲, and watch
Outlook Express send the message. Note that you may also receive new messages at this point. You'll learn how to access and read new messages shortly.
If you want to change this setting, click Tools, click Options, click the Send tab,
click the Send messages immediately check box, and then click OK to indicate that you want outgoing mail sent immediately.

TROUBLE? If Outlook Express requests a password, you might need to enter a
password before you can send and receive your mail messages.

The time it takes to send an e-mail message depends on the size of the message, the
speed of your Internet connection, and the quantity of Internet traffic at that time. When
you send an e-mail, your outgoing mail server examines the host name in the e-mail address,
locates the host, and delivers the message to that host. Because your mail server is not connected to every other host, e-mail is rarely sent along a direct path to the recipient. Instead,
the message is handed from one host to another until the e-mail reaches its destination.
Figure 5-45 shows how the Internet routes a message from a student at the University of
Alaska to a student at the University of the Virgin Islands.

Figure 5-45   INTERNET E-MAIL ROUTES

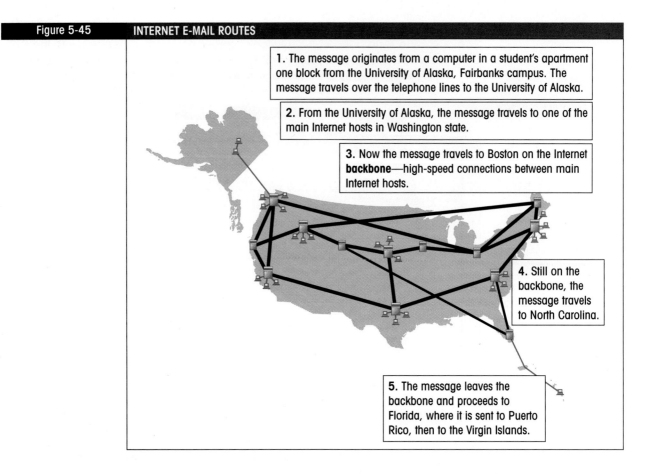

1. The message originates from a computer in a student's apartment one block from the University of Alaska, Fairbanks campus. The message travels over the telephone lines to the University of Alaska.

2. From the University of Alaska, the message travels to one of the main Internet hosts in Washington state.

3. Now the message travels to Boston on the Internet **backbone**—high-speed connections between main Internet hosts.

4. Still on the backbone, the message travels to North Carolina.

5. The message leaves the backbone and proceeds to Florida, where it is sent to Puerto Rico, then to the Virgin Islands.

Receiving E-Mail

How you receive e-mail depends on your account. For example, if you are using a Web-based account, you connect to your provider's Web page and view your messages there. If you are using a POP account, your mail server collects your mail and holds it until your mail program contacts the mail server and requests any mail addressed to your user ID. Your mail program then downloads any waiting messages to your computer. (Remember that the Outlook Express mail program allows you to set up a Hotmail account so that it too can receive local mail delivery.)

You can check your e-mail at any time by clicking the Send/Recv button 📧 in Outlook Express. Your mail server delivers any e-mail messages that have arrived since you last checked and sends any messages currently in the Outbox. Some people check for new e-mail messages sporadically during the day, while others check at regular intervals, such as every hour or every morning and evening. If you are always connected to the Internet, Outlook Express automatically checks for messages at a specified interval. You can set this interval on the General tab of the Options dialog box. You access the Options dialog box from the Tools menu.

Remember that you sent a copy of your e-mail to yourself for the purpose of completing this tutorial. You'll now check to see whether the copy arrived.

To check for incoming mail:

1. Click the **Send/Recv** button 📧. If a dialog box opens requesting your password, enter your password and follow the instructions in the dialog box.

2. Click **Inbox** in the Folders list. New messages appear in the message list, and a number in parentheses appears, indicating the number of new messages you've received. See Figure 5-46. Your Inbox folder might contain additional e-mail messages from other people.

Figure 5-46	RECEIVING MESSAGES

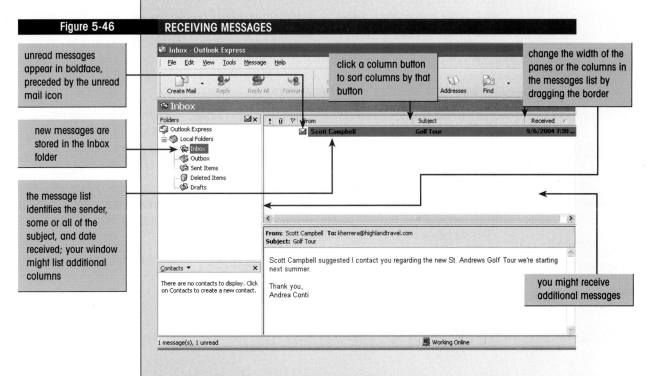

unread messages appear in boldface, preceded by the unread mail icon

new messages are stored in the Inbox folder

the message list identifies the sender, some or all of the subject, and date received; your window might list additional columns

click a column button to sort columns by that button

change the width of the panes or the columns in the messages list by dragging the border

you might receive additional messages

TROUBLE? If you receive a returned mail message in addition to the copy of your message to Katie, don't worry. This happens because the e-mail address you are using for Katie Herrera is fictional. You'll learn more about returned mail shortly.

TROUBLE? If enough time has elapsed since you sent the message, Outlook Express might have checked for incoming mail already. If that's the case, the copy should already appear. If no messages appear, your mail server might not have received or sent the messages yet. Occasionally, some mail servers cause mail to be delayed. Check later to see if your mail has arrived, or consult your technical support person.

Unread messages appear in boldface, preceded by the unread mail icon 📧. The message list displays a message header for each message, which identifies the sender, subject (truncated if it's too long), and date received. Your window might list additional columns. You can change the width of the columns in the message list by dragging the column header border in the appropriate direction. You can also click a column button to sort columns by that button. For example, if you click the From button, Outlook Express sorts messages in the current folder alphabetically by name. The default sort order is by date and time received, with newest messages at the top. Note that the sender shown in Figure 5-46 is Scott Campbell. The sender on your computer will differ.

The message list displays a variety of icons that help you determine the status of the message. For example, ✉ tells you the message has been read; ✉ tells you the message has not been read; ✉ tells you the message is in progress in the Drafts folder.

You can view a message in its own window or in the preview pane. If you click to select an e-mail message from the message list, the contents of that message appear in the preview pane. If you double-click a message from the message list, a separate message window opens. Either way, after a predetermined number of seconds, the message header no longer appears in boldface, indicating that you've opened, or displayed, the message. You already saw how you can hide the preview pane if you want to view only the message list. You can also resize the preview pane by dragging its upper border up or down. For example, to enlarge the preview so you can see more of a message, drag the top border of the pane up.

Your Inbox should contain the copy of the message you sent yourself. Read it now.

To read an e-mail message:

1. If necessary, click the message you sent yourself, which has the subject "Golf Tour" in the message list. The contents of that message appear in the preview pane. After a few seconds (five seconds is the default), the Unread icon ✉ changes to Read ✉, and the message no longer appears in boldface.

2. Now try adjusting the column widths. You can use the same technique you used when you resized the panes in the Windows Explorer window. Point to the vertical line that forms one of the column borders until your pointer changes to ↔.

3. Drag the pointer slightly to the right to see more of the column, or to the left to see less.

   TROUBLE? Your window may show additional columns. You can determine what information to display by clicking View, clicking Columns, and then removing the check from the box of the column display you wish to suppress.

By successfully viewing the copy of the message you sent to yourself, you've verified that Outlook Express is configured properly on your computer.

Handling **Undelivered Messages**

Sometimes you send an e-mail message to an Internet address that is no longer active, for example, when a person switches to a different ISP. When an outgoing mail server cannot locate a recipient's address, it sends an undeliverable mail message to the sender. This is similar to the postal service returning a letter because the street address is incorrect.

Because Katie's e-mail address is fictional, you will probably receive a returned mail message from the mail delivery subsystem of your outgoing mail server, telling you that the host was not found. Check for this message now.

To read a returned mail message:

1. Click the **Send/Recv** button 📧.

2. Click a message with "Returned mail" or something similar in the Subject column.

> **TROUBLE?** If no such message appears now, check again later. It might take a few minutes for the message to be routed to you.
>
> **3.** Read the message. It should inform you that the e-mail address had an unknown host.

If e-mail messages you send are returned undelivered, you should verify the e-mail addresses that you used. Make sure that everything is typed correctly and that the person is still using that e-mail address.

Replying to a Message

Often, you'll want to respond to an e-mail message. Although you could create and send a new message, it's easier to use the Reply feature, which automatically inserts the e-mail address of the sender and the subject into the proper lines in the message window. The Reply feature also "quotes" the sender's text to remind the sender of the message to which you are responding. When you reply to an e-mail message, you can respond to the original sender of the message, or to the sender and everyone else who received the message.

You're first going to view the message you sent yourself, this time in its own window, and then you're going to practice replying to it. To open a message in its own window, double-click the message in the message list. This allows you to display more of the message at once.

Note that this is a practice reply. Normally, you would not reply to yourself! Rather, you would reply to someone who sent you a real message.

To open a message in its own window and then reply to it:

1. Double-click the **Golf Tour** message in the Sent Items list. The message opens in its own window. Maximize this window if necessary.

2. Click the **Reply** button 🖳. The message window opens, with your name in the To box (because you're replying to your own message) and the original message's subject in the Subject box, preceded by "Re:", which means "regarding." The message quotes your original message.

3. Type the following reply in the message area. (The insertion point automatically blinks at the beginning of a blank line.)

Thanks for the information.

(your name)

4. If necessary, scroll down to see how the original text of the message is quoted after the reply you just typed. See Figure 5-47.

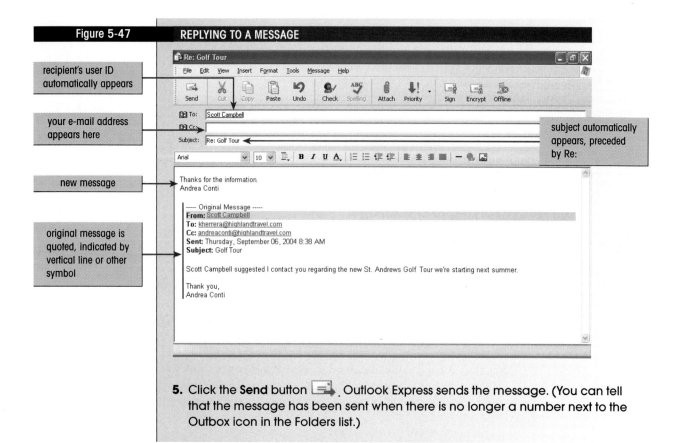

| Figure 5-47 | REPLYING TO A MESSAGE |

recipient's user ID automatically appears

your e-mail address appears here

subject automatically appears, preceded by Re:

new message

original message is quoted, indicated by vertical line or other symbol

5. Click the **Send** button. Outlook Express sends the message. (You can tell that the message has been sent when there is no longer a number next to the Outbox icon in the Folders list.)

Deciding whether to quote the sender's original message when you reply to a message depends on several factors. If the recipient might need to be reminded of the message content, it's appropriate to quote. However, long messages take longer to download, so whenever possible you should delete quoted material from your messages.

Printing a Message

You can print an e-mail message using the File menu's Print command. You decide to print the message you received from yourself.

To print an e-mail message:

1. Make sure the message you received is either open in its own window or selected in the message list.

2. Click **File** on the menu bar, and then click **Print**.

3. Check the print settings in the Print dialog box, and then click the **Print** button. The message prints on the printer specified in the Print dialog box.

4. If necessary, click the **Close** button to close the message.

5. Close Outlook Express.

By default, Outlook Express formats messages using HTML. When you print a message formatted in HTML, it includes lines and boldface headings. However, if the message you are printing uses plain text instead of HTML, the printout will not contain formatting, and some of the lines might be uneven. You can change this setting by clicking Tools, clicking Options, and then specifying HTML on the Send tab. Your messages will then be sent formatted. If you need a high-quality printout of a plain text message, you can save the message as a text file, open it in a word processor, and edit it there so that it looks professional.

Scott has now finished your training on e-mail. As you continue to work with Outlook Express, you'll see other ways in which e-mail can be integrated with the workings of Windows XP and the Web.

Session 5.3 QUICK CHECK

1. What is a mail server?

2. Identify the user ID portion and the host name portion of the following e-mail address: pcsmith@icom.net.

3. How can you view your mail account properties in Outlook Express?

4. Where can you find a copy of a message you sent?

5. Why shouldn't you type your messages in all uppercase letters?

6. Name two advantages the Reply feature has over the New Mail feature when you are responding to an e-mail.

REVIEW ASSIGNMENTS

1. *History of the Internet and the World Wide Web* Computers have been around for several decades now, but how did the Internet and the World Wide Web get started? Microsoft considered the Internet an important enough development to incorporate many of its features into the Windows XP operating system. Go to the library or use the Internet itself to locate books or articles on the Internet, and write a single-page essay on the history of the Internet. Answer questions such as:
   a. What role did the ARPANET play in the development of the Internet?
   b. What role did CERN play in the development of the World Wide Web?
   c. Over what period of time did the Internet grow? What about the World Wide Web?
   d. When did browsers first become available?

2. *Connecting to the Internet over a Modem* This tutorial mentioned that home computer users can connect to the Internet using a dial-up connection via an account with an ISP. Assume you have your own computer, and you want to connect to the Internet from home. Contact at least three ISPs in your area, ask for their rates and services, and then write a single-page essay describing your findings. Which ISP would you choose, and why?

3. *Exploring Your Home Page* In this tutorial, the figures showed the MSN home page as the home page. Your home page might be different—take some time to explore.
   a. Start the Internet Explorer browser, and print your home page.
   b. Click one of the links on your home page, and continue to click any interesting links that you encounter. Clicking whatever links interest you is often called "surfing." On your printout, circle the link you followed. Write in the margin where it took you.

    c. Use the Home button to return to your home page, click another link, and then go where it leads you. Again, circle the link on your printout, indicate where you ended up, and write what you saw along the way.

4. *Connecting to Specific Web Sites* You learned in this tutorial that you can enter a URL in the Address box of your browser to connect to a specific Web site. Using the Internet Explorer browser, enter the following URLs and print the first page of each URL.

    a. http://www.usps.gov
    b. http://www.nps.gov
    c. http://www.cnn.com
    d. Using any one of these pages as a starting point, follow links until you locate a page with frames. Record the URL of the page you found.

5. *Web Page Desktop Background* Because he will be placing the Highland Web page on your desktop soon, Scott wants you to practice using a Web page as a desktop background.

    a. Apply the Highland Web page (not the folder), located in the root directory of your Data Disk, as your desktop background.
    b. Observe the background carefully and work with the objects that are incorporated into this Web page.
    c. Connect to the Active Desktop Gallery, and add a desktop item that would add to the usefulness of this desktop.
    d. Using the Highland desktop you just created as an example, write two paragraphs describing what a Web page background offers that a graphic image file, such as you used in Tutorial 4, does not. Give detailed information about the purpose of each element on the desktop.
    e. Restore your computer's background to its original state.

Explore

6. *E-Mailing a Web Page and a Link* Scott wants you to share the Highland Travel Home Page with some potential clients. Internet Explorer provides tools to easily e-mail either the entire Web page or a link to the page.

    a. Connect to the Internet and open the Highland Travel Home Page in Internet Explorer.
    b. Click the Mail button 🖂 on the Standard Buttons toolbar, and click Send a Link to send a link to the home page to your instructor.
    c. Click the Mail button 🖂 , and send the entire Web page to your instructor.
    d. What problems might there be in sending a Web page to a user? What should you know about the user's e-mail program before attempting to send the page?

Explore

7. *Editing the Links Toolbar* Scott tells you that the Links toolbar is another place, besides the Favorites folder, where you can place shortcuts to your favorite Web sites. The Links toolbar is one of the Internet Explorer toolbars that displays icons for specific Web sites. Scott wants you to learn how to use it.

    a. Start Internet Explorer and display the Links toolbar in the Web browser. (Click View on the menu bar, click Toolbars, and then click—if necessary—to place a check mark next to Links.)
    b. Click the double arrow on the right side of the Links toolbar, and then click the Customize Links icon.
    c. Print the Web page.
    d. Using the information on this Web page, add a link to the Highland Travel Home Page to the Links toolbar.
    e. Display the Links toolbar on the Windows XP taskbar, making sure that the icon for the Highland Travel home page is visible.
    f. Using the techniques from Tutorial 2, print a copy of your screen with the revised Links toolbar.
    g. Remove the icon for the Highland Travel home page from the Links toolbar.

Explore

8. *Using Rich Text Formatting in E-Mail* Scott tells you that with Outlook Express you can use special fonts and formats to liven up your e-mail messages. You decide to test this by sending an e-mail message to Katie Herrera, telling her of your interest in working on the St. Andrews project.

   a. Start Outlook Express and compose an e-mail message to your instructor with the subject line "St. Andrews Project".

   b. In the message area, enter (in your own words) your interest in the project and willingness to participate.

   c. Turn on formatting for the message by clicking Format on the menu bar of the mail message window and then clicking Rich Text (HTML). In the message area, boldface at least one word and italicize at least one word. To boldface a word, you select it and then click the Bold button **B**. To italicize it, you select it and then click the Italic button *I*.

   d. Now color one word red: select the word, click the Font Color button **A**, and then click the color red.

   e. Send the message to your instructor.

PROJECTS

1. Internet Explorer and Windows Explorer share many of the same menus, commands, and toolbars. In fact, you can modify Windows Explorer to look and operate exactly like Internet Explorer.

   a. Open Windows Explorer.

   b. In the Address bar, enter the URL of your Home page (or use www.msn.com if you don't know the URL of your home page), and then press the Enter key. Connect to the Internet if you are not already connected.

   c. Modify the Explorer Bar so that it displays the Favorites pane.

   d. Using techniques shown in Tutorial 2, print a copy of your screen.

   e. Open the same Web page in Internet Explorer, and display the Favorites pane in that program. Compare the displays of Internet Explorer and Windows Explorer. Can you see any difference between the two?

   f. Microsoft's goal with Windows XP was to create a "single Explorer." Why do you think Microsoft set this goal? What advantages or disadvantages does the single Explorer have?

Explore

2. You have a friend who has used Windows Explorer extensively for managing his own files and folders, and you mention to him that he can also use Windows Explorer as a browser. Test this yourself first by starting Windows Explorer, opening the Favorites pane, and then clicking a link to a Web page. Observe what happens. Write a note to your friend, which you'll e-mail to him, that describes how to use Windows Explorer as a browser. Make sure you describe what happens to elements such as the left and right panes, the Address bar, the activity indicator, and the status bar.

3. In this tutorial, you learned how to access information on the Web when you either knew the URL or used a link to jump there. Internet Explorer also includes the Search Companion pane (like Windows Explorer), which helps you find the Web pages you need. Use Internet Explorer's online Help to learn about the Search Companion pane and about the general topic of searching the Web.

   a. How would you search for information on a given topic?

   b. Once the Search feature displays a list of search results, what should you do to display the Web page containing the information?

   c. Follow the directions you studied in the Help file to search for information on one of your hobbies, such as snowboarding. While you are using the Search Explorer bar, write down the exact steps you take. Was your search successful? Write down the URL of the page you connected to.

4. Internet Explorer also includes the Media pane (like Windows Explorer), which helps you find music, videos, and other multimedia files. Use Internet Explorer online Help to learn about the Media pane and about the general topic of multimedia on your PC.

   a. What kind of information can you find on the Media pane?
   b. What are multimedia files? How can you use them?
   c. Follow the directions you studied in the Help file to find one of your favorite music files. While you are using the Media Explorer bar, write down the exact steps you take. Did you successfully find the music you wanted? Write down the URL of the page you connected to.

5. You just went to California for a three-week vacation with some friends. On returning, you decide to "capture the moment" by downloading a graphic image that will remind you of your vacation activities.

   a. Use what you learned in Project 3 to locate a graphic image of surfing, rock climbing, wine tasting, or some other vacation activity, and download it to your Data Disk. (If you skipped Project 3, connect to the Highland site or your home page, and download a graphic from there.)
   b. Send an e-mail to your instructor containing the image. (You can paste the image into the e-mail document by clicking Insert on the New Message window's title bar.) Then click Picture, click Browse, locate and click the file, and then click OK.

6. Because most labs cannot accommodate subscriptions, you probably will need your own computer to complete this project. Your dream is to plan your investments so you can retire by age 55. To keep yourself posted on the stock market:

   a. Locate a Web site that contains stock market information. You could try http://www.nasdaq.com or http://www.djia.com.
   b. Place this Web page on your desktop as an Active Desktop item. (You can add the Web dialog sheet of the Display Properties dialog box.)
   c. Set up a synchronization schedule for the Web page so that it is automatically updated every morning at 8 AM.
   d. Create a log in Notepad (perhaps using the LOG feature you learned about in Tutorial 4) to record information such as the closing value of an index such as NASDAQ or the Dow on a given day.
   e. When you have recorded three days' worth of information in the log, open the log window and your synchronization schedule, and print your screen so your instructor can see which Web page you subscribed to and what information you gained. Make sure you unsubscribe from the Web page after the three days.

LAB ASSIGNMENTS

The Internet: World Wide Web

The Internet: World Wide Web

One of the most popular services on the Internet is the World Wide Web. This lab is a Web simulator that teaches you how to use Web browser software to find information. You can use this lab whether or not your school provides you with Internet access. See the Read This Before You Begin page for information on starting the lab.

1. Click the Steps button to learn how to use Web browser software. As you proceed through the steps, answer all of the Quick Check questions that appear. After you complete the steps, you will see a Quick Check Summary Report. Follow the instructions on the screen to print this report.

2. Click the Explore button on the Welcome screen. Use the Web browser to locate a weather map of the Caribbean Virgin Islands. What is its URL?

3. A scuba diver named Wadson Lachouffe has been searching for the fabled treasure of Greybeard the pirate. A link from the Adventure Travel Web site www.atour.com leads to Wadson's Web page called "Hidden Treasure." In Explore, locate the Hidden Treasure page, and answer the following questions:

   a. What was the name of Greybeard's ship?
   b. What was Greybeard's favorite food?
   c. What does Wadson think happened to Greybeard's ship?

4. In the steps, you found a graphic of Jupiter from the photo archives of the Jet Propulsion Laboratory. In the Explore section of the lab, you can also find a graphic of Saturn. Suppose one of your friends wanted a picture of Saturn for an astronomy report. Make a list of the blue, underlined links your friend must click, in the correct order, to find the Saturn graphic. Assume that your friend will begin at the Web Trainer home page.

5. Enter the URL http://www.atour.com to jump to the Adventure Travel Web site. Write a one-page description of this site. In your paper, include a description of the information at the site, the number of pages the site contains, and a diagram of the links it contains.

6. Chris Thomson is a student at UVI and has his own Web pages. In Explore, look at the information Chris has included on his pages. Suppose you could create your own Web page. What would you include? Use word-processing software to design your own Web page. Make sure you indicate the graphics and links you would use.

Web Pages & HTML

It's easy to create your own Web pages. There are many software tools to help you become a Web author. In this lab, you'll experiment with a Web-authoring Wizard that automates the process of creating a Web page. You'll also try your hand at working directly with HTML code. See the Read This Before You Begin page for information on starting the lab.

1. Click the Steps button to activate the Web-authoring Wizard and learn how to create a basic Web page. As you proceed through the steps, answer all of the Quick Check questions. After you complete the steps, you will see a Quick Check Summary Report. Follow the instructions on the screen to print this report.

2. In Explore, click the File menu, then click New to start working on a new Web page. Use the Wizard to create a home page for a veterinarian who offers dog day-care and boarding services. After you create the page, save it on drive A or C, and print the HTML code. Your site must have the following characteristics:

   a. Title: Dr. Dave's Dog Domain
   b. Background color: Gold
   c. Graphic: Dog.jpg
   d. Body text: Your dog will have the best care day and night at Dr. Dave's Dog Domain. Fine accommodations, good food, playtime, and snacks are all provided. You can board your pet by the day or week. Grooming services also available.
   e. Text link: "Reasonable rates" links to www.cciw.com/np3/rates.htm
   f. E-mail link: "For more information:" links to daveassist@drdave.com

3. In Explore, use the File menu to open the HTML document called Politics.htm. After you use the HTML window (not the Wizard) to make the following changes, save the revised page on drive A or C, and print the HTML code. Refer to Figure 5-48 for a list of HTML tags you can use:

Figure 5-48

HTML TAGS	MEANING AND LOCATION
<HTML></HTML>	States that the file is an HTML document; opening tag begins the page; closing tag ends the page (required)
<HEAD></HEAD>	States that the enclosed text is the header of the page; appears immediately after the opening HTML tag (required)
<TITLE></TITLE>	States that the enclosed text is the title of the page; must appear within the opening and closing HEAD tags (required)
<BODY></BODY>	States that the enclosed material (all the text, images, and tags in the rest of the document) is the body of the document (required)
<H1></H1>	States that the enclosed text is a heading
 	Inserts a line break; can be used to control line spacing and breaks in lines
<UL></UL> <OL></OL>	Indicates an unordered list (list items are preceded by bullets) or an ordered list (list items are preceded by numbers or letters)
<LI>	Indicates a list item; precedes all items in unordered or ordered lists
<CENTER></CENTER>	Indicates that the enclosed text should be centered on the width of the page
<B></B>	Indicates that the enclosed text should appear in boldface
<I></I>	Indicates that the enclosed text should appear in italics
<A HREF="*URL*"></A>	Indicates that the enclosed text is a hypertext link; the URL of the linked material must appear within the quotation marks after the equal sign
<IMG SRC="*filename*">	Inserts an inline image into the document where *filename* is the name of the image
<HR>	Inserts a horizontal rule

   a. Change the title to Politics 2000.

   b. Center the page heading.

   c. Change the background color to FFE7C6 and the text color to 000000.

   d. Add a line break before the sentence, "What's next?"

   e. Add a bold tag to "Additional links on this topic:"

   f. Add one more link to the "Additional links" list. The link should go to the site http://www.elections.ca, and the clickable link should read "Elections Canada".

   g. Change the last graphic to display the image "next.gif".

4. In Explore, use the Web-authoring Wizard and the HTML window to create a home page about yourself. You should include at least a screenful of text, a graphic, an external link, and an e-mail link. Save the page on drive A, then print the HTML code. Turn in your disk and printout.

Quick | Check Answers

Session 5.1

1. A home page is the Web page designated by the browser as your starting point, the Web page that an organization or business has created to give information about itself, or a personal Web page with information about an individual.

2. URL

3. Type the URL in the Address box, then press Enter.

4. It is an educational site.

5. site

6. Open the History pane in Internet Explorer. You can then try to locate the page by viewing the list of pages you accessed on a particular day, or you can search the contents of the History pane to locate it.

7. False

8. Right-click the image, click Save Picture As, enter a filename and destination folder, and then click Save. Or click the Save as button on the shortcut toolbar, enter a filename and destination folder, and then click Save.

Session 5.2

1. With offline viewing, your computer can access a Web page or file from a network so that you can view it later without being connected to the network.

2. Push technology allows both Web site authors and subscribers to gain more control over content delivery and schedule.

3. Active Desktop item

4. Synchronization is a process by which an offline file is updated with the most recent version of the network file.

5. Right-click the object and open its Properties dialog box. On the Schedule dialog sheet, add 24 new schedules, one for each hour of the day.

6. Hypertext Markup Language, the underlying language of Web documents

7. You can add special items such as animated graphics, links to files and Web pages, and applets to run programs for you from the desktop.

Session 5.3

1. A mail server is a computer on a network that manages the storage and delivery of electronic mail.

2. User ID: pcsmith; host name: icom.net

3. Click Tools, click Accounts, click the Mail tab, click the account with your name, and then click the Properties button.

4. the Sent Items folder

5. The recipient might interpret the uppercase letters as shouting—considered rude in most e-mail exchanges.

6. The recipient's e-mail address is automatically inserted, the subject is automatically inserted, and the original message is automatically quoted.

OBJECTIVES

In this tutorial you will:

- Find files by name, contents, and location using several methods, including wildcards

- Open and work with files from the Search Results window

- Limit a search to a specific folder

- Locate files by date, type, and size

- Search for information on the Internet

- Search for people and maps on the Internet

- Change search preferences

SEARCHING
FOR INFORMATION

Using the Search Feature to Locate Files for a Speechwriter

CASE

Speechwriter's Aide

Like thousands of other college students who are graduating soon, you've been visiting the campus job center regularly. Today, you notice that Senator Susannah Bernstein's speechwriter has posted an advertisement for an aide. When you call to inquire, Carolyn King, the senator's speechwriter, asks you to come by the next morning. Your interview goes very well. You learn that the job primarily involves locating information that Carolyn could use in writing the senator's speeches. Carolyn explains that her previous aide collected and organized information in a filing cabinet. In addition to the paper archive, the previous aide started an electronic quotations archive that includes over 100 files on a 3½-inch disk. These files contain anecdotes, jokes, and commentaries on a variety of subjects.

You explain to Carolyn that you could retrieve information efficiently if you had a computer running Windows XP with an Internet connection. Windows XP includes a powerful search tool called **Search** that helps you find files on local or network drives and helps you search for information on the Internet. The Internet contains a vast number of computers and networks that store information, which you can find and retrieve using the Search tool. With Windows XP and an Internet connection, you can use your office computer to access information from around the world. Carolyn is intrigued and by the end of the interview, she offers you the job.

After a week of training and orientation, Carolyn assigns you office space that includes a computer running Windows XP and an Internet connection. She promises that your first assignment will come soon and in the meantime, asks you to become familiar with the information on the quotations archive disk. You will use the Windows XP Search tool to do this.

SESSION 6.1

In this session, you will learn techniques for searching for files by their filenames, by the text they contain, and by file date, type, and size.

Search Strategies

As you install programs and store data on your computer, the number of files and folders you have increases. You have already learned to use My Computer and Windows Explorer to organize your files and folders. Windows XP offers another tool to help you find files so you can access the information they contain. Use the **Search tool** to find any kind of file, whether you know its complete name, partial name, or other facts, such as text the file contains, the file type (for example, a WordPad document or a Paint graphic), or the date the file was created or modified.

The Search tool provides many options that help you define and narrow your search so you can quickly find one or more files. Before you use Search, you should develop a strategy for finding the files you want. Determine what you already know about the files, and then choose the appropriate Search option. Figure 6-1 lists the search methods you can use to find files, and guidelines for when to choose a particular method.

Figure 6-1	SEARCH STRATEGIES	
SEARCH BY	**DESCRIPTION**	**WHEN TO USE**
Filename	Provide all or part of the filename	You know some or all of the filename Example: You want to find all the files related to the Hawthorne Company and know that the filenames include "Hawthorne," but don't know where the files are stored
Keyword	Provide text that appears in the file's contents	You know text that the files contain Example: You want to find a file that contains quotations by Albert Einstein but don't remember the name of the file
Location	Identify the drive or folder containing the file	You know where you stored the files you want Example: You want to find all the budget files in the budget 2004 folder but don't want to navigate your computer's file system
Date	Specify a date or range of dates when files were created, modified or accessed	You know when the files were created, modified, or accessed Example: You want to find a file you created last week but can't remember its name or location
Size	Specify the size of the files	You know the approximate or exact size of the files Example: You want to find files that are larger than 1 MB but don't know where they are stored
Type	Identify the file type, such as .doc or .bmp	You know the file type Example: You want to find an Excel (.xls) file but don't remember its filename

Note that you also can use the search strategies in combination. For example, if you are looking for a file you modified last month in a folder called "Budgets," you can speed the search by providing both a date and a location.

You can access the Windows XP Search tool when you're working in the My Computer or Windows Explorer window. When you do, the **Search Companion** pane opens in the Explorer bar. The Search Companion guides you through your search, offering options that change depending on your search strategy. For example, when you are searching for files, the Search Companion asks you questions about the file's name, contents, type, location, and date. Your responses help the Search Companion find the files you want. You can also access the Search tool from the Start menu. In this case, the Search Results window opens, displaying the Search Companion in the left pane. The Search Results window will be familiar to you because it includes the same features as the My Computer window, such as the Standard Buttons toolbar and similar menus on the menu bar.

Before you prepare to show Carolyn the Search tool, you browse through the quotations archive disk to learn more about its content and organization. You discover that the data on the disk is organized into several folders. You open a few files and find quotes from a wide variety of people—historical figures such as Eleanor Roosevelt and Gandhi, as well as more modern personalities such as Jay Leno and Alice Walker. As you read a file, Carolyn stops by and asks if you could look for appropriate material for a speech on successful leadership that the senator will deliver next week at Stanton College. You see that the quotations archive disk contains so many files that opening and reading all of them would be time-consuming, so you decide to use the Search tool to locate quotations on the topic of leadership.

Starting the Windows XP Search Tool

To start using the Search tool from My Computer or Windows Explorer, you can click the Search button 🔍 on the Standard Buttons toolbar in either of these windows, or you can right-click the folder or device you want to search and then click Search on the shortcut menu. You also can start the Search tool by clicking the Search command on the Start menu.

You didn't create the quotations files, and you know very little about them, so Search is just the tool to help you locate quotations for Senator Bernstein's speech. You'll start Search from the Start menu.

To start Search and specify that you want to search for files or folders:

1. Make sure your Data Disk is in drive A, click the **Start** button 🎛 start on the taskbar, and then click **Search**. The Search Results window opens, as shown in Figure 6-2. Resize the Search Results window if necessary, so your screen matches the figure.

Figure 6-2	THE SEARCH COMPANION PANE IN THE SEARCH RESULTS WINDOW

menus, toolbar, and Address bar are the same as in My Computer

Search Companion pane

list of items for which you can search

click to set preferences, such as hiding the animated Search character

results of your search appear in the right pane

animated Search character

The Search Results window is divided into two sections. In the left pane (the Explorer bar) is the Search Companion, which lists the information and objects you can find. After you conduct a search, the results appear in the right pane. You can use the same tools you use in My Computer to explore the search results. For example, you can change the view, sort the results, and open files. You can also change the Explorer bar so it displays a different pane, such as the Folders pane or History pane, if necessary.

Figure 6-3 describes the information you can find using the Search Companion.

Figure 6-3	SEARCH COMPANION OPTIONS
SEARCH OPTION	**DESCRIPTION**
Pictures, music, or video	Finds files that contain images, such as drawings, pictures, and photographs; sound, such as music or spoken word; and video, such as animation or movies
Documents (word processing, spreadsheets, etc.)	Finds files that were created in a program such as a word-processing program. If you know the type of file you are looking for, this option takes fewer steps than searching for All files or folders.
All files and folders	Finds files or folders, including system folders and program files, on local or network drives
Computers or people	Finds computers on your network, people in your Address Book, or people on the Internet
Information in Help and Support Center	Opens the Search tab in the Help and Support Center so you can find Help topics
Search the Internet	Finds information on the Internet
Change Preferences	Lets you customize the way the Search tool finds information and change the appearance of the Search Companion pane

To find information, you respond to questions in the Search Companion pane. These responses are **search criteria**, one or more conditions that information must meet to have Search find it. For example, you could provide search criteria specifying all or part of a file-name and the drive containing the file. Search then locates and displays every file that matches those criteria. You can specify the criteria shown in Figure 6-4.

Figure 6-4	SEARCH CRITERIA	
OPTION	**DESCRIPTION**	**SEARCH STRATEGY**
All or part of the filename	Search for files or folders that contain the specified text	Filename
A word or phrase in the file	Search for files that include the specified words or phrases in their contents (not in the filename)	Keyword
Look in	Search a particular location, such as a computer, drive, or folder	Location
When was it modified?	Search for files that were created or last modified on a particular date or within a range of dates	Date
What size is it?	Search for files that are small, medium, large, or a specific file size	Size
More advanced options	Search for files of a particular type and select search settings, such as whether to search subfolders or perform a case-sensitive search	Type

In the next section, you'll search by filename and location to find a file.

Searching by Name and Location

To find any type of file by its name, you need to provide the Search Companion with as much of the filename as possible. In many cases, you will know the exact name of the file you want to locate but not recall where the file is stored. However, in those instances where you do not know the complete filename, you can use a word or phrase that may be part of the filename to search for the file. Any letters or words you type to define the search are called a **search string**. By default, Search Companion is not case sensitive when searching for filenames, so you can type the search string in either uppercase or lowercase letters.

REFERENCE WINDOW   **RW**

<u>Searching for a File by Name</u>
- Click the Start button and then click Search.
- In the Search Companion, click All files and folders.
- In the All or part of the filename text box, type the complete filename or a word or phrase the file-name contains.
- Click the Look in list arrow, and then click the drive or folder you want to search, or click My Computer to select all the drives on your computer.
- Click the Search button in the Search Companion pane.

For the most part, people name their files with names that reflect the files' contents. You assume that the previous aide would have named files related to leadership with a filename that contained the word "leadership." Therefore, you decide to conduct a search of files and folders on your disk using the search string "leadership."

To begin searching for files containing "leadership" in their filenames:

1. In the What do you want to search for? list in the Search Companion pane, click **All files and folders**. See Figure 6-5.

Figure 6-5   SEARCHING FOR FILES BY NAME

type a search string in this text box

your Look in text box might show a different device or folder

If you know the full name of the file you are trying to locate, you can supply the Search Companion with the complete filename in the All or part of the file name text box. If you do not know the complete filename but perhaps know only one or two words of it, the Search Companion can work with that information to locate the file. In this case, you do not know the filename but are looking for files that contain the word "leadership" in their filenames.

2. In the All or part of the file name text box, type **leadership**.

Now that you've entered a criterion for the filename, you can specify a file location. When you start Search, a folder or drive name, such as Local Hard Drives (C:), appears in the Look in list box, which specifies where Search will look for the file. If your computer has multiple drives and you aren't sure which drive contains the file, you can search your entire computer by clicking My Computer in the Look in list box. However, if you know which drive contains the file, you can speed your search by limiting the search to that drive. All the files you are looking for are located on your Data Disk, so you can specify your floppy drive as the search location.

To search for files by location:

1. Click the **Look in** list arrow in the Search Companion pane, and then click **3½ Floppy (A:)**. Windows XP will now search only the files on your Data Disk.

2. Click the **Search** button in the Search Companion pane. Windows XP searches for all files on drive A whose names contain the search string you entered. Then it displays any matching files in the Search Results pane.

TROUBLE? If nothing appears, Windows XP might not be including subfolders in its search. Click the Back button 🔙, scroll the Search Companion pane, click More advanced options, and then make sure the Search Subfolders check box is selected. This ensures that Search will search all folders on the Data Disk, not just the files contained in the root directory. Click the Search button again to show the results.

3. Click **View** on the menu bar, and then click **Details** if necessary to ensure that you are viewing file details. See Figure 6-6.

Figure 6-6	SEARCH RESULTS

if you didn't find the file you wanted, select an option in the Search Companion pane to improve the search

the only file on the disk in drive A that contains "leadership" in its filename

TROUBLE? If your results show .txt extensions after the filenames, your computer is set to show file extensions. Showing or hiding file extensions does not affect the Search tool. If you want to hide file extensions, click Tools on the menu bar, click Folder Options, click the View tab, select the Hide file extensions for known file types check box, and then click the OK button.

The Search Results list shows one file, Leadership. The In Folder column shows the file location, A:\Topics. The location begins with the drive—in this case, A. If the file is in a folder, a backslash (\) separates the drive from the folder name. In this case, files in A:\Topics are in the Topics folder on drive A. If a folder contains subfolders, additional backslashes separate the folders from one another. Figure 6-7 shows how this notation works on a disk in drive A that contains two folders, Politics and Speeches, both of which have subfolders.

Figure 6-7   **FILE LOCATIONS**

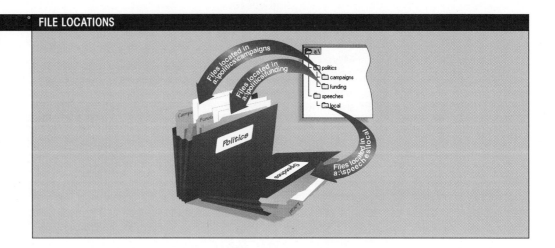

Experimenting with Search Strings

You wonder if you would find more files using a different search string. One rule of thumb is to use the root of your search word as your criterion. For example, if you decide to search for files on political topics for Senator Bernstein's speech, using "politics" as your search string would not find a file named Politician, for example. However, using the root "politic" without the added "s" as your search string would yield files named Politician, Political Quotations, or Politics. Figure 6-8 shows several examples of search strings that use the root of a word. (You don't need to try any of these now.)

Figure 6-8   **CHOOSING EFFECTIVE SEARCH STRINGS**

TOPIC	USE THIS SEARCH STRING:	FINDS THESE FILENAMES:
politics	politic	Politics, Politicians, Political Quotations
education	educ	Education, Educational Issues, Educators
computers	comput	Computers, Computing, Computerization

Of course, if the root of the word is very general, Search might find files you don't want. Searching for "lead" instead of "leader" would display a filename such as "Lead Corrosion." Fortunately, it's easy to adjust your search string until you find only those files you want.

Now that you know the archive disk has a file containing quotations specifically about leadership, you look for files on leaders, using "leader" as your search string. To perform a new search, you can change the existing criteria, add a new criterion, or start a new search. You want to change the search string from "leadership" to "leader" but still search only the disk in drive A. You will change only the filename instead of starting a new search.

To search for files containing the search string "leader" on drive A:

1. Click **Change file name or keywords** in the Search Companion pane. See Figure 6-9.

Figure 6-9   CHANGING SEARCH CRITERIA

the Search Companion pane asks you to enter part or all of the filename

2. Type **leader** in the text box in the Search Companion pane.

   TROUBLE? If an entry is already selected in a text box, you can type to replace its contents. If an entry is not selected, double-click the text box to select the contents, and then type. You also can click once and then edit the text box contents.

3. Click the **Search** button in the Search Companion pane. The right pane in the Search Results window now lists three files that might contain information on leadership. See Figure 6-10.

Figure 6-10 **RESULTS OF AN EXPANDED SEARCH**

the Search Results pane now lists more files

You decide to open the Leadership file to see if it contains any quotes the senator might find useful.

Opening a File Located by Search

Once you locate a file using the Search Companion, you can open it directly, as you would from My Computer or Windows Explorer. You can right-click the file, and then click Open on the shortcut menu, or click it and then press Enter, or you can double-click it. Windows XP locates and starts the program that created the file and then it opens the file. If Windows XP cannot open your file, you might not have the necessary program for that file type installed on your computer. In this case, Windows XP prompts you to select the program you want to use to display the file.

To open a file from the Search Results window:

1. Double-click the **Leadership** file in the right pane of the Search Results window. The file opens in Notepad.

   TROUBLE? If the text of the quotations extends beyond the right border of the Notepad window, click Format on the menu bar, and then click Word Wrap.

2. Browse through the contents of the file, and note that it contains several quotations on leadership. When you are finished, click the Notepad **Close** button ☒ to close Notepad. Click **No** if you are prompted to save your changes.

You show Carolyn the files you found for the speech at Stanton College. Carolyn is pleased that you found helpful material for her. She says that Senator Bernstein will be participating in an atomic energy symposium next month, so anything you can find on that topic would be also useful. You decide to check the quotations archive disk to see if it has any files containing quotations by Albert Einstein, but you can't remember how to spell his name. If you make a spelling error, Search won't locate the files you want.

Using Wildcards

Wildcards are characters that you can substitute for all or part of a filename in a search string. For example, you can use wildcards to approximate a filename. You can also use wildcards to locate a group of files whose names follow certain specific patterns, such as all files that begin and end with certain characters, or all files with a specified string in a specified location.

Search recognizes two wildcards: the asterisk and the question mark. The * (asterisk) wildcard stands in place of any number of consecutive characters in a filename. With the search string "m*n" for example, Search locates files with names that start with "m" and end with "n, "such as Men, Magician, or Modern, but not Male or Women. When you use the asterisk wildcard in a search string, the Search tool allows additional characters only in those places indicated by the wildcard. Search does not include filenames with characters before the "m" or after the "n." If this is not what you want, you can use additional wildcards. If you specify the search string "*m*n*" Search includes Men, Magician, Modern, Women, and Mention, but not Male. These files have the letter "m" in common, which appears somewhere in the name, followed later by "n."

You can also use the ? (question mark) as a wildcard to select files when one character in the filename varies. For example, the search string "m?n" locates Men or Man but not Mistaken or Moon. Files that match the "m?n" criteria must have the letters "m" and "n" in their filenames, separated by a single character. Unlike the asterisk wildcard, however, the question mark wildcard does not cause Search to exclude files with characters before or after the "m" or "n." So although "m*n" excludes Women and Mental, "m?n" does not, because both of these files contain "m" and "n" separated by a single character. The question mark wildcard is often used to locate files whose names include version numbers or dates, such as Sales1, Sales2, and Sales3, or Tax2001, Tax2002, and Tax2003.

You decide to search for only those files beginning with "e" and ending with "n" because you know those are the first and last letters of Einstein's name, although you aren't sure what letters are in between. To perform this search, you use "e*n" as your search string. Try this search now.

To locate files using the asterisk wildcard:

1. Click **Change file name or keywords** in the Search Companion pane.

2. In the text box, type **e*n** and then click the **Search** button in the Search Companion pane. The Search Results pane displays files on your Data Disk whose names start with "e" followed by any number of characters and then the letter "n." Two of the files found are named Einstein. See Figure 6-11.

Figure 6-11   **SEARCHING WITH THE ASTERISK WILDCARD**

the Search Results pane lists files whose names start with "e" and end with "n"

your search found two files named Einstein; your icons and file order may differ

You make a mental note that the files on Einstein might be appropriate for the atomic energy symposium, and plan to print them for Carolyn before your next meeting with her.

Finding Files by Keyword

You've found two files on Einstein, and you wonder if any files specifically mention atomic energy. You search for files named "atomic" or "energy" but don't find any. You know, however, that this doesn't necessarily mean there are no quotations about atomic energy in the files. Besides searching for a file based on its name, you can also use the Search Companion to search for a word or phrase in the contents of a file. To use this feature, you search for a keyword. A **keyword** is a search string—a word or a phrase—contained anywhere in a file. The Search Companion searches through the entire text of every file to find the keyword.

When you search based on a keyword, you can specify whether your search is case sensitive. For example, if you want to find a letter you wrote to Brenda Wolf, you could enter "Wolf" as your keyword and then select a case-sensitive search to locate only files containing Wolf with an initial uppercase letter. The Case sensitive option affects only keywords you enter in the A word or phrase in the file text box—not the search strings you enter to search for files by name. The Case sensitive option is an advanced option that you can select by starting a new search, selecting the advanced options, and then clicking the Case sensitive check box.

You decide to search for the keywords "atomic energy" to try to find more files containing quotations Carolyn could use in writing her speech for the atomic energy symposium.

To look for the keywords "atomic energy" within a file:

1. Click **Start a new search** in the Search Companion pane. You want to search only the files and folders on your Data Disk.

2. Click **All files and folders**.

3. If necessary, press the **Delete** key to delete the text in the All or part of the file name text box. Note that the Look in list arrow still shows the 3½ Floppy (A:) drive as the location from your last search.

4. Click the **A word or phrase in the file** text box, and then type **atomic energy**. Because you aren't sure what case the quote might be in, you want to make sure Search isn't set to perform case-sensitive searches.

5. Scroll to the bottom of the Search Companion pane if necessary, and then click the **More advanced options** double arrow button to display the advanced search options.

   TROUBLE? If the advanced search options already appear, such as the Case sensitive check box, you don't have to click the More advanced options double arrow button.

6. Make sure the **Case sensitive** check box is not checked. If it is, click it to remove the check mark. Otherwise Search might not locate the file if the search string text is not all lowercase. If necessary, change any other settings to match the ones shown in Figure 6-12.

Figure 6-12	PREPARING TO SEARCH BY KEYWORD

7. Click the **Search** button in the Search Companion pane. Search locates one file, Technology, located in the Topics folder. This file contains the keywords "atomic energy" in its contents.

   TROUBLE? If Search did not locate a file, check to make sure you typed the keywords "atomic energy" correctly and that drive A is selected.

Searching by keyword can be time-consuming, even on a floppy disk. To speed the search, you can index your search location.

Indexing to Speed Searches

When Windows XP searches for a file, it checks every file in the specified location to see if the file meets your search criteria. If you are searching your entire computer, for example, the search can take a long time. You can speed the search process by using the Indexing Service to **index** a disk. To index a disk, the Indexing Service reads through your files and extracts basic information, such as the name and location of your files, and organizes it in a way that makes access to that information quick and easy. After you index a disk once, Search can refer to the index to find files instead of scanning every file on your computer. The Search tool lets you enable the Indexing Service to speed your searches, which is particularly helpful if you are searching a disk containing large amounts of information or if you will search the same disk repeatedly.

You anticipate that you'll be using the Search tool often as Carolyn's aide, so you decide to use the indexing service to search more quickly.

To speed searches using the indexing service:

1. In the Search Companion pane, click **Yes, but make future searches faster** to respond to the question, "There was one file found. Is it what you wanted?"

   TROUBLE? If you do not see the "Yes, but make future searches faster" option, the Indexing Service is already enabled on your computer. You can skip Steps 1 and 2.

2. Click the **Yes, enable Indexing Service** option button, and then click the **OK** button.

Besides indexing, you also can speed a search by narrowing the search criteria so that Search looks for fewer files—for example, by specifying a folder rather than an entire drive.

Searching for Files in a Specific Folder

You can search all drives and folders available to your computer or, as you saw when you selected the drive containing your Data Disk, you can search only a single drive. You can also narrow your search by specifying a folder on your own computer or on a shared network computer.

REFERENCE WINDOW RW

Searching for Files in a Specific Folder
- Start Search and then click All files and folders in the Search Companion pane.
- Click the Look in list arrow.
- Click Browse at the bottom of the list.
- In the Browse for Folder dialog box, click the plus box next to the drive containing the folder you want to search.
- If the folder is in the root directory of the drive, click the folder icon. If the folder is a subfolder, navigate to the appropriate folder.
- Click OK and then click the Search button in the Search Companion pane.

You report to Carolyn that you've found files containing quotations on atomic energy and on Albert Einstein. She's pleased you found them so quickly and asks you to find quotations by Woody Allen, one of the senator's favorite comics. You noticed a Comedy folder earlier, and you wonder whether it contains quotes by Woody Allen. You decide to use the Search Companion to search the Comedy folder for appropriate material.

To specify the Comedy folder, you navigate a folder tree similar to the one in Windows Explorer.

To search the Comedy folder on drive A for files that contain "woody allen":

1. Click **Start a new search** in the Search Companion pane, if necessary, to return to the What do you want to search for? list. Now you can specify that you want to search all the files in the Comedy folder.

2. Click **All files and folders**.

3. Click the **Look in** list arrow, and then click **Browse** at the bottom of the list. The Browse For Folder dialog box opens, displaying a list of devices, drives, and folders.

4. Click ⊞ next to My Computer, and then click ⊞ next to 3½ Floppy (A:). The folders on drive A appear. See Figure 6-13.

| Figure 6-13 | SELECTING A FOLDER |

folders on the disk in drive A

Comedy folder

TROUBLE? Your list of devices, drives, and folders might look different, depending on your computer's drives and network.

5. Click the **Comedy** folder.

6. Click the **OK** button. The Look in list box in the Search Companion pane now shows Comedy. Next, specify the keyword you want to find.

7. Select the text in the **A word or phrase in the file** text box, and then type **woody allen**. This criteria tells Search to look only in the Comedy folder on drive A (and in any subfolders the Comedy folder might contain) for files whose contents include "woody allen."

8. Click the **Search** button in the Search Companion pane. Search locates two files.

You imagine that Carolyn will want you to find other quotations by author and decide to search the disk for any files or folders whose filenames contain the term "author."

Working with Search Results

Up until now, the file lists in the Search Results panes have been short and manageable. When your search yields many files, you can adjust the Search Results pane to display the information in a more organized format.

You noticed a folder named Author earlier and anticipate that using the search string "author" could find many files. You'll start by searching for files or folders whose filenames contain "author," and then look for ways to organize the search results.

To search for files and folders named "author" on drive A:

1. Click the **Back** button in the Search Companion pane to enter new search criteria—you want to search for files whose names contain the word "author."

2. Type **author** in the All or part of the file name text box in the Search Companion pane. Because you are not looking for files based on keywords, you will delete the text in the next text box.

3. Delete the contents of the **A word or phrase in the file** text box.

4. Click the **Look in** list arrow, and then click **3½ Floppy (A:)** to search all folders on the disk, not just the Comedy folder.

5. Click the **Search** button in the Search Companion pane. The Search Results pane displays all files and folders that have the word "author" in their file-names. Your Data Disk has 28 such files.

You can view the files in the Search Results pane by Thumbnails, Tiles, Icons, List, or Details, and you can resize columns by dragging their borders. These options are the same as in My Computer and Windows Explorer. To change the view, you can click the Views button or the View menu. Details view, the default view, is probably the most useful view because it gives you all the information you need (name, location, size, type, and date modified of each file) to verify that you've found the file you want. Just as in My Computer and Windows Explorer, you can sort the files in the Search Results pane by any of these criteria.

You see files whose names indicate that they contain quotations from authors, labeled by last name. For example, the D-Author document contains quotations from people whose last names start with D. You decide to sort the files by name to see if the Data Disk folder contains a file for every letter of the alphabet.

To sort the files by name:

1. Make sure the Search Results list appears in Details view. If it doesn't, click the **Views** button ⊞ ˅ on the Standard Buttons toolbar, and then click **Details**.

2. Click the **Name** button shown in Figure 6-14 until the files are arranged in ascending alphabetical order by name.

Figure 6-14	SORTING THE SEARCH RESULTS LIST

Name button

folder, then files, appear in alphabetical order

3. Scroll down the Search Results list, and note that there are files for most letters of the alphabet.

If you wanted to find quotations by a given author, you could try the file for the author's last name, located in the Alphabet folder. What else can you learn from the Search Results pane? The Type column shows that the first item on the list is a folder and that the rest of the files are text documents. You could sort by size to find that the largest file is 15 KB. You could sort the files by date modified (scroll to the right to see this option) to observe that these files were developed in the years 1994–2001.

Refining a Search

So far you've searched for files with particular filenames or keywords. You can also locate a file using criteria other than the filename or contents, including size, date, and type. With these criteria, you can answer questions such as: Are any files more than a few years old? Which files were created using a certain program? Which files are larger or smaller than a specified size? You enter the characteristic you want to study, and then Search lists all files that share that characteristic, such as all files created after 2002, all Microsoft Word files, or all files larger than 50 KB.

You can use these criteria alone or in combination with filenames and keywords.

Finding a File by Date

Searching for files by date is useful when you want a file that you were working with on a given date, but you can't remember where you stored it. You could get information about file dates quickly by opening Windows Explorer or My Computer and sorting the files in a folder by date. However, when the files are scattered among folders, Search can display files from any of those folders that meet your date criteria, whereas Windows Explorer and My Computer can display the contents of only one folder at a time.

Carolyn says that the previous aide spent the most time developing the quotations archive during the years 1994 to 1996. You decide to see whether the archive disk still has any files that were created then and note that those files might need to be updated. To do so, you'll search for files by date.

To search for files created between 1994 and 1996:

1. Click **Start a new search** in the Search Companion pane.

   TROUBLE? You might have to scroll in the Search Companion pane to see the Start a new search option.

2. Click **All files and folders**.

3. Press the **Delete** key to delete text in the All of or part of the file name text box, make sure 3½ Floppy (A:) still appears in the Look in text box, and then scroll down to click **When was it modified?** and display the options related to searching by date. You use these options to set date criteria. For example, you can find files modified in the last week, month, or year. You want to find files created within a different range of dates, so you can specify those dates.

4. Click the **Specify dates** option button. Now you can enter and select date criteria, including whether to search by modified date, created date, or accessed date (when a file was last opened, for example). You also specify the start and end dates in the from and to list boxes.

5. Click the **Specify dates** list arrow, and then click **Created Date**.

6. In the **from** text box, enter **1/1/1994** as the start date, and in the **to** text box, enter **12/31/1996** as the end date. See Figure 6-15.

Figure 6-15 **SPECIFYING START AND END DATES**

enter the start date of the range

select Created Date to find files created on the dates you specify

enter the end date of the range

7. Click the **Search** button in the Search Companion pane. The Search Results list shows 16 files in that range of dates.

You'd like to get an overview of the types of files on the quotations archive disk to see whether you have the software on your computer to open them. To do this, you can search the files on the disk by file type.

Finding a File by Type

You can use the Search Companion to look for files by their general file type or by the program that created them. The list of file types from which you can choose includes text files, sound files, bitmaps, Word documents, Web documents, and so on, depending on the resources on your computer.

You already know the archive disk has many text files, but you'd like to know how many to estimate the number of quotations it provides. Each text file has an average of 10 quotations. If the disk contains 20 text files, you can estimate that you have about 200 quotations. You decide to use file type criteria to find the number of text files on the archive disk.

To find files by type:

1. Click the **Back** button in the Search Companion pane to change your search criteria.

2. In the "When was it modified?" section, click the **Don't remember** option button to clear the dates you specified earlier. You specify file type in the advanced options section.

3. Locate and click the **More advanced options** double arrow button to display the advanced search options, if necessary. You use the Type of file text box in the More advanced options section to select the file type for which you want to search.

4. Click the **Type of file** list arrow, and then scroll down the alphabetical list to locate "Text Document."

5. Click **Text Document** and then click the **Search** button in the Search Companion pane. The Search Companion and status bar indicate that your disk has 92 text files. The disk contains about 920 quotations.

TROUBLE? If your list is much shorter, you might have forgotten to click the Don't remember option button to turn off the Date setting. Scroll up to the "When was it modified?" section, click the Don't remember option button, and then click the Search button in the Search Companion pane.

You also wonder whether the archive disk contains sound files that the senator could use in a multimedia presentation. Many spoken-word files are created in a file format called AU Format Sound. You can search for files of that type to see if the archive contains any spoken-word files.

To find one type of sound file:

1. Click the **Back** button in the Search Companion pane, and then click the **Type of file** list arrow again under More Advanced Options. Click **AU Format Sound**.

2. Click the **Search** button in the Search Companion pane. The Search Results list includes two AU Format Sound files.

Now you want to know if the archive disk contains other types of sound files besides those in the AU Format Sound format. The senator could also use music in a multimedia presentation. In addition to searching for files by type, the Search tool lets you search for files in a particular category, such as all sound files, which include MIDI and MP3 files, for example.

To find all types of sound files:

1. Click **Start a new search** in the Search Companion pane. Categories of file types appear in the Search Companion pane, including Pictures, music, or video, and Documents.

2. Click **Pictures, music, or video** in the Search Companion pane. Now the Search Companion shows the three types of files you can find—Pictures and Photos, Music, or Video. Although you can select some or all of these types, you only want to find music files.

3. Click the **Music** check box to select it. Windows XP will search the entire hard disk unless you specify where to search. To do so, you must first display the advanced search options.

4. Click **Use advanced search options**.

5. If necessary, scroll down the Search Companion pane, click the **Look in** list arrow, and then click **3½ Floppy (A:)**.

6. Click the **Search** button in the Search Companion pane. Switch to Details View, if necessary. Windows XP finds three files—the two spoken-word files you found earlier, and one MIDI Sequence file. Figure 6-16 shows the Search Results window in Details view.

| Figure 6-16 | **FINDING ALL SOUND FILES** |

your options may differ

your search found three sound files—two AU Format Sound files and one MIDI Sequence file

Another way to find files is based on their size. You'll try that type of search next.

Finding a File by Size

You know that sound and music files are usually bigger than text files or word-processed documents. If you are short on disk space, you'll want to identify the largest files so you can move them to free up space. You can find this information by looking for a file by its size. If disk space becomes a problem on the quotations archive disk, you can find all files that are at least 25 KB and then move them to a hard disk. Try that search now.

To search for files by size:

1. Click **Start a new search** in the Search Companion pane, and then click **All files and folders**. You need to use the advanced options to search by size.

2. Click the **More advanced options** double arrow button to display the advanced search options, if necessary. Click the **Type of file** list arrow, and then click **(All Files and Folders)**, the first item in the list.

3. Click **What size is it?** to display the options related to file size.

4. Click the **Specify size (in KB)** option button, and then make sure the "at least" option is selected.

TROUBLE? If the "at least" option is not selected, click the Specify size list arrow and then click at least.

5. Enter **25** in the second text box.

6. Click the **Search** button in the Search Companion pane. The Search Results list shows the files that are 25 KB or more. You can sort these files to identify the largest more easily. You'll sort in descending order so that the largest files appear at the top of the list.

7. Click the **Size** button until the files are sorted by size in ascending order, and then click the **Size** button again to sort in descending order, with the largest files first. Not surprisingly, three of the largest files are sound files. See Figure 6-17.

Figure 6-17	SEARCHING FOR FILES BY SIZE

Now that you know how to find a file based on size, type, or date, you can further refine a search by using a combination of these criteria.

Finding a File Using Multiple Criteria

Carolyn is now working on the second draft of Senator Bernstein's speech at Stanton College. Carolyn informs you that because Stanton College is a women's college, Senator Bernstein is interested in having a quote on leadership by a woman. If you specify multiple criteria, such as a likely filename and keyword, you might be able to pinpoint such a quote.

You remember that some files on the archive disk have filenames containing the search string "women." You guess that a quotation about leadership probably contains the word "leader," so you could specify the root "leader" as your keyword. Search uses all the criteria you enter to perform the search.

To find a file with multiple criteria:

1. Click the **Back** button in the Search Companion pane. Try looking for files whose names contain "women."

2. Click the **All or part of the file name** text box, and then type **women**.

3. Click the **A word or phrase in the file** text box, and then type **leader**. Next, be sure to clear all the criteria you've entered before so you don't add unnecessary information to the search.

4. Scroll to the "What size is it?" section, and then click the **Don't remember** option button. The search criteria you have entered indicates that you want to find files of any size that contain "women" in their filenames and "leader" in their contents.

5. Click the **Search** button in the Search Companion pane. One file matches your criteria. See Figure 6-18.

Figure 6-18	USING MULTIPLE CRITERIA TO FIND A FILE

6. Double-click the **Women** file in the right pane to open the file in Notepad. You see a quotation on leaders by Mother Teresa that the senator might want to use in her speech.

7. Close Notepad.

You've learned how to refine a file search by specifying date, type, size, or a combination. When you develop effective criteria, you can save your search settings in case you want to perform that same search again.

Saving Search Settings

After you enter criteria to find files and other information, especially if you are using multiple criteria, you might want to save your search settings. For example, if you regularly search sales documents for sales from the West region, you can create criteria to search a disk for files created in the last month containing the keyword "West." If you save your search settings, you can perform that search every month without re-creating the search criteria.

You save search settings in a file in the Saved Search format. To perform the search again, you can open the Saved Search file to start the Search tool and conduct a new search using the same criteria.

As you create other quotations disks, you might need to find other files containing quotations on women's leadership. You can save the search settings so you don't have to enter the multiple criteria again.

To save and test your search settings:

1. In the Search Results window, click **File** on the menu bar, and then click **Save Search**. The Save Search dialog box opens. This dialog box works just like the standard Save As dialog box—you specify the name and location of the file you want to save and then click the Save button.

2. Click the **Save in** list arrow, and then select **3½ Floppy (A:)**.

3. In the File name text box, type **women leaders** and then click the **Save** button. This saves the search settings in a file named "women leaders" on the root directory of your floppy disk.

4. Close the Search Results window. Next, you will open the file to make sure it performs the search correctly.

5. Open My Computer and navigate to the drive containing your Data Disk.

6. Double-click **women leaders**. The Search Results window opens and displays the saved search criteria.

7. Click the **Search** button in the Search Companion pane. This time the search finds two files—the one containing quotations by women and the saved search file called women leaders. Both meet your search criteria.

8. Close the Search Results and My Computer windows.

In this session, you used the Windows XP Search Companion to search for files by name and location, keyword, type, and size. You learned how to use wildcards and refine your search, and how to save your search settings to conduct future searches.

Session 6.1 QUICK CHECK

1. To search for a file only on drive A, what do you do in the Search Companion pane?

2. True or False: The right pane in the Search Results window displays only the files whose names exactly match the search string you entered.

3. What is a wildcard? What is the difference between the asterisk wildcard and the question mark wildcard?

4. How do you display the files in the Search Results list in alphabetical order?

5. If you want to use the Search Companion to display only the bitmapped images on your floppy disk, what should you do?

6. If the Search Results list shows the file you were looking for, how do you open the file for editing?

7. What is a keyword?

SESSION 6.2

In this session, you will learn how to use the Search Companion to search the Internet, including searching for Web pages that contain specific kinds of information. You'll learn how to narrow your search to focus on Web pages relevant to the information you want to find. You'll also learn to search for people and maps on the Web, and how to modify your search preferences.

Searching for Information on the Internet

The Internet has vast resources, and to locate the information you want, you need to search for it. However, searching for a piece of information on a Web page can be a daunting task—the Internet provides access to millions and millions of Web pages. To simplify and speed an Internet search, you can use a **search service**, a Web site that helps you find information on the Internet. Most search services use software, called the **search engine**, that searches through Internet documents and compiles a list of Web pages. It organizes and indexes this list by topic. When you use the search service to find Web pages on a specific topic, the service's search engine checks the index and provides links to all the pages it finds on that topic. Because the Internet is changing so quickly, the indexes change regularly, too. If you don't find information one day, it might be available the next. Moreover, because each search service can use a different search engine to compile its Web page index, you might find different results for the same search when using different search services. Some search services also provide specific types of information. If you cannot find what you want with one search service, such as MSN, you can try another, such as Google. Figure 6-19 lists popular search services, and the types of information their indexes provide.

Figure 6-19	POPULAR SEARCH SERVICES
SEARCH SERVICE	**DESCRIPTION**
AltaVista	One of the largest and most comprehensive search engines available, AltaVista searches for keywords anywhere on a Web page
Ask Jeeves	A **meta search engine**, which searches the indexes of other search engines and eliminates redundant listings
Direct Hit	Designed to find the most popular Web sites
Google	One of the largest and fastest search engines, Google is also designed to find Web sites that directly relate to your search
HotBot	Sorts results by date
MSN	Focuses on general-interest Web sites
Northern Light	Sorts results into appropriate search folders related to content
Yahoo!	Provides a directory of Web pages, organized by categories

By default, the Windows XP Search Companion pane uses the MSN search service to help you narrow your search criteria to find pages related to the topic or question you have in mind. You can change the default search service if you like.

Searching for Web Pages with the Search Companion

When you enter search criteria to find a Web page and click the Search button in the Search Companion pane, the Search Companion pane lists categories of information that meet your search criteria. For example, if you enter "colleges," the Search Companion pane lists categories related to colleges, such as "Find a college's Web site," and "Find information about a college." You choose the category of information you want to search, and the Search Companion pane sends the search criteria to the MSN search engine. If possible, the Search Companion then asks for more information to refine the search. For example, if you select the "Find information about a college" category, the Search Companion pane asks, "For which college?" Then it sends the refined search criteria to the MSN search engine. As you provide progressively more detailed information in the Search Companion pane, the list of topics found by the search engine grows smaller. For example, at the beginning of the college search, MSN would probably find thousands of college Web sites. After you enter a college name, MSN would list fewer, making it easier to find the information you want.

Because Senator Bernstein often visits college campuses, you want to expand the set of quotations on the quotations archives disk to include quotations about higher education. You start by searching the Internet for Web sites that include quotation collections.

To search for Web sites using the Search Companion:

1. Make sure you are connected to the Internet.

2. Click the **Start** button ⊌ start on the taskbar, and then click **Search**. In the Search Companion pane, click **Search the Internet**. The Search Results window opens. See Figure 6-20.

| Figure 6-20 | SEARCHING THE INTERNET WITH THE SEARCH COMPANION |

type search criteria here...

...or click a link in the Search Companion pane

3. Maximize the Search Results window, if necessary.

TROUBLE? If America Online (AOL) is installed on your computer, your Search Companion pane may look different than the one shown in Figure 6-20. To make your Search Companion pane match the one shown in the figure, and to be able to complete the following steps, click Change preferences in the Search Companion pane, click Internet Search Behavior, and then make sure the With Search Companion option button is selected and the default search engine is MSN. Click OK in the Search Companion pane.

4. In the Search Companion pane text box, type **quotations**, and then click the **Search** button. The Search Results window changes to the Internet Explorer window—note that the title bar shows the Internet Explorer icon 🗐, the Standard Buttons toolbar includes additional buttons, such as Mail and Print, and the Address bar shows the URL of the MSN Web Search page, which opens in the right pane, listing the first 15 Web sites that feature quotations. The Search Companion stays open in the left pane. See Figure 6-21.

Figure 6-21   **FINDING LINKS TO WEB SITES CONTAINING QUOTATIONS**

the window changes
from Search Results to
Internet Explorer

the Search Companion
pane includes options to
improve your search

click to highlight your
search words in the
results

the right pane shows the
default search service

your search found over
1,000 pages that
contain "quotations"

Note that your search found over 1,000 Web pages related to quotations. To reduce this list to only pages about education quotations, you can now enter more information in the Search Companion pane to further refine the search. When you find a Web page that lists quotations about education, you can save it on your Data Disk.

To find and save a Web page containing education quotations:

1. In the Search Companion pane, click **Find a quotation**.

2. In the Who said it or what is it about? text box, type **education**.

3. Click the **Search** button in the Search Companion pane. In the right pane, a page opens containing links to quotations about education. See Figure 6-22.

Figure 6-22	FINDING WEB PAGES WITH EDUCATION QUOTATIONS

this search found fewer Web pages because you refined the search criteria

link to a quotation about education

The right pane shows a Web page from the Bartleby.com Web site, a site that provides access to reference texts and great books. The page now lists summaries of quotations about education with links to the complete quotations.

4. Click one of the links in the right pane. A page opens displaying the complete quotation.

5. Scroll the page to read the quotation. Now you can save the education quotation in a file on your Data Disk.

6. Click **File** on the menu bar, and then click **Save As**. In the Save Web Page dialog box, navigate to the drive containing your Data Disk.

7. Type **Education** as the name of the new file, click the **Save as type** list arrow, click **Web Page, HTML only (*.htm, *.html)**, and then click the **Save** button to save the education quotation on your Data Disk.

8. Close the Search Results window.

Now that you've found an appropriate quotation, you can search the Internet for other types of Web pages, such as those that contain information about people.

Searching for People on the Internet

Besides finding Web pages, you also can use the Search tool to search for information on the Internet about specific people. To do so, you can use the Search Companion pane to enter a query such as "Find a person's address." The Search tool then connects to Web sites that host people search services such as Bigfoot and AnyWho. These people search services operate like electronic telephone books—you enter a name and the service looks up the mailing address, e-mail address, or telephone number. For common names the list is very long; for some names no information is available. Many people search services also let you perform reverse name searches—you enter telephone numbers, mailing addresses, or e-mail addresses to find a name.

Carolyn asks you to find contact information for sources she's using to prepare Senator Bernstein's speech. You've found some contact information by searching through journal articles written by the sources, but you also want to use the Internet as an alternate method of finding information about people. You decide to test the search service by attempting to locate information on yourself.

To use a search service to find information about a person:

1. Click the **Start** button ⊞ start on the taskbar, and then click **Search** to start a new search. Maximize the Search Results window, if necessary.

2. In the Search Companion pane, click **Search the Internet**, type **find a person's address** in the What are you looking for? text box, and then click the **Search** button. The window changes to Internet Explorer, and Windows XP uses the default search engine, MSN, to open a page containing links to people search services. The Search Companion remains open in the left pane.

3. In the Search Companion pane, click **Find contact information for a person**. The Search Companion pane displays text boxes where you can enter criteria to find a person. See Figure 6-23.

| Figure 6-23 | SEARCHING FOR PEOPLE ON THE INTERNET |

in the Search Companion pane, enter details about the person whose address you want to find

the search service lists links to address directories

4. In the What is the first name? text box, type your first name. In the What is the last name? text box, type your last name. In the In which city? text box, enter your city. Then click the **In which state?** list arrow and select your state.

5. Click the **Search** button in the Search Companion pane. If MSN has any address or phone number information on people with your name, it appears in a list.

TROUBLE? If MSN could not find the information you requested, click the Back button in the Search Companion pane, and then repeat Steps 3 through 5 using a different name, such as your instructor's name, or using a more common name and a large city. You can also click an option to view results from another search service, such as the AnyWho.com White Pages Address Finder.

Carolyn mentions that one common source of information for Senator Bernstein's speeches are speeches made by other members of Congress. She wonders if you could find a list of the current members of the U.S. Congress on the Internet. To find an organization, you can use the same techniques that you used to find a person.

To search for an organization:

1. In the Search Companion pane, click the **Back** button until you return to the "What are you looking for?" section.

2. In the Search Companion text box, type **find members of U.S. Congress**, and then click the **Search** button. See Figure 6-24.

Figure 6-24	FINDING MEMBERS OF CONGRESS

click a link in the Search Companion to refine the search; your list of links may differ

click a link in the right pane to open a Web page

Now you could use the Search Companion to refine the search, if necessary. For example, you could click the Find information about political agencies link to find other political organizations. However, the links you found contain relevant information, so you can explore those.

3. Click one or two links to locate a list of members of the U.S. Congress, and then close the Internet Explorer window.

Now that you have found information about people and organizations on the Internet, Carolyn asks you to help her search for maps on the Internet. She wants to find a map to Stanton College, which Senator Bernstein will visit next month. You can learn how to search the Internet for maps by finding one that shows your address.

Searching for a Map

In Windows XP, you find a location on an electronic map by providing addresses or other search criteria in the Search Companion pane of the Search Results window. The Search tool connects to a map service on the Internet. A **map service** provides street maps for addresses you enter into a search form. The Search tool uses the MSN map service by default, although you can send the search to other search services just as you can when you look for quotations. Once the map you want appears in the right pane of the Search Results window, you can zoom in to view more local detail or zoom out to view more of the surrounding area. To get familiar with searching for maps, try searching for your own address.

To locate a map:

1. Start the Search tool and then click **Search the Internet** in the Search Companion pane.

2. In the Search Companion, type **find a map** and then click the **Search** button. The window changes to Internet Explorer, and the MSN search service appears in the right pane, listing links to Web sites containing maps. The Search Companion remains in the left pane. MSN lists many types of maps to find, so you should refine your search.

3. In the Search Companion pane, click **Find a map of a place**.

4. Enter your address, city, and country in the appropriate text boxes.

5. Click the **Search** button in the Search Companion pane. The Expedia.com Find a Map page opens.

6. In the Best Match text box in the right pane, click an address and then click **Find a map** at the bottom of the page. (You might have to scroll the right pane to see this link.)

The map of the place you selected appears in the right pane.

7. Scroll the right pane and then click a zoom level to see more details in the map. See Figure 6-25.

Figure 6-25   **FINDING A MAP**

a map meeting your search criteria appears in the right pane

click an option in the Search Companion pane to send the search to another map service

your list of options may differ

click to zoom in and see a more detailed map

click to zoom out and see more of the surrounding area

TROUBLE? If the address you tried does not yield a map, try a different address.

8. Click the **Close** button ☒ to close the window.

You show Carolyn the map you found and explain that finding an electronic map is similar to finding any other kind of information on the Internet—you enter search criteria and then use a Web search service to locate the information you want. Now Carolyn wonders if you can change the default search service. She uses Google most often and is very comfortable with how it works. You can change the default search service from MSN to Google by changing search preferences.

Changing **Search Preferences**

You can customize the way the Search tool finds information and the appearance of the Search Companion pane itself. For example, as you become more experienced with creating effective search criteria, you might not want to enter additional criteria in text boxes in the Search Companion pane. You can turn off the Search Companion feature that prompts you for successively more detailed search information by choosing to use the Classic search style instead of the Search Companion. The Search Companion guides you step by step through the search process, whereas in a Classic search, you select categories and enter search queries, which use special rules to create detailed search criteria. If you are familiar with a previous version of Windows, you might prefer the Classic search style. You also probably noticed the animated character that appears at the bottom of the Search Companion pane. If that character becomes distracting, you can turn it off or change it.

Another feature you can customize is the search engine the Search tool uses to search the Internet. By default, this is MSN, but you can change this to another search engine with which you are more familiar, such as Yahoo! or InfoSeek. Carolyn wants you to change the default search service from MSN to Google.

To change search preferences:

1. Click the **Start** button on the taskbar, and then click **Search**.

2. In the Search Companion pane, click **Change preferences**. A list of features you can customize appears in the Search Companion pane. See Figure 6-26.

Figure 6-26	CHANGING SEARCH PREFERENCES

click to change the default search service and other Internet search options

your settings might differ

Figure 6-27 describes the search preference options.

Figure 6-27	SEARCH PREFERENCE OPTIONS

SEARCH PREFERENCE	DESCRIPTION
With or without an animated screen character	Show or hide the animated character at the bottom of the Screen Companion pane
With a different character	Select a different animated character to show at the bottom of the Screen Companion pane
With or without the Indexing Service	Use the Search Companion with or without using the Indexing Service to speed your searches
Change files and folders search behavior	Change how you search for files and folders, such as to manually specify search criteria
Change Internet search behavior	Change the default search service and how you search for Web sites
Show or don't show balloon tips	Show or hide ScreenTips that appear in balloons as you work in the Search Companion
Turn AutoComplete off or on	Let the Search Companion suggest entries for text you have typed before, or complete entries without suggestions

3. Click **Change Internet search behavior**. The Search Companion pane lists the Internet search behavior you can customize. Note that here you can choose to use the Classic Internet search style instead of the guided series of prompts in the Search Companion pane.

4. In the list of search engines, click **Google**. If you click the OK button now, the Search tool will now use Google as the default search service. Because you should leave the Search tool in its default state for the next person who uses your computer, you won't click the OK button now.

5. Click the **Cancel** button and then close the Search Results window.

You have searched for quotations, people, and maps, and customized the search preferences. You're confident that you can use Windows XP and its Search tool to find just about any information Carolyn needs.

Session 6.2 QUICK CHECK

1. What kind of software searches through Internet documents and compiles a list of Web pages it locates on the Internet?

2. True or False: If you don't find the information you want using Yahoo!, you probably won't find the same information using MSN.

3. If your Internet search finds thousands of Web pages, what can you do to refine the search?

4. If you are using a search service and want to find information on the movie *The Wizard of Oz*, but you don't want any pages on the book *The Wizard of Oz*, what search operators can you use?

5. How can you use Windows XP to find an e-mail address for your state's governor?

REVIEW ASSIGNMENTS

1. *Using a Search String to Find a File* The governor has asked Senator Bernstein to represent the state in meetings with representatives of Taiwan who want to set up a student exchange program. In any international exchange, language is an issue. You remember a funny story about the translation of an ad for Coca-Cola into another language. Does the quotations archive disk contain that anecdote? To find out:

   a. In the Search Companion, use the All Files and Folders option, and enter likely search strings. Make sure you select the drive containing your Data Disk. If you're having trouble locating a file, try using only part of the search string or a different search string.

   b. Once you find a file you think looks promising, open it from the Search Results window.

   c. When you've found what you want, select the text, copy it, and then paste it into a new Notepad document. Type your name in the document you just created. At the end of the document, write a few sentences listing the search string you used and the name of the file(s) you located. Print the document and then close Notepad and the Search Results window. Don't save the Notepad document.

2. *Learning More About Files* On a sheet of paper, write the answers to the following questions about the files on the Data Disk. You can answer all the questions by examining the filenames.

    a. How many files contain the text "comedy" in their filenames?

    b. How many files and folders in total are on the disk? What did you do to find the answer? (*Hint*: You can find the answer to this question with a single search.)

    c. Which letters of the alphabet are missing in the filenames of the alphabetically organized Author files?

    d. How many files are on friendship? What search string did you use to find this answer?

3. *Using Wildcards* What search strings could you use to produce the following results? Write the search strings on a piece of paper. Use a wildcard for each one. For example, a results list of Budget2000.xls, Budget2001.xls, and Budget2002.xls could come from the search string "Budget200?.xls".

    a. Comedy1.doc, Comedy2.doc, Comedy3.doc

    b. Social.txt, Society.txt, Socratic Method.txt

    c. PhotoWorks, Network, Files for Work

4. *Searching for Files by Date* You can answer the following questions about the Data Disk by using the Date option. Write the answers on a sheet of paper. Return all settings to their defaults when you are done.

    a. How many files did Carolyn's previous aide modify in 1999?

    b. How many files did the aide modify in August, 1999?

    c. Which file(s) did the aide modify on August 31, 1999?

5. *Locating Files by Size* How many files of 1 KB or less does the Data Disk contain? How many files of 15 KB or more? Return this setting to its default when you are done.

6. *Locating Files by Contents* You enjoy Dave Barry's columns. Search the contents of the files on the Data Disk to see how many of them contain the text "barry", and then record that number. Write down the name of the file that seems to contain the most Dave Barry quotations. Open the file from Search. When you are done, delete the criteria you entered.

7. *Experimenting with Search Criteria* You decide to search for appropriate quotations for Senator Bernstein's upcoming speech topics. For each speech topic, write down the criteria you used to locate a file, and then write down the file location as it appears in the In Folder column of the results list. If you find more than one file, write down the first one in the list.

    a. Senator Bernstein has been invited to give the toast at a football brunch hosted by the president of Riverside College.

    b. *death* The family of a deceased friend has asked Senator Bernstein if she'd like to contribute any thoughts to a written memorial.

    c. Senator Bernstein is cochairing this year's Renaissance Festival downtown. The festival will *shakespeare* feature outdoor performances of three of Shakespeare's plays, including a performance by the Young Shakespeareans Guild, a troupe of children under age 18. She's promised to give the opening remarks at the festival.

Explore

8. *Opening Files from Search* You learned how to open a text document from Search in this tutorial. You can open other types of files the same way, as long as your computer contains the program that created the file.

    a. Search for Sound Clip files on your Data Disk. Right-click one of them and then click Play. What did you hear? Click the Close button when the sound file is done playing. If you don't hear anything, your computer might not have speakers, or they might be off.

    b. Search for Video Clip files on your computer's hard drive. If you find any, right-click one of them and then click the Play button. Describe what you see. Click the Close button when the video clip is done playing.

9. *Searching and Viewing File Contents* Find the answers to the questions below. You will probably need to search for a keyword in the file's contents. For each answer, write the name of the file you used to find the answer. (*Hint*: Once you've located and opened the file, you can scroll through it to find the answer, or open it in Notepad, click Edit on the Notepad menu bar, and then click Find. Type the keyword in the Find what box, and then click the Find Next button.)

    a. What did Elsa Einstein think about her husband Albert's theory of relativity?

    b. Do you think cartoonist Jim Borgman is an optimist or a pessimist? Why?

    c. What was Helen Keller's opinion of college?

    d. How many children did Erma Bombeck recommend that one have? (Look carefully at the filenames in the results list so you don't open more files than necessary.)

    e. What did Elbert Hubbard have to say about books? (Look carefully at the filenames in the results list so you don't open more files than necessary.)

Explore

10. *Locating Information on the Internet* Carolyn asks that you help locate information on Taiwan for Senator Bernstein's upcoming participation in establishing a student exchange program.

    a. Use the Search Companion pane to locate information on transportation in Taiwan. Write down the search criteria you use to find specific information. Write down the URL of a page on transportation in Taiwan.

    b. Send the search to the AltaVista search engine. When you find a page of specific information, write down its URL.

    c. Locate a Web page for one of Taiwan's universities. Write down the name of the university and the URL of its Web page.

11. *Locating People on the Internet* Use two different people search services and the Find People dialog box to locate the e-mail address of the president of your university. Were you able to find it in any of them? Did the search services have e-mail addresses for other people with the same name?

12. *Locating a Map* Locate and then print a map of your home address.

PROJECTS

1. On which drive is your Windows folder? Start to search for files and folders. In the Search Companion pane, specify My Computer in the Look in list, and then search for "Windows." Write the answer on a piece of paper. If there are too many files in the results list, sort the files by name so that folders named "Windows" appear near the top.

2. Can you locate the e-mail address of the president of the United States? What is the e-mail address?

3. Specify the following search strings, and, searching your Data Disk, examine the results list for each search string very carefully. What generalizations about wildcards can you make from your observations?

men
men.*
men.
men*.*
men?
men?.*

4. You can use Search to learn about the files on your hard drive. Record how many files of each of the following types exist on your hard disk.

a. Application. Write down the names of five application files in the Windows folder of your hard drive.

b. Bitmap Image. Which folders on your hard drive store the most bitmapped images?

c. Screen Saver. Write down the location of a screen saver on your hard drive.

d. Text Document. Once the results list shows all the text documents on your hard drive, order them by Name. Are any files named README? Write down the locations of two of them. Software programs often come with a README text file that lists known software problems and answers to common questions.

5. Write down the names of 10 documents recently accessed on the hard disk.

Explore

6. You can use the Search Companion pane to locate computers on a network. If you are on a network, click "Computers or people" in the Search Companion pane. Your instructor will give you the name of a computer for which to search on your network. Enter this name in the Computer Name box, and then click the Search button. Once Search has located the computer, open it from the results list. Take a screen print of the window that opens, and then paste that in a WordPad document. Include your name and the current date in the WordPad document.

Explore

7. Search the Data Disk for pictures or photos of Abraham Lincoln. If you don't find any, search the Internet. When you locate one, try to find the size of the picture or photo file. (*Hint*: The Web page might show the size near the image. If it doesn't, try right-clicking the image and then clicking Properties.) When you find a file that is less than 300 KB, save it on your Data Disk. To do so, right-click the image, click Save Picture As, and then use Abe Lincoln.jpg as the filename.

Explore

8. Use the "Documents (word processing, spreadsheets, etc.)" option in the Search Companion pane to find only text documents (.txt) on your Data Disk. Write down the number of .txt files you find. Then use the same option to find files with a .doc extension. Write down the number of .doc files you find.

QUICK CHECK ANSWERS

Session 6.1

1. Click the Look in list arrow, and then click 3½ Floppy (A:).

2. False

3. A wildcard is a symbol that stands in place of one or more characters. The asterisk wildcard substitutes for any number of characters; the question mark substitutes for only one.

4. Click the Name button in Details view.

5. Click All files and folders (if necessary), open the More advanced options list, click the Type list arrow, click Bitmap Image, and then click the Search button.

6. Right-click it and then click Open, double-click it, or click it and then press the Enter key.

7. A keyword is a search string—a word or a phrase—contained anywhere in a file.

Session 6.2

1. search engine
2. False
3. Refine the search by entering more detailed search criteria.
4. "Wizard of Oz" NOT book or "Wizard of Oz" -book
5. Search the Internet using the Search Companion pane to find a person's e-mail address.

New Perspectives on

MICROSOFT®
WINDOWS XP

Read This Before You Begin

To the Student

Data Disks

To complete the Level III tutorials, Review Assignments, and Projects, you need two Data Disks. Your instructor will either provide you with these Data Disks or ask you to make your own.

If you are making your own Data Disks, you will need **two** blank, formatted high-density disks. You will need to copy a set of files and/or folders from a file server, standalone computer, or the Web onto your disks. Your instructor will tell you which computer, drive letter, and folders contain the files you need. You could also download the files by going to **www.course.com** and following the instructions on the screen.

The information below shows you the Data Disks you need so that you will have enough disk space to complete all the tutorials, Review Assignments, and Projects:

Data Disk 1

Write this on the disk label:
Data Disk 1: Windows XP Tutorial 7

Data Disk 2

Write this on the disk label:
Data Disk 2: Windows XP Tutorial 8

When you begin each tutorial, Review Assignment, or Project, be sure you are using the correct Data Disk. Refer to the "File Finder" chart at the back of this text for more detailed information on which files are used in which tutorials. See the inside front or inside back cover of this book for more information on Data Disk files, or ask your instructor or technical support person for assistance.

Course Labs

The Windows XP Level III tutorials feature interactive Course Labs to help you understand Internet concepts. There are Lab Assignments at the end of Tutorial 8 and Tutorial 10 that relate to these Labs.

To start a Lab, click the **Start** button on the Windows taskbar, point to **Programs**, point to **Course Labs**, point to **New Perspectives Course Labs**, and then click the name of the Lab you want to use.

Using Your Own Computer

If you are going to work through this book using your own computer, you need:

- **Computer System** Microsoft Windows XP must be installed on your computer. This book assumes a typical installation of Microsoft Windows XP Professional Edition.

- **Data Disk** You will not be able to complete the tutorials or exercises in this book using your own computer until you have your Data Disks.

- **Course Labs** See your instructor or technical support person to obtain the Course Lab software for use on your own computer.

Visit Our World Wide Web Site

Additional materials designed especially for you are available on the World Wide Web.
Go to **www.course.com/NewPerspectives**.

To the Instructor

The Data Disk Files and Course Labs are available on the Instructor's Resource Kit for this title. Follow the instructions in the Help file on the CD-ROM to install the programs to your network or standalone computer. For information on creating Data Disks or the Course Labs, see the "To the Student" section above.

You are granted a license to copy the Data Files and Course Labs to any computer or computer network used by students who have purchased this book.

OBJECTIVES

In this tutorial you will:

- Start Paint and explore the Paint window

- Open a graphic in Paint

- Crop and edit a graphic

- Save a graphic in a different bitmapped graphic format

- Draw with a variety of drawing tools, including the Pencil, Brush, Airbrush, Line, and Ellipse tools

- Magnify and edit a graphic using the grid and a thumbnail

- Copy and paste portions of a graphic

- Flip and stretch a graphic

- Add color to an existing graphic, and draw portions of a graphic in color

- Add and format text in a graphic

WORKING WITH GRAPHICS

Creating Advertisement Graphics at Kiana Ski Shop

CASE

Kiana Ski Shop

Cross-country ski enthusiast Joe Nitka owns Kiana Ski Shop in the heart of the northern Wisconsin Chequamegon National Forest, near the site of the world-class Birkebeiner cross-country ski race. Joe is one of the local promoters of the race. He gathers and distributes information on lodging and transportation for competitors, the media, and spectators. So far, Joe has been using a word processor to create brochures that contain this information but hasn't added graphics or color. An avid cross-country skier yourself, you volunteer to help Joe create his Birkebeiner brochures and to make them look more professional. You tell him his brochures would capture more attention if they included a few graphics, such as a skier or a picture of the race logo.

Joe agrees and says he could photocopy some drawings from a clip-art collection of images and pictures at the library. You tell him using a computer instead offers several advantages: computer graphics can be resized more easily, pasted seamlessly into a word-processed document, and edited. You think you can find some eye-catching graphic images on the Internet that you can customize, or you could even create a graphic or two from scratch. Joe is interested and explains that his first priority is the announcement that he needs to send to local motel and hotel owners, asking if they'd like to advertise their services in his brochures.

You spend a little time on the Internet before Joe arrives, and you find a graphic file called Sports, which includes several sports-related images. The Web page containing the Sports graphic indicates that the file is not copyrighted, which means you can download it free of charge.

SESSION 7.1

In this session, you will open a graphic in the Windows XP graphics program, Paint. You will crop a portion of the graphic, save it in a new file, and then edit the graphic to meet your needs and save it in monochrome (black and white) and color bitmapped graphic formats. For this tutorial, you will need the Data Disk for Tutorial 7.

Working with Paint

Drawings and pictures on a computer are called **graphic images** or **graphics**. Some graphics are created using a **scanner**, which converts an existing paper image into an electronic file that you can open and work with on your computer. You can also use a digital camera to create graphics from pictures you take. To create a graphic from scratch, you use a **graphics program**, software that includes drawing and graphic editing tools. Windows XP includes a basic graphics program called **Paint**, which lets you create, edit, and manipulate graphics. Graphics come in two fundamental types: bitmapped and vector. A **bitmapped graphic** is made up of small dots that form an image, whereas a **vector graphic** is created by mathematical formulas that define the shapes used in the image. Computer graphics can come in either type, although vector graphics are more precise than bitmapped because of their mathematical foundation. Many software packages come with collections of graphics called **clip art**. Clip-art images are usually in vector format because they are easier to manipulate in that format. Paint, however, handles only bitmapped graphic formats, not vector graphic formats. Because the Sports graphic you found is a bitmapped graphic, you will use Paint to create graphics for Joe's promotions. In this session, you'll work with an existing graphic, and in Sessions 7.2 and 7.3, you will work with a graphic you create from scratch.

You decide to start Paint and introduce Joe to the Windows XP graphics tools.

To start Paint:

1. Click the **Start** button [start] on the taskbar.

2. Point to **All Programs** and then point to **Accessories**. The Accessories menu opens.

3. Click **Paint**. The Paint window opens. If necessary, maximize the Paint window. See Figure 7-1.

Figure 7-1   PAINT WINDOW

Within the Paint window is a blank white area like an artist's canvas, where you work with your graphic. At the bottom of the window is the color palette, which displays available colors or shades for the foreground and background of your graphic. To the left of the color palette are two additional overlapping boxes, the top for the foreground color and the bottom for the background color of any object you might draw. The status bar at the bottom of the window provides information about the tools you select and about the location of the pointer when it's on the canvas.

To the left of the canvas is the **toolbox**, a collection of tools that you use to draw and edit graphics. The tools all work the same way: you click a tool, the pointer changes to a shape representing the tool, and then you either click or drag on the canvas to draw with the tool. Some tools offer different widths or shapes, which are identified in a **Style box** that appears below the toolbox. You will use the Style box in Session 7.2.

Figure 7-2 shows the available tools, along with the pointer shape that appears when you use the tool.

You'll work with some of the editing tools in this session, with the drawing tools in Session 7.2, and with the color and text tools in Session 7.3.

Figure 7-2   PAINT TOOLS

TOOL	BUTTON	DESCRIPTION	POINTER
Free-Form Select		Select a free-form portion of a graphic	
Select		Select a rectangular portion of a graphic	
Eraser/Color Eraser		Erase a portion of a graphic	
Fill With Color		Fill an enclosed area with the selected color	
Pick Color		Pick up an existing color in the graphic so you can apply it to another area of the graphic	

Figure 7-2	PAINT TOOLS (continued)		
TOOL	**BUTTON**	**DESCRIPTION**	**POINTER**
Magnifier	🔍	Change the magnification	
Pencil	✏️	Draw a free-form line or draw one pixel at a time	
Brush	🖌️	Draw using a brush in a variety of widths	
Airbrush		Draw using an airbrush in a variety of widths	
Text	**A**	Insert text into a graphic	
Line	╲	Draw a line	
Curve	︵	Draw a curve	
Rectangle	▢	Draw a rectangle or square	
Polygon	▱	Draw a polygon	
Ellipse	⬭	Draw an ellipse or circle	
Rounded Rectangle	▢	Draw a rectangle or square with rounded corners	

Opening a Graphic in Paint

Joe wants to take a look at the Sports graphic to see if it contains images that might work for his announcement. To open an existing graphic in Paint, you use the Open command on the File menu. The Sports graphic is located on your Data Disk.

To open the Sports graphic:

1. Click **File** on the menu bar, and then click **Open**. You use the Open dialog box in Paint to open a file just as you do in any other Windows XP program.

2. Click the **Look in** list arrow, and then click the drive containing your Data Disk.

3. Click **Sports** and then click the **Open** button.

   TROUBLE? If Sports appears as Sports.bmp, your computer is set to display file extensions as part of the filename. Click Sports.bmp, click Open, and then continue to Step 4.

4. If necessary, scroll to the bottom of the graphic and then to the right. See Figure 7-3. The Sports graphic contains a number of sporting figures.

Figure 7-3	SPORTS GRAPHIC

color palette shows monochrome colors

skis

TROUBLE? If you can't see the entire graphic image, resize the Paint window or the canvas as necessary.

Note the color palette at the bottom of the Paint window. It no longer offers the array of colors shown in Figure 7-1. Instead, the color palette includes only black, white, and patterns of black and white that give the illusion of gray shading. You tell Joe that the Sports graphic is a monochrome graphic, that is, a graphic with only two colors—black and white—available to it.

Before working with the Sports graphic, you think Joe needs to learn some basic concepts about bitmapped graphics and how Paint handles these types of images.

Working with Bitmapped Graphics

A computer screen is a grid work of small dots of light called **pixels**, which is short for "picture elements." The pixels form images on the screen by displaying different colors (including black and white), much as a television does. Buttons on the taskbar, for example, are formed by the pixels shown in Figure 7-4.

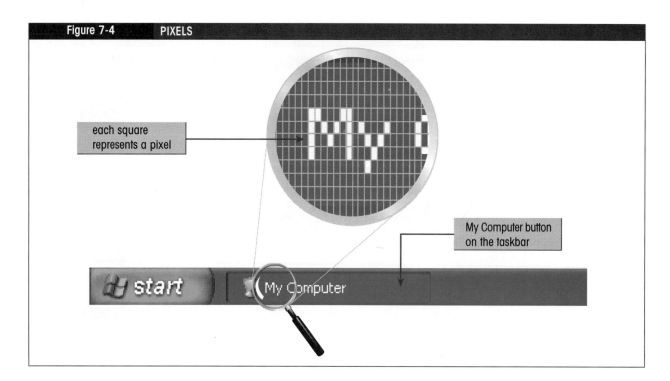

Figure 7-4 **PIXELS**

each square represents a pixel

My Computer button on the taskbar

Each pixel has a color, and the individual colored pixels form the graphics you see on your computer screen. To understand how a graphic can be created from pixels, imagine a piece of graph paper on which each square represents a pixel. To draw a straight line, you color in a row of squares; to draw a circle, you fill in the squares to approximate a curve, as shown in Figure 7-5. In this drawing, every pixel within the circle's border is black, and every pixel outside the border is white. Your computer uses 0's and 1's as a code for the color of each pixel. Each 0 or 1 is called a **bit**. Your computer maps, or assigns, a color to each code or bit, hence the term "bitmap." To determine the color of each pixel in a black-and-white drawing, you need only one bit, because a bit can be either off or on—black or white.

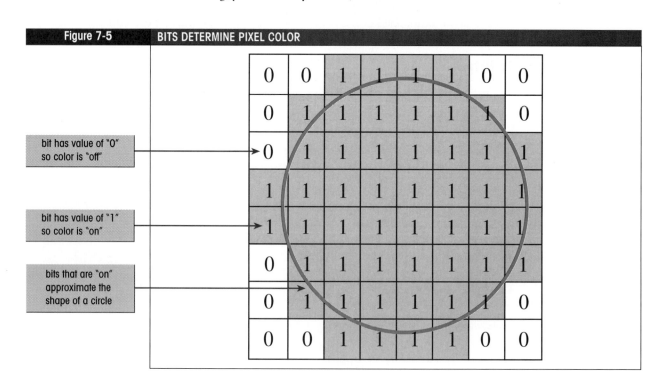

Figure 7-5 **BITS DETERMINE PIXEL COLOR**

bit has value of "0" so color is "off"

bit has value of "1" so color is "on"

bits that are "on" approximate the shape of a circle

A 1-bit graphic, such as the one in Figure 7-5, is also known as a **monochrome bitmap**. The Skis image is such a graphic. If your graphic contains more colors, the computer needs to use more bits. Paint provides four bitmap types: 1-bit (monochrome), 4-bit (up to 16 colors), 8-bit (up to 256 colors), and 24-bit (up to over 16 million colors). As the number of bits increases, so does the number of available colors and the size of the graphic file. Figure 7-6 summarizes the bitmap file types that Paint allows, the number of bits per pixel, the number of distinct colors each type can display, and the size of a file that starts out as a 4KB monochrome bitmap and then is saved in each type.

Figure 7-6	PAINT FILE FORMATS		
FILE TYPE	**NUMBER OF BITS**	**NUMBER OF COLORS**	**SAMPLE FILE SIZE**
Monochrome	1	2	4 KB
16 Color Bitmap	4	16	13 KB
256 Color Bitmap	8	256	27 KB
24-bit Bitmap	24	16.7 million	77 KB

Because increasing colors also increases the size of the file, you might not want to select a bitmap type with more colors than you need. For a simple black-and-white graphic, monochrome is the best choice.

By default, Paint stores its graphics with the .bmp file extension—the standard Windows XP file format for bitmapped graphics. However, if you have Microsoft Office installed, you can also choose to save your file as GIF, PNG, or JPEG images. These image types are often used for graphics placed on Web pages. You can also save and open TIF files, a common file type for displaying and producing detailed printed images. If you want Paint to work with graphics that have other file extensions, or if you do not have Microsoft Office, you need to use a software program called a **graphics converter** to change the file to a format that Paint can work with.

Joe comments that he's heard people complain about how bitmapped graphics can look rough around the edges. A bitmapped image needs to be the appropriate size to look good. Recall that a bitmapped graphic is defined by pixels. Because you cannot change the size of an individual pixel, resizing the overall image tends to distort it. For example, when you try to enlarge a bitmapped graphic, Paint duplicates the pixels to approximate the original shape as best it can—often resulting in jagged edges. On the other hand, when you shrink a bitmapped graphic, Paint removes pixels, and the drawing loses detail. In either case, you distort the original graphic. Sometimes the resized bitmapped graphic will look fine, as when it contains many straight lines, but just as often the resized graphic's image quality suffers. For example, if you were to enlarge the Sports graphic, the result might look like Figure 7-7.

Figure 7-7 ENLARGED PART OF THE SPORTS GRAPHIC

baseball edges are rough

How do you get around this problem? In Paint, there is no easy solution to resizing graphics, because they are all bitmapped. If you work with graphics that require resizing— for example, if you want a graphic that will look good on a small business card and a large poster—using vector graphics is a better choice. Because vector graphics are mathematically based, you can resize them as necessary without sacrificing image quality. However, you will need to buy a graphics program that allows you to work with vector graphics.

Now that Joe has had a chance to learn more about working with bitmapped graphics, he is ready to select an appropriate image for his announcement from the Sports graphic. He immediately notices the pair of skis at the bottom. He thinks that the skis alone would look great in the announcement. You tell Joe you can capture just that portion of the graphic by **cropping**, or cutting out, everything around it.

Cropping a Portion of a Graphic

To crop a graphic, you use either the Select tool or the Free-Form Select tool. With the **Select tool**, you draw a rectangle, called a **selection box**, around the area you want to crop. With the **Free-Form Select tool**, you draw any shaped line around the area. Once you have selected the portion of the graphic you need, you can manipulate it. For Joe's announcement, you want to save the selection in a separate file. The separate file will contain only the cropped area—in Joe's case, the pair of skis.

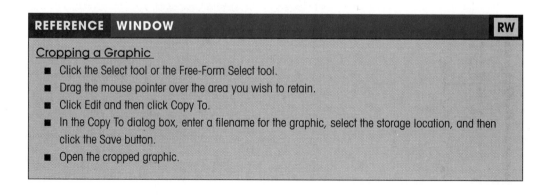

REFERENCE WINDOW **RW**

<u>Cropping a Graphic</u>
- Click the Select tool or the Free-Form Select tool.
- Drag the mouse pointer over the area you wish to retain.
- Click Edit and then click Copy To.
- In the Copy To dialog box, enter a filename for the graphic, select the storage location, and then click the Save button.
- Open the cropped graphic.

In this section, you'll use the Select tool because it's easier to manipulate than the Free-Form Select tool. However, because the sailboat and the bowling ball images are so close to the skis, when you crop you will probably include portions of those graphics. In the next section, you'll learn how to erase parts of a graphic that you don't want. In the Review Assignments, you'll have an opportunity to use the Free-Form Select tool to avoid the extra step of erasing. You're ready to select the skis.

To crop the skis from the Sports graphic:

1. Locate and click the **Select** tool ▫ in the toolbox. The Select tool is the first tool in the second column of tools in the toolbox.

2. Move the pointer over the canvas. The pointer looks like ╀. Next, you need to drag a selection box around the pair of skis.

3. Point to the white space above the upper-left part of the skis and poles. Press the left mouse button and hold it down while you drag to the lower-right corner of the skis. As you drag, a selection box appears. See Figure 7-8. The selection box can include parts of the sailboat and bowling ball because you will erase these unwanted images next.

| Figure 7-8 | SELECTING AN AREA TO CROP |

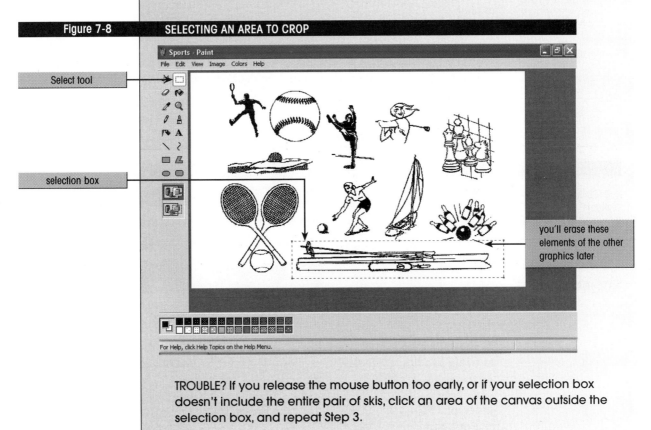

Select tool

selection box

you'll erase these elements of the other graphics later

TROUBLE? If you release the mouse button too early, or if your selection box doesn't include the entire pair of skis, click an area of the canvas outside the selection box, and repeat Step 3.

Now that you selected the skis, you can use the Copy To command to save the selected area in a new file, thereby cropping it from the Sports graphic.

To save the selected area in a new file:

1. Click **Edit** on the menu bar, and then click **Copy To**. The Copy To dialog box opens.

TROUBLE? If the Copy To dialog box doesn't open, you probably clicked the Copy command instead of the Copy To command. Repeat Step 1.

2. Type **Skis** in the File name text box. Make sure that the Save in text box shows your Data Disk.

3. Click the **Save** button. The file is saved on your Data Disk with the filename "Skis."

The Sports graphic is still open in Paint, and the Skis graphic is in a separate file. In Paint, you can work with only one graphic file at a time. If you try to open another graphic or create a new graphic, Paint closes the current one, prompting you to save it if necessary. If you want two Paint graphics open at the same time, you must start a separate Paint session, so that two Paint windows are open with one graphic in each. You don't need the Sports graphic for now, so you'll open the Skis graphic and let Paint close the Sports graphic.

To open the Skis graphic:

1. Click **File** on the menu bar, and then click **Open**.

2. In the Open dialog box, click **Skis** and then click the **Open** button. If Paint asks if you want to save the changes to the Sports file, click the **No** button. The Skis graphic opens. See Figure 7-9.

| Figure 7-9 | SKIS IMAGE CROPPED FROM THE SPORTS GRAPHIC FILE |

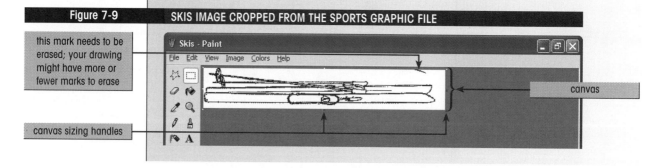

this mark needs to be erased; your drawing might have more or fewer marks to erase

canvas sizing handles

canvas

Notice that the canvas now takes up only a small portion of the Paint window. The canvas sizing handles, the small boxes shown in Figure 7-9, allow you to resize the graphic if necessary.

Joe notices the stray lines from the sailboat and bowling ball graphics at the top of the Skis graphic. You tell him you can use the Eraser/Color Eraser tool to erase unneeded portions of a graphic.

Erasing Parts of a Graphic

The **Eraser/Color Eraser tool** erases the area over which you drag the pointer. If you erase more than you intended, you can use the **Undo** command on the Edit menu, which reverses one or more of your last three actions, depending on how many times you click Undo (up to three times.) You'll show Joe how to erase the stray marks in the skis image.

To erase the portions of the graphic that you don't want:

1. Click the **Eraser/Color Eraser** tool . When you move the pointer over the graphic, it changes to ☐.

2. Drag the ☐ pointer over the areas at the top of the Skis graphic that show parts of the bowling ball and the sailboat to erase them. As you drag, the unwanted parts of these images disappear. See Figure 7-10.

| Figure 7-10 | ERASING UNWANTED PORTIONS OF A GRAPHIC |

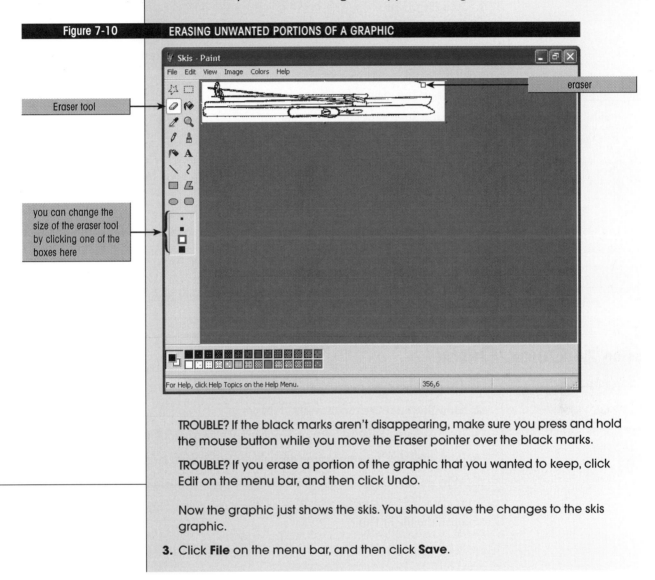

TROUBLE? If the black marks aren't disappearing, make sure you press and hold the mouse button while you move the Eraser pointer over the black marks.

TROUBLE? If you erase a portion of the graphic that you wanted to keep, click Edit on the menu bar, and then click Undo.

Now the graphic just shows the skis. You should save the changes to the skis graphic.

3. Click **File** on the menu bar, and then click **Save**.

You ask Joe if he would like to make any other changes to the skis graphic before he inserts it in his announcement. He looks it over and wonders if he could format in color. You remind Joe that this skis graphic is a monochrome file, and explain that to add color, he must save the graphic with a different file format that supports more colors.

Saving a Bitmapped Graphic in a Different File Type

When you save a graphic in a different file type in Paint, the graphic's appearance doesn't change. The pixels that were black stay black, and those that were white stay white. However, the number of bits that defines each color changes, and so the file changes in size. When you are ready to color the graphic, you'll find a new set of colors available to you. Instead of the black, white, and pattern boxes that you see now in the color palette, you will see colors. You decide to save the Skis graphic as a 256 Color Bitmap, because this format provides a wide array of colors but doesn't take up as much space as the 24-bit Bitmap format.

To save the graphic file as a 256 Color Bitmap:

1. Click **File** on the menu bar, and then click **Save As**. The Save As dialog box opens.

2. Click the **Save as type** list arrow, and then click **256 Color Bitmap**.

   Next you can change the name of the graphic so you remember that it is the color version.

3. Type **Skis256** in the File name text box.

4. Click the **Save** button.

   Notice the change in the color palette. Paint now offers an array of colors instead of the various shades of gray, white, and black. You tell Joe that if he wants to come back another time and add color to the Skis graphic, he can. For now, you are finished working with the skis graphic, and you can close Paint.

5. Click the **Close** button ⊠ to close the Paint window.

So far, you have learned the basics of working with Paint, including how to open a graphic, crop a portion of a graphic, and erase parts of it. You also learned what to consider before resizing a bitmapped graphic, and how to save a Paint image in a different file format.

Session 7.1 QUICK CHECK

1. Describe how you save a portion of a graphic in a separate file.

2. How do you resize the canvas?

3. True or False: You can open only one graphic in Paint at a time.

4. The small dots on your screen are called _____.

5. Why do color graphics use more file space than monochrome graphics?

6. If you have a graphic in a file format that Paint doesn't support, what can you do to open the file in Paint?

SESSION 7.2

In this session, you will learn to edit an existing graphic and draw new graphics with the collection of drawing tools in Paint. You'll use the Pencil, Line, Brush, and Ellipse tools, and you will flip and stretch your graphics. You'll also learn techniques that make drawing easier, such as controlling the magnification, editing one pixel at a time, using the grid and a thumbnail, and copying and pasting parts of a graphic.

Drawing with the Pencil Tool

You use the **Pencil tool** to draw a line or image one pixel at a time. Once you select the Pencil tool, you can click the canvas to draw pixel-size dots, or you can drag over the canvas to draw a line that is one pixel wide. The Pencil tool is effective when you want to edit details of an image to smooth lines or eliminate unnecessary dots, for example. You can also use the Pencil tool to draw free-form images, such as jagged lines or irregular shapes.

Joe drops by a few days after your initial computer session with a problem: the Skis graphic isn't right for the Birkebeiner announcement because it shows a downhill ski, not a cross-country ski. The bindings for the two ski types are different, as shown in Figure 7-11.

| Figure 7-11 | PROBLEM WITH THE SKIS GRAPHIC |

You tell Joe you can fix this problem by erasing unwanted portions of the graphic—the bindings—and then using the Pencil tool to draw a heel plate using free-form dots or lines. You decide to show Joe how to draw with the Pencil tool before you fix the Skis graphic.

To experiment with the Pencil tool:

1. Make sure your Data Disk is in drive A, start Paint, and then maximize the Paint window. Paint opens an empty canvas.

2. If necessary, click the **Pencil** tool , and then move the pointer onto the canvas. The pointer looks like a shape.

3. Hold the mouse button down, and drag over the canvas, drawing a line. See Figure 7-12.

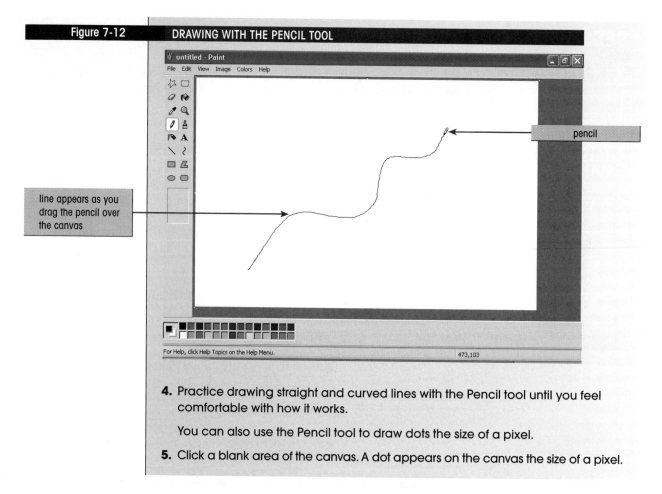

Figure 7-12 — DRAWING WITH THE PENCIL TOOL

pencil

line appears as you drag the pencil over the canvas

4. Practice drawing straight and curved lines with the Pencil tool until you feel comfortable with how it works.

You can also use the Pencil tool to draw dots the size of a pixel.

5. Click a blank area of the canvas. A dot appears on the canvas the size of a pixel.

Now that you've shown Joe how easy it is to draw lines or dots with the Pencil tool, you are ready to edit the Skis graphic. You first must erase the parts of the binding that are for downhill skis, and then you will add a heel plate for the cross-country ski binding.

Magnifying a Drawing

The changes you need to make to the Skis graphic require careful erasing and redrawing—a task made easier when you magnify the view of the image. The **Magnifier tool** allows you to view a graphic at several magnification levels. The default magnification is 100%, also called **Normal view**. If you click the Magnifier tool and then click the graphic, Paint displays it at 400%. You can select a different magnification using the Style box that appears below the toolbox when you click : 1× (Normal view), 2× (200% magnification), 6× (600% magnification), and 8× (800% magnification). The **Custom Zoom dialog box** (which you open by clicking View, pointing to Zoom, and then clicking Custom) adds the 400% zoom option. Increasing the magnification is called **zooming in**.

If you are magnifying the view to edit a few pixels at a time, you can use the grid to help you navigate. The **grid** is a checkerboard background similar to a piece of graph paper, on which each square represents a pixel. The grid guides your drawing so your lines are straight and your shapes are precise.

REFERENCE WINDOW **RW**

<u>Magnifying a Graphic</u>
- To zoom in, click the Magnifier tool and then click the graphic to zoom to the default magnification of 400%, or click one of the magnifications in the Style box below the toolbox.
- To view gridlines, switch to a magnified view, click View, point to Zoom, and then click Show Grid.
- To view a portion of the magnified graphic in Normal view, switch to a magnified view, click View, point to Zoom, and then click Show Thumbnail.

You need to first open the Skis graphic, zoom in to the highest magnification, and then show the grid so you can more easily edit the graphic.

To change the view for editing:

1. Click **File** on the menu bar, click **Open**, and then locate and open the **Skis256** file on your Data Disk. Click **No** if you are prompted to save changes to the untitled graphic you were just working with. Now save the file with a new name, so the original file remains intact, in case you need to work through these steps again.

2. Click **File** and then click **Save As**. Make sure the Save in text box displays the drive containing your Data Disk and that the Save as type text box shows 256 Color Bitmap. Type **XCountry Skis** in the File name text box, and then click the **Save** button. Click **Yes** when you are asked whether you want to replace the existing file.

3. Click the **Magnifier** tool 🔍 , and move the pointer over the canvas. The pointer changes to 🔍, and a box appears that shows the portion of the graphic Paint will magnify.

4. Click the far-left side of the graphic to zoom in on that portion of the picture. The Magnifier tool is using the default 400% magnification.

5. Click **View** on the menu bar, point to **Zoom**, and then click **Show Grid**. You can see the individual pixels, as in Figure 7-13. The boxes are too small to work with easily, so you decide to use the Custom dialog box to zoom in even more.

Figure 7-13   MAGNIFIED VIEW WITH GRID SHOWING

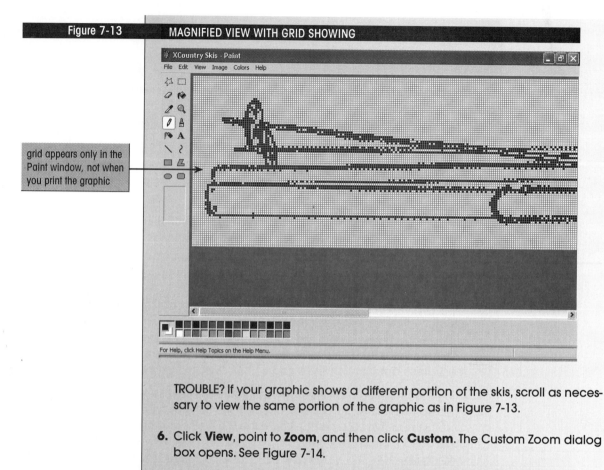

grid appears only in the Paint window, not when you print the graphic

TROUBLE? If your graphic shows a different portion of the skis, scroll as necessary to view the same portion of the graphic as in Figure 7-13.

6. Click **View**, point to **Zoom**, and then click **Custom**. The Custom Zoom dialog box opens. See Figure 7-14.

Figure 7-14   CHOOSING A DIFFERENT MAGNIFICATION

click to increase the magnification

7. Click the **800%** option button, and then click the **OK** button. Now the grid boxes are larger, and you can easily edit individual pixels.

When you're zoomed in this closely, you sometimes lose sight of the picture's appearance. You can view a **thumbnail**, a small box that shows in Normal view the area you're zooming in on. Thumbnails are especially handy for editing. You decide to view a thumbnail of the area you're working on.

To view a thumbnail:

1. Click **View** on the menu bar, and then point to **Zoom**.

TROUBLE? If the thumbnail already appears, skip Steps 1 and 2.

2. Click **Show Thumbnail**. A thumbnail of the area you're examining appears on the Paint window. See Figure 7-15.

Figure 7-15	VIEWING A THUMBNAIL OF THE MAGNIFIED AREA

thumbnail of magnified area

TROUBLE? If the thumbnail appears in a different area of the Paint window and it obscures an area you want to examine, move it to a different location.

Now that you can see each pixel, and you have a thumbnail view for monitoring how your changes affect the larger picture, you're ready to start editing.

Erasing in a Magnified View

Once you zoom in, you can erase unwanted portions of a graphic a few pixels at a time. To erase, you drag the Eraser tool over the appropriate pixels. The Eraser tool comes in several sizes; select the size according to the number of pixels you need to erase. The largest size lets you erase large sections of a graphic in 10×10 boxes (100 pixels at a time). The smallest size lets you erase in 4×4 boxes (16 pixels at a time). The Eraser tool does not erase one pixel at a time. You can, however, use the Pencil tool to accomplish the same purpose: choose white as your drawing color, and then any pixel you click will turn white.

Now you can use the Eraser tool on Joe's graphic to erase the portions of the binding that are for downhill skis.

To erase the parts of the ski binding you don't need:

1. Using Figure 7-11 as a guide, scroll the Paint window until you see the binding. Watch the thumbnail to see where the binding is located, and then click the **Eraser** tool.

TROUBLE? If the thumbnail is in the way, drag it to the lower-right corner of the screen. Resize the window as necessary.

2. Click the **smallest box** in the Eraser tool Style box. See Figure 7-16.

| Figure 7-16 | SELECTING THE SMALLEST SIZE OF THE ERASER TOOL |

drag thumbnail out of the way, if necessary

smallest eraser size

use Eraser tools to erase pixels within the ski and below the ski

3. Point to the pixels inside the ski, hold down the left mouse button, and then drag the **Eraser** tool ⬚ to erase the pixels inside the ski and below the ski, as shown in Figure 7-17. Scroll as necessary to complete the erasures. The pixels that you should erase are shown in red in Figure 7-17.

| Figure 7-17 | PIXELS THAT NEED TO BE ERASED |

pixels you need to erase are shown in red

ski after you are finished erasing

TROUBLE? If you erased an area you didn't want to erase, click Edit and then click Undo. If you need to start over, do so without saving your changes.

4. Click the **Magnifier** tool 🔍 , and then click **1x** in the Style box to return to Normal view. The grid and thumbnail are both hidden.

In Normal view you can see how your erasures have changed the look of the ski. It looks good. You are now ready to draw the heel plate, which has a trapezoidal shape. You'll use the Pencil tool to draw it a few pixels at a time.

Drawing in a Magnified View

You've already seen how to use the thumbnail to orient yourself in the Paint window. Paint offers one other feature to help you identify and control your location as you draw. The **pixel coordinates** in the status bar specify the exact location of the pointer on the canvas relative to the pixels on your screen. Paint displays the pixel coordinates in an (x,y) format (x representing the horizontal location and y the vertical location). Pixel coordinates of 138,25, for example, indicate that the pointer is 138 pixels from the left edge of the screen and 25 pixels from the top. In the next set of steps you will use pixel coordinates to add the heel plate in just the right location.

You'll use the Magnifier tool to zoom back in, this time to only 600%, because the work isn't as meticulous. A lower magnification also lets you view a little more of your graphic.

To create the heel plate:

1. Click the **Magnifier** tool 🔍 , and then click **6x** in the Style box.

2. Scroll to the binding area of the ski.

3. Point to any pixel and then note the pixel coordinates that appear in the status bar. Move the pointer and observe how the pixel coordinates change accordingly.

4. Click the **Pencil** tool ✏ , and then position the pointer at pixel coordinate **155,57**. See Figure 7-18 for the location of this pixel.

5. Click the **155,57** pixel and then click the **155,58** pixel. Drag to fill in the rest of the pixels shown in Figure 7-18.

Figure 7-18   USING PIXEL COORDINATES TO DRAW THE HEEL PLATE

(159,55)

(155,57)

(155,58)

(159,60)

pixel coordinates
of pointer

TROUBLE? If you draw in an area you didn't intend to, click Edit and then click Undo.

6. Click 🔍 and then click **1x** in the Style box to return to Normal view. See Figure 7-19. Joe is satisfied with the skis, so you decide to save the file.

Figure 7-19   FINISHED SKI

heel plate

7. Click **File** on the menu bar, and then click **Save**.

Joe asks about creating new graphics that he could use for advertising Kiana Ski Shop. Joe sketches a few ideas, and you decide to draw the sketch in Figure 7-20.

Figure 7-20   IDEA FOR A KIANA GRAPHIC

to create this ski . . .

. . . you'll draw this ski and copy it

Next, you'll show Joe how to create this new graphic using the Brush tool.

Drawing with the Brush Tool

Unlike the Pencil tool, the Brush tool offers a variety of widths and brush styles you can use to draw. To create the skis shown in Figure 7-20, you can use an angular style brush. To create the letter "K," you can use a rounded brush. (You can add letters by typing rather than drawing by using the Text tool, which you'll learn to use in Session 7.3.)

To create this new graphic, you need a blank canvas, which you can obtain in one of three ways. Assuming you have first saved the existing image on the canvas, you can erase the contents of the canvas using the Eraser tool, and then save the file under a different filename; you can choose Clear Image from the Image menu to clear the canvas and then save the file under a different filename; or you can choose New from the File menu to open a new file.

To create a new file and begin drawing with the Brush tool:

1. Click **File** on the menu bar, and then click **New**. An empty canvas opens.

2. Click the **Brush** tool 🖌 . Notice the brush styles in the Style box. The current brush style is highlighted.

3. Drag the brush pointer over the canvas. A thick rounded line appears.

   Now try a different brush style.

4. Click the leftmost **angular line** brush style in the third row of the Style box, as shown in Figure 7-21, and then drag the brush pointer over the screen. You create a line like the one in Figure 7-21.

Figure 7-21   BRUSH STYLES

line drawn with rounded brush

Angular brush style is selected

Angular brush pointer

line drawn with Angular brush

5. Drag the brush pointer around a small corner, and then draw a straight horizontal line. You will erase the drawing shortly, so feel free to experiment.

Now that you have an idea of how the brush tools work, you can clear the screen and try drawing Joe's image. This time, rather than using the New command to open a blank canvas, you'll use the Image menu's Clear Image command, which erases the entire image all at once and lets you start over with an empty canvas.

To clear the graphic and then draw the ski:

1. Click **Image** on the menu bar, and then click **Clear Image**. Your drawings disappear as Paint clears the canvas.

2. Now try drawing the ski near the bottom of the canvas. This time try to make it look like the ski in Figure 7-22. Click **Edit** on the menu bar, and then click **Undo** if you aren't satisfied, and try again.

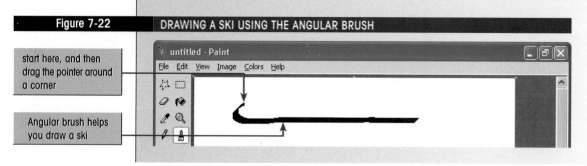

Figure 7-22   DRAWING A SKI USING THE ANGULAR BRUSH

start here, and then drag the pointer around a corner

Angular brush helps you draw a ski

> **TROUBLE?** If you have a difficult time holding the mouse steady to draw the straight line, you could try controlling the pointer with the arrow keys rather than the mouse. Use the MouseKeys option available through the Accessibility Options dialog box in the Windows XP Control Panel. (Click Start, click Control Panel, and then click Accessibility in Category view, or double-click Accessibility Options in Classic view.) You could also try drawing just one section of the ski at a time. The goal is to become familiar with the Brush tool; you won't be saving this file, and you'll learn another technique for drawing straight lines later in this session.

Once you have drawn a satisfactory ski, you need to draw a second ski that has the same size and shape as the first ski. To ensure a consistent look, you can make a copy of the first ski and then paste it on the graphic as the second ski.

Copying, Pasting, and Moving a Portion of a Graphic

To copy a portion of a graphic, you select it and then you select the Copy command on the Edit menu. Your selection is copied to the Clipboard. You can then use the Edit menu's Paste command to paste the copy into the graphic, where it "floats" in the upper-left corner of the canvas until you drag it to the desired location.

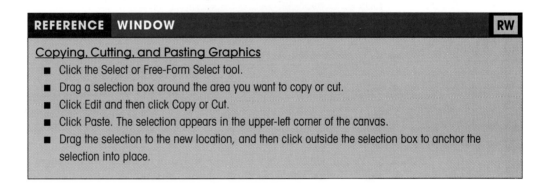

REFERENCE WINDOW **RW**

Copying, Cutting, and Pasting Graphics
- Click the Select or Free-Form Select tool.
- Drag a selection box around the area you want to copy or cut.
- Click Edit and then click Copy or Cut.
- Click Paste. The selection appears in the upper-left corner of the canvas.
- Drag the selection to the new location, and then click outside the selection box to anchor the selection into place.

You are ready to copy the first ski, paste it, and then move it just above the existing ski. So that your drawing will match the one shown in the figures, you'll open a copy of the drawing of the ski, which is stored on your Data Disk in the Brush file. You'll then save this file with the name "Kiana."

To copy and paste the first ski and then position it:

1. Click **File** on the menu bar, click **Open**, and then locate and open the **Brush** file on your Data Disk. Click **No** if you are prompted to save changes to the untitled graphic you were just working with.

2. Click **File** and then click **Save As**. Make sure the Save in text box displays the drive containing your Data Disk and that the Save as type list box shows 256 Color Bitmap. Type **Kiana** in the File name text box, and then click the **Save** button.

3. Click the **Select** tool ⬚.

4. Draw a selection box around the ski. A dashed outline appears around the ski.

5. Click **Edit** on the menu bar, and then click **Copy**. The ski is copied to the Clipboard.

6. Click **Edit** and then click **Paste**. The ski appears in the upper-left corner of the Paint window.

7. Place the pointer over the pasted ski. Make sure the pointer looks like ✛.

8. Drag the ski so that it is above and slightly to the right of the first ski. See Figure 7-23.

Figure 7-23   MOVING THE PASTED SKI

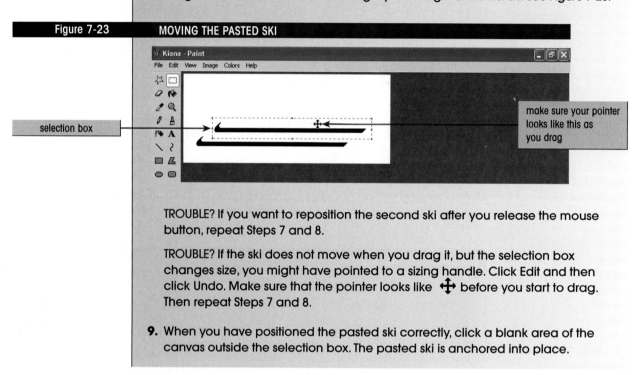

selection box

make sure your pointer looks like this as you drag

TROUBLE? If you want to reposition the second ski after you release the mouse button, repeat Steps 7 and 8.

TROUBLE? If the ski does not move when you drag it, but the selection box changes size, you might have pointed to a sizing handle. Click Edit and then click Undo. Make sure that the pointer looks like ✛ before you start to drag. Then repeat Steps 7 and 8.

9. When you have positioned the pasted ski correctly, click a blank area of the canvas outside the selection box. The pasted ski is anchored into place.

When you and Joe look at the skis, you decide you want them to point in the other direction. You can do this by flipping both images.

Flipping a Graphic

You can flip a graphic using the Flip/Rotate option on the Image menu. This option lets you reverse a graphic or rotate it by a specified number of degrees.

To flip the skis so they point in the other direction:

1. Click **Image** on the menu bar, and then click **Flip/Rotate**. The Flip and Rotate dialog box opens. See Figure 7-24.

Figure 7-24	FLIP AND ROTATE DIALOG BOX

make sure this option button is selected

Use the Flip horizontal option to flip a graphic from right to left, use the Flip vertical option to flip a graphic from top to bottom, or use the Rotate by angle option to rotate a graphic by 90, 180, or 270 degrees.

2. If necessary, click the **Flip horizontal** option button. Selecting this option will flip the graphic so that the skis are pointing to the right rather than the left.

3. Click the **OK** button. The skis now point in the other direction.

4. Click **File** on the menu bar, and then click **Save** to save the graphic.

Now you're ready to create the letter "K." You think you can create the look you want by using the rounded brush style, which is in the first row of brush styles in the Style box.

To create the letter K:

1. Click the **Brush** tool , and then click the **largest circle** in the top row of the Style box.

2. Draw the letter K following the steps shown in Figure 7-25.

Figure 7-25	DRAWING THE LETTER K

use these three brush motions to draw

TROUBLE? If you make a mistake, use the Undo command or erase what you've drawn and start over.

Now you want to make the K look as if it's moving. One way to do this is to add straight lines behind the K to create the impression of movement.

Drawing a Straight Line

You can use the Line tool to draw straight lines, which you can place in your graphic to give the illusion of movement. You can create a horizontal, vertical, or diagonal line by pressing Shift while you drag the Line pointer in one of those directions. You can, of course, draw a line using the Pencil tool, but it's difficult to keep the line straight. You are going to draw a single line behind the K, and then you'll copy it and paste it a few times to add several "movement" lines.

To add straight lines to your drawing:

1. Click the **Line** tool ◥. Notice that the Style box displays several line widths. In this case, you want to use the narrowest line style (the default).

2. Press and hold the **Shift** key while you draw a horizontal line behind the K, as shown in Figure 7-26.

Figure 7-26	DRAWING A STRAIGHT LINE WITH THE LINE TOOL

draw a line like this

Line tool

line widths

3. Release the mouse button and then release the **Shift** key. The line is perfectly straight. You can copy and paste this line several times to create several movement lines that are all the same size.

4. Click the **Select** tool ▢, and then draw a selection box around the line you just drew. Keep the selection box as close to the line as possible to avoid copying the surrounding white space. You're ready to copy and paste the line.

5. Click **Edit** on the menu bar, click **Copy**, click **Edit**, and then click **Paste**. The copy of the line appears in the upper-left corner of the Paint window.

6. Move the line you just pasted so that it is below and slightly to the right of the original line.

7. Click **Edit** and then click **Paste** to add another line, moving it to the lower-right of the other lines. Paste and move another line so that the two new lines match the positions of those shown in Figure 7-27.

Figure 7-27   ADDING MOVEMENT LINES TO THE KIANA GRAPHIC

pasted lines

8. Click a blank area of the canvas to anchor the last line into place.

As a final touch, you decide to stretch the graphic to see if that effect enhances the illusion of movement.

Stretching a Graphic

You can stretch a graphic either horizontally or vertically using the Stretch/Skew option on the Image menu. You specify a percentage and Paint expands or contracts the graphic by that percentage in the direction (horizontal or vertical) that you specify.

To stretch the skis graphic:

1. Click **Image** on the menu bar, and then click **Stretch/Skew**. The Stretch and Skew dialog box opens.

2. If necessary, click the **Horizontal** percentage box in the Stretch pane, and then type **140**.

3. Click the **OK** button. The graphic is stretched in the horizontal direction. Your graphic now looks like Figure 7-28.

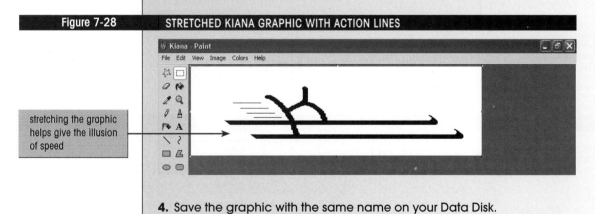

Figure 7-28   STRETCHED KIANA GRAPHIC WITH ACTION LINES

stretching the graphic
helps give the illusion
of speed

4. Save the graphic with the same name on your Data Disk.

You'll add the text to the Kiana graphic in the Review Assignments at the end of this tutorial.

Joe suggests that you create another image for use in his promotions, such as a few mountains on a sunny day. You can do this using the Paint shape tools.

Creating Shapes

The shape tools include the Line, Curve, Rectangle, Polygon, Ellipse, and Rounded Rectangle. These tools let you draw predetermined shapes. When you click one of the shape tools, a collection of styles appears in the Style box. You can choose the shape as an outline, a filled shape with a border, or a filled shape without a border. For example, Figure 7-29 shows the style options for the Rectangle tool.

| Figure 7-29 | FILL AND BORDER STYLES FOR THE RECTANGLE TOOL |

Joe quickly sketches what he'd like to see, as shown in Figure 7-30, and asks if you can draw it.

| Figure 7-30 | IDEA FOR A SCENIC GRAPHIC |

To create the mountains, you can use the Line tool, which you've already used, and to create the sun you can use the Ellipse tool. Once you have drawn the shapes, you will color them and add text in Session 7.3.

You want to start by giving Joe a quick overview of the shapes you can draw.

To draw with a variety of the Paint shapes:

1. Click **File** on the menu bar, and then click **New** to open a new canvas. Click **Yes** if prompted to save changes.

2. Point to the lower-right sizing handle on the canvas until the pointer changes to ↖, and then drag down and to the right to increase the size of the canvas. You need a larger canvas to draw the next three shapes.

3. Click the **Rectangle** tool 🔲, and then drag a rectangle.

4. Click the **Ellipse** tool 🔘, and then drag an ellipse.

5. Click the **Rounded Rectangle** tool 🔲, and then drag a rounded rectangle. Compare your screen to Figure 7-31.

Figure 7-31   SHAPE TOOLS

Rectangle tool

Ellipse tool

Rounded Rectangle tool

TROUBLE? Your Paint window might not match Figure 7-31. However, make sure you try the Rectangle, Ellipse, and Rounded Rectangle tools before continuing.

You can use the Shift key to draw a perfect circle using the Ellipse tool, just as you used the Shift key to draw a straight horizontal line using the Line tool. Likewise, if you use Shift with the Rectangle tool, you can draw a perfect square. When you draw a shape, you can use the **sizing coordinates**, immediately to the right of the pixel coordinates, to determine the size of the shape you are drawing. For example, when you draw a circle, you might start at pixel coordinates 15,15 and drag with sizing coordinates of 30 × 30—so your circle has a 30-pixel diameter.

Now you're ready to create the new graphic. To save you time, the mountains have already been drawn for you. They are stored in a file named Mountain. All you need to do is add the sun.

To open the Mountain file and add the sun:

1. Click **File** on the menu bar, click **Open**, and then locate and open the **Mountain** file on your Data Disk. Click the **No** button if you are prompted to save changes. Now save the file with a new name to keep the original file intact, in case you need to perform these steps again.

2. Click **File** and then click **Save As**; in the Save As dialog box, change the file-name to **Mountain and Sun**, and then click the **Save** button.

3. Click the **Restore** button 🗗 to resize the Paint window and reduce the amount of gray workspace surrounding the canvas. Resize the window, if necessary, so that you can see all of the canvas. Decreasing the size of the window makes it easier to watch the pixel coordinates change as you draw.

4. Click the **Ellipse** tool ⬭. You will use this tool to draw a circle for the sun. Because the sun needs to be a perfect circle, you will press the Shift key as you drag the pointer to draw the image.

5. Press the **Shift** key and then drag a circle starting at pixel coordinates 15,15. Drag to sizing coordinates of 30 × 30 (look to the right of the pixel coordinates on the far-right side of the status bar), and then release the mouse button and the **Shift** key. See Figure 7-32.

Figure 7-32   **DRAWING A CIRCLE**

Now that you added a sun to the graphic, you can save and close the file.

6. Click **File** and then click **Save**.

7. Click the **Close** button ☒ to close Paint.

Joe now has three graphics to choose from: the Skis graphic, the Kiana graphic, and the Mountain and Sun graphic. In the next session, you will enhance two of these graphics by adding text and color.

Session 7.2 QUICK CHECK

1. How wide is the line you draw with the Pencil tool, in pixels?

2. When you view the grid, what does each box represent?

3. What option can you use to view the magnified portion of your graphic in Normal view while retaining the magnification on the canvas?

4. Name three ways to clear a canvas.

5. How do you draw a perfect circle?

6. What is the diameter in pixels of a circle drawn to 50×50 sizing coordinates?

SESSION 7.3

In this session, you will work with color and text. You'll begin by filling enclosed areas with color using the Fill With Color tool. Then you'll apply color with the Airbrush tool and work with background and foreground colors. Finally, you'll add text with the Text tool and format it using the Fonts toolbar. After you finish your graphic, you will learn how to display thumbnail preview images of the graphic file.

Filling an Area with Color

You can add color to a graphic in one of two ways: choosing colors as you draw or applying color to shapes after you have finished drawing them. Before you use a drawing tool, you can select a color for the line or shape. You'll practice choosing colors as you draw later in this session. If you want to add color to an existing image or color a large area of an image, you use the Fill With Color tool. First you click the Fill with Color tool 🪣, click a color in the color palette, and then click an enclosed area in the graphic with the Fill With Color pointer 🪣. The area within the borders of the enclosure fills with color. When you use the Fill With Color tool, make sure the area you click is a fully enclosed space. If it has any openings, color will "spill out" of the boundaries of the area you are trying to color.

REFERENCE WINDOW	RW

Filling an Area with Color
- Click the Fill With Color tool.
- Click the desired color in the color palette.
- Make sure the tip of the paint pouring out of the bucket is within the border, and then click inside the border of the area you want to color.

Joe is interested to see how color affects his graphics. You decide to color the Mountain and Sun graphic using a mix of blues and purple. You can use the Fill With Color tool to apply a different color to each mountain range to give the impression of distance and shadow.

To fill the Mountain and Sun graphic with color:

1. Start Paint and then make sure your Data Disk is in drive A.

2. Click **File** on the menu bar, click **Open**, and then locate and open the **Mountain and Sun** file on your Data Disk.

3. Click the **Fill With Color** tool ⬛. The pointer changes to ⬛. You'll color each layer of mountains a different color. Start by filling the top mountain range with dark blue.

4. In the color palette at the bottom of the screen, click the **dark blue** color in the top row, seventh from the left.

   TROUBLE? This color might appear as a different shade of blue or purple on your monitor. Make sure it is the seventh from the left in the top row.

5. Click inside the border of the top mountain range with the Fill With Color pointer ⬛. The mountain range turns blue. See Figure 7-33.

Figure 7-33	FILLING THE FIRST MOUNTAIN RANGE WITH COLOR

Fill With Color tool

active part of pointer is the tip of the paint drop

dark blue color for first mountain range

TROUBLE? If the sky turns blue instead of the mountain range, you clicked the sky instead of the mountain range. You must click the area to be colored with the active part of the Fill With Color pointer, which is the tip of the paint pouring out of the can. Click Edit, click Undo, and then repeat Step 5, making sure the tip of the paint can is within the border of the mountain range.

6. In the color palette, click the **purple** color in the top row, eighth from the left, and then click the **front-left single mountain** to color it purple.

7. In the color palette, click the **bright blue** color in the bottom row, seventh from the left, and then click the **front-middle mountain range**.

8. In the color palette, click the **periwinkle** color in the bottom row, third from the right, and then click the **right mountain range**.

9. Finally, click the **yellow** color in the bottom row, fourth from the left in the color palette, and then click the **sun**. See Figure 7-34.

| Figure 7-34 | MOUNTAIN AND SUN GRAPHIC IN COLOR |

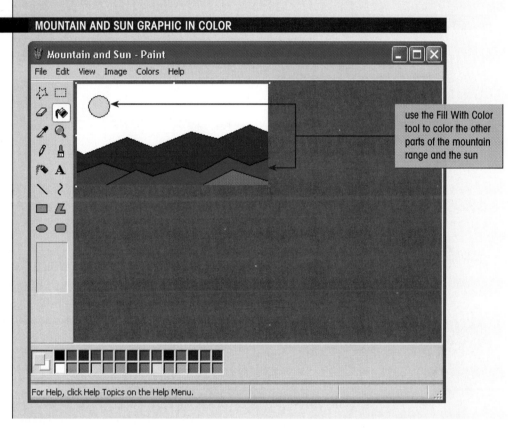

Joe likes the graphic with the colors you chose.

Coloring **with the Airbrush Tool**

You have one more idea to enhance the Mountain graphic. You can sprinkle "snow" on the top range of mountains using the Airbrush tool, which scatters color a few pixels at a time over the area you "brush." When you use a drawing tool such as the Airbrush, you can select a color in the color palette and then apply that color wherever you click or drag the tool.

To use the Airbrush tool:

1. In the color palette, click the **white** color, the first color in the second row.

2. Click the **Airbrush** tool . Note that the Airbrush tool has three different sizes available in the Style box. The small size scatters color most thickly, whereas the largest size sprinkles it more sparingly. You'll use the largest size to sprinkle the top mountain range with snow.

3. Click the **largest Airbrush style** in the Style box. You choose this size to create the effect of a light dusting of snow on the mountains.

4. Drag the **Airbrush** pointer over the top range of mountains. The Airbrush tool scatters white pixels over the blue mountains. See Figure 7-35.

Figure 7-35	USING THE AIRBRUSH TOOL

Airbrush tool

largest airbrush style

Airbrush tool leaves pixel sprinkles as you drag

5. Click **File** on the menu bar, and then click **Save**.

The airbrushed parts of the picture add texture to the graphic. In looking over the graphic, you decide you don't like the stark contrast between the sun's black border and yellow fill color. You think a different border and fill color will look better. You can control the border and fill colors by selecting the foreground and background colors.

Using **Foreground and Background Colors**

You've already seen how to color as you draw when you sprinkled the mountains with white snow using the Airbrush tool. When you draw a shape, Paint can use two colors instead of one. The foreground color is used for lines, borders of shapes, and text. The background color determines the fill of the inside of enclosed shapes and the background of text frames. It also appears when you use the eraser. To set the foreground color, you click a color with the left mouse button. The foreground color palette changes to that color. To set the background color, you click a color with the right mouse button. The background color palette changes to that color.

You can draw your shape using one of the three options located in the Style box: only a border using the foreground color, a border using the foreground color and a fill using the background color, or only the fill using the foreground color. For example, to draw a rounded rectangle with a red border and no fill color, select the Rounded Rectangle tool with the border only style, use the left mouse button to click red in the color palette, and then drag on the canvas to draw a rounded rectangle. See Figure 7-36. To add a rounded rectangle with a red border and a teal fill to the drawing, select the border and fill style, right-click teal in the color palette, and then drag on the canvas to draw the second rounded rectangle. To add a solid red rounded rectangle with no border to the drawing, select the fill only style and then drag on the canvas to draw the rounded rectangle.

Figure 7-36	EXAMPLES OF FOREGROUND AND BACKGROUND COLORS

Note that you can reverse the colors by using the right mouse button instead of the left to draw the shape. For example, if you use the settings shown in Figure 7-36 (red foreground color, teal background color, and rounded rectangle with a border only style), you can hold down the right mouse button as you drag to create a rounded rectangle with a teal border and no fill.

You decide to draw the sun with a foreground color of brown and a background color of red. First, you'll need to erase the sun you've already drawn and colored. You could use the Eraser tool, but when the area you want to erase is isolated, where no other parts of the drawing interfere, it can be quicker to select the area and then delete it using the Delete key.

To draw a sun with different foreground and background colors:

1. Click the **Select** tool ⬚, and then drag a selection box around the sun.

2. Press the **Delete** key.

Now you can draw a new sun using brown as the foreground color for the border and yellow as the background color for the fill.

3. In the color palette, click the **brown** color in the top row, farthest to the right, with the left mouse button. Notice that the foreground box turns brown. See Figure 7-37.

Figure 7-37 | **SELECTING A FOREGROUND COLOR**

foreground color turns brown when you click brown with the left mouse button

brown color

For Help, click Help Topics on the Help Menu.

4. Using the right mouse button, click the **orange** color in the bottom row, farthest to the right. The background color changes to orange.

TROUBLE? If you clicked with the left mouse button in Step 4, you changed the foreground color instead of the background color. Repeat Steps 3 and 4.

5. Click the **Ellipse** tool ⬭.

6. Click the **fill and border** option in the Style box (the middle option). This option lets you create a circle with a border (foreground) color that's different from the fill (background) color.

7. Press **Shift** and then drag a circle from pixel coordinates 15,15 and sizing coordinates 30 × 30.

The new sun has a brown border and an orange fill. However, the orange looks too dark; you decide that the original yellow color looked better.

As you've already seen, you can color an enclosed area using the Fill With Color tool. When you filled in the mountain ranges earlier with this tool, you clicked an area with the left mouse button, and Paint then applied the foreground color to the area. You can apply the background color by clicking the area with the right mouse button. Notice that this is different from drawing a shape from scratch—in that case, the foreground color determines the border, and the background color determines the fill. When you use the Fill With Color tool on an already existing shape, you are working only with the fill, and you can switch between foreground and background colors using the left or right mouse button. You decide to change the fill color back to yellow.

To select a new background color and use it to fill a shape:

1. In the color palette, right-click the **yellow** color in the bottom row, fourth from the left, to set the background color to yellow.

2. Click the **Fill With Color** tool 🪣 and then right-click the **sun**. The fill color of the sun changes to yellow, the background color you just set. This sun, yellow with a brown border, looks good.

Note that foreground and background colors take on different roles, depending on whether you're drawing an object from scratch, using a shape tool, or coloring in an object using the Fill With Color tool. Remember that when you draw an object from scratch, the foreground color is the border, and the background color is the fill. When you are coloring an object with the Fill With Color tool, Paint uses the foreground color if you left-click and the background color if you right-click.

You and Joe are satisfied with the coloring of the Mountain and Sun graphic. Now you're ready to add the text.

Using the Text Tool

Joe included the phrase "It's Ski Time!" on his sketch. To add words to the graphic, you can draw letters as you did for the "K" earlier, or you can use the **Text tool**. You first use the Text tool to create a text box, and then you type your text in this box. By default, the Text toolbar, also called the Fonts toolbar, appears when you select the Text tool so you can select a font, style, and size for the text. If your text exceeds the length and width of the selection box, you can drag the sizing handles to enlarge the selection box.

REFERENCE WINDOW RW

Adding Text to a Graphic
- Click the Text tool and then drag a text box on the canvas.
- If the Text toolbar does not appear, click View and then click Text Toolbar.
- Use the Text toolbar to select a font, font size, or attributes (bold, italic, or underline).
- Type the text in the text box, using the sizing handles to resize the text box, if necessary.
- Adjust the font, font size, or attributes (bold, italic, or underline), and resize the text box as necessary.
- Click outside the text box.

You decide to type "It's Ski Time!" just to the right of the sun in the Mountain and Sun graphic, and you want the text to appear in the same shade of dark blue you used in the first range of mountains.

To select the text color and create the text box:

1. With the left mouse button, click the **dark blue** color in the top row, seventh from the left in the color palette.

2. With the right mouse button, click the **white** color in the bottom row, farthest to the left of the color palette, to restore the background for the text box to white.

3. Click the **Text** tool **A** .

4. Create a text box by dragging from pixel coordinates 54,15 to a size of 185 × 30 and then releasing the mouse button. Make sure you don't make the box any larger than this, or it will obscure the mountains. After you've created the text box, the Fonts toolbar appears. See Figure 7-38.

Figure 7-38 | **TEXT BOX AND FONTS TOOLBAR**

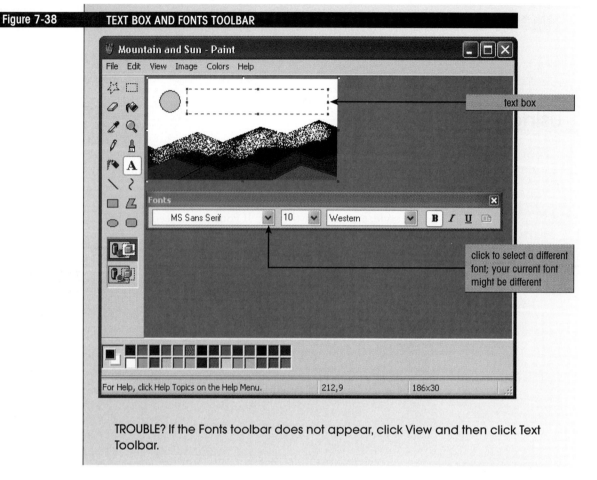

TROUBLE? If the Fonts toolbar does not appear, click View and then click Text Toolbar.

Any letters you type into the text box will appear with the font style, size, attributes, and language shown in the Fonts toolbar. The font size of the letters is measured in points, where a single point is $\frac{1}{72}$ inch. Thus, a one-inch tall character would be 72 points, and a half-inch tall character would be 36 points. Attributes are characteristics of the font, including bold, italic, and underline. You can change the font, font size, font attributes, and language using the Fonts toolbar before you type, after you type, or as you edit the text. Once you are satisfied with the text and its appearance, you click outside the text box. The text box disappears and the text is "anchored" into place, becoming a part of the bitmapped graphic. Once text is anchored in a graphic, you can change the font or its attributes only by deleting the text and starting over with the Text tool.

You decide to use an Arial 12-point font. Arial is the name of a common font that comes with Windows XP.

To choose the Arial 12-point font and insert the text:

1. Click the **Font** list arrow. The list of fonts available on your computer opens. See Figure 7-39. Your list will probably be different.

Figure 7-39   FONT LIST

Font list box; your list
might show
different fonts

2. Scroll the Font list until you locate Arial, and then click **Arial**.

3. Click the **Font Size** list arrow, and then click **12**.

4. Make sure the Bold and Italic buttons are not selected; if they are, click to deselect them.

5. Click inside the text box.

6. Type **It's Ski Time!** Your text appears in the text box in the Arial 12-point font. See Figure 7-40.

Figure 7-40	ADDING TEXT USING THE TEXT TOOL

font is Arial

text appears in the text box

point size is 12

TROUBLE? If nothing appears when you type, you might have clicked the color white with the left mouse button instead of the right mouse button in the previous set of steps. White text will not appear against a white background. Make sure the foreground color is dark blue and the background color is white.

Joe would like to use a more interesting font. You decide to experiment with several fonts, sizes, and attributes to find the look you want. Windows XP comes with a standard set of fonts, including Arial and Times New Roman, but most users add fonts so they can format text in a variety of styles. The fonts that appear on your computer will most likely differ from those shown in the figures.

To experiment with the font:

1. Click the **Font** list arrow on the Fonts toolbar.

2. Scroll the Font list until you locate Times New Roman, and then click **Times New Roman**. The text in your text box changes to the new font.

   TROUBLE? If your Times New Roman font appears many times with a number of different styles, click any one of the Times New Roman fonts, such as Times New Roman (Baltic).

3. Click the **Bold** button **B** on the Fonts toolbar to see how the text looks in bold format.

4. Click the **Italic** button I on the Fonts toolbar. You like the look of both bold and italic, though you'd like to keep looking at other font styles.

5. Continue to select different fonts and attributes, as shown in Figure 7-41.

| Figure 7-41 | EXPERIMENTING WITH DIFFERENT FONTS |

Bookman Old Style

Comic Sans MS

Impact

Verdana

TROUBLE? If you can't find the fonts shown in Figure 7-41, experiment with fonts available on your computer. Your computer might provide more than the standard fonts that come with Windows XP.

Joe likes bold and italic Verdana Baltic best, so you will use that font.

6. Select **Verdana** as the font, using both the Bold and Italic attributes.

TROUBLE? If you do not have Verdana in your list of fonts, click one of your favorites. You can also leave the font as Times New Roman.

Now enlarge the font to make the text more prominent.

7. Click the **Font Size** list arrow, and then click **16**.

TROUBLE? If you are using a font that is especially large, 16 points might cause some of the letters to disappear. Repeat Step 7, but this time pick a smaller point size.

8. Click a blank area of the canvas outside the text box to anchor the text. The text box and Fonts toolbar disappear, and the text is anchored into place. See Figure 7-42.

| Figure 7-42 | COMPLETING THE GRAPHIC WITH TEXT |

> **9.** Save the Mountain and Sun graphic.
>
> **10.** Click the Paint **Close** button ☒.

Now that you've created a number of graphics for Joe, you can view them in My Computer or Windows Explorer.

Viewing Your Pictures in Thumbnail View

As you create graphic files, you'll want to browse quickly through them to locate the file you want. Windows XP lets you view file lists in Thumbnail view, in which smaller "preview" images of the graphic file appear in the My Computer or Explorer window. You decide to show Joe how to use Thumbnail view to browse his files.

To use Thumbnail view:

1. Open **My Computer**.

2. Double-click the **3½ Floppy (A:)** icon for your Data Disk.

3. Click **View** on the menu bar, and then click **Thumbnails**. Size and scroll the window as necessary to see the images. Windows XP displays thumbnail images of the files on the Data Disk. (This may take a moment.) See Figure 7-43.

| Figure 7-43 | VIEWING GRAPHIC FILES IN THUMBNAILS VIEW |

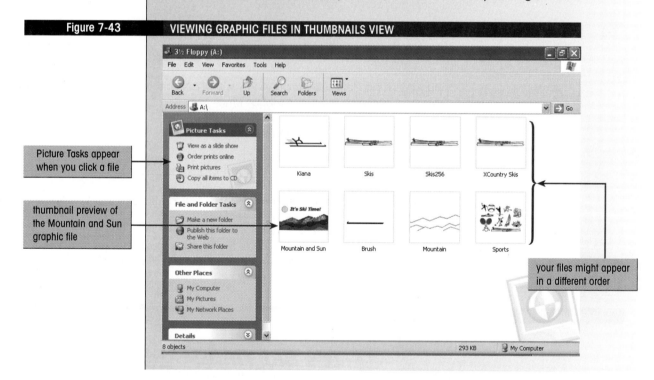

Picture Tasks appear when you click a file

thumbnail preview of the Mountain and Sun graphic file

your files might appear in a different order

Joe appreciates the ability to preview images that Windows XP provides for him. If Joe wants to organize his graphic files better, he can use the My Pictures folder, a subfolder of the My Documents folder that Windows XP provides for graphic files. The My Pictures folder is the default location for files created by Paint and also for files created by digital cameras connected to your computer.

Joe has enjoyed watching you work with the Paint program. You've showed him how to use the Fill With Color tool to fill enclosed areas with color, paint with the Airbrush tool, and work with background and foreground colors. You also added text with the Text tool and formatted it using the Fonts toolbar. After you finished the graphics, you displayed thumbnail preview images of the graphic files. Now that Joe has a few usable graphics, he looks forward to creating more announcements and promotional materials for the Birkebeiner ski race.

Session 7.3 QUICK CHECK

1. To change a shape's fill color, you use the _____ tool.

2. What does it mean to say that a font is "10 points?"

3. What font attributes can you work with in Paint?

4. You just opened a graphic containing text, and you'd like to change the font of the text. Describe your options.

5. When you draw an object from scratch, the foreground color controls an object's _____, whereas the background color controls its _____.

6. If you select the Fill With Color tool and then right-click an enclosed area, which color is applied, the foreground or the background?

REVIEW ASSIGNMENTS

1. **Cropping a Graphic**   Joe is the coordinator for a university students' bowling league, and he asks you to help create a graphic for an informational promotion he is preparing.

   a. Open the **Sports** graphic in Paint.
   b. Use the Select tool to select the bowling ball hitting the bowling pins in the lower-right corner of the Sports graphic.
   c. Use the Copy To command to save the cropped graphic on your Data Disk as a monochrome graphic with the name **Bowling Ball**.
   d. Open the **Bowling Ball** graphic, and, if necessary, erase any portions of it that aren't part of the graphic.
   e. Save and print the graphic, and then close Paint.

Explore   2. **Cropping a Graphic with the Free-Form Select Tool**   You're designing league jackets for the Community Tennis League. You want to crop the tennis rackets in the lower-left corner of the Sports graphic. In Session 7.1, you used the Select tool to crop part of a graphic, but the selection box included portions of other images that you had to erase. To avoid this extra step, use the Free-Form Select tool to draw a line of any shape around the area you want to crop.

   a. Open the **Sports** graphic in Paint.
   b. Use the Free-Form Select tool to draw around the tennis rackets and ball in the lower-left corner of the Sports graphic. When you are done drawing around the rackets, a selection box appears, similar to the one you used with the Select tool. However, when you save the selection in another file, Paint will not include any areas in the box that were not included when you used the Free-Form Select tool.
   c. Use the Copy To command to save the cropped graphic on your Data Disk as a monochrome graphic with the name **Tennis Rackets**.

d. Open the **Tennis Rackets** graphic, and ensure that you didn't include any unwanted portions of the Sports graphic. Erase any unwanted marks, if necessary.

e. Save and print the **Tennis Rackets** graphic, and then close Paint.

3. **Drawing in Color** One of the Birkebeiner participants was in the most recent Winter Olympics, and Joe's promotion highlights the fact that the Birkebeiner attracts top-notch competitors. Joe asks you to create a graphic of the Olympic rings. The top three rings are blue, black, and red. The bottom two rings are yellow and green. Save the file on your Data Disk as a 256 Color Bitmap graphic with the name **Rings**, and print the file. If a dialog box informs you that you could lose color information before you save, click the Yes button to continue. Here are techniques to use to help you complete this assignment:

- Use the Shift key with the Ellipse tool to draw perfect circles.
- Use the sizing coordinates to ensure that each circle is the same size.
- Draw each new circle in a blank area of the canvas, and then use the Select tool to select the circle and drag it into place.
- Use the pixel coordinates to ensure that you place all rings in each row on the same level.

Figure 7-44 shows such a drawing.

Figure 7-44

4. **Adding Text to the Kiana Graphic** You and Joe decide to finish the Kiana graphic. You need to add the rest of the word "Kiana." First open the **Kiana** file that you created earlier in this tutorial and saved on your Data Disk. Save the file as **Kiana2**.

a. Use the Text tool to insert a text box near the graphic K, type the letters "iana," and then select a font and font size that you like.

b. Use the Fill With Color tool to fill each letter with a different color.

c. Make the graphic take less room on your disk by selecting the entire drawing and dragging it up to the corner of the canvas. Then resize the canvas to fit the drawing.

d. Give the graphic a background color that complements the letter colors. Compare your figure to Figure 7-45.

Figure 7-45

e. Save the file as a 256 Color Bitmap, print the graphic, and then close Paint.

Explore

5. **Editing Graphic Images** Joe wants his promotions to look more professional. He wants you to connect to the Internet and locate another ski graphic. He'd like the graphic to have the word "Birkebeiner" on it.

   a. Connect to the Internet and use Yahoo!'s subject guide to search for Web pages that make graphic images available. (*Hint*: Try the Computers and Internet category and the Graphics subcategory.)

   b. Once you have located a graphics page, search for a Sports category and locate clip art showing a skier graphic. The file you choose must have a format that Paint supports: bmp, gif, jpeg, tif, or png. The file must also be less than 100KB. Note that when you use computer graphics, you must make sure they are not copyrighted. Only graphics that are in the public domain may be downloaded and used freely. (Look for a notice on the Web page that indicates the graphics are in the public domain—many clip art files are.) If you can't find a graphic image on the Internet, use the Skis graphic you used in this tutorial, and save it as **Skier**.

   c. Download the skier graphic you located on the Web to your Data Disk, and save it with the name **Skier**.

   d. Open the Skier graphic in Paint, and add the word "Birkebeiner" to the graphic. (*Hint:* If there is no blank area in which to add this word, resize the canvas as necessary.)

   e. Save and print the graphic, and then close Paint.

PROJECTS

1. You work for Jensen Telecommunications, which is hosting an engineering conference to share ideas on making high-speed fiber-optic data lines available to homes. You're helping host the conference banquet, and you'd like to create a classy design to imprint on the cocktail napkins and coasters. Use the Brush tool to draw the graphic, as shown in Steps a through f, and then save it as a Monochrome Bitmap graphic.

   a. Create a vertical line as shown, using the largest angular brush style in the third row.

   b. Copy the vertical line and paste it as shown.

   c. Draw the horizontal line to hook up with the vertical line.

   d. Copy the horizontal line and paste it on top.

   e. Copy a short section of the horizontal line, and paste it in the middle.

   f. Save the image as **Letter J** on your Data Disk, print it, and then close Paint. If a dialog box informs you that you could lose color information before you save, click the Yes button to continue.

2. You work for a commercial graphic design company, Ace Design Group (ADG). ADG has just landed a contract to create a new font style for the materials of the American Statistical Association's annual conference. Your boss has asked you to start drafting possible designs. You use Paint to create a few sample letters, specifically, an uppercase and lowercase "a" and "f." You'll probably want to use a combination of drawing tools for this assignment. You'll need to zoom in and edit, using the grid, to ensure consistency from letter to letter. The previous project showed you how to draw a letter. When you are finished drafting a few ideas, save your file as **Fonts** using the monochrome Bitmap file type, print it, and then close Paint.

3. You're preparing a flyer for a Sailing Club, and you need a graphic that shows a sailboat. You plan to print your flyer in color, so you need a graphic with color.

   a. Open the **Sports** graphic and copy the sailboat image to a new file named Sailboat on your Data Disk. Save the file as a 24-bit Bitmap image named **Sailboat**. (If you use the regular Select tool, make sure you erase any parts of the Sports graphic that aren't part of the sailboat.)

   b. Use the Fill With Color tool to color the sails of the sailboat red.

   c. Add the words "Time to Sail!" to the sailboat graphic.

   d. Save the graphic on your Data Disk, print it, and then close Paint.

4. You coordinate the Chess Club at Stanton Junior High. You want to create a simple graphic for a tournament brochure. Use the Rectangle tool and your copy and pasting skills to create the chessboard in the following Steps a through f.

   a. Use the Rectangle tool with the Shift key to create a perfect square with sizing coordinates of 35 × 35. Don't forget to use the Shift key.

   b. Copy the square, and then paste it and drag it so that the edges overlap, using the samples shown to the right as a guide. Do this three times to create the first four squares.

   c. Copy the four squares and then paste that image and drag it to the right of the first four squares.

   d. Copy those eight squares and then paste that image and drag it to the right of the existing eight squares.

   e. Copy those 16 squares and paste and drag them three times to create the rest of the chessboard.

   f. Save the image as **Chess** on your Data Disk using the 256 Color Bitmap file type, print it, and then close Paint. If a dialog box informs you that you could lose color information before you save, click the Yes button to continue.

5. You just completed the Chess graphic in Project 4. You now want to add text and color.

   a. Color every other square, using the Fill With Color tool and colors you choose, to create a chessboard.

   b. Add the words "Stanton Chess Club" to the top of the chessboard. Choose a font style and size that complement the colors and board you drew.

   c. Add the word "Tournament" below the chessboard.

   d. Now use the Select tool to select just the word "Tournament." Then rotate the word and drag it to the right side of the chessboard, as shown in Figure 7-46. Using the Flip/Rotate command on the Image menu, click Rotate by angle, and then click 270. Your graphic should look like Figure 7-46, but will vary depending on the font you chose.

   e. Save the graphic on your Data Disk as a 256 Color Bitmap called **Chess with Text**, print it, and then close Paint.

Figure 7-46

Quick Check Answers

Session 7.1

1. Select the portion you want to save, click Edit, then click Copy To, enter a name and location in the Save As dialog box, then click the Save button.
2. Drag the sizing handle.
3. True
4. pixels
5. Color graphics require more bits to define the colors.
6. Convert it to a format Paint does support, using a graphics converter.

Session 7.2

1. a single pixel
2. a single pixel
3. thumbnail
4. the Eraser tool, the Clear Image command on the Image menu, or the New command on the File menu
5. Press Shift and use the Ellipse tool.
6. 50 pixels

Session 7.3

1. Fill With Color
2. Its size is $10 \times \frac{1}{2}$ inch.
3. bold, italic, and underline
4. You must erase or cut the text, then click the Text tool and enter new text with the font you want.
5. border, fill
6. background

OBJECTIVES

In this tutorial you will:

- Create a WordPad document into which you will insert data from other documents

- Use the Cut, Copy, and Paste commands to transfer data

- Use the Calculator accessory

- Use object linking and embedding (OLE) to insert a graphic and a video clip into a WordPad document

- Examine numerous methods of using OLE: Paste, Paste Special, Insert Object, and Link

- Edit and update OLE objects

- Explore Windows XP multimedia accessories

LAB

Multimedia

OBJECT LINKING AND EMBEDDING

Creating a Multimedia Document for the Jugglers Guild

CASE

Preparing for the Jugglers Guild Convention

The Tenth Annual Jugglers Guild Convention is scheduled for this summer in New Orleans. Maria Arruda, secretary of the Jugglers Guild, is chairing the convention, aided by a committee of which you are a member. Maria has assigned tasks to each committee member—yours is to gather materials that will promote the event. Maria would like you to hire a designer to create a graphics file that can serve as a logo for informational flyers, posters, and convention T-shirts. Maria asks you also to look for an eye-catching video clip that will run on the computer screens used at the convention. A **video clip** is a file that contains a very short movie, either real-life or animated.

You hire a graphic designer to design the logo and a computer animation company to create an animated video clip. Once you receive the disks containing the graphics file and video clip, you give them to Maria so she can evaluate them. The next day she returns the disks and says she likes the logo and the animation, but she'd like feedback from the rest of the committee. She asks you to create a single WordPad document that will contain the graphics file and the video clip—she'll ask the committee members to add their comments to the document. A document that includes a variety of media, such as text, graphics, and video, is called a **multimedia document**.

Windows XP provides three ways to combine data from a variety of sources into a single multimedia document: pasting, embedding, and linking. You'll learn about pasting in Session 8.1, embedding in Session 8.2, and linking in Session 8.3. How do you decide which method to use in a given situation? It depends on what you need to do with the information after you've inserted it into the multimedia document—whether you need to use the tools in the program that originally created the data and whether you are likely to change the data once you've inserted it. As you work through these three sessions, notice how the pasting, embedding, and linking techniques offer you different options to meet these needs.

SESSION 8.1

In this session, you will learn how to work with the Windows XP Clipboard to make data from one source available to another document or program, using the Edit commands available in most Windows XP programs. To perform the steps of this tutorial, you need the Data Disk for Windows XP Tutorial 8. To complete the Review Assignments and Projects, you will need a second blank 3½" disk.

Creating a WordPad Document

You'll start by creating the WordPad document that will contain the data you want other members of the committee to review. You'll format the document as a memo, beginning with a standard memo heading that includes To, From, Date, and Subject headings.

To start a new WordPad document:

1. Click the **Start** button ⊞ start on the taskbar, point to **All Programs**, point to **Accessories**, and then click **WordPad**.

2. Type the following memo heading into the WordPad document. Press the **Enter** key twice after each line, and press the **Tab** key twice after the first three colons. (Just press the **Tab** key once after the SUBJECT colon.)

   MEMO

   TO: **Jugglers Guild Convention Committee**

   FROM: **Maria Arruda**

   DATE: **3/18/2004**

   SUBJECT: **Tenth Annual Jugglers Guild Convention**

3. If you haven't already done so, press the **Enter** key twice after typing the SUBJECT line. Now you should save the file with an appropriate name.

4. Click **File** on the menu bar, and then click **Save As** to open the Save As dialog box. Type **Feedback** in the File name text box, and select the **Rich Text Format** in the Save as type list box, if necessary. You are selecting Rich Text Format (RTF) as the file type because many word-processing programs besides WordPad can open this file type. The Rich Text Format also preserves basic text formatting such as bold and italic, no matter what type of program you use to open the file.

5. Click the **Save in** list arrow, and then click the drive containing your Data Disk.

6. Click the **Save** button.

Now that you have created and saved the memo for the committee members, you can insert the information Maria wants them to review. This information is already saved in other documents. Instead of retyping text or recreating the graphics and video, you can use Windows XP tools to transfer the information into the Feedback document.

The Clipboard

Windows XP offers several ways to transfer data from one document to another; the most basic technique is **Paste**, which lets you cut or copy data from one document and then place it into another. This procedure uses the **Clipboard**, an area in your computer's memory that temporarily stores the data you cut or copy. For example, suppose you have an e-mail message that contains information you want to paste into a WordPad document. Figure 8-1 illustrates how you can copy the message to the Clipboard and then paste it into your document.

Figure 8-1	USING THE CLIPBOARD

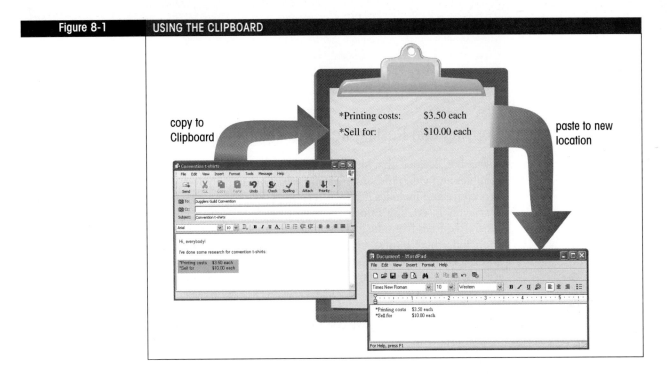

The Clipboard is part of the operating system and is available in most Windows programs. In Windows XP accessory programs, such as WordPad and Paint, you cannot view or open the Clipboard to see the information you cut or copied, although you often can in other Windows XP programs, such as Microsoft Word. Also, the Clipboard for the accessory programs can store only one item at a time. When you use the Cut, Copy, and Paste commands in any Windows program, you are using the Clipboard. Figure 8-2 shows the menu, toolbar, and keyboard methods you can use to cut, copy, and paste data within a document or from one document to another.

Figure 8-2	CUT AND PASTE OPTIONS

OPERATION	MENU COMMAND	TOOLBAR BUTTON	KEYBOARD SHORTCUT
Cut	Edit then Cut	✂	Ctrl+X
Copy	Edit then Copy	🗐	Ctrl+C
Paste	Edit then Paste	📋	Ctrl+V

When you paste data from the Clipboard into a document, you do not remove the data from the Clipboard; you can continue to paste the data as many times as you want, into as many documents as you want. The Clipboard stores the data until you cut or copy new data because the Clipboard can hold only one piece of data at a time.

If the Clipboard contains a large amount of data when you close a program, Windows XP might prompt you to clear the Clipboard contents to free your system's memory. The Clipboard's contents are also cleared when you shut down your computer.

REFERENCE WINDOW   **RW**

Using Paste to Transfer Data from One Document to Another
- Select the data you want to transfer, and then click Edit on the menu bar.
- Click Cut to remove the data from the document to the Clipboard, or click Copy to place a replica of the data on the Clipboard while leaving the original document intact.
- Switch to the second document, and then place the insertion point where you want to paste the data.
- Click Edit and then click Paste.

Copying and Pasting from the Calculator Accessory

Maria has decided that she wants the committee members to give their feedback on the graphics and video files in a specific way. She drafts a document that outlines the feedback procedure and includes her own reactions. She gives you a copy of this document and suggests you insert any information you need into your Feedback document. You've also received quotes from the graphic designer and computer animation company, and you want to include these quotes and the total estimate in the document. Maria mentions that one way to calculate totals is to use the Windows XP Calculator. Besides performing mathematical computations, you can copy the results of calculations from the Calculator into another Windows XP program.

You'll explore the Calculator in a moment. First, you decide to start by opening the copy of the document Maria gave you to see what it contains.

To open Maria's document:

1. In WordPad, open the document named **Maria** located on your Data Disk. Because you can open only one document at a time in WordPad, the Feedback document closes.

   TROUBLE? If you are asked if you want to save changes, click No.

   TROUBLE? If the Maria document does not appear in the Open dialog box, select "All Documents (*.*)" in the Files of type list box.

2. Maximize the WordPad window, if necessary, and then scroll through the document to view its contents. Figure 8-3 shows Maria's document.

Figure 8-3 **MARIA'S DOCUMENT**

price estimate
information goes here

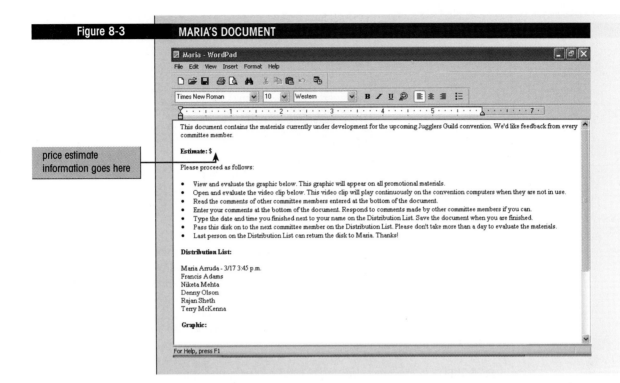

You see that Maria has left room to insert both the graphic and the video clip. Then you notice she also left room for a price estimate at the top. The quotes you received from the two vendors are $235 for the graphic and $390 for the video clip. The graphic design vendor is also offering a 12 percent discount if you use its services to print and duplicate your convention materials. As Maria suggested, you will use the Windows XP Calculator to calculate the total estimate.

The **Calculator** is a Windows XP accessory that looks and functions just like a handheld calculator. You can display it in two views: **Standard** view, which provides basic arithmetic operations, or **Scientific** view, which includes a variety of algebraic, trigonometric, and statistical functions. When you are including calculations and their results in a document, use the Calculator to perform the math for you. Because the Calculator includes a Copy command that copies the current entry to the Clipboard, you can transfer the entry to any program that uses the Windows XP Clipboard. If you are adding a column of numbers, for example, you are less likely to make a mistake entering the total into your document if you use the Clipboard to copy the data from the Calculator to your document, instead of typing it.

To calculate the total, you multiply 235 by .88 to calculate the price of the graphic discounted by 12 percent, and then add 390.

To open the Calculator and copy the total to Maria's document:

1. Click the **Start** button *start* , point to **All Programs**, point to **Accessories**, and then click **Calculator**. See Figure 8-4.

Figure 8-4   CALCULATOR ACCESSORY

TROUBLE? If your Calculator window appears twice this size, your Calculator opened in Scientific view. You can perform the calculations in Scientific or Standard view. To change to Standard view, click View on the menu bar, and then click Standard.

2. Type (or click the appropriate buttons in the Calculator window) **0.88*235+390=** to calculate a total value of 596.8.

TROUBLE? If you are using the numeric keypad on your keyboard and it doesn't work, press the NumLock key and then try again.

3. Click **Edit** on the Calculator menu bar, and then click **Copy**. With the Calculator, you don't have to select the data you want to copy. Even though the text does not appear highlighted, the Calculator automatically copies the entry in the results box. Notice that when you copy, the information is not removed from the program. You have simply placed a copy of it on the Clipboard, although you cannot see or verify that the information is stored there.

4. Click the **Close** button ☒ to close the Calculator. The information remains on the Clipboard.

The Clipboard now contains the value 596.8. You need to paste this value into Maria's document.

To paste the total into Maria's document:

1. Click then scroll to the top of Maria's document, and then click to the right of the **$** next to the **Estimate:** heading.

2. Click the **Paste** button 📋. See Figure 8-5. Notice that there is no "0" in the cents position of the total estimate.

Figure 8-5	PASTING THE CALCULATED ESTIMATE

TROUBLE? If the WordPad toolbar containing the Paste button doesn't appear, click View on the menu bar, and then click Toolbar.

3. Type **0** to complete the currency format.

You copied the results from the Calculator to Maria's document using the Clipboard. The next step in your project is to insert the information from the Maria document into your document. Maria gave you a copy of her document, and not the original, so you can move the text to avoid maintaining two versions of the same information, which could be confusing in the future. Because you want to move the information from one place to another, you should cut and paste. Doing so deletes the information from one document and stores it on the Clipboard until you paste it in another location.

Cutting and Pasting Between Two WordPad Documents

When you copy information from one file to another, the information remains in the source file—you paste a copy of that information into a different file. However, when you cut, you permanently remove the information from the original document. Because you want to move Maria's feedback from the copy of her document to the Feedback document, you decide to cut the text from the Maria document and paste it into yours.

To cut the contents from the Maria document and move it to the Clipboard:

1. Click **Edit** on the menu bar, and then click **Select All**. The entire document is selected.

2. Click the **Cut** button on the toolbar. Windows XP removes the selected material from Maria's document and places it on the Clipboard.

The Clipboard now contains the data from the Maria document. It will stay there until you copy or cut something else (because the Clipboard can contain only one cut or copied selection at a time), until you manually clear the Clipboard, or until you shut down your computer (which clears the memory, including the Clipboard). You can now open your Feedback document and insert the contents of the Clipboard.

To insert the contents of the Clipboard into your Feedback document:

1. Click **File** on the menu bar, and then click **A:\Feedback**, which appears near the bottom of the File menu.

TROUBLE? If A:\Feedback does not appear and you have left the computer since you were working with the Feedback document in the WordPad window, other, more recently opened files might appear at the bottom of the File menu. If this is the case, open the Feedback file on your Data Disk using the Open dialog box.

2. Click **No** when WordPad prompts you to save changes to Maria's document; this leaves the document intact in case you want to repeat this tutorial.

3. Press **Ctrl+End** to position the insertion point at the end of the Feedback document (below the Subject line). Any text you type or paste will appear at the insertion point.

TROUBLE? If the insertion point appears at the end of the last line, press the Enter key twice so the text doesn't appear on the same line as the existing text.

4. Click the **Paste** button 🖺 to paste the information from the Maria document into your Feedback document.

5. Scroll back to the top of the document. See Figure 8-6.

Figure 8-6	FEEDBACK DOCUMENT WITH PASTED INFORMATION

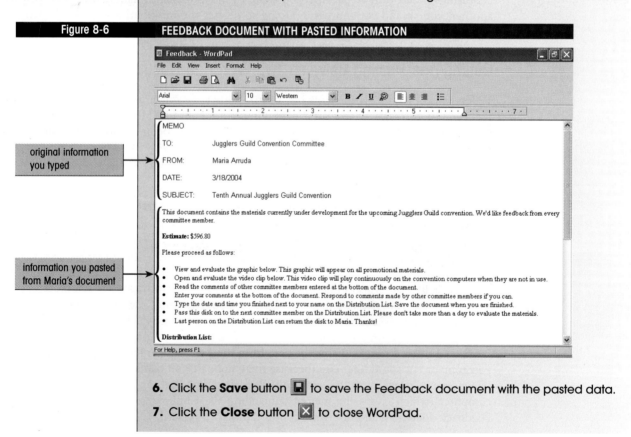

original information you typed

information you pasted from Maria's document

6. Click the **Save** button 🖫 to save the Feedback document with the pasted data.

7. Click the **Close** button ⊠ to close WordPad.

In this session, you have learned one way to transfer data from one document to another. Using the Edit commands, you copied data from the Calculator accessory and pasted the data into a WordPad document. Then you cut data from one WordPad document and pasted it into another.

Session 8.1 QUICK | CHECK

1. What is the Clipboard?

2. What happens to the selected text in the original document when you cut it? When you copy it?

3. What keyboard shortcuts can you use to cut, copy, and paste?

4. True or False: Once you paste the contents of the Clipboard into a document, that content is no longer available to be pasted into other documents.

5. Why would you use the Copy and Paste commands to transfer answers from the Calculator or similar programs into other documents?

SESSION 8.2

In this session, you'll learn how object linking and embedding (OLE) extends your ability to transfer data between files. You'll focus on embedding: you'll learn to embed a graphic object, change its size, and edit the embedded object. Then you'll display the embedded object as an icon, change its name, and change the icon that represents it.

Understanding **Object Linking and Embedding (OLE)**

So far you have pasted text into your WordPad document, first from the Calculator accessory and then from another WordPad document. The text you pasted actually became part of the Feedback document, and you can work with it in the same way you work with text you typed into the document—using the tools provided with WordPad. However, a multimedia document like the one you're creating can contain data from many different sources—graphics from Paint, charts from a spreadsheet, and sounds from an audio file, for example—as well as text. These types of data are often referred to as **objects**.

In your multimedia document, how can you work with objects that come from programs with different tools? For example, your WordPad document offers only text-editing tools. If you place a Paint graphic in this document, you cannot use the WordPad tools to edit that object. Windows XP provides the tools you need through a process called **object linking and embedding**, or **OLE** (pronounced "oh LAY"). OLE lets you insert an object into a document and access tools to manipulate the object (usually the tools of the program that were used to create the object).

With OLE, you place objects into documents using either of two methods: you embed them or you link them. In this session, you'll learn how to embed objects, and in Session 8.3 you'll learn how to link objects.

To understand both embedding and linking, you need to understand the terms listed in Figure 8-7.

Figure 8-7	OLE TERMS
TERM	**DEFINITION**
Source program	The program that created the original object
Source file	The file that contains the original object
Destination program	The program that created the document into which you are inserting the OLE object
Destination file	The file into which you are inserting the OLE object

Figure 8-8 applies the terms in Figure 8-7 to the document Maria wants you to create. Paint and Media Player are the source programs, and the Pins graphic and Video video clip are the source files. WordPad is the destination program, and Feedback is the destination file.

Figure 8-8   MULTIMEDIA DOCUMENT MARIA WANTS YOU TO CREATE

Embedding **an Object Using Paste**

You are ready to place the graphic into the Feedback document, but you want to be able to work with the graphic by using the tools from the program that originally created it—in this case, Paint. When you want to use the tools from the source program within the destination file, you should embed the object into the destination file. **Embedding** places a copy of an object into a document and "remembers" which program created the object, although it doesn't remember the name of the source file. Compare this technique to copying, which simply places the copy of the data in the new program with no reference to its source program. There are several ways to embed an object. If both the source and destination programs feature OLE technology, you can paste the object from one to the other. Many of the programs designed for Windows feature OLE.

The graphic provided by the graphic design company is called Pins, and they used the Windows XP graphics program, Paint, to create it. You want to embed a copy of this graphic into the Feedback document.

To copy the Pins graphic to the Clipboard:

1. Make sure your Data Disk is in the appropriate drive, click the **Start** button ⏚ **start** on the taskbar, point to **All Programs**, point to **Accessories**, and then click **Paint**.

2. Open the **Pins** file on your Data Disk. The Paint window displays an image of bowling pins. To embed this image into the Feedback document, you first must select it.

3. Click **Edit** on the menu bar, and then click **Select All**. A selection box appears around the graphic.

4. Click **Edit** on the menu bar, and then click **Copy**. Paint copies the graphic to the Clipboard.

5. Click the **Close** button ☒ to close Paint.

The graphic is now copied to the Clipboard. To embed it, you open the Feedback document in WordPad and then use the Paste command in WordPad.

To embed the Pins graphic into the Feedback document:

1. Start WordPad and open the **Feedback** document stored on your Data Disk.

2. Scroll the Feedback document until you locate the **Graphic:** heading. You will embed the Pins graphic below this heading.

3. Click a **blank line** below the Graphic: heading.

4. Click the **Paste** button 📋. The Pins graphic is embedded in the Feedback document, and it appears in a selection box. See Figure 8-9.

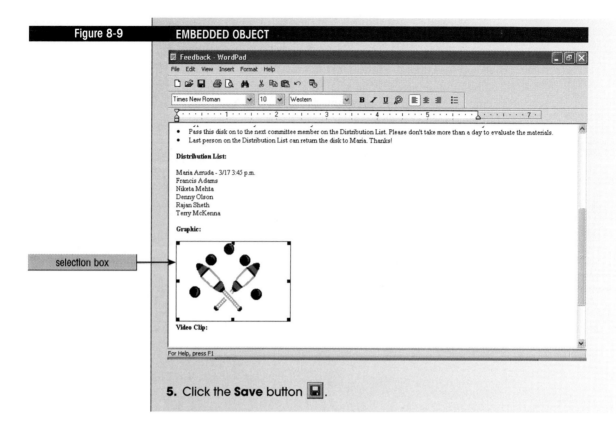

Figure 8-9   EMBEDDED OBJECT

selection box

5. Click the **Save** button.

The Paste command can be confusing because it seems to function differently with different objects. In Session 8.1, Paste simply pasted text, but here Paste embeds an object. How can you tell what Paste is doing? No hard and fast rules regulate how each program takes advantage of the OLE technology, although the following generalization can be helpful: When you use Paste to transfer data from one document to another that contains data of the same type (as it did when you transferred text into WordPad), the Paste command inserts the data without embedding. However, when you are transferring data from one document to another that contains no data of that type, and both the source and destination programs use OLE, the Paste command usually embeds the data. When you copy and paste between Windows XP programs, it's a good idea to examine what you've pasted so you can see how the program uses the Paste command. One clue is that if a selection box appears when you click the pasted data, it is embedded and you can edit the data with the tools from the source program.

Resizing an Embedded Object

After you embed an object, you can manipulate it as you would any other part of the source document. For example, you can move the embedded object, copy it, delete it, or resize it.

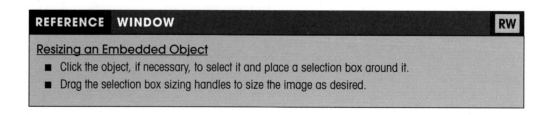

REFERENCE WINDOW   RW

Resizing an Embedded Object
■ Click the object, if necessary, to select it and place a selection box around it.
■ Drag the selection box sizing handles to size the image as desired.

As you examine the embedded graphic, you wonder if it might be easier to evaluate the image if it were bigger.

To enlarge the embedded graphic:

1. Make sure the embedded graphic is still selected. (Click the graphic, if necessary, to select it.)

2. Drag the lower-right sizing handle down and to the right. The pointer changes to ↖ when you point to the sizing handle. The embedded object is now larger. See Figure 8-10.

Figure 8-10	ENLARGED EMBEDDED OBJECT

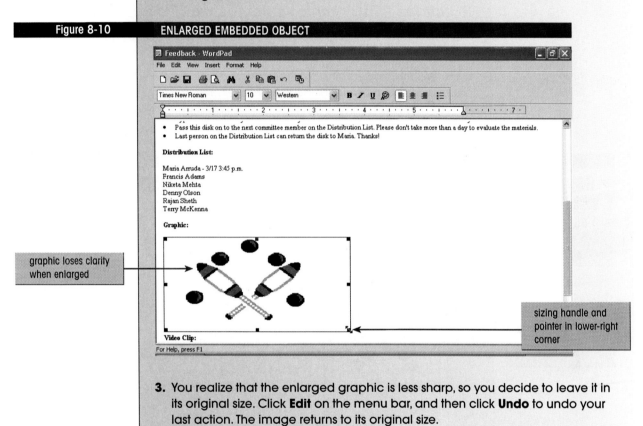

graphic loses clarity when enlarged

sizing handle and pointer in lower-right corner

3. You realize that the enlarged graphic is less sharp, so you decide to leave it in its original size. Click **Edit** on the menu bar, and then click **Undo** to undo your last action. The image returns to its original size.

The Pins graphic is in place in the Feedback document, but you decide that before the other committee members see it, you want to enhance it by adding color. Besides changing the size of an embedded object, you can also edit it to change its content.

Editing an Embedded Object

You can edit an embedded object using the source program's editing tools. Editing an object that has been embedded into a different program's document is called **in-place editing**—it gives you access to the source program's tools without making you leave the destination program. In-place editing is a valuable Windows XP data-transfer feature, because it brings the tools you need to work with your document right to you, rather than making you retrieve them.

When you use in-place editing, you might lose track of which program you are using. In that case, remember that the title bar identifies the program that contains your destination document, whereas the menus and toolbars identify the program you're using to edit the OLE object.

REFERENCE WINDOW   RW

<u>In-Place Editing</u>
- Right-click the embedded object, point to Object on the shortcut menu (this usually appears with the object type, such as Bitmap Image Object), and then click Edit—or double-click the object.
- Edit the object using the source program tools that appear in the destination program window.
- Click outside the selection box to return to the tools of the destination program.

To edit the Pins graphic within the WordPad document:

1. Right-click the **Pins** graphic, point to **Bitmap Image Object** on the shortcut menu, and then click **Edit**.

   The graphic appears inside a selection box, the Paint tools appear along the left and bottom border of the WordPad window, and the menu bar changes to reflect the Paint menus—but the title bar indicates that you are still in WordPad. See Figure 8-11.

| Figure 8-11 | USING IN-PLACE EDITING |

- title bar shows WordPad
- Paint tools
- selection box has thicker borders to indicate the object is ready for editing
- red color square
- Fill With Color tool
- scroll bars may not appear

2. Click the **Fill With Color** tool, click **red** (second row, third box from the left in the Color palette), and then click the farthest ball on the left. The ball turns red.

3. Click each ball, one at a time, to color them red.

   TROUBLE? If you mistakenly click an area outside a ball, or if you click one of the small swirls inside a ball, click Edit, click Undo, and then click the ball again.

   TROUBLE? If you can't see the entire image within the selection box, scroll to the right until you can.

4. Click outside the selection box in the WordPad document. The WordPad menus and window reappear.

5. Click the **Save** button 🖫 to save the Feedback document with the edited embedded Pins graphic.

As you'll see in Session 8.3, one of the important features that distinguish embedding from linking is that when you edit an embedded object, you do not affect the source file. You are accessing the tools that created the object, not the original file. You can verify that the original graphic remains unchanged by opening the original Pins graphic in Paint.

To see that the original Pins graphic has not changed:

1. Click the **Start** button 🏁 *start*, point to **All Programs**, point to **Accessories**, and then click **Paint**.

2. Open the **Pins** file on your Data Disk. Notice that the original Pins graphic has not changed.

3. Click the **Close** button ☒ to close the Pins file and exit Paint.

Now that you've learned how to embed an object using the Edit commands and then work with the embedded object in the destination document, you're ready to learn other ways to embed an object.

Embedding an Object Using Insert Object

To cut or copy an object in order to paste it into a different document, the object must be open in its source program and appear on the screen. However, most Windows programs that offer OLE technology also offer the Insert Object command, which lets you embed an object without having to open it and copy it to the Clipboard.

The Insert Object command embeds the entire file, without giving you the option to embed just a part of it, such as a single paragraph of text or a single table or chart. To embed only part of a file, you must use the Paste Special command, or open the file, select the data you want, cut or copy it, and then paste it into the new document.

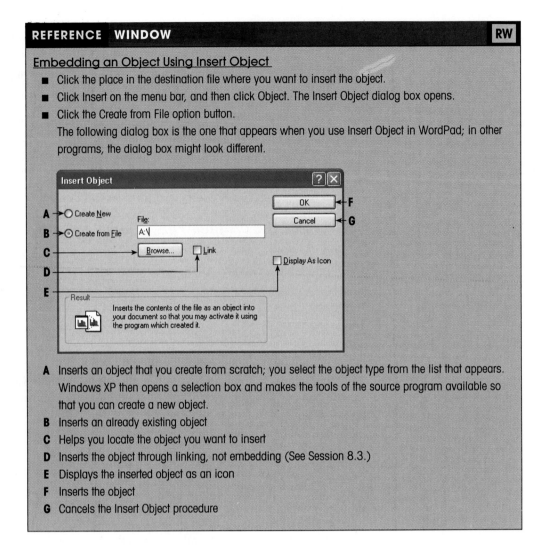

REFERENCE   WINDOW   RW

Embedding an Object Using Insert Object
- Click the place in the destination file where you want to insert the object.
- Click Insert on the menu bar, and then click Object. The Insert Object dialog box opens.
- Click the Create from File option button.

  The following dialog box is the one that appears when you use Insert Object in WordPad; in other programs, the dialog box might look different.

A Inserts an object that you create from scratch; you select the object type from the list that appears. Windows XP then opens a selection box and makes the tools of the source program available so that you can create a new object.

B Inserts an already existing object

C Helps you locate the object you want to insert

D Inserts the object through linking, not embedding (See Session 8.3.)

E Displays the inserted object as an icon

F Inserts the object

G Cancels the Insert Object procedure

When you talked to the graphic designer on the phone the other day, you mentioned that it might be nice to include the number "10" in the graphic, for tenth anniversary. The designer has just delivered a new disk with the revised file, called Pins10. You decide to embed Pins10 into the Feedback document, using the Insert Object command.

To embed an object using the Insert Object command:

1. If the Feedback document is not open, open it from your Data Disk. Click it, if necessary, to make it the active document.

2. Scroll down the Feedback document until you see the **Video Clip:** heading. You'll embed the new Pins10 graphic above this heading.

3. Click to the left of the **Video Clip:** heading.

4. Press the **Enter** key twice to add two new lines, and then press the **Up Arrow** key twice. Make sure the insertion point appears on a blank line between the Video Clip: heading and the embedded Pins graphics.

5. Click **Insert** on the menu bar, and then click **Object**. The Insert Object dialog box opens.

6. Click the **Create from File** option button. This option lets you insert an object that has already been created and saved in a file.

7. Click the **Browse** button and then locate and click the **Pins10** file on your Data Disk.

8. Click the **Open** button. The filename is inserted into the File text box.

9. Verify that the Link and Display As Icon check boxes are not selected, as shown in Figure 8-12. If you check the Display As Icon box, you see an icon instead of the actual object. You'll change the object to an icon in the next section. If you select the Link check box, you will not embed the object. You will learn more about linking in Session 8.3.

Figure 8-12	INSERT OBJECT DIALOG BOX

10. Click the **OK** button in the Insert Object dialog box. The object appears in the Feedback document.

Maria stops by and looks over the Feedback document. She mentions that the committee members might be confused by the two versions of the Pins graphic and asks you to differentiate them somehow. One way to do this is to display one graphic as an icon.

Controlling the Appearance of an OLE Object

When you place a graphic image in a document, your computer might take longer to display the document than if it contained only text. For example, when you scroll up and down the Feedback document, depending on the speed of your computer and the size of the graphics, the computer might take significantly longer to redraw the graphics as you scroll. For this reason, some users prefer to display OLE objects as icons, especially during the draft phases of creating a multimedia document. Like most Windows XP objects, your embedded object has a property sheet that lets you work with the object. You decide to display the first graphic you embedded, the red Pins graphic, as an icon.

To display the embedded Pins graphic as an icon:

1. Scroll up the Feedback document so you can see the first graphic you embedded, the Pins graphic with the red balls.

2. Right-click the **Pins** graphic and then click **Object Properties** on the shortcut menu. The Bitmap Image Properties dialog box opens. You want to change a setting that affects the appearance of the embedded object—the View tab contains those settings.

3. Click the **View** tab.

4. Click the **Display as icon** option button, and then click the **OK** button. An icon appears that represents the graphic. See Figure 8-13.

Figure 8-13	DISPLAYING AN OBJECT AS AN ICON

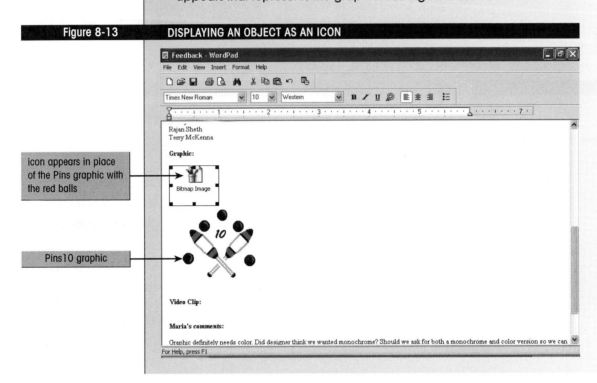

icon appears in place of the Pins graphic with the red balls

Pins10 graphic

Because you changed the graphic to an icon and can no longer identify the contents of the embedded object, you decide to change the label of the icon to make it more descriptive.

Changing the Display Icon

You can change the icon for the embedded object by selecting a different image for the icon and by entering a new label for it. You will change the icon label using the embedded object's property sheet and then change the appearance of the icon itself.

REFERENCE WINDOW RW

Changing an Icon

- Open the icon's property sheet. You usually do this by right-clicking the existing icon to open its object menu and then clicking Properties, although for embedded objects the command appears as Object Properties.
- If necessary, click the tab in the Properties dialog box that contains the Change Icon button.
- Click the Change Icon button.
- Click one of the icons that appears in the Change Icon dialog box. You could also click Create From File, click the Browse button, and then locate and select the file containing the icon. (Switch the Files of type list to All Files if you are looking for a file with an extension other than .ICO, the default type that appears.)
- Click the OK button in the Change Icon dialog box and in the Properties dialog box.

To change the label of the icon:

1. Right-click the icon representing the embedded Pins graphic.

2. Click **Object Properties** on the shortcut menu. The Bitmap Image Properties dialog box opens. You'll use the View tab again to change the icon label.

3. Click the **View** tab.

4. Click the **Change Icon** button. The Change Icon dialog box opens, showing the current icon image, the default icon image, and the current icon label. You can also use this dialog box to select a different icon from a file. You want to change the icon label, which you do using the Label text box.

5. Delete the contents of the Label text box at the bottom of the dialog box, and then type **Pins Graphic**. See Figure 8-14.

Figure 8-14 **CHANGE ICON DIALOG BOX**

enter new icon label here

label appears as Bitmap Image until you click the OK button

6. Leave the Change Icon dialog box open.

If the final format of your multimedia document includes icons, you can use the property sheet to change the icon representing the embedded object. Incidentally, you can use this method to change the appearance of many icons, including some icons on the desktop.

You decide to change the icon representing the Pins graphic to a more meaningful icon. Your Data Disk contains a bitmap graphics file called Icon that you will use as the icon.

To change the appearance of the icon:

1. In the Change Icon dialog box, which should still be open, click the **From File** option button, and then click the **Browse** button. These options let you find and select a different icon image from a file stored on your computer.

2. In the Browse dialog box, click the **Look in** list arrow, and then click the drive containing your Data Disk.

3. Click the **Files of type** list arrow, and then click **All Files**.

4. Click **Icon** and then click the **Open** button. The new icon image appears as the Current icon image in the Change Icon dialog box.

5. Click the **OK** button in the Change Icon dialog box, and then click the **OK** button in the Bitmap Image Properties dialog box. The new icon appears in the document. Click outside the selection box. See Figure 8-15.

| Figure 8-15 | NEW ICON FOR EMBEDDED OBJECT |

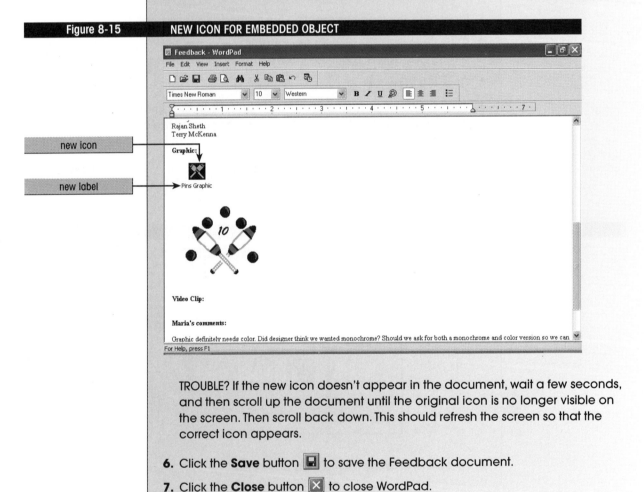

new icon

new label

TROUBLE? If the new icon doesn't appear in the document, wait a few seconds, and then scroll up the document until the original icon is no longer visible on the screen. Then scroll back down. This should refresh the screen so that the correct icon appears.

6. Click the **Save** button 🖫 to save the Feedback document.

7. Click the **Close** button ⊠ to close WordPad.

You could reduce the size of the icon image to take even less space; in this example, it's not much smaller than the original graphic. However, displaying objects as icons is a useful skill to remember if your computer is low on memory and you are working with a document with multiple embedded objects.

Embedding **with Paste Special**

When you want to embed only a portion of a file, such as part of a Paint graphic, you cannot use the Insert Object command, because Insert Object inserts an entire file. To embed part of a file, you can use **Paste Special**, a command commonly found on the Edit menu of programs that support OLE.

Maria wants to include part of the Jugglers Guild logo at the top of the memo. She gives you a Paint file named JG Logo that contains an image and text; she wants to include only the text part of the logo. To accomplish this, you'll copy the text in the Paint file and then use the Paste Special command in WordPad. Because you'll embed the graphical text instead of pasting it, you'll be able to double-click the text in WordPad and then use the Paint tools to edit it.

To use Paste Special to embed part of a file:

1. Start Paint and open the **JG Logo** file on your Data Disk.

2. Click the **Select** tool [□], and then drag to draw a dotted rectangle around the Jugglers Guild text. This selects the text in the graphic.

3. Press **Ctrl+C** to copy the text to the Clipboard.

4. Close Paint.

5. Start WordPad and open the **Feedback** document stored on your Data Disk.

6. With the insertion point in the first line, press the **Enter** key to insert a new line. Then press the **Up Arrow** key to move the insertion point back to the first line. This is where you'll insert the text part of the Jugglers Guild logo.

7. Click **Edit** on the menu bar, and then click **Paste Special**. The Paste Special dialog box opens. See Figure 8-16.

Figure 8-16   PASTE SPECIAL DIALOG BOX

paste the text from the Jugglers Guild logo here

available formats

make sure Bitmap Image is selected

8. Make sure that Bitmap Image is selected as the type of object you are pasting, and then click the **OK** button. The text from the JG Logo file appears. You can center the text to format it more attractively.

TROUBLE? If Bitmap Image does not appear in the Paste Special dialog box, click the Cancel button, open the JG Logo file again in Paint, repeat Steps 2 through 4, switch to the Feedback WordPad document, and then repeat Step 7.

9. Make sure the Jugglers Guild object is selected, and then click the **Center** button.

Now you can make sure that the Paint menu and tools appear when you double-click the logo. This indicates that you embedded the Paint object and did not simply paste it.

10. Double-click the **Jugglers Guild logo text**. The Paint menu and tools appear in the Feedback—WordPad window, indicating you can edit the graphic within the WordPad document.

11. Close the Feedback document and click the **Yes** button when asked if you want to save your changes.

Now you can edit the logo, if necessary, in the Feedback document without leaving WordPad to open Paint.

REFERENCE   WINDOW   **RW**

Using Embedding Methods

- **Paste Special** Using Paste Special allows you to embed the objects or parts of objects in specialized formats. Open the source file, select the object you want to embed, click Edit, and then click Copy. Then open the destination file, click Edit, and then click Paste Special. Select the file format option you want to use, and then click the OK button.
- **Insert Object** This method is faster than Paste when you are embedding an entire file, because you don't need to open the source file first. If you need to embed an entire file, such as a graphic image or video clip, click Insert, click Object, and then click Create from File. Locate the file you want to embed, and then click the OK button.

Some programs might not feature OLE or the Clipboard. When you attempt to transfer data from other programs and the process doesn't seem to work as you expect, the program probably doesn't support OLE. When using such programs, you must depend on the data transfer commands that they provide—commands that often appear on the File menu as Import or Export.

In this session, you embedded an object using the Paste command, changed an embedded object, embedded an object using Insert Object, changed a display icon, and embedded an object using the Paste Special command.

Session 8.2 QUICK | CHECK

1. What is OLE?

2. You just embedded text from a WordPad document into a PowerPoint presentation. Which is the source program, and which is the destination program?

3. Name two ways to embed an object with OLE. Under what circumstances might you use these different methods?

4. What is in-place editing?

5. True or False: You can use the Clipboard to transfer data between any two programs.

SESSION 8.3

In this session, you will link a new version of the Pins graphic into your Feedback document. Then you'll work with the original file to see how linking lets you update the linked information in the source document. You'll learn how to delete OLE objects from your document. Then you'll link a video clip to the Feedback document and work with the Windows XP Media Player.

Understanding Linking

The graphic designer you have been working with has supplied you with another version of the Pins graphic, called Pins2, which makes better use of color. You want the committee members to see this new graphic and plan to distribute a new version of the Feedback document to them. Maria also wants you to update and distribute the document whenever you receive any other new versions of the graphic that the designer might submit. You don't want to have to re-embed the graphic every time you receive a new version. Therefore, you decide to link the Pins2 graphic to your Feedback document rather than embed it.

Linking is another way to insert information into a document, but with linking you insert a representation of the object—a link to an object that is stored somewhere else. When you edit a linked object, you are editing the original object—the source file itself— whether you are working with the source or destination file. For example, if you change the color of the balls in a linked object, you are changing the color of the balls in the source file itself. Notice how this differs from embedding. With embedding, you place a copy of the object into the destination file; it does not connect to the source file, so any changes you make to the embedded object are not reflected in the source file. With linking, however, you maintain a connection between the source file and the destination file, and a change to one object changes the other object. See Figure 8-17.

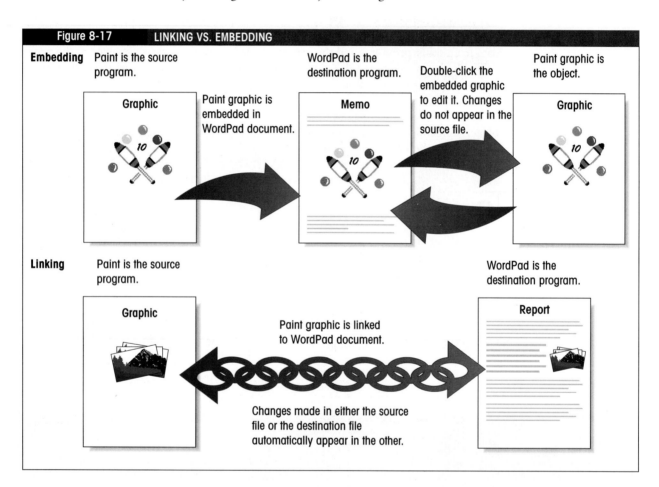

You link an object when you want to maintain only one copy of the object. For example, you might want to use an object in several documents. When you update the object, all the documents use the updated version. However, when you give someone a document that contains links, make sure to include the source files. Otherwise, she won't be able to see the linked objects—she needs the source files to do so. Note also that links target specific locations on a disk, so if you move the linked object source, the destination document will no longer be able to display it (although you can update a link by right-clicking it, clicking Object Properties, clicking the Link tab in the Linked Bitmap Image Properties dialog box, and then clicking the Change Source button).

Another difference between linking and embedding involves file size. A file that contains a linked object needs less disk space than a file that contains an embedded version of the same object. This is because a link to an object contains only a representation of the object and information about where to access it, whereas an embedded object is a copy of the original object. If the file size of the original object is large, as is the case with graphics, the size of the file containing the embedded object increases accordingly.

Linking a Graphic File to a WordPad Document

You need to link Pins2 to the Feedback document. As with embedding, you can use the Insert Object or the Paste Special command to link objects. Insert Object allows you to insert an entire file, while Paste Special allows you to insert a portion of a file.

REFERENCE WINDOW   **RW**

Linking an Object

- To use Insert Object, click the location in the destination file where you want to insert the object. Then click Insert, click Object, and then click Create from File in the Insert Object dialog box. Next click Browse to open the Browse dialog box, locate and select the file, click the Link check box, and then click the OK button twice.
- To use Paste Special, first open the source file and select the information you want to insert. Click Edit and then click Copy. Open the destination file and click the location where you want to insert the object. Click Edit, and then click Paste Special. In the Paste Special dialog box, click Paste Link and then click the OK button. Note that Paste Special does not always allow you to paste with a link.

You'll use the Insert Object command to link the Pins2 graphic because you want to link the entire file, not just a portion of it.

To insert the Pins2 graphic as a linked object:

1. Start WordPad and then open the **Feedback** file stored on your Data Disk.

2. Scroll down the Feedback document, click to the left of the **Video Clip:** heading, press the **Enter** key twice to insert two new lines, and then press the **Up Arrow** twice. This is where you'll insert the link to the Pins2 graphic.

3. Click **Insert** on the menu bar, and then click **Object**. The Insert Object dialog box opens.

4. Click the **Create from File** option button, click the **Browse** button, click the **Look in** list arrow in the Browse dialog box, click the drive containing your Data Disk, click **Pins2**, and then click the **Open** button. So far, you've followed the same steps you followed when you embedded a graphic. This time, however, you'll check the Link check box to indicate that you want to insert a link to the source file.

5. Click the **Link** check box to place a check mark in it, and then click the **OK** button. The multicolored Pins2 graphic appears in the Feedback document.

6. Save the Feedback document.

You like the look of the color graphic, but you think it would look better if all the balls were one color. You decide to edit the source file, Pins2, in Paint, but you want to see the effect on your WordPad document at the same time. You could resize and drag the windows into place, or you could use the Tile or Cascade commands on the taskbar shortcut menu. You'll try these commands in the next section.

Arranging Windows Using Tile and Cascade

The **Tile** commands on the taskbar shortcut menu arrange open windows so that they are all visible. You can tile vertically (side by side) or horizontally (one above the other). The **Cascade** command arranges all open windows so that they overlap each other and all their title bars are visible. Figure 8-18 shows horizontally tiled windows and cascading windows.

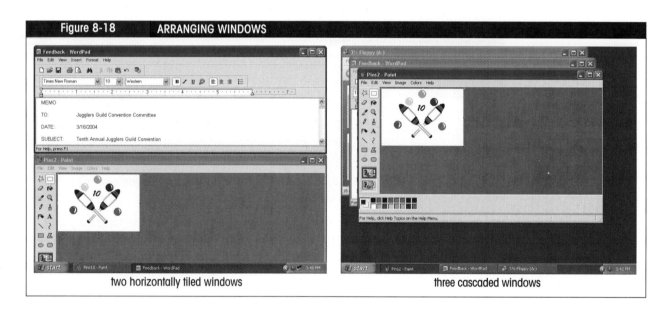

Figure 8-18   ARRANGING WINDOWS

two horizontally tiled windows   three cascaded windows

Tiling is useful when you have two or three open windows, whereas cascading is useful when you have many open windows. Arranging windows can be helpful when you transfer data, because you are often working with more than one open program, and you want to see what's happening in all the programs at the same time. You decide to tile the WordPad and Paint windows vertically.

To open and tile the Paint and WordPad windows:

1. Click the **Start** button, point to **All Programs**, point to **Accessories**, and then click **Paint**.

2. Open the **Pins2** file on your Data Disk. This is the file you just linked to the Feedback document.

3. Right-click a blank area of the taskbar to open the taskbar menu. See Figure 8-19.

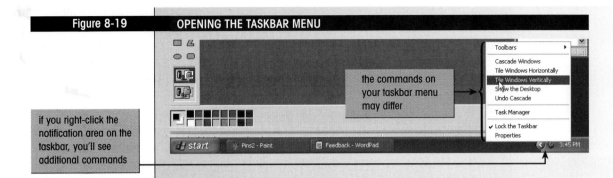

Figure 8-19   OPENING THE TASKBAR MENU

if you right-click the notification area on the taskbar, you'll see additional commands

the commands on your taskbar menu may differ

TROUBLE? If program buttons fill your taskbar, right-click the space between two program buttons until your menu looks like the one in Figure 8-19.

4. Click **Tile Windows Vertically**. The two windows appear side by side.

5. Scroll down the WordPad window, if necessary, so that you can see the multi-colored Pins2 graphic.

Now that you can see the Feedback document and the Pins2 graphic, you can edit the linked object—the Pins2 graphic in Paint—and then check the effects of your editing in the Feedback document.

Editing a Linked Object in the Source Program

The object you just inserted is linked, so you can change it in either the source or destination file, and your changes will be stored in the original file. You decide to color the balls red in the original Pins2 file.

To edit the Pins2 graphic in Paint:

1. In Paint, click the **Fill With Color** tool 🖌.

2. Click the **red** box (second row, third box from left in the Color palette), and then click each of the four balls that aren't already red. All five balls should be red when you finish.

3. In Paint, click **File** and then click **Save**.

Now that you've changed the source file—the Pins2 graphic in Paint—you can update the graphic in the Feedback document so it reflects these changes.

Updating a Linked Object

If the destination file is closed when you change the source file, any linked objects will usually update automatically the next time you open the file, or you'll be given the option to update the links when you next open the file. If the destination file is open when you change the source file, you have to update it manually, using the Links command. This opens the Links dialog box, which gives you control over the links in your document.

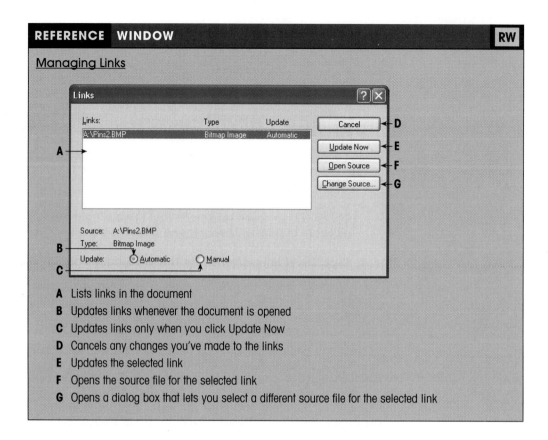

REFERENCE WINDOW   RW

Managing Links

A Lists links in the document
B Updates links whenever the document is opened
C Updates links only when you click Update Now
D Cancels any changes you've made to the links
E Updates the selected link
F Opens the source file for the selected link
G Opens a dialog box that lets you select a different source file for the selected link

You decide to update the link between the Pins2 source file and the Feedback destination file so you can verify that the changes take place.

To update the link in the WordPad document:

1. If necessary, click the multicolored **Pins2** graphic in the WordPad window to select it.

2. Click **Edit** on the WordPad menu bar, and then click **Links**. The Links dialog box opens, displaying all links in the current document. (In this case, there is only one.) See Figure 8-20.

Figure 8-20	LINKS DIALOG BOX

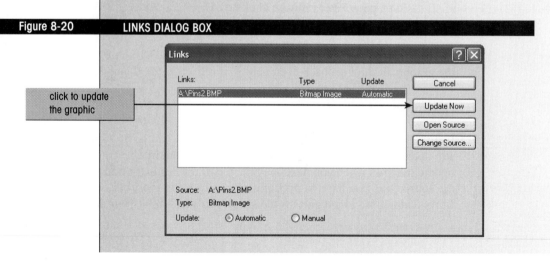

click to update
the graphic

> **3.** Click the **Update Now** button, and then click the **Close** button to close the Links dialog box.
>
> The graphic is updated.
>
> **4.** Click the **Close** button ☒ to close Paint.
>
> **5.** Maximize the WordPad window.

You have included all the graphics you need in the Feedback document. Maria suggests you review the document before you prepare to insert a video clip.

Deleting **an OLE Object**

If you insert an OLE object you no longer need, you can delete it from a document the same way you delete text or any other information—first select the object and then press the Delete key.

As you look over your document, you notice that you have now inserted three graphic objects into the Feedback document. The first two are both older versions of the graphic. You decide you don't need to include them in the Feedback document, so you can delete them.

> *To delete the two old embedded graphics, Pins and Pins10:*
>
> **1.** Scroll up the Feedback document until you see the icon representing the first Pins graphic.
>
> **2.** Click the **Pins Graphic** icon. A selection box appears around the icon, indicating it is selected.
>
> **3.** Press the **Delete** key. This removes the Pins graphic from the Feedback document.
>
> **4.** Click the **Pins10** graphic (the monochrome one). A selection box appears around it, indicating it is selected.
>
> **5.** Press the **Delete** key. This removes the Pins10 graphic from the Feedback document.
>
> **6.** Delete two blank lines below the **Graphic:** heading.
>
> **7.** Save the Feedback document.

Now you are ready to turn your attention to the next object you want to show to the committee members: the video clip. You decide to link the video clip to your Feedback document so that if the computer animation vendor sends you an updated file, you won't have to reinsert the file.

Linking **and Playing a Video Clip**

You can link a video clip in the same way you linked a graphic—using Insert Object. You can use this method because you are linking an entire file and not just a portion of a file. (Recall that if you want to link only part of a file, you use the Paste Special command on the Edit menu.)

To link a video clip to a document:

1. Scroll the Feedback document until you locate the **Video Clip:** heading.

2. Click the line above the Maria's comments: heading. This is where you will insert the video clip.

3. Click **Insert** on the menu bar, and then click **Object**. The Insert Object dialog box opens. You want to insert an object contained in a file, so you'll use the Create from File option.

4. Click the **Create from File** option button.

5. Click the **Browse** button to find the video clip file Video on your Data Disk.

6. If necessary, click the **Look in** list arrow in the Browse dialog box, and then click the drive containing your Data Disk.

7. Click **Video** and then click the **Open** button. Because you want to link the video clip to the Feedback document and not embed it, you use the Link option.

8. Click the **Link** check box to place a check mark in it, and then click the **OK** button.

The video clip looks like a graphic object, but of course it isn't. You can play the video clip by double-clicking it, or by right-clicking it and using the Play Linked Video Clip Object command. Because it is a linked object using OLE technology, you don't have to leave WordPad or start a separate program to play it.

To play the video clip:

1. Right-click the video clip and then point to **Linked Video Clip Object** on the shortcut menu.

   TROUBLE? If this appears as "Linked Media Clip Object," point to that instead.

   TROUBLE? If a message appears warning you that Windows XP couldn't launch the server application, ask your instructor or lab manager to install the multi-media accessories.

2. Click **Play**. The video clip plays in a small window. It might play once very quickly and then stop, perhaps even before it appears to reach the end, or it might play continuously and then close. You'll learn momentarily how to control the way the video clip plays. See Figure 8-21.

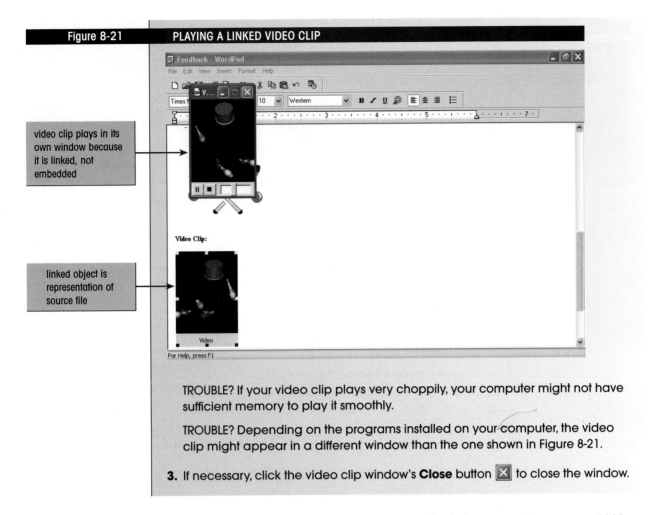

Figure 8-21	PLAYING A LINKED VIDEO CLIP

video clip plays in its own window because it is linked, not embedded

linked object is representation of source file

Video Clip:

TROUBLE? If your video clip plays very choppily, your computer might not have sufficient memory to play it smoothly.

TROUBLE? Depending on the programs installed on your computer, the video clip might appear in a different window than the one shown in Figure 8-21.

3. If necessary, click the video clip window's **Close** button ☒ to close the window.

You've now inserted the video clip into the Feedback document. However, you'd like to refine the way it plays. To do that, you need to work with the Windows XP multimedia tools.

Exploring the Windows XP Multimedia Tools

The window that opened when you played the video clip was part of Windows XP Media Player, one of the accessories Windows XP provides that handles multimedia files. The Windows XP multimedia accessories, listed in Figure 8-22 and available on the Entertainment submenu of the Accessories menu, let you create, edit, and play multimedia clips. Some of the accessories, such as DVD Player, won't appear if you don't have the appropriate hardware. Others might appear elsewhere on the Start menu, depending on how your computer was set up during installation.

Figure 8-22	MULTIMEDIA ACCESSORIES
ACCESSORY	**DESCRIPTION**
ActiveMovie Control	An Internet Explorer component that enhances the playing of audio and video files on a Web page
MovieMaker	Lets you create movie files by combining audio, video, and still images
CD Player	Plays music CDs

Figure 8-22	MULTIMEDIA ACCESSORIES (continued)
ACCESSORY	**DESCRIPTION**
DVD Player	Plays DVD discs or regular CDs from a DVD drive
Media Player	Plays audio and video clips on your computer and on the Internet
Sound Recorder	Records, mixes, edits, and plays audio files
Mulitmedia Sound Schemes	Provides different sounds that you can attach to Windows XP events (such as exiting a program)
Volume Control	Adjusts your speaker volume

Multimedia clips can use sound, video, or both. To play a clip that uses sound, you need a sound card and speakers. If your computer doesn't have these hardware devices, you can still hear sounds through your computer's internal speaker—such as the "beeps" you hear when the computer alerts you to something. The internal speaker, however, is inadequate for playing most sound files.

The **Sound Recorder** accessory uses the **WAV** (which is short for waveform-audio) file format to store and record sounds as realistically as possible. The **Media Player** accessory, on the other hand, can play many types of audio files, including those in the **MIDI** (short for Musical Instrument Digital Interface) and **MP3** (short for Motion Picture Experts Group Audio Layer-3) formats. MIDI files use artificial, synthesized sounds to mimic real sounds and hence are usually much smaller than WAV files. Although you can't use MIDI files to store voices, you can use them very effectively to store the synthesized sounds of special MIDI instruments. MP3 files are compressed to maintain low file size but still have a high sound quality. The Media Player can open as a standalone accessory or as a window you use to control and play linked and embedded multimedia files.

To play a video clip, you don't need a sound card or speakers, but the quality of the video depends on your computer's video card capabilities and its speed and memory capacity. You use the Media Player accessory to play many types of video files, including those in the **AVI** (short for Audio Video Interleaved) format. This format is sometimes called "Video for Windows." AVI files can contain both images and sound. (Of course, if you want to hear the sound you'll need a sound card and speakers.) Media Player lets you scroll back and forth through a video clip, but you cannot use Media Player to edit the clip itself.

Using Media Player

When you played the juggler video clip, it might have played only once and then stopped, or it might have played continually. You want to control the way it plays. To do this, you need to start Media Player and edit the video's settings. Media Player plays a video one frame at a time, just as a filmstrip is shown. A slider appears that shows you which frame is appearing at any given moment, so you can move forward or backward through individual frames. Media Player also includes a set of buttons that resemble the buttons on a CD player or a VCR, as described in Figure 8-23.

Figure 8-23	MEDIA PLAYER BUTTONS	
BUTTON	**NAME**	**DESCRIPTION**
▶	Play	Plays the multimedia clip; turns into the Pause button when multimedia clip is playing
‖	Pause	Pauses a playing clip; turns into Play button when mulitmedia clip is paused or not playing
■	Stop	Stops the clip at its current frame or track
▲	Eject	Appears only when you are playing a clip from a CD; ejects the CD
◄◄◄	Previous Mark	Moves to the previous mark (like a track on a CD)
◄◄	Rewind	Moves backward in increments as you click
►►	Fast Forward	Moves forward in increments as you click
►►►	Next Mark	Moves to the next mark (like a track on a CD)
⤓	Start Selection	Starts the selection (if you select just a few frames to play)
⤒	End Selection	Ends the selection (if you select just a few frames to play)

You decide you want to make sure the video plays continually. You can either start Media Player from the Start menu and then open the video clip source file, or you can start Media Player from within the Feedback document by opening the video clip for editing.

To make changes to the video clip's settings:

1. Right-click the video clip, point to **Linked Video Clip Object** on the shortcut menu, and then click **Edit**. Media Player opens. See Figure 8-24.

Figure 8-24	MEDIA PLAYER

Media Player program window for working with a linked or embedded object

2. Click **Edit** on the menu bar in the Media Player window, and then click **Options**. First see how the video plays when it is not set to Auto Repeat.

3. If necessary, click the **Auto Repeat** check box to deselect it, and then click the **OK** button.

TROUBLE? If Auto Repeat is already deselected, skip Step 3. See Figure 8-25.

| Figure 8-25 | MEDIA PLAYER OPTIONS |

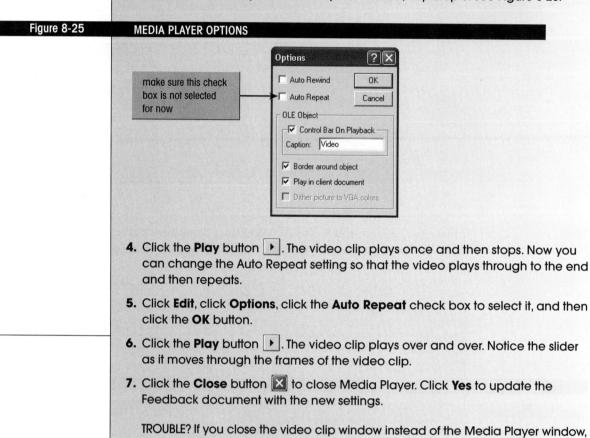

4. Click the **Play** button ▶ . The video clip plays once and then stops. Now you can change the Auto Repeat setting so that the video plays through to the end and then repeats.

5. Click **Edit**, click **Options**, click the **Auto Repeat** check box to select it, and then click the **OK** button.

6. Click the **Play** button ▶ . The video clip plays over and over. Notice the slider as it moves through the frames of the video clip.

7. Click the **Close** button ☒ to close Media Player. Click **Yes** to update the Feedback document with the new settings.

TROUBLE? If you close the video clip window instead of the Media Player window, repeat Step 7 to close Media Player.

The Feedback document now contains no embedded objects and two linked objects: the graphic and the video clip. You can send the document, along with the two source files, to the committee members for their feedback. They can easily view both objects and can then add their comments to the bottom of the document.

To save your work and close all open windows:

1. Click the **Save** button 🖫 to save your Feedback document.

2. Click the **Close** button ☒ to close WordPad.

Your final version of the Feedback document used only linking, not embedding, because you decided that both objects were likely to undergo further revision, and you wanted to be able to update the document easily without having to reinsert the objects. As you created the Feedback document, you used the Insert Object dialog box to link graphic files to the document. You edited one of the linked graphics in Paint and then updated the link in WordPad. You also linked a video clip to the Feedback document and then used the Media Player to play and control the video.

Session 8.3 QUICK CHECK

1. What is the difference between linking and embedding?

2. If you want to share a document containing embedded objects with another person, do you need to include the source files? Explain why or why not.

3. When you use the Insert Object method to insert an object into a document, do you first need to open the source file?

4. What's the difference in appearance between tiling and cascading windows?

5. True or False: Media Player plays only video, not audio, clips.

6. Describe these three file types: WAV, MIDI, and AVI.

REVIEW ASSIGNMENTS

1. **Copying and Pasting Text**   A friend of yours owns a small tailor shop and wants to advertise his services in the local telephone company's Yellow Pages. He wants feedback from his employees and friends on his advertisement and wonders if you'd share Maria's feedback process with him. You write him a note and then paste it in the steps of your process.

   a. Start WordPad and then open the **Maria** file on your Data Disk.
   b. Select the bulleted list and then copy it to the Clipboard.
   c. Open the **Tailor** file on your Data Disk, and then scroll to the boldfaced "Follow this Procedure" heading. Add a few blank lines below the heading, and then paste the copied information. Replace the name "Jan" with your name.
   d. Print and save **Tailor** and then close WordPad.

Explore 2. **Pasting Text into Paint**   In this tutorial, you pasted a Paint graphic into WordPad. Now you'll try pasting in the other direction. You are designing a banner that announces the names of incumbent officers running for reelection for the Jugglers Guild. You have created a Paint graphic called Election. You want to insert the names of the five officers into that graphic.

   a. Start Paint and open the **Election** graphic on your Data Disk.
   b. Start WordPad, open the **Maria** file, and then copy the last five names (not including Maria Arruda) in the Distribution List to the Clipboard. These are the five officers running for reelection.
   c. Close WordPad. Paste the names into the **Election** graphic. Click Yes if Paint asks if you want to enlarge the bitmap.
   d. Drag the pasted names so they are centered below the heading.
   e. Print and save the **Election** graphic, and then close Paint. Now experiment with the pasted information. Can you use the source program tools from within Paint?
   f. On your printout, write a paragraph answering the following questions: Is the text you just pasted inserted as an embedded object into the Paint graphic? How can you tell? How does the process you just completed differ from the way you pasted a Paint graphic into a WordPad document in Session 8.2?

3. **Linking and Editing a Graphic** You work as a clown named Chester, and you are attending the juggling convention. You want to distribute a flyer at the convention that advertises your clowning services. You have created the flyer in the WordPad document named Clowning, and you want to link a graphic file to that document.

   a. Open the WordPad document named **Clowning** on your Data Disk.
   b. Use the Insert Object command to insert the graphic named **Chester** into the bottom of the **Clowning** document. Make sure you insert the object with a link.
   c. After you've inserted the **Chester** graphic, open it for editing by right-clicking the object, pointing to Linked Bitmap Image Object, and then clicking Edit. Change Chester's hair color to brown. Close Paint, saving the changes to **Chester**, and then return to the WordPad document.
   d. Update the link, if necessary, and then print and save the **Clowning** document. On the printout, write a paragraph about how editing a linked object from the destination document differs from editing an embedded object. Close WordPad.

Explore ▶ 4. **Using Sound Recorder** If you have a microphone, a sound card, and speakers, you can create your own sound file, using the Sound Recorder accessory that comes with Windows XP. You want to send a colleague an electronic "Happy Birthday" message, so you decide to sing the Happy Birthday song into the microphone, save it as a sound file, and then embed it into a message.

   a. Click the Start button, point to All Programs, point to Accessories, point to Entertainment, and then click Sound Recorder.
   b. Click the Record button on the far right of Sound Recorder.
   c. Sing "Happy Birthday" into the microphone. (Sing just the first few words to keep the size of the audio clip small.) Click the Stop button when you are finished singing.
   d. Save the document as **Happy Birthday** on a new, blank, formatted disk—not your Data Disk. Label this disk "OLE Disk." (You need a second disk because if you complete all the Review Assignments and Projects, you won't have room on your Data Disk.)
   e. Play the **Happy Birthday** sound file.
   f. Compose a birthday message in WordPad, and embed the **Happy Birthday** sound file into this message.
   g. Print the message and save it as **Birthday Message**. If you have access to e-mail and you know how to send a file, you could send the WordPad file to a friend who's celebrating a birthday.

PROJECTS

1. You work for the Internal Revenue Service and have been using Notepad to draft a brochure to inform taxpayers about online tax filing. Notepad, however, does not offer any text-formatting options, and you'd like to format your document. You decide to move the text into a WordPad document.

   a. Start Notepad and then open the **IRS** file on your Data Disk.
   b. Start WordPad and then open the **New** file on your Data Disk.
   c. In Notepad, select and then copy the entire document. Close Notepad.
   d. In the WordPad window, click below the Online Tax Filing heading, and then paste the text. Type your name at the top of the document.
   e. Print and save the WordPad document on your OLE disk, and then close WordPad.

2. You are a member of the Tokunta Construction Company. You are developing a training manual for new employees. You need to link a graphic that illustrates a construction principle, but you want to display it as an icon.

   a. Open the **House** document in WordPad on your Data Disk.
   b. Use the Insert Object command to insert the **House** graphic at the end of the document. Make sure you link the graphic.

c. Change the graphic display so that it displays an icon.

d. Change the icon to the Tools icon on your Data Disk.

e. Change the label of the icon to Cantilever.

f. Print and save the **House** document on your OLE disk.

3. Your Data Disk includes a sound file from J.F. Kennedy's inaugural speech. You'd like to link this sound file to a WordPad document that you are creating for a linguistics class, in which you are studying American accents. Kennedy's sound clip exemplifies a Boston accent.

a. Create a new WordPad document, and type "Linguistics, Bostonian accent" at the beginning. Make sure you type your name. Save the document as **Linguistics** on your OLE Disk.

b. Use the Insert Object command to insert the Kennedy sound file into your document. Make sure you insert it with a link.

c. You'll be able to complete this task only if you have a sound card and speakers. Use the linked object's shortcut menu to first play the object and then open it for editing. When you open it for editing, what accessory does Windows XP use?

4. You work at CarpetMaster, a company that specializes in residential and commercial carpet cleaning and restoration. A customer wants an estimate of costs for repairing an Oriental rug that was damaged in a recent fire. You need to draw a rectangle in Paint that proportionally approximates the carpet size and indicate the area that you'll be repairing. Then you need to embed that graphic into a WordPad document that gives the estimate.

a. Create a Paint graphic that shows the carpet and the damaged area. Save this graphic as a 16-color bitmap file named **Carpet** on your OLE Disk. Close Paint. Figure 8-26 shows an example of a graphic with the marked portion of damaged carpet.

Figure 8-26

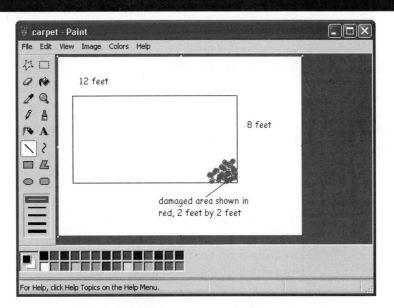

b. Create a WordPad document that uses appropriate text for an estimate and includes a description of the necessary repairs. Save the document as **CarpetMaster Estimate**.

c. Open Calculator and calculate 6.5 hours at $47/hr. Paste this amount into the WordPad document.

d. Use the Insert Object command to embed the **Carpet** graphic in the WordPad document.

e. Print and save the WordPad document.

5. If you have access to other software programs, such as a word processor, a spreadsheet program, or a database program, experiment with the data transfer operations available in those programs. Create new documents in these programs, add sample data, and then save the documents on your disk. Then try to copy and paste data between the programs. Next try embedding and linking. Write a short essay that answers the following questions:

a. What programs did you test? In what situations were you able to copy and paste?

b. In what situations did Paste embed the data? In what situations did Paste simply transfer the data without embedding?

c. In what situations were you able to do in-place editing?

d. Were there any situations in which you were unable to link?

e. Based on your experiments, what conclusions can you draw about whether or not your programs support OLE?

Explore

6. You own Circle K Ranch, a working ranch that welcomes families, summer campers, and groups for weekly stays, so they can experience life on a ranch. You are working on a flyer that you will mail to former clients and travel agents.

a. Create a WordPad document called **Ranch Flyer** on your OLE Disk. Write a brief description of the ranch. Mention that you are working on the summer schedule and that people should make their reservations as soon as possible.

b. Use Calculator to calculate this year's weekly rate. To make an acceptable profit, you need to earn $15,000 this summer from your visitor income. There are 12 weeks in the summer, and you have room for eight guests each week. To calculate a room charge per person per week, click 15000 / 12 / 8 = in the Calculator window. Paste the Calculator results into your document.

c. Use the Insert Object command to create a new bitmapped image in your advertisement. The Create New option button should be selected, with an object type of Bitmap Image. Create a small Paint graphic that shows a letter K in an interesting font with a circle around it.

d. Print and save the flyer on your OLE Disk.

LAB ASSIGNMENTS

Multimedia

Multimedia brings together text, graphics, sound, animation, video, and photo images. In this lab, you will learn how to apply multimedia and then have the chance to see what it might be like to design some aspects of multimedia projects. See the Read This Before You Begin page for information on installing and starting the Lab.

1. Click the Steps button to learn about multimedia development. As you work through the Steps, answer all of the Quick Check questions that appear. After you complete the Steps, you will see a Quick Check report. Follow the instructions on the screen to print this report.

2. How many videos are included in the Multimedia Mission Log? The image on the Mission Profile page is a vector drawing. What happens when you enlarge it?

3. Listen to the sound track on Day 4. Is this a WAV file or a MIDI file? Why do you think so? Is this a synthesized or a digitized sound? Listen to the sound track on the first page. Can you tell if this is a WAV file or a MIDI file?

4. Suppose you were hired as a multimedia designer for a multimedia series targeting fourth- and fifth-grade students. Describe the changes you would make to the Multimedia Mission Log so it would be suitable for these students. Also, include a sketch showing a screen from your revised design.

5. The Multimedia Mission Log does not contain any hyperlinks. Suppose that you were hired to revise the design of this product and to add hyperlinks. Provide a list of five specific instances where you would use hyperlinks, and indicate to what sort of information each would link.

6. Multimedia can be effectively applied to projects such as encyclopedias, atlases, and animated storybooks; computer-based training for foreign languages, first aid, or software applications; games and sports simulations; business presentations; personal albums, scrapbooks, and baby books; and product catalogs and Web pages.

7. Suppose you were hired to create one of these projects. Write a one-paragraph description of the project you would be creating. Describe some of the multimedia elements you would include. For each of these elements, indicate its source and whether you would need to obtain permission for its use. Finally, sketch a screen or two showing your completed project.

QUICK | CHECK ANSWERS

Session 8.1

1. an area in your computer's memory that stores data you cut or copy

2. When you cut selected text, it is removed from the original document and placed on the Clipboard. When you copy it, a replica of the data is moved to the Clipboard, but the original document remains intact.

3. Ctrl+X to cut, Ctrl+C to copy, Ctrl+V to paste

4. False

5. It is more accurate than typing.

Session 8.2

1. object linking and embedding—a technology that allows you to transfer data from one program to another and retain the ability to access tools from the original program

2. WordPad is the source program; PowerPoint is the destination program.

3. Paste, Paste Special, or Insert Object. Paste allows you to embed a selected portion of a file, Paste Special allows you to embed a selected portion with more control, and Insert Object allows you to embed an entire file without having to open it first.

4. editing an embedded object using the source program tools without ever leaving the destination document

5. False; older programs might not support Clipboard technology.

Session 8.3

1. Linking places a representation of the source file, whereas embedding places a copy of the source file into the destination document.

2. No. Embedded objects have been copied into the document.

3. No.

4. Tiling arranges open windows so they are all visible. Cascading overlaps open windows so their title bars are visible.

5. False

6. The WAV format records and stores sounds as realistically as possible. The MIDI format uses artificial sounds to mimic real sounds. The AVI format is the Windows video clip format.

EXPLORING YOUR NETWORK

Using Network Resources at Millennium Real Estate

CASE

OBJECTIVES

In this tutorial you will:

- Gain an understanding of networks and network terminology

- View your network using My Network Places

- Consider network security and access rights issues

- Log on to and log off a network account

- Access network resources, including folders and printers

- Share a resource on the network

- Work with network resources offline

Millennium Real Estate

You are a real estate agent who recently joined Millennium Real Estate Company, a small firm consisting of a real estate division and a land development division. Recently, Millennium connected all its computers to form a network. A **network** is a collection of computers and other hardware devices linked together so that they can exchange data and share hardware and software.

Networks offer a company such as Millennium many advantages. Groups of computers on the network can use the same printer, so Millennium doesn't have to purchase a printer for each computer. Networks facilitate group projects because one person can save a document in a folder that other users on other computers can access. A network also improves communication in a company because co-workers can easily share news and information.

Joan Alvarez, the company's owner, wants you to learn to use the Millennium network effectively, and she would like you to spend the next several hours exploring it. She decides to start by giving you an overview of the basic concepts of networking. Once you know the fundamentals, Joan will show you how to use Windows XP to be productive on the company's network. You will share an office with Anjali Gregory, one of the Millennium agents, so Joan decides to use the computer in Anjali's office to show you how to access and use the network.

SESSION 9.1

In this session, you'll explore basic network concepts. Then you will learn about some of the Windows XP tools that help you understand, view, and work with a network.

Network Concepts

Recall that a network is composed of computers and other hardware devices linked together. Each device on a network is called a **node**. A node can be a computer, a printer, or any other kind of hardware that can be accessed over a network. Nodes are typically connected to each other by means of network cables, although you can also establish connections using phone lines, satellites, and infrared signals. If the network nodes are close together, as they would be in a computer lab at your school or the Millennium office suite, the network is called a **local area network**, or **LAN**. LANs are most often simply connected with network cables. Figure 9-1 shows a typical LAN.

Figure 9-1   A LOCAL AREA NETWORK

cable connects nodes on the network

printer can be made available to all computers on the network

each computer on the network is a node

If the nodes are spread out over a wider area, such as across a state or nation, the network is often called a **wide area network**, or **WAN**. For example, an insurance company with offices in many large cities might be on a WAN, so that an office in Detroit can access information about a client whose insurance history is located on a computer in the San Antonio office. In contrast to a LAN connected by network cables, a WAN often uses satellite connections to exchange data among the nodes, but it might also use phone lines.

Not only can computers be connected to form networks, but networks can also be connected together to form larger networks. In these situations, each network (sometimes referred to as a **subnet** for subnetwork) is given a **domain name**, so that other networks can identify it. Just as information can be shared among nodes in a network, so too can information be shared among computers in different domains. The largest and most well-known example of this is the Internet, which is sometimes called a "network of networks." With Internet access, a computer in one domain can communicate with a computer in a different domain, if a path connects the two networks and these two networks communicate using the same standards and conventions that the Internet uses. Many WANs connect to the Internet to transfer data and share resources.

Because Millennium's computers are located in the same building, they are configured as a local area network. People follow one of two models to set up LANs: the hierarchical model or the peer-to-peer model.

Hierarchical Client/Server Network

In a network based on the **hierarchical model** (often called the **client/server model**), computers called **servers** provide access to resources such as files, software, and hardware devices. A computer that uses these resources is called a **workstation** or **client**. Figure 9-2 illustrates the hierarchical model.

Figure 9-2	HIERARCHICAL NETWORK MODEL

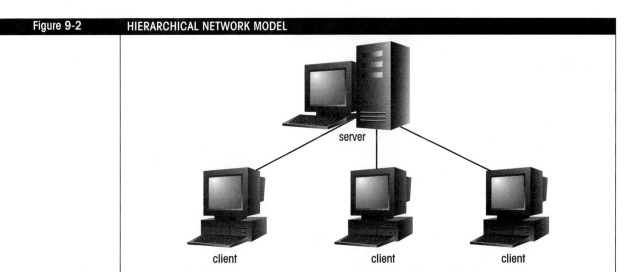

Servers offer many resources to the clients on the network. For example, a server might store a database, making it accessible to many workstations. A server might also handle electronic mail, faxes, or printing for a network. If a network is large, it often has several servers, with each server dedicated to the needs of a separate group of users or to a specific task. Most university networks use a hierarchical model, with students, faculty, and staff using workstations to access files and resources stored on servers across campus.

A hierarchical network requires special software on the server. This software, called a **network operating system**, manages the operations of the entire network. In addition, client computers must also have an operating system, such as Windows XP, that lets them communicate with the server. Windows XP comes in two different editions, each of which provides different client/server network capabilities. As an end user, you work with the Windows XP Home or Professional Edition. The Home Edition lets you connect to a network and access its resources from your workstation. With the Professional Edition, you can perform all the tasks in the Home Edition plus access security, management, and networking features designed for business users. For example, you can use any Windows computer to work with all of the settings and documents on your workstation while you are away from your office. You can access files and folders you saved on a network drive even when you are disconnected from the server. Windows XP Professional also lets you disguise sensitive data, which is especially helpful for laptop users who want to protect the information stored on their hard disks.

Peer-to-Peer Network

A second kind of network model is the peer-to-peer model. In a network based on the **peer-to-peer model**, nodes can act as both clients and servers, with each node sharing specified resources with other nodes on the network. You can use Windows XP Professional as the operating system for any peer computer, but not the Home Edition. Figure 9-3 shows the layout of a typical peer-to-peer network.

Figure 9-3	PEER-TO-PEER NETWORK MODEL

In a large peer-to-peer network, the network administrator often organizes nodes into workgroups. A **workgroup** is a group of computers that performs common tasks or belongs to users who share common responsibilities and interests. A network administrator for a business, for example, might organize computers used by the office staff into an Office workgroup and computers used by upper management into a Management workgroup. Organizing the network in this fashion makes it easier for the network administrator to manage the differing needs of each group.

An advantage of the peer-to-peer model for Windows XP Professional users is that the network can be set up without purchasing a network operating system. Everything needed to create a peer-to-peer network is built into Windows XP Professional. However, one disadvantage of peer-to-peer networks is that performance of individual nodes can deteriorate as they manage tasks for other computers as well as perform their own duties. Moreover, a peer-to-peer network does not have the same extensive network management and security features offered by network operating systems under the hierarchical model. For these reasons, peer-to-peer networks are usually used for smaller networks with just a few nodes. This is the case at Millennium Real Estate.

A network and its components are usually designed, installed, and maintained by an individual called the **network administrator**. The administrator is ultimately responsible for how you interact with the network. The network administrator tries to create a network structure that best meets the needs of the users, sometimes including elements from both the hierarchical and peer-to-peer models to create a hybrid. How a user interacts with the network can also vary from network to network and from user to user on the same network. The network administrator will limit the ability of some users to work on the network based on their job needs, whereas other administrators will give users great flexibility in sharing and accessing network resources. You will learn more about the role of the network administrator in Session 9.2.

Joan wants you to understand that what you see on the Millennium peer-to-peer network might not necessarily apply to other networks you encounter. Also, because every network is different, some of the topics in this tutorial will not apply to your network. If you are using the Windows XP Home Edition, you will not be able to work with offline files. If you are using the Windows XP Home Edition, you should still review those tasks to further your understanding of the networking capabilities of Windows XP.

Network **Protocols and Standards**

You tell Joan you've had some experience using networks because your college computer system was a network. Joan is glad to hear this but says that there are so many variations of how a network can be set up that you are bound to find differences between what your college network could do and what the Millennium network does. To best understand how to use any network, you should know how a network operates. Windows XP uses four components to provide network access: a network adapter, a communications protocol, a client, and a service component. See Figure 9-4.

Figure 9-4	NETWORK COMPONENTS

A **network adapter** is the hardware device on your computer that enables it to connect to the network. Adapters are usually cards, called **network interface cards**, or **NICs**, inserted into a slot in the back of your computer. The card includes a port into which a network cable is inserted. Figure 9-5 shows an example of a network interface card.

Figure 9-5	NETWORK INTERFACE CARD

cable connects
computer to
network

Each NIC uses a **network standard**, which is the manner in which data is handled as it travels over the network cable. Network standards are often compared in terms of how fast they transfer data. The faster a standard can transfer data, the more efficiently the network can share resources among its pool of users. Ethernet is one of the most widely used network standards. The **Ethernet** standard transfers data at 10 megabits per second—much faster than data is transferred over a phone line. Another popular network standard is the **Token Ring** standard. Developed by IBM, the Token Ring standard can transfer data at rates up to 16 megabits per second. As demands on networks increase, so do demands for new standards that support faster transfer speeds. The newer standards **Fiber Distributed Data Interchange (FDDI)** and **Asynchronous Transfer Mode (ATM)** can transfer data at 100 megabits per second and faster. Another standard, called **Fast Ethernet**, also can transfer data at 100 megabits per second.

Your computer doesn't have to have a NIC and a network cable to connect to a network—you can also connect using a modem. In these situations, Windows XP uses the modem as a **dial-up adapter**, with the phone line acting as a network connection. A phone line does not transmit data nearly as fast as the combination of the NIC and network cable, but for many users phone lines are the only choice. For example, if you have a computer at home and you have an account with an Internet service provider, you most likely use your phone line to connect to the network. More information about connecting to the Internet over a phone line is included in Appendix A, "Connecting Computers over a Phone Line."

The second component of network access is the communications protocol. A **communications protocol** determines how computers recognize each other on the network and what rules they use to transfer data. For example, the communications protocol sets the rules for determining how fast data is sent. Different network operating systems use different protocols. Computers that connect to the Internet use **Transmission Control Protocol/Internet Protocol (TCP/IP)**. With the popularity of the Internet and the World Wide Web, TCP/IP is becoming the protocol of choice. Windows XP uses TCP/IP protocol, for example, as do the latest releases of NetWare and UNIX.

The third component of your network setup is the **client** component, the client software that gives your computer the ability to access shared resources on the network. Each network operating system requires a different client component to be installed on the computers connected to the network. Windows XP includes client components to support the Novell NetWare and Microsoft networks, for example.

The final component of your network setup is the **service** component, software that enables your computer to share its resources with the network. It also lets a network administrator manage the software and hardware installed on your machine from a remote location. The service component is used primarily in peer-to-peer networks, in which each user controls how his or her computer shares its resources with the network. On many hierarchical networks, the network administrator will not make this component available to users.

Understanding which network components have been installed on your computer helps you understand the capabilities and limitations of your computer as it interacts with the network.

Viewing Your Network

To view the contents of your network, you open an icon on the desktop called **My Network Places** 🖥. My Network Places is a window similar to the My Computer window that allows you to view and access the nodes on the network. It also helps you view your network's structure and see how your computer fits into it.

REFERENCE WINDOW   **RW**

Viewing Your Network
- Open My Computer.
- In the left pane of the My Computer window, under Other Places, click My Network Places.
- To view the computers in your workgroup or domain, click View workgroup computers under Network Tasks.
- To view computers outside your workgroup or domain, make sure the computers in your workgroup or domain are listed in the right pane of the My Network Places window, and then click Microsoft Windows Network under Other Places in the left pane.

Note that the steps and figures in this tutorial show the settings and options for the Millennium network. Your screen will reflect the settings and options that apply to the network on which you are working.

To view the My Network Places window:

1. Open the My Computer window. In the left pane of the My Computer window, under Other Places, click **My Network Places**. The My Network Places window opens. Switch to Details view, if necessary, to see detailed information about the items in this window. See Figure 9-6.

Figure 9-6	MY NETWORK PLACES WINDOW

network places you can access from your computer

lists the tasks you can perform in the My Network Places window

lists other locations you can access from this window

your details might be different

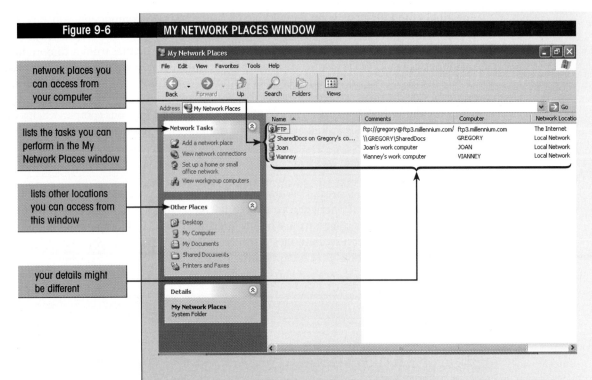

TROUBLE? If the My Network Places option does not appear under Other Places or if the My Network Places window does not open, it could be that your computer is not set up to use a network, or that the network administrator has not given you permission to view and access the network. Talk to your instructor or technical support person for assistance.

TROUBLE? Depending on how your network is set up, your My Network Places window may appear different from the one shown in Figure 9-6.

The left pane of the My Network Places window contains links to network tasks and other places you can access with your computer. (The links in your window might be different.) For example, under Network Tasks, you can click the Add Network Place link to create a shortcut to a folder on your network and store the shortcut in the My Network Places window. You can also create shortcuts to folders on the Internet, such as Web folders or FTP sites. Use the View workgroup computers link to view only those computers located in your workgroup or domain. When you are viewing the computers in your workgroup or domain, click the Microsoft Windows Network link under Other Places, and then click the Entire Network link to view the entire structure of your network, including any workgroups or domains that you can access. Figure 9-7 lists links that usually appear in the left pane of the My Network Places window.

Figure 9-7	MY NETWORK PLACES LINKS

NAME	DESCRIPTION
Add a network place	Add a shortcut to a network folder to the right pane of the window
View network connections	Open the Network Connections window to view network connections
Set up a home or small office network	Use the Network Setup Wizard to plan and set up a home or small business network
View workgroup computers	Display the computers in your workgroup in the right pane of the window
Other Places	Display the contents of the desktop, My Computer, the My Documents folder, the Shared Documents folder, or the Printers and Faxes window

Viewing Your Network's Structure

Joan suggests that you next use My Network Places to explore the structure of Millennium's computer network. You'll start by viewing other computers in your workgroup and then view the workgroups on your network.

To view the structure of the network:

1. In the left pane of the My Network Places window, under Network Tasks, click **View workgroup computers**. Windows XP displays a list of workstations and other objects in your workgroup or domain. You'll examine this window shortly; for now, note the other computers in your workgroup, and then continue to Step 2.

TROUBLE? If you are working on a domain network, the My Network Places window shows the computers in your domain by default, and the left pane does not include a View workgroup computers link. Skip Step 1 and start with Step 2.

2. In the left pane under Other Places, click **Entire Network**, and then click **Microsoft Windows Network**. Windows XP displays a list of the domains and workgroups available on your network. See Figure 9-8.

Figure 9-8	WORKGROUPS ON THE MILLENNIUM NETWORK

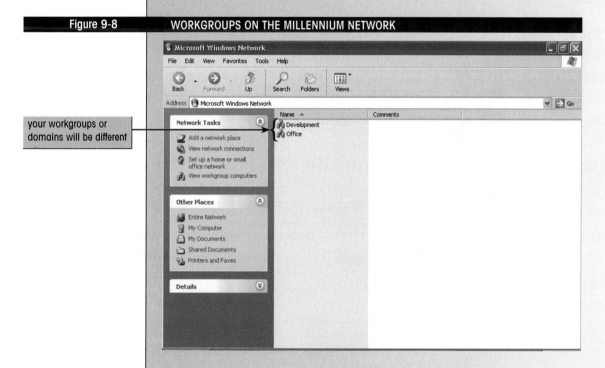

your workgroups or domains will be different

TROUBLE? Depending on your network's configuration, you might have to click other icons to view the entire structure of your network.

The Millennium network has two workgroups: Office and Development. Now you can see which computers these workgroups contain and to which workgroup your computer belongs.

Viewing the Contents of a Workgroup or Domain

To determine which computers a workgroup or domain contains, you can double-click a workgroup or domain icon to open it. You can open the Office workgroup to see which computers it includes and then view the properties of one of those computers.

To view the contents of a domain or workgroup:

1. Double-click a workgroup or domain icon.

The computers in the workgroup or domain appear. See Figure 9-9.

| Figure 9-9 | COMPUTERS IN A WORKGROUP |

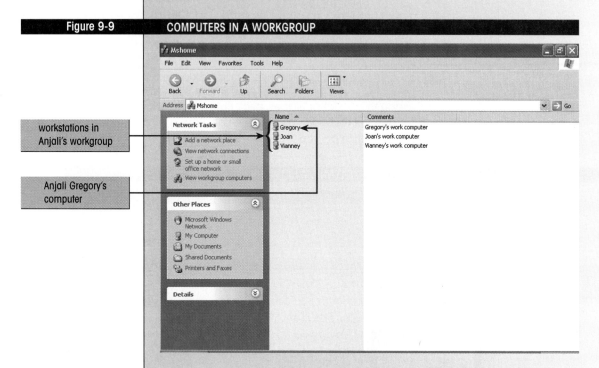

workstations in
Anjali's workgroup

Anjali Gregory's
computer

TROUBLE? Your list of computers will be different from the one shown in Figure 9-9.

TROUBLE? On some networks, you will be asked to enter a password before you can access another domain or workgroup. See your instructor or technical support person if this is the case with your network.

Note that this is the same window you opened when you clicked the View workgroup computers link earlier. The computer you're working on—Anjali Gregory's computer, identified as Gregory—is a member of the Office workgroup.

The three computers in Anjali's workgroup have the following names:

■ Gregory—named for real estate agent Anjali Gregory. This is the computer Joan and you are using to explore Millennium's network.

■ Joan—named for the owner of Millennium Real Estate, Joan Alvarez

■ Vianney—named for the Millennium office assistant, Jacques Vianney

You can find additional information on these workstations by viewing the Properties dialog box for each workstation.

To view a workstation's properties:

1. Right-click the icon representing one of the workstations in your workgroup or domain.

2. Click **Properties** on the shortcut menu.

   Figure 9-10 shows the Properties dialog box for the Joan workstation located on Millennium's network.

Figure 9-10 **PROPERTIES OF JOAN'S WORKSTATION**

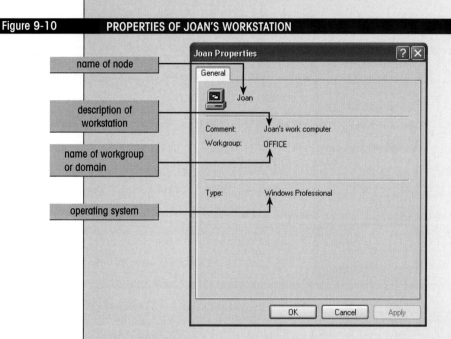

name of node

description of workstation

name of workgroup or domain

operating system

TROUBLE? If the Properties command is not available on your shortcut menu, your network administrator might not allow you access to the Properties dialog box.

3. Click the **OK** button to close the Properties dialog box.

You learn that Joan's computer uses the Windows Professional operating system. The Properties dialog box also shows the name of the computer and the workgroup to which it belongs.

Identifying Your Computer on the Network

Recall that the computers in the Office workgroup are named Gregory, Joan, and Vianney. Windows XP limits the computer name to 15 characters and does not allow blank spaces. Depending on the control you have over your computer and how it interacts with the network, you can change this name and the workgroup or domain to which your computer belongs.

To see the information Windows XP uses to identify your computer on the network, you open the System Properties dialog box and then click the Computer Name tab. You can access this dialog box from the Control Panel or from the Network Connections window. You can easily open the Network Connections window from your current view of the My Network Places window.

To view your computer on the network:

1. In the left pane under Network Tasks, click the **View network connections** link. The Network Connections window opens. See Figure 9-11.

| Figure 9-11 | NETWORK CONNECTIONS WINDOW |

network connection devices; yours may differ

click to diagnose and solve network device problems

The Network Connections window shows the connections your computer uses to connect to the Internet, a network, or another computer. You can use this window to gain access to network resources and to set up your network connections. You use the Network Identification command on the Advanced menu to see how Windows XP identifies your computer on the network.

2. In the Network Connections window, click **Advanced** on the menu bar, and then click **Network Identification**. The System Properties dialog box opens.

3. Click the **Computer Name** tab, if necessary.

Figure 9-12 shows the Computer Name property sheet in the Systems Properties dialog box. Your network administrator usually assigns a name and domain or workgroup for your computer. He or she might let you use commands and options on this sheet to change the computer's name and select a different domain or workgroup to join.

Figure 9-12   **IDENTIFYING THE COMPUTER ON THE NETWORK**

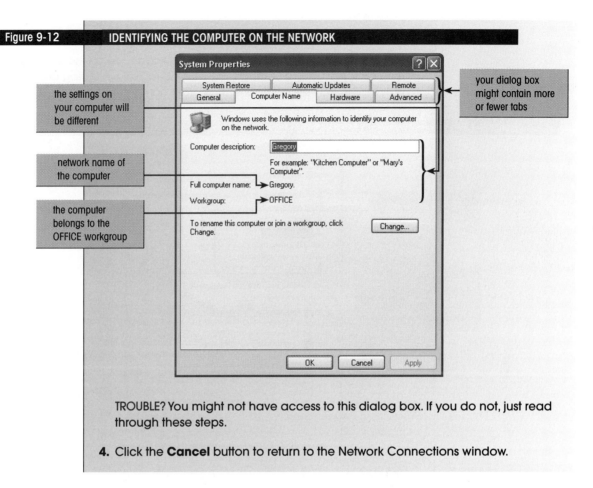

TROUBLE? You might not have access to this dialog box. If you do not, just read through these steps.

4. Click the **Cancel** button to return to the Network Connections window.

Besides using the Network Connections window to view the network identification for your computer, you can also use it to view the network components your computer contains.

Viewing Network Components

Recall that your computer must contain certain network components to be part of a network. These are the adapter, communications protocols, client software, and possibly service components that Windows XP needs to provide network access to your computer. Next you will view the advanced settings of your network connection to see which components that connection uses.

REFERENCE WINDOW   **RW**

Viewing Network Components
- Click Start, point to Connect To, and then click Show all connections to open the Network Connections window, or click the View network connections link from any My Network Places window.
- Click Advanced on the menu bar, and then click Advanced Settings.
- View the installed components information in the Advanced Settings dialog box.

To view network components:

1. In the Network Connections window, click **Advanced** on the menu bar, and then click **Advanced Settings**. The Advanced Settings dialog box opens, displaying the network components on your computer. See Figure 9-13.

Figure 9-13	ADVANCED SETTINGS DIALOG BOX

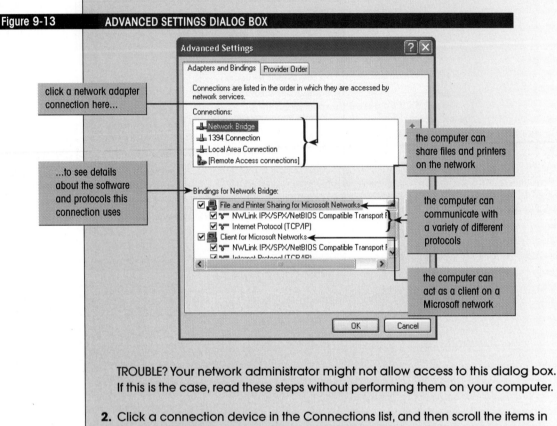

click a network adapter connection here...

...to see details about the software and protocols this connection uses

the computer can share files and printers on the network

the computer can communicate with a variety of different protocols

the computer can act as a client on a Microsoft network

TROUBLE? Your network administrator might not allow access to this dialog box. If this is the case, read these steps without performing them on your computer.

2. Click a connection device in the Connections list, and then scroll the items in the lower list box, if necessary, to see which network components are associated with this device.

3. Click the **OK** button to close the dialog box.

4. Close the Network Connections window.

In this session, you explored basic network concepts, including the difference between a hierarchical and peer-to-peer network. You learned about the four components Windows XP uses to provide network access. Finally, you viewed your network's structure and contents, identified your computer on the network, and examined your network components.

Session 9.1 QUICK CHECK

1. What is a network?

2. Define the following terms:
    a. node
    b. LAN

    c. WAN

    d. server

    e. client

3. Name the two types of network models, and then briefly describe each.

4. Name three tasks a network server might have to perform.

5. What are the four components needed to set up a Windows XP machine to work on a network?

6. What is a communications protocol? Give an example of a communications protocol, and describe what it is used for.

SESSION 9.2

In this session, you will learn how Windows XP manages users' access to the network and the network resources through user accounts and access rights. You will also learn how to log on to your network. You'll learn how to access network resources such as folders and printers. Finally, you'll see how to share a folder on your computer with others on your network.

Network Security and Access Rights

You mention to Joan that when you were at the university, you were not allowed to perform a number of tasks on the network. Joan replies that similar restrictions are in place on the Millennium network. She explains that these restrictions are part of an overall plan for maintaining security on the Millennium network. **Network security** involves controlling the people who can access the network and the actions they are allowed to perform on the network once they are connected. At Millennium, Joan explains, the network administrator wants to make sure that only Millennium employees use the network and that each employee has access only to those parts of the network that apply to his or her job. Figure 9-14 shows a partial roster of Millennium employees and the network rights they have.

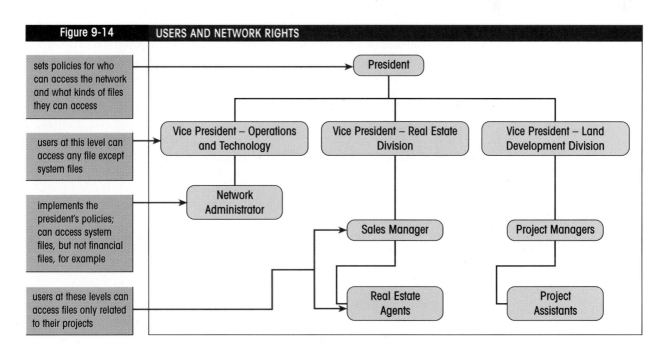

Figure 9-14   USERS AND NETWORK RIGHTS

Different networks require different types of network security. If you have a small network set up in your home, you probably don't need a sophisticated security system controlling who can access the network. You are there to monitor your computers and can control who gets into your home. However, the network requirements for a small business are probably different. A small business might want to follow security guidelines that control who can access the network; once employees receive authorization, however, they might have free access to all network resources.

A large network with hundreds of people working on different projects involving confidential information is another matter. For example, a university network server that stores student grades and records needs tight security over who can access the system and what information they can view once they gain access. Likewise, a network at a hospital must have rigorous restrictions in place to limit access to patient data and to ensure the integrity of the doctor-patient relationship.

In addition to restricting access to data, network administrators must also restrict access to hardware. For example, suppose the graphic arts department on campus purchased an expensive high-quality color laser printer and wants to prevent students from other departments from using it. The network administrator might therefore limit access to that printer to students and faculty in the graphic arts department.

Network administrators control who can access the network—and what users are allowed to do once they are connected—through network accounts and access rights. A **network account** is the collection of information about you and the work that you do on the network. Before you can use the network, the network administrator creates an account for you that identifies you as an authorized user of the network. In a network that has several servers, you might have several network accounts. For example, an engineering student who is taking a class in the art department might have two network accounts, one in the engineering department and another in the art department.

Network administrators limit access to network data, software, and hardware through the use of user IDs and passwords. Your **user ID**, or **username**, identifies you to other users on the network. A user ID might be your first name, a number such as 445228, or a word. On some systems, user IDs are limited to eight characters and cannot include spaces or special symbols.

Along with your user ID, you usually must enter your password to log on to a network. Your **password** is a string of symbols, letters, and/or numbers, known only to you and the network administrator, and shows that you are the legitimate user of the account. A password is a security device to prevent other people who might know your user ID from using your account. Once you have entered the user ID and password, the server checks to see if these are valid by matching them to your user account information before allowing you network access.

Once you're connected to the network, your ability to use network resources is controlled by a set of guidelines or **access rights** set up by the network administrator. Access rights can be limited to **read-only access**, which allows you to view the contents of a file but not to edit or delete it. For example, you would have read-only access if you were a physician who needed to review patient records stored on a hospital network database. The hospital network administrator might grant you read-only access so that you could view the files without accidentally changing or deleting a record. In other situations, you might need **read and write access**, which allows you to view and edit files but not delete them, or **full access**, which lets you view, edit, and delete a file. Read and write access is often granted on networks where your data files are stored in folders located on a network server, rather than a folder on your workstation's hard disk.

Logging on to Your Account

The process of accessing your account is called **logging on** or **logging in**. If your computer is on a network and network security is in place, a **logon dialog box** requesting your user ID and password appears when you start Windows XP. You might have to press the Ctrl,

Alt, and Del keys simultaneously to display the logon dialog box. Correctly entering your user ID and password allows you to access the Windows XP operating system and the network on which your computer resides.

You can also use the Windows XP logon dialog box in situations where a single workstation is shared by several people. Windows XP allows each user to customize the desktop settings to his or her needs and stores these settings in a file called a **user profile**. Logging on to Windows XP accesses your user profile and loads the settings for your customized desktop. You will learn more about user profiles in Tutorial 10.

The logon dialog box is the most secure way to log on. If you are working on a home network or another type of network that doesn't need high security, your computer might not be set up to display the logon dialog box. The Windows XP Welcome screen appears instead, listing the users with accounts established on your computer. In that case, you log on by clicking your account name and entering a password, if necessary.

The following steps show how to use the logon dialog box to log on to a Windows XP client computer on a network. If you have already logged on, you don't need to repeat these steps—you can read the steps to make sure you understand the process.

To log on to Windows XP:

1. If your computer is not running, turn it on. If necessary, press the **Ctrl+Alt+Del** keys. The logon dialog box appears.

   TROUBLE? If you do not see the logon dialog box after you press the Ctrl+Alt+Del keys and another dialog box, such as the Windows Task Manager, opens instead, close the dialog box, click the Start button, and then click Log Off to open the logon dialog box. If you still do not see the logon dialog box, ask your instructor or technical support person how to log on to your computer.

2. In the User Name text box, type your user name and then press the **Tab** key.

3. In the Password text box, type your password. Your password appears as a series of bullets, so your actual password remains secure.

4. Click the **OK** button. The Windows XP desktop appears.

Your network administrator usually provides a password for you to use when you log on, although you may be able to create your own or change your password after you've used it for a few months. Next, you'll learn some guidelines for creating secure passwords.

Password Protection

You have already seen how network administrators enforce network security through the use of user IDs and passwords. If you are allowed to create your own password for your account, you should keep the following principles in mind:

- Do not use fewer than seven characters in your password.
- Do not use your name, birth date, nickname, or any word or number that an unauthorized user might be able to guess.
- Try to include numbers or special symbols (!@#%&*) in your password, because they make it harder for other users to guess your password.
- Never write your password where others can see it or share your password with other users.

You also should change your password every few months. On some networks, this is a requirement and the network administrator will set up an automatic prompt that appears when it is time for you to change your password. When changing your password, you will be prompted to enter your old password and then to enter your new password twice. You enter the new password twice to reduce the possibility of a typing error.

Changing Your Password

If your computer is part of a network, changing your password means you change the way you access the network and its resources. You should therefore make sure your network administrator approves of your password change before you make it. If you are working on a network without a network administrator (or if you are working on a standalone computer that is not part of a network), you can add and change your password so that only you can access your data and settings.

Joan tells you that password protection is one of Millennium's network security measures and that you will be required to change your password every two months. Joan suggests that you review the dialog box you will use to do this.

REFERENCE WINDOW **RW**

Changing Your Windows XP Password
- Click the Start button and then click Control Panel.
- In Category View, click User Accounts. In Classic View, double-click User Accounts.
- Click the account you want to change.
- Click Change My Password.
- Type your old password in the Type your current password text box.
- Type your new password in the Type a new password text box and then again in the Type the new password to confirm text box.
- If necessary, type a word or phrase to use as a password hint.
- Click the Change Password button to save the new password.

If you are in a university computer lab, you may not be able to change your password. Your lab may also use a different network operating system, which means the process of setting up and changing your password is probably different. You should ask your instructor or technical support person about your network policies for changing passwords. In the next set of steps, you will be directed to click the Cancel button to prevent you from making any changes to your current password.

To change your Windows XP password:

1. Click the **Start** button (start), and then click **Control Panel**. The Control Panel window opens. If the Control Panel window opens in Classic View, click **Switch to Category View** in the left pane.

2. Click **User Accounts**. The User Accounts window opens, listing tasks you can perform and user accounts you can change.

3. Click your user name. The User Accounts window lists the tasks you can perform to change your account.

4. Click **Change my password**. The Change your password window opens. See Figure 9-15.

| Figure 9-15 | CHANGE PASSWORD WINDOW |

type your current password here

click a link to learn more about passwords

type your new password once to enter it and again to confirm it

5. In the Type your current password text box, type your current password.

6. In the Type a new password text box, type the new password. Type the password again in the Type the new password again to confirm text box.

Because this is just an example, you should close this dialog box without saving your changes.

7. Click the **Cancel** button.

8. Close the User Accounts window, and then close the Control Panel window.

Now that you know how to change your password when necessary, Joan suggests you try ending your session on the workstation by logging off from your account.

Logging off from Your Account

When you're done using a workstation, you should log off. Logging off is the process of closing your account on the server and preventing others from using your account. It does not necessarily involve turning off the computer. Some servers allow only a limited number of users to be logged on at any given time, and network administrators want to avoid tying up servers with nonactive users. Depending on your network, your network administrator might want you to leave the computer on for others who need to use it, so make sure you understand the procedures for your computer lab before you follow any of the instructions here.

When you are ready to stop working with Windows XP on your workstation, you will have some or all of the following options:

- **Log off your account**: On the Start menu, select the Log Off command to leave the Windows XP operating system running and the computer on, but close any active programs or network accounts. The logon dialog box appears. When the computers on the network are shared among several users, the network administrator often requests that you use this option for shutting down your account.

- **Turn off**: On the Start menu, select the Turn Off Computer command to close the Windows XP operating system and shut down the computer. The next user will have to restart the workstation and reload the Windows XP operating system. You should check with your instructor to see whether this option is allowed on your network. Many network administrators request users not to shut down individual workstations.

- **Restart**: In the Turn Off Computer dialog box, select the Restart command to shut down and then reload the Windows XP operating system. The next user will have to enter his or her user ID and password in the logon dialog box before using the computer.

- **Standby**: On the Start menu, select the Standby command to put your workstation in a low-power state so that you can quickly resume your Windows XP session later. When you want to use the computer again, it comes out of standby quickly, and your desktop is restored exactly as you left it. The Standby command is also useful for laptops running on batteries that need to go into Standby mode to conserve power.

- **Hibernate**: If your hardware supports Hibernate mode, the Turn off computer dialog box also includes the Hibernate option, which conserves energy much like the Standby option. When you choose Hibernate, Windows XP saves everything in memory on disk, turns off your monitor and hard disk, and then turns off your computer. When you restart your computer, your desktop appears exactly as you left it. Note that it takes longer to bring your computer out of hibernation than out of standby.

You should talk to your instructor or network administrator to determine which of these options you should select when you're finished working with Windows XP. At Millennium, the network administrator prefers the first option: that you log off from your account but keep the Windows XP operating system loaded. Joan shows you how to log off from Windows XP using this option.

To log off from your account:

1. Click the **Start** button ⊞ *start* , and then click **Log Off**.

TROUBLE? If the Log Off option does not appear, click ⊞ *start* and then click Shut Down.

Depending on how your user accounts are set up, either the Log Off Windows dialog box opens, asking whether you're sure you want to log off, or the Shut Down Windows dialog box appears. See Figure 9-16.

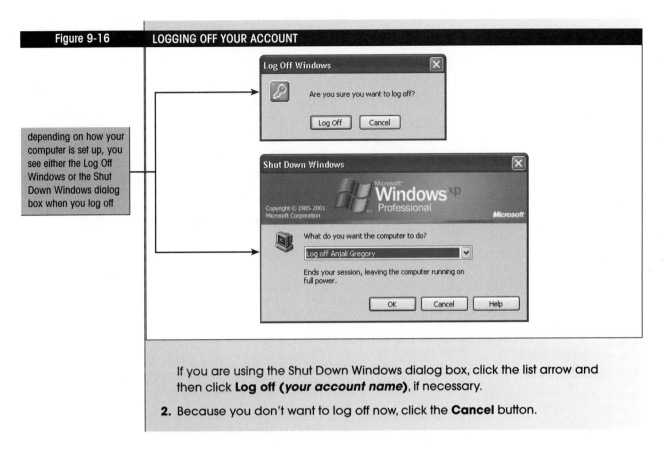

Figure 9-16   **LOGGING OFF YOUR ACCOUNT**

depending on how your computer is set up, you see either the Log Off Windows or the Shut Down Windows dialog box when you log off

If you are using the Shut Down Windows dialog box, click the list arrow and then click **Log off (*your account name*)**, if necessary.

2. Because you don't want to log off now, click the **Cancel** button.

Joan emphasizes that you should remember to log off from your account when you're done working. If you leave the workstation running, and still connected to your network account, other users could access your work, and this would be a breach in network security.

Using **Network Resources**

A network resource is any part of a computer system or network, such as a disk drive, printer, or memory, that you can use when running a program or performing another computer process, such as managing files and folders. A **shared resource** is any resource that is made available to network users, such as folders, files, and printers. Shared resources are stored on any computer that is attached to the network. You use the My Network Places window to view and access network resources, including shared resources. Windows XP adds a bar under the icon for a resource that you can share. For example, the icon for a shared printer is 🖨.

Now that you've seen how to work with your user account, Joan wants to show you some of the available resources on the Millennium servers. Currently, you're logged on to the Gregory computer; Joan wants to show you how to access some of the resources on her computer from the Gregory computer.

Recall that the steps and figures in this tutorial show the settings and objects for the Millennium network, but yours will differ because you are working on a different network. When possible, substitute the corresponding settings and objects on your network as you perform these steps. For example, in the following steps, instead of double-clicking the icon for Joan's computer, double-click the icon for any computer on your network that is connected to a shared printer or other shared resource.

To access a resource on another workstation:

1. Open the My Network Places window.

2. In the left pane under Network Tasks, click **View workgroup computers** to view the computers in your workgroup in the right pane.

3. Double-click the icon for Joan's computer. You know that this computer contains at least one shared resource. A list of resources on the computer appears in the window. Switch to Tiles view, if necessary, so you can easily identify the shared resources icons. Figure 9-17 shows the shared resources on Joan's computer at Millennium.

| Figure 9-17 | SHARED RESOURCES ON JOAN'S COMPUTER |

shared folders on Joan's computer

a shared printer

TROUBLE? If you can't tell from the icon whether the computer has a shared resource or not, ask your instructor or technical support person to locate a workstation that you can access and that has a shared resource.

TROUBLE? If you are prompted for a username or password before you can access the resources of the workstation, see your instructor or technical support person about obtaining access privileges.

Figure 9-17 shows two types of icons. Folders on the network computer are represented by the ![folder icon] icon. A printer is represented by a ![printer icon] icon. Folders placed on servers and made available to the network are called **network folders**. Folders on your own computer are called **local folders**. You can work with the files in a network folder using the same techniques you apply to files in your local folders. For example, you could click one of the files, and Windows XP would open the file in the appropriate software program.

Joan has made three folders on her computer available to other network users. Two of these (labeled C and D) access most of the contents of her C drive and her D drive, respectively. Note that although you can share a folder or a drive, Windows XP uses the shared folder icon for both. Also, Windows XP does not let you access certain locations on a drive, such as the Windows system folder. Joan's third shared folder (labeled CD on Joan) accesses the contents of her CD-ROM drive. Joan has also made her printer available to the network (labeled HP2000C).

To view the contents of a network folder:

1. Double-click an icon representing a network folder in the window. Windows XP opens the contents of the folder. See Figure 9-18.

Figure 9-18   **CONTENTS OF JOAN'S C DRIVE**

2. Close the network folder window.

When you are using recently released software programs, you can share and access files located on a network through My Network Places, as Joan has. However, to make a network file available to an older software program, you must first "map" the drive or folder that contains the file you want.

Drive Mapping

Drive mapping provides another way to connect to a network resource and serves the same purpose as sharing a folder or drive in My Network Places. When you work with shared folders, you must first navigate a sometimes complex folder structure in My Computer or My Network Places to find the files you want. If you map a network drive to your computer instead, the drive appears at the top level of the My Computer window, just as your local drives do.

In addition, some software, such as older database programs, might run in Windows XP but not recognize shared network folders. Instead of transferring the files you need from the network to your computer, you can map the network drive to your computer so that you can use the database program or other software to open and save the files.

When you map a drive, you simply assign a drive letter to a network drive or folder, such as Z or Y. Windows XP recognizes the drive letter and gives you direct access to the files it contains. You map a drive to connect your computer to a folder or drive on another computer. (Note that you can map a drive only after the user of the computer or the network administrator has given you access to the drive).

REFERENCE WINDOW   RW

<u>Mapping a Network Folder</u>
- Locate the network folder in the My Network Places window.
- Right-click the folder and then click Map Network Drive on the shortcut menu.
- In the Map Network Drive dialog box, specify a drive letter for the network folder, and indicate whether you want to reconnect to this folder the next time you log on.
- Click the OK button.

Mapping a Network Folder

When you map a drive, a letter is assigned to it, which you can change if necessary. Windows XP assigns network drives letters from Z to A, to distinguish them from local drives (the hard drives and removable storage devices on your workstation), which are assigned letters from A to Z. You can change the letter of the mapped drive, if you like, to keep all your drive letters in sequence.

Joan suggests that you map her C drive as the drive letter "Z" on your workstation.

To map a network folder:

1. Using My Network Places, view the resources of a workstation on your network.

2. Right-click a network folder icon 🗀 in the right pane, and then click **Map Network Drive** on the shortcut menu.

3. The Map Network Drive dialog box opens, as shown in Figure 9-19.

Figure 9-19   THE MAP NETWORK DRIVE DIALOG BOX

Windows XP suggests a drive letter for the network folder. You can choose a different drive letter from the list box. When you map a drive, the Map Network Drive dialog box shows the location of the drive you are going to map in the Folder list box. This location is called the file's **pathname**. Windows XP pathnames follow the **Universal Naming Convention**, or **UNC**, an accepted set of rules for expressing pathnames, including those for mapped drives and network folders. The general form is \\server\sharename, where sharename is the name or drive letter you used when sharing the folder. Thus the pathname to Joan's network folder is \\Joan\C, indicating a shared resource named C located on the server named Joan. By default, you can access the selected network drive only during this Windows XP session. If you want to access the network drive every time you log on, you can select the Reconnect at logon check box. Finally, Windows XP assumes that you want to connect to this network folder using your username and password. You can specify a different account, as long as the account exists and has access rights to the network folder.

4. Click the **Finish** button to map the network folder to the drive letter.

Windows XP opens the network folder, now mapped with the drive letter.

For example, if you map Joan's C drive to the drive letter Z, it appears almost as if you've added a new hard drive (labeled Z) to your computer. You can treat it the same way. You are not limited to mapping network folders; you can also map folders on the Internet or an intranet, such as Web folders and FTP sites.

Removing Drive Mapping

When you no longer plan to use a mapped drive, you should remove the drive mapping to maintain security—an unauthorized user might gain access to your files through the mapped drive. When you remove drive mapping, you disconnect the drive from your computer. You can also assign a computer or shared folder to a different drive letter by disconnecting from the drive and then reassigning it a new drive letter. When you are ready to remove drive mapping, you can do so from the My Computer window.

REFERENCE WINDOW   **RW**

Removing Drive Mapping
- Open the My Computer window.
- Right-click the mapped drive and click Disconnect on the shortcut menu.

To remove drive mapping:

1. Under Other Places, click **My Computer** to open the My Computer window.

2. Right-click the icon for your mapped drive, and click **Disconnect** on the shortcut menu.

3. Close the My Computer window and the network folder window.

The drive letter associated with the network folder is removed from your system.

Creating a Network Place

Another way of quickly accessing a folder on the network is to create a network place. A **network place** is a shortcut to a folder stored on the network. The icon for the shortcut will appear in the My Network Places window, although the file is saved on another computer, not on your computer's hard disk. You can create network places by using the Add Network Place Wizard, which you access from the My Network Places window.

REFERENCE WINDOW   **RW**

Creating a Network Place
- Open the My Network Places window.
- Under Network Tasks, click Add a network place.
- On the Welcome to the Add Network Place Wizard window, click the Next button.
- On the Where do you want to create this network place? window, select a location and then click the Next button.
- Type the pathname of your network folder, or locate it using the Browse button. Click the Next button.
- Type a name for the network place, and then click the Finish button.

Joan suggests that you create a network place for drive C on her computer.

To create a network place:

1. Open the My Network Places window.

2. In the left pane under Network Tasks, click **Add a network place**.

   Windows XP starts the Add Network Place Wizard.

3. On the Welcome to the Add Network Place Wizard window, click the **Next** button.

   The Where do you want to create this network place? window opens, listing locations where you can add a network place. You do this using the Choose another network location option.

4. Click **Choose another network location** if necessary, and then click the **Next** button.

   The What is the address of this network place? window opens. At this point, you could click the Browse button and locate the network folder by moving through your network's hierarchy. However, if you know the pathname of your network folder, you can also type it in directly.

5. In the Internet or network address text box, type the pathname of the network resource for which you want to create a network place. For example, type **\\Joan\C**. See Figure 9-20.

Figure 9-20	ADDING A NETWORK PLACE

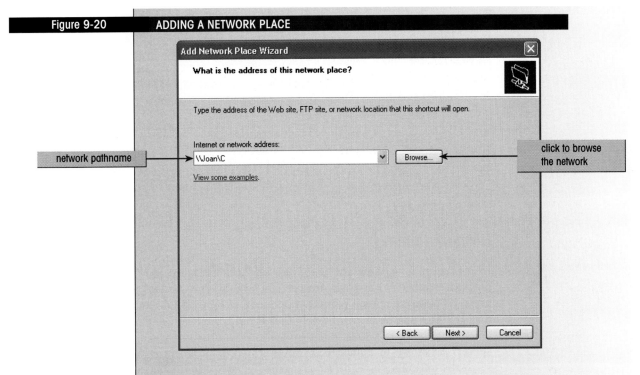

network pathname

click to browse
the network

6. Click the **Next** button.

7. Type a name for the network place, such as **Drive C on Joan**, and then click the **Next** button. The Completing the Add Network Place Wizard opens.

Figure 9-21 shows the My Network Places window with the newly created network place—a shortcut pointing to drive C on Joan's computer.

Figure 9-21	A NEW NETWORK PLACE

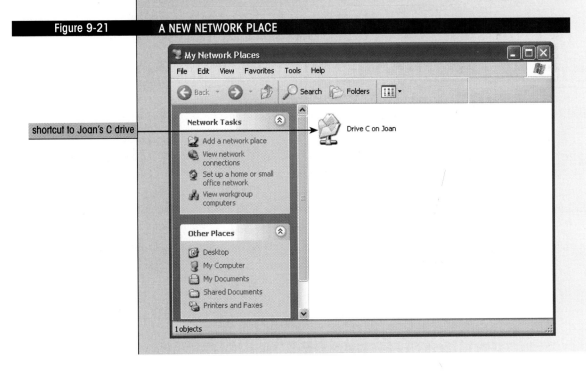

shortcut to Joan's C drive

> Now that you've seen how to create the shortcut to her folder, Joan asks you to delete it.
>
> **8.** Click the **Finish** button.
>
> **9.** Click the icon for the network place you created, and then press the **Delete** key. Click the **Yes** button in the message box to confirm that you want to delete the shortcut.
>
> **10.** Close all open windows.

So far you've learned from Joan how to access files on her computer. You can also access other network resources from her computer, including the network printer.

Network Printing

Joan would like to show you one other important resource on Millennium's network: the network printer. A **network printer** is a printer that handles printing jobs for network users. By contrast, a **local printer** is one that is connected directly to your computer. Note that any one computer can have both a local printer and a network printer (or printers) available. The operation of a network printer is often managed by a server called a **print server**. As shown in Figure 9-22, when a user wants to print a document, Windows XP sends the information needed to print the document to the network print queue located on the print server. A network print queue keeps track of the order in which print jobs are received and sends them, in order, to the network printer.

| Figure 9-22 | PRINT SERVER QUEUES PRINT JOBS |

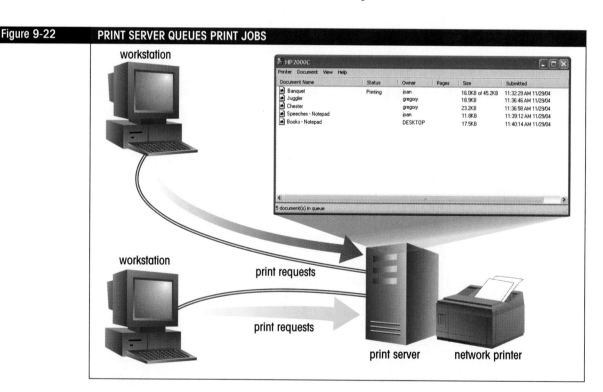

One of the printers available on the Millennium network is a color printer. It is usually reserved for final reports and special projects. Joan tells you that you can access this printer using the same techniques you use to access a local printer. Windows XP lists all available printers, both local and network , in the same Print dialog box. To send a print job to a network printer, you select the printer name from the list of printers, as shown in Figure 9-23.

| Figure 9-23 | SELECTING A NETWORK PRINTER |

Note that the name of the printer gives you an indication of where it is located. For example, the color printer in Figure 9-23 is named "HP2000C," and it's located on the JOAN workstation. If you were to write the network pathname to this particular resource, it would be \\JOAN\HP2000C.

Sharing a Resource with the Network

Up to now, you've worked with the resources available on other computers on the network. If the network administrator has given you the capability, you can make the resources of your own computer available to others on the network as well. This is a process called **sharing**, and you can share resources such as individual folders, entire drives, or printers. The process by which you share a resource is the same for any resource.

REFERENCE WINDOW **RW**

__Sharing a Folder with the Network__
- Right-click the folder and then click Sharing and Security on the shortcut menu.
- On the Sharing sheet of the Properties dialog box, make sure the Share this folder on the network box is checked.
- Enter a name for the shared folder in the Share name text box.

You have a second hard drive labeled "G:" on your computer. Joan suggests that you try to share your G drive with the Millennium network.

To share a drive:

1. Open the My Computer window.

2. Right-click the icon for the drive you wish to share, and then click **Sharing and Security** on the shortcut menu. Because you are sharing a drive, Windows warns you that sharing the root directory of a drive is a security risk.

3. Click **If you understand the risk but still want to share the root of the drive, click here**. The Properties dialog box for the selected drive opens to the Sharing sheet. See Figure 9-24.

Figure 9-24   **THE SHARING PROPERTY SHEET**

TROUBLE? If the Sharing and Security command does not appear on the menu or is dimmed, you don't have permission to share folders on your computer, or the Share feature has not been enabled. Talk to your instructor or technical support person to see if you can share files. If you cannot, continue reading through the following steps without duplicating them on your computer.

When you first attempt to share a drive or folder, you see the dialog box in Figure 9-24. The dialog box seems to indicate that the drive is already shared, and in a sense it is, but only with the network administrator. If you want to share your resource with a wider audience, you have to create a new share. In sharing your resource, you have to give it a share name that network users will see when they browse the network, provide a share comment that describes the resource, and indicate the number of users who can access it at one time.

To create a new share:

1. If necessary, click the **Share this folder on the network** check box to select this option.

2. Click the **Share name** text box if necessary, enter a name for the shared resource (such as **SharedDrive**), and then press the **Tab** key.

TROUBLE? If you are sharing a folder on your network, talk to your instructor or technical support person about the names and comments you should enter here.

You can let other network users change the files on the shared drive or folder.

3. If necessary, click the **Allow network users to change my files** check box to insert a check mark. See Figure 9-25.

Figure 9-25	CREATING A NEW SHARE

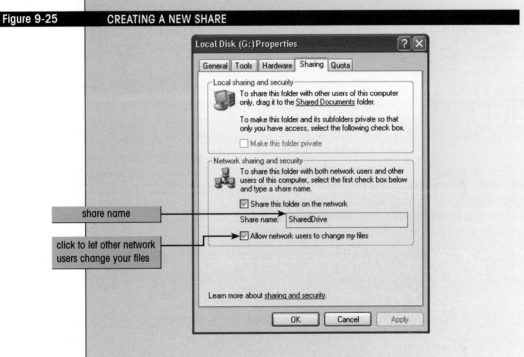

share name

click to let other network users change your files

4. Click the **OK** button to share your folder with the network.

If your network uses workgroups, once you give your drive a name and specify that users can connect to it, you can share the drive or folder on the network. If your network uses domains, you must specify which users can connect to the shared resource. You can limit the resource to specific users or to a specific class of users called a **user group**. You can also control what users can do when they access your drive, such as whether they can edit your files or simply view them.

Joan tells you that the system administrator will also have access to your workstation and can control the access to your computer's resource. You can always tell when a device such as a drive or printer is shared, since the icon will have a handle added to it. For example, the icon for a shared folder is 🖐 rather than 📁.

In this session, you have learned how to log on and off the network, how to access resources stored on the network, and how to share resources and data stored on your computer with other users on the network. In the next session, you will learn how to work on a networked computer offline.

Session 9.2 QUICK | CHECK

1. List four guidelines you should follow when choosing a password.

2. What is the difference between logging off and shutting down your computer?

3. What is drive mapping and under what circumstances must you use it?

4. What is the pathname for a printer named Work that is located on the GREGORY workstation?

5. To make a resource on your computer available to other network users, you can _____ the resource.

6. True or False: You cannot make both a local printer and a network printer available to your computer.

SESSION 9.3

In this session, you learn the value of working with offline folders on a network. You create an offline folder, use it to access offline files, and synchronize the files to make sure they are all up to date. Finally, you will remove the offline folder and its contents from your computer. *Note*: You can only work with offline folders if you are using Windows XP Professional. If you have Windows XP Home Edition installed on your computer, you will not be able to complete the steps in this session. Read through the session to learn the concepts.

Working Offline

If you want to access network files when you are not connected to the network, you can use a Windows XP Professional feature called **offline viewing** to copy and save shared network files from the network in a special folder on your computer's hard drive called the **Offline Files folder**. Then you can work with the shared network files on your portable or stand-alone computer as you normally do. When you reconnect to the network, you can have Windows XP update the network files with any changes that you made while working offline. You can also have Windows XP update the files when you log off the network. This updating process is called **synchronizing**.

You can synchronize files whenever you copy and save network files on your computer. When you first create an Offline Files folder, Windows XP simply transfers files from the network to that folder on your hard disk. After that, when you connect to the network folder that contains the files you've also stored offline, Windows makes sure that both the Offline Files folder and the network folder contain the most recent versions of the files.

If you share folders on your computer with others on the network, they can also work offline with those folders. You can protect files in your shared folders by specifying whether other users can change your documents or only view them. You can also control which shared files users can access offline.

Joan explains that, in most cases, you'll use the offline files feature to work with portable computers. For example, if your laptop has a network connection, once you leave the office with your laptop, the connection is lost and you must work with offline versions of the network files. In other cases, if the workstation storing the network file or folder has been turned off, you can't access the network file or folder even when you're connected to the network. Joan suggests that to practice with the offline feature, you should make an offline version of some of her files. Then she'll turn off her computer, allowing you to work with the offline version.

Creating an Offline Folder

To start working with offline files, you first set up your computer to use offline files. Then you locate and select the network file or folder with which you want to work offline, and select the Make Available Offline command from the shortcut menu. When you do, Windows XP also creates an Offline Files folder on your hard disk. The first time you try to make an item available offline, the Offline Files Wizard starts to guide you through the process. You follow the steps of the wizard to choose options for how you want to work with the offline files.

REFERENCE WINDOW **RW**

Setting Up Offline Folders

- Open the My Computer window.
- Click Tools on the menu bar, and then click Folder Options.
- Click the Offline Files tab in the Folder Options dialog box.
- Click the Enable Offline Files check box to select it, and then click OK to close the Folder Options dialog box.
- Locate the network folder in the My Computer window.
- Right-click the folder and then click Make Available Offline on the shortcut menu.
- If this is the first time you are making the folder available offline, follow the steps in the Offline Files Wizard to create an offline folder and set options for working with offline files.

Before you can make a network folder available offline, you have to make sure that Windows XP Professional is set up to create and use offline folders.

To set up your computer to use offline files:

1. Open the My Computer window.

2. Click **Tools** on the menu bar, and then click **Folder Options**. The Folder Options dialog box opens.

3. Click the **Offline Files** tab to display the Offline Files property sheet.

4. Write down which check boxes have been selected in the dialog sheet. You'll want to restore these settings later.

   TROUBLE? If a message regarding Fast User Switching appears on the Offline Files property sheet, your computer is set up to let users switch to another user when they log off. You cannot use offline files if your computer is set to allow Fast User Switching. Ask your instructor or technical support person for permission to change this setting, close the Folder Options dialog box, open the Control Panel, open the User Accounts window, and then click Change the way users log on or off. Click the Use Fast User Switching check box to remove the check mark, close the Control Panel windows, and then repeat Steps 1 through 4.

5. If necessary, click the **Enable Offline Files** check box to select it. See Figure 9-26.

Figure 9-26   SETTING UP THE OFFLINE FILES FEATURE

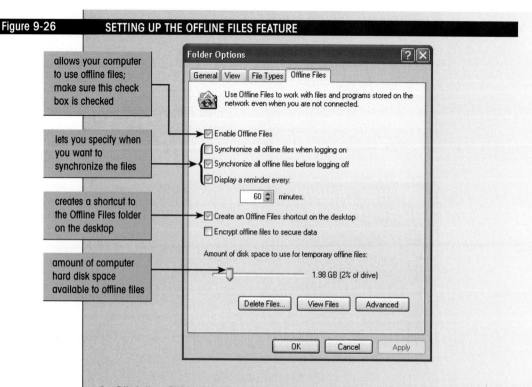

allows your computer to use offline files; make sure this check box is checked

lets you specify when you want to synchronize the files

creates a shortcut to the Offline Files folder on the desktop

amount of computer hard disk space available to offline files

6. Click the **OK** button to close the Folder Options dialog box, and then close the My Computer window.

Now that your computer is set up to use offline files, Joan suggests that you create an offline version of the files in her shared Millennium Documents folder. First you have to locate this folder on the Millennium network, and then you can make it available offline.

To make a network folder available offline:

1. Open the My Computer window, and then locate the network folder or individual files that you want to make available offline.

TROUBLE? Talk to your instructor or technical support person before setting up an offline folder. You want to make sure you pick a folder that does not have a lot of files in it. Every file in the folder (and all its subfolders) will be copied to your computer in the form of offline files.

2. Right-click the folder or file, and then click **Make Available Offline** on the shortcut menu. The Offline Files Wizard starts.

TROUBLE? If the Make Available Offline command does not appear on the shortcut menu, make sure you are using Windows XP Professional and that your network administrator will allow you to create an offline folder. Then repeat Steps 1 through 6 in "To set up your computer to use offline files."

3. In the Welcome to the Offline Files Wizard window, click the **Next** button.

First, you choose when you want Windows XP to synchronize the offline files with the network files. Synchronizing when you log on and when you log off ensures that you have the most current version of every shared network file that you work with offline.

4. Click the **Automatically synchronize the Offline Files when I log on and log off my computer** check box to select it, and then click the **Next** button.

   On the next page of the wizard, you can choose to create a shortcut to the Offline Files folder on your desktop. Doing so will give you quick access to your offline files.

5. Click the **Create a shortcut to the Offline Files folder on my desktop** check box to select it, and then click the **Finish** button. The Confirm Offline Subfolders dialog box opens so you can verify that you want to make the subfolders in the Millennium Documents folder available offline.

6. Make sure the Yes make this folder and all its subfolders available offline option button is selected, then click the **OK** button.

   Windows XP transfers the files to your computer and adds a Shortcut to Offline Files folder on your desktop.

7. Close the My Computer window that displays the contents of the workstation.

You've created and stored an offline copy of the files from Joan's Millennium Documents folder on your hard disk.

Working with an Offline File

Now you are ready to work with an offline file. Joan will now turn off her computer, disconnecting from the network, so that you can try to access the offline versions of her files. The offline versions will appear in the same location in the network hierarchy, exactly as if her workstation was still attached to the network. However, each offline folder and file will have a double-arrow symbol, indicating that it is an offline folder (or file) and not the original.

To access the offline files:

1. On your desktop, double-click the **Shortcut to Offline Files** icon 📁.

   The Offline Files Folder window opens. Figure 9-27 shows the folder containing offline files on Joan's computer.

Figure 9-27	THE OFFLINE MILLENNIUM DOCUMENTS FOLDER

offline folder has a double arrow symbol

TROUBLE? If you receive a message saying that the computer wasn't available, try it again a few minutes later. If you still cannot connect to the offline folder, ask your instructor for assistance.

2. Double-click an **offline folder** to see the offline files.

Figure 9-28 shows that the Millennium Documents folder contains two files (named Financial and Minutes). Note that both file icons have double-arrow symbols, indicating that they are offline objects.

Figure 9-28	OFFLINE FILES IN THE MILLENNIUM DOCUMENTS FOLDER

offline files also have the double-arrow symbol

3. Close the Offline Files Folder window.

If you made any changes to the files, when your folder is available again on the network, Windows XP will synchronize the two versions of this file, incorporating your changes into Joan's original files on her workstation. Now Joan will reconnect to the network so you can synchronize the offline files.

Synchronizing Offline Files

You synchronize your offline files to reconcile any differences between the files stored on your computer with those stored on the network. For example, if you worked on the Financials file offline and changed its contents, you can update the network version of the Financials file the next time you connect to the network. If you change the Financials file while you are working on the network and want to work with it later offline, you synchronize again to save the updated version of the Financials file in your Offline Files folder on your hard disk.

Depending on the settings you selected when you set up the offline files, Windows XP can automatically synchronize your offline files when you log on to your account, when you log off, or both. In any of these cases, Windows examines your offline files and the corresponding network versions to determine the differences. Then it updates both sets of files, if necessary. When you are connected to the network, you can also manually synchronize an offline file by right-clicking the file you want and then clicking Synchronize on the shortcut menu. If you and someone else on the network changed the same file, Windows XP displays the Resolve File Conflicts dialog box that you use to save your version of the file on the network, keep the original version, or save both.

Windows XP also notices when your network connection is active again (in this case, when Joan turns on her computer again) and will prompt you to synchronize.

Joan goes back to her office, turns on her workstation, and reconnects to the Millennium network. After a few minutes, Windows XP on your computer notices that her workstation is back online. The icon in the taskbar notification area changes to a 🖳 to indicate that there is a change in the offline status. When you move the mouse pointer over the icon, a ScreenTip appears reading "Offline Files—Computer(s) available for reconnection." You can now synchronize the local file with the network file.

To synchronize the offline files:

1. If necessary, turn the workstation on again, and wait a few minutes for Windows XP to note that the workstation is back online.

   TROUBLE? Talk to your instructor or technical support person to get directions on how to follow these steps with your network.

2. Double-click the **Offline Files** icon 🖳. The Items to Synchronize dialog box opens. See Figure 9-29.

Figure 9-29   ITEMS TO SYNCHRONIZE DIALOG BOX

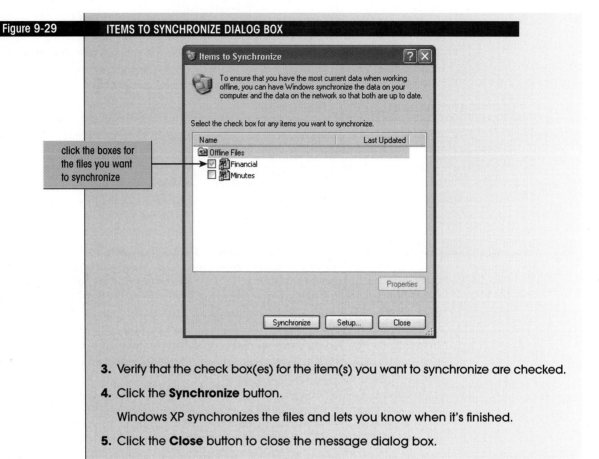

click the boxes for the files you want to synchronize

3. Verify that the check box(es) for the item(s) you want to synchronize are checked.

4. Click the **Synchronize** button.

   Windows XP synchronizes the files and lets you know when it's finished.

5. Click the **Close** button to close the message dialog box.

Note that the Offline Files icon 🖥 disappears from the taskbar notification area because you're no longer working offline.

You ask Joan how Windows XP synchronizes files. What sort of rules does it follow? What if she had made changes to the same offline files you had edited? How would Windows XP handle the differences? Joan outlines some principles that Windows XP follows when synchronizing. Recall that before Windows XP synchronizes files, it examines them to find any differences. If both the offline copy and the online copy of the file have changed, Windows pauses to ask you what you want to do.

■ If the original network version of the offline file hasn't changed, your changes are copied to the network version.

■ If someone else has made changes to the network file, Windows XP gives you the choice of saving your offline version on the network, keeping the network version and leaving your offline version on your computer, or saving both on the network. If you save both, your version is given a different filename, and both versions will appear in both locations.

■ If someone deletes the network version while you are working offline, Windows XP offers the option of saving your version on the network or deleting it.

■ If a new file is added to a network folder while you are working offline, the new file will be added to the offline folder.

Note that online etiquette dictates that unless you have created a file and have sole responsibility for it, you should not overwrite someone else's version of a network file. In this case, save your version of the file on your computer so you can still access it, or check with the other user to discuss which file should be saved on the network.

You can change the synchronization settings, if necessary. For example, instead of synchronizing automatically, you can choose to have Windows XP ask you whether you want to synchronize. Joan suggests you select this setting so you can approve any synchronizations.

To change the synchronization settings:

1. Open My Computer and then click the **Offline Folder** icon.

2. Click **Tools** on the menu bar, and then click **Synchronize**. The Items to Synchronize dialog box opens, the same dialog box you used to synchronize files in the last set of steps. This time, however, you will change the synchronization settings instead of synchronizing files.

3. Click the **Setup** button. The Synchronization Settings dialog box opens, as shown in Figure 9-30.

Figure 9-30	SYNCHRONIZATION SETTINGS DIALOG BOX

check both boxes to have Windows synchronize when you log on and log off

click to have Windows ask whether you want to synchronize the selected items

4. Click the **Ask me before synchronizing the items** check box, if necessary.

5. Click the **OK** button.

6. Click the **Close** button to close the Items to Synchronize dialog box.

Now Joan suggests that you remove the offline Millennium documents because you're finished practicing with the Offline Files feature.

Removing an Offline Object

When you no longer want to work with a network file offline, you can remove it. This removes the local version of the network file but does not affect the network version. Joan asks you to remove the local version of her Millennium Documents folder.

To remove an offline file:

1. Open the My Computer window, and navigate through your network to the location of the network file or folder.

2. Right-click the network file or folder that you've made available offline, and then click **Make Available Offline** on the shortcut menu to deselect this option. See Figure 9-31.

Figure 9-31   REMOVING AN OFFLINE FILE OR FOLDER

3. If necessary, click the **Yes** option button in the message box to indicate that you no longer want the offline folder's subfolders available either, and then click the **OK** button.

4. Close the workstation or network folder.

As Joan concludes your training on using the Millennium network with Windows XP, she explains that in the next few days she'll set up an account for you on your own workstation and will provide you with your own user ID and password. She then reminds you of the importance of keeping your password secret so unauthorized users cannot access your account. Once you're set up on your workstation, you should be able to access many of the resources that the network offers you.

Session 9.3 QUICK CHECK

1. What are local folders, network folders, and offline folders?

2. Under what circumstances would you create an offline folder?

3. What does Windows XP do when it synchronizes files?

4. When you are connected to the network, how do you know you need to synchronize the offline and network files?

5. If you edit an offline file and in the meantime the network file is deleted, what happens when you try to synchronize the offline file?

6. True or False: Windows XP only synchronizes files when you log on to the network.

REVIEW ASSIGNMENTS

1. **Diagramming Your Network** One way to understand your network is to sketch a diagram of the network layout. Figure 9-32 shows a sample schematic drawing. Create a schematic drawing of the network you use. Identify the servers and the resources they share. If there are a large number of workstations on your network, show only a few of them, identifying them by their node names. Talk to your technical support person or instructor to get the information you need.

Figure 9-32

2. **Reporting Your Network Configuration** Write a description of your network. Include the following information in your report:
   a. the number of nodes on the network
   b. the network model (peer-to-peer, hierarchical, or mixed)
   c. the network operating system
   d. the network standard
   e. the communications protocol used

3. **Password Protection** Part of creating good passwords is understanding how password protection can be overcome by people trying to break into a system. Use the Internet or your library to learn the methods used to bypass password protection. Write a one-page report summarizing these techniques, and include some suggestions for ways to protect yourself against them.

4. **Transferring a File from the Network Folder** (*Note to Instructor: You must place a file onto a network server that your students can retrieve so they can complete Review Assignment 4.*) Your instructor has placed a file in a network folder for you to work with in this assignment. With the filename and name of the folder given to you by your instructor, use My Network Places to copy the file to your Data Disk. Enter your name in the document, and then print the file.

5. **Mapping a Network Folder to a Drive Letter** (*Note to Instructor: For students to complete this assignment, you must indicate to which folder they should apply drive mapping.*) You can map network folders from the My Network Places window. Open the My Network Places window, and select the network folder indicated by your instructor. Map the folder to the drive letter U. Open the My Computer window to verify that the network folder has been mapped to drive U. Print an image of the My Computer window. (Press the PrintScreen key, open WordPad, click the Paste button, and then print the WordPad file; close WordPad without saving the file.) Remove the drive mapping when you are finished.

PROJECTS

Explore

1. In this project, you will survey organizations in your area to determine whether they use a network, what type of network they use, and for what purpose. Complete the following tasks:

   a. Identify two to three businesses, schools, or other organizations in your area that use networks. For example, contact an insurance company, a community college, an Internet service provider, or an advertising agency. Ask questions to determine the type of network used and for what purpose. For example, ask whether the network is a client/server or peer-to-peer network, how the network is structured, how many users it supports, and how security is maintained.

   b. Select one network from your survey, and create a diagram that shows how the network is set up.

   c. Prepare a one-to-two page report that outlines the information you found in your survey.

Explore

2. (*Note to Instructor: If the network your students work on is not connected to the Internet, they will not be able to complete parts a and b of Project 2.*) Many university computers are now connected to the Internet. The Internet uses the TCP/IP communications protocol. Try to discover whether your computer has the TCP/IP protocol component installed. Prove your findings by creating a printout of the Local Area Connection Properties dialog box for your computer. Examine the properties for the TCP/IP protocol component, and answer the following questions:

   a. What is your computer's IP address? (This is the address that other Internet nodes use to identify your computer.)

   b. What is the domain for your node? (*Hint*: Look on the DNS Configuration property sheet in the TCP/IP Properties dialog box. The domain is the name of your network.)

Explore

3. (*Note to Instructor: For your students to complete this project, you must give them the name of the server to find.*) You can use the Windows XP Search command to find network servers as well as files. To access the Search command, open the My Network Places window, view the entire network, and click the Search button on the Standard Buttons toolbar. The Search Companion pane opens in the My Network Places window. In the Computer name text box, type the name of the network server given to you by your instructor, and then click the Search button in the Search Companion pane. Print a copy of the Search Results window, using the techniques described earlier in Review Assignment 5.

4. (*Note to Instructor: For your students to complete this project, you must make a network folder available to them.*) Use the offline feature of Windows XP to create an offline folder of a network folder specified by your instructor. After you've created the folder, use My Computer to open the folder and view the files in it. (Click Tools, click Folder Options, click the Offline Files tab, and then click the View Files button.) Print a copy of the View Files dialog box, using the techniques described in Review Assignment 5. Remove the offline folder when you are finished.

QUICK | CHECK ANSWERS

Session 9.1

1. a collection of computers and other hardware devices linked together so that they can exchange data and share hardware and software resources

2. node: a device on a network; LAN: local area network, a network in which the nodes are located close together; WAN: wide area network, a network in which the nodes are spread over a wide area such as a state or nation; server: a computer that provides access to its resources to other computers; client: a computer that uses the resources of a server

3. the hierarchical model, in which servers provide resources to the network and clients use those resources; the peer-to-peer model, in which each computer can act as both client and server

4. store a database, handle electronic mail, manage printing, etc.

5. adapter, client, protocol, and service

6. A communications protocol determines how computers recognize each other on the network and what rules they use to transfer data. TCP/IP is used on the Internet. IPX/SPX is used in NetWare networks. NetBEUI is used in a Windows NT network.

Session 9.2

1. Do not use fewer than seven characters in your password; do not use a word or number that someone might be able to guess; include numbers or special symbols; never write down your password or share it with others.

2. Logging off is the process of closing your account on the server and preventing others from using your account. It does not necessarily involve turning off the computer. Shutting down means to close the Windows XP operating system and shut down the computer. The next user will have to restart the workstation and reload the Windows XP operating system.

3. Drive mapping is the process of assigning a drive letter to a network folder. Drive mapping is used to make it easier (and quicker) to access network folders. Also, many older programs cannot access network folders directly and require a drive letter.

4. \\GREGORY\Work

5. share

6. False

Session 9.3

1. Local folders are the folders on your local computer, network folders are located on network workstations, and offline folders are folders on your local computer that are duplicates of network folders.

2. if you were using a portable computer that was only temporarily connected to the network, or if the source of the network file was occasionally unavailable to network users

3. When Windows XP synchronizes, it reconciles any differences between the files stored on your computer with those stored on the network.

4. An Offline Files icon appears in the taskbar notification area.

5. You would be given the option of saving your version on the network or deleting it.

6. False

In this tutorial you will:

- Back up files on your hard drive

- Restore files from backup media

- Monitor and record system performance

- Create alerts to track system performance

- Manage services running on the computer

- Create and manage user accounts and user groups

- Manage security and accounting policies

LAB

Data Backup

MANAGING WINDOWS XP

Using Administrative Tools at Copy City Copiers

CASE

Copy City Copiers

You've just been hired by Copy City Copiers, a copy shop in Springdale, Illinois. Copy City Copiers provides a wide range of desktop publishing, printing, and copying services to its customers. Part of your job is to manage the computers at Copy City. This includes backing up data, monitoring system performance, and managing groups of users. You plan to schedule and perform periodic backups of the data on the computers, especially those that managers use. Their computers store data that the shop depends on to run the business, such as customer records and vendor information. If a computer were damaged or if its hard disk failed, Copy City Copiers could not afford to interrupt its operations. Regular backups are a good way to prevent a business interruption, because they let you quickly restore the data to the same or another computer. Copy City Copiers has recently purchased CD-RW drives and writeable CDs for creating backup copies of its data.

Another part of your job is to minimize and resolve hardware and software problems. These types of problems often first appear as a decline in performance, usually the computer running more slowly than normal. You need to monitor the computers' performance to make sure they are running efficiently and track activities that could affect performance, such as a program requiring more than 75 percent of available computer resources.

Copy City Copiers uses a peer-to-peer network with three types of computer users. Employees use some of the computers to control large print jobs, while customers use other computers for their own printing and copying needs. Managers use another group of computers for administrative tasks, such as payroll, scheduling, and accounting.

The last part of your job is to organize these groups of users and set permissions for the tasks they can perform. Anyone should be able to use the customer computers, but only a few managers should be able to configure them. Customers should not be able to change any of the computer settings or install their own programs. The computers used for the large print jobs should be available to all of the Copy City employees but not to the customers. Finally, the computers used for administrative tasks should be available only to employees who are responsible for managing the payroll and accounting software.

Your supervisor, Bruce Clemons, has recently installed Windows XP Professional on all of the Copy City Copiers computers. He has heard that Windows XP has several features that allow you to perform periodic backups, monitor system performance, and create and manage user groups. Bruce asks you to explore using Windows XP to perform these tasks on the computers at Copy City Copiers.

SESSION 10.1

In this session, you'll learn the principles of backing up files on your computer. You'll learn the different types of backups and when to apply them. You will use the Backup program in Windows XP Professional to back up files from your hard drive onto a floppy disk. You'll then restore the files from the floppy disk to the hard drive.
Note: You will need a blank floppy disk for this session.

Computer Backups

Data Backup

No one is safe from computer problems that result in data loss. Problems such as a power surge, a power loss, a failed section of a hard disk, or a computer virus can occur at any time. Rather than risk disaster, you should make copies of your important files regularly. You have already learned how to copy data from one 3½-inch disk to another. Making a copy of a disk or a file on a disk is one way to protect data.

To protect data on a hard drive, however, you should use a backup program instead of a copy or disk-copy procedure. A **backup program** copies and then automatically compresses files and folders from a hard disk into a single file, called a **backup file**. The backup program stores this file on a **backup medium** such as a tape cartridge, Zip disk, or writeable CD or DVD. (If you are backing up only a small amount of data, such as a few files, you can use a 3½-inch floppy disk as your backup medium.) Bruce explains that Windows XP Professional provides such a software program, called Backup. (If you are using Windows XP Home Edition, you must install the Backup accessory after you install Windows XP.) You can purchase and use a third-party backup program and use the same backup strategies to back up your files.

Backing up a set of files with the Windows XP Backup program involves the following steps:

1. You designate the folders and files you want to back up.

2. The Backup program creates a **backup job**, which lists the files you want to back up and tells your computer how, when, and where to perform the backup.

3. The Backup program copies the files and folders listed in the backup job, compresses them, and stores them in a backup file.

4. The Backup program stores the backup file on the backup medium you specify.

5. Information about the backup, including a list of the files and folders that have been saved, is stored in a file called a **catalog**.

Suppose you store all of your important files in three folders on drive C, named Projects, Accounts, and Clients. Figure 10-1 shows how Backup backs up the files in these folders.

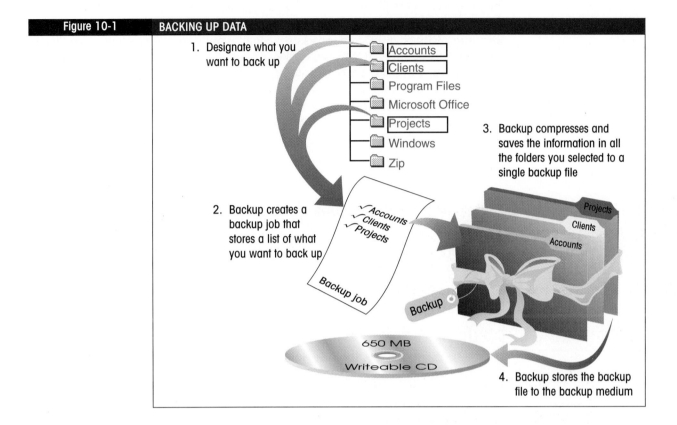

Figure 10-1   BACKING UP DATA

1. Designate what you want to back up

- Accounts
- Clients
- Program Files
- Microsoft Office
- Projects
- Windows
- Zip

2. Backup creates a backup job that stores a list of what you want to back up

✓ Accounts
✓ Clients
✓ Projects

Backup job

3. Backup compresses and saves the information in all the folders you selected to a single backup file

Projects
Clients
Accounts

Backup

650 MB Writeable CD

4. Backup stores the backup file to the backup medium

This process is different from copying files, because Backup copies files into a single, compressed file, whereas copying simply duplicates the files. Figure 10-2 points out the differences between copying and backing up, showing why backing up files is a better data-protection method than copying files.

Figure 10-2   COPYING VS. BACKING UP FILES

COPY	BACKUP
A copy of a file occupies the same amount of space as the original file. For this reason, making a copy of all the files on a hard disk is impractical.	Because it is compressed, a backup of a file is usually much smaller than the original file, depending on the file type
It would take a lot of time and effort to copy all the files on a hard disk to 3½-inch disks—not least because of the time it would take to swap disks in and out of the floppy drive. Copying 800 MB of data would require more than 560 3½-inch disks.	Backups are much quicker. If you have a tape drive, you can back up 800 MB of data to a single tape in a matter of minutes.
Because you can't split a large file over two 3½-inch disks, you must manually break up the file into smaller parts and then copy them to separate 3½-inch disks.	Backup is designed to split files across disks.
Every time you want to back up your data, you must either copy all the files on your disk again or you must painstakingly locate and then copy only those files that have changed.	Backup can automatically detect and back up only those files that have changed since your last backup.
If you do lose data because of a computer failure, there is no easy way to locate a file you need.	The Backup program keeps track of the files you have backed up in a catalog, and it's very easy to find and recover a file.

Placing Files on the Hard Disk to Back Up

The Windows XP Backup accessory is designed to back up the contents of a hard disk (or several hard disks). In this tutorial, you will simulate backing up files to a 3½-inch disk; however, using 3½-inch disks as your backup medium is impractical if you have more than just a few files to back up. As mentioned earlier, a more practical solution is to purchase a drive such as a Zip, CD/DVD rewriteable drive, or tape drive that lets you back up your data to larger storage devices. Note that tape cartridges are most often used by businesses, while individuals use CD, DVD, and Zip drives for backing up.

Because Bruce wants you to learn how to perform a real backup, you must first place some data on the hard disk, which you can then back up onto a blank formatted disk. You will place three new files in a new folder you'll create in a moment. You will then back up the files to your blank disk.

To create new files on your hard disk:

1. Right-click an empty area on your desktop, point to **New** on the shortcut menu, and then click **Folder**. Remember that any folders and files on the desktop are actually stored on the hard drive.

   TROUBLE? If you are in a computer lab and are not permitted to save files on your computer's hard disk, ask your instructor or technical support person where you should create files to back up.

2. Type **Copy City Copiers** and then press the **Enter** key.

3. Open the **Copy City Copiers** folder.

4. Click **File** on the menu bar, point to **New**, and then click **Text Document**. Type **Test1.txt** for the name of the text file, and then press the **Enter** key.

5. Repeat Step 4 twice, creating two additional empty text documents named **Test2.txt** and **Test3.txt**.

6. Close the Copy City Copiers folder window.

Now you are ready to back up the three text files from the hard disk to a floppy disk. Before you do that, however, you should learn about common backup strategies and the types of backups you can perform.

Backup Strategies

You start the backup process by designating which files and folders you want to back up. In this simulation, you will indicate the Copy City Copiers folder as the item the backup program will back up. However, Bruce explains that when you are backing up many files or a complete hard disk, choosing the files you want to back up is a little more complicated because it is part of a larger backup strategy.

A **backup strategy** is a plan you develop to ensure that you back up all the files on your computer in their most current version. The foundation of a backup strategy is a **full backup**, a compressed copy of all the files on your computer. A full backup can contain the Windows XP operating system, all your system files, all your program files, and all the data files stored on your hard disk when you performed the backup. Some people don't include their operating system or other software programs in a full backup because they know they can reinstall the software from the original disks, if necessary.

Once you have a full backup, you can perform **partial backups**, which back up only the files that have changed since the last time you backed up your data. There are two kinds of partial backups: differential and incremental. In a **differential backup**, the backup program searches for and backs up only those files that have changed since the last full backup. In an **incremental backup**, the backup program searches for and backs up only those files that have changed since the last backup, regardless of whether it was a full or partial backup. Figure 10-3 will help you understand the difference.

Figure 10-3   **PARTIAL BACKUP TYPES**

Incremental backups are generally faster and take less space, but restoring from an incremental backup can be slow. Differential backups, on the other hand, are generally slower and require more space, but restoring is quicker.

You might think that to be on the safe side, you should perform a full backup every time you back up your data. However, a full backup can take several hours, depending on how many hard disks you have and how big they are. For this reason, most users perform a full backup only once a week or once a month, depending on how substantially their files change from day to day. Many of your files don't change at all over the course of weeks or months. Your program files, for example, change only when you install a new version of the software.

How often should you perform full and partial backups? It's best to develop a backup strategy based on a schedule. For the user in Figure 10-3, a backup strategy begins with a full backup at the beginning of the week. Then this user performs a partial backup on a daily basis. Perhaps the last thing he or she does before shutting down the computer for the evening is to run the backup software to back up any files changed during the day.

Some users might want to perform more frequent backups—especially those who can't afford to lose even a few hours worth of work. They might perform a partial backup more than once a day—at lunchtime, after work, and then at midnight, for example. You don't want to overdo it, however. Even a partial backup can slow your productivity—even if the backup program is running in the background, it uses system resources. Ideally, you should schedule backups while are not using your computer. The goal is to back up your data often enough so that if your computer fails, you can restore most of your data from your backup files.

Backing Up Files

Although you generally back up a hard disk, in some cases, you might want to back up only the contents of one or several folders. For example, suppose you store all the files you work with on a daily basis in the My Documents folder. If you back up only that folder, you speed up the daily backup process because Backup doesn't have to search your entire computer for changed files. Users who perform more than one backup a day might especially profit from selecting just a few folders for backup.

In this simulation, you are not going to perform a full backup. Instead, you are going to perform a backup of only one folder: the Copy City Copiers folder. If you are using Windows XP Professional, Backup was automatically installed when you installed Windows XP. If you are using Windows XP Home Edition, you must install Backup yourself.

To install Backup if you are using Windows Home Edition:

1. Insert the Windows XP Home CD into your CD drive, and then click the **Exit** button to close the Welcome to Microsoft Windows XP dialog box.

2. Open My Computer and navigate to the Windows Home CD. Open the **VALUEADD** folder, open the **MSFT** folder, and then open the **NTBACKUP** folder.

3. Double-click the **NTBACKUP.MSI** file icon to start the Wizard for installing the Backup accessory.

4. Follow the instructions in the Wizard, and then click the **Finish** button when you are done.

REFERENCE WINDOW   **RW**

Performing a Windows XP Backup

- Click the Start button, point to All Programs, point to Accessories, point to System Tools, and then click Backup.
- Click the Next button to start the Backup or Restore Wizard.
- Click the Back up files and settings option button, and then click the Next button.
- Select what you want to back up, and then click the Next button.
- If you are specifying the items you want to back up, select the drive, folders, or files that you want to back up, and then click the Next button.
- Specify a name, location, and backup type, if necessary, and then click the Next button.
- Click the Advanced button, if necessary, to specify the type of backup to perform and the time when the backup should occur.
- Click the Finish button.

Now you're ready to start Backup.

To start Backup:

1. Click the **Start** button ![start], point to **All Programs**, point to **Accessories**, point to **System Tools**, and then click **Backup**. The Backup or Restore Wizard opens, as shown in Figure 10-4.

| Figure 10-4 | STARTING THE BACKUP OR RESTORE WIZARD |

TROUBLE? If the Backup or Restore Wizard does not start, you might have to be logged on as an administrator. If your instructor or network administrator cannot allow you to log on as an administrator, read through the steps to understand the concepts.

TROUBLE? If a message appears warning you that there is no backup device (other than the floppy drive), click No to acknowledge the message and continue with the steps. This message appears the first time you start Backup if you don't have a backup device such as a CD or DVD drive installed.

TROUBLE? If Backup does not appear as an option on the System Tools menu, then you cannot complete this session until the Backup program is installed. Check with your instructor or technical support person for directions.

2. Click the **Next** button to open the Backup or Restore window, where you specify whether you want to back up files or restore them.

3. Click the **Back up files and settings** option button if necessary, and then click the **Next** button to open the What to Back Up window, where you can choose to back up your documents and settings, the documents and settings for all the users on this computer, all the information on this computer, or only those files you specify. When you are backing up your own computer or one that you manage, you select one of the first three options. For this tutorial, however, you want to specify which files to back up.

4. Click the **Let me choose what to back up** option button, and then click the **Next** button.

The next Backup or Restore Wizard dialog box allows you to select the items you want to back up. Before you do so, take a moment to examine this dialog box and understand how to make your selections.

Selecting Files and Folders to Back Up

To select the files or folders you want to back up, you navigate through the hierarchy of objects and folders on your computer. To include a folder in the backup job, you click the empty box ☐ next to the folder to place a check mark in it. A blue check mark ☑ indicates that the entire folder or file will be backed up. A gray check mark ☑ indicates that only part of the contents of that folder or drive will be backed up. If you want to include only selected files in a folder, you click the folder's icon in the Folders list and then click the empty boxes for only those files.

You want to select the Copy City Copiers folder on your desktop to back up.

To select the Copy City Copiers folder:

1. Click the empty box ☐ to the left of the Copy City Copiers folder. A blue check mark appears in the box, indicating that all contents of the folder have been selected for backup. See Figure 10-5.

Figure 10-5   **SELECTING THE COPY CITY COPIERS FOLDER TO BACK UP**

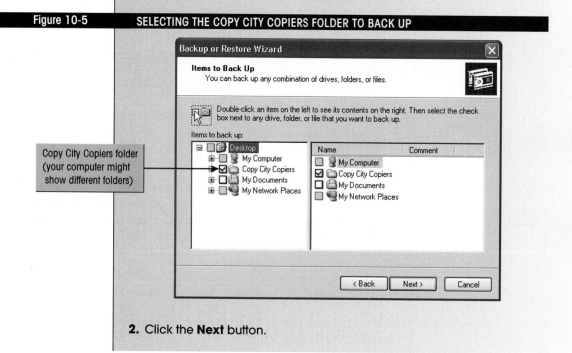

Copy City Copiers folder (your computer might show different folders)

2. Click the **Next** button.

The next step of the Wizard will determine where you want to store the backup file. Depending on the hardware devices on your system, you might see different dialog boxes. If you have a CD rewriteable drive, you will see an option to use that device. In this case, you'll write the backup to a file on your floppy disk.

To continue with the Backup Wizard:

1. If necessary, select **File** in the Select backup type list box, and then select **3½ Floppy A:** in the Choose a place to save your backup list box, if necessary.

2. In the Type a name for this backup text box, type **CCC Backup**. See Figure 10-6. Then, click the **Next** button.

Figure 10-6	SPECIFYING A BACKUP FILENAME

this list box is unavailable if you are only backing up files, and not settings or devices

name of the backup file

TROUBLE? If you don't have a drive that Backup can use for the backup medium, such as a ZIP or CD rewritable drive, the Backup media type list box will be dimmed, meaning this option is inactive.

The Backup program will now create a backup file named CCC Backup on your floppy disk.

Setting Advanced Backup Options

You've reached the end of the Backup or Restore Wizard. At this point, you can finish the wizard, accepting the backup defaults that the wizard has chosen for you. You can also specify some of the advanced options. This includes specifying whether you are performing a full, differential, or incremental backup. You can have the Backup program verify the backup, which involves comparing the files on the backup medium to the source files on the hard disk. Verification takes longer but ensures that the files you've backed up are stored correctly on the backup medium.

You can also use the Advanced options to run the Restore Wizard or the Automated System Recovery Wizard. You'll learn about and run the Restore Wizard shortly. You use the Automated System Recovery Wizard to save your system settings on a floppy disk and to save your system files on a larger medium, such as a Zip disk or CD. You can use these disks to restore your system in the event of a major system failure. It's a good idea to run the Automated System Recovery Wizard shortly after you install Windows XP.

Bruce suggests that you review the advanced backup options.

To review the advanced options:

1. Click the **Advanced** button. The Type of Backup dialog box opens.

The Type of Backup dialog box allows you to specify the type of backup you want to perform. Normal is the default selection, which is equivalent to a full backup.

2. Click the **Next** button.

The next step allows you to verify the backup. Bruce suggests that this is a good idea, as long as time is not a concern, which it isn't with such a small backup.

3. Click the **Verify data after backup** check box, and then click the **Next** button.

Next, you can specify whether to append the backup file to the backup medium or to overwrite previous backup files with this one. This option is most appropriate for backup tapes, in which the backup files are stored in a sequential order. When you're backing up to a floppy disk, the issue of appending or replacing the file is not relevant. The default option is to append to the backup medium.

4. Click the **Replace the existing backups** option button, and then click the **Next** button.

Finally, you can specify whether to back up now or at a scheduled time. The default is to back up immediately.

5. Verify that the **Now** option button is selected, and click the **Next** button.

6. Place a blank formatted disk in your floppy disk drive, and then click the **Finish** button.

The Backup program starts. After a few seconds, the backup job is complete, and the Backup Progress dialog box opens, as shown in Figure 10-7.

Figure 10-7	COMPLETING THE BACKUP JOB

7. Click the **Close** button.

Once you have the backup, keep it in a safe place. You should not store backup media near your computer. A fire that destroys your computer will probably destroy your backups as well. If a thief wants your data, it's quicker to steal your backups than your computer. Many computer owners rent safe deposit boxes at banks and store their backups there. Business owners sometimes store their backups off-site at their own homes. Backup storage is part of your overall backup strategy. You need to decide how often you will put your backup media into storage. Many users maintain two backup disks: they store the backups for a single week, and then at the end of the week, they put the backups in storage. They use the other disk for the following week, and then at the end of the week, they swap the backups.

Restoring Files

If you need to use the files you backed up, you must restore them from the backup file—you cannot simply copy the backup file to your hard disk. When you **restore files**, Windows XP extracts the files you want from the backup job and then copies them to a location you specify. In addition to selecting the files and folders you want to restore and specifying where you want to restore them, you can also set other restore options. For example, you can specify that you do not want Windows XP to replace any current files on your computer, or to replace files only if the ones on the hard disk are older. Either option prevents you from overwriting files you might need.

Bruce asks you to imagine that disaster has just struck. Your hard disk has failed, and your computer maintenance person believes data recovery is hopeless—you're going to have to reformat your hard disk. "I hope," says your maintenance person, "you made a backup." Your backup disk will allow you to easily restore the files you lost.

Bruce says that to simulate a file restoration, you'll first delete the Copy City Copiers folder from your desktop. In a real-life situation, these files might have been ruined in a power failure, by a disk defect, by a virus, or by some other misfortune.

To delete the Copy City Copiers folder from the desktop:

1. Right-click the **Copy City Copiers** folder icon on the desktop, and then click **Delete**.

2. Click the **Yes** button to confirm you want to delete this folder.

Bruce notes that at this point you could recover the folder and its contents from the Recycle Bin, but he asks you to imagine that you emptied the Recycle Bin after deleting the Copy City Copier folder to free disk space.

You are ready to use Backup to restore the folder to your hard disk. You must first identify the backup that contains the Copy City Copiers folder. In this simulation, your floppy disk contains only one backup file: the CCC Backup file you created earlier. Usually, however, the backup disk contains many backup files, especially if you run backup jobs regularly. How you restore data depends on what kind of loss you suffered. If you lost only a single file, you can choose the backup that you made after you changed the file. If the file or folder you want to restore is not in that backup, that means you haven't worked with it since the last backup, in which case you'll have to check another backup. If you lost all the data on your disk, how you recover it depends on what kind of partial backups you use. If you use incremental backups, you will need to use all the backups you've created since your most recent full backup. You would start by restoring the full backup and then restoring each backup, one at a time, beginning with the oldest. If you use differential backups, you restore the full backup and then the most recent differential backup.

You are ready to restore the Copy City Copier folder.

To select the files to restore from the backup media:

1. Start the Backup or Restore Wizard again, and then click the **Next** button.

2. Click the **Restore files and settings** option button, and then click the **Next** button.

   The wizard displays the backup file on the floppy disk. This is the CCC Backup file that you created earlier. From this file, you select the files and folders that you want to restore. To do so, you have to work down through the hierarchy of objects in the backup media.

3. Click the **plus box** ⊞ next to File.

4. Click the ⊞ next to CCC Backup.bkf.

At this point, you can select the C folder (or whichever folder contains the original files) to restore the files. (You don't have to navigate through the rest of the folder hierarchy.)

5. Click the **box** ☐ next to the drive C icon (or other hard drive icon). See Figure 10-8.

Figure 10-8	SELECTING THE FILES TO RESTORE

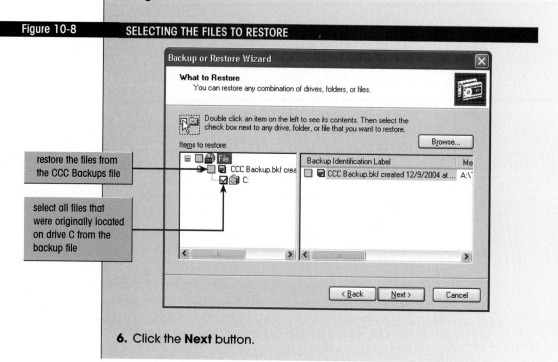

restore the files from the CCC Backups file

select all files that were originally located on drive C from the backup file

6. Click the **Next** button.

Now you can restore the files to the original locations. If you want to select a different location for the files, you can use the advanced restore options. The advanced options also allow you to specify whether you want files from the backup media to overwrite files on the hard disk. Bruce suggests that you examine the advanced restore options.

To view the advanced restore options:

1. Click the **Advanced** button.

The first dialog box lets you specify a location for the restored files. If you select Alternate Location from the Restore files to list box, you will be prompted for the new location. The default is to restore the files to the original location, which you'll accept.

2. Click the **Next** button.

If you're restoring files that also reside on the hard drive, you can either (1) leave the files on the hard disk untouched, (2) overwrite the files on the hard disk if the file on the backup medium is a newer version, or (3) always replace the hard disk files. In this case, you won't be restoring over any existing files, so you can safely continue with the Wizard.

3. Click the **Next** button.

The last advanced option allows you to restore special system files or security files. None of these options apply to the files you created in the Copy City Copiers folder.

4. Click the **Next** button.

You've finished reviewing the advanced options. Now you can complete restoring the backed up files.

To restore the files:

1. Make sure your floppy disk is in the appropriate drive, and click the **Finish** button.

After a few seconds, the files are restored. Windows XP displays the Restore Progress dialog box shown in Figure 10-9.

Figure 10-9	COMPLETING THE RESTORE PROCESS

To maintain a permanent record of the backup and restore information, you can generate a report and then print it. You'll open the report to examine the information it contains.

2. Click the **Report** button.

The backup report opens in Notepad and shows what you restored and when you restored the files.

3. Close the Notepad window and then click the **Close** button to close the Backup window.

4. Verify that the Copy City Copiers folder has been restored to the desktop. (The icon might be in a different location than it was originally.)

5. Delete the **Copy City Copiers** folder to return the desktop to its original state.

Bruce tells you that if you're lucky, you'll never have to use Restore to recover lost data. Then he tells you that backup is probably one of the most important topics he's discussed with you. Practically everyone who has been using computers for very long has a data-loss story to tell. Many computer owners who now make regular backups learned the hard way how important protecting data is. If you are a computer owner, put a backup strategy planning session at the top of your list, and then stick to your strategy scrupulously.

Session 10.1 QUICK CHECK

1. How does copying a disk differ from backing up a disk?

2. What is the difference between a backup job and a backup?

3. What is a partial backup? Identify and differentiate between two kinds of partial backups.

4. Why would you use a partial backup rather than perform a full backup?

5. When you select the folders and files to back up, Backup uses colored check marks to indicate which files and folders will be backed up. If a folder has a blue check mark in front of it, will the entire folder be backed up?

SESSION 10.2

In this session, you'll look at some of the tools that Windows XP provides to help you manage system performance. You'll see how to track the performance of key components of your computer using the Performance Monitor and log files. You'll see how to set up an alert to warn of certain behavior on your computer. Finally, you'll learn about the various services that constantly run on your computer. You'll see how to access those services and control them.

Note: You will need a blank, formatted floppy disk for some of the steps in this session.

Monitoring System Performance

Part of your job at Copy City Copiers is to make sure that the computers are running at peak efficiency and to help resolve any hardware and software difficulties. One user reports that lately his computer has been running slowly. A number of problems could cause this loss of performance. The user may have too many programs running at the same time. The computer may be low on memory. Or the computer may need to have its processor upgraded to a faster one. To determine the cause, you need to measure the performance of the system.

One way of accomplishing this task is to use the Windows XP Performance Monitor, which can display the amount of system resources that your computer is using at any time. Bruce suggests that you run the Performance Monitor on the user's computer. Note that it's easiest to access Performance Monitor and other system management tools by using the Control Panel in Classic View.

To start the Performance Monitor:

1. Open the Control Panel in Classic View, and then double-click the **Administrative Tools** icon.

2. In the Administrative Tools window, double-click the **Performance** shortcut icon.

The Performance window opens, as shown in Figure 10-10.

Figure 10-10	THE PERFORMANCE MONITOR

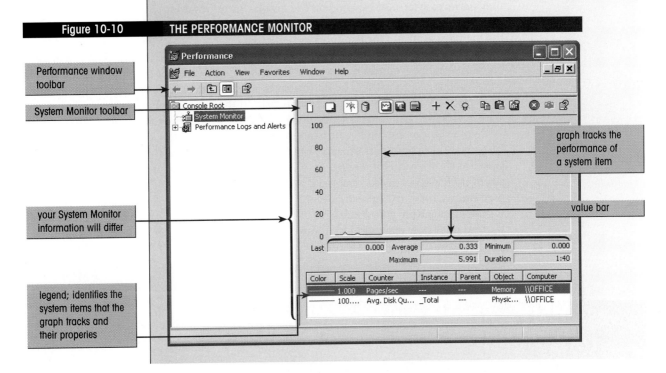

Performance window toolbar

System Monitor toolbar

your System Monitor information will differ

legend; identifies the system items that the graph tracks and their properies

graph tracks the performance of a system item

value bar

You can use Performance Monitor to produce a graph that reflects system performance. Figure 10-11 describes the tools and information the Performance window provides.

Figure 10-11	ELEMENTS OF THE PERFORMANCE WINDOW

PERFORMANCE WINDOW ELEMENT	DESCRIPTION
System Monitor icon	Click to monitor the performance of your system
Performance Logs and Alerts icon	Click to record performance information in a log file to set an alert that warns you of a potential performance problem
Performance window toolbar	Contains buttons that let you work with the Performance window or access online Help
System Monitor toolbar	Contains buttons that let you perform system monitoring tasks; for example, you can clear the graph, add or delete graphed system items, change the view of the graph, and set system monitor properties
Graph area	Tracks the performance of system items listed in the legend
Value bar	Shows the last, minimum, maximum, and average values for the selected system item
Legend	Shows the names and associated information for the system items you select

Graphing System Performance

To obtain performance data, Windows XP monitors the components in your computer, such as the processor, memory, and the physical hard disk. Components generate data as they perform system tasks, and you can graph this information in the Performance window. For example, you can graph performance data about the processor on your system or about the memory available for handling system tasks.

Each system item you can track provides **counters** that represent the data you are graphing. For example, you can track the % Processor Time Counter to determine the activity of your computer's processor. The Performance window then shows the percentage of time that your processor is busy performing system tasks. If the values the Performance window graphs are near 100 percent, that could mean the processor is struggling to handle a heavy workload.

Before you can use the Performance Monitor, you must select a counter to track a particular part of the system performance. Once you do, the values of the counter are shown in the graph, as shown earlier in Figure 10-10. The counter is updated at intervals you specify—usually every few seconds. You can track performance indicators such as the amount of time your processor is not idle (a measure of how busy your system is) and the speed of the computer in retrieving data from your hard drive. If your computer is acting as a print server for a network, you can track how many print requests it receives and the number of pages it has printed.

REFERENCE WINDOW   **RW**

Graphing System Performance

- Open the Control Panel in Classic View, open the Administrative Tools window, and then double-click the Performance shortcut icon.
- Click the System Monitor icon in the left pane of the Performance window, if necessary.
- Click the Add button on the System Monitor toolbar.
- In the Add Counter dialog box, select an item from the list of performance objects and a counter from the counter list.
- Click the Add button and then click the Close button.

Tracking performance information can locate the source of trouble in a slow system and may help you determine what needs to be done to speed up the system. Bruce suggests that you track the amount of time the computer's processor is in use. If you find that a process is using a high percentage of processor time, you could upgrade to a faster processor or install an additional processor to speed the system.

To track processor time:

1. In the left pane of the Performance window, click the **System Monitor** icon, if necessary. The Performance window shows the System Monitor toolbar and a graphing area.

2. If the Performance window already lists counters below the graphing area, click the right pane and then press **Ctrl+E** to clear the counters. If the Performance window contains a graph, press **Ctrl+D** to clear the window.

3. Click the **Add** button ⊞ on the System Monitor toolbar. The Add Counters dialog box opens.

4. Select **Processor** in the Performance object list box if it's not already selected.

5. Verify that the **Select counters from list** option button is selected. Selecting this option button means that you can isolate one counter to see if it shows the performance problem.

6. Click **% Processor Time** in the list of counters if it's not already selected.

7. Click the **Explain** button. See Figure 10-12.

Figure 10-12	SELECTING AN ITEM TO TRACK

A short description of the item you're about to track appears at the bottom of the Add Counters dialog box. In this case, you'll be measuring the percentage of time that the processor is busy performing system tasks. A value near 100 percent will suggest that the processor is almost never idle. If so, that indicates the processor might be so busy that it can't perform tasks efficiently.

8. Click the **Add** button and then click the **Close** button.

TROUBLE? If your System Monitor is already set to track % Processor Time, a message appears informing you that this counter is already selected. Click OK to continue.

The System Monitor starts tracking the percentage of time that the processor is in use each second. See Figure 10-13.

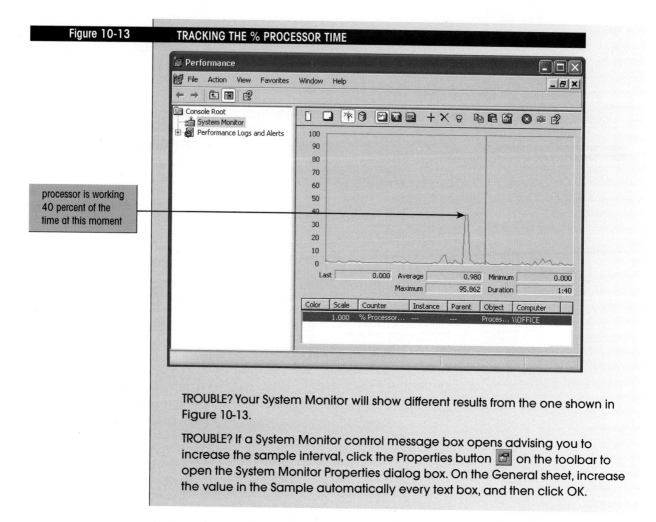

Figure 10-13   TRACKING THE % PROCESSOR TIME

processor is working 40 percent of the time at this moment

TROUBLE? Your System Monitor will show different results from the one shown in Figure 10-13.

TROUBLE? If a System Monitor control message box opens advising you to increase the sample interval, click the Properties button 🖼 on the toolbar to open the System Monitor Properties dialog box. On the General sheet, increase the value in the Sample automatically every text box, and then click OK.

From the results shown in Figure 10-13, you note that the processor use does not approach 100 percent during the time the System Monitor tracks it. If the processor use on your computer jumped to 100 percent at any point, you should examine the types of programs that the computer is running. It's possible that one of these programs is causing a heavy load on the system and slowing it down.

Bruce has enough information on the performance of the processor, so you can turn off the % Processor counter.

To turn off the counter:

1. If necessary, click to select the **% Processor Counter** in the list below the graph.

2. Click the **Delete** button ⊠ on the System Monitor toolbar located above the graph area.

The System Monitor stops tracking the performance of the processor.

In addition to creating an on-screen graph of system performance, you can also record the information in a file, which you'll do next.

Logging System Performance

Sometimes you will find it useful to have a permanent record of the results from the System Monitor. For example, you can create a **baseline chart**, which is a chart of the computer's performance when it's running at a normal level. When the system has problems, administrators can create another performance chart to compare to the baseline one. Using baseline charts, administrators can anticipate and then prevent problems.

You create a baseline chart by first creating a **log file**, a text file that contains all the performance values shown in the graph. You save the log file on your computer so you have a record you can use for troubleshooting. Bruce asks you to create a log file of the processor score and to store the log file on a floppy disk that you can give to him later.

To create a log file of the performance values:

1. Place a blank, formatted floppy disk in your floppy disk drive.

2. In the left pane of the Performance window, click the **plus box** [+] next to the Performance Logs and Alerts icon.

3. Click the **Counter Logs** icon. A sample log icon and file description appear in the right pane of the Performance window. If necessary, you can examine this sample log file to determine how to set up your own file. For now, you can continue creating a log file without opening the sample.

4. Click **Action** on the menu bar, and then click **New Log Settings**. The New Log Settings dialog box opens, displaying a text box where you can type a name for the log file.

5. Type **Processor Performance** in the Name text box, and then click the **OK** button.

   A dialog box appears in which you can specify which items you want to track in the log file.

6. Click the **Add Counters** button to open the Add Counters dialog box.

7. Verify that the **% Processor Time** counter is selected in the Select counters from list box, click the **Add** button, and then click the **Close** button.

   In addition to using the System Monitor Properties dialog box, you can also use the Processor Performance dialog box to determine how often the system will monitor the performance of the processor. You decide to sample the performance every five seconds.

8. Enter **5** in the **Interval** spin box to set the interval value to five seconds. See Figure 10-14.

Figure 10-14	SPECIFYING DATA TO SAVE IN A LOG FILE

the path for your
filename may
be different

performance
item to track

sample the % Processor
Time every 5 seconds

Next, you'll specify where you want to save the log file. In this case, you'll save the log file on your floppy disk so you can give it to Bruce.

To save the log file:

1. Click the **Log Files** tab in the Processor Performance dialog box. You use the Log Files property sheet to select the log file type and name. You use the binary file type if you want to log data continuously to a single file, overwriting previous data with new data. If you were using the log file outside of the Performance tool, you could save it as a text file and open it using Notepad, for example. Bruce wants to use the same file continuously, so you can leave the type set to Binary. You do, however, need to change where you want to save the file.

2. Click the **Configure** button.

    The Configure Log Files dialog box opens, with text boxes where you can specify the location and name of the file.

3. Click the **Location** text box, if necessary, and then type **A:** (or the drive letter of your floppy drive). See Figure 10-15.

Figure 10-15	SPECIFYING A FILE NAME AND LOCATION FOR THE PERFORMANCE LOG

Configure Log Files

Location:
A:

File name:
Processor Performance

Log file size
○ Maximum limit
○ Limit of:
1   MB

if necessary, you can set a limit for the log file size

OK   Cancel

4. Click the **OK** button to return to the Log Files property sheet.

   Notice the End file names with check box that appears on this property sheet. Each filename can end with a series of numbers or dates so that you can create several performance log files, with the files distinguished by either the date on which they were created or the order in which they were created. In this case, because you are creating only one log file, you'll remove that feature from the log filename.

5. If necessary, deselect the **End file names with** check box.

   The log file will be stored in the file named "Processor Performance.blg" on your floppy disk. (Windows XP adds the file extension.)

6. Click the **OK** button.

7. In the right pane of the Performance window, click the **Processor Performance** icon 🟥.

When you click the Processor Performance icon, Windows XP starts tracking performance data and changes the Processor Performance icon from 🟥, which means inactive, to 🟩, which means the log file is active. Every five seconds after that, new performance data will be sampled and then stored on the log file on your floppy disk. This will continue until you manually stop the sampling or the floppy disk is full.

To stop sampling:

1. Wait about half a minute to obtain a good sample.

2. In the right pane of the Performance window, right-click the **Processor Performance** icon 🟩, and then click **Stop** on the shortcut menu. The icon returns to red, indicating that it is again inactive.

   TROUBLE? If you receive an error message indicating that the Processor Performance log or alert has not stopped, click the OK button and wait for the sampling to stop. If it does not stop sampling after a few moments, repeat step 2.

If you were to look at the contents of your floppy disk, you would see a file named "Processor Performance.blg." You could take this file to Bruce for him to examine, or you could file it as a permanent record of the processor performance of this particular computer.

To view the contents of the log file, you open it within the Performance Monitor. Try this now.

To view the contents of the Processor Performance log file:

1. In the left pane of the Performance window, click the **System Monitor** icon ![icon].

2. Click the **View Log Data** button ![button] on the System Monitor toolbar. To select a log file, you must first add it to the Log files list.

3. Click the **Log files** option button, and then click the **Add** button.

4. In the Select Log File dialog box, click the **Processor Performance** file located on your floppy disk, and then click the **Open** button.

5. Click the **OK** button to close the System Monitor Properties dialog box.

    A log file can contain several different items, so you have to select which item you want to display on the monitor.

6. Click the **Add** button ![+].

7. Verify that **Processor** is the selected performance object (it has to be, since that is the only item you've logged), click the **Add** button, and then click the **Close** button.

    The Performance Monitor shows the contents of the log file, as shown in Figure 10-16. (Your graph will be different.)

Figure 10-16	VIEWING THE PROCESSOR PERFORMANCE LOG FILE

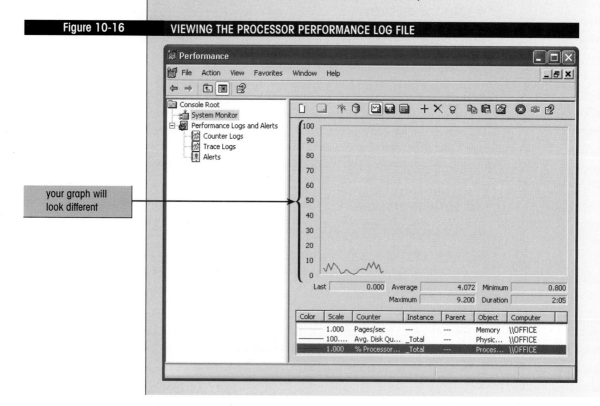

your graph will look different

Now that you've created the log file, you should delete the Processor Performance item from the list of counter logs. Deleting the Processor Performance item does not affect the log file you just created.

To delete the Processor Performance icon:

1. In the left pane of the Performance window, click the **Counter Logs** icon 🖾.
2. In the right pane of the Performance window, click the **Processor Performance** icon 🥟.
3. Click the **Delete** button ☒ on the System Monitor toolbar.
4. Remove your floppy disk from the drive.

Bruce can store this log file in his office and use it in the future as a baseline against which other performance charts can be compared.

Creating a Performance Alert

Often you will not want to monitor your system's performance every second; instead, you will want to monitor in the background, with the system alerting you if certain conditions are met. To do this, you create a performance alert. Bruce suggests that you create an alert to let you know when the percentage of non-idle processor time exceeds 75 percent. The process of creating an alert is similar to the one for creating a log file. Note that running System Monitor in the background can slow processing time on its own.

To create an alert:

1. In the left pane of the Performance window, click the **Alerts** icon 🗒.
2. Click **Action** on the menu bar, and then click **New Alert Settings**.

   The Processor Alert dialog box opens, where you can enter a name for the new alert.
3. Type **Processor Alert** in the New Alert Settings dialog box, and then click the **OK** button.
4. Type **Alert when processor usage exceeds 75%** in the Comment text box.

   Now that you have named and described the alert, you can select the object and counters you want to track.
5. Click the **Add** button to select the object and counters you want to track.
6. In the Add Counters dialog box, verify that **Processor** is selected in the Performance object list box and that **% Processor Time** is selected in the list of counters.
7. Click the **Add** button and then click the **Close** button. Now you can set the conditions that specify when to generate an alert.
8. In the Processor Alert dialog box, click the **Alert when the value is** list arrow, and then click **Over**, if necessary.
9. Type **75** in the Limit text box.

Figure 10-17 shows the completed dialog box.

Figure 10-17 **SETTING AN ALERT WHEN THE % PROCESSOR TIME RISES ABOVE 75 PERCENT**

describes the alert
you're creating

specific conditions
for the alert

Now that you've defined the conditions under which an alert will occur, you have to specify the action that the operating system will take. You can choose any or all of four possibilities:

- Place an entry in the application event log.
- Send a message to a specific user on the system.
- Start logging the performance of the item in a log file.
- Run a specific program.

You'll choose the first option, which places an entry in the system's application event log. (You'll learn what this log does shortly.)

To specify an action for the event:

1. In the Processor alert dialog box, click the **Action** tab.

2. Verify that the **Log an entry in the application event log** check box is selected and that no other check box is selected.

3. Click the **OK** button.

4. Click the **Processor Alert** icon 📚 , if necessary, to select it in the right pane of the Performance window. This starts the performance alert log. When the conditions of the alert are met, Windows XP will record this fact in the application event log.

5. Close the Performance window.

Note that logging events does not do anything to address the reason that the events are occurring—it merely records the fact that the events did occur. Many system administrators choose to run a utility program (the last option in the previous bulleted list), such as a virus checker, when the conditions of an alert are met to further diagnose or solve the problem.

Tracking Events on Your System

As you work on your computer, Windows XP is constantly tracking **events**—any significant activity in the system or an application that requires Windows to notify users of a situation or problem, or to add an entry to a log. When an event occurs, Windows records it in a file called an **event log**. You can use these event logs to help you diagnose problems on your system. Figure 10-18 shows three types of event logs created by Windows XP.

Figure 10-18	TYPES OF EVENT LOGS

EVENT LOG	DESCRIPTION
Application	Contains events logged by applications or programs
System	Contains events logged by the Windows XP operating system, such as the failure of a hardware driver to load upon startup
Security	Records events related to system security, such as valid and invalid logons and account lockouts

Managing the computers at Copy City Copiers, you'll occasionally have to search through event logs, especially in situations where a system has crashed and you need to discover the reason for it. What sorts of things were happening before the system failed? An event log might provide valuable information.

REFERENCE WINDOW   **RW**

Viewing the Event Log
- Open the Control Panel in Classic View, and then double-click the Administrative Tools icon.
- In the Administrative Tools window, double-click the Event Viewer shortcut.
- Double-click the icon for the type of event log you want to view.

For Copy City Copiers, you created an alert condition in the performance monitor, and you're using the application event log to store the times when and situations in which the alert is triggered. You decide to open the application event log to see if an alert has been logged.

To view the application event log:

1. In the Administrative Tools window, double-click the **Event Viewer** shortcut icon 🖳. The Event Viewer window opens; like the Performance window, it lists objects in the left pane. When you click an object in the left pane, detailed information about that object appears in the right pane.

   TROUBLE? If the Administrative Tools window is not open, reopen the Control Panel in Classic View, and then double-click the Administrative Tools icon 🖳.

2. In the left pane of the Event Viewer window, click the **Application** icon 📇.

A list of events that have been generated by applications is shown in the right pane. Your list will differ. See Figure 10-19.

Figure 10-19   **EVENT VIEWER WINDOW**

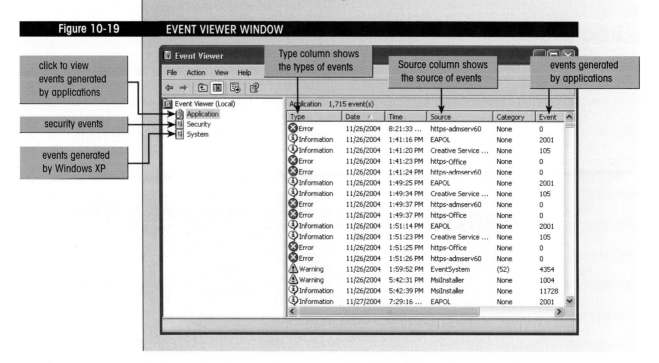

Depending on your computer, you may or may not have activated the alert for percent processor time above 75 percent. However, one event that is sure to be logged is the event that started the alert monitor in the first place. This will be one of the more recent alerts in the list, identified by the Information icon ⓘ, indicating that the event is logged for your information only. A Warning icon ⚠ indicates that the event may cause problems in the future, for example, low disk space. On the other hand, an Error icon ⊗ indicates a significant problem, possibly resulting in lost data or the failure of an application.

To view information on an event:

1. Double-click one of the **Information** event icons ⓘ in the list of events. The Event Properties dialog box opens.

Figure 10-20 shows the event in which the conditions of the processor alert have been met. (Your event dialog box will probably show something else.)

Figure 10-20	PROPERTIES OF AN EVENT

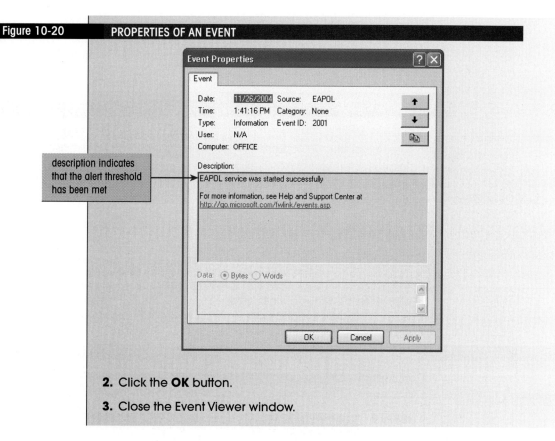

description indicates that the alert threshold has been met

2. Click the **OK** button.

3. Close the Event Viewer window.

Now that you've seen how the event log works, you should remove the processor alert that you created earlier.

To remove the processor alert:

1. In the Administrative Tools window, double-click the **Performance** icon , click the **plus box** ⊞ next to Performance Logs and Alerts, if necessary, and then click **Alerts**.

2. Select the **Processor Alert** icon 🗃 in the list of alerts, and then click the **Delete** button ⊠ on the toolbar.

3. Click **OK** if you are asked to confirm the deletion.

4. Close the Performance window.

Viewing **the Service List**

The event log is an example of a **service**, a small program controlled by Windows XP and designed to manage one or more tasks to support other programs. Services often run in the background as you are working with your computer. Event logs, the print spooler, and the ability to detect a plug-and-play device are all examples of services.

Services either start automatically when Windows XP starts (as in the case of the event log), or you start them manually when you run an application or select a command. Sometimes the system administrator will want to have control over the services on the computer in order to shut down an active service or manually start one.

Bruce suggests that you "take a look under the hood" of Windows XP to see how this process works. To do this, you can open the Services window, another Windows XP administrative tool that you use to control various services on your computer.

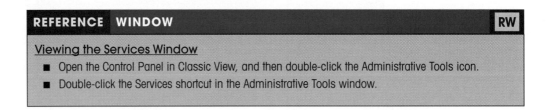

REFERENCE WINDOW RW

Viewing the Services Window

■ Open the Control Panel in Classic View, and then double-click the Administrative Tools icon.

■ Double-click the Services shortcut in the Administrative Tools window.

To access the list of services:

1. In the Administrative Tools window, double-click the **Services** shortcut icon.

The Services window opens, displaying the list of services in the right pane. Maximize the window if necessary. See Figure 10-21. Notice that one of the services in the list is Event Log, the service that automatically logs all events.

Figure 10-21	LIST OF SERVICES

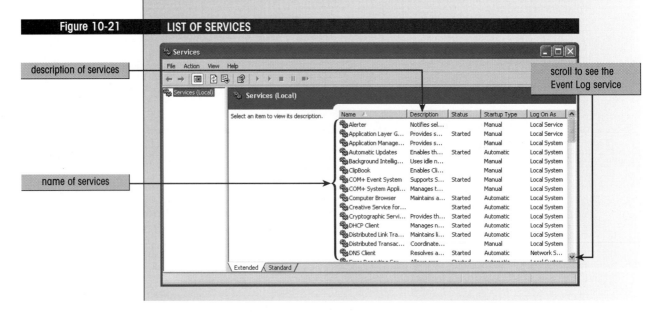

In the Status column, you can see which services have already started. To see more detailed information about a service, you can double-click its icon in the list. Bruce suggests that you do this with the Event Log service but take care not to change any of the settings.

To view information about a service:

1. Locate and double-click the **Event Log** service in the Services list.

The Event Log Properties (Local Computer) dialog box opens, as shown in Figure 10-22.

Figure 10-22   PROPERTIES OF THE EVENT LOG SERVICE

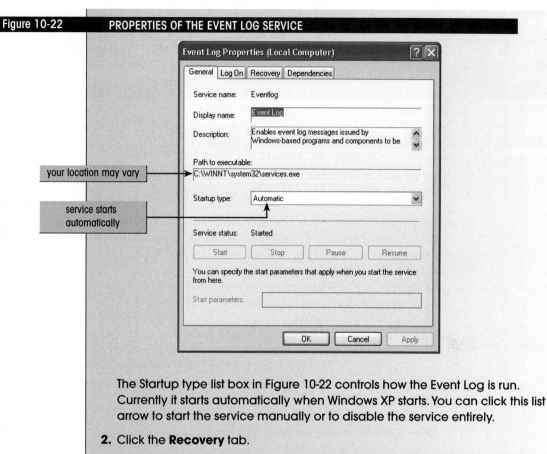

your location may vary

service starts
automatically

The Startup type list box in Figure 10-22 controls how the Event Log is run. Currently it starts automatically when Windows XP starts. You can click this list arrow to start the service manually or to disable the service entirely.

2. Click the **Recovery** tab.

From this property sheet, you can control what happens when a service fails to start. In this case no action is taken, but in some situations you will want Windows XP to try to restart the service or reboot the computer.

3. Click the **Cancel** button.

4. Close the Services window, close the Administrative Tools window, and then close the Control Panel.

You're finished with the administrative tools that allow you to monitor and alter the behavior of your computer. In the next session, Bruce will show you how to manage the users of the Copy City Copier computers.

Session 10.2 QUICK CHECK

1. What would you use the Performance Monitor for?

2. What does the % Processor Time Counter measure?

3. How would you set up your computer to alert you when the % Processor Time Counter rises above 95%?

4. What are three types of events that your system tracks?

5. What is a service?

6. How would you turn off a service?

SESSION 10.3

In this session, you'll learn how to create and manage user accounts and user groups on your computer. You'll examine the different kinds of user groups you can establish on your system and how those groups relate to system security. You'll learn how to control access to your system using security policies. Finally, you'll lock your computer to prevent unauthorized access.

Understanding Users, User Groups, and Accounts on Your Computer

In Tutorial 9, you learned about users and user groups as they pertain to a computer network. Recall that a **user group** is a group of users who share the same rights and privileges on a computer or network. These privileges could include the ability to install and remove programs, perform system backups, or change hardware settings. There are two types of user groups: global and local. A **global** or **domain group** is a user group that is part of a network and is managed by a network administrator. The network administrator determines which rights and privileges a domain group has when using the network computers. Domain groups are the user groups you studied in Tutorial 9.

In this session, you will learn about local user groups. A **local group** is a user group created for a specific computer. Most of the time, this computer is a workstation attached to a network, but it could also be a stand-alone computer that is not attached to a network. The administrator of that individual computer determines which rights and privileges the local group has when working with the computer. Administrators often set up user groups to organize users, such as to organize different types of employees at a company. Note that if you use Windows XP Home Edition, all users on a single computer are the same—they are all administrators, so they all have unlimited privileges. You can read the information in this session about types of user groups, but it does not apply to Windows XP Home Edition computers.

While the administrator can determine whether a user belongs to a group, every user on a network or stand-alone computer must have an **account**, a collection of information about the user, including all the information that defines the user to Windows XP or to the network, such as a user name and password. When you log on to Windows XP, for example, and enter a user name and password, Windows checks to see which account has that user name and password and then opens the desktop associated with the account.

Windows XP Professional Edition provides three types of user accounts for a workgroup or stand-alone computer—Administrator, Limited, and Guest. Figure 10-23 describes these types of user accounts.

Figure 10-23	WINDOWS XP USER ACCOUNT TYPES

ACCOUNT TYPE	DESCRIPTION
Administrators	Administrators have full control over all computer operations and system settings.
Limited	Limited users can perform most common tasks, such as running programs, saving files, and shutting down the system. Limited users cannot install software or hardware or change account names or types.
Guests	Guests do not have a user account or password on the computer but can log on to use programs and save files. Guests cannot install software or hardware, change accounts, or access system settings.

When you install Windows XP Professional Edition, you first log on to the computer as the administrator and then create a user account for yourself and for each person who will use the computer; you will do that in the next section. Users of workgroup and stand-alone computers have rights and permissions associated with their accounts. For example, only users with an Administrator account type can install new hardware. On the other hand, users of network domain computers have rights and permissions associated with their user group. The network administrator assigns each account to a user group, which determines the tasks that user can perform on the system. In this way, a user group on a network computer is similar to a user account on a stand-alone computer. For example, members of the Administrator group can set up or change any system setting. You will learn more about user groups later in this session.

To complete the steps in this session, you need to be logged on to your computer as an administrator. If you are in a lab and the computer you are using is part of your school's network, an account with limited permissions has been set up for you. Most likely, your account is not part of the Administrator group. To perform the steps in this tutorial, your instructor or technical support person must ensure that you can log on to the computer as an administrator. If you cannot log on as an administrator, read through the following sections for reference.

Adding a New User

If you log on to a computer as an administrator, you can set up and manage accounts for everyone who uses the computer. For example, on your home computer, you could add an account for each member of your family. Then each user could have a different desktop design, screen saver, and other personalized settings and preferences, such as their own Favorite lists and protected access to files and folders.

When you add a new user to a workgroup or stand-alone computer, you add a new user account. Users can perform tasks as defined by their account type. A user with an Administrator account has a role on that computer similar to the role a network administrator has on a network. An administrator can control the rights and privileges of the other users of the computer and can control various computer settings, including the security settings for the computer. Windows XP must have at least one administrator, who is usually the computer's owner, and can have more. For example, if you are using Windows XP Professional on a home computer, you and your spouse could have separate Administrator accounts, meaning that both of you could perform administrative tasks such as changing system settings and installing hardware.

Administrators can also assign other users to a Limited account. Users with a Limited account can use installed programs, save documents, and change their passwords, but they can't perform administrative tasks such as creating user accounts, adding or removing hardware, and changing system files. Using a Limited account works best in a business setting, where someone responsible for the computer serves as the administrator and others who only use its resources have a Limited account.

The Guest account is intended for someone who has no user account on the computer but wants to log on quickly to check e-mail or browse the Internet, for example. The administrator can choose whether to use the Guest account by turning it on or off. (It is turned off by default.)

Copy City Copiers has a new employee, Joyce Tallent, who will be working as an assistant in the payroll department. She will share a computer with Wai Chen and needs to have her own account on the computer. Bruce wants you to set up an account for her. She should have the same permissions as Wai, which are to run programs and create files but not modify the settings of the computer. Bruce wants you to assign her to the Limited group, which will give her these limited privileges. Note that the following steps apply to a workgroup or stand-alone computer, not one on a domain network.

REFERENCE WINDOW   **RW**

Adding a New User
- Log on to the computer as an administrator.
- Open the Control Panel in Classic View, and then double-click the User Accounts icon.
- In the User Accounts window, click the Create a new account link.
- Enter a name for the new user in the Type a name for the new account text box.
- Click the Next button and then specify a user group for the new user.
- Click the Create Account button.

To create a new user:

1. Log on to your computer as an administrator.

    TROUBLE? If you are working on a stand-alone computer that is not attached to a network, and you are the sole user of the computer, then you are automatically logged on as the Administrator. If you don't know how to log on with administrative privileges, talk to your instructor. If you can't get administrative privileges, review the material in this session without performing the steps.

2. Click the **Start** button *start* , and then click **Control Panel**.

3. If necessary, switch to Classic View by clicking the **Switch to Classic View** link in the left pane of the Control Panel window.

4. Double-click the **User Accounts** icon 👥.

    The User Accounts window opens, listing the user accounts set up on the computer. See Figure 10-24.

| Figure 10-24 | THE USER ACCOUNTS WINDOW |

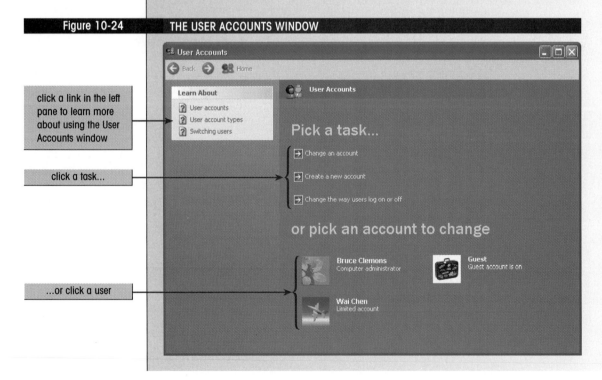

5. Click the **Create a new account** link.

6. Type **Joyce Tallent** in the Type a name for the new account text box. See Figure 10-25.

Figure 10-25	SPECIFYING A NAME FOR A NEW USER

type the user name here

7. Click the **Next** button.

Next, you specify a user group for the new user. You'll place Joyce Tallent in the Limited group.

8. Click the **Limited** option button. See Figure 10-26.

Figure 10-26	SPECIFYING THE ACCOUNT TYPE FOR A NEW USER

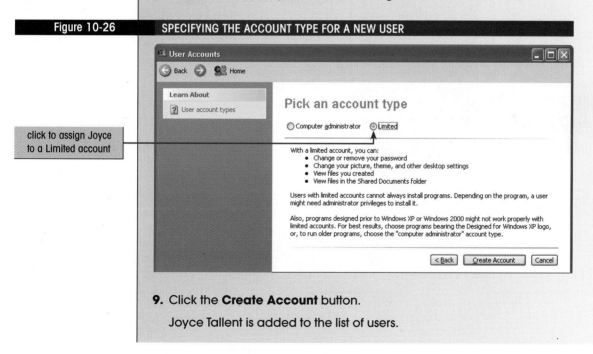

click to assign Joyce to a Limited account

9. Click the **Create Account** button.

Joyce Tallent is added to the list of users.

Once you add a user, you can set properties for the account. In the next section, you'll set up a password for Joyce.

Changing a User Account

After you add a user, you can change the basic properties of the account. You use the User Accounts window to change the name, picture, or account type, set a password for the user, or delete the account.

Bruce asks you to set a password for Joyce. When she logs on, she must identify herself to the system by using this password. You'll use the User Accounts window to set a password for Joyce, which you'll give to her on her first day on the job.

To change the basic properties of an account:

1. In the User Accounts window, click **Change an account**.

Now the User Accounts window lists all the accounts on this computer so you can select the one you want to change.

2. Click **Joyce Tallent**.

The User Accounts window lists the account properties you can change, including setting a password. See Figure 10-27.

Figure 10-27	CHANGING BASIC USER ACCOUNT PROPERTIES

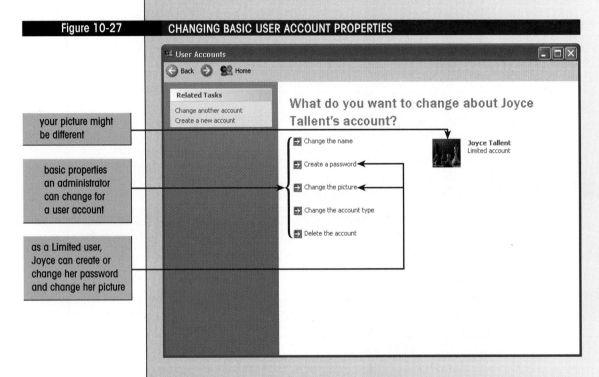

your picture might be different

basic properties an administrator can change for a user account

as a Limited user, Joyce can create or change her password and change her picture

3. Click **Create a password**. Now you can use the User Accounts window shown in Figure 10-28 to enter and verify a password. You can also include a password hint, which is a word or phrase to help Joyce remember her password.

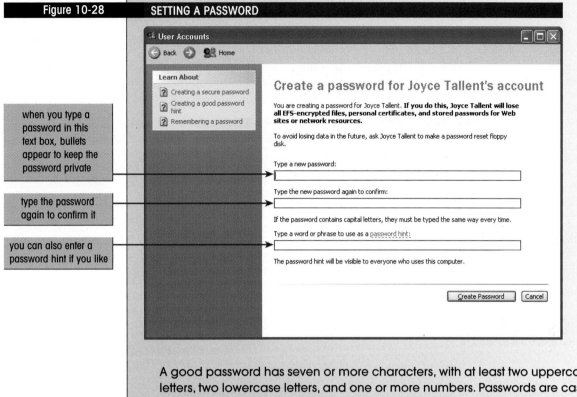

Figure 10-28 SETTING A PASSWORD

when you type a password in this text box, bullets appear to keep the password private

type the password again to confirm it

you can also enter a password hint if you like

A good password has seven or more characters, with at least two uppercase letters, two lowercase letters, and one or more numbers. Passwords are case sensitive, so ButterFly09 is not the same as butterFly09.

4. In the Type a new password text box, type **ButterFly09**. Notice as you type the password, the characters appear as bullets. This is to protect your password from people passing by your computer.

5. Press the **Tab** key and then type **ButterFly09** again to confirm the password.

You don't need to enter a password hint. Because Joyce must use her password every day when she logs on, she is not likely to forget her password. Also, the hint would appear on the Welcome window, which Bruce feels is a security risk.

6. Click the **Create Password** button. Note that the User Accounts window now indicates Joyce's account is password protected.

7. Close the User Accounts window, and return to the Control Panel.

As a member of the Limited group, Joyce can change or remove the password later and select a different picture to associate with her account. However, she cannot change her account name or account type, nor can she delete her account. Only an administrator can make these kinds of changes to her account.

In addition to setting basic properties for an account, an administrator can also set advanced properties. For example, to enhance security, you can prevent users from changing their own passwords. To set advanced user properties, you work in the Computer Management window, not the User Accounts window.

Using the Computer Management Window

Many of the tools you can use to administer your system and manage the computer's hardware and software are collected in the **Computer Management** window. If you are using

Windows XP Professional, you can manage user accounts and user groups, monitor your system's performance, view the list of devices on your system, and manage your computer's hard disk(s) from a single window. You'll use the Computer Management window to work with advanced user properties and perform other administrative tasks. Note that if you are working with Windows XP Home Edition, you cannot use the Computer Management window to perform these tasks. Read through the following sections to learn the concepts.

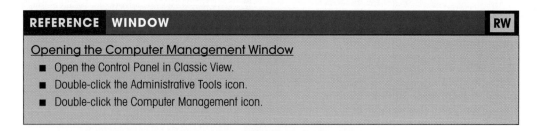

To work with advanced user properties, start by opening the Computer Management window.

To open the Computer Management tool:

1. In the Control Panel window, double-click the **Administrative Tools** icon. 🖳. The Administrative Tools window opens. This is the same window you used earlier in this tutorial to manage the performance, events, and services on your computer.

   TROUBLE? If you receive an error message when you attempt to open the Administrative Tools window, you might not be logged on to an account that has administrative privileges. See your instructor or technical support person for assistance.

2. Double-click the **Computer Management** shortcut 🖳. The Computer Management window opens. See Figure 10-29.

Figure 10-29	THE COMPUTER MANAGEMENT WINDOW

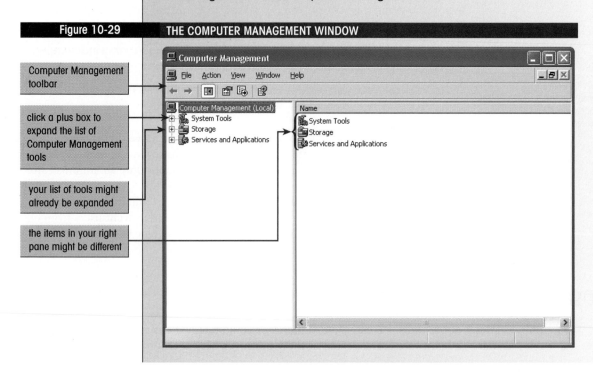

Computer Management toolbar

click a plus box to expand the list of Computer Management tools

your list of tools might already be expanded

the items in your right pane might be different

3. In the left pane of the Computer Management window, click the **plus box** ⊞ next to **System Tools**, if necessary, to expand the list.

Figure 10-30 describes the tools included in the Computer Management window.

Figure 10-30	ITEMS IN THE COMPUTER MANAGEMENT WINDOW	
COMPUTER MANAGEMENT	**DESCRIPTION**	
System Tools	Contains the Event Viewer, Shared Folders, Local Users and Groups (for Windows XP Professional users only), Performance Logs and Alerts, and Device Manager tools that you can use to manage system events and performance	
Storage	Displays storage devices installed on the computer that you are managing. You can use the Revmovable Storage, Disk Defragmentor, and Disk Management tools to manage storage devices	
Services and Applications	Contains tools to help you manage services (small programs that help Windows XP perform system tasks) and applications on your computer	
Computer Management toolbar	Contains buttons that let you change the view of the window, work with the properties of Computer Management tools, and access online Help	

Now you can access the Users folder in the Computer Management window, which contains the advanced settings for the user accounts.

Setting Advanced User Properties

In addition to basic user properties, such as name and password, you can select more advanced settings to manage user accounts. For example, on some systems users are required to change their passwords every few months to improve security. To override this setting, you can set a particular user's password so that it never expires.

You decide to open the Users folder to view the list of properties for Joyce Tallent's account. The Users folder is included as part of the Local Users and Groups tool, which is a system tool.

To access a list of advanced properties:

1. Click the **plus box** ⊞ next to Local Users and Groups.

2. Click the **Users** folder.

   A list of all the users on your computer appears in the right pane of the Computer Management window.

3. Right-click **Joyce Tallent** in the list of users, and then click **Properties** on the shortcut menu.

   The Properties dialog box opens, as shown in Figure 10-31. You can select or deselect several check boxes related to the properties that you want to set for this user. Some options might not be available because of security settings on your computer.

Figure 10-31   **USER PROPERTIES**

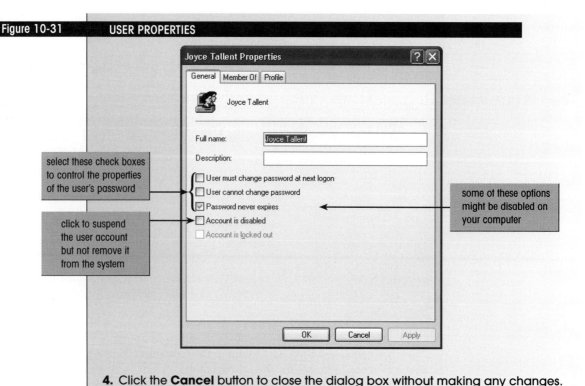

select these check boxes
to control the properties
of the user's password

click to suspend
the user account
but not remove it
from the system

some of these options
might be disabled on
your computer

4. Click the **Cancel** button to close the dialog box without making any changes.

Note that in addition to configuring an account, you can also turn off, or disable, one. A disabled user account remains on the system but is no longer usable. Often when an employee leaves a company, the employee's account is disabled rather than deleted, allowing the administrator to preserve all of the settings for the next user of the account. For example, if Joyce goes on maternity leave, the administrator could preserve the settings for the employee who temporarily performs her job.

Creating a User Group

Recall that a user group is simply a group of users who share the same rights and permissions on a system. Windows XP Professional Edition provides several standard user groups that reflect how most people use their computers. For example, Windows XP includes a Power Users group for users who can create user accounts but cannot perform most other administrative tasks.

Administrators often set up additional user groups to organize user accounts, especially on a network with many users. On a workgroup or stand-alone computer, you can also create user groups to organize accounts. For example, you could create a user group for each type of employee who uses a particular computer. This would help you more specifically define the rights and permissions of each user.

For example, recall that Joyce Tallent is a payroll assistant and will share a computer with Wai Chen, who generates the monthly payroll and backs up the payroll files. Their manager also uses the computer once a month to verify and approve the payroll. All three have Limited user accounts, meaning they can use programs and save documents on that computer but not perform administrative tasks. However, Bruce wants to differentiate the three users further. The rights and permissions of a Limited account are appropriate for Joyce, except that Bruce does not want Joyce to be able to shut down the computer. Doing so could cause problems on the network. Wai needs permission to back up files and folders, usually an administrative task. The manager also needs to access, modify, and save Wai's files, rights a Limited account usually does not have. To customize the rights and permissions of an account on a workgroup or stand-alone computer, you can assign the account to a user group and then specify which rights and permissions that user group has.

To create user groups, you open the Groups folder in the Computer Management window.

REFERENCE WINDOW | **RW**

Creating a User Group
- Log on to the computer as an administrator.
- Open the Control Panel in Classic View, and then double-click the Administrative Tools icon.
- Double-click the Computer Management icon.
- In the Computer Management window, click the Groups folder, click Action on the menu bar, and then click New Group.
- In the New Group dialog box, enter the group name and description.
- Click the Add button and then add users to the group.
- Click the OK button.

Bruce has asked you to create a user group for the office staff. You can then add Joyce Tallent to that group.

To create a user group:

1. In the left pane of the Computer Management window, click the **Groups** folder.

2. Click **Action** on the menu bar, and then click **New Group**. The New Group dialog box opens.

3. Type **Office Staff** in the Group name text box, and then type **Office staff at Copy City Copiers** in the Description text box.

4. Click the **Add** button to select the users who will be part of the Office Staff user group.

   TROUBLE? If Joyce Tallent does not immediately appear in the list of users, click the Advanced button, click the Find Now button, click Joyce Tallent, then click OK twice.

5. Click **Joyce Tallent** in the list of users, and then click the **Add** button to add Joyce to the users in the Office Staff group.

6. Click the **OK** button.

   Figure 10-32 shows the completed New Group dialog box.

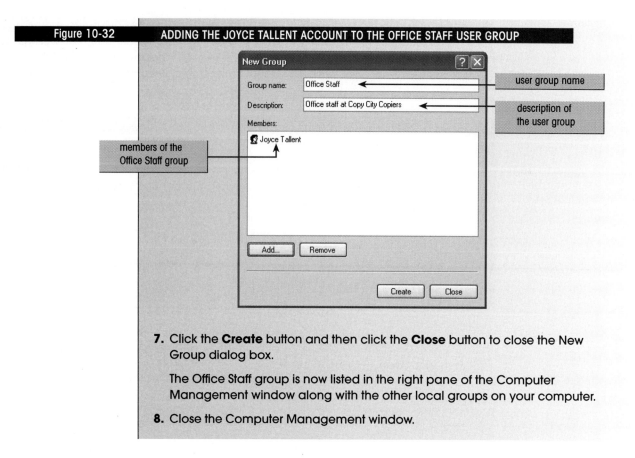

Figure 10-32   ADDING THE JOYCE TALLENT ACCOUNT TO THE OFFICE STAFF USER GROUP

7. Click the **Create** button and then click the **Close** button to close the New Group dialog box.

The Office Staff group is now listed in the right pane of the Computer Management window along with the other local groups on your computer.

8. Close the Computer Management window.

Now Joyce is part of the Office Staff group. Next, you will learn how to customize the rights of a user group.

Managing Local Security Policies

Windows XP considers the rights and permissions of user groups to be security **policies**, rules an administrator sets to control who can access parts of a system or perform certain tasks. For example, a network administrator for a business could set a policy to limit the user groups that can access a shared network folder containing financial documents. An administrator for a workgroup or stand-alone computer could allow members of a Computer Technicians group to install hardware device drivers.

To customize the rights and permissions of user groups, you work with the **Local Security Policy** tool, another Windows XP administrative tool included in the Administrative Tools window. Only Windows XP Professional users logged on as administrators can use the Local Security Policy tool. You assign privileges to users and user groups by considering what tasks they perform on the computer and what computer resources they need. For example, if part of the billing manager's job is to back up and restore billing information, she needs to belong to a user group that can perform those tasks.

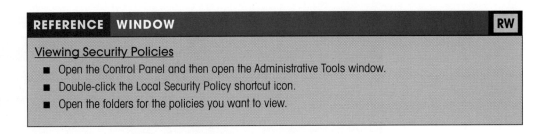

REFERENCE WINDOW RW

<u>Viewing Security Policies</u>

■ Open the Control Panel and then open the Administrative Tools window.
■ Double-click the Local Security Policy shortcut icon.
■ Open the folders for the policies you want to view.

Now you can open the Local Security policy tool. Bruce wants you to examine this window but not set any security policies right now because changing policies can make a computer vulnerable to security threats.

To open the Local Security Policy tool:

1. In the Administrative Tools window, double-click the **Local Security Policy** shortcut icon 🔾.

The Local Security Settings window opens, as shown in Figure 10-33.

Figure 10-33	LOCAL SECURITY SETTINGS WINDOW

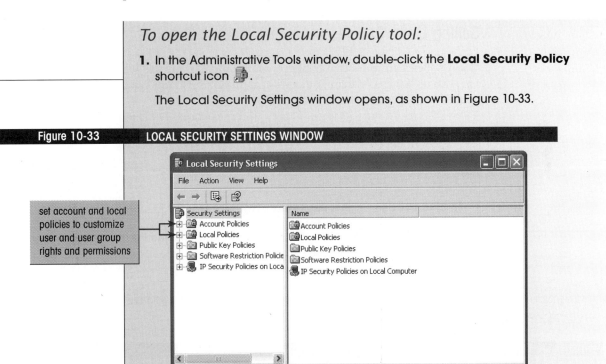

set account and local policies to customize user and user group rights and permissions

In this window, the various policies on your computer are organized into five folders: Account, Local, Public Key, Software Restriction, and IP Security. Figure 10-34 describes each folder.

Figure 10-34	SECURITY POLICIES

SECURITY SETTING OPTIONS	DESCRIPTION
Account Policies	Account policies apply to network and stand-alone computers and affect the rights and permissions of a particular account. Account policies include password rules, such as enforcement and life time settings, and account lockout rules, such as the circumstances and length of time that an account will be locked out of the system.
Local Polices	Local policies apply to the local computer on a network or to a stand-alone computer and determine which users and users groups have certain rights and permissions on the computer. You can also set audit policies to determine whether to log security events in the Event Viewer's Security log.

Figure 10-34   **SECURITY POLICIES (CONTINUED)**

SECURITY SETTING OPTIONS	DESCRIPTION
Public Key Policies	Public key policies apply only on a network domain and determine data encryption policies.
Software Restriction Policies	Software restriction policies apply only on a network domain and identify the software users can run.
IP Security Policies	IP security policies apply on a network domain connected to the Internet, and protect computers from network attacks.

Bruce suggests that you take a closer look at the Local Policies and Account folders. You use these folders to set policies that affect computer users.

Setting Local Policies

Local policies are rules that apply to your computer and are set by an administrator on a network or stand-alone computer with multiple users. You can make some of the policies accessible to specific users or user groups.

To view local policy settings:

1. In the left pane of the Local Security Settings window, click the **plus box** ⊞ next to the Local Policies folder.

2. Click the **User Rights Assignment** folder icon 📷.

   TROUBLE? If you can't see the complete names of the items in the left pane of the Local Security Settings window, drag the vertical bar dividing the two panes to the right to widen the left pane.

   A list of policies that can be assigned to specific users or user groups appears in the right pane. See Figure 10-35.

Figure 10-35   **LOCAL SECURITY SETTINGS WINDOW LISTING POLICIES**

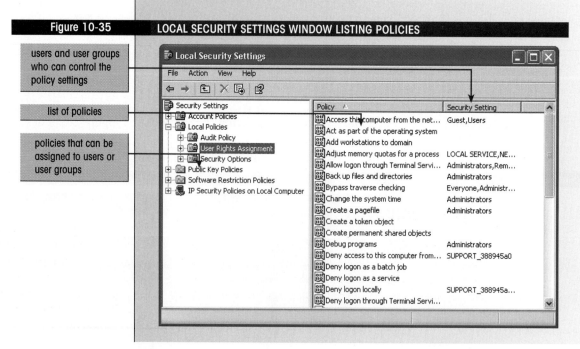

users and user groups who can control the policy settings

list of policies

policies that can be assigned to users or user groups

Many of the policies in this list are extremely technical in nature. One relatively simple policy is the ability to back up files. Bruce suggests that you open this policy to see who has access to it.

To open a policy:

1. Scroll to and double-click **Back up files and directories** in the Policy list.

   The Properties dialog box shows that only members of the Administrators group can back up files. (Your list of user groups might differ, depending on your network settings.) See Figure 10-36.

Figure 10-36	CONTROLLING THE BACKUP POLICY

user groups that can perform a backup

click to add other users or groups to the list

Bruce says that when you are ready to assign Wai Chen the right to back up files, you can create a group for users who can back up computers, assign Wai to the group, and then click the Add User or Group button on this dialog box to add that group to the list.

2. Click the **Cancel** button to close the dialog box without saving any inadvertent changes.

Account policies also affect users on a network or stand-alone computer. You'll examine those next.

Account Policies

The other types of policies that affect users are the **account policies**. These are policies that affect all of the accounts on a computer. There are two types of account policies: password policies and account lockout policies. The **password policies** determine how you want to manage passwords on your computer. For example, you can specify the minimum number of characters a password must have before it is accepted by the system or how long a password can stay on your system before it expires and must be replaced by a new password.

Lockout policies specify the conditions under which Windows XP Professional will lock out a user account. Locking out an account prevents users from accessing the account until the system administrator unlocks it. This is an added security feature that helps prevent an outsider from hacking into the system. One policy might lock out the account if someone tries to access it using a wrong password 10 times in a row (indicating that an unauthorized user might be trying to "fish around" for the correct password).

Bruce suggests that you review these policies on your computer.

To view the password policies:

1. In the left pane of the Local Security Settings window, click the **plus box** ⊞ next to the Account Policies folder icon.

2. Click the **Password Policy** folder icon 📷. The list of password policies appears in the right pane. You can examine the properties of the Maximum password age policy, which determines how long an account can use a password before it expires.

3. Double-click the **Maximum password age** policy in the Policy list.

4. The Maximum password age Properties dialog box shown in Figure 10-37 indicates that passwords expire in 42 days on this system. (Your setting may be different.) Note that a setting of 0 means the password does not expire.

Figure 10-37	MAXIMUM AGE OF PASSWORD

the system will prompt users to create a new password after 42 days

5. Click the **Cancel** button.

Now view the account lockout policy on your computer.

6. In the left pane of the Local Security Settings window, click the **Account Lockout Policy** folder icon 📷.

7. Double-click the **Account lockout threshold** policy in the Policy list.

The dialog box shown in Figure 10-38 indicates that accounts will be locked out after 16 failed logon attempts—this discourages unauthorized users from trying to guess your user name and password. You can increase or decrease this value, if necessary.

Figure 10-38	SETTING THE ACCOUNT LOCKOUT POLICY

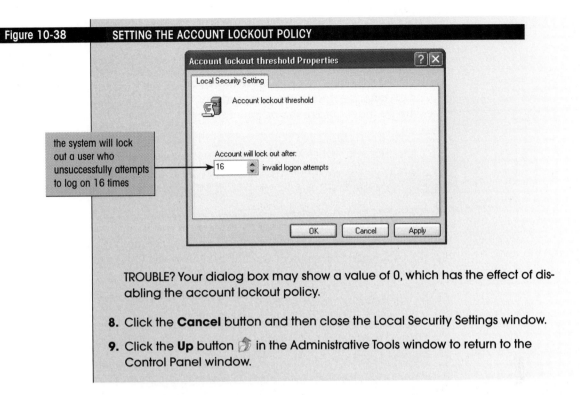

the system will lock out a user who unsuccessfully attempts to log on 16 times

TROUBLE? Your dialog box may show a value of 0, which has the effect of disabling the account lockout policy.

8. Click the **Cancel** button and then close the Local Security Settings window.

9. Click the **Up** button in the Administrative Tools window to return to the Control Panel window.

Having viewed the Local Security Settings window, you can see how you can control many of the features of the computers at Copy City Copiers. Bruce cautions you that you should not make any changes to these settings without first discussing the changes with him.

Removing **Users and User Groups**

When an employee leaves Copy City Copiers, the user account must be either disabled or removed. Recall that a disabled user account remains on the system but is no longer usable. Removing an account completely deletes it from the system. In some cases, you can save the settings and preferences associated with the account before you remove it so you can later assign them to another user. For example, if an employee leaves a company, you can save his account settings and then assign them to his replacement.

Bruce suggests that you practice removing user accounts and user groups by deleting the Joyce Tallent account you created earlier, as well as the Office Staff group.

REFERENCE   WINDOW   **RW**

Removing a User
- Log on to the computer as an administrator.
- Open the Control Panel and then open the User Accounts window.
- Select the user account you want to remove, and click Delete the account.
- To save the user's settings and other preferences in the preferences file, click the Keep Files button. To delete the preferences file, click the Delete Files button.
- To confirm you want to delete the account, click the Delete Account button.

To remove a user account:

1. In the Control Panel, double-click the **User Accounts** icon.

2. In the User Accounts window, click **Joyce Tallent** in the list of user names, and then click the **Delete the account** link. Windows asks if you also want to delete the file that contains the account settings for Joyce.

3. Click the **Delete Files** button, and then click the **Delete Account** button to confirm that you want to delete Joyce's account from your computer.

4. Close the User Accounts window.

Note that you could also use the Computer Management window to delete users. You follow similar steps to those you use to delete a user group, which you'll do next when you use the Computer Management window to remove the Office Staff user group.

To remove a user group:

1. In the Control Panel, double-click the **Administrative Tools** icon, and then double-click the **Computer Management** icon in the Administrative Tools window.

2. Click the **plus box** next to Local Users and Groups, if necessary, to expand the list in the left pane, and then click the **Groups** folder.

3. In the right pane, click **Office Staff** in the list of user groups, click the **Delete** button on the Computer Management toolbar, and then click the **Yes** button to confirm you want to delete this user group.

4. Close the Computer Management window and the Administrative Tools window.

Bruce is finished showing you how to use the Computer Management and Local Security Policies administrative tools to manage users, groups, and accounts. You are ready to perform all three parts of your job involving managing Windows XP.

Session 10.3 QUICK CHECK

1. What are two types of user accounts you can set up in Windows XP Professional Edition?

2. Give an example of an advanced user property.

3. What is a user group?

4. Why might you create a user group on a workgroup or stand-alone computer?

5. What is a policy?

6. How would you set up your computer to help lock out hackers?

REVIEW ASSIGNMENTS

1. **Performing a Backup** You would like to back up some of the Copy City Copier files on your hard disk to your backup disk. You'll need to create a folder on your hard disk, create some files in the folder, and then back them up.
   a. Open Windows Explorer and create a folder named CCC on your hard disk. Create one new Bitmap Image file named CCCLogo.bmp and two new Text Document files named CopyList.txt and EmpList.txt. Store them in the CCC folder. You don't need to enter any data in these files.
   b. Place your backup disk in the appropriate drive. Start the Backup and Restore Wizard, and specify that you want to back up only the CCC folder and its files.
   c. Select your backup disk as the backup device. Name the backup **Test Backup**.
   d. Delete the CCC folder from your hard disk. Give your backup disk to your instructor.

2. **Monitoring Hardware Interrupts** Bruce has asked you to create a baseline report on the number of hardware interrupts on your computer. The more hardware you have on your system, the more times per second the processor will be interrupted to deal with a hardware request.

   Explore
   a. Open the Performance Monitor and track the total number of hardware interrupts per second experienced by the Processor performance object. Print an image of the screen showing the real-time results from the performance graph. (To print images of the screen, press the PrintScreen key, start WordPad, click the Paste button, print the document, and then close WordPad without saving the file.)
   b. Create a log file containing the interrupts per second, sampling the data every five seconds. Sample the data for about a minute. Save the log to a file named **Interrupt.blg** on your floppy disk.

   Explore
   c. Write a short description of the interrupts/second value. What does it signify and how is it calculated?

3. **Printing an Event from the System Log** One of the computers at Copy City Copiers has been crashing a lot lately. Bruce has asked you to examine the problem. He wants you to work on the computer and print some of the entries from the event log. He wants you to pay close attention to any warning messages that have been generated by either the system or applications on the system.
   a. Open the log for system events on your computer.
   b. Open the latest warning event in the log. If there are no warning events listed, open the latest event of any kind in the list.
   c. Copy the description of the event from the event properties dialog box (you can use the Copy button), and paste the description into a Notepad file. Print the Notepad file.
   d. Repeat these steps for items in the log of application events.

4. *Explore* **Working with the Plug and Play Service** One of the computers at Copy City Copiers has just had a new video card installed. Although the card is a plug-and-play device, Windows XP did not automatically recognize the new card. Bruce wants you to track down the problem. The card may be defective, but he also wonders whether the Plug and Play service on that computer is working. Bruce asks you to examine this.
   a. Open the Services window on your computer.
   b. Open the properties for the Plug and Play service. Does the service start automatically, or must it be started manually? How does the system recover if the Plug and Play service fails?
   c. Print an image of the screen showing the properties of the Plug and Play service, including images of the General dialog sheet and the Recovery dialog sheet. (See Review Assignment 2a.)

5. **Creating a New User** Bruce has a new user account for you to create. The user's name is David Robbins, and his username will be DRobbins. He works in the copier mainte-nance department and will have a Limited account. His password should never expire.
   a. Create an account for this user on your computer.

b. Use the Computer Management window to open the advanced properties for DRobbins, and set his password never to expire. Print a screen image of the appropriate dialog box. (See Review Assignment 2a.)

c. Remove DRobbins from your system when you're finished.

6. **Creating a New User Group** Bruce wants you to create a new user group for employees in the maintenance department. The name of this user group should be "Maintenance Department."

a. Use the Computer Management window to create the Maintenance Department user group on your system. Add your own user account to the group.

b. Print an image of the screen, displaying the properties of the Maintenance Department group. (See Review Assignment 2a.)

c. Delete the Maintenance Department group from your system when you're finished.

7. **Changing a Password Policy** Some of the employees at Copy City Copiers have been complaining that it seems as if they constantly have to change their passwords. Management has decided to change the expiration time for passwords from 42 days to 66 days. In exchange for relaxing this requirement, users will be required to have at least eight characters in their passwords. Accounts with longer passwords are more difficult for hackers to break into. Bruce asks you to change the password policy on your computer to reflect this decision.

a. Open the Local Security Policy window on your computer. Note the current password policies in place on your system.

b. Change the expiration date of passwords to 66 days.

Explore

c. Change the length of password characters to eight characters.

d. Print an image of the screen displaying the changed password policies. (See Review Assignment 2a.)

e. Restore the policies to the original values.

PROJECTS

1. If you have your own computer and it has a Zip drive or writeable CD drive, you can do this project. Otherwise, just read this assignment so you can see how you would back up an entire system. Backing up your full system is an important part of a comprehensive backup strategy, but it can take an hour or more, depending on the speed of your backup drive and the size of your hard disk or disks.

a. Start the Backup or Restore Wizard.

b. Choose the All information on this computer option button.

c. When you choose the backup device, make sure you select the backup device on your computer, not a file on a 3½-inch disk.

d. Name the backup file **My Computer Backup**.

e. Follow the prompts that appear on the screen. Be prepared to wait an hour or more for the backup to finish. Print an image of the Backup summary dialog box before you close Backup, and then give this printout to your instructor.

2. You work at Hal's Food Warehouse in inventory management. You are responsible for backing up the computer system. You performed a full backup on Friday, and then on Monday you worked with a database file named Orders. You performed an incremental backup on Monday evening. On Tuesday you worked with the Orders file again, and on Tuesday evening you performed an incremental backup. When you attempt to open the Orders file Wednesday morning, you receive an error message that says the file cannot be found. How would you restore the file?

3. If you have your own computer, do you use a disk maintenance strategy? If not, now's your chance to implement one. Ask yourself the following questions, and then write a

disk maintenance strategy and schedule:

   a. How often do I install different software on my computer?

   b. How often do I work with important files, and how much are they worth to me?

   c. What would I lose if the hard disk drive failed?

4. Research the different types of backup media available, such as CD writeable drives and Zip drives. You can use the Internet or computing trade magazines as sources. Make a chart with four columns: backup medium name (such as CD drive), description of the backup medium (describe writeable CDs), brand names, and price. (Include both the price of the drive and the medium the drive uses, if applicable.) Then write a paragraph below the chart describing which device you would purchase for your own computer and why.

Explore ▷ 5. You can use the Computer Management tool to print summary information about your computer. Open the Computer Management window, and then open the System Summary folder (found under the System Information icon). Print the summary information.

6. Examine your own user account on your computer, and answer the following questions. Print the appropriate screen proving the answers you give.

   a. What is your user name?

   b. Do you belong to a user group? Which one?

   c. Can you change your password?

Explore ▷ 7. Examine the security policies on your computer, and answer the following questions. Again, print the appropriate screen to prove your answers.

   a. What is the maximum age of passwords? What is the minimum password length?

   b. Are accounts locked out after a certain number of invalid logons? If so, how many invalid logons are allowed?

   c. Which users or user groups have the right to increase disk quotas?

   d. Can users install printer drivers on the computer?

   e. How many days before the password expires will the system start prompting users to change their password?

LAB ASSIGNMENTS

Data Backup

Data Backup The Data Backup Lab gives you an opportunity to make tape backups on a simulated computer system. Periodically, the hard disk on the simulated computer will fail, which gives you a chance to assess the convenience and efficiency of different backup procedures. See the Read This Before You Begin page for instructions on installing and starting the lab.

1. Click the Steps button to learn how to use the simulation. As you work through the steps, answer all of the Quick Check questions that appear. After you complete the steps, you will see a Summary Report of your Quick Check answers. Follow the directions on the screen to print this report.

2. Click the Explore button. Create a full backup every Friday using only Tape 1. At some point in the simulation, an event will cause data loss on the simulated computer system. Use the simulation to restore as much data as you can. After you restore the data, print the Backup Audit Report.

3. In Explore, create a full backup every Friday on Tape 1 and a differential backup every Wednesday on Tape 2. At some point in the simulation, an event will cause data loss on the simulated computer system. Use the simulation to restore as much data as you can. Print the Backup Audit Report.

4. In Explore, create a full backup on Tape 1 every Monday. Make incremental backups on Tapes 2, 3, 4, and 5 each day for the rest of the week. Continue this cycle, reusing the same tapes each week. At some point in the simulation, an event will cause data loss on the simulated computer system. Use the simulation to restore as much data as you can. Print the Backup Audit Report.

5. Photocopy a calendar for next month. On the calendar, indicate your best plan for backing up data. In Explore, implement your plan. Print the Backup Audit Report. Write a paragraph or two discussing the effectiveness of your plan.

QUICK CHECK ANSWERS

Session 10.1

1. Copying a disk duplicates the disk contents, whereas backing up a disk compresses the files on the disk into a single, smaller file.
2. A backup job contains the list of files and folders you are backing up and the settings you are using; the backup itself is the compressed file that contains the data you backed up.
3. A partial backup is a backup of files that have changed since your last backup. An incremental backup backs up the files since the last backup, regardless of whether it was full or partial. A differential backup backs up the files since the last full backup.
4. It takes less time.
5. yes

Session 10.2

1. to track the performance of various tasks on the system in order to discover the source of any problems, such as a slow computer
2. It measures the percentage of time that the processor is not idle.
3. Open the Performance shortcut in the Administrative Tools window, and then open the Performance and Log Alerts icon. Create a new Alerts log, recording the % Processor Time value, specifying that values over 95 should result in an alert message sent to the application event log.
4. application, security, and system
5. A service is a small program that is run by your computer, designed to manage one or more aspects of the computer.
6. Open the Services icon in the Administrative Tools window, open the service from the list of services, and then click the Stop button.

Session 10.3

1. Administrator and Limited
2. disabling an account and changing password settings, such as preventing a user from changing a password, preventing a password from expiring, or having the user change the password at the next logon
3. A user group is a group of users who share the same rights and permissions on a system.
4. On a workgroup or stand-alone computer, you might create user groups to organize accounts and define the rights and permissions of each user more specifically.
5. A policy is a set of rules that governs an operation on your computer.
6. Set up an account policy that will count the number of invalid logons. If a certain number of invalid logons occurs within a certain time-frame for an account, the account is locked and must be manually unlocked by the administrator.

In this tutorial you will:

- Review hardware device terminology and settings

- Use the Add Hardware Wizard

- View a list of hardware devices on your system

- Add a printer to your system

- Review the properties of a printer

- Learn to use a print queue

- Learn the principles of disks and disk maintenance

- Schedule hardware maintenance tasks with the Task Scheduler

LAB

Defragmentation and Disk Operations

WORKING WITH HARDWARE

Installing and Troubleshooting Hardware at Chan & Associates

CASE

Chan & Associates

You're a new employee at Chan & Associates, a small desktop publishing company. You work for David Markham, the company's computer systems administrator. Your job is to help David maintain the hardware and software on the company's computers. This involves installing hardware, troubleshooting hardware problems, and training the employees to use their equipment.

David has a list of assignments for you on your first day. He wants you to install a network card in one of the company's new computers to allow it to share resources with other computers on the company's network. The company has also received a new color printer that has to be installed on a different computer, and David wants you to show a new employee how to use the printer.

David also wants you to learn how to manage and maintain a computer's hard disk. He wants you to explore some of the tools that Windows XP provides to make hard disks operate more efficiently and consistently. These tools provide important protection against data loss and hardware failure.

SESSION 11.1

In this session, you'll learn how Windows XP interacts with the hardware on your computer. You will study basic principles of hardware devices and resources. You'll learn how to use the Device Manager to view the hardware devices installed on your system. You'll also learn how to use Windows XP to troubleshoot common hardware problems.

Learning About Hardware

Before you start working with the hardware devices at Chan & Associates, you decide to review the basic concepts and terminology for hardware devices. **Hardware** is any physical piece of equipment, called a **device**, that is both connected to your computer and controlled by your computer. These devices include **external** equipment such as keyboards, printers, and scanners, which remain outside the case of the computer, and **internal** equipment, such as disk drives, modems, and network adapter cards, which are placed inside the case of the computer.

External Devices and Ports

An external device is connected to your computer through a **port**, as shown in Figure 11-1. Windows XP supports three different types of ports: serial, parallel, and USB.

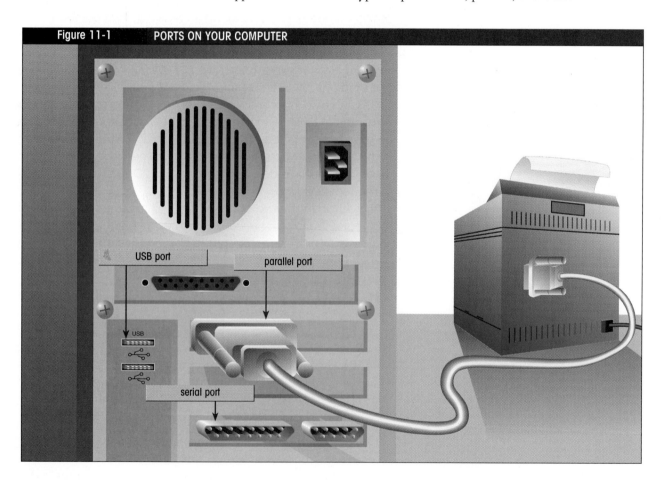

Figure 11-1   PORTS ON YOUR COMPUTER

A **serial port** is one of the older port types, usually used for a mouse, although it can be used for some printers. A computer can have up to four different serial ports, although most computers have only two. They are labeled COM1, COM2, COM3, and COM4. (COM stands for "communications.") Serial ports transfer data one bit at a time. This is in contrast to a **parallel port**, which transmits data eight bits at a time. Most computers have only one parallel port, which is usually reserved for a printer. Parallel ports are labeled LPT1, LPT2, and LPT3. (LPT stands for "line print terminal.") Usually, you use only the LPT1 port on your computer.

Because serial and parallel ports are limited in terms of speed and the number of connections they can have, a new port type called USB has been introduced in the last decade. **USB**, short for **Universal Serial Bus**, is a thin, rectangular slot that accommodates a high-speed connection to a variety of external devices, such as joysticks, scanners, keyboards, video conferencing cameras, speakers, modems, and printers. To use USB technology, your computer must have a USB port, and the device you install must have a **USB connector**, a small, rectangular plug. Windows XP supports USB devices, so that when you plug the USB connector into the USB port, Windows XP recognizes the device and allows you to use it immediately.

Using a USB port solves many problems that older technology created. For example, before the advent of USB, most printers connected to a computer through the parallel port, and most computers had only one parallel port. If you wanted to use another hardware device that also used the parallel port, such as a Zip drive, you had to cable the printer and Zip drive together and plug both into the parallel port, which usually slowed both the printer and the Zip drive. Other devices such as digital cameras and handheld computers could only connect to your PC via a serial port. Most computers had only two serial ports, and both transferred data slowly. If a device required a faster connection to your PC, it came with its own card, a small microcircuit board that had to fit in a card slot inside the computer case. The number of card slots was also limited, and installing the cards was not an easy task—you had to shut down the computer, open the case, carefully fit the card into the slot, and then restart the computer.

Owners of computers that have a USB port no longer have these problems. Almost all computer devices now come in a USB version, and any one of these can use a USB port. You install a device by finding the USB port on your computer and then plugging the USB connector into it—you don't need to open the computer case to install a card. You can "daisy chain" up to 127 devices together, meaning that you plug one device, such as a scanner, into the USB port, and then plug a second device, such as a speaker, into the scanner, so you are no longer limited by the number of ports on your computer. Instead of daisy-chaining devices, you can also connect multiple devices to a single inexpensive **USB hub**. A hub is simply a box that contains many USB ports—you plug the hub into your computer and then plug your USB devices into the hub. USB devices communicate with your computer more efficiently—a USB port transfers data 10 times faster than a serial port. You can also connect and disconnect USB devices without shutting down or restarting your computer.

Internal Devices and Expansion Slots

Internal devices are connected to the **motherboard**, a circuit board inside your computer that contains the **microprocessor** (the "brains" of your computer), the computer memory, and other internal hardware devices. Internal devices (such as the microprocessor and your memory chips) are connected either directly to the motherboard or via a socket in the motherboard called an **expansion slot**. See Figure 11-2. You can insert devices such as network adapter cards, sound cards, or internal modems into expansion slots. Devices that you insert into expansion slots are often called **expansion cards** or **adapter cards** because they "expand" or "adapt" your computer and they look like large cards. Most computers have about six expansion slots, which allow you to install up to six expansion cards in your system at any one time.

Figure 11-2   INTERNAL DEVICES

(Labels: wires and ribbon cables, power supply, floppy disk drive, hard disk drive, expansion cards, memory, expansion slots, motherboard, microprocessor chip)

If your computer needs an expansion card, it probably uses the **PCI (Peripheral Component Interconnect)** connection standard that supports high connection speeds and is easy install and configure.

Device Resources

Windows XP assigns each device a set of system resources to help it work with the computer. Windows can assign four resources to a device: an IRQ, a DMA channel, an I/O address, and a memory range. When two devices share a particular resource, a **device conflict** can occur, rendering one or both of the devices unusable. Let's consider each of these resources.

A hardware device often needs to use the microprocessor in the computer to send or receive information. When you are trying to complete several computer tasks at once (for example, when you search for a Web page while you are printing a document and playing an audio CD), the operating system needs a way to handle these simultaneous requests. It does so by assigning each device an **IRQ (interrupt request line)** number that signals the microprocessor that the device is requesting an action. Windows XP makes 16 IRQ numbers, numbered from 0 to 15, available to hardware devices. Lower numbers have higher priority and receive attention first. One common hardware headache is to have more devices than available IRQs, resulting in an IRQ conflict. If you use USB devices, however, Windows XP only uses one set of resources for all USB devices, meaning you don't have to resolve these types of IRQ conflicts.

If the device does not need to use the microprocessor, information can then be transferred directly between the device and the system's memory. This channel for transferring data is called the **DMA (direct memory access)** channel. Most computers have four DMA channels, numbered from 0 to 3, available for your devices.

When the computer receives information from one of its devices, it needs a place to store that data in the computer's memory. It does this by reserving a specific section of the computer's memory for each device. The section of the computer's memory devoted to the different devices on a computer is called the **I/O (input/output)** address. Each device requires a different I/O address.

Finally, some devices, such as video cards, require additional computer memory for their own use (not related to communicating with the microprocessor). For example, a video card needs additional memory to manage video and graphics that are not essential to the operating system. This resource is called the **memory address** or **memory range**.

Your computer uses all four types of system resources—IRQs, DMA channels, I/O addresses, and memory addresses—to communicate between hardware and software. See Figure 11-3.

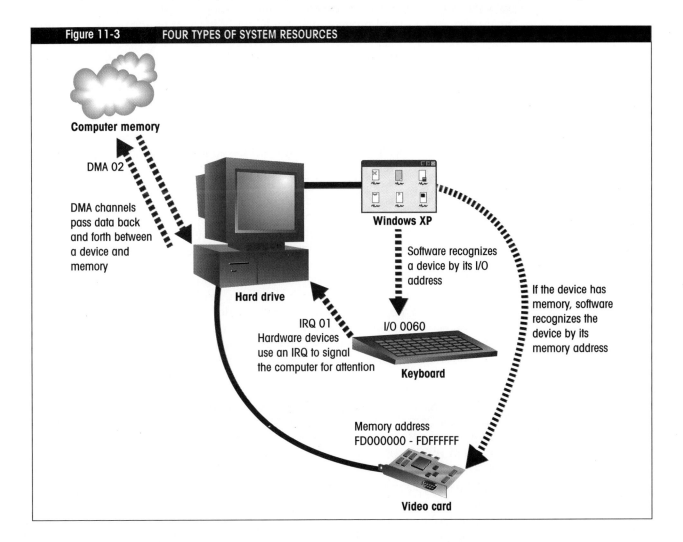

Figure 11-3   **FOUR TYPES OF SYSTEM RESOURCES**

Device Drivers

Each hardware device requires a **driver**, a software file that enables Windows XP to communicate with and control the operation of the device. In most cases, the driver comes on a disk with the hardware device, and an installation program automatically installs the driver for you. In other cases, Windows XP installs the driver when you install the operating system.

Hardware manufacturers update drivers on a regular basis to improve device performance and speed, so you should periodically check with the manufacturer to confirm that you're using the most current driver version. Most hardware manufacturers provide driver information and updated driver files on their Web sites.

Installing a Hardware Device

As far as installation is concerned, hardware devices fall into two categories: legacy and plug and play. A **legacy device** is an older piece of hardware, one whose resources you must set manually on the hardware device itself. For example, on some old adapter cards, you physically set switches to either the off or on position when you install the card. A legacy device might also have a special program that you have to run to set up the device on your computer. Windows XP supports most legacy devices, although it may take extra effort to have all of your legacy devices work together, as they are based on old specifications. You are also more likely to run into device conflicts with legacy devices.

A **plug-and-play device** uses newer technology that allows Windows XP to recognize the new device automatically the first time it is connected to the computer. Windows XP then configures the computer and the device to work together, allocating system resources and installing the best driver. In the best case, a plug-and-play device requires no intervention on your part. Occasionally you must select the appropriate device from a list of hardware to install the driver. Most USB devices are plug and play, as are most expansion cards that use a PCI connection. Because Windows XP manages the resource allocation, you are less likely to run into problems with device conflicts.

Now that you've reviewed hardware terminology, you're ready to install the new network card David gave you. The network card is plug and play, and it fits into a PCI slot inside the computer. After you turn the computer off and insert the card into the computer, you turn the computer on again. In most cases, your computer will recognize the new plug-and-play device when it loads Windows XP, and an installation wizard will start even before you get a chance to work with the operating system. In some cases, however, Windows XP won't recognize the new device, and you'll have to tell Windows XP to locate it. Let's assume that this is what occurs with the new network card: you have to run the **Add Hardware Wizard**, a series of dialog boxes in which Windows XP prompts you for information about the new device, so you can set up the device properly with Windows XP.

REFERENCE WINDOW   **RW**

Installing a New Hardware Device

- Turn off your computer.
- Plug the hardware device into your computer, either internally or externally.
- Turn on your computer.
- Follow the steps of the Add Hardware Installation Wizard.
- Open the Control Panel and then double-click the Add Hardware icon in Classic View.
- Click the Next button and then follow the steps of the Add Hardware Installation Wizard.

Most likely, you won't actually be able to work with new hardware in your lab, but this tutorial is written so you can complete most of the steps as if you had new hardware to add. Read through any steps that you cannot complete.

To run the Add Hardware Wizard:

1. Open the Control Panel.

2. If necessary, switch to Classic View by clicking **Switch to Classic View** in the left pane of the Control Panel window.

3. Double-click the **Add Hardware** icon 🐾. The Add Hardware Wizard starts and displays the Welcome window.

4. Click the **Next** button.

   Windows XP starts searching for a new plug-and-play device. If it finds one, it indicates it found a new device. See Figure 11-4.

Figure 11-4	DETECTING A NEW HARDWARE DEVICE

if Windows XP detects a new plug-and-play device, it identifies the device for you

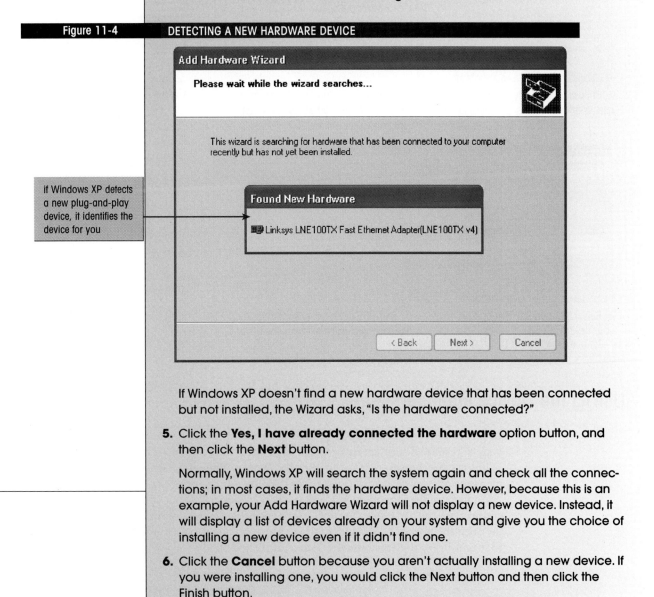

If Windows XP doesn't find a new hardware device that has been connected but not installed, the Wizard asks, "Is the hardware connected?"

5. Click the **Yes, I have already connected the hardware** option button, and then click the **Next** button.

   Normally, Windows XP will search the system again and check all the connections; in most cases, it finds the hardware device. However, because this is an example, your Add Hardware Wizard will not display a new device. Instead, it will display a list of devices already on your system and give you the choice of installing a new device even if it didn't find one.

6. Click the **Cancel** button because you aren't actually installing a new device. If you were installing one, you would click the Next button and then click the Finish button.

If you are working with a legacy device or if Windows XP doesn't locate your new device, you can still use the Add Hardware Wizard to install the device. In this case, you'll have to provide most of the information to Windows XP yourself. Figure 11-5 summarizes the steps you should follow to install a new device manually after Windows XP fails to locate it and install it for you. (Your screens may look slightly different from those shown in Figure 11-5.)

Figure 11-5   MANUALLY ADDING A NEW DEVICE TO WINDOWS XP

1. Choose to manually add a new device after Windows XP fails to locate it for you.

2. Choose the option to select the new device from a list rather than redo the search.

3. Select the device type.

4. Select the manufacturer and brand of your device.

5. Verify the device you want to install, and then click Next to install the driver files.

Using the Device Manager

In earlier versions of Windows, installing a new hardware device meant juggling all of your system resources and carefully keeping written notes about each device's settings. With Windows XP, however, you can use the **Device Manager**, a tool that makes it easier to manage your devices and the resources they use.

You've installed the network card at Chan & Associates, but you discover that you cannot connect to the company network. One possible source of trouble could be a conflict between the network card and another device on your system. You'll work with the Device Manager to try to determine the source of the problem.

REFERENCE WINDOW   **RW**

Opening the Device Manager
- Open the Control Panel.
- In Classic View, double-click the System icon. In Category View, click Performance and Maintenance and then double-click the System icon.
- Click the Hardware tab in the Systems Properties dialog box, and then click the Device Manager button.

You decide to open the Device Manager to see if there is a resource conflict.

To start the Device Manager:

1. Double-click the **System** icon in Control Panel. The System Properties dialog box opens. You use this dialog box to manage hardware information for your computer. You access the Device Manager by clicking a button on the Hardware property sheet.

2. Click the **Hardware** tab in the System Properties dialog box.

3. Click the **Device Manager** button.

   The Device Manager window opens, as shown in Figure 11-6.

Figure 11-6	LIST OF DEVICES IN DEVICE MANAGER

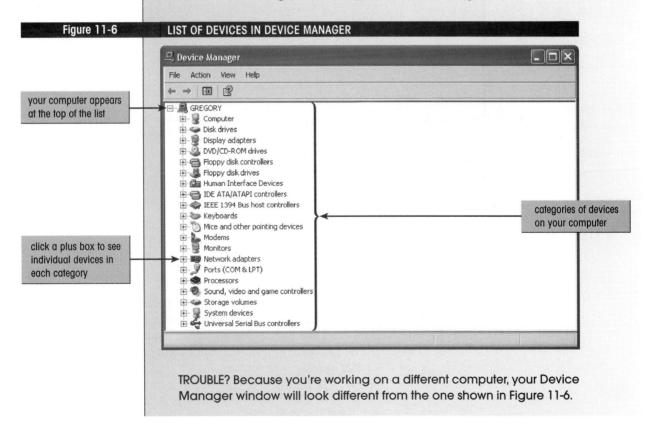

your computer appears at the top of the list

categories of devices on your computer

click a plus box to see individual devices in each category

TROUBLE? Because you're working on a different computer, your Device Manager window will look different from the one shown in Figure 11-6.

By default, the Device Manager lists all of the devices by type. You see that this computer has a CD-ROM drive, modem, mouse, and sound card, among other devices. You can also view the specific device used within these different categories. You're interested in learning about the state of the network card and whether the Device Manager indicates that the card is not working properly.

> ### To display information about a specific hardware device:
>
> **1.** Click the **plus box** ⊞ next to the Network adapters.
>
> The brand names of the network cards installed on the computer appear in the list. See Figure 11-7. (Your list will be different.)

Figure 11-7   **VIEWING SPECIFIC INFORMATION ABOUT A DEVICE ON YOUR COMPUTER**

If a device is not working properly, the Device Manager will place an ⚠ symbol on top of the device's icon. If the device has been disabled, an ✖ symbol will appear on the icon. However, the icon in Figure 11-6 shows neither of these, so there is no indication that the device is not working properly. To find out more, you have to open the Properties dialog box for the device.

Viewing the Properties of a Device

The Properties dialog box for each device on your computer contains additional information about the device, such as the resources and driver file it uses. By viewing the Properties dialog box for a device, you can learn a great deal about the status of your hardware device and continue to troubleshoot hardware problems. You'll examine the properties of the new network card to see if you can identify any problems.

To view the properties of your hardware device:

1. Click the brand name of the network card in the Device Manager window to select it.

   TROUBLE? If your Device Manager window does not list a network card, click another hardware device.

2. Click the **Properties** button 🖼 on the Device Manager toolbar.

   The Properties dialog box for the network card opens, displaying the General sheet. The General sheet shows information about the network card's brand name and manufacturer. It also displays the status of the device and indicates whether it's working properly. As shown in Figure 11-8, the Properties dialog box does not indicate a problem with the network adapter card.

| Figure 11-8 | GENERAL SHEET IN THE PROPERTIES DIALOG BOX FOR THE NETWORK ADAPTER |

device type and manufacturer

Windows XP indicates the current status of the driver

click to start the Hardware Troubleshooter

the device is enabled

If the device itself does not seem to have a problem, you should next check the drivers for the device. Hardware devices often fail to work if their drivers are out of date or if the files have been damaged.

3. Click the **Driver** tab.

   The Driver sheet, shown in Figure 11-9, displays information about the driver for the network card. From here you can uninstall the driver for the device, removing it from your system. (You would then either remove the actual device from your computer or try reinstalling the driver.) You can also update the driver if you have a more recent version of the driver file. If a new driver doesn't work with the device, you can use the Roll Back Driver button to revert to the previously installed driver.

Figure 11-9   **INFORMATION ABOUT THE CURRENT DEVICE DRIVER**

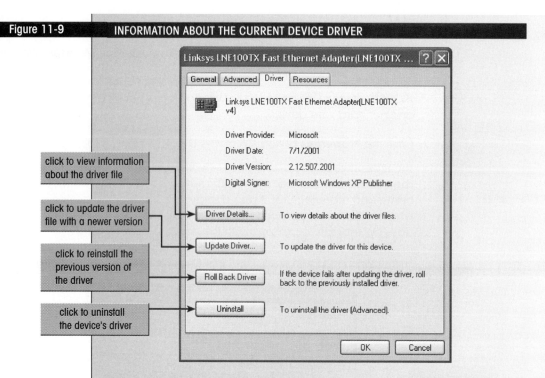

click to view information about the driver file

click to update the driver file with a newer version

click to reinstall the previous version of the driver

click to uninstall the device's driver

If you don't suspect a problem with the drivers (for example, if you have recently installed up-to-date drivers for the device), you can next check to see whether the resources your new devices uses conflict with resources for other devices. This information is provided on the Resources sheet.

4. Click the **Resources** tab.

The Resources sheet, shown in Figure 11-10, displays the current system resources used by the device and indicates whether there are any device conflicts. The network card you just installed uses IRQ 09, an I/O range of D800-D8FF, and has a memory address of FEAFF400–FEAFF7FF. None of these resources is in conflict with any other device on your system.

Figure 11-10 **RESOURCES USED BY THE DEVICE**

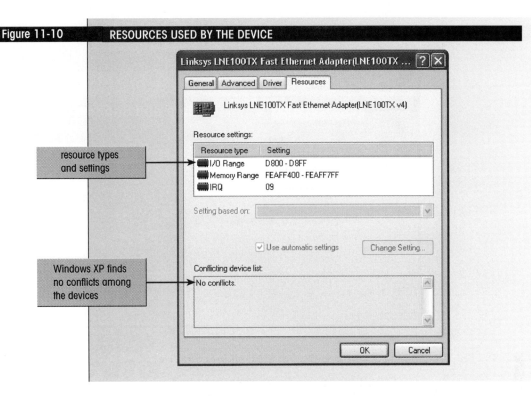

resource types and settings

Windows XP finds no conflicts among the devices

The Properties dialog box for the new network card also contains an Advanced sheet. This sheet contains advanced settings for the network card, which you should not change unless the device manufacturer instructs you to do so. Not all devices have an Advanced sheet.

Troubleshooting a Device

If you are having trouble with a hardware device—if it doesn't start, for example, or fails to work properly, you can try to locate the source of the trouble using a Windows XP Troubleshooter. A **Troubleshooter** is a sequence of dialog boxes that contain suggestions and questions about the source of your hardware trouble. By answering a series of questions, you can view tips on solving your problem.

So far, you can find no indication that the network card is working improperly, but you are still having problems connecting to the company network. This means that the problem may lie elsewhere. You decide to start the Troubleshooter for the network card.

To start the Troubleshooter:

1. Click the **General** tab in the Properties dialog box for your device.

TROUBLE? If you closed the dialog box for your device, reopen it by repeating Steps 1 and 2 in the last set of steps to view the properties of your hardware device.

2. Click the **Troubleshoot** button.

The Help and Support Center window opens, with the "I'm having a problem with my hardware device" option button selected, as shown in Figure 11-11.

Figure 11-11   STARTING THE HARDWARE TROUBLESHOOTER

3. Click the **Next** button at the bottom of the Help and Support Center window.

4. The Troubleshooter asks whether your device is on the Windows Hardware Compatibility List (HCL). Because it is, click the **Yes, my hardware is on the HCL** option button (you might have to scroll to locate this option button), and then click the **Next** button.

The Troubleshooter asks if you have recently installed a new driver. You installed a new driver when you installed the network card only a few days ago, but Windows XP might include an earlier version of the driver. The Troubleshooter provides instructions for using an earlier version of the device driver. You could follow the instructions in the Help and Support Center window, clicking the Device Manager link to open the Device Manager window. Then you could open the Properties dialog box for the hardware device, click the Driver tab, and then click the Roll Back Driver button. Leaving the Help and Support Center window open, you could try connecting to the network again and then return to the Help and Support Center window to answer the question, "Does rolling back to a previous driver solve the problem?"

5. Click the Help and Support Center window, if necessary, and then click the **Yes, this solves the problem** option button, as shown in Figure 11-12.

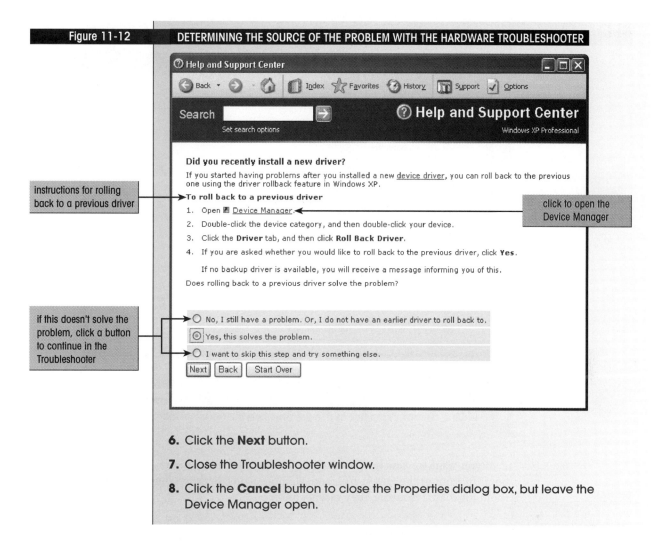

Figure 11-12 | **DETERMINING THE SOURCE OF THE PROBLEM WITH THE HARDWARE TROUBLESHOOTER**

instructions for rolling back to a previous driver

click to open the Device Manager

if this doesn't solve the problem, click a button to continue in the Troubleshooter

6. Click the **Next** button.

7. Close the Troubleshooter window.

8. Click the **Cancel** button to close the Properties dialog box, but leave the Device Manager open.

By using the Troubleshooter, you've located the source of the problem. You decide to explore other functions of the Device Manager.

Changing the Device Manager View

Sometimes you will want to change your view of the devices and resources on your system. For example, you have a limited number of IRQs on the computer. You know that the new network card you inserted uses an IRQ of 10. How many free IRQs do you have left? This information might be important if you intend to add new devices to the computer. You can find out by viewing a list of the IRQs and the devices using them.

To view your device list by resource:

1. Click **View** on the Device Manager menu bar, and then click **Resources by type**. A list of resource types appears in the Device Manager window, including DMA, IO, IRQ, and Memory.

2. Click the **plus box** ⊞ in front of the Interrupt request (IRQ) icon. See Figure 11-13.

Figure 11-13   VIEWING THE LIST OF USED IRQS

IRQs 2, 5, and 7 are free for new devices

The Device Manager displays all of the used IRQs and the devices using them. Your computer will display different IRQs and devices. In Figure 11-13, note that IRQs 2, 5, and 7 are not in the list and are therefore free for new devices.

If you want to view how your computer uses its other resources, you can click the plus boxes in front of the DMA, I/O, and Memory icons. Because your computer provides more room for these resources, they rarely conflict.

Printing a Device List

If you need a permanent record of the devices on your computer, you can print a device list. This list contains information on every device installed on the system and the resources each uses. If the computer won't start or fails for whatever reason, a printed device list might prove useful if you have to reinstall some devices.

David wants you to print a hard copy of the device list each time you install new equipment on the company computers.

To print out a device list:

1. Click **Action** on the Device Manager menu bar, and then click **Print**. The Print dialog box opens.

2. Click the **All devices and system summary** option button. See Figure 11-14.

| Figure 11-14 | PRINTING A HARD COPY OF THE DEVICES AND A SYSTEM SUMMARY |

click to print a report detailing the device types and resources they use

By clicking the All devices and system summary option button, you will create a report detailing each device type on your computer and a summary report of the resources in use.

3. Select a printer and then click the **Print** button.

The device list report prints.

4. Close the Device Manager window.

5. Click the **Cancel** button to close the System Properties dialog box, and then close the Control Panel.

You've finished your work inserting the network adapter card into the new computer. In this session, you gained an understanding of hardware on the computer, how it interacts with Windows XP, and how to troubleshoot hardware problems. Your next task on David's list is to attach a new printer to another computer and then show the user how to use the printer.

Session 11.1 QUICK | CHECK

1. List the three types of ports on a standard computer.

2. Name a type of card that can fit into your computer's expansion slots.

3. What is an IRQ? How many IRQs are available on a computer?

4. What is a driver?

5. What is the difference between a legacy device and a plug-and-play device?

6. Describe how you would view a list of devices installed on your computer.

7. Describe how you would view a list of resources being used on your computer.

<table>
<tr><td>**SESSION 11.2**</td><td>In this session, you will learn how to install a printer. You will review the properties of your printer and learn how to change those properties. You will print a test page to verify that your printer is working correctly, and you will discover how Windows XP manages your print jobs and how you can control which documents get printed when.</td></tr>
</table>

Installing a Printer

To install a printer, you first shut off the computer. Then you need to follow the manufacturer's directions for connecting the printer to the appropriate port on your computer and for plugging the printer into a power supply. After you've done this, you turn the computer on again. As Windows XP starts, it will recognize the new printer and start a Wizard that will install a driver and select appropriate resource settings for the printer. However, if no Wizard starts, you can use the Add Printer Wizard. Although you probably are not actually allowed to install a new printer in your computer lab, you can still do many of the steps in this session. The steps tell you specifically when you should cancel the procedure. If you were really installing a new printer, you would need to have the manufacturer's disks and the Windows XP installation disks handy so Windows XP could access installation data.

REFERENCE WINDOW   **RW**

Installing a Printer
- Follow the manufacturer's directions to connect the printer to the appropriate port and plug it into a power supply.
- Follow the steps of the Add Printer Wizard that starts.
- If the wizard does not start, click the Start button and then click Printers and Faxes. (If you are using Windows XP Home Edition, click the Start button, click Control Panel, click Printers and Other Hardware, and then click Printers and Faxes.)
- Under "Printer Tasks" in the left pane of the Printers and Faxes window, click Add a Printer; follow the steps of the Add Printer Wizard.

Your next job on David's task list is to install a new color printer for Sally Li. You connected a printer to the appropriate port and turned on the printer. The Add Printer Wizard did not start automatically, so you will start it yourself.

To start the Add Printer Wizard:

1. Click the **Start** button ⟪ *start* ⟫ , and then click **Printers and Faxes**. The Printers and Faxes window opens.

   TROUBLE? If the Printers and Faxes command does not appear on the Start menu, click the Start button, click Control Panel, click Printers and Other Hardware, and then click Printers and Faxes.

2. Under Printer Tasks in the left pane of the Printers and Faxes window, click **Add a printer**.

   The Add Printer Wizard starts and opens the Welcome window.

3. Click the **Next** button.

In the first step of the Add Printer Wizard, you indicate whether you are installing a local printer or a network printer. A **local printer** is one that is connected directly to your computer, usually through the LPT1 parallel port. A **network printer** is connected to another computer on your network, called a **print server**. In this example, you'll be connecting to a local printer, though in working through the tasks, you can also try to connect to a network printer if that is what your instructor wants you to do. If your local printer uses plug-and-play technology, you can have the Add Printer Wizard search for it, install the drivers, and choose resource settings for you. In this example, the local printer does not support plug and play, so you can see how to install a printer manually.

To specify the printer type:

1. Click the **Local printer attached to this computer** option button, if necessary.

   TROUBLE? If you're installing a network printer, click the option button labeled "A network printer, or a printer attached to another printer."

2. If necessary, deselect the **Automatically detect and install my Plug and Play printer** check box.

   TROUBLE? You probably haven't actually physically installed a new printer. However, you can perform the steps in the Add Printer Wizard and click the Cancel button at the end to end the Wizard without installing anything.

3. Click the **Next** button.

   The Add Printer Wizard prompts you for the port you want the printer to use. For a local printer, you are prompted for the port to which the printer is attached (LPT1, LPT2, COM1, etc.). For a network printer, you either have to enter the network address of the printer (the URL) or browse the network to locate the printer.

4. Specify the port for your printer by referring to Figure 11-15 and taking one of the following actions:

   ■ If it's a local printer, click the port name to which you've connected the printer in the Using the following port list box (usually LPT1), and then click the **Next** button.

   ■ If it's a network printer to which you connect via the Internet, click the **Connect to a printer on the Internet or on a home or office network** option button, enter the network address for the printer in the URL text box, and then click the **Next** button.

   ■ If it's a network printer to which you connect via a network connection, click the **Connect to this printer** option button, type the network location of the printer (such as \\server\printer) in the Name text box, and then click the **Next** button.

   ■ If it's a network printer and you don't know the network address, click the **Connect to this printer** option button, leave the Name text box blank, and then click the **Next** button. You can then locate printer on the network by moving through the hierarchy of network objects.

Figure 11-15	SPECIFYING THE LOCATION OF THE PRINTER

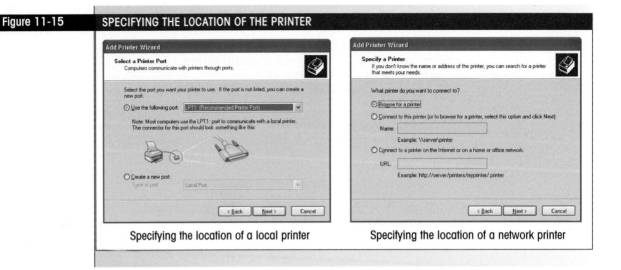

Specifying the location of a local printer   Specifying the location of a network printer

In the next step of the Add Printer Wizard, you specify the printer brand and install the appropriate driver. If you're installing a network printer, Windows XP will try to copy the driver files from the print server to your computer, saving you this step. If the print server is using driver files for a previous version of Windows or if you're installing a local printer, you will have to install the driver files yourself.

To install the printer driver:

1. In the Install Printer Software window of the Add Printer Wizard, select the name of the manufacturer in the Manufacturer list box.

2. Select the printer model in the Printers list box. See Figure 11-16.

Figure 11-16	SPECIFYING THE PRINTER MANUFACTURER AND BRAND

> TROUBLE? If you have an installation disk from the printer manufacturer, insert the disk into your computer, and then click the Have Disk button to use those driver files. It is usually best to use the drivers supplied by the hardware device's manufacturer rather than those supplied by Windows XP.
>
> TROUBLE? You may also see a Windows Update button that you can click to connect to the Internet and download the latest driver file.
>
> **3.** Click the **Next** button.

If you're installing a local printer, you'll first be prompted for the printer name, then asked whether you want to share the printer with the network, and finally asked whether you want to print a test page. If you're connecting to a network printer, the Add Printer Wizard will skip these steps. If you already have a printer, you will also be prompted to make the new printer the default printer, which means that Windows XP automatically uses that printer unless you specify one of the others. You can also choose whether to use the current printer driver or select a new one.

To specify the printer name and other properties for your local printer:

1. Enter the printer name in the Printer name text box of the Name Your Printer window of the Add Printer Wizard.

2. If you want this to be the default printer on your computer, click the **Yes** option button shown in Figure 11-17 if necessary, and then click the **Next** button.

Figure 11-17	SPECIFYING THE NAME OF THE PRINTER

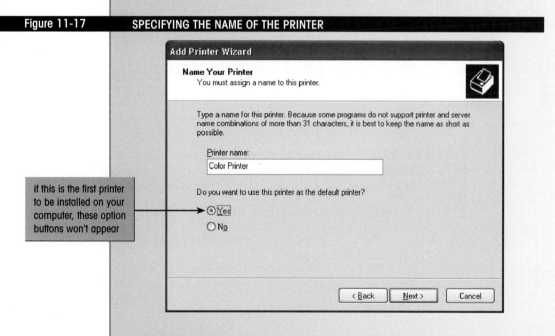

if this is the first printer to be installed on your computer, these option buttons won't appear

> TROUBLE? If this is the first printer to be installed on your computer, you will not have the option of making the printer the default. Windows XP will make it the default printer automatically.

If you are working on a network, you can next choose to share this printer with other computers on your network. At this point, you decide not to share the printer.

3. Verify that the **Do not share this printer** option button is selected, and then click the **Next** button.

TROUBLE? If you are not working on a network, skip Step 3.

Finally, you can choose to print a test page. This option allows you to confirm that the printer and the connection are working correctly. Because this is just an example, you won't create a test page, but in most cases creating a test page is a good idea.

4. Click the **No** option button, and then click the **Next** button.

5. You've completed the Add Printer Wizard. If you've been following these steps without intending to add a new printer, click the **Cancel** button. If you've actually added a new printer, click the **Finish** button to add the printer to your printer list.

If you installed the printer, an icon for the printer should now appear in the Printers and Faxes window.

You've finished installing the new printer. Your next job is to work with the new printer and review the tools that Windows XP provides to manage printers.

Managing a Printer

Windows XP provides a variety of tools to help you manage your printer. With these tools you can, among other things, update the printer driver, control how documents are sent to the printer, and change printer settings. You access these tools through the printer's Properties dialog box.

To display the printer properties:

1. In the Printers and Faxes window, right-click the icon for the printer, and then click **Properties** on the shortcut menu. If you didn't actually install a new printer in the last set of steps, use your regular printer for these steps.

The Properties dialog box opens, as shown in Figure 11-18.

Figure 11-18 THE PRINTER PROPERTIES DIALOG BOX

shows the name you provided for this printer; you can change the name here

summary of features

click to print a test page

TROUBLE? Your Properties dialog box will look different from the one shown in Figure 11-18; it will show the properties of the printer you have selected.

The number of dialog sheets in the Properties dialog box will vary for different printers. However, at least five sheets appear for every printer.

- **General** provides general information about the printer, such as its name and features.
- **Sharing** lets you choose whether to share your printer with other users or the network.
- **Ports** is for specifying the port to which your printer is connected.
- **Advanced** is for specifying the times at which the printer is available, how files are sent to the printer, and other advanced options.
- **Device Settings** is for specifying settings for the printer. (The list will vary among printers.)

The General sheet shown in Figure 11-18 indicates that the printer supports color but not double-sided printing or automatic stapling. The speed of the printer is 12 pages per minute at a maximum resolution of 600 dots per inch (dpi). In addition to the five sheets, the Properties dialog box in Figure 11-18 displays two additional sheets, Color Management and Services, that apply only to that particular printer.

Printing a Test Page

Sometimes a printer will not print correctly or will not work at all. You might be able to turn on the printer but not print documents from your computer. Or the printed page is missing text or graphics. In any case, you must determine whether the problem lies in the program that's using the printer, in Windows XP, in the printer driver, or in the printer hardware itself. For example, suppose you installed a new printer but now cannot print documents from your word-processing program. One way of locating the source of the trouble is to print a test page.

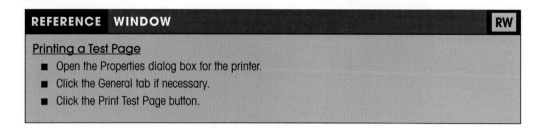

REFERENCE WINDOW | RW

Printing a Test Page
- Open the Properties dialog box for the printer.
- Click the General tab if necessary.
- Click the Print Test Page button.

If the test page prints correctly, you can eliminate the word-processing program as the problem's source. Failure to print a test page might indicate a hardware problem. A test page also provides a printed report of the printer's technical specifications.

To print a test page for your printer:

1. Click the **Print Test Page** button on the General tab of your printer's Properties dialog box.

   Windows XP displays a message telling you that a test page is being sent to your printer.

2. Click the **OK** button when the test page has finished printing, and leave the Properties dialog box open.

   TROUBLE? If the test page doesn't print, you can click the Troubleshoot button in the message box to access the Print Troubleshooter. You can then use the Troubleshooter to diagnose your problem in the same way that you used the Hardware Troubleshooter in the previous session.

While the General sheet provides basic information about a printer, such as its name and features, the Advanced sheet provides more sophisticated information and lets you fine-tune how the printer works. You'll investigate the advanced options for your printer in the next section.

Setting Advanced Options

You have probably printed documents many times in Windows XP without thinking much about what goes on behind the scenes. You might have noticed a dialog box that tells you your document is printing, or you might have seen printer icons appear on and then disappear from the taskbar. You might even have heard your hard drive spinning for a second or two when you printed a large document. David suggests that you explore how Windows XP manages your print jobs. See Figure 11-19.

Figure 11-19   PRINTING A DOCUMENT

2. spooler prepares your document for printing

3. print job is stored in a temporary file on your hard drive

1. you click OK or Print

4. print job appears in print queue

5. print queue sends job to printer

When you send a file to your printer, Windows XP prepares your document using print spooling. **Print spooling** creates a temporary file on your hard disk containing the electronic codes that control your particular printer, such as the code to move down to the next line or to eject a page. After each page is spooled, Windows XP sends the file to the printer to be processed. One of the big advantages of print spooling is that you don't have to wait for the entire document to be printed before you can continue your work at your computer. The printing goes on in the background. You can even generate more than one print job at the same time.

You can control how print spooling works on your computer using the Advanced sheet of the Properties dialog box.

> ### To view the advanced properties of your printer:
>
> **1.** Click the **Advanced** tab in your printer's Properties dialog box. See Figure 11-20.

Figure 11-20   ADVANCED PROPERTIES OF THE PRINTER

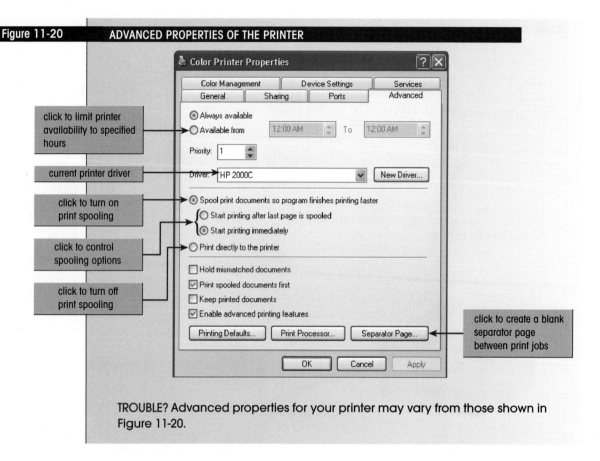

click to limit printer availability to specified hours

current printer driver

click to turn on print spooling

click to control spooling options

click to turn off print spooling

click to create a blank separator page between print jobs

TROUBLE? Advanced properties for your printer may vary from those shown in Figure 11-20.

As you can see from Figure 11-20, you can have Windows XP either spool your print jobs or send them directly to the printer without spooling. You would only use the second option if your computer lacked the resources to perform spooling. You can also have Windows XP send the print job only after all pages have been spooled. This will cause your program to "freeze" until the spooling is completed, but it also provides more system resources, such as memory, to the print job rather than sharing those resources between the program and the spooling process.

Another feature to note in Figure 11-20 is the ability to restrict access to a printer to certain hours of the day. This is useful on a network, when you don't want users to access a printer during hours that the computer attached to that printer is turned off. If someone tries to use the printer during the off hours, the print job is held until the printer is available. Finally, note that you can also create separator pages, blank pages that separate one print job from another. This is also useful on a network on which several users may generate several print jobs.

Viewing Device Settings

Each printer has its own set of unique device settings, such as the amount of memory installed in the printer, the number and type of paper trays, and the type of fonts the printer uses. Windows XP communicates with your printer to record these device settings. David tells you that sometimes the company's printers are upgraded and these settings need to be changed, so you should know how to access these device settings.

To view the printer's device settings:

1. Click the **Device Settings** tab in your printer's Properties dialog box. See Figure 11-21. The device settings for your printer will be different.

Figure 11-21   **DEVICE SETTINGS FOR A SPECIFIC PRINTER**

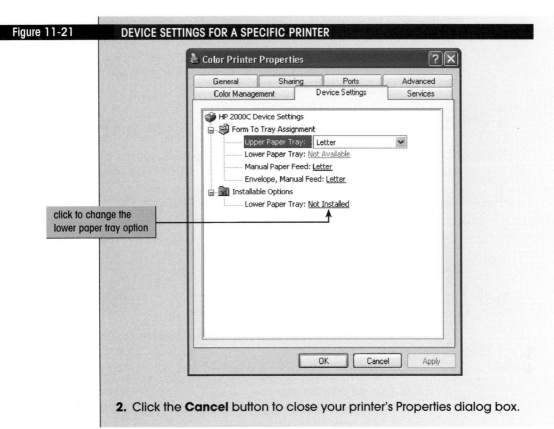

click to change the
lower paper tray option

2. Click the **Cancel** button to close your printer's Properties dialog box.

In this case, the printer has only one upgrade option—to install a lower paper tray. The company hasn't chosen to install that tray yet.

You've completed your work reviewing the properties of the new printer. Your next task is to help a new user operate the printer.

Managing a Print Queue

Sally Li, the user of the new computer you are setting up, knows all about printing a single document. However, her printer will be shared on the network with other users, and she wants to know how to manage her print jobs in such an environment. You tell her that if other print jobs are pending, many print servers will put her print job into a **print queue**, a list of jobs being sent to the printer. You can view the print queue by opening the Printers and Faxes window and then double-clicking the icon for the appropriate printer. The print job listed first in the print queue typically goes to the printer first. After the entire job is transferred into the printer's temporary memory, it disappears from the print queue.

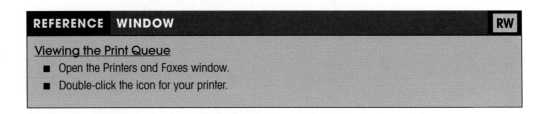

REFERENCE WINDOW   **RW**

Viewing the Print Queue
- Open the Printers and Faxes window.
- Double-click the icon for your printer.

The print queue also gives you some control over print jobs waiting to print. For example, you can pause or cancel print jobs or change their order. On a network, you must belong to a user group that has permission to manage the documents on the printer. Sally Li has been given that kind of permission. Recall that you learned how to set permissions for users and user groups in Tutorial 10.

Opening the Print Queue Window

To display the print queue for a printer, you open the printer's icon from the Printers and Faxes window.

To view the print queue:

1. Double-click the default printer icon 🖨 in the Printers and Faxes window.

2. Maximize the print queue window.

The print queue window has several columns:

- **Document Name** lists the filename of the document being sent to the printer.
- **Status** tells the current status of the print job, such as spooling, paused, or printing.
- **Owner** gives the user name of the person who sent the print job.
- **Pages** is a count of the number of pages that have printed and the total number of pages in the document.
- **Size** gives the size of the document in kilobytes.
- **Submitted** is the time and date the job was sent to the printer.
- **Port** specifies the port used by the printer.

From viewing the print queue, you can see instantly which documents are waiting to be printed, how large they are, who sent them, and other details that might help you manage print jobs.

Sally wants to see how the print queue changes when she sends a document to the printer. You suggest that she print one of the topics in Windows XP Help.

To send a job to the printer:

1. Click the **Start** button 🏁 start on the taskbar, and then click **Help and Support**.

2. In the Help and Support Center window, click **What's new in Windows XP** (under "Pick a Help Topic").

3. In the left pane, click **What's new topics**.

4. In the right pane, click **What's new in Windows XP**.

5. Click the **Print** icon 🖨 in the right pane. The Print dialog box opens.

6. If necessary, click to select the default printer icon 🖨 in the Print dialog box, and then click the **Print** button.

7. Quickly minimize the Help and Support window, so you can see the print queue window you opened earlier and observe the new entry. See Figure 11-22.

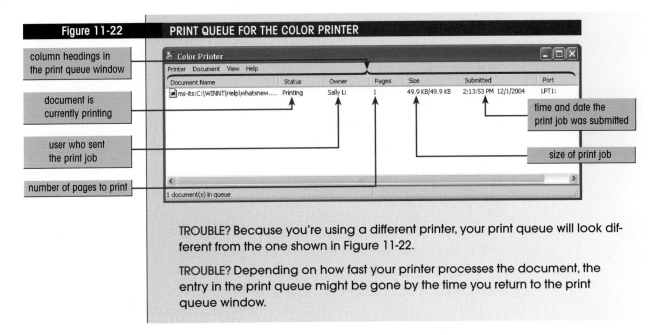

Figure 11-22   **PRINT QUEUE FOR THE COLOR PRINTER**

column headings in the print queue window

document is currently printing

user who sent the print job

number of pages to print

time and date the print job was submitted

size of print job

TROUBLE? Because you're using a different printer, your print queue will look different from the one shown in Figure 11-22.

TROUBLE? Depending on how fast your printer processes the document, the entry in the print queue might be gone by the time you return to the print queue window.

The print queue also supports drag and drop. For example, you can drag a document located at the bottom of the queue and drop it at the beginning of the queue. In this way, you can give greater priority to the documents you want printed earlier. Note that you can only do this if you belong to a user group that has permission to manage those print jobs.

Pausing the Print Queue

On occasion you might want to delay your computer from sending jobs to the printer. For example, if you want to use a specific letterhead for a print job, you have to change the paper in the printer before you print that job. Windows XP lets you pause one or all documents in the print queue so you can perform such paper changes.

REFERENCE WINDOW   **RW**

Pausing the Print Queue
- Open the print queue window for your printer.
- Click Printer on the menu bar, and then click Pause Printing.

If you want to pause the entire queue, you select the Pause Printing command on the Printer menu. This tells Windows XP to stop sending all jobs to the printer. When you restart printing, the print queue starts sending all print jobs in the order shown in the queue. To pause all of the jobs in the print queue, you must have permission to manage documents in the printer. However, you can always pause one or all of your own documents because you are their owner. If you want to pause a specific print job, you select the document you want to pause and then click the Pause command on the Document menu. Pausing a single print job halts your job while allowing other print jobs in the queue to print. Sally asks you to show her how to pause her entire print queue.

> ### To pause the print queue:
>
> 1. Click **Printer** on the print queue window's menu bar, and then click **Pause Printing**.
>
>   The word "Paused" is now on the title bar of the print queue window to show that the printer is paused.
>
> 2. Return to the Help and Support Center window, and print the What's New in Windows XP topic again.
>
> 3. Return to the print queue window. The print queue shows the new print job, but since the queue is paused, the job does not print, and nothing appears in the Status column.

You can now remove this job from the print queue because you already have a copy of it.

Removing a Job from the Print Queue

Suppose you started to print a document but then noticed an error in the document that you want to fix before printing. You might want to remove the job from the print queue to prevent it from printing. You can prevent your printer from processing a print job by deleting the job from the print queue.

REFERENCE WINDOW   **RW**

Removing Print Jobs from the Print Queue
- To remove all jobs, click Printer on the menu bar, and then click Purge Print Documents.
- To remove a single job, click the job in the print queue, either press the Delete key or click Document on the menu bar, and then click Cancel Printing.

After you attempt to remove a job, you might discover that all or part of the document prints anyway. If this happens, Windows XP already sent part of the job—maybe even all of it—to the printer before you tried to cancel the print job. Your printer has memory too, and spooling sends the print job to the printer's memory. Removing print jobs from the Windows XP print queue does not affect the parts of a print job already in the printer's memory. You can clear your printer's memory by resetting your printer. How you do this depends on what type of printer you have, but some printers have a Reset button. You decide to show Sally how to remove the print job she just sent.

> ### To remove a job from the print queue:
>
> 1. Click the document in the Document Name list in the print queue.
>
> 2. Click **Document** on the menu bar, and then click **Cancel** to remove the document from the queue.
>
> 3. When a message box appears asking if you are sure you want to cancel the selected print job, click the **Yes** button.

4. Click **Printer** on the menu bar, and then click **Pause Printing** to turn off paused printing and restart the print queue.

Because no documents are in the print queue, turning off paused printing will not cause documents to be printed.

5. Close the print queue window, the Help and Support Center window, and the Printers and Faxes window.

Sally thanks you for the help. You have installed a printer and learned how to manage a printer and a print queue. You're finished with your work on printers and print queues and are ready to start on your next task, which will be to perform some routine hard disk maintenance tasks.

Session 11.2 QUICK CHECK

1. What is the difference between a local printer and a network printer?
2. How do you print a test page?
3. What is print spooling?
4. What is a print queue?
5. How do you pause the operation of your printer?
6. How do you remove a single print job from the printer?

SESSION 11.3

In this session, you will learn some of the fundamentals of disks and disk maintenance, including how to clean your hard disk to remove unnecessary files. You will learn how to scan your disk, checking for errors and fixing them. You will also learn about fragmentation and how to defragment your disk to improve performance. Finally, you will schedule disk maintenance tasks to run automatically at specified times.

Windows XP Disk Maintenance Accessories

David tells you that disk maintenance is a critical part of your job managing hardware devices at the company. Individuals and businesses rely on computers and the data they contain. If a computer's hard disk fails, it can be disastrous.

Windows XP helps you prevent disk failure from occurring in the first place by providing some valuable disk maintenance accessories. Disk maintenance accessories are available on the Tools tab of the disk's property sheet (accessible by right-clicking the icon for the disk in the My Computer window and then clicking Properties) or via the System Tools submenu of the Accessories menu.

David suggests that you use these accessories as part of a scheduled comprehensive disk maintenance plan. You should begin your disk maintenance with a "spring cleaning," in which you delete old or unneeded files and scan the disk for **viruses**, programs that run on your computer and disrupt its operations. Many software products on the market are designed to protect your computer from viruses by regularly scanning for known viruses. Windows XP does not include a virus accessory, so if you own a computer, you should purchase virus checking software and use it regularly as part of your disk maintenance plan.

After you have ensured that your computer is free from viruses, you should check each disk on your computer to locate and repair errors, such as parts of corrupted files and damaged sections on the disk. Then you should defragment each disk. **Defragmenting** a disk organizes its files so that they are stored most efficiently. If you are responsible for maintaining a computer that is used all day, you should probably run these maintenance procedures on a weekly or even daily basis. On the other hand, if you use your computer less frequently—for example, if you use a home computer only for correspondence, games, and maintaining your checkbook—you might only need to run disk maintenance procedures once every month or so.

Removing Unneeded Files

When you work with programs and files in Windows XP, unnecessary files, such as temporary Web graphics, accumulate on your hard disk. This impairs system performance. The Disk Cleanup accessory helps you free disk space by permanently deleting these files. When you start Disk Cleanup, it searches your disk for unnecessary files and then lists the types of files it found. See Figure 11-23. When you start Disk Cleanup, you might not see all the options on this list. What you see depends on the files Disk Cleanup finds on your disk.

Figure 11-23	DISK CLEANUP OPTIONS
CATEGORY	**DESCRIPTION**
Downloaded program files	Program files downloaded automatically from the Internet when you view certain Web pages
Temporary Internet files	Web pages stored on your hard disk for quick viewing, stored in the Temporary Internet Files folder
Temporary Setup files	Temporary files created when you install a program—some programs delete these files when they are no longer needed; others leave them on your hard drive
Offline Web Pages	Web pages stored on your computer so you can view them without being connected to the Internet
Recycle Bin	Files you deleted from your computer, which are stored in the Recycle Bin until you delete them
Old CheckDisk files	Files created by CheckDisk when it locates corrupted data
Temporary files	Files generated by programs to be used temporarily; usually these are deleted when you close the program, but if the program isn't shut down properly, the temporary files remain on your disk
WebClient/Publisher Temporary Files	Files maintained by the WebClient service, which maintains a cache of accessed files on the drive
Compress Old Files	Windows XP compresses files you haven't accessed recently
Catalog Files for the Content Indexer	Files left over from the Indexing Service, which speeds up file searches by building an index of files on a disk
Windows XP Uninstall Information	Files from a previous version of Windows—these appear only if Windows XP was installed on a computer that used an older version of Windows; they can be safely deleted if you don't intend to revert to the original version

REFERENCE WINDOW   RW

Removing Unneeded Files
- Click the Start button, point to All Programs, point to Accessories, point to System Tools, and then click Disk Cleanup.
- Select the drive you want to clean.
- Select the types of files you want to remove.
- Click OK.

David provides a computer for you to see how Disk Cleanup works. At this point, he doesn't want you to change any features on the computer's hard disk, so you'll close Disk Cleanup without actually removing unnecessary files. Note that you can only clean a hard disk on a local computer or if you have permission from your network administrator.

To start Disk Cleanup:

1. Click the **Start** button [start], point to **All Programs**, point to **Accessories**, point to **System Tools**, and then click **Disk Cleanup**.

2. If your computer has more than one hard disk or has a partitioned hard disk with more than one logical drive, click the **Drives** list arrow, click **(C:)** if necessary, and then click the **OK** button.

   Disk Cleanup calculates how much space you'll be able to clean and then displays the dialog box shown in Figure 11-24.

Figure 11-24	CHOOSING FILES TO DELETE

click to remove programs and Windows XP components

click to remove the check mark if you don't want to delete these types of files

amount of space you'll gain by removing the selected file types

amount of space taken up by each file type

description of selected file type

click to view the selected file type

TROUBLE? If drive C doesn't appear or if you receive an error message, you don't have permission to clean drive C. Click the OK button to acknowledge the message, close any open windows, and then read through the rest of this section without performing the steps.

3. Check the boxes corresponding to the files you want to delete, and then notice the amount of disk space you can recover.

4. Click the **Cancel** button. If you are using your own computer and want to clean your disk, you can click the **OK** button and then the **Yes** button to confirm that you want to start cleaning the disk.

You can also use the More Options tab of Disk Cleanup to delete optional Windows components or installed programs that you do not use.

Scanning a Disk for Errors

Sections of the magnetic surface of a disk sometimes get damaged. Regularly scanning your disks for errors can be an effective way to head off potential problems that would make data inaccessible. The Windows XP Check Disk accessory not only locates errors on a disk, but it also attempts to repair them or at least to mark the defective portions of the disk so that the operating system won't try to store data there.

To understand what errors Check Disk is looking for and how it repairs them, you need to learn a little bit about the structure of a disk. When you format a disk such as a 3½-inch disk (or a hard disk), a formatting program divides the disk into storage compartments. First it creates a series of rings, called **tracks**, around the circumference of the disk. Then it divides the tracks into equal parts, like pieces of pie, to form **sectors**, as shown in Figure 11-25.

Figure 11-25	A FORMATTED DISK

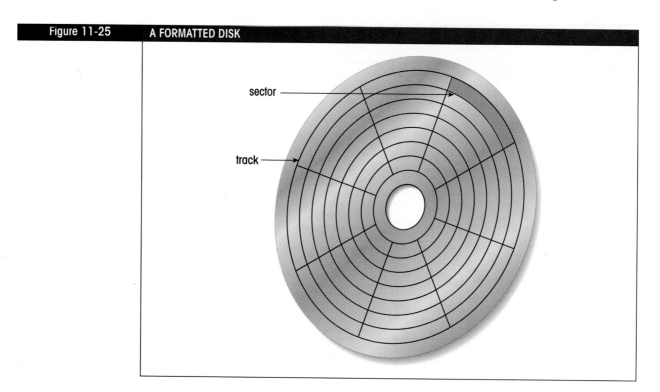

The number of sectors and tracks depends on the size of the disk. A high-density disk, such as your Data Disk, stores data on both sides of the disk. Each side has 80 tracks, and each track is divided into 18 sectors. Each sector can hold 512 bytes, for a total of 1,474,560 bytes or 1.44 Mb. (A megabyte is 1024 bytes.)

Although the physical surface of a disk is made up of tracks and sectors, a file is stored in clusters. A **cluster**, also called an **allocation unit**, is one or more sectors of storage space—it represents the minimum amount of space that an operating system reserves when saving the contents of a file on a disk. Most files are larger than 512 bytes (the size of one sector). Therefore, a file might be stored in more than one cluster. Figure 11-26 shows a file that takes up four clusters on an otherwise empty disk. A unique number identifies each cluster; the first two clusters, shown in blue, are reserved by the operating system.

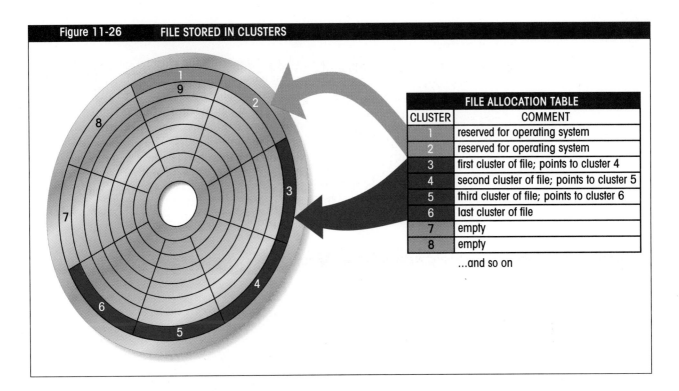

Figure 11-26   FILE STORED IN CLUSTERS

FILE ALLOCATION TABLE	
CLUSTER	COMMENT
1	reserved for operating system
2	reserved for operating system
3	first cluster of file; points to cluster 4
4	second cluster of file; points to cluster 5
5	third cluster of file; points to cluster 6
6	last cluster of file
7	empty
8	empty

...and so on

Types of File Systems

Windows XP maintains a **file allocation table (FAT)** for each disk, which lists the clusters on the disk and records the status of each cluster: whether it is occupied (and by which file), available, or defective. Each cluster in a file "remembers" its order in the chain of clusters—and each cluster points to the next one until the last cluster, which marks the end of that file.

Another type of file system supported by Windows XP is **FAT32**. Previous versions of Windows used FAT (now referred to as FAT16) to manage the data on a disk, but FAT16 could work only with hard drives smaller than 2 GB. FAT32 improves on FAT16 by using disk space much more efficiently than FAT16 and accessing hard drives up to 2 terabytes in size (a terabyte is 1,000,000,000,000 bytes). Older computers that upgraded to Windows XP might still use FAT16, but if Windows XP was installed on a new computer, it probably uses FAT32. David explains that if you are using an older computer, you can convert a FAT16 drive to FAT32 using the Drive Converter accessory on the System Tools submenu of the Accessories menu, but that once you convert a drive to FAT32 you cannot convert it back without reformatting it. For this reason, Drive Converter won't be covered in this tutorial.

The final type of file system supported by Windows XP is NTFS. **NTFS** is a file system introduced with Windows NT. NTFS supports file system recovery (in the case of a hard disk failure) and can access disk drives up to 2 terabytes in size. Generally, NTFS provides higher performance than both FAT16 and FAT32. NTFS is the preferred file system if your disk drive is larger than 32 gigabytes. Be aware that some older disk maintenance tools will not work with NTFS. So carefully consider your decision before converting your disk to NTFS.

Running Check Disk

When you use Check Disk to check your disk for errors, you can specify whether you want it to check the physical surface of the disk, the files, or both the surface and the files. Check Disk examines the disk surface, looking for damaged sectors. If it finds any, it marks those sectors and prevents data from being stored there. A damaged sector is called a **bad sector**.

Check Disk checks the files on a disk by comparing the clusters on the disk to the file allocation table. It looks specifically for lost clusters and cross-linked files. A **lost cluster** is a cluster that contains data that the file allocation table cannot match to a file. If your computer suffers a power surge, a power failure, or any problem that locks it up, the operating system might lose one or more clusters from a file that was open when the problem occurred, and you might lose the data stored in those clusters. The presence of lost clusters on a disk is not damaging, but lost clusters do take up valuable space, and too many of them can lead to further errors. Check Disk identifies lost clusters and either deletes them or saves them in a new file. Although sometimes you recover lost data from such a file, more often you won't be able to do much with the file and should simply delete it. Figure 11-27 shows how Check Disk repairs lost cluster problems on a 3½-inch disk.

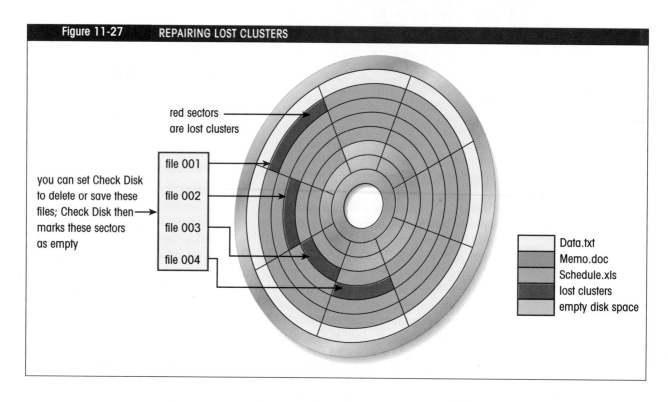

Figure 11-27 **REPAIRING LOST CLUSTERS**

red sectors are lost clusters

you can set Check Disk to delete or save these files; Check Disk then marks these sectors as empty

file 001
file 002
file 003
file 004

Data.txt
Memo.doc
Schedule.xls
lost clusters
empty disk space

Check Disk also checks for cross-linked files. A **cross-linked file** contains at least one cluster that has been allocated to more than one file in the file allocation table. Like lost clusters, cross-linked files can result when a program abruptly ends. Because a cluster should be occupied by data coming from only one file, the file allocation table becomes confused about which clusters belong to which files. You can tell Check Disk how you want it to handle such a file—by deleting it, copying it, or ignoring it. If you want to maintain the integrity of your files, it's best to allow Check Disk to copy each file to a new location on the disk and remove the original files so they are no longer cross-linked. This procedure often saves both files, although you might lose a portion of one of the files where the cross-link occurred. In most cases, the saved files can be deleted.

REFERENCE WINDOW **RW**

Running Check Disk
- Close all open windows and programs, including screen savers running in the background.
- Open the My Computer window.
- Right-click the drive you want to check, and then click Properties on the shortcut menu.
- Click the Tools tab in the Properties dialog box.
- Click the Check Now button.

David says that the first thing he wants you to do is scan a disk for errors. To save time now, you'll be performing the scan on a 3½-inch floppy disk, although this procedure is generally most useful for maintaining a hard disk. You'll have a chance to scan your hard disk in a Review Assignment.

To start Check Disk:

1. Close all open programs—if a program is in use while a disk is being scanned, you could lose data. If you are using a screen saver, right-click the desktop, point to **Properties**, click the **Screen Saver** tab, click the **Screen saver** list arrow, click **(None)**, and then click the **OK** button.

2. Open the My Computer window, and then right-click the **3½ Floppy (A:)** icon in the right pane.

3. Click **Properties** on the shortcut menu, and then click the **Tools** tab of the 3½ Floppy (A:) Properties dialog box.

4. Click the **Check Now** button.

   The Check Disk 3½ Floppy (A:) dialog box opens as shown in Figure 11-28. In this dialog box, you can specify how Windows XP handles the errors if finds. For example, you can choose to have Windows XP fix the errors as it finds them. All files and programs stored on the drive must be closed for this to happen. If the drive is already in use, Windows XP will ask you if you want to reschedule the task for the next time you restart the computer. You can also have Windows XP scan for and attempt to recover bad sectors. If you choose this option, you do not need to select the check box to fix file system errors automatically, because Windows XP will fix them when it recovers the bad sectors.

Figure 11-28 **SELECTING THE CHECK DISK OPTIONS**

click to have Windows XP scan for and attempt to recover bad sectors

5. Click the **Scan for and attempt recovery of bad sectors** check box.

6. Click the **Start** button in the Check Disk dialog box.

Windows XP takes a few minutes to scan the disk, checking for errors. When it's finished, it reports any errors that it finds on your disk.

7. When a message box appears telling you the disk check is complete, click the **OK** button, then close the Properties dialog box and the My Computer window.

Your computer might be set up to run Check Disk automatically in situations where Windows XP has been improperly shut down (for example, because of a power failure during operation). When you next launch Windows XP after such a shutdown you might be asked if you want to run Check Disk.

Defragmenting **Your Disk**

Now that you've corrected any errors on your disk, you can use Disk Defragmenter to improve the disk's performance so that programs start and files open more quickly. When you save a file, Windows XP stores as much of the file as possible in the first available cluster. If the file won't fit into one cluster, Windows XP locates the next available cluster and puts more of the file in it. Windows XP attempts to place files in contiguous clusters whenever possible. The file is saved once Windows XP has placed all the file data into clusters. Figure 11-29 shows two files that you have just saved on a new 3½-inch floppy disk: Address and Recipes.

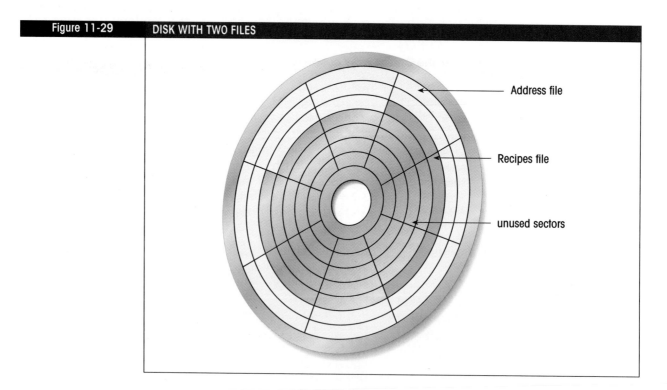

Figure 11-29   DISK WITH TWO FILES

- Address file
- Recipes file
- unused sectors

As you create and save new files, more clusters are used. If you delete a file or two, those clusters are freed. In Figure 11-30, you have saved a new file, Memo, and then deleted Recipes.

| Figure 11-30 | ADDING ONE FILE AND DELETING ANOTHER FILE |

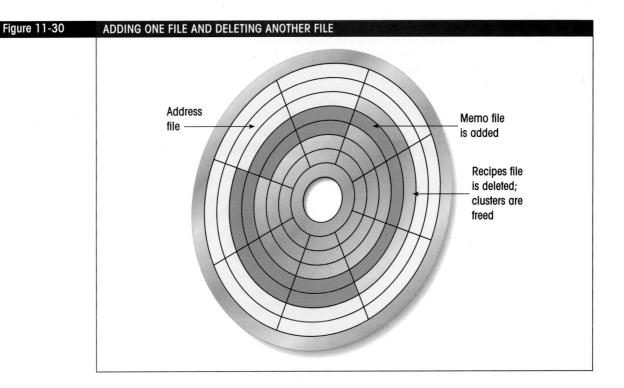

The next time you save a file, Windows XP searches for the first available cluster, which is now between two files. Figure 11-31 shows what happens when you save a fourth file, Schedule. It is saved in clusters that are not adjacent.

| Figure 11-31 | ADDING A NEW FILE IN FRAGMENTED CLUSTERS |

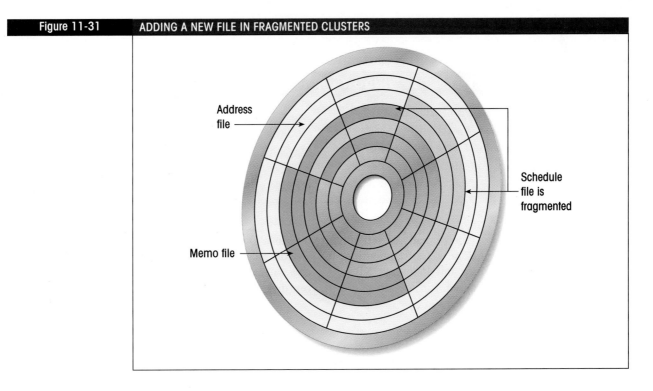

The more files you save and delete, the more scattered the clusters for a file become. A disk that contains files whose clusters are not next to each other is said to be **fragmented**.

The more fragmented the disk, the longer Windows XP takes to retrieve the file, and the more likely you are to have problems with the file. Whenever a disk has been used for a long time, it's a good idea to defragment it. Defragmenting rearranges the clusters on the disk so each file's clusters are adjacent to one another. Figure 11-32 shows a fragmented disk. When a program tries to access a file on this disk, file retrieval takes longer than necessary because the program must locate clusters that aren't adjacent.

Figure 11-32	FRAGMENTED FILES

next file to be saved will use these clusters

File #1
File #2
File #3
File #4

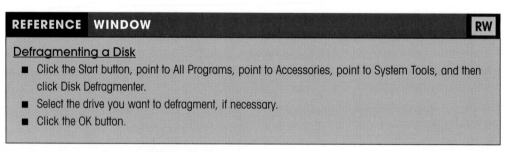

REFERENCE WINDOW   RW

Defragmenting a Disk

- Click the Start button, point to All Programs, point to Accessories, point to System Tools, and then click Disk Defragmenter.
- Select the drive you want to defragment, if necessary.
- Click the OK button.

You're ready to defragment your disk. David tells you that he can't guarantee that your disk needs defragmenting. It's possible that you'll go through the defragmenting procedure, but Windows XP won't have to make any changes because your disk is not fragmented. If this is the case with your disk, you might not be able to perform all the steps in this section.

To start Disk Defragmenter:

1. Close all open programs to prevent loss of data.

2. Click the **Start** button _start_ , point to **All Programs**, point to **Accessories**, point to **System Tools**, and then click **Disk Defragmenter**.

The Disk Defragmenter window opens, as shown in Figure 11-33.

Figure 11-33	THE DISK DEFRAGMENTER WINDOW

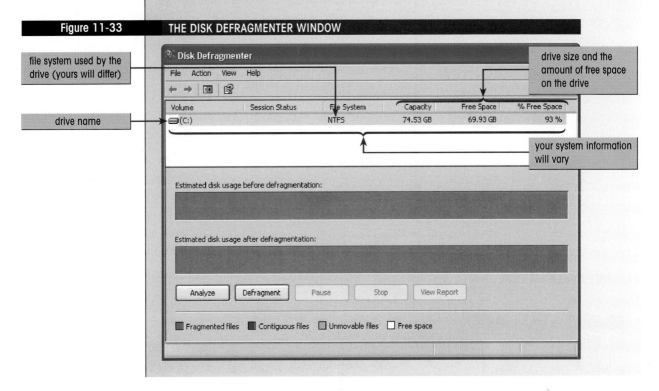

file system used by the drive (yours will differ)

drive size and the amount of free space on the drive

drive name

your system information will vary

Before attempting to defragment a hard disk, you should analyze the current state of the disk. The Disk Defragmenter produces a report to tell you how fragmented the disk is and whether Windows XP recommends that you defragment the disk. Defragmenting can be a time-consuming process, so you will not always want to defragment a hard disk immediately.

To analyze your disk:

1. Click to select a disk on your computer.

2. Click the **Analyze** button at the bottom of the window.

The analyzing process can take a few minutes. After the analysis is finished, Windows XP presents its recommendation about whether you should defragment the drive.

3. Click the **View Report** button.

The Analysis Report dialog box in Figure 11-34 shows information about the drive, including the file fragmentation and a list of fragmented files. At the top of the dialog box is the recommendation about whether to defragment the drive. In this case, Windows XP does not recommend that you defragment the disk.

Figure 11-34   FRAGMENTATION ANALYSIS REPORT DIALOG BOX

recommendation to
defragment or not
appears here

list of highly
fragmented files

scroll to view
fragmentation information

4. Click the **Close** button.

Disk Defragmenter shows a schematic diagram (see Figure 11-35) of the current state of the disk.

Figure 11-35   DIAGRAM OF HARD DISK BEFORE DEFRAGMENTATION

schematic diagram of
fragmentation on the
hard disk

You could click the Defragment button now to start defragmenting the hard disk. However, because this could take an hour or longer, you'll simply close the window without defragmenting.

5. Close the Disk Defragmenter window.

If you are working on your own computer, you can run Disk Defragmenter at a time when you won't need to use the computer for other tasks.

Scheduling Disk Maintenance Tasks

Performing disk maintenance tasks regularly will help your computer run efficiently. You can use the Windows XP Task Scheduler to schedule Windows XP to run the tasks automatically. The Task Scheduler schedules and then runs programs according to your computer's clock (if your computer is turned on). You'll use the Task Scheduler to schedule a weekly cleanup of the hard disk.

To start the Task Scheduler:

1. Click the **Start** button , point to **All Programs**, point to **Accessories**, point to **System Tools**, and then click **Scheduled Tasks**.

The Scheduled Tasks window opens. See Figure 11-36.

| Figure 11-36 | SCHEDULED TASKS WINDOW |

click to schedule a task

currently scheduled tasks

2. Double-click the **Add Scheduled Task** icon .

The Scheduled Task Wizard starts and explains the purpose of the Task Scheduler—to select a program you want Windows to run and then schedule it for a convenient time.

3. Click the **Next** button.

4. Click **Disk Cleanup** in the Application list (you may need to scroll to see it), and then click the **Next** button.

When you create a scheduled task, you give that task a name and specify when and how often the task should be performed.

To create a scheduled task:

1. Type **Clean the Hard Disk** in the task name box.

2. Click the **Weekly** option button, as shown in Figure 11-37, and then click the **Next** button.

| Figure 11-37 | CREATING A WEEKLY SCHEDULE TO CLEAN THE HARD DISK |

type the name of the scheduled task

click to clean the hard disk once a week

You decide to clean the hard disk every Friday night at 6 PM.

3. Enter **6:00 PM** in the Start Time spin box.

4. Verify that **1** is entered in the Every weeks spin box, and then click the **Friday** check box. See Figure 11-38.

Figure 11-38	SETTING THE SCHEDULE FOR EVERY FRIDAY AT 6 PM

specify when you want Windows XP to start cleaning the disk

select these options to set the frequency

5. Click the **Next** button.

Finally, you specify the user who will be credited for running the task. Because you're working on Sally Li's computer, you'll enter her name in the User Name box. On your own computer, you can enter your own user name.

6. Type *your user name* in the Enter the user name box, if necessary, and then click the **Next** button. No password is necessary.

7. Click the **Finish** button.

The Clean the Hard Disk icon appears in the Scheduled Tasks window. If you close the window now, your computer will automatically run the Disk Cleanup program at 6 PM every Friday. If the computer is off, then Windows XP will ask if you want to run Disk Cleanup the next time you turn on your computer. David suggests that you delete the task from the list until you can confer with Sally Li to make sure that running this task at that time won't interfere with her work.

To delete a task:

1. Click the **Clean the Hard Disk** icon in the Schedule Tasks window.

2. Press the **Delete** key and click **Yes** when Windows XP asks you to confirm the file deletion.

3. Close the Scheduled Tasks window.

Now that you know how to use the Windows XP disk maintenance accessories, you've completed your work with hardware and Windows XP. With the tools you've learned to use, you can manage most of the hardware problems that you might encounter in your job at Chan & Associates.

Session 11.3 QUICK CHECK

1. A destructive program that runs on your computer and disrupts its operations is called what?

2. Why should you regularly defragment your disks?

3. What is a cluster?

4. What is the purpose of the file allocation table?

5. True or False: Windows XP always stores a file in adjacent clusters.

6. How does a disk become fragmented?

REVIEW ASSIGNMENTS

1. **Exploring Your Computer** Open the Device Manager on your computer. Using the information in the Device Manager, answer the following questions. When you are finished, close all open windows.

   Explore
   a. What type of display adapter is your computer using? What resources is the display adapter using? How old is the driver for the display adapter? If there is no date for the driver, make a note of this.

   Explore
   b. What DMA numbers are being used and by which devices?
   c. What IRQ numbers are being used and by which devices?

2. **Exploring Your Printer** Open the Properties dialog box for your printer, and then answer the following questions. When you are finished, close all open windows.
   a. What is the name of your printer?
   b. What is your printer's manufacturer and brand name?
   c. Through what kind of port is your printer connected?
   d. Is the printer a local printer or a network printer?
   e. What driver does your printer use?
   f. Describe how your computer is set up to handle spooling.

   Explore
   3. **Troubleshooting a Hardware Problem** You are providing hardware support for some Windows XP users at your work. A user contacts you because of a problem he or she is having playing audio CDs on the CD-ROM player. The CD-ROM player is listed on the Windows XP Hardware Compatibility List, and you learn that the MCI CD audio driver is installed. Use the Hardware Troubleshooter to determine what you should have the user do next to determine the source of the trouble.

4. **Cleaning a Hard Disk** Upon returning from a business trip to Chan & Associates, you decide to apply some of the disk maintenance procedures you learned. You decide to use the Disk Cleanup accessory to explore the different types of files that are likely to be cluttering your disks.
   a. Close any open programs and then start Disk Cleanup to clean drive C. What appears in the cleanup list for drive C? Are there more or fewer options than those listed in Figure 11-24? If there are any differences, can you account for them?
   b. Select all of the check boxes available for drive C, and record the amount of disk space you could save by running the Disk Cleanup accessory.
   c. If you are using a lab computer, close Disk Cleanup without cleaning any disks. If you are using your own computer, proceed with the Disk Cleanup procedure to clean your hard disk.

   Explore
   5. **Defragmenting a Hard Drive** If you have your own computer or have permission from the computer lab's staff, work on defragmenting your computer's hard drive.
   a. Analyze your hard drive and then print the defragmentation analysis report.

   b. Print the screen shot of the schematic diagram of your hard disk. (Press the PrintScreen key, open Paint, paste the image, print the image from Paint, and then close Paint without saving changes.)
   c. Start the defragmentation.
   d. After the defragmentation is finished, print a screen shot of the schematic diagram. Compare the two diagrams (before and after defragmentation).

Explore 6. **Scheduling Tasks** You've learned how to schedule maintenance tasks using the Task Scheduler. You can use the Task Scheduler to schedule additional programs. Now you'd like to schedule a virus checker on your computer. If you have access to a computer with a virus checker, schedule the virus checker so that it runs whenever you log on to Windows XP. If you don't have a virus checker, choose a different program to schedule.
   a. Open the Task Scheduler and add a new task for your virus checker (or a different program if you prefer). Schedule the task to run when you log on to Windows XP. Using the techniques listed in Assignment 5 above, print a screen shot of each dialog box in the Add Task wizard.
   b. If possible, log off and then log on to Windows XP to verify that the task starts as planned.
   c. If you are working in a lab, remove the task you added from the Task Scheduler.

PROJECTS

Explore 1. You can learn a lot about your system from the System Information tool.
   a. To open the System Information window, click the Start button, point to All Programs, point to Accessories, point to System Tools, and then click System Information.
   b. Print the System Summary information.
   c. Print the component information for the Display component.

Explore 2. You can customize your hardware settings on your computer through hardware profiles. Using the Help and Support Center, read about hardware profiles and write a report describing what hardware profiles are, when you would typically use them, and how to set up a hardware profile on your computer.

Explore 3. Another way of checking the performance of your hardware is to use the System Monitor. The System Monitor displays real-time information on system usage. One of the things you may want to monitor is **% Processor Time**, which is the percentage of time that the processor is executing. It's used as a measure of the load on the system's processor.
   a. To open the System Monitor, open the Control Panel, open Administrative Tools, and then double-click Performance.
   b. Click the Add button ⊞, and add the Interrupts/sec to the list of items being monitored.
   c. Using the techniques listed in Review Assignment 5, create a screen shot of the system monitor showing the Interrupts/sec being graphed.
   d. Stop and remove the process from the System Monitor.

   4. Another type of port that your computer might be using is a SCSI port. Research the topics of SCSI ports and SCSI devices, and write a report based on your research. In your report, write what the acronym "SCSI" stands for, describe the differences between these ports and the ports described in this tutorial, and describe the advantages and disadvantages of SCSI ports and devices.

LAB ASSIGNMENTS

Defragmentation and Disk Operations In this lab, you will format a simulated disk, save files, delete files, and undelete files to see how the computer updates the FAT. You will also find out how the files on your disk become fragmented and what a defragmentation utility does to reorganize the clusters on your disk. See the Read This Before You Begin page for instructions on installing and starting the Lab.

1. Click the Steps button to learn how the computer updates the FAT when you format a disk and save, delete, and undelete files. As you proceed through the steps, answer all of the Quick Check questions that appear. After you complete the steps, you will see a Quick Check Summary Report. Follow the instructions on the screen to print this report.

2. Click the Explore button. Click the Format button to format the simulated disk. Try to save files 1, 2, 3, 4, and 6. Do they all fit on the disk?

3. In Explore, format the simulated disk. Try to save all the files on the disk. What happens?

4. In Explore, format the simulated disk. Save FILE-3, FILE-4, and FILE-6. Next, delete FILE-6. Now, save FILE-5. Try to undelete FILE-6. What happens and why?

5. In Explore, format the simulated disk. Save and erase files until the files become fragmented. Draw a picture of the disk to show the fragmented files. Indicate which files are in each cluster by using color, crosshatching, or labels. List which files in your drawing are fragmented. Finally, defragment the disk and draw a new picture showing the unfragmented files.

QUICK | CHECK ANSWERS

Session 11.1

1. parallel, serial, and USB
2. PCI
3. IRQ stands for interrupt request line, and the computer uses it to handle simultaneous requests for action from hardware. There are 16 IRQs available to use.
4. A driver is a file on your computer that enables Windows XP to communicate with and control the operation of a hardware device.
5. A legacy device is an older hardware device on your system whose settings you have to enter manually. A plug-and-play device is a hardware device that Windows XP can configure automatically.
6. Open the Control Panel, open the System icon, and click the Device Manager button to open the Device Manager window.
7. Open the Device Manager window, click View on the menu bar, and then click View and Resources by type or Resources by connection.

Session 11.2

1. A local printer is connected directly to your computer through a parallel or serial cable. A network printer is a printer connected via the network.
2. Open the Properties dialog box for the printer, and then click the Print Test Page button on the General sheet.
3. Print spooling is the process of creating a file on your hard disk containing the codes to control the operation of your printer. The file is then sent to the printer to create the printed document.
4. The print queue is a list of documents waiting to be printed on the printer.
5. Open the print queue window, and then click Pause Printing on the Printer menu.
6. Right-click the document in the print queue window, and press the Delete key.

Session 11.3

1. virus
2. to prevent files from being stored inefficiently on the disk
3. one or more sectors of storage space—the minimum amount of space that an operating system reserves when saving the contents of a file on a disk
4. The FAT keeps track of the clusters on a disk and the status of each cluster.
5. False
6. A disk becomes fragmented when it contains files whose clusters are not next to each other.

CONNECTING
COMPUTERS
OVER A
PHONE LINE

Windows XP **Dial-Up Tools**

Windows XP makes communicating with computers easier than ever because it provides tools that allow you to connect your computer to other computers and to the Internet. If you are using a computer on a university or institutional network, you are probably already connected to the Internet, and you can skip this appendix. This appendix is useful for people who are not connected to the Internet but who have their own computer with a modem and access to a phone line.

Computers at universities or large companies are likely to be connected to the Internet via expensive, high-speed wiring that transmits data very quickly. Home computer owners, however, usually cannot afford to run similar cables and wires to their homes, and instead rely on phone lines that are already in place, as shown in Figure A-1.

Figure A-1   PHONE LINE CONNECTION TO THE INTERNET

computers and networks on the Internet

modem inside your computer

phone jack on the wall

your Internet service provider maintains a server directly connected to the Internet

phone lines connect your computer to your Internet service provider's server

Phone lines use analog signals, which is one way to transmit voice and other data across wires, but a computer sends data as digital signals, a different way to transmit information. Phone lines cannot transmit digital signals, so when a modem uses an ordinary voice phone line, it must convert the modem's digital signals to analog, as shown in Figure A-2.

The receiving computer converts the analog signal back to digital. Data usually travels more slowly over phone wires than over the networking infrastructure of the Internet. If there are any problems with the phone connection, data can be lost. But regular phone lines are often the only practical choice for homes and small businesses. In some areas, **ISDN lines**, wires that provide a completely digital path from one computer to another, are dropping in price so that small businesses and homeowners can afford them. Whether you use a regular phone line or a faster ISDN line, Windows XP can help you establish a connection to the Internet. You will need to select an **Internet service provider (ISP)**, a company that provides Internet access. ISPs maintain servers that are directly connected to the Internet 24 hours a day. You dial into your ISP's server over your phone line to use its Internet connection. You pay a fee for this service, most often a flat monthly rate. When you use your computer's modem to connect to an ISP via your phone line, you are making a **dial-up connection**.

Once you've selected an ISP, you can use Windows XP to set up your dial-up connection. Figure A-2 shows the tools Windows XP includes for connecting to the Internet.

Figure A-2	WINDOWS XP CONNECTION TOOLS	
CONNECTION TOOL	**AVAILABLE FROM**	**DESCRIPTION**
Network Connections window	Connect To command on the Windows XP Start menu	Some computer users have one Internet account for home use and a different account for business use. The Network Connections window helps you manage multiple accounts that you use to connect to the Internet.
New Connection Wizard	In the New Connection window, click the Create a new connection command under Network Tasks in the left pane	The New Connection Wizard makes it easy to create an Internet account for the first time by prompting you for information through a series of dialog boxes.

The following sections show you how to use the New Connection Wizard to set up a new dial-up connection to your ISP so you can access the Internet and other networks.

Setting Up a Dial-Up Connection

There are three ways you can establish a connection to the Internet using your phone line. All three methods require the New Connection Wizard. The New Connection Wizard is a series of dialog boxes that prompt you for information your computer needs to connect to the Internet. Once you start the New Connection Wizard, you have three choices for setting up your connection. You can choose an ISP from a list Windows XP provides through the New Connection Wizard. If you have already selected an ISP and this ISP provided a setup CD-ROM with an installation program, you can use the CD-ROM to set up the connection. Lastly, you can manually set up the necessary dial-up connection.

To set up a dial-up connection using any of these methods, you first need to start the New Connection Wizard.

Starting the New Connection Wizard

You can use the New Connection Wizard to create a dial-up account. These steps assume you have signed up for an account with an ISP, but you have not set up the account yet. Before you perform the steps, you should gather any documentation from your ISP, such as phone number, user name or account name, and password.

To begin setting up a dial-up connection:

1. Click the **Start** button ⚡ start on the taskbar, point to **Connect To**, and then click **Show all connections**. The Network Connections window opens. See Figure A-3.

| Figure A-3 | THE NETWORK CONNECTIONS WINDOW |

click to use the New Connection Wizard to set up a connection to your ISP

your list of connections and other options might be different

click this link to open a Troubleshooter to help solve connection problems

after you set up a connection, it appears in the Dial-up section

the red X indicates this connection is not currently established

2. Under Network Tasks, click **Create a new connection**. The Welcome to the New Connection Wizard dialog box opens, the first dialog box in the New Connection Wizard. The wizard will guide you through the steps of setting up a new connection.

   TROUBLE? If the Location Information window opens, provide the requested information and then click the OK button.

3. Click the **Next** button. The Network Connection Type dialog box opens. You can use this dialog box to connect to the Internet, connect to a business network, set up a small or home office network, or set up an advanced connection, which is usually a direct connection to another computer. These steps show you how to connect to the Internet.

4. Make sure the **Connect to the Internet** option button is selected, and then click the **Next** button. The Getting Ready dialog box opens.

At this point in the New Connection Wizard, you can choose from a list of ISPs, use the setup CD-ROM provided by an ISP, or set up a connection manually. The following section shows you how to set up an account by selecting one from the list of ISPs provided by the New Connection Wizard. After that section come sections that explain how to use a CD-ROM that an ISP provided to set up a connection and how to set up a connection manually.

Choosing from a List of ISPs

If you use a nationwide online service as your ISP, such as MSN, Earthlink, or Prodigy, you can quickly set up an automatic Internet connection by selecting an online service from a list Windows XP provides and then entering your user name and password. You can also have the Microsoft Internet Referral Service scan its list of ISPs to locate one you can access from your geographical area. If the Referral Service finds the one you want to use, you can select it and enter your user name and password to set up an automatic Internet connection.

To set up a connection by selecting an ISP from a list:

1. Make sure the New Connection Wizard is open to the Getting Ready dialog box.

   TROUBLE? If the Getting Ready dialog box is not open, start the New Connection Wizard again. Click the Start button, point to Connect To, click Show all connections, and then click Create a new connection. In the New Connection Wizard, click Next, and then click Next to open the Getting Ready dialog box.

2. Make sure the **Choose from a list of Internet Service Providers (ISPs)** option button is selected, and then click the **Next** button. The Completing the New Connection Wizard dialog box opens. This dialog box lets you set up an Internet connection using MSN Explorer or an ISP.

3. Click the **Select from a list of other ISPs** option button, and then click the **Finish** button. The Online Services window opens. See Figure A-4.

Figure A-4	THE ONLINE SERVICES WINDOW

double-click to set up an Internet connection with an online service

double-click to sign up for Internet access using MSN Explorer

double-click to search for ISPs in your area

your list of services and options may differ

If you subscribe to one of these online services, double-click the appropriate folder and then double-click an HTML file to see setup instructions in Internet Explorer. For example, open the EARTHLN~1 folder and then double-click the EarthInk HTML document. You can also look for more ISPs.

4. If necessary, select a modem and then click **OK**.

5. Double-click the **Refer me to more Internet Service Providers** icon. The Internet Connection Wizard starts and dials the Microsoft Internet Referral Service.

   TROUBLE? If the computer you are using already has an Internet connection, a message might appear asking if you want to continue. Click the Yes button.

   After you connect to the Referral Service, the Internet Connection Wizard lists ISPs in your area.

6. Click the ISP you want to use, and then click the **Next** button. The Internet Account Information dialog box opens.

   TROUBLE? If the Referral Service does not find any ISPs in your area, you must use a different method to set up a connection. See "Using a Setup CD-ROM from your ISP" or "Setting Up a Connection Manually."

7. Type your user name and password, and then click the **Next** button. Your ISP documentation will provide you with a user name and password.

   TROUBLE? If you cannot find your user name in your documentation, it might be called the User ID, Member ID, Account Name, Login Name, or something similar.

8. Type a name for your connection, such as the name of your ISP, and then click the **Next** button.

9. Deselect the **Connect to the Internet Immediately** check box, and then click the **Finish** button.

10. Close the Online Services window. You return to the Network Connections window.

If you set up an Internet connection by choosing an ISP from the list of services Windows XP provided, you can now use the connection to dial up to your ISP and connect to the Internet. See "Using the Network Connections Window" for details. If you did not set up an Internet connection in the previous steps, you'll see how to do so in the following section by using a CD-ROM your ISP provided.

Using a Setup CD-ROM from Your ISP

Some ISPs create Setup CD-ROMs that include all the information you need to set up a dial-up connection to the ISP. In this case, you start the New Connection Wizard, indicate that you want to use a CD-ROM your ISP provided, and then typically step through a Setup Wizard that your ISP provided on the CD-ROM.

To set up a connection using a CD-ROM from your ISP:

1. Start the New Connection Wizard.

   TROUBLE? To start the New Connection Wizard, click the Start button, point to Connect To, click Show all connections, and then click Create a new connection.

2. In the Welcome to the New Connection Wizard dialog box, click the **Next** button. In the Network Connection Type dialog box, make sure the **Connect to the Internet** option button is selected, and then click the **Nex**t button to open the Getting Ready dialog box.

3. Click the **Use the CD I got from an ISP** option button, and then click the **Next** button. The Completing the New Connection Wizard dialog box opens.

4. Click the **Finish** button.

5. Insert the CD-ROM your ISP gave you in the CD-ROM drive of your computer. A Setup program should start automatically to help you connect to the Internet.

   TROUBLE? If a Setup program does not start, contact your ISP.

If you set up an Internet connection by using the CD-ROM your ISP provided, you can now use the connection to dial up to your ISP and connect to the Internet. See "Using the Network Connections Window" for details. If you did not set up an Internet connection in the previous steps, you will learn how to set up a connection manually in the following section.

Setting Up a Connection Manually

If you could not set up a dial-up connection to your ISP using an online service, an ISP from the Microsoft Internet Referral Service, or a CD-ROM your ISP provided, you can set up a connection manually. To do so, you use the New Connection Wizard to enter the phone number of your ISP and the user name and password for your account. You can add a desktop shortcut to the connection so you can easily access it when you're finished.

To set up a connection manually:

1. Start the New Connection Wizard.

TROUBLE? To start the New Connection Wizard, click the Start button, point to Connect To, click Show all connections, and then click Create a new connection.

2. In the Welcome to the New Connection Wizard dialog box, click the **Next** button. In the Network Connection Type dialog box, make sure the **Connect to the Internet** option button is selected, and then click the **Next** button to open the Getting Ready dialog box.

3. Click the **Set up my connection manually** option button, and then click the **Next** button. The Internet Connection dialog box opens, asking how you want to connect to the Internet. In addition to using a dial-up modem to connect, you can also use this dialog box to connect using a broadband connection, which is a high-speed connection using either a digital service line (DSL) or a cable modem.

TROUBLE? If your computer has more than one modem, the Select a Device dialog box opens. Click the modem you want to use and then click Next.

TROUBLE? If you are using a broadband connection, see your instructor or technical support person for instructions on completing the New Connection Wizard.

4. Make sure the **Connect using a dial-up modem** option button is selected, and then click the **Next** button. The Connection Name dialog box opens.

5. Type a name for this connection, such as the name of your ISP, and then click the Next button. The Phone Number to Dial dialog box opens.

TROUBLE? If the Connection Availability dialog box opens, click Next to continue to the Phone Number to Dial dialog box.

6. Type the phone number of your ISP, and then click the Next button. The Internet Account Information dialog box opens.

7. Type the user name and password for your ISP account. In the Confirm password text box, type the password again. As you type the password, bullets appear instead of the letters you type, as shown in Figure A-5. This is a security feature; you should keep your password secret, so that unauthorized users cannot access your account.

TROUBLE? Refer to your ISP documentation for your user name and password. If you cannot find your user name in your documentation, it might be called the User ID, Member ID, Account Name, Login Name, or something similar.

Figure A-5   **ENTERING ACCOUNT INFORMATION**

8. Click the **Next** button. In the Completing the New Connection Wizard dialog box, click the **Add a shortcut to this connection to my desktop** check box to select this option, and then click the **Finish** button.

   The Connect dialog box opens. You could use it to connect to your ISP now by clicking the Dial button. For now, you can close this dialog box.

9. Click the **Cancel** button.

Now you can use your new dial-up connection to connect to your ISP and the Internet.

Using the Network Connections Window

Once you have established a dial-up connection, you are ready to use it to connect to the Internet or another network or computer. Windows XP will try to connect to the Internet automatically whenever you start a program that requires Internet access, such as your Web browser. If you have more than one ISP, Windows XP uses the one you set as the default connection.

Other ways of establishing your Internet connection would be to double-click the shortcut icon to your ISP on your desktop, or open the Network Connections window and then double-click the icon for your ISP. This window also provides tools to change your dial-up settings or any of your network connections (through your modem or local area network).

To connect to your dial-up service through the Network Connections window:

1. Click the **Start** button ![start], point to **Connect To**, and then click **Show all connections**. The Network Connections window opens as shown in Figure A-6.

| Figure A-6 | NETWORK CONNECTIONS |

double-click the Network Connection icon on the desktop...

...or in the Network Connections window to connect to your dial-up service

click to change your dial-up settings

You can have more than one network service, in which case multiple icons appear in the Network Connections window. One connection might provide your business Internet service, another might be for home or family use, and another might access your local area network.

2. Make sure your phone line is connected to your computer's modem.

3. Double-click the icon for your ISP.

The Connecting dialog box opens and identifies the steps of establishing a connection. First it uses your modem to dial the number, then it verifies your user name and password, and finally it establishes a connection. A ScreenTip may appear, indicating that you are connected to your ISP.

4. A connection icon 🖥 appears on your taskbar that indicates you are connected. You can now start your Internet browser to view Web pages, check your e-mail, or use any of the other Windows XP online communications features.

Your dial-up account will remain connected until you leave your computer idle for several minutes, in which case your ISP may automatically disconnect you, or until you disconnect from your account yourself.

To disconnect your dial-up account:

1. Double-click the Connection icon 🖥 on the taskbar. The Status dialog box opens, shown in Figure A-7.

Figure A-7   THE STATUS DIALOG BOX

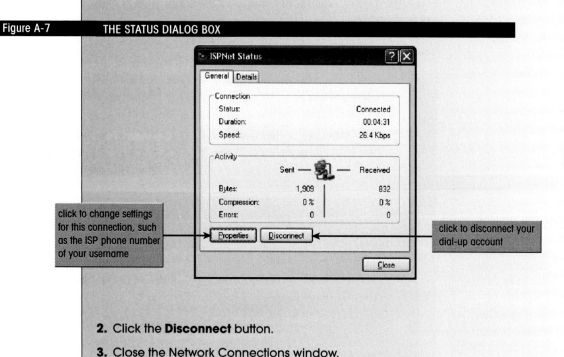

click to change settings for this connection, such as the ISP phone number of your username

click to disconnect your dial-up account

2. Click the **Disconnect** button.

3. Close the Network Connections window.

In this appendix you have learned how to set up an Internet connection using your voice phone line and an ISP service. The Internet service provider market is changing very rapidly, so make sure you compare prices and features before choosing the ISP that best suits your needs.

EXPLORING
ADDITIONAL
WINDOWS
XP TOOLS

Using **Power Management Features**

The Windows XP **power management features** allow you to control the amount of power your computer and its devices use when they are not running at full capacity. For example, if you're taking a short break, you might not want to turn your system off completely, because shutting down and then restarting the computer is time consuming. Instead, you can place the computer on **standby**, a mode that reduces the amount of power consumed by your drives and monitor but still allows you to return to work quickly because the computer is not actually turned off. Some users leave their computers on 24 hours a day to perform resource-intensive tasks in the middle of the night, or to use their computers to receive faxes or download files when they are not sitting at their computers. Windows XP can perform tasks such as these when the machine is in standby mode. This mode is also useful for conserving battery power in portable computers. You can specify one standby setting for battery power and a different setting for AC power.

If you plan to be away from the computer for an extended time or overnight, you can put the computer in hibernation mode. During **hibernation**, Windows XP saves everything in memory on disk, turns off your monitor and hard disk, and then turns off your computer. When you restart your computer, your desktop is restored exactly as you left it. Note that it takes longer to bring your computer out of hibernation than out of standby.

The power management features conserve both energy and money, but you can use these features only if your computer hardware is designed for power conservation. When you set power management options, Windows XP automatically detects what is available on your computer and shows you only the features that you can control. If the following sections describe a feature that you do not see on your computer, your hardware most likely does not support that feature. Although you may not be able to perform the steps, read through the sections to learn the power management concepts and principles. You must also be logged on to your computer as an Administrator.

Working with Power Management Schemes

You change power management settings via the Control Panel by working with **power schemes**, groups of preset power management options. For example, one power scheme sets the best power options for a laptop computer, which needs to conserve battery power. The default power scheme for a laptop computer turns off the monitor after 15 minutes of idle time and keeps the monitor blank until you move the mouse. Figure B-1 lists the power schemes that Windows XP provides by default, although you can create additional schemes for your own needs.

Figure B-1	POWER MANAGEMENT SCHEMES			
WINDOWS XP POWER SCHEME	**TURNS OFF MONITOR**	**TURNS OFF HARD DISKS**	**SWITCHES TO STANDBY MODE**	**SWITCHES TO HIBERNATION MODE**
Home/Office Desk	After 20 minutes	Never	After 30 minutes	Never
Portable/Laptop	After 15 minutes	After 30 minutes	After 20 minutes	After 3 hours
Presentation	Never	Never	Never	Never
Always on	After 20 minutes	Never	Never	Never
Minimal Power Management	After 15 minutes	Never	Never	Never
Max Battery	After 15 minutes	Never	After 20 minutes	After 45 minutes

All power schemes include settings for when to turn off the monitor and hard disk and when to put the system into standby or hibernation.

To view your computer's power management settings:

1. Click the **Start** button ⊞ start on the taskbar, and then click **Control Panel**.

2. Maximize the Control Panel window, and then click **Switch to Classic View**, if necessary, in the left pane.

3. Double-click the **Power Options** icon 🔌.

   The Power Options Properties dialog box opens as shown in Figure B-2.

Figure B-2	POWER OPTIONS PROPERTIES DIALOG BOX

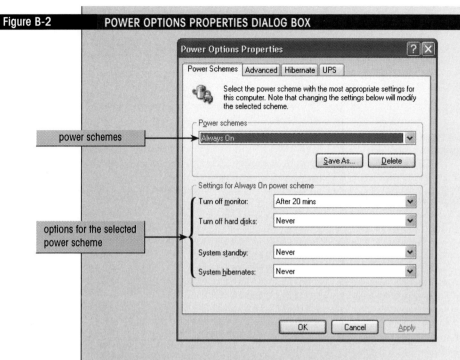

power schemes

options for the selected power scheme

4. On the Power Schemes tab, click the **Power schemes** list arrow. Note the schemes available to your computer. The settings for the selected power scheme appear below the Power schemes list box.

   TROUBLE? If you don't see the Power Schemes tab or the Power schemes list arrow, you might not have administrative control over your computer. Ask your instructor or technical support person for assistance. If you cannot get administrative control, review this material without performing the steps.

5. Click outside the list in the Power Options Properties dialog box to close the list.

Before your system can hibernate, hibernation must be enabled on your computer. In the next section, you'll make sure it is.

Using Hibernation

If your computer hardware supports hibernation, Windows XP enables it by default. However, because this feature requires a certain amount of hard disk space in which to save your work before it shuts down your computer, you can turn off hibernation if you need to save disk space. If you want your system to hibernate, make sure Windows XP is set up to enable hibernation.

To enable hibernation on your computer:

1. Click the **Hibernate** tab in the Power Options Properties dialog box.

2. If necessary, click the **Enable hibernation** check box as shown in Figure B-3.

Figure B-3	ENABLING HIBERNATION

Power Options Properties

Power Schemes | Advanced | Hibernate | UPS

When your computer hibernates, it stores whatever it has in memory on your hard disk and then shuts down. When your computer comes out of hibernation, it returns to its previous state.

Hibernate

☑ Enable hibernation ← click to turn on the hibernation feature

Disk space for hibernation

Free disk space: 70,368 MB
Disk space required to hibernate: 256 MB ← Windows XP needs this much free disk space to save the current working environment

your settings may differ

[OK] [Cancel] [Apply]

Once this feature has been enabled, your system will go into hibernation mode as defined by your current power scheme. You can also go into hibernation mode at any time by clicking the Turn Off Computer command on the Start menu to open the Shut Down Windows dialog box. Then you can click the What do you want the computer to do list arrow and select the Hibernate option. (To use the Shut Down Windows dialog box, you might have to change the way users log off. From the Control Panel, open the User Accounts window, click Change the way users log on or off, deselect the Use Welcome screen check box, and then click the Apply Options button.)

Using an Uninterruptible Power Supply

The safest way to guard your computer against the possibility of power failure (and the associated loss of data) is with an **uninterruptible power supply**, or **UPS**. When your computer experiences a power failure, the UPS immediately detects it and supplies emergency power from a battery connected to the computer through a COM port. Then you can safely shut down your computer without the loss of critical data.

You can install support for a UPS from the Power Options Properties dialog box. Note that if you were actually adding a UPS device to your system, you would perform these steps after connecting the device to your computer.

To enable support for a UPS:

1. Click the **UPS** tab in the Power Options Properties dialog box. See Figure B-4.

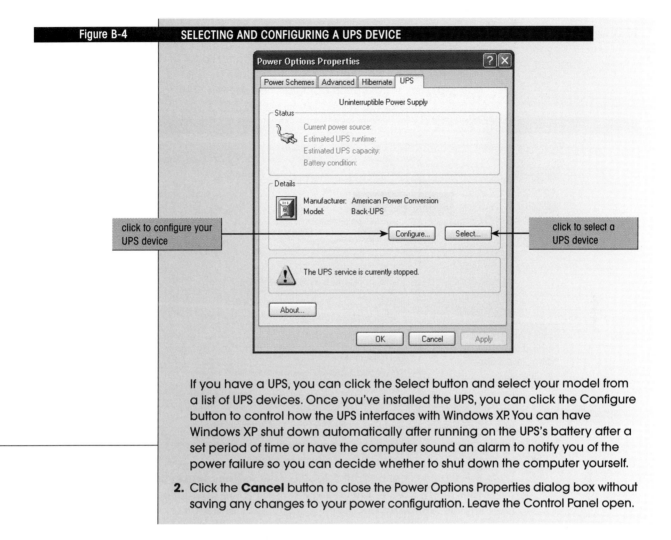

Figure B-4   SELECTING AND CONFIGURING A UPS DEVICE

If you have a UPS, you can click the Select button and select your model from a list of UPS devices. Once you've installed the UPS, you can click the Configure button to control how the UPS interfaces with Windows XP. You can have Windows XP shut down automatically after running on the UPS's battery after a set period of time or have the computer sound an alarm to notify you of the power failure so you can decide whether to shut down the computer yourself.

2. Click the **Cancel** button to close the Power Options Properties dialog box without saving any changes to your power configuration. Leave the Control Panel open.

Now that you've learned how to conserve power when you're using your computer, you can learn how to customize the mouse to suit your needs.

Customizing the Mouse

The Mouse Properties dialog box, available through the Control Panel, lets you customize the mouse settings. You can configure the mouse for the right or left hand, adjust the double-click speed, choose different pointer shapes, adjust the pointer speed, and turn on pointer **trails**, which make the pointer easier to see when you are moving it. If you have a Microsoft IntelliPoint mouse or another pointing device, you might see additional features in the Mouse Properties dialog box that are specific to that type of pointing device.

Configuring the Mouse for the Right or Left Hand

You can configure the mouse for either right-handed or left-handed users. To do so, you switch the primary and secondary buttons. Windows XP considers the left button to be the primary button, and the right button to be the secondary button. If you are left-handed, you can configure the mouse settings so the right button (the one your forefinger rests on if you are left-handed) is the primary button and the left button is secondary.

To configure the mouse for right-handed or left-handed users:

1. Double-click the **Mouse** icon 🖰 in the Control Panel to display the Mouse Properties dialog box. You can set the mouse for right-handed users or left-handed users in the Button configuration section. See Figure B-5.

Figure B-5   THE MOUSE PROPERTIES DIALOG BOX

if you are left-handed, click this check box to switch the primary and secondary mouse buttons

click to use ClickLock instead of holding down the mouse button to drag

double-click the folder icon to test your double-click speed

drag to adjust the double-click speed of your mouse

---

2. If you are left-handed, click to select the **Switch primary and secondary buttons** check box. As you change this setting, the description and picture of mouse operations change. If you are right-handed, do not select this check box.

3. If you are working on your own computer, click the **Apply** button to apply your changes, and then test the new mouse setting by dragging the Mouse Properties dialog box with the appropriate mouse button.

4. Return this setting to its original state, and then click the **Apply** button.

    TROUBLE? If Step 4 doesn't seem to reset your mouse, try using the other mouse button.

In addition to configuring the mouse buttons, you can also customize the double-click speed of your mouse.

Adjusting Double-Click Speed

Most Windows programs use double-clicking to select or open objects. Because some new users double-click more slowly or more quickly than others, Windows XP lets you set your preference so you can work comfortably with the mouse. First you can test your double-click speed to see if you need to adjust it.

To test the current double-click speed:

1. Position the pointer over the **folder icon** in the Mouse Properties dialog box.

2. Place your hand on the mouse, and double-click the mouse button as you normally do.

   TROUBLE? If you changed the mouse to left-handed operation, you will need to double-click by quickly pressing and releasing the right mouse button twice.

   If you double-click successfully, the folder icon opens.

3. Double-click the **folder icon** again to close it.

   TROUBLE? If you couldn't open the folder, you probably need to adjust the double-click speed of the mouse. You'll do so in the next set of steps.

If you have trouble double-clicking, you can slow down the double-click speed by using the Double-click speed slider.

To slow down the double-click speed:

1. Drag the **Double-click speed** slider to the left, toward Slow.

2. Double-click the **folder icon** to see if you can open it.

3. If you still cannot successfully double-click to open the folder, drag the **Double-click speed** slider even farther to the left toward Slow, and then repeat Step 2.

4. Once you can successfully double-click, try increasing or decreasing the double-click speed to find the most comfortable speed for you.

5. If you are using your own computer, click the **Apply** button to change the double-click speed to the new setting. If you are in a lab, make sure to restore this setting to its original status.

Besides setting the double-click speed, you can also set the speed of the pointer, which you'll do in the next section.

Adjusting Pointer Speed

Use the Pointer Options property sheet in the Mouse Properties dialog box to adjust the pointer speed or the relative distance the pointer moves on the screen when you move the mouse. It can be easier to use a slower speed when you need more control. Likewise, you might need faster speed if you have limited desktop space.

To adjust the pointer speed:

1. Click the **Pointer Options** tab in the Mouse Properties dialog box to display the Pointer Options property sheet. See Figure B-6.

Figure B-6	POINTER OPTIONS FOR THE MOUSE

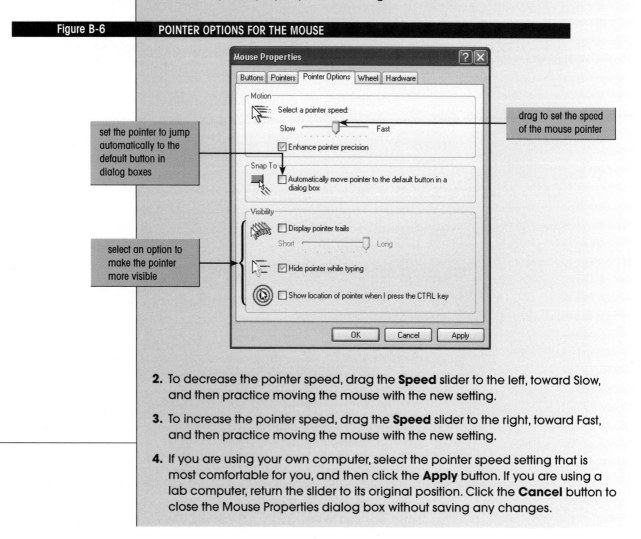

set the pointer to jump automatically to the default button in dialog boxes

drag to set the speed of the mouse pointer

select an option to make the pointer more visible

2. To decrease the pointer speed, drag the **Speed** slider to the left, toward Slow, and then practice moving the mouse with the new setting.

3. To increase the pointer speed, drag the **Speed** slider to the right, toward Fast, and then practice moving the mouse with the new setting.

4. If you are using your own computer, select the pointer speed setting that is most comfortable for you, and then click the **Apply** button. If you are using a lab computer, return the slider to its original position. Click the **Cancel** button to close the Mouse Properties dialog box without saving any changes.

You can adjust additional mouse settings using the Accessibility Options feature, as you'll see in the next section.

Using Accessibility Options

Accessibility options are Windows XP settings that you can change to make interacting with your computer easier. Although designed primarily for users with special vision, hearing, and mobility needs, users without special needs also find adjusting accessibility settings is helpful when they are working with drawing software and need more control over mouse and keyboard settings, using a portable computer with a small screen, or working in a poorly lit room.

You can change accessibility settings in two ways. You can open the Accessibility Options dialog box from the Control Panel to access individual accessibility settings, or you can use the Accessibility Settings Wizard to determine what settings you should change to work most effectively. You'll examine some individual accessibility settings and then learn how to start the Accessibility Settings Wizard.

To open the Accessibility Options dialog box:

1. Double-click the **Accessibility Options** icon ♿ in Control Panel. The Accessibility Options dialog box opens. Make sure the Keyboard tab is selected. See Figure B-7.

Figure B-7	ACCESSIBILITY OPTIONS DIALOG BOX

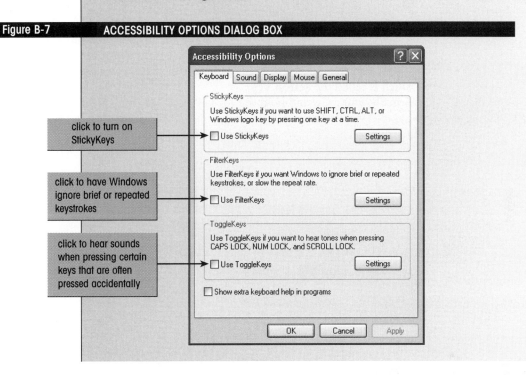

click to turn on StickyKeys

click to have Windows ignore brief or repeated keystrokes

click to hear sounds when pressing certain keys that are often pressed accidentally

The Accessibility Options dialog box has five tabs: Keyboard, Sound, Display, Mouse, and General. First you'll explore some of the most commonly used accessibility options. See Figure B-8.

Figure B-8	ACCESSIBILITY FEATURES

TAB NAME	DESCRIPTION	ACCESSIBILITY FEATURES
Keyboard	Set options for using keys and keyboard shortcuts	StickyKeys: Press modifier and then the action key separately instead of simultaneously FilterKeys: Ignore brief or repeated keystrokes or slow the rate at which keystrokes are repeated ToggleKeys: Hear tones when pressing the Caps Lock, Num Lock, and Scroll Lock keys
Sound	Set options for replacing computer sounds with text or images	SoundSentry: Generate a visual warning when your system makes a sound ShowSounds: Have programs display captions for the speech and sounds they make
Display	Set options to improve the readability of items on your computer screen	High Contrast: Use colors and fonts designed for easy reading Cursor Options: Change the speed and width of the cursor
Mouse	Set an option to control the pointer without using the mouse	MouseKeys: Control the pointer with the numeric keypad on your keyboard
General	Set options related to using accessibility features	Automatic Reset: Turn off accessibility features after a specified amount of time Notification: Display a message or play a sound when using an accessibility feature SerialKey Devices: Connect to input devices taking the place of keyboards and mice Administrative Options: Apply accessibility settings to logon desktop and to default settings for new users

Simplifying Keyboard Shortcuts with StickyKeys

You can perform many actions either with the mouse or by holding down one key while pressing another key. For example, instead of clicking the Start button to open the Start menu, you can use Ctrl+Esc. (Hold down the Ctrl key, and then press the Esc key.) Key combinations like this one are often called **keyboard shortcuts**. Some users have trouble pressing two keys at once; StickyKeys is a feature that makes it easier. You typically use one of three keys—the Shift key, the Ctrl key, or the Alt key—with another key to perform an action, such as selecting a menu command. These three keys are also known as **modifier keys**—you hold them down while pressing another key to modify the action of the second key, which is called the **action key**.

Normally, you press and hold the Alt key and then press an action key to open a menu. For example, you can press Alt+F to open the File menu. If you don't want to hold down the modifier key, such as Alt, you can turn on StickyKeys. With StickyKeys, you can press and release the modifier key and then press the action key, so you'd press Alt and then F to open the File menu.

To turn on StickyKeys:

1. Click the **Use StickyKeys** check box to select this option.

2. Click the **Apply** button to activate StickyKeys. After a few moments, the StickyKeys icon 🎛 appears in the taskbar notification area.

Now you can test the effect of StickyKeys by using a keyboard shortcut to open the File menu.

To test the effect of StickyKeys:

1. Click the **Control Panel** button on the taskbar to activate the Control Panel window.

2. Press and release the **Alt** key. A sound indicates that you pressed a StickyKey. The sound and the icon indicate that the next key you press will be combined with the Alt key.

   TROUBLE? If you didn't hear a sound, sounds might not be enabled on your StickyKeys settings or on your computer. To enable sounds, click the Settings button on the Keyboard property sheet, and select the desired sound settings.

3. Press the **F** key. The File menu opens again. Because StickyKeys was activated, you did not have to hold down the Alt key while you pressed the F key.

4. Press the **Esc** key twice to close the File menu.

5. Click the **Minimize** button ⬜ to minimize the Control Panel window.

6. In the Accessibility Options dialog box, click the **Use StickyKeys** check box to remove the check mark, and then click the **Apply** button to deactivate StickyKeys. The StickyKeys icon disappears from the taskbar.

Note that you can also start StickyKeys by pressing the Shift key on your keyboard five times in succession.

Using MouseKeys to Control the Pointer

All users occasionally have trouble using the mouse to control the pointer, especially when using drawing or graphics programs. You can turn on **MouseKeys**, a feature that lets you control the pointer with the numeric keypad as well as with the mouse. This is also a useful feature if you have a hand injury.

To see how MouseKeys works, you'll start Paint, turn on MouseKeys, and then use the keys on the numeric keypad to draw on the Paint canvas.

To start Paint and turn on MouseKeys:

1. Click the **Start** button, point to **All Programs**, point to **Accessories**, and then click **Paint**. Minimize the Paint window.

2. In the Accessibility Options dialog box, click the **Mouse** tab.

3. Click the **Use MouseKeys** check box to insert a check mark.

4. If number lock is not on, press the **NumLock** key on your keyboard.

5. Click the **Apply** button to activate MouseKeys. After a short time, the MouseKeys icon 🔘 appears in the taskbar notification area. See Figure B-9.

| Figure B-9 | ENABLING MOUSEKEYS |

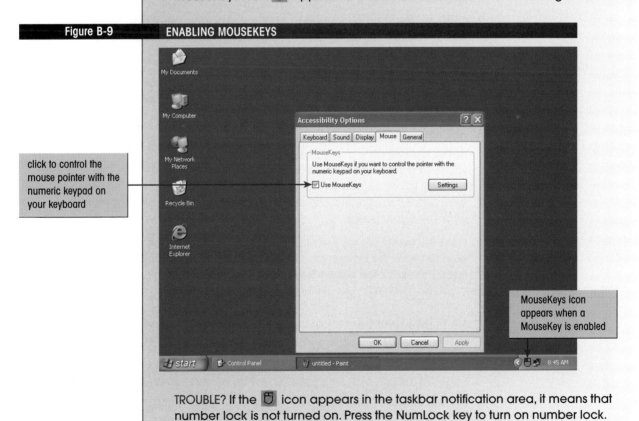

click to control the mouse pointer with the numeric keypad on your keyboard

MouseKeys icon appears when a MouseKey is enabled

TROUBLE? If the 🔘 icon appears in the taskbar notification area, it means that number lock is not turned on. Press the NumLock key to turn on number lock.

Before you try working with MouseKeys, study Figure B-10, which describes some of the mouse actions you can duplicate using keys on the numeric keypad.

Figure B-10	MOUSEKEYS AND CORRESPONDING KEYS
MOUSE ACTION	**CORRESPONDING NUMERIC KEYPAD KEY**
Move pointer horizontally	Press 4 to move left, 6 to move right
Move pointer vertically	Press 8 to move up, 2 to move down
Move pointer diagonally	Press 7, 1, 9, and 3
Click	Press 5
Double-click	Press + (plus)
Right-click	Press – (minus), then press 5 (pressing – assigns the right-click function to 5; when you are done right-clicking, press / to restore 5 to clicking)
Begin dragging after pointing to object	Press Insert and then press arrow keys
End dragging	Press Delete to release mouse button
Move a single pixel at a time	Press and hold Shift, then use directional keys

To practice using MouseKeys:

1. Click the **Paint** program button on the taskbar, and then use the numeric key-pad to move the pointer over the **Paint** program window. The 8 key moves the pointer up.

   TROUBLE? Most keyboards have two keypads: one with only arrows and one with numbers and arrows. Make sure you are using the keypad with arrows and numbers.

   TROUBLE? If MouseKeys isn't working, Windows XP might be set to turn off accessibility options after a specified amount of time. Return to the Mouse property sheet, and then reset MouseKeys by clicking the Apply button. Then click the General tab to see if the Turn off accessibility features after idle for check box is selected. If it is, click the check box to deselect this option for now, and then click the Apply button.

2. Press the **Insert** key on the numeric keypad to start drawing. Press the number keys to move the pointer and draw precise vertical, horizontal, and diagonal lines. Then click the **Delete** key to stop drawing.

If you've used Paint before, you might notice that this is a much slower method of drawing, but it is more precise. Now close Paint and deactivate MouseKeys.

To use MouseKeys to close the Paint window:

1. Use the keys on the numeric keypad to move the pointer over the **Close** button ☒ in the Paint window.

2. Press the **5** key to click ☒.

3. Use the keys on the numeric keypad to move the pointer over the **No** button in the Paint dialog box, and then press the **5** key to close Paint.

4. In the Accessibility Options dialog box, click the **Use MouseKeys** check box to turn off this feature, and then click the **Apply** button.

While you can use MouseKeys to move the pointer more precisely, you'll use another feature in the next section to see items on the screen more clearly.

Enabling High Contrast

The Display property sheet in the Accessibility Options dialog box lets you set the screen display to high contrast.

By default, high contrast uses large white letters on a black background and increases the size of the title bar and window control buttons, making objects and text stand out. If you have limited vision or if you're in a dark office, high-contrast mode can make it easier to see what's on your screen.

Before you turn on high contrast, you can select a high contrast scheme, a collection of colors and text sizes to use for the desktop, windows, and other on-screen elements.

To turn on high contrast:

1. Click the **Display** tab in the Accessibility Options dialog box to see the display properties.

2. Click the **Settings** button to open the Settings for High Contrast dialog box. You can click the list arrow on this dialog box to choose a high contrast scheme.

3. Click the **Your current high contrast scheme is** list arrow, and then click **High Contrast Black**.

4. Click the **OK** button to close the Settings for High Contrast dialog box.

5. In the Accessibility Options dialog box, click the **Use High Contrast** check box to select this option.

6. Click the **Apply** button to activate the high contrast settings. After a short time, the screen shows the high contrast settings. See Figure B-11. Note that on screens set to a lower resolution, high contrast can make the desktop appear crowded.

| Figure B-11 | THE HIGH CONTRAST SETTING |

The high contrast setting affects all programs, but it does not affect the contents of the document window in a program. Now you should return the setting to its original state.

To turn off the high contrast setting:

1. Click the **Use High Contrast** check box to remove the check mark.

2. Click the **Apply** button to apply the new setting. After a short time, the screen returns to the normal display.

   TROUBLE? If the Apply button is hidden behind the taskbar, drag the Accessibility Options dialog box up until you can see the Apply button.

   TROUBLE? If clicking Apply does not return the desktop to its normal display, right-click a blank area of the desktop, click Properties, click the Appearance tab, click the Windows and buttons list arrow, and then click Windows XP style.

Next you will set the accessibility features to turn off automatically after a specified period of idle time.

Turning Off Accessibility Options Automatically

You also use the Accessibility Options dialog box to set accessibility features to turn off automatically after the computer sits idle for a period of time. This is ideal for situations such as computer labs, where you want to use accessibility options, but other users don't. In the following steps, you'll select this setting and then close the dialog box without saving your changes in case you are working in a lab and should not change the settings on your computer.

To make sure that the accessibility options turn off after a specified period of time:

1. Click the **General** tab in the Accessibility Options dialog box.

2. If the **Turn off accessibility features after idle for** check box is not checked, click it to activate this feature.

3. You can click the minutes list arrow to select a period of time from 5 to 30 minutes, after which the accessibility features turn off automatically. Refer to Figure B-12 to see how you would make sure that the accessibility features turn off after a specified period of time. Don't make this change, however, if you are using a lab computer.

Figure B-12	SETTING ACCESSIBILITY OPTIONS TO TURN OFF AUTOMATICALLY

the number of minutes before the accessibility options disengage

4. Click the **Cancel** button to close the Accessibility Options dialog box without saving your changes.

Next, you'll examine the other options in the Accessibility Options dialog box and learn how to start the Accessibility Wizard.

The Accessibility Options Wizard

If you want to further refine your accessibility settings, you can use the Accessibility Wizard. You can use the Wizard to set the size of screen text and other items on your screen, and let Windows XP configure settings according to special vision, hearing, and mobility needs. Figure B-13 describes the options you can set only with the Accessibility Wizard.

Figure B-13	ACCESSIBILITY WIZARD FEATURES

ACCESSIBILITY WIZARD PAGE	DESCRIPTION OF FEATURES TO SET
Text size	Select a font size that you can comfortably read
Display settings	Set the font size of on-screen text, use a lower screen resolution, use Microsoft Magnifier to increase the size of text you point to with the Magnifier pointer, and disable personalized menus
Set Wizard options	Select an option to configure Windows XP to your vision, hearing, or mobility needs
Scroll bar and window size	Vision-impaired users can set the size of the scroll bars and window borders
SoundSentry	Hearing-impaired users can display visual warnings instead of system sounds
StickyKeys	Mobility-impaired users can use StickyKeys instead of pressing keys simultaneously
Set automatic timeouts	Administrators can set timeouts for StickyKeys, FilterKeys, ToggleKeys, and High Contrast features

Another feature users often want to customize is the fonts on their computer. You'll learn how to view and install fonts next.

Working with Fonts

From the Control Panel you can open the Fonts window, which you use to manage the fonts on your computer. As you probably know, a **font** is the design of a collection of numbers, symbols, and characters. All the fonts in the Fonts window are available for use in all your Windows programs. You can use the Fonts window to open fonts to look at their style and print a test page. You can also install or delete fonts.

To view the fonts installed on your computer:

1. Return to the Control Panel window.

2. Double-click the **Fonts** icon 🗎. The Fonts window opens.

3. To display more details about the fonts installed on your computer, click the **Details** button 🔲 on the Standard Buttons toolbar. See Figure B-14.

Figure B-14	VIEWING FONT DETAILS

4. Scroll down the list of fonts to see which fonts are installed on your computer.

In Details view, the Fonts window shows you the name of the font, its filename, and its type, among other information. The next section explains how those three font characteristics are related.

Font Types

When you view the Fonts window in Details view, you see detailed information about the font files on your computer. A **font file** contains the information Windows XP needs to display the font on the computer screen or to print the font. A font file's name is not necessarily the same as the name of the font itself, as you can see in Figure B-14. The Arial Bold font, for example, is stored in a file named ARIALBD.ttf.

Scroll through the Fonts window, and notice the filenames. Some filenames have a TTF extension, while others have an FON extension. The extensions indicate that these are different types of fonts. Those with a TTF extension are TrueType fonts (or OpenType, an updated extension of TrueType), which Windows XP uses to both display text on your computer screen and to print text on a printer. Those font files with FON extensions are screen fonts, which Windows uses only to display text on your screen. The Fonts window does not show printer fonts you might have installed when you installed a printer. These fonts reside in the printer or on a font cartridge. They do not appear in the Fonts window, but they do appear in the Font list of Windows programs, such as WordPad. Figure B-15 describes the types of fonts your computer can use.

Figure B-15	FONT TYPES
FONT TYPE	**DESCRIPTION**
Screen fonts	Fonts used by your computer monitor to display the text that appears in dialog boxes, menus, buttons, and icons. Screen fonts are also used when you preview how your document will look when printed, although they do not always perfectly match the fonts your printer uses. This can cause your printed documents to look slightly different than you expect.
TrueType and OpenType fonts	Fonts capable of both being displayed on your monitor and being printed on your printer with minimal change in appearance. Windows XP includes many of these fonts. You can also scale a TrueType font—enlarge or shrink it without its losing its shape and appearance—and rotate a TrueType font.
Printer fonts	Fonts built into your printer. These are not stored in files on your computer and therefore do not appear in the Fonts window.
Postscript fonts	Fonts developed by a company called Adobe that are described by a special language called Postscript. You can scale and rotate Postscript fonts, but they require an extra software utility called the Adobe Type Manager to be converted into a form that a computer monitor can display. Postscript fonts are a special type of printer font.

As you scrolled through the Fonts window, you might have noticed that some fonts have one base font and a number of variations. For example, Times New Roman is a base font and has three variations: Times New Roman Bold, Times New Roman Bold Italic, and Times New Roman Italic. Times New Roman uses the Times.ttf file, while each variation uses a separate file: Timesbd.ttf, Timesbi.ttf, and Timesi.ttf, respectively. When you choose an attribute such as bold or italic from within a program, you are actually choosing an alternate font file. To reduce the number of fonts listed in the Fonts window, you can use the Hide Variations command on the View menu to show only the font names, not all the variations.

Opening a Font

You can open a font in the Fonts window to see its characteristics and how it will look in a variety of sizes. One of the fonts that comes with Windows XP is Comic Sans MS.

To open the Comic Sans MS font:

1. Right-click the **Comic Sans MS** font, and then click **Open** on the shortcut menu.

A window displays the font in different sizes, along with information about the font and its creator at the top of the window. See Figure B-16.

TROUBLE? If the Comic Sans MS font does not appear in your Fonts window, select a different font to complete these steps.

information about the font and font file

samples of the different font characters

font samples in increasing size

click to print a hard copy of the font window

2. Click the **Done** button to close the Comic Sans MS window.

In addition to using the fonts that Windows XP or your printer provides, you can also find fonts on the Internet or in font collections on disk or CD-ROM. Before you can use such fonts, you must install them.

Installing a Font

When you install a font, you place it in the Fonts folder on your hard disk, and Windows XP makes it available to other programs. You can install a font using the Install New Font command found on the File menu in the Fonts window.

To install a new font:

1. Click **File** on the menu bar, and then click **Install New Font**. The Add Fonts dialog box opens. See Figure B-17.

font files in the selected folder

selected folder

current drive

select this option to copy the font file to the Fonts folder on the hard disk

> If you needed to install a font, you would select the drive and folder containing the font. It would then appear in the List of fonts box. You would click it and then click the OK button.
>
> 2. Click the **Close** button to close the Add Fonts dialog box without installing a font, and then close all open windows.

In addition to viewing and installing fonts, you can also delete the fonts you no longer use.

Deleting a Font

As you add fonts to your computer, you might find you have many that you don't use often. Fonts take valuable disk space, so you should periodically delete those you don't need. You can delete a font by clicking the font icon in the Fonts window and then pressing the Delete key.

Before you delete a font, make sure no documents you need use that font. Documents that do would no longer print correctly. You also should not delete fonts with the ◢ icon, because you might inadvertently delete a font that Windows XP needs to display objects on the screen. If you are working in a computer lab, it is unlikely that you will be able to delete fonts. You've completed your work with the Control Panel, so you can close it.

> ### *To close the Font window and the Control Panel:*
>
> 1. Click the **Close** button ☒ .

One other Windows XP tool that you will use often is the Recycle Bin. The following section explains how to delete and restore files with the Recycle Bin.

Working **with the Recycle Bin**

Deleting a file is a two-step process. First, you delete the file using a tool such as My Computer. The file no longer appears in the contents of the folder or device from which you deleted it. However, Windows XP has not actually removed it from the hard disk. It remains on the disk, and the information about its original location is stored in the Recycle Bin. To delete a file completely from your hard drive, you must empty the Recycle Bin by right-clicking its icon 🗑 in My Computer or on the desktop and then clicking Empty Recycle Bin. Emptying the Recycle Bin frees disk space, but do not choose this option unless you are absolutely sure you will no longer need the files. You can also open the Recycle Bin window from Windows Explorer or the desktop.

You can restore a deleted file to its original location by opening the Recycle Bin window, right-clicking the filename, and selecting the Restore command from the shortcut menu. Note however, that you cannot restore files you deleted from a floppy disk or from a network drive, because these are not stored in the local drive's Recycle Bin. Once you empty the Recycle Bin, it is almost impossible to recover the file.

> ### *To restore a file from the Recycle Bin:*
>
> 1. Right-click the **Recycle Bin** 🗑 on your desktop, and click **Open**.
>
> The Recycle Bin window opens as shown in Figure B-18.

Figure B-18	THE RECYCLE BIN WINDOW

click to empty all items in the Recycle Bin, permanently deleting them

click to restore all files to their original locations

2. Right-click the file you want to restore in the right pane, and click **Restore** on the shortcut menu.

   The file is restored to its original location in your computer.

3. Click the **Close** button ⊠ to close the Recycle Bin window.

In this appendix, you learned how to use common Windows XP tools that you can find in the Control Panel and on your desktop. You learned how to use the Control Panel to customize the power management features, mouse settings, accessibility options, and fonts on your computer, and to use the Recycle Bin to delete and restore files.

TASK	PAGE #	RECOMMENDED METHOD
Accessibility options, set	WIN B.09	Open the Control Panel in Classic View, double-click Accessibility Options
Active Desktop item, add from Web Gallery	WIN 5.26	In Control Panel, click Appearance and Themes, click Change the desktop background, click the Customize Desktop button, click the Web tab, click the New button, click the Visit Gallery button, click the Add to Active Desktop button for the item you want, click Yes, click OK
Active Desktop item, close	WIN 5.29	Point to an item, wait for a title bar to appear, click ☒
Active Desktop item, delete from desktop	WIN 5.35	In Control Panel, click Appearance and Themes, click Change the desktop background, click the Customize Desktop button, click the Web tab, click the item you want to remove, click the Delete button
Active Desktop item, move	WIN 5.29	Point to an item, wait for the title bar to appear, drag the title bar
Active Desktop item, resize	WIN 5.29	Point to an item, wait for a border to appear, drag the border or the border corner
Active Desktop item, schedule an update for	WIN 5.34	See Reference Window: Scheduling an Update
Active Desktop item, synchronize	WIN 5.31	See Reference Window: Synchronizing an Active Desktop Item
Active Desktop item, view an update schedule	WIN 5.32	Point to an item, wait for a title bar to appear, click the down arrow in the upper-left corner of the title bar, click Properties, click the Schedule tab
Back up files	WIN 10.06	See Reference Window: Performing a Windows XP Backup
Backup, restore files from	WIN 10.11– 10.13	Start the Backup or Restore Wizard, click Next, click the Restore files and settings option button, click Next, then complete the wizard
Backup or Restore Wizard, start	WIN 10.06	Click 🍱 start , point to All Programs, point to Accessories, point to System Tools, click Backup
Calculator, start	WIN 8.05	Click 🍱 start , point to All Programs, point to Accessories, click Calculator
Character, insert	WIN 2.07	Click where you want to insert the character, type the character
Computer, identify on a network	WIN 9.12	Open My Network Places, click View network connections, click Advanced on the menu bar, click Network Identification, click the Computer Name tab
Computer Management window, open	WIN 10.36	See Reference Window: Opening the Computer Management Window
Control Panel, open	WIN 4.16	Click 🍱 start , click Control Panel
Data, transfer using Cut, Copy, and Paste	WIN 8.04	See Reference Window: Using Paste to Transfer Data from One Document to Another
Desktop, access	WIN 1.14	Click 🖼 on the Quick Launch toolbar

TASK	PAGE #	RECOMMENDED METHOD
Desktop appearance, save as theme	WIN 4.28	In Control Panel, click Appearance and Themes, click Change the computer's theme, click the Theme list arrow, click My Current Theme, click the Save As button, type a filename, click Save
Desktop background, use HTML file for	WIN 5.38	In Control Panel, click Appearance and Themes, click Change the desktop background, click the Browse button, select the HTML file
Desktop color palette, change	WIN 4.34	In Control Panel, click Appearance and Themes, click Change the screen resolution, click the Colors quality list arrow, click the palette you want, click OK
Desktop document, create	WIN 4.04	See Reference Window: Creating a New Document Icon on the Desktop
Desktop document, open	WIN 4.06	Double-click the document icon
Desktop resolution, change	WIN 4.32	In Control Panel, click Appearance and Themes, click Change the screen resolution, drag the Screen area slider, click OK
Desktop, change appearance	WIN 4.29	In Control Panel, click Appearance and Themes, click Change the computer's theme, click the Theme list arrow, click a theme, click OK
Desktop, change background	WIN 4.20	In Control Panel, click Appearance and Themes, click Change the desktop background, select an item in the Background list, click OK
Device Manager, open	WIN 11.09	See Reference Window: Opening the Device Manager
Device, select	WIN 3.08	Click the device icon on the Explorer bar of Windows Explorer
Disk, format	WIN 2.02	Right-click the 3½ Floppy icon in My Computer, click Format on the shortcut menu, click Start
Disk, quick format	WIN 3.24	In My Computer, right-click 🖫, click Format, click Quick Format, click Start
Event log, view	WIN 10.25	See Reference Window: Viewing the Event Log
Explorer bar, view	WIN 3.04	In Windows Explorer or My Computer, click View, point to Explorer Bar, click the Explorer bar you want to open
Favorites folder, add a Web page to	WIN 5.20	See Reference Window: Adding a Web Page to the Favorites Folder
Favorites folder, organize	WIN 5.20	See Reference Window: Organizing the Favorites Folder
Favorites folder, view	WIN 5.19	In Windows Explorer, click View, point to the Explorer Bar, click Favorites
File, copy	WIN 2.28	Use the right mouse button to drag the file you want to copy, release the mouse button, click Copy Here on the shortcut menu
File, copy from one floppy disk to another	WIN 3.20	See Reference Window: Moving and Copying a File
File, delete	WIN 2.30	Right-click the file you want to delete, click Delete on the shortcut menu, click Yes in the confirmation dialog box
File, download from Web	WIN 5.23	In Internet Explorer, right-click the file you want to download, click Save As (or Save Picture As, or something similar), enter a location, click Save

TASK	PAGE #	RECOMMENDED METHOD
File, locate by contents	WIN 6.13	In the Search Companion, click All files and folders, click the A word or phrase in the file text box, type the text you want to search for, click the Search button
File, locate by date	WIN 6.18	In the Search Companion, click All files and folders, click When was it modified?, select a date option, click the Search button
File, locate in a specific folder	WIN 6.14	See Reference Window: Searching for a File in a Specific Folder
File, move	WIN 2.28	Use the right mouse button to drag the file you want to copy, release the mouse button, click Move Here on the shortcut menu
File, move or copy from floppy disk to hard disk	WIN 3.23	See Reference Window: Moving or Copying Files with the Move To Folder and Copy To Folder commands
File, move or copy with Cut and Paste	WIN 3.20	See Reference Window: Moving or Copying Files with Cut, Copy, and Paste
File, open from My Computer	WIN 2.12	Open My Computer, open the Window containing the file, double-click the file
File, open from Search Results	WIN 6.10	Locate the file using the Search tool, double-click the file in the Results list
File, open from within a program	WIN 2.13	Start the program, click [icon], select the file in the Open dialog box, click Open
File or folder, delete	WIN 3.27	Click the file or folder icon, press Delete, click Yes in the confirmation dialog box
File, preview before printing	WIN 2.15	Click [icon]
File, print	WIN 2.15	Click [icon]
File, rename	WIN 2.29	Right-click the file, click Rename on shortcut menu, type new filename, press Enter
File, save	WIN 2.08	Click [icon]
File, select	WIN 3.15	See Reference Window: Selecting Files
File, select all but a certain one	WIN 3.16	See Reference Window: Selecting All Files Except Certain Ones
Files, locate by type or size	WIN 6.19-6.20	In the Search Companion, click All files and folders, click More advanced options, click Type of file list arrow, click file type, and then click the Search button
Files, view as large icons	WIN 2.21	Click the View button, click Tiles
Files, view as small icons	WIN 2.21	Click the View button, click Icons
Files, view details	WIN 2.22	Click the View button, click Details
Files, view in list	WIN 2.21	Click the View button, click List
Files, view thumbnails	WIN 2.21	Click the View button, click Thumbnails

TASK REFERENCE

TASK	PAGE #	RECOMMENDED METHOD
Floppy disk, copy	WIN 2.31	Right-click the 💾 icon in My Computer, click Copy Disk on the shortcut menu, click Start, insert the disk you want to copy from (source disk), then click OK
Folder hierarchy, move back in the	WIN 2.26	Click ⬅
Folder hierarchy, move forward in the	WIN 2.26	Click ➡
Folder hierarchy, move up	WIN 2.26	Click 📂
Folder options, restore default settings	WIN 2.23	Click Tools, click Folder Options, click the General tab, click Restore Defaults, (or click the View tab and click Restore Defaults), click OK
Folder or device, share on a network	WIN 9.29	See Reference Window: Sharing a Folder with the Network
Folder, rename	WIN 3.11	Right-click 📁, click Rename, type the new folder name, press Enter
Folder, create	WIN 2.25	Click File, point to New, click Folder, type a folder name, press Enter
Folder, create	WIN 3.09	See Reference Window: Creating a Folder in Windows Explorer
Font, delete	WIN B.19	Select a font in the Fonts window, press Delete, click Yes in the confirmation dialog box
Font, install	WIN B.18	In the Fonts window, click File, click Install New Font, locate and install the font file
Font, open	WIN B.17	In the Fonts window, right-click the font you want, click Open
Graphic, add text	WIN 7.37	See Reference Window: Adding Text to a Graphic
Graphic, change foreground or background color	WIN 7.36	In Paint, click color in color box with left mouse button to change foreground color or with right mouse button to change background color
Graphic, color	WIN 7.31	See Reference Window: Filling an Area with Color
Graphic, copy, paste, and move portions	WIN 7.23	See Reference Window: Copying, Cutting, and Pasting Graphics
Graphic, crop	WIN 7.08	See Reference Window: Cropping a Graphic
Graphic, embedded, resize	WIN 8.12	See Reference Window: Resizing an Embedded Object
Graphic, erase	WIN 7.11	In Paint, click 🖊, drag area you want to erase
Graphic, flip	WIN 7.24	In Paint, click Image, click Flip/Rotate, click option button you want, click OK
Graphic, magnify	WIN 7.15	See Reference Window: Magnifying a Graphic
Graphic, save in a different format	WIN 7.12	Click File, click Save As, click Save as type list arrow, click the file type you want, type filename, click Save
Graphic, stretch	WIN 7.27	In Paint, click Image, click Stretch/Skew, enter a stretch or skew percentage, click OK

TASK	PAGE #	RECOMMENDED METHOD
Grid, show in magnified view	WIN 7.15	In Paint, click View, point to Zoom, click Show Grid
Hard disk, check	WIN 11.37	See Reference Window: Running Check Disk
Hard disk, defragment	WIN 11.40	See Reference Window: Defragmenting a Disk
Hard disk, schedule maintenance	WIN 11.43–11.45	Click ⊞ start , point to All Programs, point to Accessories, point to System Tools,, click Scheduled Tasks; double-click 🕐 , click Next, select maintenance task
Hardware device list, print	WIN 11.16	Open Device Manager, click Action, click Print
Hardware device properties, view	WIN 11.11	Open Device Manager, right-click device icon, click Properties
Hardware device, install	WIN 11.06	See Reference Window: Installing a New Hardware Device
Hardware device, troubleshoot	WIN 11.13	Open the Properties dialog box for the hardware device, click the General tab, click Troubleshoot
Help, display topic from the Home page	WIN 1.30	In Help and Support, click Home in the navigation bar
Help, display topic from the Index page	WIN 1.31	In Help, click Index in the navigation bar, scroll to locate a topic or type a keyword, click the topic, click Display
Help, find topic	WIN 1.33	In Help, click in the Search box, type word or phrase, click →
Help, start	WIN 1.29	Click ⊞ start , click Help and Support
Hibernation, use	WIN B.03	Open the Control Panel in Classic View, double-click Power Options, click the Hibernate tab, click the Enable hibernation check box
High Contrast, use	WIN B.13	Open the Control Panel in Classic View, double-click Accessibility Options, click the Display tab, click the Use High Contrast check box
History pane, display	WIN 3.34	In Windows Explorer, click View, point to Explorer Bar, click History
History pane, display objects by most visits	WIN 3.36	In the History pane, click View, click By Most Visited
History pane, display recently opened files	WIN 3.35	In the History pane, click View, click By Order Visited Today
Icon, change	WIN 8.19	See Reference Window: Changing an Icon
Insertion point, move	WIN 2.06	Click the location in the document to which you want to move
Internet Connection Wizard, start	WIN A.04	Open My Network Places, click View network connections, click the Create a new connection link
Internet Explorer, start	WIN 5.06	See Reference Window: Starting Internet Explorer
Links, manage and update	WIN 8.28	See Reference Window: Managing Links
List box, scroll	WIN 1.26	Click the list arrow for the list box to display the list of options; click the scroll down or up arrow; or drag the scroll box
Log file, create	WIN 4.06	In Notepad, type .LOG

TASK	PAGE #	RECOMMENDED METHOD
Menu option, select	WIN 1.23	Click the option on the menu; for submenus, point to an option on the menu
Mouse double-click speed, set	WIN B.07	Open the Control Panel in Classic View, double-click Mouse, click the Buttons tab, set the double-click speed, click OK
Mouse pointer, change	WIN B.08	Open the Control Panel in Classic View, double-click Mouse, click the Pointers tab, select a mouse pointer, click OK
Mouse properties, view	WIN B.06	Open the Control Panel in Classic View, double-click Mouse
MouseKeys, use	WIN B.11	Open the Control Panel in Classic View, double-click Accessibility Options, click the Mouse tab, click the Use MouseKeys check box
My Computer, open	WIN 2.12	Double-click the My Computer icon on the desktop
My Network Places window, open	WIN 9.07	See Reference Window: Viewing Your Network
Network components, view	WIN 9.13	See Reference Window: Viewing Network Components
Network folder, map to drive letter	WIN 9.24	See Reference Window: Mapping a Network Folder
Network folder, remove drive mapping	WIN 9.25	See Reference Window: Remove Drive Mapping
Network folder, view	WIN 9.22	Open My Network Places window, double-click network workstation, if necessary, double-click
Network, log off	WIN 9.20	Click , click Log Off
Network place, create	WIN 9.26	See Reference Window: Creating a Network Place
Object, display as icon	WIN 8.18	Right-click object, click Object Properties, click View tab, click Display as Icon, click OK
Object, edit in place	WIN 8.14	See Reference Window: In-place Editing
Object, embed using Insert Object	WIN 8.16	See Reference Window: Embedding an Object with Insert Object
Object, embed using Paste	WIN 8.11	Select object, cut or copy to the Clipboard, click desired location in destination document, click
Object, embed with different methods	WIN 8.23	See Reference Window: Methods of Embedding
Object, link	WIN 8.25	See Reference Window: Linking an Object
Object, resize	WIN 8.12	See Reference Window: Resizing an Embedded Object
Objects, display or hide in the Folders pane	WIN 3.06	See Reference Window: Displaying or Hiding Objects in the Folders Pane
Offline folder, access	WIN 9.35	Double-click , and then double-click an offline folder
Offline folder, remove	WIN 9.40	Open the My Computer window, locate and right-click the offline folder, deselect Make Available Offline
Offline folder, set up	WIN 9.33	See Reference Window: Setting Up an Offline Folder

TASK	PAGE #	RECOMMENDED METHOD
Outlook Express, receive e-mail from	WIN 5.53	Click 📧
Outlook Express, reply to e-mail from	WIN 5.55	Click 👤↵
Outlook Express, send e-mail from	WIN 5.50	See Reference Window: Sending an E-mail Message
Outlook Express, set up an e-mail account for	WIN 5.44	See Reference Window: Setting up an E-mail Account
Outlook Express, start	WIN 5.41	Click *start*, point to All Programs, if necessary, click Outlook Express
Paint, start	WIN 7.02	Click *start*, point to All Programs, point to Accessories, click Paint
Paint tools, use	WIN 7.03	See Figure 7-2
Panes, adjust width	WIN 3.11	See Reference Window: Adjusting the Width of the Exploring Window Pane
Password, change	WIN 9.18	See Reference Window: Changing Your Windows XP Password
People, locate on the Web	WIN 6.30	In the Search Companion, click Search the Internet, enter search criteria, click the Search button
Power option properties, view	WIN B.03	Open the Control Panel in Classic View, double-click Power Options
Print queue, pause	WIN 11.29	See Reference Window: Pausing the Print Queue
Print queue, remove jobs from	WIN 11.30	See Reference Window: Removing Print Jobs from the Print Queue
Print queue, view	WIN 11.27	See Reference Window: Viewing the Print Queue
Printer, install	WIN 11.18	See Reference Window: Installing a Printer
Printer properties, view	WIN 11.22	Right-click the icon for the printer, click Properties
Program, close	WIN 1.12	Click ☒
Program, close inactive	WIN 1.15	Right-click the program button on the taskbar, click Close
Program, start	WIN 1.11	*See* Reference Window: Starting a Program
Program, switch to another	WIN 1.14	Click the program button on the taskbar
Properties, view	WIN 4.20	Right-click an object, click Properties
Recycle Bin, open	WIN B.19	Double-click 🗑 on the desktop
Recycle Bin, restore file from	WIN B.20	Double-click 🗑, right-click the file you want to restore, click Restore
Results list, sort	WIN 6.16–6.17	In the Search Results window, display the file list in Details view, click the title buttons on the top of the file list
Screen, print	WIN 3.17	Press PrintScreen, start WordPad, click 📋, click 🖨
Screen saver, activate	WIN 4.30	In Control Panel, click Appearance and Themes, click Choose a screen saver, click the Screen Saver list arrow, select a screen saver, click OK

TASK	PAGE #	RECOMMENDED METHOD
ScreenTips, view	WIN 1.05	Position pointer over an item
Search Companion pane, open	WIN 6.03	Click **start**, click Search
Search, locate file by name	WIN 6.05	See Reference Window: Searching for a File by Name
Search the Internet	WIN 6.26	In the Search Companion pane, click Search the Internet
Security policy, view	WIN 10.41	See Reference Window: Viewing Security Policies
Send To command, copy files with	WIN 3.25	Right-click the file icon, point to Send To, select the destination of the file
Service list, view	WIN 10.28	See Reference Window: Viewing the Service Window
Shortcut, create	WIN 4.09	See Figure 4-9: Methods for Creating Shortcuts
Shortcut icon, delete	WIN 4.15	Select the shortcut icon, press Delete, click Yes
Start Menu, add an item to	WIN 4.46	See Reference Window: Adding an Item to the Start Menu
Start menu, open	WIN 1.06	Click **start**
Start Menu, remove an item from	WIN 4.50	See Reference Window: Removing a Start Menu Item
Subfolders, view or hide	WIN 3.07	Click ➕ or ➖
System performance alert, create	WIN 10.23	Open the Control Panel in Classic View, double-click Administrative Tools, double-click 📷, double-click 📷, right-click 📷, click New Alert Settings, enter the name of the alert, and then click OK
System performance, graph	WIN 10.16	See Reference Window: Graphing System Performance
System performance log, create	WIN 10.19	Open the Control Panel in Classic View, double-click Administrative Tools, double-click 📷, right-click 📷, click 📷, add an item to track, click the Log Files tab, enter a name for the log file, click OK
Taskbar, move and resize	WIN 4.36	See Reference Window: Moving and Resizing the Taskbar
Taskbar toolbar, create	WIN 4.40	See Reference Window: Displaying a Taskbar Toolbar
Taskbar toolbar, modify the appearance of	WIN 4.42	Right-click the taskbar, click Properties, modify the properties that apply to the taskbar's appearance
Taskbar toolbar, remove	WIN 4.44	Right-click a blank area on the taskbar, point to Toolbars, click the taskbar toolbar you want to remove
Taskbar, set properties	WIN 4.39	Right-click the taskbar, click Properties
Test page, print	WIN 11.24	See Reference Window: Printing a Test Page
Text, select	WIN 2.06	Drag the pointer over the text
Thumbnail, show in magnified view	WIN 7.19–7-20	In Paint, click View, point to Zoom, click Show Thumbnail
Thumbnails, view your graphic files as	WIN 7.42	In My Computer or Windows Explorer, click View, click Thumbnails

TASK	PAGE #	RECOMMENDED METHOD
Toolbar button, select	WIN 1.25	Click the toolbar button
Toolbars, control display	WIN 2.20	Click View, point to Toolbars, select the toolbar options you want
Unneeded files, delete	WIN 11.32	See Reference Window: Removing Unneeded Files
UPS device, configure	WIN B.04–B.05	Open the Control Panel in Classic View, double-click Power Options, click the UPS tab, select UPS options, click OK
User group, create	WIN 10.39	See Reference Window: Creating a User Group
User properties, advanced, set	WIN 10.38	Open the Computer Management window, click ✚ next to Local Users and Groups, click the Users folder, right-click user, click Properties
User properties, basic, set	WIN 10.35	Open the Control Panel in Classic View, double-click User Accounts, click Change an account, click account, click an option
User	WIN 10.32	See Reference Window: Adding a New User
User, remove	WIN 10.46	See Reference Window: Removing a User
Video clip, change settings	WIN 8.33	Right-click video clip, point to Video Clip Object, click Edit or, if it's an OLE object, click Linked Video Clip Object and then click Edit, change the settings, and then close the editor
Video clip, play	WIN 8.31	Right-click video clip, point to Video Clip Object, click Play or, if it's an OLE object, click Linked Video Clip Object, and then click Play
Workstation properties, view	WIN 9.11	Right-click the workstation icon, click Properties
Web page, activate link	WIN 5.12	In Internet Explorer, click a link on a Web page
Web page, open with URL	WIN 5.09	See Reference Window: Opening a Page with a URL
Web page, return to previous	WIN 5.16	In Internet Explorer, click ⬅
Wildcards, use to find files by name	WIN 6.11	In the Search Companion, click All files and folders, type search string using ? in place of single characters and * in place of multiple characters
Window, close	WIN 1.12	Click ✕
Window, maximize	WIN 1.20	Click ◻
Window, minimize	WIN 1.20	Click ▬
Window, move	WIN 1.21	Drag the title bar
Window, resize	WIN 1.21	Drag ⬏
Window, restore	WIN 1.21	Click ❐
Windows Explorer, start	WIN 3.02	Click ⊞ start , point to All Programs, point to Accessories, click Windows Explorer
Windows XP, shut down	WIN 1.15	Click ⊞ start , click Turn Off Computer, click the Turn Off button
Windows XP, start	WIN 1.02	Turn on the computer

Windows XP Level I File Finder

Location in Tutorial	Name and Location of Data File	Student Saves File As...	Student Creates New File
WINDOWS XP LEVEL I			
Tutorial 1	No Data Files needed		
Tutorial 2 Session 2.1			Practice Text.txt
Session 2.2 *Note*: Students copy the contents of Disk 1 onto Disk 2 in this session	Agenda.rtf Beck.asx Holiday.bmp Iceberg.jpg Logo.bmp New Logo.bmp Proposal.rtf Resume.rtf Salinas Family.eml Stationery.bmp Vinca.jpg Practice Text.txt *(saved from Session 2.1)*		
Review Assignments and Projects *Note*: Students continue to use the Data Disks they used in the Tutorial. For certain Assignments, they need a third blank disk		Woods Resume.rtf	Letter.rtf Song.rtf Poem.rtf

Windows XP Level II File Finder

Location in Tutorial	Name and Location of Data File	Student Saves File As...	Student Creates New File
WINDOWS XP LEVEL II			

Tutorial 3
Session 3.1
	[16 files]
	Clients (folder)
	  Advanced (folder)
	    [4 files]
	    Alpine (folder)
	      [3 files]
	    Ice (folder)
	      [2 files]
	    Sport (folder)
	      [2 files]
	    Basic (folder)
	      [4 files]
	  Gear (folder)
	    [3 files]
	  Guides (folder)
	    [3 files]
		[16 files]
		Clients (folder)
		  Advanced (folder)
		    [4 files]
		    Alpine (folder)
		      [3 files]
		    Ice (folder)
		      [2 files]
		    Sport (folder)
		      [2 files]
		    Basic (folder)
		      [4 files]
		  Gear (folder)
		    [3 files]
		    Hardware (folder)
		    Ropes and Harnesses (folder)
		  Guides (folder)
		    [3 files]
			Gear (folder)
			  Hardware (folder)
			  Ropes and Harnesses (folder)

Session 3.2	*(Continued from Session 3.1)*	[4 files]
		Clients (folder)
		  Advanced (folder)
		    [4 files]
		    Alpine (folder)
		      [5 files]	

Location in Tutorial	Name and Location of Data File	Student Saves File As...	Student Creates New File
		Ice (folder) [2 files] Sport (folder) [2 files] Basic (folder) [13 files] Gear (folder) Hardware (folder) Ropes and Harnesses (folder) [5 files] Guides (folder) [3 files]	
Session 3.3	No Data Files needed		
Review Assignments and Projects			C:\My Documents\Advertise A:\All Clients
Tutorial 4			
Session 4.1	Same files used as in Session 3.2.		Phone Log.txt
Session 4.2	Logo.bmp		
Session 4.3	No Data Files needed		

Review Assignments and Projects			Classes.txt
			A:\Sally (folder)
			  Smith.txt
			  Arruga.txt
			  Kosta.txt
			A:\My Signature.bmp

Tutorial 5			
Session 5.1	No Data Files needed		Lake.jpg
Session 5.2	Highland.htm [15 supporting files]		
Session 5.3			Highland.htm [15 supporting files]
Tutorial 6			
Session 6.1	Alphabet (folder) [25 files] Authors (folder) [25 files] Comedy (folder) [18 files] Images (folder) [2 files] Social (folder) [16 files] Topics (folder) [19 files]		
Session 6.2	No Data Files needed		
Review Assignments and Projects	Same as Session 6.1		

Windows XP Level III File Finder

Location in Tutorial	Name and Location of Data File	Student Saves File As...	Student Creates New File
Tutorial 7			
Session 7.1	Sports.bmp		Skis.bmp Skis256.bmp
Session 7.2	Skis256.bmp (saved in Session 7.1) Brush.bmp Mountain.bmp	XCountry Skis.bmp Kiana.bmp Mountain and Sun.bmp	
Session 7.3	*Continued from Session 7.2*		
Review Assignments	Sports.bmp Kiana.bmp	Kiana2.bmp	Bowling Ball.bmp Tennis Rackets.bmp Rings.bmp Skier
Projects	Sports.bmp		Letter J.bmp Fonts.bmp Sailboat.bmp Chess.bmp Chess with Text.bmp
Tutorial 8			
Session 8.1	Maria.rtf		Feedback.rtf
Session 8.2	Pins.bmp Pins10.bmp Icon.bmp JG Logo.bmp		
Session 8.3	Pins2.bmp Video.avi		
Review Assignments	Maria.rtf Tailor.rtf Election.bmp Clowning.rtf Chester.bmp		Happy Birthday.wav Birthday Message.rtf
Projects	IRS.txt New.rtf House.rtf House.bmp Kennedy.wav		Linguistics.rtf Carpet.bmp CarpetMasterEstimate.rtf Ranch Flyer.rtf
Tutorial 9			
Session 9.1	No Data Files needed		
Session 9.2	No Data Files needed		
Session 9.3	No Data Files needed		
Review Assignments and Projects	Instructor will supply Data Files		
Tutorial 10			
Session 10.1			Test1.txt Test2.txt Test3.txt CCC Backup.bkf
Session 10.2	Need a blank formatted disk		Processor Performance.blg
Session 10.3	No Data Files needed		
Review Assignments and Projects			Interrupt.blg
Tutorial 11			
Session 11.1	No Data Files needed		
Session 11.2	No Data Files needed		
Session 11.3	Use the Tutorial 8 Data Disk		
Review Assignments and Projects	No Data Files needed		
Appendix B	No Data Files needed		